Hungarian Yearbook of International Law and European Law 2019

Hungarian Yearbook of International Law and European Law 2019

MARCEL SZABÓ
(EDITOR-IN-CHIEF)
LAURA GYENEY
PETRA LEA LÁNCOS
(EDITORS)

international publishing

Published, sold and distributed by Eleven International Publishing
P.O. Box 85576
2508 CG The Hague
The Netherlands
Tel.: +31 70 33 070 33
Fax: +31 70 33 070 30
email: sales@elevenpub.nl
www.elevenpub.com

Sold and distributed in USA and Canada
Independent Publishers Group
814 N. Franklin Street
Chicago, IL 60610, USA
Order Placement: +1 800 888 4741
Fax: +1 312 337 5985
orders@ipgbook.com
www.ipgbook.com

Eleven International Publishing is an imprint of Boom uitgevers Den Haag.

ISBN 978-94-6236-979-5
ISBN 978-94-6094-424-6 (e-book)
ISSN (print): 2666-2701
ISSN (online): 2666-271X

Printed in The Netherlands

TABLE OF CONTENTS

CONTRIBUTORS

Editors:

Laura Gyeney (Pázmány Péter Catholic University, Budapest)

Petra Lea Láncos (Deutsches Forschungsinstitut für Öffentliche Verwaltung, Speyer; Pázmány Péter Catholic University, Budapest)

Editorial Assistants:

Kinga Debisso (Ministry of Justice of Hungary; Pázmány Péter Catholic University, Budapest)

Zsuzsanna Máthé-Fäller (Constitutional Court of Hungary)

Balázs Tárnok (National University of Public Service, Budapest)

International Advisory Board:

Roger O'Keefe (University College London)

Dinah Shelton (George Washington University Law School)

David Turns (Cranfield University, UK)

Ottavio Quirico (University of New England)

Christina Binder (University of Vienna)

Franziska Sucker (University of the Witwatersrand, South Africa)

Legal, Ethical and Economical Impacts of Intergenerational Equity (Editorial Comments)

Foreword to Vol. 7 (2019) of the Hungarian Yearbook of International Law and European Law

Marcel Szabó[*]

International law reflects the values shared by states and has helped them face the most consequential challenges of the day. After World War II, the most significant challenge was to preserve international peace and security, as well as to guarantee basic human rights. In the 21st century, states are facing a new challenge: climate change and its consequences, and, ultimately, the survival of mankind. Unfortunately, the consequences of climate change are highly visible – *e.g.* extreme weather conditions (droughts, heat waves and devastating storms, floods in areas where people have never experienced similar events before), melting ice in the Arctic and the extinction of some native plant and animal species and the appearance of unknown invasive species in the same area.[1]

While climate change impacts can be localized, the main means of intervention against such impacts is through international law since, once these rules have been properly ratified, states are responsible for applying the provisions of international law fully and unconditionally within their own legal systems. This, however, requires intensive cooperation among the various fields of study. So, *e.g.* in politics and economy (including both the level of individual companies and that of the national economy), scholars and decision-makers alike accept that preservation of the environment and the responsible management of resources are as important as short-term political and economic advantages.

In determining the scope of interventions for preserving the environment, the latest results of research in natural sciences must also be taken into account. In this context, jurisprudence shall elaborate upon and apply new regulatory methods that encourage

---

[*] Marcel Szabó: editor-in-chief; professor of law, Pázmány Péter Catholic University, Budapest; justice, Constitutional Court of Hungary.
1 *Living Planet Report 2018*, pp. 11, 90 and 119 at https://wwf.panda.org/knowledge_hub/all_publications/living_planet_report_2018/; Camilo Mora & Peter Sale, *Ongoing Global Biodiversity Loss and the Need to Move Beyond Protected Areas: A Review of the Technical and Practical Shortcomings of Protected Areas on Land and Sea*, Marine Ecology Progress Series, 2011, pp. 251-255.

economic operators, consumers and public authorities to manage resources responsibly and reward them for such responsible management. Such new regulatory methods can include supporting the introduction of new technologies, encouraging consumer awareness and conscious economic behavior through tax incentives or otherwise and applying consistently the 'polluter pays' principle as one of the oldest principles of international environmental law.

A further significant consideration is that the Earth's population continues to increase. Currently, the Earth's population is at approximately 7.5 billion, but according to UN estimates it may exceed 11 billion persons by 2100.[2] Population growth will require an increase in food production and agricultural lands, which may occur to the detriment of forests. According to a FAO report, the size of forests in tropical states decreased by 7 million hectares annually between 2000 and 2010, whilst the size of agricultural lands increased by 6 million hectares annually.[3] At the same time, the reduction of forests automatically entails the increase of carbon dioxide in the atmosphere as forests play a particularly important role in carbon sequestration.

In its special report, the Intergovernmental Panel on Climate Change (IPCC) confirmed that the rate of global warming will reach the threshold of 1.5 degree Celsius between 2030 and 2052,[4] and an increase of the temperature by 2 degrees Celsius is the maximum increase that humankind can tolerate. In case of an increase by 2.2 degrees Celsius, large African mammals are expected to become extinct, while an increase by 2.8 degrees Celsius would result in the destruction of Amazon rainforests and the coral reefs around Australia. An increase by approximately 4 degrees Celsius would result in the destruction of all mankind as in natural circumstances humans can tolerate a maximum temperature of approximately 35 degrees Celsius (the so-called wet bulb temperature).

At the same time, global warming triggered by the reduction of forests also decreases the average production of agricultural lands, therefore in order to maintain the production rates in the regions that are most affected by global warming and are overpopulated, additional lands must be subjected to agricultural production or production must be intensified by monoculture production and fertilizer use leading to a rapid depletion of soils.

It is, therefore, particularly important for today's generations to take into account the interests of future generations in all areas of life. Furthermore, it is essential to raise awareness about the fact that climate change is not an issue in the unforeseeable future, affecting generations that are yet to be born. On the contrary, the global consequences of current environmental changes will be felt within the next years or decades, so they also

---

2   *World Population Prospect 2019*, at https://population.un.org/wpp/.
3   *State of the World's Forests*, FAO, 2016, p. x.
4   *Special Report on Global Warming of 1.5 C, Summary for Policymakers*, IPCC, 2018, p. 6.

will affect today's generations. This also means that if the circumstances remain unchanged, today's generation will not be able to fully enjoy the results of economic development in the next 30 years. In relation to the fight against climate change, the most important political guideline may be that "after a flood, it only matters who made the ship on time." Thus, while the history of past centuries centered on wars and conquests, today's statesmen may gain recognition and respect from next generations by thinking and acting responsibly in the interest of future generations instead of turning to the use of arms. In this context, policy and lawmakers need to take into account the interests of future generations mainly in the fields of ethics, law and economy.

1   ETHICAL ASPECTS OF INTERGENERATIONAL EQUITY

For centuries, the main driving force of human history has been that the world is gradually getting better and better, under the guidance of wise people. Technical means are becoming ever more perfect, the environment surrounding us is improving, and the quality of life is increasing, so everyone will live an increasingly better life and be able to consume more and more. This approach, however, may only be valid if it is assumed that resources are endless and can be used without limits. The phenomenon of climate change, however, has clearly shown that such an assumption does not hold true. Future generations will hardly be able to increase their use of resources and consume more than today's generations. On the contrary, a significant decrease of available resources for consumption is expected in terms of both their absolute value and their value *pro capita*. However, it follows from the responsibility of today's generations for future generations that we pose a fundamental question: if it is already certain that we cannot improve our lives and living conditions what sacrifice must we make in order not to impair the living conditions of our children and grandchildren and to provide them with the opportunity of free choice? Even though today's generations' responsibility for future generations is set out in an increasing number of legal documents, this issue can be considered primarily to be an ethical one.

Furthermore, the responsibility for future generations sheds light on an additional issue. The concept of future generations is linked to specific societies instead of specific individuals, therefore, responsibility for future generations can be understood as the responsibility of the entire society rather than that of specific individuals. However, the question of whether preserving the living conditions for future generations requires the same level or at least the same proportion of sacrifice from all members of today's generations regardless of whether they are citizens of a developed or a developing country remains unaddressed. In this situation, differences among living and other conditions in developed and developing countries should be taken into account in determining the scope of the responsibility for next generations. Intragenerational equity requires each nation to ensure the survival of their own descendants, knowing and hoping that the other nations are also subject to similar responsibility and sacrifice in connection with their own future generations. While ethically it may be expected that everyone will take necessary measures in the interests of their own descendants, the approach requiring action from today's generations in the interest of future generations of nations living in other parts of the world is undermined by significant economic, geographical, political and other objective differences.

The cornerstone of thinking about future generations is that members of a nation answer together the question of identity, shared cultural and ethical values that will be left to their children and grandchildren, and the question of how to change consumption patterns and lifestyles to allow these values to be passed on. In his encyclical letter *Laudato si'*, Pope Francis underlines that the sense of today's generations' life may be questioned if they leave an unlivable world to subsequent generations.[5]

It is generally true that the community is more willing to make a larger sacrifice where there is already a direct and institutionalized link between today's generation and the future generation. While international law introduced *inter alia* the category of intergenerational equity, it still lacks real means to support the implementation of such equity. On the contrary, the national laws of certain states already contain institutions (mostly falling within the scope of the social care system) which are aimed at implementing intergenerational cooperation. Such institutions include, *e.g.* old-age pensions or childbirth allowances. Therefore, while institutions of international law are suitable for determining the scope of intergenerational equity, nations and states should be responsible for determining its content.

2   LEGAL ASPECTS OF INTERGENERATIONAL EQUITY

Although responsibility for future generations may primarily be assessed at the national level, an approach beyond the state level must be applied in relation to the protection of human rights, including for the so-called second and third generation human rights. Article 1 of the ICESCR provides that "[a]ll peoples may [...] freely dispose of their natural wealth and resources [...]. In no case may a people be deprived of its own means of subsistence." While state are required to enforce basic human rights within their own territories (with due consideration to their respective legal systems and cultures), the same states may fail to take into account whether, within their jurisdiction, economic operators (including in particular multinational companies) respect basic human rights in their foreign operations.

---

5   *Encyclical Letter Laudato si' of the Holy Father Francis on Care for Our Common Home*, 2015, para. 206.

Similarly, where a state adopts a specific regulation in respect of its resident citizens or resident legal entities, such a regulation will not necessarily take into account the global impacts resulting therefrom. For example, a direct link exists where rules on water resources have an impact on neighboring states using the water base or where the emissions of pollutants effect the territory of neighboring states. An indirect link exists, however, if the effect on other states and citizens can only be demonstrated as a secondary impact. In this context, an international legal environment that allows for establishing responsibility not only for direct links but also in case of scientifically substantiated indirect links would also be suitable for enforcing responsibility for future generations, thereby promoting the responsible management of resources. In this case, taking into account the 2001 Draft Articles on Responsibility of States for Internationally Wrongful Acts, state responsibility may be based on non-compliance with the due diligence obligations[6] in addition to responsibility for specific human rights violations.

Certain international agreements, primarily those on the environment or human rights, already apply monitoring requirements and from time to time analyze contracting parties' practices in relation to a treaty regime's terms.[7] Extending the monitoring system beyond the purely human rights context to the specific issues of climate change and therefore to the issue of responsibility for future generations can provide the basis for a kind of global solidarity, thereby reducing intragenerational inequality.

Furthermore, determining the applicable legal consequences is a significant element of regulating the responsibility for future generations. The current rules of international law, in particular those relating to climate change, are much more focused on remedying the damage that has arisen than preventing damage or restoring the original condition (if applicable). So, for example, the inclusion of persons fleeing from impossible living conditions requires significant economic and social resources from the states concerned. With careful planning, such resources could also be used for preventing the reasons underlying the flight of populations and/or solving problems at their source. This is important because, while the living conditions of billions of people may become impossible due to climate change, the number of refugees the EU may be able to receive is not proportional to the climate activity of this organization.

Intragenerational solidarity, however, requires changing today's perspective that is primarily, and in many cases exclusively, based on economic interests. The classic liberal economic policy of Adam Smith and David Ricardo is based on the self-regulating power of the market and assumes that free market processes which are free from government

---

6   Timo Koivurova, 'Due diligence', *in Max Planck Encyclopedia of Public International Law*, 2010, at https://opil.ouplaw.com/view/10.1093/law:epil/9780199231690/law-9780199231690-e1034.

7   Examples of monitoring: regular country visits by elected or appointed experts; ad-hoc inspections on-site by experts; evaluations based on questionnaires; written reporting, done by the member states themselves (self-assessment).

interventions create an economic order that is ideal for everyone. While it is unquestionable that the extension of economic cooperation was successful in several instances (*e.g.* the EU or the WTO), intragenerational solidarity requires state and international law intervention and subjecting classic free market processes to legal and ethical constraints.

Two issues arise in this respect. On the one hand, legal and ethical constraints are missing from these systems. For example, it its hardly justifiable from a legal or ethical point of view that in the framework of the WTO, mineral water is a commodity just like any other product,[8] therefore, based on market processes and interests only, the water resources of a developing country may also be used for supplying a developed country so that it may keep its own water resources 'in reserve'. Furthermore, the regulatory state (or, as the case may be, the community of states) should be strong enough even when, due to the rationalization of economic processes and the increased efficiency of production, the business interests of market players turn out to be contrary to the applicable legal and ethical rules and their lobbies try to soften such rules.

Similar trends apply where agricultural lands are acquired or leased by foreign market players. International law and EU law, as well as the national law of several states, allow for the lease and acquisition of arable land by foreigners, and certain developed countries may satisfy the needs of their citizens by using the resources of other states, thereby sparing their own arable lands. The importance of such an approach is well demonstrated by the fact that, for example, within the EU arable lands are regulated as an investment vehicle in connection with the free movement of capital and the Member States may only exceptionally subject them to restrictions. Furthermore, EU Member States shall allow for the acquisition of their arable lands by the citizens of other Member States, according to the provisions of EU law.

Another example of the conflict between legal and ethical aspects of intergenerational equity is the regulation and practices concerning the prohibition of child labor.[9] In principle, all states support the prohibition of child labor, however certain states and international organizations have failed to take truly efficient action against multinational companies that obtain advantages on the market through the indirect use of child labor. Currently, action against such market players is primarily driven by the ethical stance of society.

This also holds true for the obligation to preserve natural resources for future generations. Several natural resources may be fully exhausted within the next decades if the level of their current use is maintained. Although several decades is a short period compared to human history, in the world of short political objectives, it is sufficient time for this

---

8   Mike Muller & Christophe Bellmann, *Trade and Water – How Might Trade Policy Contribute to Sustainable Water Management?*, International Centre for Trade and Sustainable Development, 2016, pp. 14-17.

9   The relevant ILO Conventions and Recommendations concerning child labor are available at www.ilo.org/ipec/facts/ILOconventionsonchildlabour/lang--en/index.htm.

issue to be put into the focus of political thinking. For example, in its Decision No. 28/2017. (X. 25.) AB, the Hungarian Constitutional Court found that the obligation to preserve biological diversity is "a peremptory norm of the international law and it reflects also the intention of the international community as a whole."[10] Legal solutions employing similar, existing legal means to preserve natural resources may serve as an example for legislators, those applying the law and courts (constitutional courts) globally.

Further to strategic documents, several national parliaments have a body which is mainly responsible for taking into account sustainable development (or, in a broader sense, the interests of future generations), including for example the National Council for Sustainable Development in Hungary, which was set up in 2008, headed by the president of Parliament. It is a consultative and advisory body of Parliament on matters relating to sustainable development.[11] What is common to such bodies is that their members come from professional and scientific research institutes, universities and civil society organizations in addition to politics, and they are responsible for *inter alia* taking positions on whether legislative bills comply with the concept of sustainable development and may, where appropriate, initiate legislative processes. Unfortunately, even though such institutions exist in several states, their findings are in many cases fully ignored by legislators.

Where certain strategic documents are to be adopted only at the national level, protection of the interests of future generations may also be realized universally. Several international civil society organizations requested the creation of a position similar to that of an ombudsman or high commissioner as an element of UN's reform at the Rio+20 summit. Even though such an institution has not been established yet, the UN Secretary General was invited to prepare a report on the situation of future generations within the auspices of the UN.[12]

3   ECONOMIC ASPECTS OF INTERGENERATIONAL EQUITY

Today's economic model is based on increasing consumption and production and on the assumption that the continuous development thereof can satisfy the needs of an ever-increasing world population. The major weakness of this model is that the Earth's resources are limited. While citizens of developed states already use the natural resources very intensively in order to ensure their own well-being and quality of life, citizens of developing countries also aspire to reach such level of well-being. This effort, however, will result in

---

10   Decision No. 28/2017. (X. 25.) AB, Reasoning [38].
11   *See* in detail at www.parlament.hu/web/ncsd/national-council-for-sustainable-development.
12   *Intergenerational Solidarity and the Needs of Future Generations*, Report of the Secretary General, A/68/100, 2013.

an unsustainable situation already in the short-term, by 2050 according to certain pessimistic forecasts. According to Principle 8 of the 1992 Rio Declaration,

> "To achieve sustainable development and a higher quality of life for all people, States should reduce and eliminate unsustainable patterns of production and consumption and promote appropriate demographic policies."

Therefore, it can be said that due consideration of the interests of future generations and responsible management of the Earth's resources require changing the ethical and legal approach, as well as revisiting the basic economic approach. A key element may be decoupling,[13] that is, separating the economic concept of growth from natural growth in terms of consumption. Although statistical growth is virtually unlimited, at least in theory, the Earth's limited resources constitute an absolute limit to physical growth.

Implementation of decoupling is by no means impossible. Decoupling would be supported, *e.g.* by making public administration eco-friendly, by the obligatory recycling of raw materials in the construction of infrastructure or obligatory consideration of calculations regarding the efficiency of certain investments and proper accounting of their efficiency. However, the issue in this respect is how to obtain stakeholders' joint support. Market players will refrain from adopting a different market practice as long as they consider its introduction to be a competitive disadvantage, as otherwise they would threaten their own market position.

According to this approach, we should not consider ecological services as being externalities when establishing product value.[14] Furthermore, discounting is also essential in today's economic approach. By recognizing future damage at a smaller current value, discounting creates a link between ecological damage certainly arising in the distant future and a financial advantage that may certainly be realized in the immediate future.[15] This approach itself, however, also prefers current economic advantage to mid-term and long-term damage.

Meanwhile, a great deal of work is being done today to advance greener, more sustainable economics.[16] Green economics takes into account also ecological services and assigns a value to them, thereby considering them in the analysis of economic processes. Although

---

13 *Indicators to measure decoupling of environmental pressure from economic growth. The OECD Environment Programme, Executive Summary*, pp. 1-3, at www.oecd.org/environment/indicators-modelling-outlooks/1933638.pdf.

14 *See* in general: *The Economics of Ecosystems and Biodiversity. TEEB Report for Business*, at www.teeb-web.org/wp-content/uploads/Study%20and%20Reports/Reports/Business%20and%20Enterprise/TEEB%20for%20Business%20Report/TEEB%20for%20Business.pdf.

15 Cedric Philibert, *Discounting the Future*, Internet Encyclopaedia of Ecological Economics, 2003.

16 Cameron Allen & Stuart Clouth (eds.), *A Guidebook to the Green Economy*, UN Division for Sustainable Development, 2012.

this approach may continue to be pushed to the background by mainstream economic studies today, it is also clear that reform ideas which would be suitable for achieving a more sustainable development and a responsible management of environmental resources against the unconditional achievement of short-term economic advantages, also exist in the field of economics.

4   LESSONS FOR INTERGENERATIONAL EQUITY AND ENVIRONMENTAL LAW IN VOL. 7 OF THE HUNGARIAN YEARBOOK

The thematic chapter of this year's Hungarian Yearbook of International Law and European Law is dedicated to the role of legal sciences and jurisprudence in responding to climate change and environmental challenges. In the 2019 volume seven articles deal with the question of the protection of the environment and the interests of future generations.

Ludwig Krämer examines EU Directive 2001/42 on the assessment of the effects of certain plans and programs on the environment based on the case-law of the CJEU and highlights a number of legal questions which were not yet discussed by the CJEU. *Marie-Claire Cordonier Segger* introduces sustainable development in foreign investment law and policy related to renewable energy and climate change mitigation and adaptation.

Based on Article P of the Fundamental Law of Hungary – which underlines that national resources shall be protected, maintained and preserved for future generations by the state and everyone – the Constitutional Court of Hungary has a solid case-law concerning the protection of the environment and the interests of future generations. *Gyula Bándi* provides us with an overview of the recent decisions of the Constitutional Court, including the principle of non-derogation (non-regression), firstly recognized in Decision No. 28/1994. (V. 20.) AB. *Marcel Szabó* demonstrates how the precautionary principle became a constitutional cornerstone in the Hungarian constitutional practice and dialogue. In the field of environmental policy, the principle of 'think globally – act locally' has special relevance. *László Fodor* analyzes how Hungarian municipalities deal with environmental issues within their powers (including, among others, the question of air protection, waste management, or the protection of the built environment).

Gábor Baranyai evaluates the resilience assessment of European water law from the perspective of the management of hydrological variability and, last but not least, *Ágnes Váradi* tries to define the role of the Aarhus Convention as part of national, and international and EU law at the same time.

On behalf of the editors, I wish you a good read and hope you enjoy the current thematic chapter and our other 'traditional' chapters (Developments in international law; Developments in EU law; Hungarian state practice; Case notes; Conference reports; Book reviews).

I also hope to welcome you among the authors of the next volume of the Hungarian Yearbook of International Law and European Law. For more information (including current and past volumes, call for papers and submission guidelines, current news *etc.*) please do not forget to check our brand new homepage at www.hungarianyearbook.com, launched in October 2019.

PART I
THE ROLE OF LEGAL SCIENCES AND JURISPRUDENCE IN RESPONDING TO CLIMATE CHANGE AND ENVIRONMENTAL CHALLENGES

1 AN IMPORTANT PLANNING INSTRUMENT: STRATEGIC ENVIRONMENTAL ASSESSMENT (EU DIRECTIVE 2001/42)

*Ludwig Krämer**

Keywords
environmental impact assessment, Directive 2001/42, strategic planning, assessment of plans, environmental report

Abstract
Directive 2001/42 requires the elaboration of an environmental impact assessment, before certain national, regional or local plans or programs related to the environment are adopted. The paper presents the content of the Directive and summarizes the case-law of the CJEU on the Directive. Furthermore, it raises a number of legal questions hitherto left undiscussed by the European courts.

1.1 INTRODUCTION

Directive 2001/42[1] requests EU Member States to provide for an environmental impact assessment for certain plans or programs, before these plans or programs are adopted by the public authorities or before they are submitted for adoption to the local, regional or national legislator. Although the term 'strategic environmental assessment' (SEA) or a similar term is not used in Directive 2001/42, it is generally applied to the assessment under Directive 2001/42, in order to distinguish this assessment from the environmental impact assessment for specific projects under Directive 2001/92.[2]

---

*   Ludwig Krämer: Derecho y Medio Ambiente S.L., Madrid.
1   Directive 2001/42 on the assessment of certain plans and programmes on the environment.
2   Directive 2011/92 on the assessment of the effects of certain public and private projects on the environment.

1.2   THE EU LEGISLATIVE FRAMEWORK

When in 1980 the EU Commission made a proposal for a directive on the assessment of the environmental impact of certain projects, it announced this as a first step which would be followed by a proposal on the assessment of plans and programs.[3] It then took until 1996 before such a proposal was submitted[4] and until 2001, before the 'Directive on the assessment of the effects of certain plans and programmes on the environment' (SEA Directive) was adopted. Member States had to apply it by 21 July 2004.

The Directive provides that certain plans or programs shall, before being adopted, undergo an environment impact assessment. This concerns plans and programs for certain sectors[5] which set the framework for granting a planning permission (development consent) for projects that come under the Directive on the environmental impact assessment of certain projects,[6] plans or programs which require an assessment under Directive 92/43,[7] other plans and programs where screening reveals that they may have a significant impact on the environment, and also small plans or programs at local level,[8] where screening shows that they may have a significant impact on the environment. The elaboration of plans or programs must be foreseen under legislative or administrative provisions (Article 2a).

The environment impact assessment consists of the elaboration of an environmental report which identifies, assesses and evaluates the likely significant effects of the plan or program on the environment, including reasonable alternatives (Article 5). Other authorities and the public concerned shall be consulted on the draft plan or program; the results of the consultation shall be taken into consideration in the final version of the plan or program (Article 8). The final plan or program is to be made public (Article 9). The significant effects of the plan or program shall be monitored (Article 10).

In December 2004, the Commission opened formal procedures against 15 Member States for failure to transpose the Directive in time into national law;[9] five cases ended before the CJEU. The Court found that Belgium (Flanders), Luxemburg, Italy, Finland

---

3   COM(1980) 313, Recital (4).
4   COM(96) 511.
5   The Directive enumerates the sectors of agriculture, forestry, fisheries, energy, industry, transport, waste management, water management, telecommunication, tourism, town and country planning and land use.
6   Directive 85/337, now replaced by Directive 2011/92.
7   Directive 92/43 on the conservation of natural habitats and of wild fauna and flora.
8   The term 'small plans' has to be understood in a purely quantitative form; and 'local level' refers to the administrative authority which is charged to adopt local plans, *see* Judgment of 21 December 2016, *Case C-444/15, Associazione Italia Nostra Onlus v. Comune di Venezia and Others (Italia Nostra),* ECLI:EU:C:2016:978.
9   COM(2009) 469, p. 2.

(Aaland Islands) and Portugal had not transposed the Directive in time;[10] by 2009, all member States had transposed the Directive. No case was decided by the CJEU regarding the incorrect transposition of the Directive into national law. However, by mid-2019, the CJEU gave 20 preliminary judgments on the Directive upon request of national courts;[11] these will be discussed below.

The Commission reported in 2009 and 2017 on the Directive's implementation.[12] It issued, probably in 2003 and then in 2013, two non-binding guidance documents.[13] Member States submitted to the Commission, according to the Commission's website, overall 230 pieces of legislation which transposed the Directive's requirements into national law.[14] The titles of the relevant national legislation are available on the Commission's website, but not the text of the national legislation itself; as the references are vague and translations uncertain, these texts cannot be retraced.

The Directive remained unamended until mid-2019. However, in 2008, the EU concluded the 'Protocol on strategic environmental assessment to the UNECE Espoo Convention for environmental impact assessment in a transboundary context'[15] which became, according to Article 216(2) TFEU, integral part of EU law and prevailed over secondary EU legislation. The Protocol obliges contracting parties to make an environmental impact assessment for plans or programs which are required by legislative, regulatory or administrative provisions and subject to the preparation and adoption by an authority or prepared for adoption, through a formal procedure, by a parliament or a government.[16] As a contracting party, the EU is therefore obliged to submit EU plans or programs to an environmental impact assessment. Although the Espoo Convention itself refers to transboundary projects only, the Protocol to the Convention is not limited to plans or programs which have a transboundary impact.

---

10   Judgment of 7 December 2006, *Case C-54/06, Commission v. Belgium*, ECLI:EU:C:2006:767; Judgment of 26 October 2006, *Case C-77/06, Commission v. Luxemburg*, ECLI:EU:C:2006:689; Judgment of 8 November 2007, *Case C-40/07, Commission v. Italy*, ECLI:EU:C:2007:665; Judgment of 27 October 2006, *Case C-159/06, Commission v. Finland*, ECLI:EU:C:2006:694; Judgment of 24 May 2007, *Case C-376/06, Commission v. Portugal*, ECLI:EU:C:2007:308.

11   Ten of these 20 cases were submitted by Belgian courts.

12   COM(2009) 469 and COM(2017) 234.

13   Commission, Implementation of Directive 2001/42, undated [2003]; Guidance on integrating climate change and biodiversity into SEA, 2013.

14   The number of the pieces of national legislation is as follows: Belgium 19, Bulgaria 3, Czechia 1, Denmark 10, Germany 34, Estonia 4, Ireland 6, Croatia 1, Spain 2, France 7, Greece 7, Italy 2, Cyprus 1, Latvia 2, Lithuania 27, Luxemburg 1, Hungary 2, Malta 5, Netherlands 3, Austria 47, Poland 6, Portugal 1, Romania 1, Slovenia 6, Slovakia 4, Finland 21, Sweden 2, United Kingdom 6.

15   Decision 2008/871.

16   Protocol, Article 2(5).

Furthermore, in 2005, the EU concluded the Aarhus Convention[17] which contains relevant provisions on public participation in environmental decision-making which prevails over EU secondary legislation. Consequently, EU institutions[18] and EU Member States are obliged to apply the provisions of the Convention, when they make assessments according to the provisions of Directive 2001/42. Finally, the EU concluded the 'Protocol on strategic environmental assessment to the Convention on environmental impact assessment in a transboundary context'[19] which must also be applied.

1.3 THE CJEU'S INTERPRETATION OF DIRECTIVE 2001/42

Directive 2001/42 concerns plans and programs which are elaborated or adopted by an authority at national, regional or local level [Article 2(a)]. The CJEU clarified that also those plans or programs were covered by this provision which were adopted by the legislature.[20] The terms 'plan' or 'program' are not defined, neither in Directive 2001/42 nor elsewhere in EU law,[21] and are used, in EU law, without differentiation. In case C-225/13, the CJEU referred to plans as 'an organized and coherent system' for achieving the objectives of waste management.[22] This excluded the possibility to consider a single legislative provision which contained conditions under which derogation for landfills could be authorized as a plan. The amendment of a plan is also covered by Directive 2001/42 [Article 2(a)].[23] Such plans or programs are covered by the Directive, when they establish,

> "by defining rules and procedures for scrutiny applicable to the sector concerned, a significant body of criteria and detailed rules for the grant and

---

17   Decision 2005/370; the Aarhus Convention on access to information, public participation in decision-making and access to justice in environmental matters is reproduced in the Annex to that decision.

18   There are no binding provisions on the making of an environmental impact assessment of plans and programs that the EU institutions elaborate. However, the provisions of the Aarhus Convention regarding public participation also apply to EU plans and programs that are related to the environment, as the EU has ratified the Aarhus Convention which thus forms integral part of EU law [Article 216(2) TFEU], *see* Judgment of 8 March 2011, *Case C-240/09, Lesoochranárske zoskupenie VLK v. Ministerstvo zivotného prostredia Slovenskej republiky*, ECLI:EU:C:2011:125.

19   Decision 2008/871.

20   Judgment of 17 June 2010, *Joined Cases C-105/09 and C-110/09, Terre wallonne ASBL and Inter-Environnement Wallonie ASBL v. Région wallonne (Terre wallonne)*, ECLI:EU:C:2010:355, para. 41; Judgment of 22 September 2011, *Case C-295/10, Genovaité Valciukiene and Others v. Pakruojo rajono savivaldybé and Others (Valciukiene)*, ECLI:EU:C:2011:608. *See* also Article 4(1) of the Directive.

21   *See* Ludwig Krämer, *Casebook on EU Environmental Law*, London, 2002, p. 264.

22   Judgment of 9 April 2014, *Case C-225/13, Ville d'Ottignies-Louvain-la-Neuve and Others v. Région wallonne*, ECLI:EU:C:2014:245, para. 29.

23   *See also* Judgment of 10 September 2015, *Case C-473/14, Dimos Kropias Attikis v. Ypourgos Perivallontos, Energeias kai Klimatikis Allagis*, ECLI:EU:C:2015:582.

> implementation of one or more projects likely to have a significant effect on
> the environment."[24]

The term 'body of criteria and detailed rules' has to be understood qualitatively, not quantitatively, in particular in order to avoid attempts to circumvent the Directive's application by splitting the planning into several smaller parts.[25] The CJEU consistently held that the Directive's objective, to contribute to the objective of a high level of environmental protection, means that the provisions of the Directive have to be interpreted broadly and, consequently, any exception provided for has to be interpreted narrowly.[26] This approach led the Court to conclude that a plan or program is also 'required', when its adoption is not compulsory, but when the relevant legislative or regulatory provisions regulate details of the plan, such as the determination of the competent authorities or the procedure to be followed for the preparation of the plan. An exclusion of such cases would, in the opinion of the Court, unduly restrict the practical effect of Directive 2001/42 and would undermine the overall objective to ensure a high level of environmental protection.[27] For the same reasons, the Court concluded that the repeal of a plan or program could also have significant effects on the environment and was therefore covered by the Directive's provisions.[28]

When the national authority dealing with environmental matters which is, according to Article 6(3) of the Directive, to be consulted on the plan, is identical to the authority that elaborates the plan, the Member State in question is not obliged to set up, for the purposes of that consultation, a new body. However, responsibilities within the public authority for drawing up the plan and for giving expert advice during the consultation phase, must be functionally separated, in order to comply with Article 6(2).[29]

The CJEU held that the diversion of a course of a river did not constitute a 'plan', since it did not define criteria or detailed rules for the development of land or the implementation of subsequent projects.[30] In contrast, a decree which fixed a specific area, within which it was procedurally easier to realize infrastructure projects, was a 'plan' which was covered

---

24   *C-290/15, Valciukiene*, para. 69; settled case-law.

25   Judgment of 8 May 2019, *Case C-305/18, Associazione "Verdi Ambiente e Societá – Aps Onlus" (VAS) and "Movimento Legge Rifiuti Zero per l'Economia Circolare" Aps v. Presidente del Consiglio dei Ministri and Others (Verdi Ambiente)*, ECLI:EU:C:2019:384, para. 50; settled case-law.

26   *See e.g.* Judgment of 7 June 2018, *Case C-671/16, Inter-Environnement Bruxelles ASBL and Others v. Région de Bruxelles-Capitale (Inter-Environnement Bruxelles)*, ECLI:EU:C:2018:403.

27   Judgment of 22 March 2012, *Case C-567/10, Inter-Environnement Bruxelles ASBL and Others v. Région de Bruxelles-Capitale (Inter-Environnement Bruxelles)*, ECLI:EU:C:2012:159; settled case-law.

28   Id.

29   Judgment of 10 October 2011, *Case C-474/10, Department of the Environment for Northern Ireland v. Seaport (NI) Ltd and Others*, ECLI:EU:C:2011:681.

30   Judgment of 11 September 2012, *Case C-43/10, Nomarchiaki Aftodioikisi Aitoloakarnanias and Others v. Ypourgos Perivallontos, Chorotaxias kai Dimosion ergon and Others (Acheloos)*, ECLI:EU:C:2012:560.

by the Directive.[31] Likewise, a decree which concerned the regional and district planning of wind turbines, was considered to be a plan, as it set technical standards such as operating conditions ('shadow flicker'), measures to prevent accidents and fires, and the restoration of the landscape.[32] Furthermore, the CJEU considered provisions concerning the areas around buildings, the size and layout of buildings, construction-free areas, courtyards and garden areas, fences, hedges, boarding walls, the collection of rainwater, and vehicle access to buildings as indications that the measure under scrutiny in fact is a (town and country) plan. It held that such measures could influence the lighting, the wind inside agglomerations, the urban landscape, air quality, biodiversity, water management, emissions and the sustainability of buildings.[33]

The fact that a plan only covered one specific sector – in the specific case pig-rearing installations – did not exclude it from being covered by Directive 2001/42.[34] As regards a plan which affects a natural habitat or a bird habitat, the CJEU held that such a plan is only excluded from the scope of Directive 2001/42 and does not necessitate an environmental impact assessment, when it can be ascertained, 'on the basis of objective information' that the plan has no significant impact on the habitat.[35] The CJEU also pronounced itself on the consequences of a plan having been adopted without proper environmental impact assessment. It held that

> "courts, before which actions are brought in that regard [a plan or program having been adopted without an environmental impact assessment] must adopt, on the basis of their national law, measures to suspend or annul the 'plan' or 'program' adopted in breach of the obligation to carry out an environmental assessment."[36]

Consequently, it clarified that a provision of national law providing that a plan which had been adopted without the required environmental assessment, should nevertheless remain in force, was incompatible with Directive 2001/42, since it undermined the Directive's effects.[37]

31   Judgment of 7 June 2018, *Case C-160/17, Raoul Thybaut and Others v. Région wallonne*, ECLI:EU:C:2018:401.
32   *C-290/15, Valciukiene.*
33   *C-671/16, Inter-Environnement Bruxelles*, para. 57.
34   Id.
35   Judgment of 21 June 2012, *Case C-177/11, Syllogos Ellinon Poleodomon kai Chorotakton v. Ypourgos Perivallontos, Chorotaxias & Dimosion Ergon and Others (Syllogos Ellinon)*, ECLI:EU:C:2012:378.
36   Judgment of 28 February 2012, *Case C-41/11, Inter-Environnement Wallonie ASBL and Terre wallonne ASBL v. Région wallonne (Inter-Environnement Wallonie)*, ECLI:EU:C:2012:103, para. 46; Judgment of 18 April 2013, *Case C-463/11, L. v. M.*, ECLI:EU:C:2013:247, para. 43.
37   *C-463/11, L. v. M.*

In case *C-379/15*, the CJEU held that, exceptionally, a national decree which constituted a plan, but had not complied with the requirements of Directive 2001/42, could nevertheless be maintained in force for a specific period, for overriding environmental reasons. Otherwise, different implementing measures and decisions which had been based on the decree would also have to be annulled, which would run the risk of an increased impairment of the environment. The Court set, however, detailed restrictive conditions for such an exceptional possibility to maintain illegal national provisions in effect.[38] Similarly, the Court upheld a plan that dealt with the reduction of nitrogen in the environment under Directive 91/676[39] and complied with the requirements of that directive, but which had not been the subject of an environmental impact assessment under Directive 2001/42.[40] The Court insisted, however, that such a plan could only be maintained in force for the time necessary to make the impact assessment, and that its remaining in force was owed to the fact that its annulment would result in a legal vacuum, that it had no negative effects on the environment and that Directive 91/676 was complied with.

This Court jurisprudence does not answer all those questions which the monitoring of Directive 2001/42 raises. Some of these questions will be discussed below, without however providing an exhaustive discussion of all problems.

1.4   DEFINITION OF A PLAN

The general approach of the CJEU that the provisions of the Directive are to be interpreted broadly, in order to ensure a high level of environmental protection, means that in case of doubt and depending on their content, circulars and other measures may well be considered to be 'plans' in the meaning of the Directive.[41] The mentioning by the Court that a plan constitutes an organized and coherent system to achieve a certain result, completed by the requirement that rules and procedures are set for granting or the implementation of one or several projects, are essential elements in the definition of a plan. These aspects differentiate a plan (or program) from general legislation which regulates one or more sectors, but which does not necessarily set the framework for subsequent planning permissions for projects and which has, among others, informative and coordinating functions.[42]

---

38   Judgment of 28 July 2016, *Case C-379/15, Association France Nature Environnement v. Premier ministre és Ministre de l'Écologie, du Développement durable et de l'Énergie*, ECLI:EU:C:2016:103.

39   Directive 91/676 concerning the protection of waters against pollution caused by nitrates from agricultural sources.

40   *C-41/11, Inter-Environnement Wallonie.*

41   *See e.g.* the facts of the application for a preliminary ruling of the CJEU in case *C-24/19, A. and Others* (pending).

42   *See* also Advocate General Kokott in *Case C-43/18, Compagnie d'entreprises CFE SA v. Région de Bruxelles-Capitale, and C-321/18, Terre wallonne ASBL v. Région wallonne*, ECLI:EU:C:2019:56, para. 97.

A timetable, within which the objectives of the plan or program are to be attained, does not appear to be necessary. First, there may also be plans which have a permanent objective, for example plans to protect against floods. Second, if a time frame were required in order to have a plan come under the scope of Directive 2001/42, it would be easy to circumvent the application of the Directive, by not providing for such a timetable.

Directive 2001/42 addresses the Member States. It does not apply to plans or programs which are adopted by EU institutions. However, the Protocol to the Espoo Convention, mentioned above, concluded by the EU in 2008 and which forms thus part of EU law, provides for strategic environmental impact assessments for plans and programs that are required by legislative, regulatory or administrative provisions and which set the framework for future planning permissions (development consents) for projects.[43] If one applies also to such plans the above-mentioned jurisdiction by the CJEU setting forth when a plan is 'required',[44] numerous plans and programs adopted by EU institutions must undergo an environmental impact assessment, before they are adopted. Examples would be plans for energy-saving, programs in the agricultural sector or, generally, programs related to EU structural funds, plans for trans-European networks or on industrial standardization *etc.* In particular, Article 2(a) of Directive 2001/42 clarifies that also measures which are adopted by national or EU legislative acts, are covered by the Directive. An example for this is case *C-305/18*, where the CJEU declared a national legislation which laid down the framework for the construction of waste incineration installations, to be a plan under Directive 2001/42 which thus required an environmental impact assessment.[45] The relevance of this provision becomes clear, when the jurisdiction of the CJEU, also mentioned above, is taken into consideration, according to which a plan is illegal and must normally be declared void, if it was adopted without respecting the requirements of Directive 2001/42.[46]

The plan must be adopted by a public authority, an administration, a government or another legislative authority. Plans which are adopted by private bodies are not covered by Directive 2001/42. However, sometimes private bodies have quasi-public functions and may therefore be considered to be 'public authorities' under Directive 2001/42. The CJEU considers in its settled case-law a body to be associated to a public authority, when it fulfills a public service and was given, in order to fulfill its functions, specific powers which the body would normally not possess under private law.[47]

---

43   The list of projects which require such an environmental impact assessment, is slightly different from the list of projects under Directive 2011/92. The impact assessment of EU plans or programs will not further be discussed here.

44   *Case C-567/10, Inter-Environnement Bruxelles.*

45   *Case C-305/18, Verdi Ambiente.*

46   *Case C-463/11, L.v. M.*

47   Judgment of 19 December 2013, *Case C-279/12, Fish Legal and Emily Shirley v. Information Commissioner and Others*, ECLI:EU:C:2012:853; settled case-law.

1.5   ASSESSMENT OF PLANS AND ASSESSMENTS OF PROJECTS

Article 11 of Directive 2001/42 explicitly provides that an environmental impact assessment under the Directive shall be 'without prejudice' to any requirement under Directive 85/337 – now Directive 2011/92. This is logical, as the latter directive applies to specific projects, whereas Directive 2001/42 applies to plans and programs. Nevertheless, the distinction between a plan and a project is not always easily made. Examples for such a possible overlap are projects – all enumerated in Annex II to Directive 2011/92 – for urban development, the restructuring of rural land holdings, coastal work to combat erosion or holiday villages. The CJEU considered that a river diversion did not establish criteria and detailed rules for the development of land use which normally concerned multiple projects, and was therefore not subject to an assessment under Directive 2001/42.[48] In contrast, plans such as those which limit nitrates in waters,[49] waste management plans, noise reduction plans or plans to reduce the risk of floods may well be covered by Directive 2001/42.[50]

With regard to plans and programs that are mentioned in Article 6 of Directive 92/43, the CJEU clarified that the assessment under Directive 92/43 is limited to the question, whether the plan or program has a significant effect on the habitat in question.[51] If such an effect cannot be excluded on the basis of objective information, an impact assessment has to be made. However, all other potential effects which the plan or program may have outside the habitat – on air, water, land use, noise *etc.* – are not assessed by the assessment under Article 6 of Directive 92/43. Therefore, these effects must be the subject of another impact assessment under Directive 2001/42. An example could be an urban development plan outside a natural habitat, which may, however, have some impact on the protected site.

In contrast, a regulatory act which designates, under Directive 92/43, a special area of protection, setting objectives for the conservation of that area and certain measures of prevention, does not constitute a plan which comes under Directive 2001/42.[52]

---

48   *Case C-43/10, Acheloos*, referring to *C-567/10, Inter-Environnement Bruxelles*, para. 30.
49   *Joined Cases C-105/09 and C-110/09, Terre wallonne.*
50   COM(2017) 234, part 3. Relationship with other EU legislation and policy areas.
51   *Case C-177/11, Syllogos Ellinon.*
52   Judgment of 12 June 2019, *Case C-43/18, Compagnie d'entreprises CFE SA v. Région de Bruxelles-Capitale*, ECLI:EU:C:2019:483; similarly (when the regulatory act only sets conservation objectives for a habitat): Judgment of 12 June 2019, *Case C-321/18, Terre wallonne ASBL v. Région wallonne*, ECLI:EU:C:2019:484.

1.6   THE ENVIRONMENTAL REPORT

The environmental report that must be elaborated according to Article 5 of Directive 2001/42, shall 'identify, describe and evaluate' the likely significant effects that the implementation of the plan may have on the environment, as well as reasonable alternatives to the plan. Annex I to the Directive enumerates the aspects which are to be considered in the report. Of particular relevance is the fact that the 'significant effects' include "secondary, cumulative, synergistic, short, medium and long-term permanent, temporary, positive and negative effects" of the plan.[53]

As far as national plans are concerned, such requirements can hardly ever be complied with, unless a book is published on each plan. For example, the German plan to finish coal mining and the use of coal as fuel by 2038 at the latest, is certainly a plan that comes under Directive 2001/42, as regards the closing of coal and lignite mines. However the economic, social and environmental impact, its interrelationship with the ending of using nuclear energy, the construction of renewable energy installations, the electricity transport networks, the relocation of people, the land use including expropriations *etc.*, furthermore the impact of coal and alternative energies on soil, water, landscape, nature conservation, town and country planning, the mitigation measures envisaged, the zero alternative (not realizing the plan), all this over a period of some twenty years makes full compliance of the impact report with Article 5 and Annex I to the Directive something of a wishful thinking.

Of course, one might argue that the German plan to abandon coal as an energy source is not 'required'. However, Germany ratified the Paris Agreement on fighting climate change, is bound by numerous EU regulations and directives to reduce its greenhouse gas emissions and has itself several times publicly declared that it would renounce on the use of coal as quickly as possible. All this constitutes, in this author's opinion, a 'requirement' to take measures that reduce the use of coal in Germany. The Commission does not examine, whether the requirements of Article 5 are complied with.

1.7   PARTICIPATION AND CONSULTATION

Article 6 of Directive 2001/42 provides for the consultation on the draft plan of authorities concerned and of the public. This consultation shall take place early and shall be effective to allow the authorities and the public to express an opinion on the draft within appropriate time frames. The main problem with this provision is that it does not take into consideration the amendments which the Aarhus Convention brought to EU law. As mentioned, the provisions of that Convention are binding on the EU institutions and the Member States.

---

53   Directive 2001/42, Annex I.

The Convention requires the participation of the public in the elaboration of plans or programs, not only their consultation. 'Participation' constitutes, in contrast with 'consultation', a bilateral process: the public concerned shall be informed early, "when all options are open and effective participation can take place."[54] 'Effective participation' means that the information regarding the draft is made available to the public concerned in the language of the public, not only in English.[55] No discrimination as to nationality may take place[56] which means that Article 7 of Directive 2001/42 is not in accordance with other legal obligations arisen from EU law and international law. Indeed, this provisions suggests an intergovernmental consultation on plans which may affect the environment of another EU Member State – not any other neighboring State –, since citizens of the planning Member State are directly consulted; therefore, also the public of any neighboring country Party to the Aarhus Convention has the right to obtain appropriate information, the possibility to read the draft plan and the opportunity to issue an opinion on it, directly and not only via its Government. Finally, 'participation' means that the opinions of the public concerned are taken into consideration and that the final plan mentions why these comments were taken into consideration, or why not.

1.8   PLANS FOR THE TRANS-EUROPEAN NETWORKS

A particularly problematic area with regard to environmental impact assessments of plans and programs concerning energy and transport are the trans-European Network (TEN) plans and programs. Their legal bases are Articles 170 to 172 TFEU. For the implementation of these provisions, regulations were elaborated to establish a trans-European energy infrastructure[57] and a trans-European transport network.[58] Both Regulations, required under Article 172 TFEU, establish a framework for the realization of projects of common EU interest: energy projects are proposed by one of the twelve regional groups, in which Member States and the EU decide on the proposals to make: the proposals are then inserted into an EU-wide list of projects of common interest. Transport projects of EU common interest are listed directly in Regulation 1315/2013. The Regulations lay down procedures for realizing the projects and provide for financial means that are made available by the EU for such projects.

---

54   Aarhus Convention, Articles 7 and 6(4).
55   The EU Commission's consultations normally take place via internet and in one language only.
56   Aarhus Convention, Article 3(9).
57   Regulation (EU) No 347/2013 on the establishment of a framework for the identification, planning and implementation of energy projects of common [EU] interest.
58   Regulation (EU) No 1315/2013 on Union guidelines for the development of the trans-European transport network.

Both regulations thus fulfill the criteria of being plans that are related to the environment and should therefore, according to Article 7 of the Aarhus Convention and Directive 2001/42, have been the subject of a strategic environment impact assessment. The same applies to the proposals which are made by the regional groups of Member States for energy projects of EU interest, as these proposals are integrated into the general legislative EU plan. Insofar, a Commission Regulation on energy projects limits itself to state that, among others, environmental organizations were consulted on the proposals[59] – without any indication as to whether the public was consulted, when the consultations had taken place, what the content of the observations had been *etc.* In general, it is fair to state that the trans-European energy and transport projects have never been the subject of a strategic environmental impact assessment. A subsequent possible impact assessment of the specific project at national level cannot remedy this omission, as the lines, corridors and sometimes even the location of the projects have already been determined by the trans-European procedure at EU level. In 2003, the Commission had suggested to make, for trans-European projects, an EU-wide environmental impact assessment,[60] but this proposal had not been accepted by Member States.

An illustration of the problem is Commission Decision 2019/1118 on the linking of the rivers Seine (France) and Scheldt (Belgium).[61] The Decision lays down a considerable number of work on inland waterways in France and in Belgium, in particular the construction of a canal 'Seine-Nord Europe'; the construction of such a canal comes under Annex I or II to Directive 2011/92 on the environmental impact assessment of projects.

Decision 2019/1118 lays down in great detail what kind of work has to be carried out in France and in Belgium, enumerating overall 39 different work activities which have to be executed. For the canal, it determines the precise dates (months and year), in both countries, for the granting of a single environmental authorization, the start of the main work, the completion of the work and the commencement of the operation of the canal. In substance, the Decision constitutes a 'plan' according to Directive 2001/42. However, it does not contain any information on an environmental impact assessment having been made, or any consultation or participation of the public. It is an illusion to believe that the impact assessment will be made following the Commission Decision, as the agenda set for the different activities does not foresee the elaboration of an impact report, the consultation with the public *etc.*

---

59   *See e.g.* Commission Delegated Regulation (EU) 2018/540 as regards the Union list of energy projects of common interest, Recital (5).
60   COM(2003) 742.
61   Decision 2019/1118 on the Seine-Scheldt cross-border project.

1.9   MONITORING AND REPORTING

Article 10 of Directive 2001/42 provides that the Member States monitor the implementation of the plans and programs falling under the scope of the Directive, in order to identify in particular any unforeseen negative effects and to be able to take the appropriate remedial measure. However, Member States do not have any obligation to inform the Commission or the public on the results of their monitoring. Article 12(1) only provides that the Member States and the Commission exchange experience on the implementation of the Directive. Nothing is said on the frequency of such an exchange and nothing is known about the results of such an exchange.

The Commission was to report in 2006 and then every seven years on the implementation and effectiveness of the Directive [Article 12(3)]. Such reports were made in 2009 and 2017.[62] Both Commission reports are very vague as to the implementation of Article 10. The 2017 report does not record on any concrete monitoring measures undertaken such as the methodology used or the bodies entrusted with the monitoring, but only indicates that most Member States were unable to indicate the frequency of their monitoring measures and that Member States 'tend to use', where applicable, the monitoring systems set up under other directives.[63] The problem is that no information is available either on the monitoring of these other directives. It can thus be concluded with some certainty that the monitoring of Directive 2001/42 according to Article 10 does not take place in most Member States.

The Commission also reported that many Member States consider that the Directive is more effective when it comes to small scale or regional plans than for national plans.[64] This is plausible, as already the consultation process and the taking into consideration of opinions that were voiced by the public raise almost unsurmountable organizational difficulties with large projects.

Directive 2001/42 also applies to the plans and programs which Member States adopt under the EU Structural Funds.[65] In this regard, Regulation 1303/2013[66] provides that, where appropriate, the Member States shall take into consideration the requirements of Directive 2001/42 when they make an ex-ante evaluation of the programs which are to be co-financed by the EU. The Regulation does not provide for any specific sanction, so that the 'sanctions' of Directive 2001/42 apply: according to the CJEU a plan or program that was adopted without the impact assessment under the Directive having been made, is normally to be declared void. The Commission reported that 'most' of the national plans

---

62   COM(2009) 469 and COM(2017) 234.
63   The report mentions the water framework Directive, Directive 92/43 and the industrial emissions Directive.
64   COM(2017) 234, part 5. Effectiveness of the SEA Directive.
65   Directive 2001/42, Article 3(9).
66   Regulation 1303/2013 laying down common provisions on the EU Structural Funds, Article 55.

and programs under the Structural Funds complied with the requirements of Directive 2001/42,[67] without giving the slightest details on the number of plans and programs, the number of impact assessments made and the number where such an impact assessment was not made, the public consultation, the publication of the impact report *etc*. Of course, the Commission also failed to report, whether it took any measures, when a Member State had failed to carry out the environmental assessment under Directive 2001/42.

1.10   Concluding Remarks

According to the Commission, there is a general conviction within the EU that the environmental impact assessment procedure, established by Directive 2001/42 "is more effective, if there is the political will to effectively influence the planning process."[68] The general broad formulation of Directive 2001/42 and the general character of several of its provisions certainly lead to the conclusion that this statement is correct. Directive 2001/42 shares, in this regard, the impact of numerous pieces of EU environmental legislation: if there is a political will in the administrative, political and judicial instances of the Member States – at national, but also at regional and local level – to effectively apply the provisions of EU environmental law, this law has the capacity of preserving and significantly improving the protection of the environment, *i.e.* of water, air and soil, fauna and flora, climate, cultural heritage *etc.*, including, last but not least, the health and well-being of humans. When this political will is lacking, EU environmental directives and regulations offer ample opportunities to avoid the protection obligations. The enforcement powers of EU institutions are not strong enough to counterbalance any such lack of political will.

Article 12(3) of Directive 2001/42 evokes the eventuality of an amendment of the Directive in light of the experience made with its application. After more than fifteen years of application, the question might be posed, what amendments to the Directive would appear timely and reasonable. Some proposals are submitted hereafter.

i.   The first aspect that springs to mind is the accountability of the Member States. Member States should be obliged to report at regular intervals – Article 12 of the directive refers to an interval of seven years – on the application of the Directive and of their national transposing provisions. This report need not necessarily be sent to the European Commission, but should be made public,[69] so that the interested or

---

67   Commission, COM(2017) 234, Section 4.
68   Id. Section 5.
69   *See* also Article 5(5) of the Aarhus Convention: "Each Party shall take measures within the framework of its legislation for the purpose of disseminating, *inter alia*: *(a)* [...] progress reports on their [legislation and policy documents] implementation." Directive 2003/4 on public access to environmental information,

concerned public is aware, if and to what extent the provisions of Directive 2001/42 are actually applied.

ii. Also, the legislation adopted by the Member States to transpose Directive 2001/42 into the national legal order should be made available to the public. In the electronic age, it is not comprehensible, why the Commission does not make these texts available on its website. As there is a question of EU legislation and its implementation, it is not sufficient that the transposing texts are available in national or regional official publication. Indeed, the question, whether the Directive was properly implemented is of interest to all EU citizens.

iii. The anachronistic provision of Article 7 of the Directive on transboundary consultations which is, as mentioned above, not in compliance with the provisions of the Aarhus Convention, should be replaced by a version which gives citizens in a neighboring country – be it an EU Member State or not – which are likely to be significantly affected by a plan or a program, the direct right to give an opinion or voice objections to a draft plan. It is wrong to pass via the neighboring government for such a consultation. After all, the environment has no frontiers.

iv. It should be clearly stated in an amended text that a plan or program which is covered by the Directive, but which was adopted without an environmental assessment, is as a main rule not valid. This consequence, already clearly pronounced by the CJEU, would act as a powerful deterrent to disregard the requirements of the Directive.

It can be gleaned from the above that none of these suggestions intends to change the planning responsibility of the Member States in favor of the EU. The suggestions rather intend to better clarify, what the different responsibilities are. Already today, a responsible Member State could implement the different suggestions in its national legislation.

Directive 2001/42 is a useful planning instrument which helps integrate environmental requirements into the elaboration and implementation of sectoral policies, such as agriculture, fisheries, energy, transport, town and country planning *etc.* At a time, when the environmental challenges for the Member States, the EU itself and even for the whole planet are greater than ever in the past, the full use of this instrument by all planning authorities would be a sign of determination to effectively try protect our common heritage which constitutes the environment.

Article 7(2): "The information to be made available and [systematically] disseminated shall be updated as appropriate and shall include at least: […] *(c)* progress reports on the implementation of […] Community, national, regional and local legislation on the environment or relating to it."

2   SUSTAINABLE DEVELOPMENTS IN FOREIGN INVESTMENT LAW AND POLICY

Related to Renewable Energy and Climate Change Mitigation and Adaptation

Marie-Claire Cordonier Segger*

Keywords
sustainable development, climate change mitigation, Paris Agreement, renewable energy law, ICSID

Abstract
Sustainable development is gradually integrated into policies worldwide, meanwhile, government authorities and policymakers, alongside public and private enterprises, are signaling the growing scope and scale of investment opportunities in this field. Capital cuts and decreasing generating costs are fueling the market in renewable technologies. At the same time, bilateral and multilateral treaties are being negotiated, which set the framework for expanding sustainable solutions: treaty regimes increasingly encourage and promote trade and investment for more sustainable energy development, responding to global concerns on climate change. Investment protection litigation offers new insights into trends in jurisprudence, demonstrating how this field of law can be instrumental not only for protecting undertakings' interests, but holding countries to their commitments under international treaties for the protection of the environment.

2.1   INTRODUCTION

The risks and global impacts of climate change are gaining significance and priority throughout the world, with the majority of countries and enterprises working to redirect investment flows towards more sustainable, low-carbon development pathways, while others face a rising tide of potentially costly litigation on climate change. As reflected in

---

*   Marie-Claire Cordonier Segger: senior director, Centre for International Sustainable Development Law (CISDL); professor of law, University of Waterloo, Canada. Sincere thanks and recognition are due to Sean Stephenson, CISDL research fellow, for his excellent legal research, substantive insights, and significant contributions to drafting this piece. Thanks and acknowledgements are also due to Natalia Kubesch, CISDL researcher, for her excellent legal research and insights on current trends in climate litigation and in the interpretation of the Paris Agreement on climate change.

the Paris Agreement on climate change and its new Katowice Rulebook,[1] the growing global importance of harnessing higher levels of investment and financing renewable energy and climate mitigation technologies, as well as climate adaptation and resilience, has never been clearer nor more pressing. Indeed, as specific investment needs are being defined and refined in the National Determined Contributions (NDC) that each country intends to achieve under the Paris Agreement,[2] many government authorities and policy-makers, alongside public and private enterprises, are signaling the growing scope and scale of investment opportunities in this field.

In 2017, for the 8th year running, global investment in renewable energy exceeded USD 240 billion. Last year's total of USD 279.8 billion was 2% higher than the 2016 equivalent, but still significantly lower than the all-time high in 2015 of USD 323.4 billion. Drastic reductions in capital and generating costs for renewables have been instrumental in creating a bigger market for these technologies.[3] Thus, renewable generation capacity increased by +8.3%, continuing the trend of 8-9% annual capacity growth in recent years.[4]

In its landmark report 'Investing in Climate – Investing in Growth,' the OECD noted that to meet the targets set out in the global Sustainable Development Goals (SDGs), and to achieve the high international ambition of the Paris Agreement, exponential increases are essential for investment in low-carbon green growth, including climate-smart projects and infrastructure, particularly in developing countries.[5]

2.2 INNOVATIONS IN INVESTMENT LAW & POLICY RELATED TO CLEAN ENERGY, CLIMATE CHANGE AND SUSTAINABLE DEVELOPMENT

An intriguing and observable trend of investment law innovations can be tracked in multilateral, bilateral and national policy in relation to clean energy and climate change. Moreover, several important investment awards were rendered related to renewable energy and the environment, sending key signals to markets.

---

1   Paris Agreement, signed on 12 December 2015, entry into force on 4 November 2016, Article 2.1(c).
2   For the interim NDC Registry *see* https://unfccc.int/process/the-paris-agreement/nationally-determined-contributions-ndcs#eq-2.
3   UNDP & Bloomberg Finance and Frankfurt School, *UNEP Centre Global Trends in Renewable Energy Investment 2018*, at http://fs-unep-centre.org/sites/default/files/publications/gtr2018v2.pdf.
4   International Renewable Energy Agency (IRENA), *Renewable capacity highlights, March 2018*, at http://sun-connect-news.org/fileadmin/DATEIEN/Dateien/New/RE_capacity_highlights_2018.pdf.
5   OECD, *Investing in Climate, Investing in Growth, June 2017*, at https://read.oecd-ilibrary.org/economics/investing-in-climate-investing-in-growth_9789264273528-en#page3.

2.2.1   Treaty & Policy Developments

Several bilateral treaties are under negotiation and entering into force, including chapters and provisions of specific relevance to SDG 7 on access to affordable and clean energy and SDG 13 on bold action on climate change. Many other provisions in these treaties, among a growing collection of further 'next generation' regional and bilateral trade and investment treaties being crafted this decade, also seek to contribute to various other targets of the 17 SDGs.[6]

The Comprehensive Economic and Trade Agreement (CETA) between Canada and the EU provisionally entered into force in 2017,[7] and includes a chapter linking trade and sustainable development, in which Parties

> "recognize that economic development, social development and environmental protection are interdependent and mutually reinforcing components of sustainable development, and reaffirm their commitment to promoting the development of international trade in such a way as to contribute to the objective of sustainable development, for the welfare of present and future generations,"[8]

and also related chapters on trade and the environment[9] and on trade and labor.[10] Several provisions are of direct relevance to clean energy and climate change. At 22.1.3, Parties commit to

> "enhance enforcement of their respective labor and environmental law and respect for labor and environmental international agreements; [and to] promote the full use of instruments, such as impact assessment and stakeholder consultations, in the regulation of trade, labor and environmental issues and encourage businesses, civil society organizations and citizens to develop and implement practices that contribute to the achievement of sustainable development goals."

---

6   Marie-Claire Cordonier Segger, *Crafting Trade and Investment Agreements for Sustainable Development: Athena's Treaties*, Oxford University Press, 2019 (forthcoming).

7   For a list of the provisions that entered into force *see* Canada Gazette, Vol. 151(1), Order Fixing 21 September 2017 as the Day on which the Act Comes into Force, other than Certain Provisions, at http://gazette.gc.ca/rp-pr/p2/2017/2017-09-07-x1/html/si-tr47-eng.html.

8   *Canada-European Union Comprehensive Economic and Trade and Agreement* (CETA) signed October 30, 2016, provisionally entered into force on 21 September 2017, Chapter 22 Trade and Sustainable Development.

9   CETA, Chapter 24 Trade and Environment.

10   CETA, Chapter 23 Trade and Labor.

Further, under Article 22.3.2 Parties affirm that "trade should promote sustainable development. Accordingly, each Party shall strive to promote trade and economic flows and practices that contribute to enhancing decent work and environmental protection […]." Further, at 22.3.3, they highlight the importance of assessing the potential economic, social and environmental impacts of possible actions under the treaty, taking account of stakeholder views. Each Party "commits to review, monitor and assess the impact of the implementation of this Agreement on sustainable development in its territory in order to identify any need for action" also opening the possibility for joint assessments.[11]

Of direct relevance, under 24.9.2, the Parties commit, consistent with their international obligations to

> "pay special attention to facilitating the removal of obstacles to trade or investment in goods and services of particular relevance for climate change mitigation and in particular trade or investment in renewable energy goods and related services."

In addition, under 24.12.1, the Parties prioritize

> "trade-related aspects of the current and future international climate change regime, as well as domestic climate policies and programs relating to mitigation and adaptation, including issues relating to carbon markets, ways to address adverse effects of trade on climate, as well as means to promote energy efficiency and the development and deployment of low-carbon and other climate-friendly technologies; […] trade and investment in environmental goods and services, including environmental and green technologies and practices; renewable energy",

and also "promotion of life-cycle management of goods, including carbon accounting and end-of-life management…" They also undertake, under 24.10.2a,

> "in a manner consistent with their international obligations to: *(i)* encourage trade in forest products from sustainably managed forests and harvested in accordance with the law of the country of harvest; *(ii)* exchange information, and if appropriate, cooperate on initiatives to promote sustainable forest management, including initiatives designed to combat illegal logging and related trade […]",

---

11   *See* Markus Gehring *et al.*, 'Sustainability Impact Assessments as Inputs and as Interpretative Aids in International Investment Law', *Journal of World Investment and Trade*, Vol. 17, 2017, p. 155.

an innovation that if implemented, to incentivize investment and trade, could deliver co-benefits for climate change.[12] They seek "improved understanding of the effects of economic activity and market forces on the environment; and exchange of views on the relationship between multilateral environmental agreements and international trade rules." Taken together, these commitments suggest CETA's potential to support the implementation of Article 2.1c of the Paris Agreement on climate change under the UN Framework Convention on Climate Change (UNFCCC) and related provisions,[13] as well as other accords that seek to promote climate action and sustainable development of renewable energy.[14] To encourage implementation, under Article 24.13 Parties commit to take into account the activities of relevant multilateral environmental organizations, and establish a mechanism whereby the new Committee on Trade and Sustainable Development serves as a focal institution within the organization for discussion, cooperation and implementation of these provisions.

In Chapter 22, Parties also emphasize that the rights and obligations outlined in the labor and environmental chapters are to be taken into account by the Parties as part of an integrated approach on trade and sustainable development.[15] This guides interpretation, for instance in the context of future investment disputes.[16] The Vienna Convention requires that treaties be interpreted in light of their object and purpose,[17] and the Parties' objectives for the CETA encompass the promotion of sustainable development. In the treaty, Parties also reinforce the need for transparency,[18] and commit to an ongoing dialogue on trade and sustainable development,[19] creating a Committee on Trade and Sustainable Development which will oversee the implementation of the environment and labor chapters.[20] This Committee can refer implementation to a Panel of Experts established to examine any

---

12   For further discussion *see* Marie-Claire Cordonier Segger *et al.*, 'REDD+ Instruments, International Investment Rules and Sustainable Landscapes', *in* Christina Voigt (ed.), *Research Handbook on REDD+ and International Law*, Edward Elgar, 2016, pp. 347-389.

13   *See e.g.* Marie-Claire Cordonier Segger, 'Advancing the Paris Agreement on Climate Change for Sustainable Development', *Cambridge International Law Journal*, Vol. 5, Issue 2, 2016, p. 202; Marie-Claire Cordonier Segger, 'Sustainable Development through the 2015 Paris Agreement', *Canadian International Lawyer*, Vol. 11, Issue 2, 2017, p. 124.

14   Although CETA does not explicitly mention reducing fossil fuel subsidies in the same as, for instance, the EU-Singapore FTA, Chapter 12, Section C, & Annex 12-A at Article 13.11(3). *See* Markus Gehring *et al.*, *Climate Change and Sustainable Energy Measures in Regional Trade Agreements (RTAs): An Overview*, at www.ictsd.org/sites/default/files/downloads/2013/08/climate-change-and-sustainable-energy-measures-in-regional-trade-agreements-rtas.pdf.

15   CETA, Article 22.1(2).

16   Id. Article 29.17.

17   Vienna Convention on the Law of Treaties, entered into force 27 January 1980, *see* Marie-Claire Cordonier Segger, 'Inspiration for Integration: Interpreting International Trade and Investment Accords for Sustainable Development', *Canadian Journal of Comparative and Contemporary Law*, Vol. 3, Issue 1, 2017, p. 159.

18   CETA, Article 22.2.

19   Id. Article 22.3.

20   CETA, Chapter 26, at Article 26.2.1(g).

concerns and provide recommendations for their resolution. If the final report of the Panel of Experts determines that a Party has not complied with its obligations, the Parties shall engage in discussions and shall endeavor, within three months of the delivery of the final report, to identify an appropriate measure or, if appropriate, to decide upon a mutually satisfactory action plan. Such provisions suggest that the approach of Europe and Canada has evolved from earlier trade and investment plus environment/labor, into a more nuanced focus on cooperation and integrated commitment to incentivize trade and investment that will support sustainable development, sending important signals to investors and others that the treaty seeks to encourage climate-related trade and investment. In essence, rather than staying mute or ignoring challenges, treaty regimes increasingly explicitly encourage and promote trade and investment for more sustainable energy development and are expected to respond to global concerns on climate change.

2.2.2   Investment Treaty Disputes

Several interesting investor-state awards are also being issued, including an important award in relation to European renewable energy disputes, as well as awards related to counterclaims based on human rights violations and environmental damage. Moreover, among the still pending cases, in two disputes the investors are challenging the governments' decision to introduce restrictions on offshore oil and gas activity.[21]

Investment disputes relating to European renewable energy continue to emerge, with new claims also becoming public. In these cases, claimants had invested significantly in renewable energy programs which would arguably further global SDGs related to climate change mitigation (SDG 13) and clean, affordable energy (SDG 7). When these programs were substantially changed or administered in a manner contrary to treaty standards by governments that had committed to incentivize renewables, the investors pursued their economic rights to enforce standards of conduct and government behavior.

To date there have been at least 40 cases brought against Spain in the wave of litigation by solar power and other eco-investors,[22] and with many cases of important relevance for

---

21   *Rockhopper Exploration Plc, Rockhopper Italia S.p.A. and Rockhopper Mediterranean Ltd v. Italian Republic*, ICSID Case No. ARB/17/14; *Lone Pine Resources Inc. v. The Government of Canada*, ICSID Case No. UNCT/15/2.

22   *OperaFund Eco-Invest SICAV PLC and Schwab Holding AG v. Kingdom of Spain*, ICSID Case No. ARB/15/36; *EDF ENERGIES NOUVELLES (France) v. Kingdom of Spain*; *FREIF Eurowind Holdings Ltd v. Kingdom of Spain* SCC, Case No. 2017/060; *Green Power K/S Y Obton A/S (Denmark) v. Kingdom of Spain*, SCC, Case No. V2016/135; *Greentech Energy System A/S, Foresight Luxembourg Solar 1 S.A.R.L., Foresight Luxembourg Solar 2 S.A.R.L., GWM Renewable Energy I S.P.A, GWM Renewable Energy II S.P.A v. Kingdom of Spain*; *The PV Investors v. Spain*, UNCITRAL; *Charanne (the Netherlands) and Construction Investments (Luxembourg) v. Spain*, SCC; *Isolux Infrastructure Netherlands B.V. v. Spain*, SCC; *Eiser Infrastructure Limited and Energia Solar Luxembourg S.à.r.l. v. Spain*, ICSID Case No. ARB/13/36; *CSP Equity Investment S.à.r.l. v.*

the security of renewable energy investments.[23] There are also at least seven disputes against the Czech Republic,[24] and at least seven disputes against Italy.[25] Non-legal NGO commentators suggest that such cases, were they to be resolved for the full amounts claimed, would be worth over USD 9.5 billion.[26] As such, these disputes are a warning for states looking to encourage foreign investment in their renewable energy sectors.[27] The cases suggest that even in the absence of specific representations by the state, an investor may rely on the fair and equitable treatment standard when subjected to fundamental changes in the state's

Spain, SCC; _RREEF Infrastructure (G.P.) Limited and RREEF Pan-European Infrastructure Two Lux S.à.r.l._ _v. Spain_, ICSID Case No. ARB/13/30; _Antin Infrastructure Services Luxembourg S.à.r.l. and Antin Energia Termosolar B.V. v. Spain_, ICSID Case No. ARB/13/31; _Masdar Solar & Wind Cooperatief UA v. Spain_, ICSID Case No. ABR/14/01.

23   _NextEra Energy Global Holdings B.V. and NextEra Energy Spain Holdings B.V. v. Spain_, ICSID Case No. ABR/14/11; _InfraRed Environmental Infrastructure GP ltd. et al. v. Spain_, ICSID Case No. ABR/14/12; _RENERGY S.à.r.l. v. Spain_, ICSID Case No. ABR/14/18; _Stadtwerke München GmbH, RWE Innogy GmbH et al. v. Spain_, ICSID Case No. ARB/15/1; _RWE Innogy GmbH and RWE Innogy Aersa S.A.U. v. Spain_, ICSID Case No. ARB/14/34; _STEAG GmbH v. Spain_, ICSID Case No. ABR/15/4; _9REN Holding S.a.r.l v. Spain_, ICSID Case No. ARB/15/15; _BayWa r.e. Renewable Energy GmbH and BayWa r.e. Asset Holding GmbH v. Spain_, ICSID Case No. ARB/15/16; _Cube Infrastructure Fund SICAV and Others v. Spain_ ICSID Case No. ARB/15/20; _Matthias Kruck and Others v. Spain_, ICSID Case No. ARB/15/23; _KS Invest GmbH and TLS Invest GmbH v. Spain_, ICSID Case No. ARB/15/25; _JGC Corporation v. Spain_, ICSID Case No. ARB/15/27; _Cavalum SGPS, S.A. v. Spain_, ICSID Case No. ARB/15/34; _E.ON SE, E.ON Finanzanlagen GmbH and E.ON Iberia Holding GmbH. v. Spain_, ICSID Case No. ARB/15/35; _SolEs Badajoz GmbH v. Spain_, ICSID Case No. ARB/15/38; _Hydro Energy 1 S.à.r.l. and Hydroxana Sweden AB v. Spain_, ICSID Case No. ARB/15/42; _Watkins Holdings S.à.r.l. and Others v. Spain_, ICSID Case No. ARB/15/44; _Landesbank Baden-Württemberg and Others v. Spain_, ICSID Case No. ARB/15/45; _Eurus Energy Holdings Corporation and Eurus Energy Europe B.V. v. Spain_, ICSID Case No. ARB/16/4; _Alten Renewable Energy Developments BV v. Spain_, SCC; _Sun-Flower Olmeda GmbH & Co KG and Others v. Spain_, ICSID Case No. ARB/16/17; _Infracapital F1 S.à.r.l. and Infracapital Solar B.V. v. Spain_, ICSID Case No. ARB/16/18; _Sevilla Beheer B.V. and Others v. Spain_, ICSID Case No. ARB/16/27; _Portigon AG v. Kingdom of Spain_, ICSID Case No. ARB/17/15; _Novenergia v. Spain_, SCC; _DCM Energy GmbH & Co. Solar 1 KG and Others v. Kingdom of Spain_, ICSID Case No. ARB/17/41.

24   _Antaris Solar and Dr. Michael Göde v. Czech Republic_, PCA; _Jürgen Wirtgen, Stefan Wirtgen, Gisela Wirtgen and JSW Solar (zwei) GmbH & Co. KG v. Czech Republic_, PCA Case No. 2014-03; _Natland Investment Group NV, Natland Group Limited, G.I.H.G. Limited, and Radiance Energy Holding S.A.R.L. v. Czech Republic_; _Voltaic Network GmbH v. Czech Republic_, PCA; _ICW Europe Investments Limited v. Czech Republic_, PCA; _Photovoltaik Knopf Betriebs-GmbH v. Czech Republic_, PCA; _WA Investments-Europa Nova Limited v. Czech Republic_, PCA.

25   _VC Holding II S.a.r.l. and Others v. Italy_, ICSID Case No. ARB/16/39; _ESPF Beteiligungs GmbH, ESPF Nr. 2 Austria Beteiligungs GmbH, and InfraClass Energie 5 GmbH & Co. KG v. Italy_, ICSID Case No. ARB/16/5; _Eskosol S.p.A. in liquidazione v. Italy_, ICSID Case No. ARB/15/50; _Belenergia S.A. v. Italy_, ICSID Case No. ARB/15/40; _Silver Ridge power BV v. Italy_, ICSID Case No. ARB/15/37; _Blusun SA, Jean-Pierre Lecorcier and Nichael Stein v. Italy_, ICSID Case No. ARB/14/03; _Greentech Energy Systems and Novenergia v. Italy_, SCC 2015.

26   Luke Peterson, 'As Another Spain Award Looms, Four More Previously-Confidential Renewable Cases Surface; Potential Liability For All Pending Claims Now Exceeds $9.5 Billion', _Investment Arbitration Report_, 7 February 2018.

27   Richard Power & Paul Baker, 'Energy Arbitrations', _The European Arbitration Review_, 2018, at https://globalarbitrationreview.com/insight/the-european-arbitration-review-2018/1148943/energy-arbitrations.

regulatory regime. Thus, states ought to be careful not to alter their regulatory landscapes in the renewable energy sectors too drastically so as not to unreasonably withdraw promised incentives or fail to provide investors with the time necessary to meet new standards.[28]

In the decisions in *Charanne*[29] and *Isolux*[30] in 2016, Spain was successful in defending its measures against the claims made by investors. These were followed shortly by the *Eiser* decision in 2017, however, in which the claimant was successful and was awarded USD 140 million in lost profits from their investment in a Concentrated Solar Power (CSP) project.[31] The tribunal considered that the continuous regulatory changes approved by the Spanish Government, including the sudden cuts to the Feed-in Tariff regime for the photovoltaic sector introduced by the Spalma-Incentivi Decree, were in violation of Article 10(1) of the Energy Charter Treaty (ECT).[32] The Tribunal noted that although the ECT did not grant Eiser the right to expect a fixed legal regime, they did have a legitimate expectation that regulatory measures would not destroy the value of their investment. The evidence showed that Spain had changed its regulatory regime in 2013/2014 in a drastic fashion. It adopted and implemented an entirely new regulatory approach, "applying it to existing investments in a manner that washed away the financial underpinnings of the claimants' investments."[33] The new regime was based on different assumptions, and utilized a new and untested regulatory approach, all intended to significantly reduce subsidies to existing plants.[34]

Moreover, a decision was rendered for some of the claims against Czech Republic relating to its solar program. In *Jürgen Wirtgen, Stefan Wirtgen, Gisela Wirtgen and JSW Solar (zwei) GmbH & Co. KG v. Czech Republic*, the Czech Republic successfully defended its measures against further claims, despite arbitrator Gary Born's strong dissent.[35] In an

---

28   *See* at www.wfw.com/wp-content/uploads/2017/06/Investor-succeeds-in-ECT-renewable-energy-arbitration-Eiser-v-Spain.pdf.

29   *Charanne B.V. and Construction Investments S.a.r.l. v. Spain*, SCC Case No. 062/2012.

30   *Isolux Infrastructure Netherlands B.V. v. Kingdom of Spain*, SCC Case No. 2013/153.

31   *Eiser Infrastructure Limited and Energia Solar Luxembourg v. Spain*, Award of 4 May 2017, Annulment Application registered 28 July 2017.

32   *Eiser Infrastructure Limited and Energia Solar Luxembourg S.A.R.L v. Kingdom of Spain*, Award, ICSID Case No. ARB/13/36, 26 April 2017. The Award was recognized in the Southern District of New York through an *ex parte* procedure, although in November of 2017 the order recognizing the award in New York was challenged and vacated. Judge Lewis A. Kaplan relied on two second circuits decisions that found that the Foreign Sovereign Immunities Act did not permit the use of summary *ex parte* enforcement procedures, and that the Petitioners were, instead, required to file a plenary action to enforce their ICSID award; *see Mobil Cerro Negro, Ltd. v. Bolivarian Republic of Venezuela*, 863 F.3d 96, 2d Cir., 2017, *Micula v. Government of Romania*, 2d Cir., 23 October 2017.

33   *Eiser Infrastructure Limited and Energia Solar Luxembourg S.A.R.L v. Kingdom of Spain*, Award, ICSID Case No. ARB/13/36, 26 April 2017, para. 389.

34   Id. paras. 389-393.

35   *Jürgen Wirtgen, Stefan Wirtgen, Gisela Wirtgen and JSW Solar (zwei) GmbH & Co. KG v. Czech Republic*, PCA Case No. 2014-03.

attempt to encourage the production of electricity from renewable sources of energy, the Czech Republic issued a Support Scheme providing incentives of a guaranteed feed-in tariff (FIT), originally for 15 and later 20 years and tax incentives. According to the claimants, they made investments in solar photovoltaic plants relying on the explicit guarantees and incentives in this scheme. In 2009 and 2010 the Czech Republic amended the Support Scheme, the amendments consisted of 26 per cent solar levy and withdrawal of tax exemption. The Claimants argued that the amendments gave rise to breaches of their legitimate expectations, guaranteed inter alia under the FIT clause. The tribunal held that there could only be a violation if legitimate expectations generated by specific commitments are affected.[36] The majority, however, held that there was no separate guarantee of an absolute FIT price level, set independently of the guarantees of a payback of capital expenses and an annual return on investment. The tribunal held that the guarantees of return to investors as the groundwork of the renewable energy promotion regime had been complied with by the Czech Republic and as such the majority held there was no breach of legitimate expectations: the claimants continued to receive a level of revenue that ensured a payback of capital expenses and a return on investment over a period of 15 years.[37] In his dissent, Born rejected the majority's finding. He argued that the Czech Republic had provided a plain and unequivocal statutory guarantee for a fixed FIT for the duration of the investment and the claimants invested relying on this guarantee. The entire regime was a commitment guaranteed by the state and should therefore not be amended.

Finally, in addition to the renewable energy cases, Ecuador's successful counterclaim in *Burlington Resources v. Ecuador* for environmental damage has important implications for the consideration of climate change in investment disputes.[38] Burlington Resources acquired and operated the exploration and development of oilfields in Ecuador. While the jurisdiction of the counterclaim was initially challenged, it was later agreed by the parties to adjudicate the counterclaim to limit parallel proceedings and multiple decisions.[39] The tribunal found that domestic Ecuadorian law was applicable, notably as contained in several Ecuadorian Supreme Court decisions and that this contained a strict liability provision for environmental damage. The tribunal found damage at 40 sites across two oil fields and in its damages, analysis assessed the cost of remediation. In total Ecuador was awarded USD 41 million for infrastructure and environmental damage.[40] Notable in this case is the tribunal's willingness to engage in a substantial analysis of Ecuadorian environmental law remediation obligations.

---

36 Id. paras. 436-437.
37 Id. para. 469.
38 *Burlington Resources Inc. v. Republic of Ecuador, Decision on Counter-Claims*, ICSID Case No. ARB/08/5, 7 February 2017.
39 Id. para 6.
40 Id.

These renewable energy cases are emerging as a forceful reminder of the importance of an integrated and balanced approach to achieving sustainable development, indicating that investment law can act to frustrate but also to foster sustainable energy investment. Further, these cases raise questions about how to provide legal frameworks necessary to catalyze renewable energy investment, while avoiding unduly costly corporate subsidies, and allowing public policies to respond to changing circumstances in terms of government priorities, fiscal constraints, and market dynamics. They suggest that investment law is solely neither sword nor shield for measures to respond to climate change and to promote clean, renewable energy. Rather, in each dispute, there is a need to make a sound case.[41]

2.3   RECENT CLIMATE LAW & POLICY TRENDS AFFECTING INVESTMENTS

The UNFCCC negotiations on modalities and guidelines for Paris Agreement implementation are important for both future development of investment law and for climate and energy policy. While the guidelines are not yet concluded and agreed by the 'Conference of the Parties serving as the Meeting of the Parties to the Paris Agreement' (CMA), certain advances have been achieved, particularly with regards to climate mitigation, adaptation and transparency.[42]

On transparency actions, the Paris Agreement in Article 13 requires that all Parties 'shall' provide national inventory reports and submit information that allows tracking the progress towards achievement of their Nationally Determined Contributions to the objectives of the treaty. Parties 'should' further provide information on climate change related impacts and adaptation. Parties' reports on mitigation action and support will undergo technical expert view. In Paris, the Parties accepted that "the transparency framework shall provide flexibility" to developing countries.[43] However, in Bonn, Parties were divided as to whether the transparency framework should be a single system, with

---

41   For further discussion *see e.g.* Marie-Claire Cordonier Segger & Markus Gehring, 'Overcoming Obstacles with Opportunities: Trade and Investment Agreements for Sustainable Development', *in* Stephan W. Schill *et al.* (eds.), *International Investment Law and Development: Bridging the Gap*, Edward Elgar, 2015; Marie-Claire Cordonier Segger, 'Innovative Legal Solutions for Investment Law and Sustainable Development Challenges', *in* Yulia Levashova *et al.* (eds.), *Bridging the Gap Between International Investment Law and the Environment*, Eleven International Publishing, 2015. *See* also Marie-Claire Cordonier Segger & Markus Gehring, 'Climate Change and International Trade and Investment Law', *in* Rosemary Reyfuse & Shirley V. Scott (eds.), *International Law in the Era of Climate Change*, Edward Elgar, 2013. And *see* Marie-Claire Cordonier Segger *et al.*, 'Conclusions: Promoting Sustainable Investment through International Law', *in* Marie-Claire Cordonier Segger *et al.* (eds.), *Sustainable Development in World Investment Law*, Kluwer Law International, 2012.

42   This analysis is due to the helpful legal research and excellent scholarly drafting work of Natalia Kubesch, researcher at CISDL.

43   Paris Agreement, Article 13(2).

all countries working to meet the same standings, or whether it should be an extension of existing UNFCCC transparency arrangements, with separate rules and processes for developed and developing countries.[44] Alternatively, only some obligations could be common to all, such as those on reporting and technical review.[45] While the Parties were able to agree on one document in Bonn, they were unable to reduce the number of possible options for the future transparency framework.[46]

Overall, adaption-related information has certain advantages for investors, and for public investment authorities seeking to encourage financial flows to key sectors. For instance, such transparency can help Parties understand whether international adaptation finance is effective and to learn from each other on how to increase infrastructure, agriculture, renewable energy or other investments to levels required for meeting climate mitigation and adaptation objectives.[47] During the negotiations in Bonn in May 2017, 29 countries were undergoing peer review. These countries publicly answered questions about the steps they are taking to reduce greenhouse gas emissions and build resilience. For instance, India offered an intervention on the benefits of this "facilitative sharing of views", presenting an ambitious target to achieve renewable energy capacity of 175,000 MW by 2022 mostly solar power plants, with the Jawaharlal Nehru National Solar Mission (100,000 MW) being central to achieving this target. Developed and developing countries alike were interested in how India advanced this energy policy in a short timeframe and how the federal government was working with local governments and the private sector, including investors.[48]

Moreover, greater transparency encourages confidence and trust among Parties to the Paris agreement enabling the learning from experiences in an open way.[49] As such, allowing for discretionary reporting may be problematic for investment in case it impedes the emergence of a clear picture of the international climate finance landscape.[50] Furthermore, greater transparency can also impact dispute settlement processes. The Paris Agreement assists states to consider and verify each other's contributions to climate change, and as

44 Romain Weikmans & J. Timmons Roberts, *Pocket Guide to Transparency under the UNFCCC*, ECBI, 2017, p. 36.

45 Sumit Prasad *et al.*, *Enhanced Transparency Framework in the Paris Agreement: Perspective of Parties*, Council on Energy, Environment and Water, New Delhi, 2017.

46 Ad Hoc Working Group on the Paris Agreement Fourth part of the first session Bonn, 7-15 November 2017, Agenda items 3-8, FCCC/APA/2017/LA/Add.3, 15 November 2017.

47 Weikmans & Roberts 2017, p. 36.

48 Jennifer Huang, 'Why Transparency Makes the Paris Agreement a Good Deal', *Center for Climate and Energy Solutions July 2017*, at www.c2es.org/2017/07/why-transparency-makes-the-paris-agreement-a-good-deal/.

49 Kate Cook, 'Chapter 15', *in* Wendy Miles (ed.), *Dispute Resolution and Climate Change: The Paris Agreement and Beyon*d, International Chamber of Commerce, 2017.

50 Weikmans & Roberts 2017, p. 34.

such heightens accountability.[51] State actions increasingly come under scrutiny, as the transparency framework provides countries and wider stakeholders with information on national decisions, on regulations, investments, and measures to protect local populations or the way companies are regulated. States or private entities may decide to study and rely on this information in challenging states' failure to comply with their responsibilities under the Paris Agreement, or to otherwise provide reasonable measures to address climate change. For investors, the implication is centrally one of increased risk for those still insisting on obsolete technologies and fuels. As such, greater transparency can trigger dispute settlement proceedings regarding state's non-compliance with mitigation/adaptation commitments. Indeed, there is the possibility that the transparency required under climate agreements can facilitate claims under investment treaties by private investors based on failure to abide by mitigation/adaptation-related commitments.

However, in terms of investor-state arbitration, the question arises whether this dispute settlement process will further or impede the objectives of the Paris Agreement.[52] Although disputes directly challenging environmental standards are rare, as the climate space continues to grow, climate related or adjacent disputes related to contract and market mechanisms may expand. One question that remains is whether disputes between states and private entities will drive fragmentation in international law, and not give sufficient weight to the importance of delivering tailored, country specific NDCs.

In addition, regarding compliance, Article 15 establishes a mechanism 'to promote compliance' with the Agreement. This mechanism should take the form of a geographically balanced twelve-member Expert Committee. Overall, Parties generally appear to agree that the compliance procedure should be "facilitative, transparent, non-adversarial and non-punitive."[53] However, in 2017, there were conflicting views as to whether the Committee should have a more active role, should receive information directly or through other bodies or be able to define its own rules.[54] Several Parties made it clear that they do not seek the Committee to act as a dispute resolution or judicial system and/or apply penalties or sanctions.[55] The concern appears to be that a strong compliance mechanism could restrict national climate change policy decisions, or, for developing countries, that developed countries use such mechanisms – especially when containing the possibility of sanctions – to adversely impact their economic development and opportunities for investments that

---

51 Kate Cook, 'Arbitration and Climate Change – Wendy Miles QC, Kate Cook and Angeline Welsh', *The Law of Nations Podcast*, November 2017.

52 Id.

53 Paris Agreement, Article 15(2).

54 Wolfgang Obergassel *et al., An Assessment of the 23rd Climate Conference COP23 in Bonn*, Wuppertal Institut für Klima, Energie GmbH, February 2018, p. 7.

55 Id.

would negatively impact on the world's climate.[56] The lack of compliance mechanisms and as such the voluntary non-binding nature of NDCS, arguably allows for the rapid scaling up of commitments over time as compared to binding, enforceable obligations.[57]

Finally, in Bonn in 2017, certain Parties seemed comfortable with the idea of a self-trigger, *i.e.* Parties initiating cases with respect to themselves, but less so with allowing Parties to bring one another before the Committee.[58] Thus, the questions of if and how this Committee will respond to cases of non-compliance remain still unsettled. The negotiation rounds indicate that the Committee will lack compulsion except through reputational costs arising from its reports. As such, the Committee does not provide a forum for conflict resolution, either for state-state or investor-state disputes. To some, such a compliance mechanism coupled with a self-trigger and discretionary transparency obligations raises the concern that Parties may be able to evade their obligations under the Paris Agreement.

Further, other international treaty regimes and institutions continued to foster climate friendly investment. For example, the Kigali Amendment to the Montreal Protocol, which directly seeks to discourage investments in ozone-depleting substances that are also likely to have serious effects on global climate change,[59] passed its ratification threshold in 2017. The accord, which seeks to phase down climate-warming hydrofluorocarbons (HFCs) under the Montreal Protocol on Substances that Deplete the Ozone Layer, will enter into force on 1 January 2019. Firms that produce and use coolants in their products will need to develop alternative technologies in order to gain access to a new global market for replacement coolants and continue to participate in the growing market for refrigerators and air conditioning. States committed to phase out HFCs gradually by more than 80 percent over a 30-year period, along four tracks of 'Article 5 Parties' which reflect nuanced differences between nations, particularly their varying economic circumstances, reliance on HFC technologies, and the cost of alternative technologies. Many high-income countries will cut HFCs from 2019, consuming no more than 15 percent of their 2011-2013 averaged baseline emissions by the year 2036. States will receive support through the Montreal Protocol's Multilateral Fund. Montreal Protocol transitions from controlled substances to new alternatives have often been completed ahead of schedule. The incentive for countries to ratify and comply with the Kigali Amendment is strong. Following the Montreal Proto-

---

56 Peter Lawrence & Daryl Wong, 'Soft Law in the Paris Climate Agreement: Strength or Weakness', *Review of European, Comparative & International Environmental Law*, November 2017.

57 Id.

58 Centre for Climate and Energy Solutions, *'Outcomes of the U.N. Climate Change Conference in Bonn'*, December 2017, at www.c2es.org/site/assets/uploads/2017/11/outcomes-of-the-u-n-climate-change-conference-in-bonn.pdf.

59 Kigali Amendment, Montreal Protocol to the Vienna Convention on Substances that Deplete the Ozone Layer.

col's practice of restricting trade in controlled substances between parties and non-parties, the amendment foresees implementing trade restrictions on HFCs with non-parties by 2030, provided that at least 70 countries have ratified the deal. The protocol's trade element is an innovative feature that has ensured very broad support for the accord and all its amendments, as ICTSD has noted.[60] The Kigali Amendment is estimated to prevent up to 0.5 degrees Celsius in global warming above pre-industrial levels by the end of the century.

As an additional note, the International Civil Aviation Organization (ICAO) further progressed in its climate investment policy. This included advances in the negotiation and refinement of a new Carbon Offsetting and Reduction Scheme for International Aviation (CORSIA), which has the potential to raise important revenues for climate finance, and to change the direction of future investments in aviation towards the adoption of renewable fuels and practices.[61]

2.4   RECENT TRENDS IN CLIMATE CHANGE LITIGATION

Of potential relevance to investors, and international law on investment, several major climate change litigations are being advanced, with the first few 'wins' in a growing flood of lawsuits. Indeed, some 884 climate change cases had been filed by March 2017 in 24 countries in Africa, Asia, Pacific, Europe and the Americas. The US had the highest number of cases (654) according to the survey carried out by the UN Environment Programme and the University of Columbia Law School's Sabin Center for Climate Change Law.[62]

A new wave of cases is emerging which query the roles of states, as well as public and private enterprise, in implementing climate change laws and policies to prevent dangerous impacts.[63] The judicial decisions and court filings reveal several trends with implications for investment policies.

First, a tendency to focus claims on the failures of institutions and nations to respond adequately to climate change can be observed.[64] The Paris Agreement is emerging as a novel anchorage for lawsuits of this kind, giving shape and legal significance to national

---

60   ICTSD reporting, 'Montreal Protocol Celebrates Another Milestone as Agreement to Reduce Climate-Warming Gases Is Set to Enter into Force in 2019', *UN Environment*, 20 November 2017; 'McKenna Says Amendment Signed to Montreal Protocol', *CBC News*, 20 November 2017; 'Treaty to Phase Out 'Greenhouse Gasses on Steroids' to Enter Force', *The New York Times*, 17 November 2017; 'Kigali Amendment to the Montreal Protocol Enters into Force in 2019', *The New York Times*, 19 November 2017.
61   ICAO, CORSIA, at www.icao.int/environmental-protection/Pages/market-based-measures.aspx.
62   Sabin Center for Climate Change Law, Climate Change Database: US and Non-US Climate Change Litigation.
63   Wendy J. Miles QC & Nicola K. Swan, 'Climate Change and Dispute Resolution', *Dispute Resolution International*, Vol. 11, Issue 2, 2017, pp. 117-132.
64   Jacqueline Peel, 'Issues in Climate Change Litigation', *Carbon & Climate Law Review*, Vol. 5, 2011, pp. 15-24.

mitigation commitments.[65] Moreover, the Agreement seems to provide momentum within a growing climate law and governance community.[66] Examples of cases falling within this category include the *Vienna Schwechat Airport Expansion*[67] case, where several NGOs persuaded the Austrian Administrative Court that the expansion of the Vienna airport would jeopardize the emission reductions targets set forth *inter alia* in the Paris Agreement.

This case illustrates how domestic lawsuits may be used as 'climate swords' to promote more progressive climate law and regulation. These domestic legal actions, whatever their outcomes, can provide certainty and predictability on domestic climate frameworks on which investors may base investment decisions. If successfully challenged, states are obligated a further honor international obligation towards climate change mitigation and may, as a result, incentivize investments into renewable energy or discourage or even ban investment activities that prove to be harmful to the environment. While concerns may be raised that domestic climate lawsuits could trigger investment claims if judicial decisions generate legal changes that disadvantage fossil fuel industry players, since a successful outcome could oblige a government to suspend guarantees or promises made to investors, there are questions about whether a carbon-intensive investment, in light of the Paris Agreement and other discussions above, is truly in 'like circumstances' to investment which supports renewables and other low-carbon pathways.[68]

Second, cases are increasingly focusing on constitutional rights to a clean and healthy environment, seeking to hold authorities accountable for violation of universal values of human rights, and more specifically, domestic climate policies.[69] Thus, recent lawsuits on climate change have not only provided a judicial forum to further greater 'physical and social understanding of climate change',[70] but also indicate a trend towards a human rights framework and approach.[71] However, the success rate of these cases has been mixed. While

---

65 Id.

66 *The Status of Climate Change Litigation – A Global Review*, UNEP, May 2017, p. 10.

67 *Vienna Airport Expansion*, W109 2000179-1/291E, Federal Administrative Court, Austria, 2 February 2017.

68 For further discussion, *see e.g.* Cordonier Segger & Gehring 2013; Marie-Claire Cordonier Segger & Markus Gehring, 'Making Progress? Climate Change, Sustainable Development and International Trade and Investment Law', *in* David Freestone & Charlotte Streck (eds.), *Legal Aspects of Carbon Trading: Kyoto, Copenhagen and Beyond*, Oxford University Press, 2009, and Marie-Claire Cordonier Segger, 'Sistemas de inversión y comercio para economías bajas en emisiones de carbono más sustentables', *in* Pilar Moraga Sariego (ed.), *Nuevo Marco Legal para el Cambio Climático*, LOM, Santiago, 2009.

69 Climate Law & Governance Initiative (CLGI), in partnership with the UN Framework Convention on Climate Change (UNFCCC), at www.climatelawgovernance.org/. *See* also *Policy Brief: Global Trends in Climate Change Legislation and Litigation 2017*, Grantham Research Institute on Climate Change and the Environment, March 2017. This repository of climate litigations worldwide pegs the number of cases globally at 250 across 25 different jurisdictions.

70 Elizabeth Fisher, 'Climate Change Litigation, Obsession and Expertise: Reflecting on the Scholarly Response to Massachusetts v. EPA', *Law and Policy*, Vol. 35, Issue 3, 2013, pp. 236-260.

71 Jacqueline Peel and Hari M. Osofsky, 'A Rights Turn in Climate Change Litigation?', *Transnational Environmental Law*, Vol. 7, Issue 1, 2018, pp. 37-67.

national courts may find for the climate and for peoples' rights in accordance with the local law, some remain reluctant to find violations by governments. This trend, of course, could be directly relevant to risk analysis among investors already facing concerns and reputational losses in relation to their human rights records. For instance, in March 2017 an Irish environmental charity challenged a council's decision to issue a five-year extension to the Dublin Airport Authority for their planning permission to construct a new runway.[72] While the Court recognized "a personal constitutional right to an environment under the Irish Constitution", it did not find any violation of this right. It was observed that the exercise of powers in the present case did not constitute any departure from the objectives set out in the Climate Action and Low Carbon Development Act 2015, which the petitioners had alleged to be breached by the impugned conduct. Similarly, in *Greenpeace Norway v. Government of Norway*, the Oslo District Court rejected the NGO's argument that Norway's oil and gas exploration in the Arctic violates citizens' right to a clean environment, despite finding that such right was protected by the Constitution.[73] In contrast, South Africa's High Court accepted the claimants' argument that in failing to consider climate change-related impacts when approving the building of a coal plant, the government had violated fundamental rights. It therefore invalidated the plant's approval.[74] This sends a message to governments and developers/investors proposing projects, especially in the fossil fuel sector, with potentially significant climate change impacts in South Africa, that permission for such projects is contingent upon proper climate change impact assessments.

Overall, these cases raise questions as to the extent to which relying on rights-based approaches is becoming more common among those challenging governments' failure to mitigate climate change, the impact of which may even be exacerbated by state decisions to allow private entities to conduct environmentally harmful activities. Significantly, these cases reveal a potential tension between state's constitutional obligations towards their citizens as interpreted by domestic courts, and their investment treaty commitments towards international investors.

Third, claimants have brought cases against individual emitters, alleging that their environmentally harmful activities have caused them particular injuries. This category encompasses cases brought by private individuals and by state authorities against private corporations. In *Lliuya v. RWE*, a Peruvian farmer sued the German energy firm RWE, seeking USD 21,000 towards flood damage prevention from glacial melt caused by the company's contribution to climate change. On appeal in November 2017, his demand was held "admissible", allowing the case to proceed into the evidentiary phase.[75] The case sug-

---

72 *Friends of the Irish Environment CLG v. Fingal County Council*, 21 November 2017, No. 201 JR.
73 *Föreningen Greenpeace Norden & Natur og Ungdom v. The Government of Norway through the Ministry of Petroleum and Energy*, Case No. 16-166674TVI-OTIR/06.
74 *Earthlife Africa Johannesburg v. Minister of Environmental Affairs and Others*, ZAGPPHC (2017) 65662/16.
75 Beschluss des 5. Zivilsenats des Oberlandesgerichts Hamm vom 01.02.2018 in dem Rechtsstreit Lliuya.

gests that private companies can be held liable for climate change-related damages of their greenhouse gas emissions. This recognition may prove to be significant to a number of recently filed climate litigation cases in the US. In these cases municipalities and state or provincial governments are suing private enterprises for their contribution to climate change, or non-governmental organizations or individuals sue governments or public enterprises for failing to fulfill climate obligations under national and international laws and conventions respectively.[76] Notable cases include New York City suing Shell, Exxon Mobil Corporation and others, claiming that they are responsible for damage caused due to flooding during storm Sandy;[77] and *County of San Mateo v. Chevron Corp* involving an action by Californian local governments seeking damage and other relief from fossil fuel companies for sea level rise, focusing on Chevron[78] and British Petroleum.[79] Such cases generated high interest during the UNFCC 23rd Conference of the Parties in 2017, presided by Fiji in Bonn, Germany, including the Climate Law and Governance Day symposium, where negotiators and senior officials from highly climate vulnerable countries and legal advisors to investors and the climate finance community, debated the implications for investment flows in relation to risk, liability and due diligence.

Overall, the willingness of domestic courts to hear cases against corporations causing climate-related damage adds pressure for change in industry practices and implicates investment decision-makers. Indeed, as a result of growing pressure from civil society, governments and the judiciary, investment and capital markets have begun to feature climate change as a significant risk factor. Certain enterprises and analysts characterize the systemic nature of climate risk by exploring multiple avenues through which risk or threat of climate change materializes, highlighting 'litigation risks' in particular.[80] While some might posit that markets shall simply adjust themselves or make necessary amends to accommodate the new pressures and risk categories, for instance deciding liability for fiduciary duties owed to investments,[81] more research is needed to uncover the influence of climate litigation on investment decision-making. Both public and private enterprises

---

76 Dena P. Adler, *U.S. Climate Change Litigation in the Age of Trump: Year One*, Sabin Center for Climate Change Law, Columbia Law School, 2018.

77 *New York City Sues Shell, ExxonMobil and Other Oil Companies Over Climate Change*, at www.washington-post.com/news/energy-environment/wp/2018/01/10/new-york-city-sues-shell-exxonmobil-and-other-oil-majors-over-climate-change/?utm_term=.95770433c1d8.

78 *County of San Mateo v. Chevron Corp and Others*, Case No. 17 CIV 03222, Cal, filed 17 July 2017.

79 *People of the State of California v. BP PLc and Others*, Case No. 3:17-cv-06012-WHA.

80 *Cf. Navigating Climate Risk*, CERES, September 2013, at https://static1.squarespace.com/static/57c0a650197aea879e3a81ef/t/58261ad3e6f2e16e929e1130/1478892253649/Navigating+Climate+Risk-+Ceres'+Primer+for+Family+Offices.pdf; *Climate Change Scenarios – Implications for Strategic Asset Allocation*, Mercer, 2011, at www.ifc.org/wps/wcm/connect/6b85a6804885569fba64fa6a6515bb18/ClimateChangeSurvey_Report.pdf?MOD=AJPERES.

81 Sarah Barker *et al.*, 'Climate Change and the Fiduciary Duties of Pension Fund Trustees – Lessons from the Australian Law', *Journal of Sustainable Finance and Investment*, Vol. 6, Issue 3, 2016, p. 211.

and institutional investors among others, are placing priority on understanding and responding to climate litigation risks, including through changes in investment decisions.[82] For example, the Task Force on Climate related Financial Disclosure,[83] set up by the G20, post-Paris Agreement, recommended that corporations should disclose their climate-related financial risk alongside other financial and securities risks. This recommendation has been seconded by the EU High Level Expert Group on Sustainable Finance,[84] and the UK Green Finance Task Force[85] both of which are looking to bring these recommendations into law in the next few years. In addition, shareholder activism, including shareholder resolutions requiring enterprise to reduce greenhouse gas emissions, to divest from fossil fuels, or to switch to clean energy, may be further shaping investment decision-making.[86]

State actions ranging from the introduction of climate laws, to the promotion of collaborative policies to decelerate investment in obsolete fossil fuels such as coal, suggest states' growing interest in decoupling economic development from emissions, with more participation from the private sector, including investors. Such polices include encouraging investments in renewables, providing subsidies and scaling up funding for innovation in clean energy technologies, and other actions.[87] A twenty-fold increase in legislation on climate change is reflective that the public in many countries supports, indeed is driving this trend.[88] While some may accuse courts of judicial overreach, the vast increase in climate litigation on all continents suggests that citizens and consumers in many countries expect the judiciary to hold governments, private and public enterprises accountable, in the absence of any other mechanism.

2.5   CONCLUSIONS

Certain sustainable development progress is being made in international investment law, as international law and policy further prioritized the need to make finance flows consistent with a pathway towards low greenhouse gas emissions and climate- resilient development,

---

82   Sarah Barker & Kurt Winter, 'Temperatures Rise in the Boardroom: Climate Litigation in the Commercial Arena', *Australian Environment Review*, Vol. 32, Issue 3, 2017, p. 62.

83   *See* at www.fsb-tcfd.org/.

84   *See* at https://ec.europa.eu/info/publications/180131-sustainable-finance-report_en.

85   *See* at http://greenfinanceinitiative.org/workstreams/green-finance-taskforce/.

86   Mark Allen *et al., Climate Change and Capital Markets*, The Steyer-Taylor Center for Energy Policy and Finance, 2015, pp. 22-23.

87   *Cf. Investment Grade Climate Change Policy: Financing the Transition to the Low Carbon Economy*, UNEP Finance Initiative, 2011, at www.unepfi.org/fileadmin/documents/Investment-GradeClimateChangePolicy.pdf; *Briefing Paper Submitted to G7 and G20: 'Governments Urged to Maintain Momentum on Climate Action'*, CERES, July 2017, at www.ceres.org/sites/default/files/Briefing-Paper-for-G20.pdf.

88   *Policy Brief: Global Trends in Climate Change Legislation and Litigation 2017*, Grantham Research Institute on Climate Change and the Environment, March 2017.

as per the UNFCCC Paris Agreement, and to take bold action on climate change, as outlined in the global Sustainable Development Goals. New investment-related developments in trade, climate change, ozone and aviation instruments, also renewables and climate related investment arbitrations and domestic litigations, illustrate both progress and remaining gaps in climate law and governance.

More broadly, recent developments suggest that the world has reached the crossroads. All sectors of society can either contribute to the solutions, or become obsolete and increasingly, face litigation for the harm that they cause. International law and policy have the power and the potential to either foster or frustrate prompt and effective action on climate change. There is an important opportunity to strengthen and bolster investment in climate, renewable energy, and as such, to support sustainable development. In this regard, it is critical to continually update international and domestic legal regimes to ensure that they are supportive of renewable, green and sustainable development in a carbon-constrained world. With multiple sustainable developments in international investment law and policy, as well as in climate law and policy, there is an opportunity to bolster investment in renewable energy, and climate mitigation and adaptation. It is hoped, taking the risks and urgency emphasized by the IPCC in its recent Report on the need to keep warming below 1.5 degrees worldwide, that nations will seize the day.

3   The Case of the Hungarian Constitutional Court with Environmental Principles

From Non-Derogation to the Precautionary Approach

*Gyula Bándi**

Keywords

Constitutional Court of Hungary, environmental issues, non-derogation principle, precautionary principle, Article P of the Fundamental Law of Hungary, right to a healthy environment

Abstract

Principles influence legislation, implementation and enforcement of the law to a great extent. This is especially the case with those fields of law, which are relatively new and subject to constant changes, such as environmental law. Principles have legal value, among others to fill legal gaps or to assist proper interpretation. It is always expedient to have a high-level judicial forum for legal interpretation at national level this would be a constitutional court or a supreme court. Legal interpretation can be particularly tricky when principles are combined with human rights. Constitutional courts, such as the Hungarian Constitutional Court are the preferred choice for such legal interpretation, since human rights are normally enshrined in the constitutions. In Hungary both the previous (1989) Constitution and the currently effective Fundamental Law of 2011 contain express and rather similar provisions regarding the right to environment, the content of which need clarification. Beside this similarity, the Fundamental Law has several other additional provisions supporting interpretation in the interests of the environment. This paper only presents – as examples of necessary interpretation – two principles to illustrate what the right to environment actually means. These are the non-regression (non-derogation) and the precautionary principles, which will be described both in general and in light of their current Hungarian interpretation. Non-regression (non-derogation) basically represents a decent minimum that should not be contravened, while precautionary principle is more

---

*   Gyula Bándi: Jean Monnet professor of law, Pázmány Péter Catholic University, Budapest; Ombudsman for future generations.

in flux, a moving target, focusing on likely consequences, with scientific uncertainty at its core. Both principles will be introduced through the decisions of the Hungarian Constitutional Court.

3.1 30 YEARS OF THE CONSTITUTIONAL COURT, 25 YEARS OF HIGHLIGHTING ENVIRONMENTAL RIGHTS

2019 marks the 30th anniversary of the establishment of the Constitutional Court of Hungary. The 1949 Constitution was amended in October 1989 in order to create the foundations of democratic change, among others to insert this new institution into the system of public institutions and law. Act XXXII of 1989 on the Constitutional Court entered into force on 30 October 1989. The Court commenced its activity on 1 January 1990. Here I do not wish to discuss neither the history, nor case-law of the Court in detail, but restrict myself to analyzing its practice in the field of environmental rights. More specifically, I shall focus on two major legal principles emerging as constitutional principles of the past 25 years since the first environmental case of the Court was decided in 1994. These two principles aptly illustrate the vision of the Court in connection with the interpretation of the right to environment: *(i)* the non-derogation principle, which has been present already at the very beginning of Hungarian constitutional jurisprudence and still mentioned in almost all environmental related cases. This principle may also be articulated as the minimum, the baseline of requirements, a threshold not to be crossed. Meanwhile, *(ii)* the precautionary principle manifested in 1992 as Principle 15 of the Rio Declaration[1] and enshrined in Article 130r(2) of the Maastricht Treaty at the same year and emerges in the most recent cases of the Court. In contrast with the former principle, the precautionary approach represents a different vision, a moving target, requiring more activity, changing the well-known direction of legal interpretation.

3.2 THE VALUE OF LEGAL PRINCIPLES IN THE FIELD OF ENVIRONMENTAL PROTECTION

Before going into the details of the Court's practice regarding these principles, it is worth recalling in a nutshell, why legal principles are imperative in the field of environmental law. "The legal principles reflect an overarching concept that environmental protection is a matter of public or common concern."[2] Or from another perspective:

---

1   The Rio Declaration on Environment and Development, at www.unesco.org/education/pdf/RIO_E.PDF.
2   Alexandre Kiss & Dinah Shelton, *Manual of European Environmental Law*, Grotius Publications, 1993, p. 36.

"[a] principle 'expresses a general truth, which guides our action, serves as a theoretical basis for the various acts of our life, and the application of which to reality produces a given consequences'."[3]

Certainly, the most intriguing question is the true legal character of these principles. Although doubts[4] may remain about the binding nature of principles, most legal scholars agree that

"A principle is undoubtedly a candidate for legal effect, if it is contained in a law or sublegal norm. The legislator must however have intended to give the principle such effect."[5]

De Sadeleer takes a similar approach when considering the significance of principles: they have a guiding, orienting role, beyond their purpose as a theoretical backdrop.[6] The CJEU, placing a general emphasis on the role of principles in connection with the water framework directive, underlined the importance of principles of law in general, including principles of national law:[7]

"34.[…] In particular, the existence of general principles of constitutional or administrative law may render superfluous transposition by specific legislative or regulatory measures provided, however, that those principles actually ensure the full application of the directive by the national authorities and that, where the relevant provision of the directive seeks to create rights for individuals, the legal situation arising from those principles is sufficiently precise and clear and that the persons concerned are put in a position to know the full extent of their rights and, where appropriate, to be able to rely on them before the national courts."

---

3   Philippe Sands, *Principles of International Environmental Law*, Cambridge 2003, p. 233. (referring to the *Gentini* case of 1903).

4   "As regards the principles of Art. 174(2.2) EC, they constitute, in my opinion, general guidelines for Community environmental policy, but not binding rules of law which apply to each individual Community measures; nor do they contain an obligation to take specific measures in favor of the environment." Ludwig Krämer, *EC Environmental Law*, Sixth Edition, Thomson-Sweet and Maxwell, London, 2007, p. 15.

5   Gerd Winter, 'The Legal Nature of Environmental Principle in International, EC and German Law', *in* Richard Macrory *et al.* (eds.), *Principles of European Environmental Law*, Europa Law Publishing, Groningen, 2004, p. 13.

6   Nicolas de Sadeleer, 'Environmental Principles, Modern and Post-modern Law', *in* Id. p. 232.

7   Judgment of 30 November 2006, *Case C-32/05, Commission v. Grand Duchy of Luxemburg*, ECLI:EU:C:2006:749.

3.3 FROM THE 1989 AMENDMENT OF THE CONSTITUTION TO THE FUNDAMENTAL LAW – THE NON-DEROGATION PRINCIPLE

After these brief introductory remarks, I come back to the right to environment, mentioned first as a potential human right in Hungary in the first environmental act – Act II of 1976. Section 2(2) reads: "Every citizen has the right to live in an environment worthy of man." This unprecedented provision had never been implemented before or even interpreted by any forum; yet it constitutes the first reference to such a human right in Hungary. Following many years of silence on this issue, the amended Constitution in 1989[8] provided for the right to environment in two separate articles: *(i)* Article 18 stated that "The Hungarian Republic recognizes and implements everybody's right to a healthy environment.", while *(ii)* Article 70/D(2) also mentioned environmental protection as an instrument for safeguarding the right to the highest level of mental and physical health, together with healthy working conditions, the management of the health care system and ensuring the conditions for regular physical training.

Due to their general phrasing, these articles had to be interpreted in order to give them teeth, *i.e.* enforceable legal consequences. The only forum empowered to interpret constitutional provisions such as the ones cited above, was the newly established Constitutional Court. The first and most important case, where the Court interpreted the right to a healthy environment was Decision No. 28/1994. (V. 20.) AB.[9] The case in question concerned a plea of unconstitutionality of statutory provisions that had the potential to curtail nature conservation areas. Furthermore, it threatened natural resources by opening up nature conservation areas for privatization without foreseeing any limitations or obligations to balance environmental interests. The Court stated that although private ownership of nature conservation areas in itself is legal, the act in question was lacking the necessary obligations and limitations on the use of such property.

A major argument was found in environmental rights. According to the Court the level of protection in the field of environment and nature conservation should not be restricted, unless the implementation of other constitutional values or fundamental rights are the issue. Thus, the Court held that there must be a balance between environmental rights and other constitutional values or fundamental rights. The entire decision hinged on the constitutional right for environment.

The decision states that the right to a healthy environment constitutes an obligation for the state to establish and maintain the specific system of institutions to protect this

---

8   *See* the English translation of the former Hungarian Constitution at www2.ohchr.org/english/bodies/cescr/docs/E.C.12.HUN.3-Annex2.pdf.

9   Decision No. 28/1994. (V. 20.) AB, ABH 1994, 134, *see* in English at https://huncourt.hu/uploads/sites/3/2017/11/en_0028_1994.pdf.

right. These legal and organizational institutions are necessary for the implementation of this right as the mere stipulation of the right is far from enough. The decision also emphasizes that the real subject of the right is humanity and nature. This very first environment-related decision also stresses that the level of protection is not at the discretion of the state, since this protection constitutes the foundations of human life and the harm to the environment is usually irreparable. The necessity of a certain level of protection requires a strict legal regime. Consequently, while the state is free to choose from the means and methods of protection, it enjoys no freedom in allowing for any form or even risk of environmental degradation.

One paragraph of the decision explains that prevention takes priority over sanctions in the field of environmental protection. Prevention as a requirement can only be effective in case the legal framework for effective protection is in place. The lack of such preventive measures was one of findings of the decision. As to the merits of the case, it meant that private ownership of nature conservation areas could not be considered unconstitutional in itself, but taken together with the lack of necessary legal institutions to replace the special protection regime guaranteed by the controlled and central management of state ownership, it may well contravene nature conservation interests. Sanctions and mere prohibitions in this situation are insufficient, however, since guarantees to help avoid environmental degradation are lacking. Limiting or risking the given level of protection through unclear privatization rules and property relations, without a system of preventive measures is unconstitutional. This is known as the prohibition of setback or step backwards (non-derogation principle).

Several other decisions could also be mentioned from the Constitutional Court's jurisprudence, such as for example, Decision No. 48/1997. (X. 6.) AB.[10] This case was also related to nature conservation. The Court stated among others that the need to protect natural resources is based on objective conditions. Damage to nature may destroy finite resources, which often cannot be restored. As such, the lack of protection may trigger irreversible processes. Therefore, the qualitative or quantitative adaptation of protection to changing economic and social conditions is not permissible (in contrast with social and cultural rights, where temporary restrictions may later be remedied). The implementation of the right to environment requires not only that the present level of protection is maintained, but also that the state should never take a step backwards in the level of protection, *i.e.* towards liability-based protection instead of preventive measures.

An additional element enshrined in Decision No. 48/1998. (XI. 23.) AB[11] should also be mentioned, conveying the very same message. This decision dealt with the protection

---

10   Decision No. 48/1997. (X. 6.) AB, ABH 1997, 502.
11   Decision No. 48/1998. (XI. 23.) AB, ABH 1998, 333, *see* in English at https://huncon-court.hu/uploads/sites/3/2017/11/en_0048_1998.pdf.

of fetal life, but at the same time, it made comparisons with other human rights. The Constitutional Court referred to the right to environment as an analogue concept, which is also rooted in the right to life. According to the Court both the right to health and the right to a healthy environment serve the health of future generations. The right to a healthy environment sets forth the duty of the state as a constitutional right. These types of rights preclude any oscillation, unlike for example social rights, the implementation of which may well depend on the wealth and financial capacity of the state at any given time. Meanwhile, other rights, such as the right to environment, may not ebb and flow with changing circumstances.

Some decisions discussed the problems of conflicting human rights, such as the conflict between property rights and the right to environment. In its Decision No. 106/2007 (XII. 20.) AB,[12] the Court examined the possibilities for the constitutional limitation of human rights. The Court underlined that the proportionality/necessity test must be carried out in each and every case, where there is a likelihood of a limitation of a human right. The only constitutional justification for a limitation is the need to protect another fundamental right or to enforce another constitutional objective. An example would be the limitation of property rights, interpreted by the Court "not as an absolute right, since it may be limited in a proportionate way, if warranted by public interest."[13] Limiting property rights may prove to be necessary for the protection of nature conservation interests, as emphasized by the Court in Decision No. 33/2006. (VII. 13.) AB.[14]

3.4 THE NON-DEROGATION PRINCIPLE IN A COMPARATIVE PERSPECTIVE

Before turning to the next stage of Hungarian constitutional development, it is worth examining the principle of non-derogation in general. Pope Francis provided important theoretical underpinnings for this principle:

"194. [...] It is not enough to balance, in the medium term, the protection of nature with financial gain, or the preservation of the environment with progress. Halfway measures simply delay the inevitable disaster. Put simply, it is a matter of redefining our notion of progress. A technological and economic develop-

---

12   Decision No. 106/2007. (XII. 20.) AB, ABH 2007, 900.
13   Decision No. 64/1993. (XII. 22.) AB, ABH 1993, 373.
14   Decision No. 33/2006. (VII. 13.) AB, ABH 2006, 447.

ment which does not leave in its wake a better world and an integrally higher quality of life cannot be considered progress. [...]"[15]

Consequently, halfway legal measures are not acceptable either. The way forward is to combine the above moral concept with the interpretation of the right to environment, if we wish to come closer to the solution.

> "More than 100 constitutions throughout the world currently guarantee a right to a clean and healthy environment, impose a duty on the state to prevent environmental harm, or mention the protection of the environment or natural resources as a national goal."[16]

Thus, the right to a healthy environment as a fundamental concept provides the necessary legal basis for further action. However, it does not suffice to introduce the new right and monitor its implementation, we must also change the ethos of governance, our vision of the world. Environmental protection – and sustainable development in its wider context – may only be realized through the reform of existing governance and regulatory mechanisms. Human rights can only bolster this effort. And as we move towards a human rights concept, regression as a threat immediately comes into focus:

> "Framing environmental protection as a human right eliminates those trade-offs that would lead to retrogression from existing levels of environmental protection or would prevent states from providing a minimum core environmental quality. The human rights perspective thus adds legitimacy to the demand for making environmental protection the primary goal of policymaking. Moreover, there is an international human rights edifice that promotes awareness and offers the possibility of remedies to individuals deprived of these rights. The explicit recognition of a right to a healthy environment might therefore provide new tools for civil society to hold governments accountable for ensuring access to the right."[17]

---

15 *Encyclical Letter Laudato Si' of the Holy Father Francis: On Care for Our Common Home*, 2015, at http://w2.vatican.va/content/francesco/en/encyclicals/documents/papa-francesco_20150524_enciclica-laudato-si.html.

16 Dinah Shelton, 'Whiplash and Backlash – Reflections on a Human Rights Approach to Environmental Protection', *Santa Clara Journal of International Law*, Vol. 13, Issue 1, 2015, p. 17.

17 Rebecca M. Bratspies, 'Do We Need a Human Right to a Healthy Environment?', *Santa Clara Journal of International Law*, Vol. 13, Issue 1, 2015, p. 36.

But what does regression exactly mean and what are its possible consequences? Originally, this principle was not conceived for environmental purposes, but as a principle of constitutional law.[18]

> "The principle of non-derogation holds that there is a core of fundamental rights that may not be infringed or limited, even in an emergency. Although it is often conceded in many constitutions, as it is in international human rights instruments, that the state may derogate from its obligations in an emergency, it is also acknowledged that certain essential protections and rights cannot be derogated from (*i.e.* those protections/obligations are non-derogable). First instance, the right against torture is generally regarded as a principle of *ius cogens* [...]"[19]

Turning now to environmental interests, the Report of the Special Rapporteur on the human right to safe drinking water and sanitation[20] may be cited as an example. It reads:

> "14. A retrogressive measure is one that, directly or indirectly, leads to backward steps in the enjoyment of human rights [...] 7. There is a clear link between non-regression and sustainability. [...] retrogressive steps will perpetuate unsustainable practices and create a constant threat to the full realization of economic, social and cultural rights in general and the rights to water and sanitation in particular."[21]

Non-derogation may also be considered from a more general perspective, that is, the limitation of any right – as set forth, among others, in the EU Charter of Fundamental Rights.[22]

---

18   *See e.g.* John C. Jeffries Jr. & Daryl J. Levinson, 'The Non-regression Principle in Constitutional Law', *California Law Review*, Vol. 86, Issue 6, 1998, pp. 1211-1250.

19   Mark Tushnet *et al.* (eds.), *Routledge Handbook of Constitutional Law*, Routledge, 2013, p. 91.

20   Report of the Special Rapporteur on the human right to safe drinking water and sanitation, Catarina de Albuquerque, A/HRC/24/44, at www.ohchr.org/EN/HRBodies/HRC/RegularSessions/Session24/Documents/A-HRC-24-44_en.pdf.

21   The same report provides a summary of the conditions and the constraints: "15. From a human rights standpoint, retrogressive measures are prohibited if they deliberately interfere with the progressive realization of rights. States must justify such measures according the following criteria: *(a)* There must be a reasonable justification for the steps taken and the subsequent regression in the implementation of rights. The measure must be necessary and proportionate [...]; *(b)* In addition to meeting core obligations as a matter of priority, maximum available resources must be fully used to progressively realize all levels of human rights in a way that guards against retrogressive steps or impacts and/or maintaining the status quo [...]; *(c)* Measures must not be discriminatory [...]; *(d)* Meaningful participation of affected groups and individuals [...]; *(e)* Retrogressive measures should be temporary and short term in nature [...]; *(f)* There should be accountability mechanisms in place [...]; *(g)* The State has the burden of proof regarding compliance with the above criteria."

22   *See* Article 52.

Several similar conditions are listed in the Siracusa Principles on the Limitation and Derogation of Provisions in the ICCPR (2001)[23] which may be referred to in the ambit of environmental rights. Finally, similar conditions are enshrined in the Guide on Article 15 ECHR – Derogation in time of emergency.[24]

Prieur made several efforts to elaborate on the merits of non-regression in environmental law. According to Prieur, environmental law is under numerous threats coming from politics, the economy or human nature. The latter means that the huge scope of environmental standards is complex and difficult to understand. Also, regression takes many forms:

> "Internationally, it can take the form of refusing to adhere to universal environmental treaties, boycotting their implementation, or even denouncing them. [...] In EU environmental legislation, regression is diffuse and appears the most when certain directives are revised. National environmental legislation is subject to increasing and often insidious regression: changing procedures so as to curtail the rights of the public on the pretext of simplification; repealing or amending environmental rules, thus reducing means of protection or rendering them ineffective. [...]"[25]

In Hungarian literature Fodor describes the different types of non-derogation as follows: changes of substantial norms, changes of procedural provisions and changes to organizational structures.[26] In addition, we may also mention a fourth approach, namely, the order of priority. This means that we understand environmental interests as taking priority over other – political, economic, social – interests.

3.5   THE FUNDAMENTAL LAW OF 2011 AND THE ENVIRONMENTAL VALUES ENSHRINED IN IT

Turning to the current era of the constitutional interpretation of the non-derogation principle, it is worth introducing the new constitutional provision reflecting this principle.

---

23   Siracusa Principles on the Limitation and Derogation of Provisions in the International Covenant on Civil and Political Rights Annex, UN Doc E/CN.4/1984/4 (1984), at www.uio.no/studier/emner/jus/human-rights/HUMR5503/h09/undervisningsmateriale/SiracusaPrinciples.pdf.
24   *Guide on Article 15 of the European Convention on Human Rights, Derogation in Time of Emergency*, 2019, at www.echr.coe.int/Documents/Guide_Art_15_ENG.pdf.
25   *See e.g.* Michel Prieur, 'Non-regression in Environmental Law', *Surveys and Perspectives Integrating Environment and Society*, Vol. 5, Issue 2, 2012, pp. 53-54.
26   László Fodor, 'A környezethez való jog dogmatikája napjaink kihívásai tükrében' *Miskolci Jogi Szemle*, Vol. 2, Issue 1, 2007, pp. 5-19.

Probably the most interesting and by far the most significant element of the recent development of the Hungarian legal system is the new Fundamental Law, which entered into force on 1 January 2012. The new Fundamental Law contains more environmental references and a more positive theoretical foundation for the protection of environmental interests than the previous constitutions. The National Avowal (preamble) sets forth three major concepts that are essential from the point of view of the environment: *(i)* national assets or national heritage, extended not only to assets within the boundaries of Hungary, but also in the whole Carpathian basin – there is a certain similarity between the concepts of "common heritage of mankind" and "common concern of humanity"; *(ii)* mention is made of future generations and *(iii)* human dignity, as these may best be protected together with the natural environment and environmental protection in a wider context. One cannot separate human dignity from the fact that humanity forms a part of nature.

The next chapter of the Fundamental Law is entitled "Foundation" including Article P providing a very complex summary of heritage, using the definition in a broad context and referring yet again to future generations:

> "All natural resources, especially arable land, forests and drinking water supplies, biodiversity – in particular native plant and animal species – and cultural assets shall form part of the nation's common heritage, and the State and every person shall be obliged to protect, sustain and preserve them for future generations."

This article provides a list of the elements of our common heritage, without it being exhaustive, allowing for further elements to be added to the list. A vital question here is whether this legal basis gives rise to obligations or is merely a reference to rights.

"Freedom and Responsibility" is the human rights chapter of the Fundamental Law, containing general civil rights, from among which I would like to mention those which may considered as environmental rights. There are two articles focusing on the right to environment, similar to the provisions of the previous constitution. Article XX is formulated less directly, connecting the protection of the environment to public health. Here, environmental protection is understood as a tool for safeguarding public health. Article XXI is the specific article on environmental rights, the first paragraph of which until recently has been the major legal basis for environmental protection cited by the Constitutional Court: "Hungary shall recognize and enforce the right of every person to a healthy environment." According to the fourth amendment of the Fundamental Law

> "Those decisions of the Constitutional Court which had been issued before the entering into force of the Fundamental Law are repealed. This provision does not have an effect on those legal consequences, evolved by these decisions."

In fact, this means that the Constitutional Court may not legitimately and formally refer to its own reasoning laid down in the abovementioned remarkable decisions, unless a close link between the former and the current constitutional provision is proven. Fortunately, the continuity in the wording of environmental rights is clear and easy to prove. In what follows, I evaluate some new decisions of the Constitutional Court demonstrating this textual relationship.

3.6   THE NON-DEROGATION PRINCIPLE AND THE JURISPRUDENCE OF THE CONSTITUTIONAL COURT AFTER 2011

An important environmental decision of the Constitutional Court is Decision No. 16/2015. (VI. 5.) AB, underlining primarily that the level of environmental protection hinges on the efficiency of legal guarantees. According to the decision, even the risk of derogation from the original level of protection is unconstitutional. There are several other elements of the judgment that are worth mentioning, such as the possibility of limiting property rights or the strong interrelationship between the protection of life and the environment. The issue at the core of the case was the use of state-owned land in harmony with nature conservation interests. Normally, agricultural uses are given priority over nature conservation aspects, with no effective guarantee for the latter. In Reasoning [104] the Court pointed out the unbalanced situation, *i.e.* that property interests can receive an immediate and direct protection, while nature conservation interests may only be protected in a reactive, posterior way.

In connection with the non-derogation principle the Court emphasized[27] that the lack of effective implementation or even disregard for nature conservation interests may result in long-term negative externalities, cause expenses or even damage for society, contrary to what is stipulated by Article P(1) and Article XXI(1) of the Fundamental Law.

> "When the legislator gives nature conservation tasks to such an organ which is primarily business oriented, special substantial and procedural guarantees shall also be defined in order to avoid putting nature conservation aims second to primarily profit-making functions."

The Constitutional Court, while a bit hesitant on certain other issues, is relatively active in interpreting the cases involving the right to a healthy environment and is broadening its approach to cover even more aspects than before.

---

27   Decision No. 16/2015. (VI. 5.) AB, Reasoning [104].

The next in the line of this new trend in Constitutional Court decisions is Decision No. 28/2017. (X. 25.) AB, related again to nature conservation, more specifically to Natura 2000 protection *versus* agricultural uses. According to the Court, some new provisions facilitating agricultural uses limited the opportunities and the efficiency of nature conservation. Meanwhile, these new measures did not mean to set forth any necessary conditions or prerequisites for the protection of other fundamental human rights or constitutional values. The Court did not intervene directly in the regulatory process but restated that the legislator made an omission. Nevertheless, the Court listed several important references, which may be invoked to bolster similar legal arguments. The Court underlined the significance of biodiversity, the special status of Natura 2000 sites, referred to the common heritage of the nation and emphasized yet again the non-regression (or in other words, non-derogation) principle. According to the Court, while environmental protection places an obligation on everyone, the responsibility of the state is much greater, as the state is in a position to create the underlying legal conditions for effective environmental protection.

In this decision the Court also interpreted what the obligation towards future generations means, as articulated in the preamble and Article P of the Fundamental Law. This encompasses a threefold obligation: *(i)* to ensure the chance for having options, *(ii)* to maintain the quality of the environment and *(iii)* to provide the chance for access. All three together shall be interpreted in a way as to protect the interest of future generations. In the given case this meant that a purely economic approach towards the utilization of Natura 2000 sites cannot be accepted. Finally, the Court clearly stated that the state, when making various decisions in connection with nature conservation, must consider the *precautionary principle*. The precautionary principle has been considered as forming part of the constitutional right to a healthy environment. We shall come back to the precautionary principle below.

The next decision worth mentioning is Decision No. 3223/2017. (IX. 25.) AB. While rejecting the motion itself, the Court interpreted the principle of non-derogation or non-derogation in the most comprehensive way. What are the major lessons learnt from more than 20 years of Court's case-law?[28] *(i)* From the very beginning (1994) the core element is the clear duty of the state, not to reduce the level of protection, unless such reduction is unavoidable in order to enforce other constitutional rights or interests; *(ii)* the possible reduction must be tested for proportionality and it must also be necessary for the protection of other constitutional rights; *(iii)* the reason for such requirements is mostly based on the fact that the failure to protect the environment and nature may trigger irreversible processes; *(iv)* therefore, the principles of prevention and precaution must also be taken into consideration, when legal rules are designed; *(v)* the requirement may cover substantive, procedural and organizational provisions, one-by-one or in any combination; *(vi)* the legislator

---

28   Id. Reasoning [27]-[28].

and those tasked with enforcement must share this long-term vision, reflecting the quality of the given living conditions, extending from codification to planning to cover the different legislative or governance periods; and *(vii)* the principle also governs individual enforcement and administrative actions taken by public authorities.

One of the most recent decisions, Decision No. 13/2018. (IX. 4.) AB is based upon the constitutionality initiative of the President of the Republic, referring to a large extent to the arguments of the Ombudsman for Future Generations. The main issue is water management, more specifically, the unlimited drilling and use of groundwater wells, down to a depth of 80 meters. The ensuing decision combined the references to future generations and the right to environment with the questions of state property or with a growing number of national assets[29] – such as water resources belonging to this scope.

The non-derogation principle is underlined yet again, as being based on the provisions of the Fundamental Law, combined with the precautionary principle. The necessity-proportionality test must be applied in both cases, with the protection of the environment converging towards the protection of various other human rights. Since the proposed law aimed to eliminate the permitting or notification requirements for wells without replacing this with other guarantees, the Court could not accept this regression of protection. The Court also drew attention to the fact that the protection of water resources is a strategic task of the state. The legislator could not point to any other human rights or constitutional interests which could justify the limitation of environmental rights.

3.7   The Precautionary Principle in the Decisions of the Constitutional Court

From the very beginning, prevention has always formed part of the Constitutional Court's environmental jurisprudence, but the precautionary approach has become more prevalent in the past years, after the 2015 revitalization of the case-law of the Court.

The precautionary principle is undoubtedly the most defining principle of environmental protection. It brought about a conceptual change in the general perception reactive legal measures. It was the UNCED in 1992 and Principle 15 of the Rio Declaration[30] that summarized the essence of the precautionary approach:

> "In order to protect the environment, the precautionary approach shall be widely applied by States according to their capabilities. Where there are threats of serious or irreversible damage, lack of full scientific certainty shall not be

---

29   Article 38 of the Fundamental Law of Hungary.
30   *See* www.unesco.org/education/pdf/RIO_E.PDF.

used as a reason for postponing cost-effective measures to prevent environmental degradation."

It is worth stressing that the precautionary principle was already applied by the CJEU in practice[31] before it was officially included in the text of the Maastricht Treaty. Article 130r(2) enshrined the principle, without providing any further guidance.

I do not wish to introduce the complete range of cases and views related to this principle, nevertheless a few basic comments are justified. Perhaps the most well-known case was the so-called *BSE* case,[32] the main consideration underlying it being the likely connection between the BSE-disease of cows and the Creutzfeldt-Jakob disease appearing in humans. The United Kingdom considered the limitation measures of the Commission (export ban) to be extreme. Concisely put:

"61. In the present case, the publication of new scientific information had established a probable link between a disease affecting cattle in the United Kingdom and a fatal disease affecting humans for which no known cure yet exists.
[…]
98. At the time when the contested decision was adopted, there was great uncertainty as to the risks posed by live animals, bovine meat and derived products.
99. Where there is uncertainty as to the existence or extent of risks to human health, the institutions may take protective measures without having to wait until the reality and seriousness of those risks become fully apparent."

The general nature of the precautionary principle was first pronounced in the *Artegodan* case, referring to it as a general principle,

"requiring the competent authorities to take appropriate measures to prevent specific potential risks to public health, safety and the environment, by giving precedence to the requirements related to the protection of those interests over economic interests."[33]

---

31 Judgment of 14 July 1983, *Case C-174/82, Criminal proceedings against Sandoz BV*, ECLI:EU:C:1983:213.
32 Judgment of 5 May 1998, *Case C-180/96, United Kingdom v. Commission*, ECLI:EU:C:1998:192.
33 Judgment of 26 November 2002, *Joint Cases T-74,76,83-85,132,137 & 141/00, Artegodan GmbH and Others v. Commission*, ECLI:EU:T:2002:283, para. 184.

The main reasons underlying the wide use of the precautionary principle are the following:[34]

> "According to the principle, when there are credible threats of harm, precau-
> tionary action should be taken, even when full understanding of the effects of
> a proposed activity is lacking. In other words, the precautionary principle
> combines the ethical notion of duty to prevent harm with the realities of the
> limits of scientific understanding. […] The principle is based on recognizing
> that people have a responsibility to prevent harm and to preserve the natural
> foundations of life, now and into the future. The needs of future generations
> of people and other species and the integrity of ecosystems are recognized as
> being worthy of care and respect. […] Precaution gives priority to protecting
> these vulnerable systems and requires gratitude, empathy, restraint, humility,
> respect and compassion."

The major elements of precautionary principle or approach are the following. (i) The situation has the potential for a high risk of adverse effects, endangering interests that are
commonly accepted to take priority (e.g. human health, environment, animal health, or
similar); (ii) these adverse effects must be serious with the potential for being irreversible;
(iii) there is a scientific probability, but a lack of full scientific certainty, justifying the need
for a risk assessment; (iv) the necessary measures should not be unreasonable or discriminatory, but must be effective and proportionate; (v) finally, the burden of proof is reversed,
the person wishing to carry out an activity must prove that it does not cause harm.

The precautionary principle has been better articulated in Decision No. 27/2017. (X. 25.)
AB, strictly connected with its counterpart,[35] both related to issues of land use. Here the
Court clearly stated:

> "According to the precautionary principle – widely accepted in environmental
> law – the state must guarantee that the state of environment is not deteriorated
> as a consequence of a given measure […]."[36]

Decision No. 13/2018. (IX. 4.) AB has also been discussed above. Here too, as in its earlier
decisions, the Court referred to the Fundamental Law, taking its reference to sustainable
development seriously, underlining that the state has a great responsibility when dealing
with the environmental resources and interests. The Court claims:

---

34   Ted Schettler & Carolyn Raffensperger, 'Why Is a Precautionary Approach Needed?', in Marco Martuzzi
& Joel A. Tickner (eds.), *The Precautionary Principle: Protecting Public Health, The Environment and The
Future of Our Children*, WHO Europe, 2004, p. 66.
35   *See* Decision No. 28/2017. (X. 25.) AB.
36   Id. Reasoning [49].

"The responsibility towards future generations, following from the provisions of the Fundamental Law requires that the legislator evaluate and consider the likely consequences of its measures on the basis of scientific information, according to the principles of prevention and precaution."[37]

According to the Court the non-derogation principle, together with the precautionary principle and prevention have their foundations in the Fundamental Law.

„[…] in case of measures which formally do not constitute a derogation, but which may influence the state of the environment, the measure is limited by the precautionary principle, according to which it is the constitutional obligation of the legislator to take into consideration when making its decisions those risks which are likely to or will definitely arise [...]"[38]

The state shall consider non-derogation on the basis of proportionality and necessity, balanced with the possible enforcement of other rights. The Court also underlined that the repeal of authorization for, or notification of the drilling of wells is only a tool and not the purpose of protection. Consequently, the restriction of the right to a healthy environment was not necessary for the protection of other constitutional rights.[39] The main message in connection with water management is that the state should only manage the underground water supplies, belonging to the common heritage of the nation, in a way that not only the water demand of today, but also that of the future be guaranteed in a sustainable way. "The available water resources can only remain accessible in the future, in case qualitative and quantitative protection is provided for."[40]

The Hungaroring (a racetrack made for Formula 1 races) is a major attraction in Hungary, however, it has several unfavorable consequences for the people living in the neighborhood. The legal background of noise abatement was the subject matter of Decision No. 17/2018. (X. 10.) AB, first summarizing the non-derogation principle.[41] According to the decision, the principle should be interpreted together – 'in unity' – with the principles of precaution and prevention. The Court also foresees that the legislator implements these principles when the possibility of restricting the right to a healthy environment arises. The Court underlined that the principle of non-derogation prohibits those derogations which may lead to the irreversible damage of the environment or nature, while the precautionary principle and prevention examines the risk, *i.e.* the likelihood of any such damage. "The

---

37   Id. Reasoning [13].
38   Id. Reasoning [20].
39   Id. Reasoning [50].
40   Id. Reasoning [69].
41   Id. Reasoning [87].

constitutional protection of the environment and nature have common roots: both protect the conditions of (human) life."[42] Noise should be understood as a longer process the consequence of which may be the irreparable harm.

Finally, the Court had to deal with the reorganization of the system and competences of public authorities in its Decision No. 4/2019. (III. 7.) AB. This was raised by MPs in 2015, and in my capacity as an ombudsman I also issued a 13-page statement (amicus curiae) in 2018, trying to influence the decision. In my opinion the Court did not want to decide against the restructuring, referring to the primary responsibility of the Government to design public administration and applicable procedural provisions. Still, the major question was, how these changes affect the right to a healthy environment, with due consideration the principles of prevention ad precaution.[43]

What is really missing, according to the Court is the lack of a clear reference in the public authorities' decisions to those environmental considerations, which have been taken into account during the procedure.[44] In fact, when all bodies entrusted with protecting the environment are dissolved and integrated into a huge administrative structure, leaving these special interests without specific protection, the necessary momentum may be lost. Thus, the decisions taken must at least refer to environmental interests. The Court took this to be an omission of the legislator, which must be resolved by mid-2019. The legislator must therefore enact provisions governing public authorities' decisions which make it clear that considerations related to the protection of environmental interests or natural resources were examined.[45]

3.8   CONCLUDING REMARKS

Principles influence legislation, implementation and enforcement to a great extent, primarily in those fields of law, which are relatively new and subject to constant change – such as environmental law. Principles thus have a legal value, a legal consequence, not only to fill the gaps, but also to assist proper interpretation. It is even more the case if the subject of interpretation is again a relatively wide field itself, a new fundamental right: the right to environment. Principles and human rights require a high-level forum of interpretation, which may either be an international forum – such as the ECtHR or the CJEU – or a national constitutional court or a supreme court. Constitutional courts are preferable, since human rights are generally enshrined in constitutions.

---

42   Id. Reasoning [91].
43   Id. Reasoning [74].
44   Id. Reasoning [79].
45   Id. Reasoning [93].

The same is true for the Hungarian Constitutional Court, which has a strong mandate, since both the previous (1989) Constitution and the current Fundamental Law contain direct references to the right to environment, the substance of which needs clarification. Also, it is an imperative point that the current constitutional provisions stipulate similar requirements as the former rules, thus, a continuity may easily be proven. Besides this similarity, the Fundamental Law has several other additional references which support interpretation in the interest of the environment.

In this paper I did not want to present all aspects of constitutional interpretation but wanted to focus only on the two extremes of protection: non-derogation on the one hand and precaution on the other. While the first has a longer, 25-year history in Hungarian constitutional jurisprudence, the latter is relatively new, going back only to the second half of the present decade.

Non-derogation represents a decent minimum in this respect, as the main idea is not to allow the actual level of protection to be reduced, or if so, with at least some guarantees, which do not tolerate too much flexibility. Reducing the level or protection must be the exception and should only be done for the sake of other and equal constitutional rights, always in a proportionate manner. So not unrestricted backsliding is allowed. This principle also differentiates between constitutional rights (and the reference to equal rights above substantiates this view): property rights or freedom of enterprise shall not be taken into consideration, as the right to environment is more closely connected to the right to life than to social rights, for example. All this has been unfolded by the Constitutional Court in the past quarter of a century. Still, it does not entail the need for improving the current level of protection. As such, non-derogation is not an active principle, does not constitute a great challenge.

By comparison, the precautionary principle is a much more active principle with a moving target. The limitations of scientific evidence or certainty are always changing. Risk assessments are always improving, tools, methods and experiences are constantly developing. Here those wishing to take risky or potentially dangerous steps, must bear the burden of proof. The precautionary principle as a legal principle is defining for contemporary environmental law, its practical application covering all areas, where the likelihood of extended risk requires intervention. The principle seems to enshrine a 'presumption of guilt' when it comes to risky undertakings. It requires the clarification of underlying conditions and guarantees, with a view to increase the balance between different interests, with the proper application of the principle proportionality. Finally, in the above presented cases, the burden of proof is on the state. With the Constitutional Court taking its first steps into that direction, we may expect a more active role for the Court in protecting the environment in the near future.

4   THE PRECAUTIONARY PRINCIPLE IN THE FUNDAMENTAL LAW OF HUNGARY

Judicial Activism or an Inherent Fundamental Principle?
An Evaluation of Constitutional Court Decision No. 13/2018. (IX. 4.) AB on
the Protection of Groundwater

Marcel Szabó*

Keywords

Constitutional Court of Hungary, Article P of the Fundamental Law, precautionary principle, judicial activism, constitutional protection of the environment

Abstract

Acting upon the motion of the President of the Republic, the Constitutional Court of Hungary ruled in its Decision No. 13/2018. (IX. 4.) AB that the regulation which would have allowed establishing new wells up to the depth of 80m without a license or notification was contrary to the Fundamental Law. The Constitutional Court found in its decision that the regulation would endanger the volume and quality of underground water in a way that, considering the precautionary principle, was no longer compatible with the protection of natural resources and cultural artefacts forming the common heritage of the nation as laid down in Article P(1) of the Fundamental Law or Article XXI(1) of the same on the right to a healthy environment. It was in this decision that the Constitutional Court first outlined in detail the constitutional significance of the precautionary principle, with this principle forming the central part of the decision's reasoning. Within the framework of this study I examine whether this decision based on the precautionary principle can be considered the 'extraction' of what is inherently present in the Fundamental Law or on the contrary, whether it was an activist approach imposing the principle on the Fundamental Law.

*   Marcel Szabó: professor of law, Pázmány Péter Catholic University, Budapest; justice, Constitutional Court of Hungary.

4.1 Antecedents of Decision No. 13/2018. (IX. 4.) AB – The Motion of the President of the Republic

On 20 July 2018 the Hungarian Parliament passed an amendment to Act LVII of 1995 on Water Management. The bill aimed to establish regulations that were to enable anyone to construct a well up to the depth of 80m without requiring a license from or a notification to authorities, in order to meet the water demand of their household. The President of the Republic did not sign the bill passed but initiated its preliminary constitutionality review by the Constitutional Court.[1] The President of the Republic was of the opinion that the bill was contrary to the obligation of the protection of water resources forming the common heritage of the nation as laid down in Article P(1) of the Fundamental Law. In particular, it was unconstitutional considering the prohibition of stepping back from an already achieved level of protection (violation of the principle of non-derogation) and the requirements following from the precautionary principle. The legislators failed to explain both in the wording of the bill and its reasoning why the legislation in force had to be amended. Likewise, they failed to formulate guarantees for the protection of drinking water or the preservation of the condition of the environment. The President of the Republic also noted in his motion that, in a statement of principle, the Ombudsman for Future Generations[2] argued against approving the regulation, in addition, eleven NGOs issued a common statement protesting against putting an end to the responsible management of water resources as well as the protection of underground waters.

4.2 The Protection of Environmental and Natural Values in the Fundamental Law

The Constitutional Court established already three years after the Fundamental Law had entered into force that the Fundamental Law further developed the environmental value system and approach of the previous Constitution.[3] According to the National Avowal of the Fundamental Law,

> "We commit to promoting and safeguarding our heritage, our unique language, Hungarian culture, the languages and cultures of nationalities living in Hungary, along with all man-made and natural assets of the Carpathian Basin. We bear

---

1   *See* in Hungarian at http://public.mkab.hu/dev/dontesek.nsf/0/cbb2386065131e71c12582da004720cb/$FILE/I_1216_0_2018_ind%C3%ADtv%C3%A1ny.002.pdf/I_1216_0_2018_ind%C3%ADtv%C3%A1ny.pdf.
2   *See* in Hungarian at www.ajbh.hu/documents/10180/2704088/Elvi+%C3%A1ll%C3%A1sfoglal%C3%A1s+a+felsz%C3%ADn+alatti+vizek+v%C3%A9delm%C3%A9ben.pdf.
3   Decision No. 16/2015. (VI. 5.) AB, Reasoning [91].

responsibility for our descendants; therefore, we shall protect the living conditions of future generations by making prudent use of our material, intellectual
and natural resources."

In this respect, the National Avowal also points out that the Fundamental Law "shall be
an alliance among Hungarians of the past, present and future." Thus, the National Avowal,
too, underlines that the decisions made by governments today will also affect future generations, in view of which current government and legislative decisions must bear the
interests of the coming generations in mind. This also means that the provision of the
National Avowal cited above establishes an interpretative framework for the Fundamental
Law and consequently, for the whole Hungarian legal system. This requires that while
considering present needs, one must take into consideration the interests of future generations, too, with equal weight. Article P(1) of the Fundamental Law stipulates:

"Natural resources, in particular arable land, forests and the reserves of water;
biodiversity, in particular native plant and animal species; as well as cultural
assets shall form the common heritage of the nation; it shall be the obligation
of the State and everyone to protect and maintain them, and to preserve them
for future generations."

In the case of the natural resources and cultural assets forming the common heritage of
the nation[4] Article P(1) clearly specifies the conduct expected of "the State and everyone":
their *(i)* protection, *(ii)* maintenance and *(iii)* preservation for future generations. In relation
to the preservation of natural resources for future generations it is the responsibility of the
current generation to preserve the opportunity of choice, preserve the opportunity of
quality and preserve the opportunity of access.[5] These principles help evaluate the interests
of current and future generations based on the same aspects and strike a balance between
them. Article P(1) of the Fundamental Law is an extremely forward-looking provision in
several respects. On the one hand, by taking the concept of common heritage of humanity
as a basis it created the category of 'common heritage of the nation', which includes both
natural and cultural values. On the other hand, it also set forth that the protection of these
values was the responsibility of "the State and everyone", that is, also that of civil society
and individual citizens.[6] While this obligation requires natural and legal persons only to
respect the regulations in force, the state is expected to clearly identify legal obligations
that both the state and private parties must observe to ensure the efficient protection of

---

4   Decision No. 3104/2017. (V. 8.) AB, Reasoning [37]-[39].
5   Decision No. 28/2017. (X. 25.) AB, Reasoning [33].
6   Decision No. 16/2015. (VI. 5.) AB, Reasoning [92].

values under Article P(1) and their implementation,[7] and finally, to guarantee and, where required, enforce compliance with these regulations.

> "Thus, from Article P of the Fundamental Law there also follows a content benchmark of an absolute nature on the state of natural resources, which sets objective requirements for the prevailing state activity."[8]

4.3 The Decision of the Constitutional Court

The Constitutional Court underlined in its Decision that the comprehensive water rights licensing system that was to be done away with by the law (opening up the opportunity to construct wells up to the depth of 80 meters without a license or notification) was indispensable for the quantitative and qualitative protection of underground waters. It serves the quantitative protection of underground waters that their use should be allowed by authorities only to the extent that does not endanger their regeneration *i.e.* does not result in their overuse. The qualitative protection of underground waters, on the other hand, is facilitated by the licensing system by ensuring the professional construction of individual wells.[9] Legislators mentioned the reduction of bureaucracy and superfluous administrative burden on citizens as the reasons underlying the regulation,[10] which argument was not considered by the Constitutional Court as a constitutional grounds which could justify a step back in the level of protection under Article I(3) of the Fundamental Law.

> "From Article P(1) of the Fundamental Law it follows that the state may manage underground waters as natural resources constituting parts of the common heritage of the nation only in a way that ensures that not only current but also future water use demands can be sustainably met. The water resources currently available can only remain available for future use provided that they are afforded quantitative and qualitative protection."[11]

The Constitutional Court underlined: by creating the opportunity to ignore provisions for the quantitative and qualitative protection of underground waters, the regulation creates a risk of deterioration which, pursuant to the precautionary principle, is incompatible with the Fundamental Law. It follows namely from the precautionary principle that the state

---

7   Decision No. 28/2017. (X. 25.) AB, Reasoning [30].
8   Id. Reasoning [32].
9   Decision No. 13/2018. (IX. 4.) AB, Reasoning [57]-[58].
10 Id. Reasoning [66].
11 Id. Reasoning [69].

must ensure that measures do not involve any deterioration of the environment as their consequence,[12] and the principle of prevention embodied in prior administrative licensing must have priority over the polluter pays principle, granting the opportunity of retrospective sanctioning.[13] The Constitutional Court found therefore that the contested regulation violated Article P(1) and Article XXI(1) of the Fundamental Law, as a result of which it could not be promulgated as an act.[14]

4.4   'EXTRACTION' AS A TECHNIQUE OF THE CONSTITUTIONAL COURT

Justice András Varga Zs. emphasized in his dissenting opinion that a significant element of the decision was 'extracting' the precautionary principle from the wording of the Fundamental Law.[15] The dissenting opinion establishes the following as regards extraction as a constitutional court technique:

> "There is no doubt that the wording of the Fundamental Law – like any other norm – requires interpretation. Through interpretation it is the obligation of the Constitutional Court to establish what the wording means in general as well as in a particular situation. The interpretation as a text is inevitably longer than the wording of the Fundamental Law. Therefore, it must be applied as restrictively as possible, expanding the original wording of the norm to the least possible extent. Thus, the interpretation may only contain new text elements (interpretation domains, principles) that are so closely related to the rights granted by or other regulations in the Fundamental Law that the wording would not prevail without these."[16]

The main difference of principle between justices of the Constitutional Court supporting the majority decision and those expressing dissenting opinions in relation to it is whether the precautionary principle is 'closely related' to Article P(1) of the Fundamental Law and/or the right to a healthy environment laid down under Article XXI(1), or the Constitutional Court in fact 'made an addition' to the Fundamental Law by its decision in an activist manner.

---

12   Decision No. 27/2017. (X. 25.) AB, Reasoning [49].
13   Decision No. 13/2018. (IX. 4.) AB, Reasoning [72].
14   About the decision *see* (in Hungarian) János Ede Szilágyi, 'Az elővigyázatosság elve és a magyar alkotmány-bírósági gyakorlat – Szellem a palackból avagy alkotmánybírósági magas labda az alkotmányrevízióhoz', *Miskolci Jogi Szemle*, Vol. 13, Issue 2, 2018, pp. 76-91.
15   Decision No. 13/2018. (IX. 4.) AB, dissenting opinion by András Varga Zs., [133].
16   Id. [134].

The extraction technique of constitutional interpretation in the practice of the Constitutional Court is summarized in the dissenting opinion of Béla Pokol to Decision No. 8/2014. (III. 20.) AB as follows:

> "if the extraction technique was used only for making certain abstract constitutional values or fundamental principles more specific (*i.e.* more specific content was fleshed out from abstract values and principles while the scope was not enlarged by adding new areas), no fault could be found with it."[17]

At the same time, Pokol finds the statement in the Decision "[t]he question what rights should be understood as 'rights enshrined in the Fundamental Law' shall be determined by the case-law of the Constitutional Court"[18] unacceptable as, in his view, after the Fundamental Law took effect the Constitutional Court may only interpret the Fundamental Law but cannot not add to it and, in particular, it cannot declare any rights 'constitutionally enshrined' in case these are not explicitly included or specified in the Fundamental Law as such.

There are five major areas of constitutional activism specified in scholarly literature: *(i)* striking down arguably constitutional actions of other branches of power; *(ii)* ignoring precedent; *(iii)* judicial legislation; *(iv)* departure from accepted interpretive methodology; and *(v)* result-oriented judging.[19] Based on these areas, it is worth considering the Constitutional Court's approach to the precautionary principle. Is Decision No. 13/2018. (IX. 4.) AB in fact activist, as outlined in the dissenting opinions to the decision, or on the contrary: did it merely flesh out content clearly inherent in the Fundamental Law, making it apparent to everyone?

4.4.1 Striking Down Arguably Constitutional Actions of Other Branches of Power

In my view, the decision of another branch of power (be it the legislative or the judiciary) may be considered 'arguably constitutional' if even in the opinion of a reasonable person it violates some provision of the Fundamental Law beyond doubt.[20] In this context it is worth quoting the dissenting opinion of Antonin Scalia in *Casey*,[21] according to which:

---

17   Decision No. 8/2014. (III. 20.) AB, dissenting opinion by Béla Pokol, [146].
18   Id. Reasoning [64]
19   Keenan D. Kmiec, 'The Origin and Current Meanings of "Judicial Activism"', *California Law Review*, Vol. 92, Issue 5, 2004, pp. 1463-1476.
20   From the practice of the US Supreme Court *see e.g. Lochner v. New York*, dissenting opinion by Oliver Wendell Holmes, 198 U.S. 45, 75-76.
21   505 U.S. 833.

"A State's choice between two positions on which reasonable people can disagree is constitutional even when (as is often the case) it intrudes upon a »liberty« in the absolute sense."[22]

In this respect the benchmark before the Constitutional Court is the test of unconstitutionality 'beyond doubt'. The consistent case-law of the Constitutional Court obviously meets this test on the whole and in every case where the Court sees the opportunity to do so, it acts by 'keeping the law in force'.[23] Where, however, a legal provision can be interpreted both in compliance with and contrary to the constitution (Fundamental Law), the Constitutional Court establishes by virtue of Section 46(3) of the Act on the Constitutional Court in a constitutional requirement

"those constitutional requirements which originate from the regulation of the Fundamental Law and which enforce the constitutional requirements of the Fundamental Law with which the application of the examined legal regulation or the legal regulation applicable in court proceedings must comply."

In cases where the regulation under scrutiny violates the constitution (Fundamental Law) not because of its substance but because of its clearly identifiable defects, the Constitutional Court may by virtue of Section 46(1) of the Act on the Constitutional Court declare an omission on the part of the lawmaker. This means a violation of the Fundamental Law, and the Constitutional Court shall call upon the body that had committed the omission to perform its task, setting a deadline for adopting the new regulation.

In my view, this was not the case in the case in question, which is clearly laid down in the decision.

"Considering namely the findings with regard to the significance of underground waters and the [role] of the licensing procedure [related to] the quantitative and qualitative protection of underground waters, it is not doing away with the licensing system but its absolute retention and efficient implementation that can be considered indispensable for the implementation of the right laid down under Articles P(1) and XXI(1) of the Fundamental Law. It follows namely from Article P(1) of the Fundamental Law that the state may manage underground waters as natural resources forming the common heritage of the nation only in a way that ensures the sustainable meeting of not only current water needs but those that may arise in the future as well. And the water resources

---

22   505 U.S. 980.
23   *See e.g.* Decision No. 20/2019. (VI. 26.) AB, Reasoning [66].

currently available will remain usable also in the future provided they are given quantitative and qualitative protection. Regulation making it possible in the case of an unspecified range of use of underground waters that use may proceed without the official notification of or control by authorities, does not meet this requirement [...]."[24]

All this means that the Constitutional Court provided, in my view, a straightforward reasoning in its decision as to why they considered the regulation to be unconstitutional beyond doubt and why there was no room for either setting a constitutional requirement or declaring an omission on the part of the lawmaker.

4.4.2   Ignoring Precedent

Provisions of the Fundamental Law – due to their concise nature in the first place – often allow for several different interpretations. In such cases it is a reasonable expectation that the (constitutional) judicial body concerned should interpret the same norm the same way in similar cases later on, or in the case they deviate from their consistent interpretation, should clearly and explicitly state the reasons for such a departure. Predictable decision-making not only enhances the prestige of the body concerned but is also an expectation following from the principles of constitutionality and legal certainty and the rule of law [as laid down under Article B(1) of the Fundamental Law of Hungary].

Formally the Hungarian Constitutional Court is not a precedent-court, but in practice (similarly to other courts) in the course of its decision-making it takes its earlier decisions into account. This is also supported by Section 41(6) of the Rules of Procedure of the Constitutional Court: "The rapporteur shall indicate any intention to deter from the established judicial practice of the Constitutional Court and justify its necessity." The same conclusion can be drawn from the fourth amendment of the Fundamental Law, which stipulates the following:

"The decisions of the Constitutional Court made prior to the entry into force of the Fundamental Law are repealed. This provision shall be without prejudice to the legal effects produced by those decisions."

By way of this provision the constitution-making power intended to avoid that in the process of interpreting the new Fundamental Law the Constitutional Court be bound by statements of principle made in relation to the former Constitution. According to the

---

24   Decision No. 13/2018. (IX. 4.) AB, Reasoning [69].

scholarly literature precedent-based decision-making involves a justification obligation for the decision-making forum: *(i)* if there is a precedent rule applicable in the case concerned, it must be applied; and *(ii)* the intention to refrain from applying the precedent rule for any reason involves the obligation to provide justification for it.[25] The reason for deviating from precedent may either be to overrule it or the case concerned is in fact in essential aspects different from the precedent case and the precedent rule is therefore not applicable. As long as it is part of everyday (constitutional) judicial practice to establish that the earlier rule is not applicable in the latter case due to significant factual differences between the two cases, explicit deviation from the earlier precedent invariably amounts to judicial activism. Probably the best-known example of deviating from earlier precedent would be the segregation practice of the US Supreme Court. In the *Plessy v. Ferguson* case[26] in 1896 the Supreme Court explicitly stipulated that the separate but equal doctrine was in compliance with the Constitution. In the *Brown v. Board of Education*[27] case of 1954, however, the Supreme Court explicitly stipulated that racial segregation at public schools in itself involved unequal opportunities and thereby violated the 14th Amendment to the Constitution.

In its Decision No. 13/2018. (IX. 4.) AB the Constitutional Court did not ignore its own earlier practice, for two reasons. On the one hand, the mere fact that the body bases its decision on a principle that it did not explicitly take into consideration previously would mean deviation from earlier precedent only if the Constitutional Court had explicitly stipulated that the precautionary principle had no constitutional relevance. On the other hand, although it is undoubtedly true that the Constitutional Court evaluated the precautionary principle in its entirety only in this decision, it in fact already made mention of the precautionary principle in previous cases concerning similar subjects.

The substance of the precautionary principle already appeared in Decision No. 16/2015. (VI. 5.) AB where the Constitutional Court found:

> "The circumstance that certain earlier prevailing and clearly identifiable scopes of authority granted by legal provisions are now missing from the regulatory environment and because of that certain duties remain unperformed results in a reduced level of legislative protection even if this involves 'only' a risk of deterioration in nature."[28]

---

25   Frederick Schauer, 'Precedent', *Stanford Law Review*, Vol. 39, Issue 3, 1987, pp. 580-581.
26   *Plessy v. Ferguson*, 163 U.S. 537.
27   *Brown v. Board of Education*, 347 U.S. 483.
28   Decision No. 16/2015. (VI. 5.) AB, Reasoning [110].

In this case the Constitutional Court had to evaluate the regulation according to which the right to manage nature protection areas was transferred from national parks (*i.e.* institutions operating with nature conservation purposes specifically) to the National Land Fund operating on a business basis. The Constitutional Court found that the amendment itself involved the risk that the level of environmental protection would be reduced by becoming less efficient compared to the former level – which basically corresponds with the precautionary principle. Furthermore, the precautionary principle was clearly formulated in Decision No. 3292/2017. (XI. 20.) and Order No. 3374/2017. (XII. 22.) AB, while Decision No. 3223/2017. (IX. 25.) AB stated that

> "The primary justification for non-derogation as a regulatory benchmark is that the failure to protect nature and the environment may launch irreversible processes, and thus legislation on environment protection is only possible by considering the principles of precaution and prevention."[29]

Similar definitions were included in Decisions No. 27/2017. (X. 25.) AB and No. 28/2017. (X. 25.) AB, according to which

> "For the sake of the protection of the environment [...] legislators must also keep the precautionary principle in mind, by virtue of which the state must certify – also taking scientific uncertainty into consideration – that a certain measure will by no means involve a deterioration in the condition of the environment as a consequence."[30]

In my view it can clearly be established on the basis of these examples that Decision No. 13/2018. (IX. 4.) AB only completed the 'extraction' of the precautionary principle, and by no means departed from the earlier case law of the Constitutional Court.

4.4.3   Judicial Legislation

In a certain sense, judicial legislation may be considered as the opposite of "striking down arguably constitutional actions". While, however, striking down arguably constitutional actions on the part of the Constitutional Court has negative effects (it results in the annulment of some legislative act or judicial decision), the direction of judicial legislation

---

29   Decision No. 3223/2017. (IX. 25.) AB, Reasoning [27].
30   Decision No. 28/2017. (X. 25.) AB, Reasoning [75].

is inevitably positive, and as a result of the Constitutional Court decision the norm concerned is given a new meaning that it did not have before.

Judicial legislation may emerge in two respects in Constitutional Court proceedings. On the one hand, when the Constitutional Court adopts a constitutional requirement or when it uses the instrument of so-called mosaic annulment. When the Constitutional Court establishes – primarily in relation to Article XV of the Fundamental Law – the discriminative nature of a provision, it is difficult to draw the line between judicial legislation meaning activism or interpretation by the Constitutional Court. It was in 2019, for instance, that the Constitutional Court dealt with the requirements of old-age benefits for permanent carers as a specific Hungarian provision of social security law. It is pensioners who cared for their permanently ill or seriously disabled child in their own households for at least 20 years who are entitled to the benefit. The Constitutional Court established in its decision that the legislator's exclusion from the benefit of carers who have more than one disabled child and cared for them for less than 20 years individually but for at least 20 years altogether was contrary to the Fundamental Law. The Constitutional Court also ruled that the provision which excluded carers from the benefit who, due to the date of birth or death of their disabled child, were unable to use certain state provisions that did not actually exist at the time concerned, violated the Fundamental Law.[31] Based on a rigid interpretation of the Constitutional Court's jurisdiction, the Court would only have had jurisdiction in this case to choose between the absolute annulment of the rule (abolishing thereby the old-age benefit for permanent carers) or the violation of the Fundamental Law manifested in the omission. According to the dissenting opinion of justice András Varga Zs.

> "The Constitutional Court may annul an existing regulation due to its violation of the Fundamental Law, may establish that the legislator caused a violation of the Fundamental Law manifested in an omission or where applicable establish in the course of the implementation of a regulation the requirements following from the Fundamental Law, which is binding for courts. It may, on the other hand, not stipulate what a regulation must be like and it may in particular not change the substance of a regulation by including provisions reflecting to its own conviction. […] A requirement may not become a new rule."[32]

While I fully agree with this statement, it is a question of principle regarding jurisdiction whether the Constitutional Court has the authority to annul elements of a regulation violating the Fundamental Law, and at the same time render the rest of the regulation in force constitutional. In my view, the jurisdiction of the Constitutional Court should be examined

---

31   Decision No. 25/2019. (VII. 23.) AB.
32   Id. dissenting opinion by András Varga Zs., [98]-[99].

case by case in this respect. If the regulation that stays in force as a result of the Constitutional Court decision is in harmony with the objective specified by the legislator which is clearly identifiable, the Constitutional Court does not in fact make new law but only remedies the 'legislative error', as was the case in Decision No. 25/2019. (VII. 23.) AB. Similarly if in the field of environmental law, in compliance with the principle of non-derogation directly following from the Fundamental Law, the Constitutional Court keeps the new regulation in force either by mosaic annulment or by applying a constitutional requirement in a way essentially applying *restitutio in integrum*. This way, the Constitutional Court restores an earlier status of the regulation, which is once again not a case of making a new law.

Another aspect of judicial legislation may arise in relation to Decision No. 13/2018. (IX. 4.) AB, namely that the Constitutional Court 'extracted' the precautionary principle from the Fundamental Law in a way that was actually not included in the law. In this approach the argumentation that the Constitutional Court only 'completed' the extraction of the principle does not hold water either, since the problem arose in connection with the Constitutional Court's approach to the wording of the Fundamental Law rather than to its own earlier decisions. Thus, the question is whether by 'extracting' the precautionary principle the Constitutional Court actually derived a new right from the Fundamental Law (for which it had no jurisdiction), or whether it performed the constitutional interpretation within the boundaries of its jurisdiction. In its already cited Decision No. 28/2017. (X. 25.) AB the Constitutional Court established with reference to the precautionary principle that

> "The precautionary principle is recognized and applied in international law (thus especially the Convention on Biological Diversity, the United Nations Framework Agreement on Climate Change promulgated by Act LXXXII of 1995, the Cartagena Protocol of the Convention on Biological Diversity promulgated by Act CIX of 2004), in international case law [ECHR, *Tatar v. Romania* (67021/01), 27 January 2009)], in EU law (especially Article 191 TFEU) as well as in Hungarian law (Act LIII of 1995 on the General Rules of Environmental Protection)."[33]

It is not mentioned in the Constitutional Court decision, but the EU practice related to the precautionary principle is especially significant.[34] Environmental law itself means the totality of norms that target the precautionary use of the environment and the prevention,

---

33   Decision No. 28/2017. (X. 25.) AB, Reasoning [75].
34   *See e.g.* Judgment of 11 September 2002, *Case T-13/99, Pfizer Animal Health SA v. Council of the European Union*, ECLI:EU:T:2002:209; Judgment of 26 November 2002, *Case T-74/00, Artegodan GmbH v. Commission*, ECLI:EU:T:2002:283.

mitigation and remedy of the consequences of human activity (or inactivity), as well as the improvement of the condition of the environment.[35]

In relation to Article P(1) of the Fundamental Law reference should be made to the reasoning of the Fundamental Law in order to directly identify the legislator's intention. According to this, Article P

> "[d]eclares that Hungary shall protect and preserve the healthy environment. Thereby it includes as a new element in the Fundamental Law the requirement of sustainability, which sets a course for the state and the economy for the responsible management of environmental values. It specifically highlights Hungary's own environmental values as well as the values of Hungarian culture, making the protection of which everybody's obligation for the sake of preservation for future generations."

The preservation for future generations of resources forming the common heritage of the nation (including underground waters) can only be realized if, as a result of the current generation's decisions resources remain available in sufficient quantity and quality for future generations. This means that respect for the fair interests of future generations sets absolute restrictions on the management of resources.[36] This is only possible if the legislator evaluates and considers "the expected impact of their respective measures on the basis of scientific knowledge, in compliance with the principles of precaution and prevention".[37] All this means at the same time that the precautionary principle undoubtedly forms a part of Article P(1) and thus, in relation to Article P, the Constitutional Court did not actually make new law by 'extracting' the precautionary principle from this article.

The situation is similar in the case of the right to a healthy environment under Article XXI(1). Already in its Decision No. 28/1994. (V. 20.) AB, the Constitutional Court pointed out that

> "the right to environment protection […] is primarily independent institutional protection in its own right, i.e. a specific fundamental right whose objective, institutional protection element is overwhelming and decisive. The right to the environment raises the guarantees for the performance of the state's environment protection obligations, including setting conditions for cutting back the attained level of protection of the environment, to the level of fundamental

---

35   Gergely Horváth, 'Az Alaptörvény környezetjogi előírásai', in Katalin Szoboszlai-Kiss & Gergely Deli (eds.), *Tanulmányok a 70 éves Bihari Mihály tiszteletére*, Győr, 2013, p. 225.

36   Decision No. 28/2017. (X. 25.) AB, Reasoning [33].

37   Decision No. 13/2018. (IX. 4.) AB, Reasoning [13].

rights. Owing to the specific features of this right, all the duties that the state performs through the vehicle of protecting substantive rights in other areas must be met in this field by way legislative and organizational guarantees."[38]

After the Fundamental Law entered into force, in Decision No. 3068/2013. (III. 14.) AB the Constitutional Court established that

"[t]he wording of the Fundamental Law with respect to the right to a healthy environment is identical with the wording of the Constitution, therefore in the interpretation of the right to a healthy environment the statements made in previous decisions of the Constitutional Court in the course of interpreting the right to a healthy environment shall be regarded as authoritative."[39]

This also means that the Constitutional Court has a consistent practice with respect to the fact that the precautionary principle as an element of performing the state obligation of environmental protection constitutes in accordance with the consistent practice of the Constitutional Court, by virtue of Article XXI(1), a part of the right to a healthy environment. Its 'extraction' from Article XXI(1) cannot be considered as an introduction of a new obligation formerly not included in the Fundamental Law, because it constitutes an integral part of the state obligation of environmental protection. A regulation that ignores the major fundamental rules governing environmental protection cannot be suitable for the preservation of the environment or for meeting the objective obligations of the state directly arising from the Fundamental Law.

Considering all these aspects it can be established that the explicit emergence of the precautionary principle in the reasoning of Decision No. 13/2018. (IX. 4.) AB cannot be considered as legislation by the Constitutional Court relative to the wording of the Fundamental Law.

4.4.4   Departure from Accepted Interpretative Methodology

Several studies in scholarly literature analyze what 'accepted interpretative methodologies' are.[40] While the respective authors' approaches vary already in the number of the interpre-

---

38   Decision No. 28/1994. (V. 20.) AB, ABH 1994, 134, 138.
39   Decision No. 3068/2013. (III. 14.) AB, Reasoning [46].
40   *See e.g.* Carl Friedrich von Savigny, *Das System des hautigen Römischen Rechts*, Veit, Berlin, 1840, pp. 213-214; Robert Samuel Summers & Michele Taruffo, 'Interpretation and Comparative Analysis', *in* Donald Neil McCormick & Robert Samuel Summers (eds.), *Interpreting Statutes*, Dartmouth, Aldershot, 1991, pp. 464-465; from the Hungarian literature *see e.g.* Béla Pokol, *Jogelmélet. Társadalomtudományi trilógia II.*, Századvég, Budapest, 2005; András Jakab, 'A bírói jogértelmezés az Alaptörvény tükrében', *Jogesetek Mag-*

tative methodologies, it can be pointed out in general that the grammatical, historical, logical, systematic, teleological and practical interpretations are all considered as generally accepted interpretative methods in the scientific literature.

Article 28 of the Fundamental Law of Hungary stipulates:

> "In the course of the application of law, courts shall interpret the text of legal regulations primarily in accordance with their purposes and with the Fundamental Law. When establishing the purpose of a legal regulation, the preamble of the legal regulation and the reasoning of the motion for establishing or amending the law shall be considered. When interpreting the Fundamental Law or legal regulations, it shall be presumed that they serve moral and economical purposes which are in accordance with common sense and the public good."

In its Decision No. 2/2019. (III. 5.) AB the Constitutional Court also underlined in relation to the interpretation of the Fundamental Law that "In the course of the interpretation of the Fundamental Law the Constitutional Court also keeps in mind the obligations following from EU membership as well as international agreements."[41]

The above also means that in the course of interpreting the Fundamental Law and on the basis of regulations in force grammatical, logical, systematic and teleological interpretations certainly qualify as 'accepted interpretative methodologies', which means that the application of these interpretative methods amount to constitutional activism only in absolutely extreme cases.

In relation to the precautionary principle, in its Decision No. 13/2018. (IX. 4.) AB the Constitutional Court referred to its reasoning related to the draft and reasoning of the Fundamental Law[42] (teleological and historical interpretation), the meaning of the precautionary principle in international law, EU law and Hungarian law[43] (systematic interpretation), as well as the earlier case-law of the Constitutional Court as regards the precautionary principle[44] (practical interpretation), in view of which we cannot speak of activism, in my opinion, with reference to either the 'extraction' of the precautionary principle or the meaning assigned to this principle. On the contrary: the Constitutional Court did in fact

---

yarázata, 2011/4, pp. 86-94; Zoltán Tóth J., 'A dogmatikai, a logikai és a jogirodalmi értelmezés a magyar felsőbírósági gyakorlatban', *MTA Law Working Papers*, 2015/17.
41   Decision No. 2/2019. (III. 5.) AB, Reasoning [38].
42   Decision No. 13/2018. (IX. 4.) AB, Reasoning [13].
43   Decision No. 28/2017. (X. 25.) AB, Reasoning [75]; Decision No. 13/2018. (IX. 4.) AB, concurring opinion by Ágnes Czine, [83].
44   Decision No. 13/2018. (IX. 4.) AB, Reasoning [20].

use the accepted interpretative methodologies with reference to both Article P(1) and Article XXI(1).

4.4.5   Result-Oriented Judging

In several respects result-oriented adjudication may be the most suitable category for evaluating the activism of a constitutional or a regular court.[45] Result-oriented adjudication is characterized by the proceeding court establishing its jurisdiction or lack of jurisdiction in a case in view of the result to be attained. Result-oriented adjudication can only be interpreted in relation to activism in the so-called 'twilight zone',[46] *i.e.* in cases where both the Fundamental Law and the Act on the Constitutional Court are silent on whether the Constitutional Court has jurisdiction in a case or what legal consequences the Constitutional Court may establish. In relation to cases where the Fundamental Law or the Act on the Constitutional Court clearly lay down the framework of the proceedings, activism does not come arise.

From the case-law of the Hungarian Constitutional Court prior to the entry into force of the Fundamental Law, an example for result-oriented adjudication is Decision No. 42/2005. (XI. 14.) AB where the Constitutional Court established its jurisdiction for reviewing decisions on the uniformity of law made by the Supreme Court of Hungary despite the fact that its jurisdiction had not been specified either in the former Constitution or in the former Act on the Constitutional Court.[47] From among the decisions after the Fundamental Law took effect, the Constitutional Court's interpretation of its jurisdiction in relation to EU law may be mentioned as an example for result-oriented adjudication. Although neither the Fundamental Law, nor the Act on the Constitutional Court empowers the Constitutional Court to examine EU law, "the Founding Treaties qualify as Hungary's international obligations"[48] and thus, via these international law commitments the Constitutional Court has, at least on a theoretical level, the power to examine certain issues related to EU law.

At the same time, Decision No. 13/2018. (IX. 4.) AB can hardly be regarded as an example for result-oriented adjudication, as there are no doubts surrounding either the jurisdictional rule constituting the basis of the decision or the legal consequence applied. Consequently, the Constitutional Court was not forced to embark upon an activist interpretation in order to attain the desired result.

---

45   András Molnár, 'Szempontok a bírói aktivizmus definiálásához', *Jogelméleti Szemle*, 2012/3, p. 76.
46   László Blutman, 'Szürkületi zóna: az Alaptörvény és az uniós jog viszonya', *Közjogi Szemle*, 2017/1, pp. 1-14.
47   Decision No. 42/2005. (XI. 14.) AB, ABH 2005, 504.
48   Decision No. 2/2019. (III. 2.) AB, Reasoning [18].

4.5   CONCLUSIONS

The significance of Constitutional Court Decision No. 13/2018. (IX. 4.) AB lies exactly in the fact that the main substance of the decision – namely the almost absolute 'extraction' of the precautionary principle from the wording of the Fundamental Law – is not a result of Constitutional Court activism. In the course of making this decision the Constitutional Court, while using the major achievements of international law, EU law and Hungarian law, did nothing else but attach the precautionary principle to the Fundamental Law. The latter being a constitution that in fact includes extremely forward-looking provisions as regards environmental protection, leaving no doubt for legislators and practitioners as to the intention of the constitution-makers. The true significance of the decision is that it clearly connected Article P(1) and Article XXI(1) of the Fundamental Law by laying down that

> "Article P(1) [...] can be regarded simultaneously as the fundamental human rights guarantee under Article XXI(1) and a *sui generis* obligation prescribing the protection of the common heritage of the nation that has general relevance beyond Article XXI(1)."[49]

Article P(1) stipulates "it shall be the obligation of the State and everyone to protect and maintain, and to preserve for future generations" the natural and cultural assets forming the common heritage of the nation. The Constitutional Court in fact performed an act of major significance: it established beyond doubt that the precautionary principle was a part of the Fundamental Law, which the state and everyone must always consider in the course of legislation and legal practice. The efficient consideration of the interests of future generations is only possible, at the same time, if the legislator "makes long-term considerations beyond governing cycles in the course of their decision-making."[50] It is the latter to which the decision drew attention, serving also as an example for other national law enforcement forums outside Hungary by demonstrating how a national institution may facilitate and, where necessary, strike down in the interest of future generations legislation implementing short-term political considerations.

---

49   Decision No. 13/2018. (IX. 4.) AB, Reasoning [14].
50   Decision No. 28/2017. (X. 25.) AB, Reasoning [34].

5 THE VALUE OF THE ENVIRONMENT IN HUNGARIAN MUNICIPALITIES

An Overview of the Legal Aspects

*László Fodor**

Keywords

environmental regulation, environmental policy, local self-governments, local actions, environmental sustainability

Abstract

In the field of environmental policy, the principle of sustainability and local actions are becoming increasingly important ('think globally – act locally'). In Hungary, the focus is – within the multi-level local government system – on the local governments of the municipalities. This study is part of a research project on the role of municipal local governments in Hungary. During our research, in addition to the research methods of the 'desktop', case studies, questionnaires, interviews and focus group interviews were used. This study presents such general conclusions that can be drawn from the partial results. It does not include the presentation of certain areas of local environmental protection (air protection, waste management, protecting the built environment *etc.*), it rather tries to present the attitude of local governments, their commitment to environmental protection and the circumstances affecting it. It shows that Hungarian local governments do not form a homogeneous group. Primarily due to the differing size of municipalities, local environmental conflicts and the financial resources available for their resolution differ from each other as well. However, certain circumstances – such as the low degree of environmental awareness of the Hungarian population, the decrease in the autonomy of the local governments, the effects of the economic crisis and the changes of central regulations – affect them equally. The environmental protection performance of local governments is generally lower than desired.

---

* László Fodor: professor of law, University of Debrecen. The study is a part of the research project No. K 115530 (Roles and instruments of local governments in the realization of ecological sustainability) and was supported by the Hungarian National Research, Development and Innovation Office. The following monograph presents the results of the research project in more detail in Hungarian: László Fodor, *A falu füstje. A települési önkormányzatok és a környezet védelme a 21. század eleji Magyarországon*, Gondolat, Budapest, 2019.

5.1   INTRODUCTION

Tackling/overcoming challenges such as the climate change and the global ecological crisis requires collaboration from the individual to the global level, including local communities.[1]

The principle of subsidiarity demands that, with the knowledge of local conditions and in the possession of means for a more effective management of problems with greater chances of actual implementation, the various norms and individual decisions be enacted at the lowest possible level (closest to the subjects, *i.e.* the citizens).[2] At the same time, the principle implies autonomy for communities; promotes social participation in the administration of local affairs.[3] I assume that the emergence of the principle of subsidiarity is limited in today's Hungary. Increasing its reach could mean a reduction of the significance of the central government and the administration of the state, at the same time it could strengthen the role and autonomy of local governments, and – along with appropriate regulation, coordination and funding – improve the state's environmental performance.[4] This is desirable since the state's environmental performance is low.

The central institutions also support solving local problems. Local governmental environmental protection, (municipal wastewater and waste management, construction affairs, noise protection *etc.*), is the subject of central – both EU and national level – regulation. Environmental protection rules are increasingly striving to take into account local conditions, and identifying various instruments (permissions, environmental impact assessments, setting up different zones *etc.*) to differentiate, individualize protection, and to be able to evaluate the characteristics of the (local) environment in a complex (holistic) manner.

All the previously mentioned instruments are important, but they are insufficient. This is because they lack the initiative of the local community, lack local development ideas for the future, as most of these decisions are not adopted by the local community (that is to say, not made at the municipal level, or by bodies elected by the population), and finally, both their accuracy and their legitimacy is low.[5] At the same time, it is obvious that decisions

---

1   Each of the individual, family, personal relationship, settlement, community, metacommunication, city (urban), national, regional, continental, and global level has its own role, and if these levels are synchronized, the chance to effectively manage the problem is multiplied. Avit Bhowmik *et al., Powers of 10: A Cross-scale Optimization Framework for Rapid Sustainability Transformation*, EarthArXiv Preprints, 2018, at https://eartharxiv.org/feaq5/.

2   Gyula Bándi, *Környezetjog*, Szent István Társulat, Budapest, 2014, pp. 175-176.

3   János Frivaldszky, 'Szubszidiaritás és az európai identitás a közösségek Európájáért', *in* János Frivaldszky (ed.), *Szubszidiaritás és szolidaritás az Európai Unióban*, OCIPE Magyarország-Faludi Ferenc Akadémia, Budapest, 2006, p. 36.

4   Gyula Bándi, 'Variációk a környezetvédelmi igazgatás témájára', *Magyar Közigazgatás*, 1995/10, p. 582.

5   At the same time – for various reasons that are mentioned in this study as well, just as in the case of decision-making mechanisms – this problem unfortunately exists in local governmental decisions, although here I

made at the local level with the involvement of local communities, can be more substantiated and more successful.[6] It is important for the municipal local governments in the field of environmental policy to receive various instruments to supplement and concretize central regulations (as is the case in some other related areas, such as construction), in order to define and enforce their own environmental policies.

Research on local strategies show that the number of municipalities that no longer expect solutions from their governments or international organizations, but formulate their own ideas, is growing all over the world.[7] The role of the settlement/municipal level in some countries is increasing, because the government does not pay enough attention to the implementation of sustainability, meaning that the issue remains with the municipalities. For example, although the US (notoriously) does not participate in certain international climate protection agreements, 200 of its city governments have declared that they will do their utmost to achieve the Kyoto targets.[8]

The number of those international networks is growing increasingly, where local governments can participate and influence global processes, defining common goals, and transferring good practices.[9]

Significant international documents that define the global framework for sustainability policies also highlight the importance of the local levels of action. Agenda 21 (Goals for the 21st Century) adopted in Rio de Janeiro (1992) is a relatively widely known document, and its Chapter 6 specifically deals with sustainable urban development and encourages local governments to develop their own sustainable development strategies.[10] Among the UN Millennium Development Goals (MDGs), in order to improve the living conditions of masses living in slums, disaster recovery, urban water and public cleanliness services take center stage.[11]

---

am referring to the limited implementation of subsidiarity and the low level of development of environmental democracy.

6   On the other hand, as public environment protection bodies are typically under-represented at the local level, the implementation and the application of central regulations and measures is difficult. This can be overcome by local actions if certain conditions are met. *Cf.* Gunilla Wingqvist Ölund *et al., The role of governance for improved environmental outcomes*, Swedish Environmental Protection Agency, Bromma, 2012, p. 25.

7   László Antal Z., 'A természet és a társadalom kapcsolata, valamint a klímabarát települések eredményei', in Orsolya Bányai & Attila Barta (eds.), *A települési környezetvédelem elméleti és gyakorlati megközelítései*, Gondolat, Budapest, 2018, p. 24. at https://gondolatkiado.hu/pdf/Kornyezetvedelem.pdf.

8   At the same time, it has to be seen in this example that the US local government system is differs from the European models, where the municipalities have a greater autonomy, and the dependence on and the interconnectedness with the center is not typical. *See* Ilona Pálné Kovács, *Helyi kormányzás Magyarországon*, Dialóg-Campus, Budapest-Pécs, 2008, pp. 89-90.

9   Laura Kovács, 'Helyi önkormányzatok hálózatainak szerepe a globális kormányzásban', *Tér és Társadalom*, Vol. 24, Issue 1, 2010, pp. 103-117.

10   János Szlávik, *Fenntartható környezet- és erőforrás-gazdálkodás*, KJK-KERSZÖV, Budapest, 2005, p. 245.

11   Goal 7 – Ensure environmental sustainability, at www.un.org/millenniumgoals/pdf/Goal_7_fs.pdf.

The World Summit on Sustainable Development (Johannesburg Summit 2002) – in light of the lack of implementation of previous plans and the worsening of global environmental problems – called for the re-evaluation of the concept of development and for a new type of international cooperation. Regarding the adopted declaration (5th), environmental protection needs to be strengthened at local, national, regional and global levels. As a result of the Summit, partnership agreements have been concluded to execute the Agenda 21 goals, where besides national governments, regional groups, local governments, NGOs, international institutions, participants of private sector *etc.* are also present.[12]

The Agenda 2030 for Sustainable Development (2015)[13] also highlights the role of municipalities and local communities in urban development and management by describing their situation in the world (34th), that has a decisive impact on the quality of life of the population. Among the UN Sustainable Development Goals (SDGs) included in the document there are several that relate to the protection of the environment (issues of water, energy, public cleanliness, infrastructure) and the local/community level. The 11th SDG is specifically aimed at rendering settlements sustainable. I emphasize the requirement of participation-based, integrated, sustainable urban development among its sub-targets, in which local governments are necessarily involved (but the same holds true for the elimination of slums, the improvement of road safety, the improvement of urban air or the improvement of connections with peri-urban areas *etc.*).

By the 7th Environment Action Program of the EU,[14] that is currently in force (2015-2020), environmental health and (in the light of urbanization trends) the typical problems of cities (air pollution, noise pollution, inadequate waste management, water shortages, high greenhouse gas emission) are also considered to be priorities. The importance of sustainable urban development and urban planning and, as also highlighted, the promotion of good practices in this field and the provision of EU funds for this purpose are also considered as EU goals.

Underlying the national environmental regulations concerning urban environmental protection, are often EU directives. According to the latest evaluation, it is rather worrying that air quality standards are not applied in urban areas,[15] as air pollution is the number

12 Zsuzsanna Horváth, *Fenntartható fejlődés: Fenntartható termelés és fogyasztás az Európai Unióban*, Dóm-Dialóg Campus, Budapest-Pécs, 2016, pp. 34-37.
13 *Transforming our world: the 2030 Agenda for Sustainable Development*, at https://sustainabledevelopment.un.org/post2015/transformingourworld.
14 Decision No 1386/2013/EU of the European Parliament and of the Council of 20 November 2013 on a General Union Environment Action Programme to 2020 'Living well, within the limits of our planet.'
15 Client Earth, an international NGO, has pointed out regarding air protection that planning is, in general, nowhere effective, meaningful, and timely. In several of its cases (by examining German and English plans) the CJEU has already confirmed this (Judgment of 19 November 2014, *Case C-404/13, Client Earth*, ECLI:EU:C:2014:2382; Judgment of 25 July 2008, *Case C-237/07, Janecek*, ECLI:EU:C:2008:447). In other countries, such as Slovakia and the Czech Republic, national courts have already ruled the same. In Hungary and Poland, the criticism of air quality plans has also started by independent, civilian experts with submitting

one environmental cause of death in the EU. Exposure to environmental noise is also typical. At the same time, in Member States a "[m]ixed progress was reported as regards energy efficiency, sustainable transport and mobility, sustainable urban planning and design, urban biodiversity and sustainable buildings."[16]

This study summarizes some of the results of the research project led by me at the University of Debrecen (2015-2019) and deals only with the Hungarian local governments. However, its findings may be interesting with regards to other countries in the region.[17] In the course of this research, I analyzed current problems and regulations in light of the changes that have taken place since 2010.[18] These include the deterioration of national environmental policy performance as a result of the economic crisis, the reforms of public law restricting the autonomy of local governments, the reform of the system of public services (decreasing the role of local governments and centralization), and the changes to the EU funding system.

At the beginning of the research, I formulated questions such as what are the environmental responsibilities of the municipalities and how do they perform? Is there a difference between central regulations and local practices? Are there local regulations that are more restrictive than the central ones and which accommodate local characteristics? Do the local governments enforce their own regulations? Do they make use of the provided legal frameworks? Do they comply with international and EU regulations? Are environmental aspects integrated into their development strategies, various (*e.g.* construction) regulations?

A variety of methods were used to answer these questions: analyzing central and local environmental policy documents, focus-group interviews, questionnaires and case studies. The research outcomes have been published in several Hungarian and English publications so far.[19] In this study, I present my overall conclusions based on the summary of the partial results.

---

appropriate proposals to the authorities. In the autumn of 2018, the Clean Air Action Group (Levegő Munkacsoport) criticized the plan on Budapest in several points. *See* www.levego.hu/sites/default/files/kozig.%20kereset_vegleges_bp.pdf.

16   Report (6 March 2018) on the implementation of the 7th Environment Action Programme [2017/2030(INI)] at www.europarl.europa.eu/doceo/document/A-8-2018-0059_EN.html.

17   László Fodor *et al.*, 'Települési környezetvédelem Magyarországon: Egy kutatás előfeltevései', *Tér és Társadalom*, Vol. 30, Issue 3, 2016, pp. 19-39.

18   *E.g.* while earlier regional waste management investments, sewerage were supported, today, energy efficiency projects are, irrespective of what is needed locally (*e.g.* water supply protection).

19   *E.g.* Mihály Fónai *et al.* (eds.), *Local Environmental Problems and Answers in Hungary and Romania*. Scientia, Cluj Napoca, 2018, at https://ceeol.com/ in the Central and Eastern European Online Library.

5.2 The Relationship of Hungarian Local Governments to Environmental Protection – Environmental Tasks and Instruments at the Municipal Level in a Nutshell

In Hungary, following the change of regime in 1989, one of the most liberal local government systems was created. This means that in the spirit of sharing of powers, constitutional guarantees ensured autonomy and the local governments were given a relatively large number of tasks and competencies. At the same time, the level of municipalities remained decisive in the Hungarian local governmental system, that came with fragmentation and significant disproportionalities. Currently there are 3178 municipal local governments. In addition to these, 19 county (territorial) local governments have been established, but their role in environmental protection matters is low; they are only entrusted with instruments of regional development and rural development.

Local governments have performed, and are performing their tasks at different levels today, because, the capital and its districts, the larger cities, and the towns and cities with tourism tend to have more financial resources. The idea of (environmental) sustainability is receiving an increased role in settlements with a population of between 1000 and 5000 people and towns with over 10,000 inhabitants. The advantage of smaller settlements is that the local conditions are still more transparent for the leaders of the settlements and the mayor's offices, while sustainability is perceived as a chance for economic development by the larger cities. As for the rest, small village settlements do not possess sufficient financial or human resources, and in the mid-sized settlements, resources are consumed by operational costs.[20]

These local governments have been facing serious difficulties in carrying out environmental tasks that require specialized professionals and instruments. The 3rd National Environmental Program (NEP), adopted in 2009, already pointed out that it would be better to organize certain tasks at micro-regional level.

Since 2010, the central government has centralized several tasks and authorities in the field of local public service provision. As far as the environmental public services (waste management, wastewater treatment) are concerned, the involvement of the state (e.g. the service charges are centrally determined, the public service provider can no longer be freely chosen by the local governments, certain tasks have been taken over by the state) has also increased. Certain administrative authorities of state administration (e.g. for air protection) have been transferred to the territorial offices of the government, that is to say the metropolitan offices of the county government offices. Several professional fields have been regulated by the Act of Parliament, reducing the opportunities for local regulation.

---

20   *Tudatos Település Útmutató*, Belügyminisztérium, Budapest, 2018, p. 36. at http://bm-oki.hu/News/View-File?fileId=1117.

From 2012, the autonomy of local governments has been removed from the new Fundamental Law of Hungary.

The 4th NEP (2015-2020), as a culmination of the process, reflects the abolition of self-government autonomy and the relationship of the local governments to the Fundamental Law. It includes local governmental tasks and environmental problems at the municipal level, but the division of tasks between the state and local governments or the relationship between local governmental and central legislation are no longer considered, just as the principles of subsidiarity or territoriality the municipality is not mentioned.

The most important environmental tasks of the local governments are: regulation and planning, organization of local public services, performance of official (authority) tasks. The first two are always interconnected, since there is a need to organize and locally regulate services. Some of the official tasks are national and some are related to local public affairs.

Local governmental ordinances regulate the cleanliness of public areas (*e.g.* the pavement in front of houses), the burning of the leaves and garden waste (the government is currently considering a national ban on the burning of these wastes), the actions to be taken in case of a smog alert, the shipment of waste (date of delivery, size of bins), wastewater treatment, townscape protection, settlement structure *etc.* The local government may decide to regulate the protection of local natural values, the felling of trees in private areas and set local requirements for noise protection.

Some bodies of the local government act as public authorities (authorize, control, sanction, and act), *e.g.* regarding illegal dumping, construction, noise pollution, animal protection, industrial authority affairs, townscape protection, smog-alert, local conservation, water protection (typically in lower priority cases).

During the research it was found that most local governments do not have any environmental protection experts and did not set up such a committee, or organizational unit that would specialize in environmental protection tasks. Many local governments have failed to carry out their planning obligations, have not taken any measures, and often have poor local regulations. At the same time, there are also good examples: local sustainability initiatives, 'green bureaus', cooperations between local governments *etc.* The picture is highly varied, and the differences cannot be explained only by objective circumstances, *e.g.* much depends on the commitment of the mayor and the local population to environmental awareness.

Due to the lack of resources, some of the small settlements would like to pass on a few of their tasks and competences to others. However, the other municipal local governments rather find the legal instruments at their disposal insufficient. Overall, we have found that the environmental policy of local governments is less determined by proactivity, but rather by the need for the management of existing conflicts instead. New (and possibly foreign) solutions that go beyond central requirements are hardly ever employed, and the precautionary principle is less effective than desirable.

In the following, substantive part of the study, I will try to illustrate the background of the phenomena and put forward arguments for the claim that the local level of environmental policy should be strengthened.

5.3   Environmental Protection Has Not Yet Become a Priority

Generally speaking, the content and the instruments of environmental policy are influenced by several different circumstances. The strongest catalyst for an effective environmental policy can be an existing environmental problem, including acute local social conflicts. From this perspective, Hungary's territory – currently – does not belong to the worst areas of the Earth. Regarding an assessment based on 50 environmental indicators, our country is considered to be one of the most vulnerable countries.[21] Vulnerability refers to several previously recognized circumstances (such as the vulnerability of our waters, the risk of water pollution from neighboring countries).

A few years ago, surveys showed that environmental issues generally do not appear among the priorities of local governments[22] (and if they do, this is owed to economic interests or subsidies). This picture is succinct, as it obscures the differences between the municipalities, and it is also changing, as in recent years – with the increase of damages, dangers, also as a result of the financial resources from tenders – environmental issues seem to be coming to the forefront of climate protection. At the same time, there are other sub-areas that could make environmental protection a priority, as air quality has deteriorated in many municipalities in recent years, mainly due to polluting heating technologies, burning waste and the aging car fleet, thereby becoming a source of significant health damage. Even before (for example, in 2010), many settlements were seriously affected by flooding after heavy rainfall, one of the reasons being the reduction in the water retention capacity of the area, in conjunction with poor land use (e.g. by building-up areas). The health effects of increasing noise exposure are insidious, just as water scarcity, not occurring simultaneously, but there are also warning signs of intimidation in these areas.

5.4   Local Governments and Environmental Sustainability

If we look at the specific statutory requirements, (the promotion of) sustainable development as such is not listed among compulsory local governmental tasks. Sustainable

---

21   Mihály Simai, *A harmadik évezred nyitánya. A zöld fejlődés esélyei és a globális kockázatok*, Corvina, Budapest, 2016, p. 320.
22   Viktor Varjú, 'A települési önkormányzatok környezetvédelmi orientáltsága', *Comitatus: Önkormányzati Szemle*, Vol. 23, Issue 213, 2013, pp. 21-36.

development – to put it simply – includes environmental protection, but also several additional aspects (integration of environmental protection into the widest range of fields, the precautionary principle, long-term forward thinking, intergenerational equity *etc.*); with their sustainable economic, social and human aspects.

In my opinion sustainability[23] is not a luxury, but a condition for the competitiveness of municipalities. However, this is recognized and applied by only a fraction of Hungarian local governments. Relatively few settlements have a local sustainable development strategy that complies with Agenda 21, and even these adopted a weak concept of sustainability.[24]

A similar result came from a survey conducted by the Ministry of the Interior in 2016 (covering one thousand settlements), that also extended to the analysis on the appearance of sustainability in local documents. According to the survey, the idea of sustainability appears only in one third of the local municipal development plans, but in the municipal environmental programs this ratio is even worse. The integrated design method is typical for smart city projects and climate strategies, but only a small part of the settlements have these.[25] It is a common problem that the idea of sustainability is mostly limited to the confines of mandatory central regulations – themselves barely fulfilling requirement of sustainability, and as such insufficient for setting the appropriate direction – and subsidies. Therefore, sustainability is barely considered, and there are no real local ideas either.

It should also be mentioned that the idea of sustainability has not been conceived at governmental level either. Neither the intent (as I have referred to this several times) nor the right knowledge is available (the guidelines for regulatory impact assessments consider sustainability to be the same as environmental and nature protection, and even the EU funds managing authority is not familiar with the fact that sustainability is not tantamount to environmental and climate protection).[26]

5.5   THERE IS VERY LITTLE ROOM FOR MANEUVER

As I have already alluded to it multiple times, there are several local sustainability initiatives in Hungary as well (where local communities strive towards environmentally conscious

---

23   In addition to the environmental aspect of sustainable development, there are also serious problems in Hungary regarding the reproduction of knowledge capital, health, social inclusion, corruption *etc. A Nemzeti Fenntartható Fejlődési Keretstratégia második előrehaladási jelentése 2015-2016*, National Council for Sustainable Development (Nemzeti Fenntartható Fejlődés Tanács), Budapest, 2017, p. 9. at www.nfft.hu/documents/1238941/1261771/NFFS_2EHJ_vegso_20171207_HU.pdf/9e88dce0-bd15-1803-9675-68e35b028019.

24   Imre Baják & Zsolt Törcsvári, 'Local Sustainable Development Programs in Hungary' *Periodica Oeconomica* 2012, pp. 81-87. at http://gti.ektf.hu/anyagok/po/2012/PO2012_Bajak_Torcsvari.pdf.

25   Helyi Versenyképesség-fejlesztési Kutatási Program, 2016, Source of the data: Tudatos Település Útmutató, Budapest, 2018, pp. 33-34. at http://bm-oki.hu/News/ViewFile?FileID=105.

26   László Fodor, 'Fenntarthatósági indikátorok a jogi szabályozás hatásvizsgálatában', *Pázmány Law Working Papers*, 2012/4, pp. 3-4. at http://plwp.eu/evfolyamok/2012/96-2012-04.

energy consumption, self-sufficiency, ecological lifestyle). We assumed that, in accordance with good practices, the local ordinances in the settlements analyzed would also apply the concept and, for example, the local requirements for the conscious, long-term management of natural resources would appear in local regulations. Instead, we found that the local regulations of such settlements do not differ significantly from those of other local governments, and that often even their ideas were not incorporated into strategic documents.[27] The creation of regulations therefore does not necessarily constitute part of the pursuit of sustainability.

The reason for this may be that the local regulations more suited to the requirements of sustainability would outweigh the legitimate maneuver room of local governments. At the same time, it shall be noted that the awareness of the inhabitants cannot be turned into a legislative commitment. Finally, in the smallest settlements the possible cost implications of planning and regulatory tasks are also a major obstacle.

By studying several local documents, questionnaire surveys and interviews I found that local governments are dissatisfied with the central regulations that do not provide adequate protection for the environment, and with it, for the citizens. There are some who would go beyond the legal constraints they face in order to act more rigorously and there are those who cannot take advantage of the room for maneuver that is granted to them under the statutory rules.

It can be stated that the centralization of regulation often leads to losses at the local level. (I found several examples for this, such as the salting of sidewalks in winter, animal husbandry and regulations regarding public service charges.)

5.6 ENVIRONMENTAL PROTECTION IS QUITE A WIDE AREA

Local governments and local communities do not see the challenge of environmental protection in its complexity. On the one hand, they lack the necessary, complex knowledge and planning, and on the other hand, for various reasons, they are forced to emphasize some environmental sub-areas and sub-goals. This is problematic because, in the absence of a comprehensive approach, environmental measures often result in harm to other environmental interests and values.

The correlation seems to be obvious. The financing of local governments is not satisfactory in all respects (for example, there are few own resources, and the centrally secured

---

27   Orsolya Bányai, 'A helyi önkormányzatok környezetvédelmi szabályozása – elmélet és gyakorlat kettőssége', *in* Orsolya Bányai & Attila Barta (eds.), *A települési környezetvédelem elméleti és gyakorlati megközelítései*, Gondolat, Budapest, 2018, p. 52.

sources of revenue decrease),[28] then local leaders strive for a narrow interpretation of environmental protection, and go beyond what is required by law only to the extent that is covered by additional available financial resources (*e.g.* EU funds). This limitation also affects the nature of tasks and the extent of environmental protection. In connection with the latter, it is worth recalling that in the 1990s there was a wider interpretation of local governmental competences. For example, the Hungarian Constitutional Court confirmed the decisions of local governments even if they were in a conflict with central regulations but facilitated the protection of the environment (an emblematic example of this was the ordinance of the city of Szarvas laying down restrictions on waterborne traffic). Nowadays, narrow interpretation (often not reflecting on the integration of environmental protection into construction, water management *etc.*) is typical, ignoring the principle of integration. Many environmental tasks can be included in other mandatory tasks (*e.g.* settlement structure planning), but this is not always supported by central regulations, that can be illustrated by several examples (*e.g.* climate protection).

In Hungary, climate protection (with the exception of a very general obligation to create a program) does not appear as a mandatory local governmental task.[29] Measures affecting the quality of municipal air (reducing emissions, increasing the proportion of green areas) could be included in the local environmental protection, but because of some elements of climate adaptation (such as construction law, agricultural regulations that cannot be established by the municipality), this interpretation faces difficulties too. Due to the global context of climate protection, it certainly cannot be interpreted solely as a part of a local environmental task. It is no coincidence that although local governments consider climate protection to be a major challenge today, the preparation and implementation of comprehensive programs is currently characteristic of only a small number of municipalities. The relevant programs and measures are motivated by the access to EU funds and by the reduction of local governmental expenditures through energy investments.

---

28   Not only environmental revenues shall be considered in this regard, but financing issues of local governments in general. For example, the fact that in Hungary a system was created where a wide range of tasks are associated with narrowish portions from the joint resources. The introduction of real property taxes known in many countries in Western Europe has faced resistance, and the independence of the financial management is increasingly restricted, and the task-financing system introduced after 2010 was specifically designed for central purposes. *Cf.* Ilona Pálné Kovács, 'Fából vaskarika: a közigazgatás racionális térszerkezete', *in* Tamás Sikos T. & Tibor Tiner (eds.), *Tájak, régiók, települések térben és időben: tanulmánykötet Beluszky Pál 80. születésnapjára*, Dialóg Campus, Budapest, 2016, p. 328; Gábor Péteri, 'Kísérletezgetünk: önkormányzati feladatfinanszírozás', *Közjavak*, 2015/1, p. 28.

29   Antal 2018, pp. 24-25.

5.7 The Chance to Achieve Sustainability

Today, the protection of the local environment can become relatively strong, where there are some additional interests, such as *e.g.* municipal marketing. This is related to the competition between the municipalities, the need for a highly trained workforce[30] and tourism, that requires a low noise level at night, a pleasant, green, waste-free environment, clean water, a well-committed municipality for the protection of the environment and so on.[31] However, these are the barely necessary, not the sufficient conditions. The answers given to our research questions have shown that access to central (EU) funds plays a crucial role.

There is a chance for a successful local environmental policy in small settlements that have already been able to adopt sustainability initiatives and are not exposed to significant environmental pressures. However, it seems that there is an even greater potential in larger cities, where we can talk about economic development, that is, where environmental protection can become part of the local municipal development, economic development and competitiveness policy. In other words, in townships where it is possible to change the economic structure. However, it is typical that only a few Hungarian cities – such as Debrecen, Miskolc, Zalaegerszeg – have a deliberate concept on investments. The Smart City and Green City programs (and related subsidies) can further strengthen their efforts at environmental protection.

Meanwhile, the appearance of a large investor can override such endeavors. Municipal marketing (competition) and local economic development do not necessarily focus on environmental aspects, instead, they often push job creation and economic growth to the forefront, that necessarily entails environmental and social losses.[32]

---

30 György Enyedi: 'A sikeres város', *Tér és Társadalom*, Vol. 11, Issue 4, 1997, p. 4. As the author points out, one of the characteristics of a successful city is the presence of a trained middle class. At the same time, not only livelihood is important for this social layer, but they have high expectations regarding their environment and the provided public services.

31 I have experienced the importance of tourism, for example in the case of Bogács. At the same time, long-term, hidden effects are already being pushed back. (I am thinking of anomalies in thermal water management.) Researches in Balatonlelle and a small town in Slovenia (Bled) have come to a similar conclusion regarding the relationship between optional tasks and tourism. Marianna Nagy *et al.*, 'A Comparative Research on Municipal Voluntary Tasks of Three Hungarian and Slovenian Municipalities', *Central European Public Administration Review (CEPAR)*, Issue 1, 2019, pp. 165-197. at http://uprava.fu.uni-lj.si/index.php/CEPAR/article/view/418/461.

32 Enyedi 1997, pp. 4-5.

5.8   THE ROLE OF ENVIRONMENTAL PLANNING

A significant part of Hungarian settlements, in contravention of the obligation laid down in Section 48/E of the Environmental Act of Hungary (Act LIII of 1995 on the General rules of environmental protection), have not had for many years or have never had an environmental program. They have no money to prepare the program, to involve experts, or if they had a program, they would have no money to execute it.

During the research I found many signs that even if there was a program, then it would not necessarily be followed by local governments, as it would make it difficult to exploit the investment and job creation opportunities that are often provided randomly. In many places, environmental protection is still juxtaposed with economic 'development'. It has to be noted again at this point, however, that local regulations are not similar in this respect, that is to say, there are several settlements – mainly larger, richer, with better abilities – where there are programs, experts, local regulations defined with respect to each other, conscious developments *etc.* even if perhaps they are not always considered ideal. Thus, the preference, sequence, and appreciation of values are also decisive in terms of the content of the municipal environmental policy.

In conclusion, sustainability presupposes an (environmentally) conscious local community, that takes initiative. However, this ideal situation exists only in a small fraction of settlements. Typically, short-term environmental problems that are the source of conflict within the community receive more attention than the problems that seem less pressing today but threaten survival in the long run. Thus, for example, in the case of a natural-spa city living on tourism, it may be an important environmental interest to reduce the night-time noise level or to create an attractive environment, while generating more and more thermal water to increase revenues and tourism. Meanwhile, the city may continue to exploit its resources wastefully, ignoring the balance of water abstraction and water supply, and the opportunities in using waste heat as energy resource.

5.9   THE CONTRADICTION OF VALUES

The term 'value creation' (otherwise taken over from the economy) is often used in the wording of the municipal local governments. For example, plants are planted, buildings are renovated, public areas are paved (asphalted), infrastructure is being built/developed, the land of the municipality is cultivated, livestock are kept (while also producing food for sale), that gives meaningful work to public workers (who therefore 'do not just mow the lawn and sweep the lawn'), meeting a variety of local needs, often in partnership with local communities (such as cooperatives, associations, companies). On the part of a local government, value creation – in contrast with the value creation of the economy – also enables the appreciation of community aspects. Therefore, and in such a way, the endeavor is respectable, but what we regard as value is, in many cases, debatable, and often the municipalities do not think about the downside of 'value creation'. While value creation meets human needs (with the help of various products and services), it leads to a loss of value and a deterioration in the natural environment.[33] Taking space away from nature is characteristic of most Hungarian settlements and the tendency is increasing. Too frequent mowing/reaping, planting of introduced species or plants with high irrigation needs, failing to protect trees in public areas under construction, covering the ground unreasonably causing soil sealing (making it incapable of soaking up rainwater), building infrastructure beyond actual needs can all be mentioned as an example. This is a serious problem. If we look at the period since the change of regime, the proportion of biologically active areas in Hungary has been dramatically decreasing, and in direct proportion the ecosystem services in the municipal environment are in a decline (as well).[34]

5.10   The Environmental Influence of the Government

It is a serious problem in Hungary that the government's environmental commitment has declined significantly in recent years. The level of protection provided by central regulations, the organizational framework of the state institutional system, and the guarantees provided in official procedures are also weakened. Furthermore, some of the subsidies provided to municipalities (and businesses) ignore environmental considerations.

While in the years following the change of regime, the value-oriented side of environmental policy became more prominent (even though it did not become the 'winning' position) and was struggling with short-term economic group interests, it has now become a driver of economic rationality (where environmental protection includes technologies, business models). The latter, however, is driven by various competing group interests and business policies. We often see that environmental measures are made depending on subsidies and financial resources. However, this is not simply a result of a lack/deprivation of funds, but a consequence of a change in the values and the logical approach.

---

33   Sándor Kerekes, 'A fenntarthatóság közgazdasági értelmezése', in Miklós Bulla & Piroska Guzli (eds.), *Fenntartható fejlődés Magyarországon*, Új Mandátum, Budapest, 2006, p. 196.

34   In addition to the environmental impacts induced at the location, correlating effects shall also be considered in a broader context, such as the declining proportion of green areas in the whole country. Also, areas without any value for ecological services (such as arable land), the growing coverage of the soil surface, and the increased use of materials and energy are such impacts. *Cf.* Gábor Bartus, 'Az érdemi és hatékony környezetpolitika körvonalai: Miért nem képesek a társadalmak megfékezni a természeti környezet pusztulását?', in András Jakab & László Urbán (eds.), *Hegymenet: Társadalmi és politikai kihívások Magyarországon*, Osiris, Budapest, 2017, pp. 444-446.

A similarly grave problem is that there are no coherent, long-term policy strategies and concepts from the outset (*e.g.* rural development, agricultural policy, energetical policy *etc.*) to which local governments can adapt their own ideas. Even where there are sectoral strategies, these are often not in line with each other, thus, there is a lack of horizontal coordination, and it is also typical that they do not emerge in concrete (legislative, budgetary, financing and other) decisions. A meaningful involvement of local governments in the drafting of national strategies has not taken place either.[35]

Perhaps the biggest shortcoming may be detected in the financing system of local governments, which does not make local governments directly concerned with the protection of their own environment or prompt them to respect the interests of other settlements affected. The rate and differentiation of communal taxes is inadequate, local business taxes do not have to be distributed among the municipalities of the impact area.[36] Although income from fines can be shared, this is not automatic, and local governments rather 'expropriate' the resources themselves rather than share them with each other. There are hardly any incentives to channel income into environmental protection, while the lack of financial resources has an adverse effect. State acquisition of public services and, in parallel, the shrinking of competencies – the loss of authority over price regulation – further reduce the involvement of local governments in protecting the environment, making them less concerned in the sustainability of related public services.

Under such circumstances, financial resources from central (governmental) tenders are particularly important. What is important is not merely that these tenders exist as such, but that they foster the complexity of the environmental policy (integration), the consideration of local specificities/needs, promote decentralized decisions, and so on. The research also pointed to several anomalies in this regard.

---

35   Miklós Bulla *et al.*, 'Fenntarthatóság – dilemmák és lehetőségek', *in* Bulla & Guzli (eds.), 2006, pp. 138 and 144.

36   Erzsébet Beliczay, 'A területfoglalást serkentő támogatások', *in* Károly Kiss (ed.), *Tiltandó állami támogatások. Környezetvédelmi szempontból káros támogatások a magyar gazdaságban*, L'Harmattan, Budapest, 2006, p. 154. One of the model examples of the problem of 'burden sharing' has appeared in our questionnaire survey. The city of Vecsés's response indicated that the problem of air traffic noise has been a problem in the settlement for decades. The noise management committee set up by the airport operator has not been able to assist this settlement problem for more than ten years of its operation. Probably, because the Liszt Ferenc International Airport is the only airport with such a heavy traffic, which is in the interest of the national economy. There would be traffic management solutions that would require burden sharing other settlements adjacent to the airport, but these settlements have been unable to resolve their differences, therefore, central intervention is necessary.

5.11   FALSE DILEMMAS AND TRAPS

The leaders of municipalities also encounter countless political traps, the recognition of which is not necessarily rewarding at the current level of public (environmental) awareness. In order to preserve popularity and the confidence of voters, environmental regulations are less likely to be enforced at several small settlements (local authorities do not act, do not sanction, regardless of their obligation under the law). At the same time, this can lead to real environmental problems, and can lead to conflicts within the local community.

The almost unquestionable dogma of economic growth also affects the values of local governments. In addition, most of the local governments in Hungary are still linking economic growth with increasing built-up areas (creating residential, economic, commercial, industrial zones),[37] despite its infrastructure development cost implications, and numerous negative effects (increased demand for mobility, soil degradation, decline in biodiversity and agricultural land, the increase of built-up density etc.).[38] Meanwhile, the utilization/rehabilitation of the brownfield belt is generally lagging behind.[39]

Fashionable developments made at the expense of the public spaces most valuable for the citizens, that is the green spaces, not only reduce sustainability and worsen the chances of climate adaptation, but also lead to misguided decisions regarding the city's assets.[40]

As far as environmental protection is concerned, local governments tend to complain about the lack of financial resources. As I have already mentioned several times, the financing system is indeed inadequate, and this affects especially villages and small towns. In addition, the contradiction is difficult to resolve when simultaneously with the latter the resources and revenues typically come from some kind of environmental exploitation (use of thermal water, tourism, sale of green space, local business tax etc.). I find it particularly anomalous when a municipality that has a significant income from the utilization of natural resources, depletes them in a way that none of the income is spent on environmental protection (if, for example, water is being produced, it is hardly compensated by planting flowerbeds in the settlement). Another problem is when the settlement does not

---

37   György Ádám Horváth, *A fenntarthatósággal kapcsolatos kihívások és újszerű megoldási lehetőségek az önkormányzati szférában*, PhD thesis, Budapest, 2017, p. 113.

38   Some case studies made in the Budapest agglomeration (Piliscsaba, Tinnye) point out that the rapid expansion associated with suburbanization may be in conflict with the interests of the existing population and trigger its resistance. There is another domestic type problem here: the fragmented inner areas that are the result of inconsiderate settlement planning. Márta Scheer *et al.*, 'A szuburbanizációs környezeti konfliktusok feloldásának lehetőségei', *in* Sándor Kerekes & Károly Kiss, *Környezetpolitikánk európai dimenziói*, MTA TK, Budapest, 2004, pp. 89-97.

39   Beliczay 2006, pp. 147-150.

40   Gábor Bartus, 'Fenntarthatóság és klímapolitika', *in Mérsékelt öv? Felelős cselekvési irányok a hatékony klímavédelemért*, Klímabarát Települések Szövetsége, Budapest, 2018, p. 56.

strive for the economic utilization of natural resources, or to achieve meaningful environmental objectives.

Larger settlements tend to realize investments and projects that favor, for example, economic development, job creation and other aspects. However, with a badly chosen location, technology, or ill selected size, these projects eventually result in environmental conflicts. As far as investments carried out in the name of protecting the environment, contradictions may also emerge (*e.g.* bypass roads).[41]

Among the limitations faced by local governments that make it more difficult to introduce innovative local ideas, there is a regrettable attitude of circumventing the regulations that is typical to the Hungarian population. Irregular constructions, well-drilling, landscaping (landfilling), uncontrolled demolition of waste *etc.* are examples. Among the services for households, black economy still represents a significant proportion, which also has environmental consequences.[42] Services performed without an invoice (*e.g.* well-drilling) are often done by inadequately trained professionals.[43]

The introduction of certain regulatory solutions is obstructed by the fact that it is not only the investors who compete for the best locations, but (typically, outside of the capital Budapest, and in certain sectors) local governments compete for investors who provide labor, pay taxes, and purchase land. Under these circumstances, there is little chance that one local government would impose stricter environmental requirements on the participants of the financial market.

Lastly, I would like to mention, that the result of a questionnaire survey showed that the potential to follow the best international/EU standards and international best practices lies mainly with large cities (cities with county rights). Meanwhile, smaller settlements demonstrate the least willingness and opportunity to follow such practices.[44] It seems that following international good practices means only paying lip service to them in local laws and strategies, or while organizing procurement and public services. It is national legislation that is rather relied upon, and this, for the most part, already applies EU (international) standards. The EU (air protection, nature conservation) regulations, or international standards (for example, because some of their territory falls under the Ramsar Convention) are examined directly only by few settlements.

---

41   Sándor Fülöp (ed.), *A jövő nemzedékek országgyűlési biztosának beszámolója 2008-2009*, OBH, Budapest, 2010, p. 108 and pp. 154-156.

42   Károly Kiss, 'Környezetvédelmi szempontból káros támogatások a magyar gazdaságban' (összefoglaló áttekintés), *in* Kiss (ed.), 2006, pp. 13-44.

43   *Tájékoztató a települési önkormányzat jegyzőjének engedélyezési hatáskörébe tartozó kutak eljárásjogi szabályairól*, Belügyminisztérium, Budapest, 2017, p. 4. at www.nak.hu/kiadvanyok/kiadvanyok/1232-tajekoztato-kutak-eljarasjogi-szabalyai/file.

44   The adoption and transfer of international good practices is also supported by international movements (such as Green Cities), local governmental alliances (International Council for Local Environmental Initiatives, Covenant of Mayors, Climate Alliance *etc.*) and competitions (*e.g.* for the Green Capital of Europe).

While it is not expected that international practices will be incorporated into local regulations (partly due to the limitations imposed by central legislation), the direct monitoring of EU standards and the follow-up of others' best practices are common in EU-funded developments.[45]

5.12 Conclusions

During the research I attempted to define the attitude of Hungarian local governments to environmental protection. However, due to the disproportion within the local governmental system (the differences between the smallest and largest municipalities), it is difficult to make general statements. Importantly, however, several factors affecting environmental protection duties and performance of municipalities have been identified. Only some of these influencing factors are central environmental protection regulations, and many other legal and non-legal factors may be identified. The degree of centralization (also, the autonomy of the local government), the method and amount of funding for tasks, access to financial resources (*e.g.* EU funds), the networks and cooperation of local governments (with NGOs, authorities, other local governments *etc.*), the commitment and political relationships of settlement leaders, the activity of local communities, and occasionally, corruption are all relevant factors.

It would be worth exploring the local level of environmental policy in other countries of Central and Eastern Europe and then comparing the typical problems, solutions and instruments. Such research should also take into account the diversity of local governmental systems;[46] first and foremost, how the obligations of local governments are determined (mandatory and optional tasks;[47] local governmental and central (state) administration

---

45 Fodor 2019, pp. 175-176.

46 The differences between Latin, Anglo-American, continental, Scandinavian, Eastern European and other local governmental systems are not only constitutional, by their nature. Behind each model, there are national traditions, socio-cultural differences, and in their grouping the division of the actual positions of power, their political and operational specificities also play a role. Ilona Pálné Kovács, 'Helyi önkormányzatok', *in* András Jakab & Balázs Fekete (eds.), *Internetes Jogtudományi Enciklopédia* (2017), p. 5. at https://ijoten.hu/ uploads/helyi-onkormanyzatok.pdf.

47 In Hungary, several tasks of the local environmental policy pertain to the mandatory tasks (*e.g.* regulation of municipal waste management, certain administration tasks in the field of industrial management, managing municipal wastewater treatment) and several to the voluntary tasks (*e.g.* nature preservation, preference for renewable energy sources, setting up a public surveillance). The provision of mandatory (obligatory) tasks are strongly preferred under Hungarian municipal law. Voluntary tasks may be funded by the own local income and revenues, and these own revenues are partly 'labeled' resources. (*E.g.* Section 36/A of Act C of 1990 on Local Taxes states that local social services and in the capital city local public transport should be primarily financed by the income from the local business tasks). The County Government Offices have new powers and duties in the field of the supervision of local governments: they can make a replacement decision if a municipality does not perform its obligatory tasks (*e.g.* in the field of delegated legislation).

powers), how the financing is done *etc.*[48] The spatial structure of public administration is also important,[49] as is the one-level or multi-level structure of the local governmental system (*e.g.* in many countries of Western Europe, or even in neighboring Romania, local governmental autonomy is not provided to small villages; and some of the tasks (such as waste management) are not delegated to the local municipal level but to regional authorities).

Therefore, municipalities have a narrow field of local policy making, especially in the field of voluntary tasks. *See* Marianna Nagy & István Hoffman (eds.), *A Magyarország helyi önkormányzatairól szóló törvény magyarázata*, HVG-ORAC, Budapest, 2016, pp. 60-62. *E.g.* in Anglo-American local governmental systems, the optional (voluntarily) assignment of tasks is conceptually excluded. Pálné Kovács 2017, p. 8; István Hoffman *et al.*, 'Önkormányzati feladatellátás vizsgálata a KÖFOP program keretében', *Jegyző és Közigazgatás*, 2018/2, p. 11.

48   Nagy *et al.* 2016, p. 166.

49   In many countries in Europe, an integrated local governmental level has been created to make it more responsive to public functions, while in other countries, the system is fragmented, where the tasks and powers are delegated to local municipal governments, although they seek to achieve optimal size through partnerships or differentiated task deployment. *See* Ilona Pálné Kovács, 'A közigazgatás térszerkezete', *in* András Jakab & Balázs Fekete (eds.), *Internetes Jogtudományi Enciklopédia* (2017), p. 4. at https://ijoten.hu/uploads/ a-kozigazgatas-terszerkezete.pdf.

6   European Water Law and Uncertainty

Managing Hydrological Variability in Shared River Basins in the EU

Gábor Baranyai[*]

Keywords

hydrological variability, transboundary water governance, EU water law, shared river basins, variability management

Abstract

Hydrological variability has been on the rise in the past decades with dramatic consequences for water management on the national and international plane alike. Yet, most legal regimes governing the use and protection of water resources reflect a high degree of rigidity presuming that hydrological conditions prevailing at the time of their conception remain stable indefinitely. The mismatch between rigid legal frameworks and rapidly changing natural conditions are likely to give rise to new types of interstate conflicts in shared river basins (or accentuate existing ones), since historically the adoption of (new) transboundary governance regimes has been very slow and reactive in character. While the EU has been praised worldwide as an exemplary model of co-riparian cooperation, its multi-layered water governance regime also deserves a comprehensive fitness check that, among others, should evaluate its ability to handle the growing uncertainty surrounding underlying hydrological circumstances. This article provides a resilience assessment of European water law from the perspective of the management of hydrological variability.

6.1   Introduction: Hydrological Variability in the Anthropocene

Much of the world's legal institutions governing transboundary water management have evolved in relatively stable hydro-climatic conditions over the past century or so. These regimes therefore reflect a high degree of stationarity, an assumption that the physical parameters of the management of international rivers are sufficiently well-known and are largely predictable. Yet, the arrival of the Anthropocene ('age of man') has brought about new phenomena that are likely to alter the natural hydrological cycle beyond recognition.[1]

---

[*]   Gábor Baranyai: senior lecturer, National University of Public Service, Budapest.
1   Paul C. D. Milly *et al.*, 'Stationarity is Dead: Whiter Water Management?' *Science*, Vol. 319, Issue 5863, 2008, p. 573.

With stationarity declared dead by natural sciences, international water governance frameworks must embark on a fundamental adaptation course so they can continue to fulfil their foundational objective: ensuring the smooth cooperation of states over the utilization and protection of shared water resources. The principal facet of this adaptation challenge is the management of increasing hydrological variability with extreme events beyond historically recorded ranges and frequencies. Variability management is, therefore, an essential token of the resilience of a given governance system as it provides a means for the political and technical masters of transboundary water management to address elements of uncertainty and surprise in an orderly fashion.

This article investigates how the four overlapping regulatory regimes governing co-riparian relations in the EU – *i.e.* EU law, the UNECE framework, basin treaties and bilateral water agreements – address the question of hydrological variability. It does so from an analytical perspective with a view to identifying regulatory lacunae that may amount to major sources of conflict in shared river basins in the EU.

6.2   The Role of Variability Management in Co-Riparian Relations

Fluctuation of flow quantities is an inherent feature of any natural river system, even in temperate basins characterized by modest intra-annual variability. The variation of high and low water levels plays an important regulating role in riverine ecology and in traditional agriculture. Yet, a high degree of natural variability may also be a precursor to transboundary water conflict. Rivers with outstanding hydrological variability display a considerable tendency to trigger or contribute to political tensions among basin states. As Wolf *et al.* conclude

> "extreme events of conflicts were more frequent in marginal climates with highly variable hydrological conditions, while the riparians of rivers with less extreme natural conditions have been more moderate in their conflict/cooperation relationship."[2]

Consequently, managing hydrological variability can be a major challenge in co-riparian relations even at the best of times. Given, however, the impact of climate change on the hydrological cycle and human responses thereto (*e.g.* more irrigation in times of drought) controlling flow variability beyond previously recorded ranges will give rise to new levels of political difficulty all over the world. Not surprisingly, the question features high in

---

2   Aaron T. Wolf *et al.*, 'Conflict and Cooperation Within International River Basins: The Importance of Institutional Capacity', *Water Resources Update*, Vol. 125, 2003, p. 31.

recent hydro-political analyses. In fact, based on a mathematical modelling of the relationship between water conflicts and treaty configurations Dinar *et al.* actually suggest that
legally defined adaptation mechanisms for hydro-variability are one of the few key factors
of the resilience of co-riparian relations.[3]

6.3   Variability Management as a Policy and Regulatory Challenge

In the broadest sense of the word, variability management is about dealing with naturally
occurring hydrological extremes, including floods, droughts and other specific variations.[4]
It must be pointed out, however, that while both floods and droughts can be considered
as extreme events, their impacts on co-riparian relations are quite different. Floods are
typically short-term phenomena with a(n almost) mechanical knock-on effect on downstream riparians. The downstream motion of water can be predicted fairly precisely by
widely available satellite-based technologies. On mid- and downstream areas, where population density tends to be the highest, these allow authorities and citizens to choose the
adequate level of protection. Droughts, on the other hand, do not follow precisely calculable
patterns and can last several months or years. Severe droughts trigger a variety of response
measures by water managers, many of them actually having a dramatic impact on water
availability downstream (typically: more irrigation). As a consequence, flood management
features among the most 'benign' collective action problems of shared river basins, while
natural or man-made water shortages or scarcity tends to be the most powerful driver of
transboundary conflict.[5] Either way, variability management is closely linked to water
quantity regulation.

The potentially very broad range of measures dealing with hydrological variability in
a transboundary context can be clustered as follows:

---

3   Shlomi Dinar *et al.*, 'Climate Change, Conflict, and Cooperation – Global Analysis of the Resilience of
    International River Treaties to Increased Water Variability', *Policy Research Working Paper No. 6916*, The
    World Bank, Washington D.C., 2014, p. 20.
4   Id. p. 8.
5   Suzanne Schmeier, *Governing International Watercourses – River Basin Organizations and the Sustainable
    Governance of Internationally Shared Rivers and Lakes*, Routledge, London, 2013, p. 68.

i. *short term measures:*

- flexible water allocation mechanisms (*e.g.* water sharing based on percentages) that require the automatic adjustment of cross-border river flow to changes in water availability;[6]
- domestic water management measures aimed to minimize the transboundary impacts of hydrological extremes (emergency use of reservoirs to store or release water, stricter irrigation procedures *etc.*);[7]
- emergency communication and cooperation mechanisms (data collection and sharing, early warning, immediate consultations, mutual assistance among riparian states *etc.*).[8]

ii. *long term measures:*

- regular review of water allocation and relevant water uses;[9]
- joint construction and/or operation of water infrastructure to increase water supply or store excess water;[10]
- joint long-term planning for and management of hydrological extremes (*e.g.* transboundary flood risk mapping);
- broadened cooperation with regards to issues that go beyond flow variability or the quantitative aspects of water.[11]

6.4 VARIABILITY MANAGEMENT IN INTERNATIONAL WATER LAW: AN OVERVIEW

Concerns about the natural variability of transboundary river flow are not a new phenomenon in international relations. As Drieschova *et al.* point out as early as 1863 the Netherlands and Belgium made allocation of water resources of the Meuse conditional upon annual variability. Yet, until relatively recently neither water treaties nor academic research have paid sufficient attention to the issue. As a result, general international water law scarcely addresses variability management in any explicit fashion. Thus, the various principles enumerated by of world's most eminent framework instrument: the 1997 UN Watercourses Convention[12] – *i.e.* equitable and reasonable utilization, the obligation not to cause significant harm and the obligation to cooperate – regulate the issue only indi-

---

6   Alena Drieschova *et al.*, 'Governance Mechanisms to Address Flow Variability in Water Treaties', *Global Environmental Change*, Vol. 18, Issue 2, 2008, p. 290.

7   Lucia De Stefano *et al.*, 'Climate Change and the Institutional Resilience of International River Basins', *Journal of Peace Research*, Vol. 49, Issue 1, 2012, p. 196.

8   Id.

9   Id.

10   Drieschova *et al.* 2008, p. 290.

11   Id. p. 291.

12   Convention on the Law of Non-navigational Uses of International Watercourses, New York, 21 May 1997.

rectly.[13] These principles imply the duty of watercourse states to manage hydrological extremes with due attention to the interests of other riparians. The Convention also calls on watercourse states to prevent and mitigate, individually and/or jointly, 'harmful conditions', *e.g.* floods, droughts or desertification that may have a negative impact on other riparian states.[14] When such conditions amount to an emergency situation, *i.e.* a sudden event actually or potentially causing serious harm to other watercourse states, the state of origin must immediately notify the (potentially affected) other riparians and take all practicable measures to prevent, mitigate or eliminate the harmful effects of the emergency.[15] Such emergency cooperation, however, does not apply to gradually unfolding events such as droughts and desertification.

In a similar fashion, the regional water governance agreement of the Southern African Development Community, the SADC Revised Protocol on Shared Watercourses[16] addresses hydrological variability only marginally, calling on riparian states to act individually and/or jointly to prevent and mitigate harmful conditions resulting from such natural causes as floods, droughts or desertification.[17]

As the scale of treaty area decreases, specific variability management schemes become more frequent. In fact, a meticulous review of 50 relevant basin treaties concluded between 1980 and 2002 by Drieschova *et al.* found that 68% of the water agreements explicitly mention flow variability.[18] *E.g.* the Mekong Cooperation Agreement[19] contains general and specific rules for water quantity management for the monsoonal wet and dry seasons.[20] In "cases of historically severe droughts and/or floods", however, the application of regular allocation rules is suspended.[21] Such exceptionally severe hydrological events are subject to early notification and the mandatory involvement of the Joint Committee of the Mekong River Commission with a view to adopting appropriate remedial action.[22] The Charter of Waters of the Senegal River[23] also foresees such consultation procedures in the event pre-

---

13   Stephen McCaffrey, 'The UN Convention on the Law of the Non-Navigational Uses of International Watercourses: Prospects and Pitfalls', *in* Salman M. A. Salman & Laurence Boisson de Chazournes (eds.), *International Watercourses – Enhancing Cooperation and Managing Conflict*, World Bank Technical Paper No. 414, Washington D.C., 1998, pp. 18-19.
14   *See* Article 27 of the Convention.
15   Id. Article 28.
16   SADC Revised Protocol on Shared Watercourses, Windhoek, 7 August 2000.
17   Id. Article 3(4)(a).
18   Drieschova *et al.* 2008, p. 287.
19   Agreement on the Cooperation for the Sustainable Development of the Mekong River Basin, Chieng Rai, 5 April 1995.
20   Id. Articles 5 and 6.
21   Id. Article 6.
22   Id. Article 10.
23   Charter of Waters of the Senegal River, 28 May 2002.

determined water allocations must be revisited due to floods, other natural disasters or water shortages of natural character.[24]

Apparently, water treaties primarily concerned with water allocation are more likely to contain some kind of mechanisms to handle extreme flow variations. For instance the 1996 Ganges Treaty between India and Bangladesh[25] calls for immediate consultations should the flow at the Farakka Dam at the border fall below a commonly agreed threshold so as "to make adjustments on an emergency basis, in accordance with the principles of equity, fair play and no harm to either party."[26]

6.5   VARIABILITY MANAGEMENT IN EUROPEAN WATER LAW

6.5.1   The Structure and Normative Features of European Water Law

Co-riparian relations in the EU are governed by a complicated system of overlapping transnational legal regimes. Such normative characteristic stems from the unique constitutional construction of the EU, under which the management of shared water resources is subjected to four levels of supranational law (hereinafter collectively referred to as European water law): *(i)* EU primary law determines the distribution of powers in the field of water policy between the EU and its Member States. It also establishes horizontal institutional requirements and broad policy environmental objectives that apply across all levels of European water law; *(ii)* international water treaties ratified by the EU: the EU is an active player in the international water policy arena. Any treaty to which the EU accedes becomes automatically binding on EU institutions and Member States, even if some Member States choose not to become a party on their own right; *(iii)* EU secondary law: the bulk of EU water law has been adopted by EU institutions, mostly in the form of directives. Any such secondary legislation must conform to primary EU law as well as to international treaties approved by the EU; *(iv)* multilateral and bilateral water treaties concluded by EU Member States: the daily practice of cross-border water management takes place through basin treaties and bilateral water agreements. These treaties do not only have to comply with all three above layers of EU law, but – under the 'doctrine of harmonious interpretation' – Member States must also interpret them in light of the letter

---

24   Id. Articles 6 and 7.
25   Treaty between the Government of the Republic of India and the Government of the People's Republic of Bangladesh on sharing of the Ganga/Ganges waters at Farakka, New Delhi, 21 December 1996.
26   Id. Article II.

and spirit of relevant EU norms.[27] It means that Member States cannot conclude agreements to deviate from general EU or specific water law.

6.5.2   EU Water Law and Variability

EU water law addresses several facets of natural hydrological variability. In fact, one of the objectives of the EU's core water legislation, the Water Framework Directive (WFD), is to contribute to mitigating the effects of floods and droughts.[28] Yet, the coverage of these phenomena by the WFD is far from comprehensive, especially in a transboundary context. One major exception however stands out: Floods Directive creates an elaborate system of flood risk mapping and management that pays particular attention to the vulnerabilities of downstream riparian states.[29] Following the above classification, the measures aimed at managing hydrological variability in the EU's existing legal toolbox can be summarized as follows.

As regards short term management of hydrological extremes all that the WFD does is to create a temporary derogation from the obligation to comply with the objectives of good water status, i.e. the overarching objective of water management under EU law. These circumstances include in particular "extreme floods and prolonged droughts" or other conditions of natural cause or force majeure that are "exceptional or could not reasonably have been foreseen."[30] If a member state intends to invoke such derogation, it must, ironically, define in advance in the relevant river basin management plan the conditions under which such 'unforeseeable' emergency situation can be declared. It also must specify what measures will have to be taken under such circumstances.[31]

As regards long term adaptation to hydrological variability the WFD goes several steps further. First, it imposed an obligation on Member States to undertake a detailed analysis of the main characteristics of each river basin by 2004 that had to contain an analysis of all relevant water uses, human and natural impacts on river flow and groundwater status, including abstractions.[32] Ever since, Member States have been required to continuously monitor any developments in these factors, including the volume and rate or level of flow.[33]

---

27   Pieter Jan Kuijper, 'It Shall Contribute to … the Strict Observance and Development of International Law…', in Allan Rossas et al. (eds.), The Court of Justice and the Construction of Europe: Analyses and Perspectives on Sixty Years of Case-law, TCM Asser Press, The Hague, 2013, p. 601.

28   Directive 2000/60/EC of the European Parliament and of the Council of 23 October 2000 establishing a framework for Community action in the field of water policy (WFD), Article 1(e).

29   Directive 2007/60/EC of the European Parliament and of the Council of 23 October 2007 on the assessment and management of flood risks (Floods Directive).

30   WFD, Article 4(6).

31   Id. Article 4(6)(b) and (c).

32   Id. Article 5, Annex II.

33   Id. Article 8.

The impacts of natural and man-made fluctuations in stream flow had to be reviewed by 2014 and appropriate adaptation measures had to be included in the revised river basin management plans and program of measures.[34] The coordination framework of the WFD, however, ensures not only the collection and exchange of information among EU Member States on hydrological variability in shared basins. Through the consultation procedures in the context of international river basins it also provides a (limited) opportunity to influence each other's plans and measures to manage existing and emerging hydrological extremes.

Finally, EU law lays down sophisticated transboundary cooperation mechanisms in relation to floods. The above-mentioned Floods Directive sets up a scheme that complements the ecological program of the WFD with regard to flood risk management. The Directive is not concerned with short term emergency cooperation among riparian states. Instead, it obliges Member States to assess, develop and coordinate their flood control activity with a long term and comprehensive focus. Thus, EU governments are required to carry out a preliminary flood risk assessment and, subsequently, to establish flood hazard and flood risk maps.[35] Based on these maps Member States must adopt flood risk management plans that are coordinated at basin or at least sub-basin level.[36] The Directive requires flood risk management plans to address all aspects of flood management from prevention to emergency preparedness. The plans may also contain long term national adaptation measures such as the promotion of sustainable land use practices, improvement of water retention or controlled emergency flooding.[37] Importantly, the Floods Directive prohibits Member States from adopting measures that are liable to significantly increase flood risks upstream or downstream in the same basin, unless it has been specifically agreed upon by the affected riparians.[38] In the case of international river basins Member States must, as a priority, produce a single flood risk management plan or a set of coordinated plans for the entire basin. Should the riparian states concerned fail to deliver joint plan(s), the Floods Directive simply calls on individual Member States to produce their own flood risk management plan. A similar procedure applies *vis-à-vis* basin states outside the EU with the difference, however, that members must only 'endeavor' to arrive at a single plan with fellow co-riparians that are not bound by the Directive.[39]

---

34 Id. Article 5, Annex VII. *See* also *River Basin Management in a Changing Climate*, CIS Guidance Document No. 24, European Commission, Luxembourg, 2009.
35 Floods Directive, Articles 4-6.
36 Id. Article 7(1).
37 Id. Article 7(3).
38 Id. Article 7(4).
39 Id. Article 8.

6.5.3   The UNECE Water Convention

The UNECE Water Convention[40] – the overarching instrument of pan-European trans-boundary water cooperation – does not directly address variability management. Nonetheless, it contains a number of obligations that require riparian states to cooperate with respect to hydrological extremes. In addition, during the past two decades the Convention bodies have developed a number of soft law documents that provide guidance on how to manage the various impacts of climate change, the primary driver of increasing hydrological variability in the EU. While the latter instruments are legally non-binding, they are seen to contribute significantly to controlling the hydro-political risks relating to intensifying river flow fluctuations.[41]

The starting point under the Convention is the general obligation to prevent, control and reduce transboundary impact.[42] Transboundary impact is defined as "significant adverse effect [...] caused by a human activity". Yet, the progressive reading of the Convention text and two decades of practice confirm that the impacts of naturally occurring hydrological extremes also fall under this obligation. This is because eventually, human acts and omissions contribute to the occurrence, magnitude or the damage potential of these phenomena.[43] Hand in hand with the prevention/mitigation obligation goes the general duty of riparian states to cooperate on a multitude of water management issues. These include the joint monitoring and regular assessment of transboundary impacts (including the quantity of transboundary waters, floods and ice drifts)[44] or the early exchange of information.[45] Also, in their basin treaties and/or bilateral arrangements riparian states have to establish warning and alarm procedures as well as contingency plans that cover hydrological extremes.[46] In case of critical situations parties are under a duty to assist each other following the procedures laid down by the Convention.[47]

In addition to the above general framework, the various Convention bodies have adopted a range of soft law instruments that provide further assistance to basin states as to the short- and long-term management of hydrological variability. First and foremost, the 2009 guidance document on water and climate adaptation is designed to assist states

---

40   Convention on the Protection and Use of Transboundary Watercourses and Lakes, Helsinki, 17 March 1992.
41   Francesca Bernardini, 'The Normative and Institutional Evolution of the Convention', *in* Attila Tanzi *et al.* (eds.), *The UNECE Convention on the Protection and Use of Transboundary Watercourses and International Lakes – Its Contribution to International Water Cooperation*, Brill Nijhoff, Leiden, Boston, 2013, pp. 43-44.
42   UNECE Water Convention, Articles 1(2) and 2(1).
43   Alexandros Kolliopoulos, 'The UNECE Model Provisions on Transboundary Flood Management', *in* Tanzi *et al.* (eds.), 2015, p. 369.
44   UNECE Water Convention, Articles 4, 9(2), 11(1) and 13(3).
45   Id. Articles 6 and 13(1).
46   Id. Articles 3(1), 9(2) and 14.
47   Id. Article 15.

in tackling a range of climate change-related water issues in a transboundary context, including flood and drought mitigation and response.[48] Equally important are the UNECE Model Provisions on Transboundary Flood Management,[49] endorsed by the Meeting of the Parties of the Convention in 2006, that provide a concrete legislative text that can be used by riparian states in their specific basin-wide or bilateral arrangements to tackle the challenges of transboundary flood control. The Model Provisions follow a similar logic as the EU's Floods Directive, but, unlike the former, they also cover short term risk assessment and emergency response.[50]

6.5.4 Multilateral Basin Treaties

Despite its primary ecological focus, the Danube Protection Convention[51] contains a number of substantive and procedural provisions that help riparian states address hydro-logical variability in a systematic and structured fashion. The preamble to the Convention directs specific attention to "the occurrence and threats of adverse effects, in the short and the long term, of changes in conditions of watercourses within the Danube River Basin".[52] It follows that the primary obligation of Danube states is to cooperate in the prevention, control and reduction of transboundary "adverse impacts and changes occurring or likely to be caused."[53] Joint action thus extends not only to man-made transboundary impacts, but must also encompasses the monitoring and evaluation of the natural water cycle and all of its components (precipitation, evaporation, surface and groundwater run-off) in the entire basin.[54] From this general objective flow a number of precisely defined obligations. First, riparian states must monitor, record and assess, jointly and individually, the conditions of the Danube's natural water resources through a number of quantitative parameters, including water balances, flood forecasts or any change in the riverine regime.[55] Second, under the general obligation to prevent, control and reduce transboundary impacts riparian states are obliged to exchange all relevant data, including the operation of existing hydrotechnical constructions (e.g. reservoirs, water power plants) and measures aimed at preventing the deterioration of hydrological conditions, erosion, inundations and sediment flow etc.[56] Regular exchange of information must be supplemented by coordinated or joint

---

48 UNECE, *Guidance on Water and Adaptation to Climate Change*, Geneva, 2009. *Also see* Bernardini 2015, p. 44.
49 UNECE, *Model Provisions on Transboundary Flood Management*, ECE/MP.WAT/2006/4.
50 Kolliopoulos 2015, p. 369.
51 Convention on Cooperation for the Protection and Sustainable Use of the Danube, Sofia, 29 June 1994.
52 Id. Recital 2.
53 Id. Article 5(2).
54 Id. Article 1(c)(g).
55 Id. Articles 5(2)(a) and 9(1).
56 Id. Articles 3(2) and 12.

communication, warning and alarm systems as well as emergency plans to address critical water conditions, including floods and ice-hazards.[57] Should such a critical situation of riverine conditions arise, riparian states must provide mutual assistance upon the request of the affected basin state.[58]

The daughter treaty of the Danube Convention, the Sava Framework Agreement[59] goes even further when it comes to managing hydrological variability. The Agreement specifically refers to droughts and water shortages as critical hazards jeopardizing the integrity of the river's water regime.[60] It therefore calls upon riparian states to establish a coordinated or joint system of "measures, activities and alarms in the Sava River Basin for extraordinary impacts on the water regime, such as [...] discharge of artificial accumulations and retentions caused by [...] flood, ice, drought, water shortage [...]."[61] To that effect, parties even committed themselves to conclude a special protocol "on the protection against flood, excessive groundwater, erosion, ice hazards, drought and water shortages."[62] Out of this ambitious variability management program, however, only a protocol on flood management cooperation was adopted by the riparian states in 2010.[63] This protocol, on the one hand, provides for the coordinated implementation of the EU Floods Directive in the basin (even though half of the riparian states are not EU members).[64] On the other hand, it creates an operative system of flood protection, comprising forecasting, warning and alarm, information exchange as well as the handling of emergency situations and mutual assistance.[65]

The Rhine Protection Convention[66] addresses variability management along similar lines, although in a far less elaborate fashion. The key objectives of the Convention – the maintenance and restoration of the natural functions of the Rhine basin waters, the environmentally sound management of water resources and general flood protection and prevention – imply broad cooperation in flood protection and other hydrological hazards.[67] Thus, riparian states must inform the competent river basin organization, the International Commission for the Protection of the Rhine (ICPR) and other riparian states likely to be affected by imminent flooding.[68] They must also draw up warning and alert plans for the Rhine under the coordination of the ICPR.[69] Rhine basin states also actively cooperate on

---

57   Id. Article 16.
58   Id. Article 17.
59   Framework Agreement on the Sava River Basin, Kranjska Gora, 3 December 2002.
60   Id. Articles 2(1) and 13.
61   Id. Article 13(1).
62   Id. Article 30(1)(a).
63   Protocol on Flood Protection to the Framework Agreement on the Sava River Basin, Gradiška, 1 June 2010.
64   Id. Articles 3-8.
65   Id. Articles 9-11.
66   Convention on the Protection of the Rhine, Bern, 12 April 1999.
67   Id. Article 3.
68   Id. Article 5(6).
69   Id. Article 8(1)(c).

certain long term variability questions such as extreme low water levels and declining water availability even in the absence of explicit treaty requirements to that effect.[70]

The Meuse Agreement[71] defines the mitigation of the effects of floods and droughts as one of the key objectives of transboundary cooperation.[72] In both cases joint riparian action should extend to the development of preventive measures.[73] To that end, the International Meuse Commission is tasked with developing recommendations on flood prevention and protection, flood management coordination as well as on the mitigation of the effects of droughts.[74] Meuse riparians are also obliged to inform each other of any major hydrological events, including imminent floods.[75]

The 1990 Elbe and the 1996 Oder Conventions make no reference whatsoever to hydrological variability, not even flood protection cooperation. The two basin commissions are, however, tasked with monitoring the general hydrological situation in their respective catchment areas.[76]

While explicit treaty justification to do so remains limited or entire missing, all relevant river basin commissions are extensively engaged in climate change adaptation and flood management. *E.g.* the International Commission for the Protection of the Danube (ICPDR) adopted, in 2012, a climate change strategy which outlines the guiding principles of adaptation and their integration in the ICPDR's activities, especially in implementing the Water Framework Directive and the Floods Directive. Similar strategies have been adopted for the Rhine or in progress for the Sava basin.[77]

6.5.5 Bilateral Water Agreements

The most comprehensive of all bilateral water agreements, the Albufeira Convention[78] between Spain and Portugal addresses hydrological variability in a substantive and sophisticated manner. The Convention expressly defines the prevention, elimination, mitigation or control of the effects of exceptional situations as a key priority of cooperation

---

70   Heide Jekel, 'Integrated Water Resources Management as a Tool to Prevent or Mitigate Transboundary Impact', *in* Tanzi *et al.* (eds.), 2015, p. 237.

71   Accord international sur la Meuse, Gent, 3 December 2002.

72   Id. Recitals (7) and (8).

73   Id. Article 2(c).

74   Id. Article 4(4)(a) and (b).

75   Id. Article 3(2)(d).

76   Convention on the International Commission for the Protection of the Elbe, Magdeburg, 8 October 1990, Article 2, Convention on the International Commission for the Protection of the Oder, Wroclaw, 11 April 1996, Article 2.

77   Jekel 2015, p. 247.

78   Convention on the Co-operation for the Protection and the Sustainable Use of the Waters of the Luso-Spanish River Basins, Albufeira, 30 November 1998.

between the parties.[79] Consequently, the Convention sets out a robust water allocation regime that caters for natural variations in river flow that also include extreme situations. (Extreme hydrological situations are determined with reference to historic precipitation levels).[80] Should such a situation emerge, parties must inform each other and the joint Commission and exchange all relevant information.[81] The Convention also sets out concrete substantive measures parties must implement in case of floods and droughts. With regards to floods the applicable regime goes further than the usual forecasting-warning-emergency-preparedness provisions most regional or bilateral similar regimes contain. It also gives upper and lower riparian states a right to demand the other party to implement pre-defined (or any other) interventions that are necessary to prevent, control or mitigate the effects of floods.[82] Even more elaborate are the measures relating to droughts and water scarcity. In this context the Convention defines a set of concrete drought management measures to prevent and control the effects of low precipitation and discharge. These relate to water demand control (abstractions for consumption), infrastructure management (impoundment, storage and release), wastewater discharges *etc.*[83] Conditions of exceptional situations – both floods and droughts – are to be defined for every two years and subsequently reviewed. The Convention also calls for the joint study of water scarcity and floods with a view to long term prevention and mitigation.[84]

Several other European bilateral water treaties make some reference to cooperation over flood prevention and protection. Most of these treaty provisions are, however, relatively basic, reinstating the general will or duty of the parties to cooperate and/or referring the subject to the activities of joint commissions.[85] In a limited number of cases bilateral water treaties contain substantive obligations parties must observe in flood protection or other emergency situations. *E.g.* the Hungarian-Ukrainian frontier water treaty[86] requires parties to refrain from permitting any interventions that may raise flood volumes above previously agreed-upon levels. In the spirit of solidarity riparian states are also obliged to provide technical assistance in times of exceptional floods upon demand (the costs of such technical

---

79   Id. Article 10(1)(f).
80   Id. Annex II to the Additional Protocol.
81   Id. Article 11.
82   Id. Article 18(5).
83   Id. Article 19(2).
84   Id. Articles 18(7) and 19(5).
85   Agreement between Finland and Sweden Concerning Transboundary Rivers, Agreement between Finland and Sweden Concerning Transboundary Rivers, Stockholm, 11 November 2009, Article 2(1)(b); Agreement between the Federal Republic of Germany and the European Economic Community, on the one hand, and the Republic of Austria, on the other, on cooperation on management of water resources in the Danube Basin, Regensburg, 1 December 1987, Articles 2(2)(b) and 6.
86   Convention between the Government of the Republic of Hungary and the Government of Ukraine on water management questions relating to frontier waters, Budapest, 11 November 1997, Articles 9(1) and 9(4).

assistance are to be borne by the beneficiary).[87] As opposed to flood protection the management of droughts rarely features in bilateral water treaties. Exceptions are those bilateral agreements that are primarily concerned with transboundary flow regimes or water allocation anyway. Thus, the 1991 Discharge Rule[88] between upstream Finland and downstream Russia for the Vuoksi river basin calls on riparian states to maintain the flow quantity of the river in a 'normal zone', defined by the Rule with reference to historically prevailing natural flow volumes. Should extreme low water levels appear discharge rates must be changed by Finland with a view to minimizing adverse effects.[89] The 1970 amendment of the 1958 French-Spanish Agreement regarding the Lake Lanoux also takes into account natural flow variations, although it does not specifically address droughts or floods. The allocation regime calls for the increased discharged towards Spain in the summer months "in order to take account of the evaporation from the enlarged surface area of the Lake."[90]

6.6 EVALUATION AND CONCLUSIONS

The four layers of European water law regulate an important aspect of variability management, notably flood prevention and protection at an exemplary level of sophistication. Given the high number of catastrophic inundations most international basins witnessed only during this millennium, the complementary regimes of the EU Floods Directive, the UNECE Model Provisions and the extensive cooperation at basin and bilateral level seem to constitute an adequate regulatory response to the collective action problems posed by excess water levels.

Less positive is the picture when it comes to long term adaptation to hydrological extremes, especially prolonged droughts. Here, the systematic review of the main characteristics of each basin, as foreseen by the Water Framework Directive, ensures that riparian states address changing hydrological conditions on a regular and substantive basis. Also, it allows riparian states to have an impact on the joint river basin management plans and, to a lesser extent, on each other's programs and measures. Yet, neither EU and UNECE law, nor basin treaties call for real adaptation interventions. The various climate change adaptation strategies developed by the river basin organizations only provide general

---

87 Anikó Raisz & János Ede Szilágyi, 'Cross Border Issues of the Hungarian Water Resources', *Rivista quadrimestrale di diritto dell'ambiente*, Vol. 1, Issue 1, 2017, p. 86.

88 Vuoksi Agreement on Discharge Rule in Lake Saimaa and the Vuoksi River, 1989.

89 Antti Belinskij, 'Cooperation between Finland and the Russian Federation', *in* Tanzi *et al.* (eds.), 2015, p. 315.

90 Exchange of Letters Constituting an Agreement between France and Spain Amending the Arrangement of 12 July 1958 relating to Lake Lanoux, 27 January 1970.

guidance as to future measures and do not address the potential of political risks prolonged droughts are likely to pose in transboundary relations.

Finally, European water law addresses the short-term consequences of prolonged low river flows only marginally. Undoubtedly, the basic principles of transboundary water cooperation (equitable and reasonable utilization and the no-harm rule) together with the various information exchange and notification procedures provide a rudimentary framework to handle such critical situations. These, however, do not amount to any operative guidance to riparian states as to the immediate adaptation measures to be taken, including adjustments in transboundary flow allocation. This shortcoming can, in part, be explained by the fact that hitherto basin-wide extreme droughts have been relatively rare (apart from the Iberian Peninsula), so there was no real need and political will to address the contentious issue of national water use restrictions or the curtailing of transboundary flows. In part, however, the root of the problem lies in the notoriously complacent approach of EU law and decision-makers *vis-à-vis* the question of transboundary water allocation.[91] This regulatory lacuna and political timidity may, in the future, turn out to be a critical hydropolitical risk, if droughts and scarcity continue to intensify in a transboundary context as projected.

---

91   Gábor Baranyai, 'Transboundary Water Governance in the European Union: The (Unresolved) Allocation Question', *Water Policy*, Vol. 21, Issue 2, 2019, p. 1.

7   Defining the Role of the Aarhus Convention as Part of National, International and EU Law

Conclusions of a Case-Law Analysis

*Ágnes Váradi**

Keywords

Aarhus Convention, principle of public participation, protection of the environment, environmental issues before national (constitutional) courts, direct applicability

Abstract

As a basic point of reference in international law the Aarhus Convention has a considerable impact on the framework of public participation in environmental matters. The fact that the Convention forms part of national legal orders of EU Member States both as part of international and EU law, the proper enforcement of its provisions makes it inevitable to draw up certain principles of interpretation. The current paper aims to analyze how the Aarhus Convention appears at the level of legal argumentation in the case-law of the CJEU and selected national constitutional courts or high courts of EU Member States, namely, Germany, France and Hungary. Those decisions are examined that refer directly and explicitly to the Aarhus Convention. The case-law analysis is completed by the reference to the relevant secondary literature. The findings can provide a synthesis about the role of the Aarhus Convention, thematic milestones can be drawn up concerning the interpretation of the obligations stemming from the Convention and they can give useful insights into the relationship of national laws, EU law and international law. Meanwhile, they contribute to the analysis of the role of civil participation in the protection of the environment. This way, the conclusions can support the emergence of a (more) general approach in EU Member States as far as public participation in environmental matters is concerned.

---

*   Ágnes Váradi: research fellow, Hungarian Academy of Sciences, Centre for Social Sciences, Institute for Legal Studies.

7.1 INTRODUCTION

"Environmental issues are best handled with the participation of all concerned citizens, at the relevant level. At the national level, each individual shall have appropriate access to information concerning the environment that is held by public authorities, including information on hazardous materials and activities in their communities, and the opportunity to participate in decision-making processes. States shall facilitate and encourage public awareness and participation by making information widely available. Effective access to judicial and administrative proceedings, including redress and remedy, shall be provided."

The goals[1] defined in Principle 10 of the Rio Declaration[2] have been further elaborated on in the Convention on Access to Information, Public Participation in Decision-Making and Access to Justice in Environmental Matters done at Aarhus, Denmark, on 25 June 1998 (Aarhus Convention or Convention).[3] It is, however, only one of the references to the importance of public participation in environmental matters at the level of international law. Further relevant phenomena are the following: *(i)* On 4 March 2018, the countries of the Latin American and Caribbean region adopted the Escazú Convention as a regional agreement on public participation in environmental matters.[4] *(ii)* In the Budva Declaration, on 15 September 2017, parties to the Aarhus Convention confirmed that the participation by stakeholders may considerably contribute to achieving the aims of sustainable develop-

---

1   "Parties shall cooperate in taking measures, as appropriate, to enhance climate change education, training, public awareness, public participation and public access to information, recognizing the importance of these steps with respect to enhancing actions under this Agreement." The wording of Article 12 of the Paris Agreement and the document as a whole proves the same approach. *See* the Paris Agreement adopted at the 21st Conference of the Parties to the United Nations Framework Convention on Climate Change, at https://unfccc.int/files/meetings/paris_nov_2015/application/pdf/paris_agreement_english_.pdf.

2   Rio Declaration on Environment and Development (1992), at www.unesco.org/education/pdf/RIO_E.PDF.

3   United Nations Economic Commission for Europe (UNECE), *Convention on Access to Information, Public Participation in Decision-Making and Access to Justice in Environmental Matters* done at Aarhus, Denmark, on 25 June 1998, at www.unece.org/fileadmin/DAM/env/pp/documents/cep43e.pdf.

4   Economic Commission for Latin America and the Caribbean, *Regional Agreement on Access to Information, Public Participation and Justice in Environmental Matters in Latin America and the Caribbean.* Adopted at Escazú, Costa Rica, on 4 March 2018, at https://repositorio.cepal.org/bitstream/handle/11362/43583/1/S1800428_en.pdf.

ment.[5] *(iii)* The Strategic Plan of the Aarhus Convention[6] foresees as a primary goal to work towards full implementation of the Convention by each Party where this has not already been achieved, to encourage and support its use by the public and to increase the impact of the Convention by increasing the number of Parties. *(iv)* The CJEU interpreted several times[7] the access to justice rights of stakeholders and these decisions obtained a high level of media attention in cases related to the protection of the environment.[8] *(v)* Recognizing these problems the European Commission issued a Notice on access to justice in environmental matters in summer 2017.[9] *(vi)* Legal standpoints of the Council of the European Union and the Compliance Committee of the Aarhus Convention show certain ruptures as regards the implementation of the Aarhus Convention in EU law.[10] Furthermore,

---

5   *Budva Declaration on Environmental Democracy for Our Sustainable Future, ECE/MP.PP/2017/ CRP.3--ECE/MP.PRTR/2017/CRP.1,* at www.unece.org/fileadmin/DAM/env/pp/mop6/in-session_docs/ECE.MP. PP.2017.CRP.3-ECE.MP.PRTR.2017.CRP.1_EN.pdf. *Governments and stakeholders strengthen commitment to environmental democracy as driver of sustainable development at Budva meetings,* at www.unece. org/info/media/presscurrent-press-h/environment/2017/governments-and-stakeholders-strengthen-commitment-to-environmental-democracy-as-driver-of-sustainable-development-at-budva-meetings/doc.html.

6   'The current Strategic Plan of the Aarhus Convention was adopted by the Meeting of the Parties at its fifth session, held in Maastricht, Netherlands on 30 June – 1 July 2014, through Decision V/5 on the Strategic Plan for 2015-2020', at www.unece.org/environmental-policy/conventions/public-participation/aarhus-convention/areas-of-work/current-work-programme-and-strategic-plan/strategic-plan-2015-2020.html, see the Strategic Plan at www.unece.org/fileadmin/DAM/env/pp/mop5/Documents/Post_session_docs/Decision_excerpts_in_English/Decision_V_5_on_the_Strategic_Plan_for_2015%E2%80%932020.pdf.

7   *E.g.* Judgment of 19 December 2013, *Case C-279/12, Fish Legal and Emily Shirley v. Information Commissioner and Others,* ECLI:EU:C:2013:853; Judgment of 11 April 2013, *Case C-260/11, The Queen, on the application of David Edwards and Lilian Pallikaropoulos v. Environment Agency and Others,* ECLI:EU:C:2013:221; Judgment of 13 January 2015, *Joined Cases C-404/12 P and C-405/12 P, Council of the European Union and European Commission v. Stichting Natuur en Milieu and Pesticide Action Network Europe,* ECLI:EU:C:2015:5.

8   *E.g.* concerning the judgment of the CJEU in joined cases C-404/12 P and C-405/12 P: *'ECJ rulings a setback for environmental democracy'* at www.clientearth.org/press-release-ecj-rulings-setback-environmental-democracy/; 'European Court of Justice blocks NGOs' access to court' at https://gmwatch.org/en/news/archive/2015-articles/15896-european-court-of-justice-blocks-ngos-access-to-court.

9   Commission Notice on Access to Justice in Environmental Matters, C (2017) 2616 final.

10   The Compliance Committee concluded in the case ACCC/C/2008/32 that EU law does not comply with the requirement of access to justice of the public; neither the relevant legal provisions, nor the case-law of the CJEU ensure the implementation of the relevant provisions of EU law. *See* the findings and recommendations of the Compliance Committee at www.unece.org/fileadmin/DAM/env/pp/compliance/C2008-32/Findings/C32_EU_Findings_as_adopted_advance_unedited_version.pdf, para. 123. On contrary, the Council stressed the specific features of EU law. In the explanatory memorandum to the Proposal for a Council Decision on the position to be adopted, on behalf of the European Union, at the sixth session of the Meeting of the Parties to the Aarhus Convention regarding compliance case ACCC/C/2008/32 [Brussels, 29 June 2017, COM(2017) 366 final, 2017/0151 (NLE)] contained a statement that "[t]he findings of the Compliance Committee case (ACCC/C/2008/32) are problematic for the EU because the findings do not recognize the EU's special legal order." However, the adopted version contains a softer formulation as follows: "The Union should explore ways and means to comply with the Aarhus Convention in a way that is compatible with the fundamental principles of the Union legal order and with its system of judicial review." At the same time, it stressed that the Council cannot give instructions or make recommendations to the Court of Justice of the European concerning its judicial activities. [Council Decision (EU) 2017/1346 of 17 July

the evaluation of the situation demonstrates the different approach from the side of both the Council and the European Commission.[11] Therefore, the interpretation of the Aarhus Convention has become a significant topic affecting both EU law, international law and their relation to national laws as well.

As these examples show, the question of public participation in environmental matters, with special regard to the provisions of the Aarhus Convention, are equally substantial questions at the level of legal regulation and political cooperation.

Instead of providing a description of the Aarhus Convention or an overall analysis of its implementation,[12] the current paper aims to analyze how the Aarhus Convention appears at the level of legal argumentation in the case-law of the CJEU and selected national constitutional courts or high courts of EU Member States, namely, Germany, France and Hungary.[13] Those decisions are examined that refer directly and explicitly to the Aarhus Convention. The countries examined and the EU are parties to the Convention; therefore, the findings can provide a synthesis about the role of the Aarhus Convention at the level of EU law and national laws, thematic milestones can be drawn up concerning the interpretation of the obligations stemming from the Convention and they can give useful insights into the relationship of national laws, EU law and international law. Meanwhile, they contribute to the analysis of the role of social responsibility in the protection of the

---

2017 on the position to be adopted, on behalf of the European Union, at the sixth session of the Meeting of the Parties to the Aarhus Convention as regards compliance case ACCC/C/2008/32.].

11 Statement by the Commission: Draft Council Decision on the position to be adopted, on behalf of the European Union, at the sixth session of the Meeting of the Parties to the Aarhus Convention regarding compliance case ACCC/C/2008/32, Brussels, 17 July 2017, 2017/0151 (NLE) at http://data.consil-ium.europa.eu/doc/document/ST-11194-2017-ADD-1-REV-1/en/pdf.

12 Suzanne Kingston (ed.), *European Perspectives on Environmental Law and Governance*, Routledge, Abingdon, 2013; Jane Holder & Maria Lee, *Environmental Protection, Law and Policy: Text and Materials*, Cambridge University Press, Cambridge, 2007, pp. 85-134; Maria Lee, *EU Environmental Law, Governance and Decision-Making*, Hart Publishing, Oxford-Portland, 2014, pp. 182-202; Gyula Bándi (ed.), *Environmental Democracy and Law*, Europa Law Publishing, Amsterdam, 2014; Joana Mendes, *Participation in EU Rule-making: A Rights-Based Approach*. Oxford University Press, Oxford, 2011; Carol Harlow *et al.*, *Research Handbook on EU Administrative Law*, Edward Elgar Publishing, Cheltenham, 2017, pp. 551-557; Attila Pánovics, *Az Aarhusi egyezmény és az Európai Unió*, IDResearch Kft. – Publikon, Pécs, 2015; Gyula Bándi *et al.*, *Az Európai Bíróság környezetjogi ítélkezési gyakorlata*, Szent István Társulat, Budapest, 2008.

13 The Compliance Committee of the Aarhus Convention analyzed besides the EU, certain aspects of the implementation of the Aarhus Convention in Germany (Decision V/9h on compliance by Germany with its obligations under the Convention, ECE/MP.PP/2014/2/Add.1; Compliance by Germany with its obligations under the Convention, ECE/MP.PP/2017/40, 2 August 2017), France (Findings with regard to communication ACCC/C/2007/22 concerning compliance by France, ECE/MP.PP/C.1/2009/4/Add.1, 8 February 2011) and Hungary (Findings and recommendations with respect to compliance by specific parties, Hungary, ECE/MP.PP/2005/13/Add.4, 11 March 2005). However, both the scope and the date of these analyses are different; they do not go into details concerning the specific situation of national law obligations with respect to EU law. Furthermore, the main focus of the current paper is the case-law of the CJEU and national courts; therefore, the conclusions of the Compliance Committee will not be elaborated on in detail in the following.

environment. This way, the conclusions can support the emergence of a (more) general approach at the levels of national law, EU law and international law as far as public participation in environmental matters is concerned.

7.2   Theoretical Framework

The general starting point of this analysis is the role of public participation in environmental matters, since it provides for the most general interpretative framework of the Convention. This concept is inherently linked to the requirement of public involvement in legislative processes, which has become a general principle of a democratic state governed by law.[14] Firstly, because it is corollary to the right of every citizen to take part in the conduct of public affairs (safeguarded among others by Article 25 ICCPR). As the Human Rights Committee stated,

> "the conduct of public affairs [...] is a broad concept which relates to the exercise of political power, in particular the exercise of legislative, executive and administrative powers. It covers all aspects of public administration, and the formulation and implementation of policy at international, national, regional and local levels."[15]

Secondly, by virtue of being a central element of transparency, public consultations support accountability, sustain confidence in the legal environment make regulations more secure and accessible, less influenced by special interests.[16]

The significant role of public consultations in enhancing civil control over governmental policies and establishing a higher legitimacy of legislative processes can also be perceived at EU level. The TEU stipulates in its Article 11(1) a general basis for civil participation in decision-making processes in all fields of EU law: "The institutions shall, by appropriate means, give citizens and representative associations the opportunity to make known and publicly exchange their views in all areas of Union action." Article 11(3) TEU gives further

---

14   Cristina Fraenkel-Haeberle *et al.*, *Citizen Participation in Multi-level Democracies*, Brill Nijhoff, Leiden-Boston, 2015.

15   UN Human Rights Committee, *CCPR General Comment No. 25 on the Right to Participate in Public Affairs, Voting Rights and the Right of Equal Access to Public Service (Art. 25), CCPR/C/21/Rev.1/Add.7.* 1996, para. 5; similarly: Office of the United Nations High Commissioner for Human Rights (OHCHR), *Rule-of-Law Tools for Post-Conflict States. National Consultations on Transitional Justice (HR/PUB/09/2)*, UN, New York-Geneva, 2009, p. 4.

16   OECD, *Better Regulation in Europe: Finland 2010. Chapter 3: Transparency Through Consultation and Communication*, 2010, at www.oecd-ilibrary.org/governance/better-regulation-in-europe_20790368, p. 71; similarly: Open Government Partnership (OGP), *Open Government Declaration. September 2011*, at www.opengovpartnership.org/open-government-declaration.

guidance: "The European Commission shall carry out broad consultations with parties concerned in order to ensure that the Union's actions are coherent and transparent."

From these statements a very specific aim of public consultations can be derived, namely the inclusion of the needs and interests of the public concerned and the special knowledge of specialized groups and organizations in order to ensure the transparency and coherence of the legislative process.

While the Treaties – as foundations of EU law – offer a clearly defined legal basis for public participation, such points of reference cannot be found in the constitutions – themselves the foundations of national legal orders – of the examined Member States.

In Germany the types and detailed rules of public consultation are regulated as procedural issues. For instance, concerning the drafting of laws, the Joint Rules of Procedure of the Federal Ministries (GGO) establishes the possibility of involving central and umbrella associations and an expert community at federal level if their interests are affected.[17] The constitutional provision on the protection of the environment[18] stipulates the responsibility for the protection of the natural foundations of life and animals. However, as far as the detailed provisions are concerned, it refers to legislation, executive and judicial actions. Since this constitutional formulation leaves a rather broad margin of appreciation for the legislator, the examination of compliance with the constitution is limited to obvious violations.[19]

In France, although a general right of public participation in decision-making procedures does not follow from the Constitution,[20] the right of public participation as regards environmental matters is laid down as a constitutional obligation in Article 7 of the Charter for the environment:

> "Everyone has the right, in the conditions and to the extent provided for by law, to have access to information pertaining to the environment in the possession of public bodies and to participate in the public decision-taking process likely to affect the environment."

---

17 "The timing, scope and selection will be left to the discretion of the lead Federal Ministry, unless specific rules stipulate otherwise", Section 47 GGO at www.bmi.bund.de/SharedDocs/downloads/DE/veroeffentlichungen/themen/ministerium/ggo.pdf;jsessionid=E2FCCC425AE1B97B68F64D7CAD32699B.2_cid295?__blob=publicationFile&v=2.

18 Article 20a of the *Grundgesetz*.

19 Andreas Glaser, *Nachhaltige Entwicklung und Demokratie*, Mohr Siebeck, Tübingen, 2006, pp. 236-237.

20 Article 39 of the Constitution only refers to the fact that "[t]he presentation of Government Bills tabled before the National Assembly or the Senate, shall follow the conditions determined by an Institutional Act". A separate piece of legislation implementing this obligation contains detailed provisions on these criteria including a report on the consultations carried out: Loi organique n° 2009-403 du 15 avril 2009 relative à l'application des articles 34-1, 39 et 44 de la Constitution, at www.legifrance.gouv.fr/affichTexte.do?cidTexte=JORFTEXT000020521873.

These rights are safeguarded through several formalized procedures laid down in *e.g.* the Code on the environment, the Code on municipalities, however, these rules are mostly related to specific projects or plans.[21]

In Hungary, Article P(1) of the Fundamental Law guarantees a similarly high-level of protection for the environment as in the two above mentioned countries:

> "Natural resources, in particular arable land, forests and the reserves of water; biodiversity, in particular native plant and animal species; and cultural artefacts, shall form the common heritage of the nation, it shall be the obligation of the State and everyone to protect and maintain them, and to preserve them for future generations."

Nevertheless, public participation – similarly to the German model – cannot be directly derived from the constitution. This statement has been confirmed by the Constitutional Court of Hungary in its Decision No. 1146/B/2005. AB in respect of the former Constitution. As the adoption of the Fundamental Law did not cause significant changes in this context, these statements can be seen even currently as points of reference.

These examples show that national constitutions reflect different ways of approaching the question of public participation in environmental matters; as such, they do not offer a solid, uniform background for public involvement. However, it is apparent from the text of the TEU that public participation is particularly important in case of environmental matters, where the social discussion is strongly linked to scientific questions, economic interests and legal regulation. The Aarhus Convention is of great importance, since it offers a specific regime for public participation in environmental matters.

7.3   THE ROLE OF THE AARHUS CONVENTION

According to Article 191(1) TFEU

> "Union policy on the environment shall contribute to pursuit of the following objectives: preserving, protecting and improving the quality of the environment, protecting human health, prudent and rational utilization of natural resources, promoting measures at international level to deal with regional or worldwide environmental problems, and in particular combating climate change."

---

21   OECD, *Better Regulation in Europe Better Regulation in Europe: France 2010*, at www.oecd.org/gov/regulatory-policy/45706677.pdf, pp. 69-86; Susan Rose-Ackerman & Thomas Perroud, 'Policymaking and Public Law in France: Public Participation, Agency Independence and Impact Assessment', *Columbia Journal of European Law*, Vol. 19, Issue 2, 2013, pp. 225-312.

Recognizing that the

> "improvement of the public's access to information and a broader participation of the public in decision-making processes and access to justice are essential tools to ensure public awareness on environmental issues and to promote a better implementation and enforcement of environmental legislation",

thus, "it contributes to strengthen and make more effective environmental protection policies", the European Community approved the Aarhus Convention.[22] This way, the Aarhus Convention has become part of the environmental policy of the EU.

> "By becoming a party to the Aarhus Convention, the European Union undertook to ensure, within the scope of European Union law, a general principle of access to environmental information held by the public authorities."[23]

Furthermore, it made the right of the public to participate in decision-making processes affecting the environment and the access to justice in environmental matters a part of EU law. At the time of approving the Aarhus Convention, the EU – in line with the goals of the Aarhus Convention and in shared competence with its Member States –

> "has already adopted a comprehensive set of legislation which is evolving and contributes to the achievement of the objective of the Convention, not only by its own institutions, but also by public authorities in its Member States"[24]

According to Article 216(2) TFEU "[a]greements concluded by the Union are binding upon the institutions of the Union and on its Member States." As such agreements – like the Aarhus Convention – form an integral part of EU law,[25] the CJEU undoubtedly has the competence to interpret them in preliminary ruling procedures.[26]

---

22 Council Decision 2005/370/EC of 17 February 2005 on the conclusion, on behalf of the European Community, of the Convention on access to information, public participation in decision-making and access to justice in environmental matters.

23 Judgment of 14 February 2012, *Case C-204/09, Flachglas Torgau GmbH v. Bundesrepublik Deutschland*, ECLI:EU:C:2012:71, para. 30.

24 Recital (7) of Council Decision 2005/370/EC.

25 Judgment of 8 November 2016, *Case C-243/15, Lesoochranárske zoskupenie VLK v. Obvodný úrad Trenčín*, ECLI:EU:C:2016:838, para. 45; similarly: Judgment of 10 January 2006 *Case C-344/04, The Queen, on the application of International Air Transport Association and European Low Fares Airline Association v. Department for Transport*, ECLI:EU:C:2006:10, para. 36.

26 Judgment of 8 March 2011, *Case C-240/09, Lesoochranárske zoskupenie VLK v. Ministerstvo životného prostredia Slovenskej republiky*, ECLI:EU:C:2011:125, para. 30.

The general formulation of Article 1 of the Convention makes it possible to consider the Aarhus Convention as a basic point of reference in all cases where the procedure is related to environmental legislation.[27] Nevertheless, according to the case-law of CJEU, such an obligation exists only with regards to environmental laws in a strict sense. Therefore, the interpretation of EU norms cannot be changed by invoking the Aarhus Convention solely on the basis that their application is related to environmental matters.[28] Furthermore, in certain decisions the CJEU denied the reference to the Convention even in cases where the EU legislator established *sui generis* rules in a certain sector of public participation in environmental matters.[29] Finally, from a specific judgment of the CJEU it is also evident that the indirect correlation to environmental matters cannot lead to an extensive interpretation of the scope of EU law either.[30] In summary, EU law falling within this scope shall be interpreted in a way that in is in line with the Aarhus Convention, and EU law shall be properly aligned with the Convention.[31]

As far as national laws are concerned, a special double-character of the Aarhus Convention may be observed. On the one hand, as an international treaty it is referred to as a part of national laws. The French Constitution stipulates in its Article 55 that "treaties or agreements duly ratified or approved shall, upon publication, prevail over Acts of Parliament." In Germany, the relationship of international law and national law is primarily determined by the principle of *'völkerrechtsfreundliche Auslegung'*, which includes the requirement of preventing or remediating violations of international law through national legislation or its application.[32] In Hungary, in turn, it is a rule of competence that clarifies the prevalence of international law over national law, since Article 24(2)(f) stipulates that the Constitutional Court "shall examine any law for conflict with any international treaties."[33]

---

27   Opinion of Advocate General Eleanor Sharpston (12 October 2017) in *Case C-664/15. Protect Natur-, Arten-und Landschaftschutz Umweltorganisation v. Bezirkshauptmannschaft Gmünd*, ECLI:EU:C:2017:760, para. 5.

28   Judgment of 16 July 2015, *Case C-612/13 P, Client Earth v. European Commission*, ECLI:EU:C:2015:486, para. 37.

29   Judgment of 22 December 2010, *Case C-524/09, Ville de Lyon v. Caisse des dépôts et consignations*, ECLI:EU:C:2010:822, para. 38.

30   Judgment of 6 March 2014, *Case C-206/13, Cruciano Siragusa v. Regione Sicilia -- Soprintendenza Beni Culturali e Ambientali di Palermo*, ECLI:EU:C:2014:126, paras. 26-30.

31   Judgment of 12 May 2011, *Case C-115/09, Bund für Umwelt und Naturschutz Deutschland, Landesverband Nordrhein-Westfalen eV v. Bezirksregierung Arnsberg*, ECLI:EU:C:2011:289, para. 41.

32   Rüdiger Wolfrum *et al.*, 'The Reception of International Law in the German Legal Order: An Introduction', *in* Erika de Wet *et al.* (eds.), *The Implementation of International Law in Germany and South Africa*, Pretoria University Law Press, Pretoria, 2015, p. 19; *BVerfG*, judgment of 23 June 1981, *Case 2 BvR 1107/77*; *BVerwG*, judgment of 29 June 2016, *Case 7 C 32.15*, para. 14.

33   At this point it should be stressed that the current paper does not aim to address the complex question of the relationship between national and international law. This question is referred to only to the extent as it is necessary to demonstrate the special position of the Convention in the legal order of the Member States.

On the other hand, it is an international treaty, which derives its binding force from being a part of EU law – and by virtue of the Member States' implementation obligation of the relevant directives transposing the Convention in EU law. In this regard, the principle of the primacy of EU law[34] ensures the enforcement of the Convention.

Based on the above, the major question is whether the Convention should be referenced by national courts as an international treaty to which the given State is party to or as an international treaty that is part of EU law as transposed by the EU legislator and interpreted by the CJEU. The first area, where this question is of decisive importance, is the problem of direct applicability.

7.4   THE QUESTION OF DIRECT APPLICABILITY

At this point, the question arises, what is the role of the Convention, if the above-mentioned proper legal alignment is lacking? Can the Convention be applied directly? Generally, it would not be contrary to EU law to apply an international treaty directly to which the EU is party, but the provisions of the given treaty must comply with the general requirements of direct applicability even in this case.[35] However, the CJEU generally excludes this possibility regarding the Convention on the basis of two factors. Firstly, because several provisions of the Convention need positive, implementing actions, such as Article 9(3) of the Convention. This provision ensures the right that, where they meet the criteria, if any, laid down in national law, members of the public have access to administrative or judicial procedures to challenge acts and omissions of private persons and public authorities which contravene provisions of their national law relating to the environment. Thus, these provisions "do not contain any clear and precise obligation capable of directly regulating the legal position of individuals",[36] thereby excluding direct applicability.[37]

Direct applicability is denied, secondly, as the wording of the Convention make the extensive consideration of the specificities of the single legal orders possible. Since the Convention addresses an issue having legal, economic and social relevance from several points of view, the wording usually ensures a broad margin of appreciation to the parties [*e.g.* Article 9(5) of the Convention]. In this context, the CJEU concluded that

---

34   Bruno de Witte, 'Direct Effect, Primacy and the Nature of the Legal Order', *in* Paul Craig & Gráinne de Búrca (eds.), *The Evolution of EU Law*, Oxford University Press, Oxford, 2011, pp. 343-346.

35   Judgment of 13 January 2015, *Joined Cases C-401/12 P, C-402/12 P and C-403/12 P, Council of the European Union and Others v. Vereniging Milieudefensie and Stichting Stop Luchtverontreiniging Utrecht*, ECLI:EU:C:2015:4, para. 54.

36   *Case C-240/09, Lesoochranárske zoskupenie VLK*, para. 45.

37   Order of the General Court of 28 September 2016, *Case T-600/15, Pesticide Action Network Europe (PAN Europe) and Others v. European Commission*, ECLI:EU:T:2016:601, paras. 53-61.

"it follows from that provision, under which each party to the Convention is obliged to 'consider' the establishment of 'appropriate assistance mechanisms' to remove or reduce financial and other barriers to access to justice, that it does not include an unconditional and sufficiently precise obligation and that it is subject, in its implementation or effects, to the adoption of a subsequent measure."[38]

From these conclusions it also follows that – although the Convention makes the accession of regional economic communities possible – its structures and institutions are more tailored to the national legal systems of single states.[39] CJEU case-law seems to be clear on the point that the provisions of the Convention cannot be applied directly in EU law.

Within the national laws, however, different conclusions can have been drawn. There are only four judgments of the Hungarian Constitutional Court that refer expressis verbis to the Convention. In one of these, Decision No. 3068/2013. (III. 14.) AB, the Constitutional Court examined whether the relevant Hungarian legislation is contrary to the Convention as an international treaty. In this context the lack of reference to EU law can be a consequence of the fact that the Hungarian Constitutional Court traditionally refrains from interpreting and applying EU law,[40] while its competence as regards the compliance of national law with international law follows directly from the Fundamental Law. In one case, however, it also referred to the Act promulgating the Convention, stating that the legislator did not fail to regulate public participation in connection to road construction affecting the environment.[41] Thus, in this single case the Constitutional Court seems to have considered the Convention to be a direct point of reference. This line of thought can be confirmed on the basis of a relevant judgment of the Hungarian Supreme Court: in case BH 2010.261. it ruled that the right of access to justice based on the Convention results in the obligation of the court to analyze the claim in detail; otherwise the court would violate international law binding the State. No further judgments containing direct references to the Aarhus Convention resort to a detailed interpretation of its provisions.[42]

A case with direct reference to the Aarhus Convention cannot be found in the case-law of the German Constitutional Court. However, the Federal Administrative Court, *Bundesverwaltungsgericht (BVerwG)*, relies on an approach where it applies the standards

---

38   Judgment of 28 July 2016, *Case C-543/14, Ordre des barreaux francophones et germanophone and Others v. Conseil des ministers*, ECLI:EU:C:2016:605, para. 55.
39   Judgment of 16 July 2015, *Case C-612/13 P, ClientEarth v. European Commission*, ECLI:EU:C:2015:486, para. 40.
40   *See* Decision No. 2/2019. (III. 5.) AB, Reasoning [20] and [35].
41   Decision No. 1418/E/1997. AB, ABH 2007, 1174.
42   Hungarian Supreme Court, Judgment of 24 June 2009, *Case Kfv.IV.37.448/2008/6*; Curia of Hungary, Judgment of 12 April 2017, *Case Pfv.IV.22.344/2016/4*.

elaborated by the CJEU with reference to the EU legal framework parallel to the indication of the relevant provisions of the Convention. However, instead of an autonomous interpretation of the Convention as a part of international law, the *BVerwG* seems to prioritize and emphasize the enforcement of an interpretation in conformity with EU law.[43] In a specific case, the *BVerwG* explicitly referred to the Convention as a background norm to the relevant EU law,[44] in another case it stressed the EU law nature of the public participation scheme in environmental matters.[45] The synthesis of these statements is offered by a judgment, in which the *BVerwG* ruled that it is clear from jurisprudence that the provisions of the Aarhus Convention do not have direct effect. National courts, however, are obliged to interpret their national laws of administrative procedure and administrative court procedure in a way that they comply with the goals set by the Convention and the principle of efficient judicial protection in a field covered by EU law.[46]

Although there is a direct constitutional link between environmental matters and public participation, the case-law of the French *Conseil Constitutionnel* does not contain an explicit reference to the Aarhus Convention. In certain cases, the *Conseil d'État* seems to refer to it when evaluating the compatibility of an administrative act with the Convention as an international treaty.[47] Furthermore, to a certain, limited extent the *Conseil d'État* has confirmed the direct applicability of the Convention as well.[48] However, in recent jurisprudence this kind of argumentation seems to be declining, with the parallel rise of the continuously broadening case-law of the CJEU. Therefore, the main doctrine of the *Conseil d'État* is that there are no rights stemming from the Convention itself which could be invoked directly;[49] the case-law rather argues for a parallel application of both implementing EU law and the Convention.[50]

It follows from these conclusions that the CJEU case-law on the lack of direct applicability of the Convention essentially defines interpretation by national courts with the result that the Convention is primarily considered as a background norm of EU law implementing

---

43   *BVerwG*, Order of 25 April 2018, *Case 9 A 16.16*, para. 60; Judgment of 19 December 2017, *Case 7 A 10.17*, paras. 29-30.
44   *BVerwG*, Judgment of 2 November 2017, *Case 7 C 25.15*, para. 19; similarly: Order of 10 October 2017, *Case 7 B 4.17*, para. 9.
45   *BVerwG*, Judgment of 1 June 2017, *Case 9 C 2.16*, paras. 17-18.
46   *BVerwG*, Judgment of 18 December 2014, *Case 4 C 35.13*, para. 61.
47   *Conseil d'État*, Judgment of 12 April 2013, *Case 342409*, para. 15.
48   *Conseil d'État*, Judgment of 9 May 2006, *Case 292398*; Judgment of 14 June 2006, *Case 293317*; for a detailed analysis *see* Julien Bétaille, 'The Direct Effect of the Aarhus Convention as Seen by the French 'Conseil d'État', *Environmental Law Network International*, Issue 2, 2009, pp. 63-73.
49   *Conseil d'État*, Judgment of 25 September 2013, *Case 352660*, para. 25; Judgment of 23 March 2011, *Case 329642*; Judgment of 23 April 2009, *Case 306242*; similarly: Judgment of 13 March 2019, *Case 414930*; Judgment of 16 October 2017, *Case 397606*.
50   *Conseil d'État*, Judgment of 28 September 2016, *Case 390111*; similarly: Judgment of 27 January 2016, *Case 386869*; Judgment of 28 March 2011, *Case 330256*.

the Aarhus Convention. As such, it is the relevant EU laws – primarily directives – and their autonomous interpretation by the CJEU that define the enforcement of the provisions on public participation in national laws.

7.5   Principles of Interpretation

As far as the specific interpretation principles of the Aarhus Convention are concerned, the following cornerstones can be identified.

7.5.1   General Principles

Firstly, also in connection to the Convention as an international agreement the principle applies that it shall be interpreted on the basis of its wording and goals. These principles of international law appear in the case-law of CJEU as well,[51] thus affecting the interpretation of the EU law implementing the provisions of the Convention:

> "[i]t follows that, for the purposes of interpreting Directive 2003/4, account is to be taken of the wording and aim of the Aarhus Convention, which that directive is designed to implement in EU law."[52]

Secondly, it also apparent that the general principles of interpretation in EU law[53] – such as the autonomous interpretation of EU law, the principles of efficiency and effectiveness,[54] the requirement of uniform interpretation in the EU[55] – are to be applied accordingly by

---

51   Judgment of the General Court of 14 June 2012, *Case T-338/08, Stichting Natuur en Milieu and Pesticide Action Network Europe v. European Commission*, ECLI:EU:T:2012:300, para. 72; similarly: *Case C-344/04, International Air Transport Association*, para. 40.

52   Judgment of 23 November 2016, *Case C-442/14, Bayer CropScience SA-NV and Stichting De Bijenstichting v. College voor de toelating van gewasbeschermingsmiddelen en biocide*, ECLI:EU:C:2016:890, para. 54.

53   De Witte 2011, pp. 323-362; Lorenzo Mellado Ruiz: 'Los principios comunitarios de eficacia directa y primacía frente a la funcionalidad del principio de autonomía procedimental: proceso de convergencia y estatuto de ciudadanía', *in* Fernando Fernández Marín & Ángel Fornieles Gil (eds.), *Derecho Comunitario Y Procedimiento Tributario*, Atelier, Barcelona, 2010, pp. 24-51; Damian Chalmers *et al.*, *European Union Law: Cases and Materials*, Cambridge University Press, Cambridge, 2010.

54   Judgment of 18 October 2011, *Joined Cases C-128/09-131/09, C-134/09 and C-135/09, Antoine Boxus and Willy Roua, Guido Durlet and Others, Paul Fastrez and Henriette Fastrez, Philippe Daras, Association des riverains et habitants des communes proches de l'aéroport BSCA (Brussels South Charleroi Airport) (ARACh), Bernard Page and Léon L'Hoir and Nadine Dartois v. Région wallonne*, ECLI:EU:C:2011:667, para. 52; similarly: Judgment of 16 February 2012, *Case C-182/10, Marie-Noëlle Solvay and Others v. Région wallonne*, ECLI:EU:C:2012:82, paras. 46-49.

55   Judgment of 18 July 2013, *Case C-515/11, Deutsche Umwelthilfe eV v. Bundesrepublik Deutschland*, ECLI:EU:C:2013:523, para. 21.

the EU and the Member States.[56] This interpretation has been confirmed – from among the examined national high courts[57] – in the case-law of *BVerwG* in relation to questions falling into the scope of application of the Aarhus Convention. At the same time, it sets the limits of the margin of appreciation in national law, as it stated that the national legislator has a room for maneuver in implementing the Convention, giving due consideration to the principles of efficiency and effectiveness.[58] In this context, *'völkerrechtsfreundliche Auslegung'* means that EU-law, to be transposed into national law shall be interpreted in light of the aims of the Convention.[59] This statement can be seen – in a more general sense – as a confirmation of the fact that the implementation obligation stemming from EU law takes priority to the enforcement of the Convention as an international agreement. In a concrete case, the Hungarian Constitutional Court used a similar formulation as regards the Convention on the Rights of Persons with Disabilities, to which both Hungary and the EU are parties.[60] Therefore, it is highly possible that the Hungarian Constitutional Court would follow a similar approach as that of the *BVerwG* in relation to the Aarhus Convention as well. Consequently, the principle elaborated by the CJEU[61] as regards the role of EU law implementing international law seems to have become an integral part of national jurisprudence, even in cases – like that of the Hungarian Constitutional Court – where the application or interpretation of EU law is not a direct obligation.

At this point, an important digression shall be made concerning the role of general principles of EU law in connection to the third pillar of the Aarhus Convention. Namely, at the time of joining the Convention, the European Community made a reservation, stating that the Member States have the primary obligation to fulfil the obligations arising from Article 9(3) of the Convention until the Community decides to adopt "provisions of Community law covering the implementation of these obligations" (Council Decision 2005/370/EC). In lack of a common regulation in the field of access to justice, the Member

---

56   *Case C-204/09, Flachglas Torgau*, para. 37.
57   The available decisions of the Hungarian Supreme Court (Curia of Hungary) do not contain substantial argumentation as regards the relationship of national, international and EU law; they refer usually to the promulgating act and seem to examine the question as the application of internal laws.
58   *BVerwG*, Judgment of 28 July 2016, *Case 7 C 7.14*, paras. 35-37; Judgment of 24 October 2013, *Case 7 C 36.11*, para. 27.
59   *BVerwG*, Judgment of 29 June 2016, *Case 7 C 32.15*, paras. 14-20; similarly: Judgment of 30 March 2017, *Case 7 C 17.15*, para. 27; Judgment of 23 February 2017, *Case 7 C 31.15*, para. 35. *See* Christoph Görisch, 'Effective Legal Protection in the European Legal Order', *in* Zoltán Szente & Konrad Lachmayer (eds.), *The Principle of Effective Legal Protection in Administrative Law*, Routledge, Abingdon, 2017, p. 37; Anna Katharina Mangold, 'The Persistence of National Peculiarities: Translating Representative Environmental Action from Transnational into German Law', *Indiana Journal of Global Legal Studies*, Vol. 21, Issue 1, 2014, pp. 223-261.
60   Decision No. 21/2018. (XI. 14.) AB, Reasoning [27].
61   Judgment of 11 April 2013, *Joined Cases C-335/11 and C-337/11, HK Danmark, acting on behalf of Jette Ring v. Dansk almennyttigt Boligselskab and HK Danmark, acting on behalf of Lone Skouboe Werge v. Dansk Arbejdsgiverforening, acting on behalf of Pro Display A/S*, ECLI:EU:C:2013:222, paras. 28-30.

States should bear significant responsibility for the implementation of the third pillar of the Convention and fulfil their obligations stemming from the Convention not only as individual parties to the Convention but as members of the EU as well. This dual character of the implementation of the third pillar, especially with regard to the *locus standi* of non-governmental organizations promoting the protection of the environment, means that considerable differences remain with respect to the individual evaluation of the Member States; however, also general standards should be defined and enforced as part of EU law. The CJEU seems to promote this by stressing the EU law aspects of litigation, mostly by referring to a background EU norm, such as the Habitats Directive[62] or the Environmental Impact Assessment Directive.[63] Nevertheless, strive for *actio popularis* in environmental matters cannot be gleaned from the case-law of the CJEU;[64] it would result in interpretation problems concerning Article 263(4) TFEU. Rather, the extensive interpretation of the general principles of EU law is a way of encouraging the establishment of a uniform minimum of access to justice in the Member States. This case also confirms the conclusion that the general obligations stemming from EU law define the framework of implementation of the Convention even in situations, where the major responsibility is placed on the Member States by EU law itself.

7.5.2   Specific Principles

Furthermore, there are principles that shall be taken into consideration specifically regarding the interpretation of the Convention. One such principle is related to the role of the Implementation Guide of the Convention.[65] In this respect, the CJEU stressed that

---

62   Judgment of 12 May 2011, *Case C-115/09, Bund für Umwelt und Naturschutz Deutschland, Landesverband Nordrhein-Westfalen eV v. Bezirksregierung Arnsberg,* ECLI:EU:C:2011:289.

63   Judgment of 7 November 2013, *Case C-72/12, Gemeinde Altrip, Gebrüder Hört GbR, Willi Schneider v. Land Rheinland-Pfalz,* ECLI:EU:C:2013:712; Judgment of 15 October 2015, *Case C-137/14, European Commission v. Federal Republic of Germany,* ECLI:EU:C:2015:683.

64   Moritz Reese *et al.*, 'The Courts as Guardians of the Environment – New Developments in Access to Justice and Environmental Litigation', *in ICLG TO: Environment & Climate Change Law 2019,* Global Legal Group, London, 2019; European Parliament, 'Implementing the Aarhus Convention Access to Justice in Environmental Matters', Briefing October 2017, at www.europarl.europa.eu/RegData/etudes/BRIE/2017/608753/EPRS_BRI(2017)608753_EN.pdf; Astrid Epiney & Benedikt Pirker, 'The Case-law of the European Court of Justice on Access to Justice in the Aarhus Convention and Its Implications for Switzerland', *Journal for European Environmental & Planning Law,* 2014/4, pp. 348-366; Ágnes Váradi, 'Facilitating the Persecution of Rights in the European Union: New Tendencies for a Better Access to Justice', *in* András Lőrincz (ed.), *Prospects for the European Union: Borderless Europe?* Institute for Cultural Relations Policy, Budapest, 2014, pp. 160-169.

65   *The Aarhus Convention: An Implementation Guide (second edition 2014)*, at www.unece.org/fileadmin/DAM/env/pp/Publications/Aarhus_Implementation_Guide_interactive_eng.pdf.

"while the Aarhus Convention Implementation Guide may be regarded as an explanatory document, capable of being taken into consideration, if appropriate, among other relevant material for the purpose of interpreting the convention, the observations in the guide have no binding force and do not have the normative effect of the provisions of the Aarhus Convention."[66]

The *BVerwG* interpreted the role of the implementation guide similarly,[67] but at the same time it stressed that the practice of the Compliance Committee may have a significant effect on national laws. Consequently, it takes these recommendations into account when evaluating whether the margin of appreciation of national law was in accordance with the principles of the Convention.[68] However, according to the case-law of CJEU the Implementation Guide of the Convention cannot be generally invoked when evaluating the legality of EU acts implementing the Aarhus Convention.[69] Compared to the restrictions following from the CJEU case-law, the approach of the *BVerwG* seems to take another stance, referring to the Convention as an international treaty.

The other, very important principle of interpretation is the presumption for public participation,[70] which is strongly related to the aims of the Convention, namely to the efficient protection of the environment.[71] Consequently, the provisions restricting public participation shall be interpreted narrowly, while other provisions ensuring the right of public involvement cannot be interpreted in a restrictive way.

"Therefore, although the national legislature is entitled, inter alia, to confine the rights whose infringement may be relied on by an individual in legal proceedings contesting one of the decisions, acts or omissions referred to in Article 11 of Directive 2011/92 to individual public-law rights, that is to say, individual rights which, under national law, can be categorized as individual public-law rights (see, to that effect, judgment in *Bund für Umwelt und Naturschutz Deutschland, Landesverband Nordrhein-Westfalen*, C-115/09, EU:C:2011:289, paragraphs 36 and 45), the provisions of that article relating to the rights to

---

66   *Case C-279/12, Fish Legal*, para. 38; similarly: *Case C-204/09, Flachglas Torgau*, para. 36; *Case C-182/10, Marie-Noëlle Solvay*, para. 28; Judgment of 23 November 2016, *Case C-673/13 P, European Commission v. Stichting Greenpeace Nederland and PAN Europe*, ECLI:EU:C:2016:889, para. 59.
67   *BVerwG, Judgment of 5 September 2013, Case 7 C 21.12*, paras. 33-34.
68   *BVerwG, Judgment of 29 June 2017, Case 3 A 1.16*, para. 28.
69   *Joined Cases C-404/12 P and C-405/12 P, Stichting Natuur en Milieu*, paras. 46 and 53.
70   For a detailed analysis of this aspect in relation to the single pillars of the Aarhus Convention *see* Ágnes Váradi, 'Az Aarhusi Egyezmény értelmezésének egyes kérdései az Európai Unió Bíróságának gyakorlatában', *Állam- és Jogtudomány*, Vol. 59, Issue 2, 2018, pp. 97-114.
71   Judgment of 15 March 2018, *Case C-470/16, North East Pylon Pressure Campaign Limited and Maura Sheehy v. An Bord Pleanála and Others*, ECLI:EU:C:2018:185, para. 53.

bring actions of members of the public concerned by the decisions, acts or omissions which fall within that directive's scope cannot be interpreted restrictively."[72]

Hence, it can be confirmed that the CJEU interprets the provisions of the Convention in light of the general principles of EU law, with regard to the EU environmental policy and the specificities of environmental matters, in an autonomous way.

This principle is confirmed in the jurisdiction of the *BVerwG* as well. However, in a concrete case it gave an important addition to this principle: the presumption for public participation and the teleological interpretation of the Convention cannot result in the broadening of the scope of application of the EU law – and thus, national law – implementing the Convention.[73] These conclusions lead back to the statements of the CJEU referred to in Part 3, namely, that indirect correlation with environmental matters cannot lead to the extensive interpretation of the scope of EU law. At the same time, they confirm the conclusion that following the EU's accession, the European law nature of the Convention has taken precedence over its role as an international treaty in the law of the Member States.

7.6   FINAL THOUGHTS

On the basis of the analysis above, it can be concluded that the interpretation of the Aarhus Convention has become an integral part of CJEU case-law as well as the jurisprudence of national courts. The case-law of the CJEU gives considerable guidance for national courts through the interpretation of EU norms transposing the Convention into the common legal order. The conclusions stemming from CJEU case-law also demonstrate that while becoming an integral part of EU law, the Convention has gained a specific interpretation, which may under certain circumstances differ from its general, original interpretation based on its nature of being an international agreement. This phenomenon can be traced back to the fact that EU environmental policy and the general principles of EU law provide a specific framework for the Convention, and these are interpreted by the CJEU in an autonomous manner, affecting the interpretation of the Convention in the national judicial practice as well.

The case-law of the national high courts of the examined countries has also expanded in the past few years. The decisions, however, show diverging attitudes of the judicial fora:

---

72   Judgment of 16 April 2015, *Case C-570/13, Karoline Gruber v. Unabhängiger Verwaltungssenat für Kärnten and Others*, ECLI:EU:C:2015:231, para. 40.

73   *BVerwG*, Judgment of 12 November 2014, *Case 4 C 34.13*, para. 18; similarly: Judgment of 19 December 2013, *Case 4 C 14.12*, para. 20.

in two of the examined countries – Germany and France – the Aarhus Convention has not been analyzed from a constitutional point of view, while the Hungarian Constitutional Court treated the question as a matter of compliance between national law and international law. The case-law of the *BVerwG* and the *Conseil d'État* demonstrates that while applying the Convention, the obligation of national courts is complex: complying with EU law standards, principles and fulfilling the aims of the Convention.[74] In this context, the requirements stemming from EU law prevail, while divergence may be detected in the context of the methods of interpretation (*e.g.* the role of the Implementation Guide in certain judgments of the *BVerwG*).

These insights into the relationship of national laws, EU law and the Convention can support the proper application of the Convention, strengthening thereby the public participation in environmental matters, thereby promoting the protection of common social interests. Furthermore, a well-elaborated interpretation of the Convention in EU law can contribute to the success of the whole Convention, as

> "[r]egional arrangements of less heterogeneous groups of States can be a way to more effectively advance in the implementation of universally recognized principles by providing for a closer, systematic cooperation in the enforcement of those principles at a decentralized level."[75]

---

74 Jan Darpö, 'Pulling the Trigger', *in* Sanja Bogojevic & Rosemary Rayfuse (eds.), *Environmental Rights in Europe and Beyond*, Hart, Oxford-London, 2018, pp. 257-258.

75 Karl-Peter Sommerman, 'Transformative Effects of the Aarhus Convention in Europe', *Zeitschrift für ausländisches öffentliches Recht und Völkerrecht*, Vol. 77, 2017, p. 337.

PART II
DEVELOPMENTS IN INTERNATIONAL LAW

8   Judge Géza Herczegh – The First Hungarian at the International Court of Justice

*Peter Tomka**

Abstract

Géza Herczegh was a Hungarian academic, justice of the Hungarian Constitutional Court and judge of the International Court of Justice (ICJ). In this paper, which commemorates the 90th anniversary of Géza Herczegh's birth, his successor at the ICJ, Judge Peter Tomka, offers his reflections on Herczegh's time at the Court. While they had only limited interaction, Judge Tomka recalls his encounters with Herczegh, both before and after Herczegh's election to the ICJ. Additionally, Judge Tomka reviews Herczegh's legacy at the ICJ, considering both the occasions when Herczegh wrote separately from the Court and his reputation amongst people familiar with the ICJ as a dedicated and open-minded judge interested in finding areas of consensus.

8.1   Introduction

I did not work with the late Judge Géza Herczegh at the International Court of Justice (ICJ). I succeeded him on the bench of the World Court when he retired, after almost ten years of dedicated service in the principal judicial organ of the UN, on 5 February 2003. However, I did have opportunities to meet him, both before his election to the Court and while he exercised his highest judicial function.

*   Peter Tomka: Member of the ICJ since 6 February 2003 (re-elected as from 6 February 2012), Vice-President of the ICJ from 6 February 2009 until 5 February 2012; President of the ICJ from 6 February 2012 until 5 February 2015.

8.2 Promotion and Dissemination of International Humanitarian Law

Our first encounter occurred in November 1986 in Prague. He came to a seminar on international humanitarian law, the third one[1] in the series organized since 1984 jointly by the International Institute of Humanitarian Law based in San Remo, Italy, led at that time by Professor Jovica Patrnogić, and the International Committee of the Red Cross (ICRC), in the then socialist countries of the Eastern bloc. Who could then have envisaged that in a few years' time, the implementation of international humanitarian law would become so topical in the context of the Balkan wars resulting from the break-up of former Yugoslavia. Professor Géza Herczegh (as he then was) was a natural choice for the organizers of the seminar to speak at the event. He was a well-respected authority in this field of international law, having actively participated at the 'Diplomatic Conference on the protection of victims of armed conflict', held in Geneva in 1974-1977, which adopted the two Additional Protocols to the Geneva Conventions. Professor Herczegh also published (in English) a monograph 'Development of International Humanitarian Law',[2] analyzing the normative achievements of the Geneva Conference in the larger context of the historical development of the rules designed to protect victims of war. The ICRC was interested not only in the dissemination of international humanitarian law but also in increasing the number of States Parties to the two Additional Protocols. While socialist countries, members of the Warsaw Pact, signed these instruments, none had ratified them. The reason was obvious: the Soviet Union had been heavily involved in the Afghan War from late 1979 until February 1989. It was only after the withdrawal of Soviet troops from Afghanistan that gradually Warsaw Pact countries ratified the Additional Protocols; Hungary did so on 12 April 1989 as the first country of the bloc, followed by Bulgaria on 26 September 1989 and three days later by the Soviet Union itself.

8.3 Professor Herczegh's Election to the International Court of Justice

The next encounter, although not personal, came in 1993. Having led the Slovak legal team at the negotiations with Hungarian experts (Dr. Király, Dr. Szénási and Professor Valki) on a Special Agreement for submission of the dispute concerning the Gabčíkovo-Nagymaros Project, which was finalized in early February 1993 in Budapest, I returned to my diplomatic post as Deputy Permanent Representative of Slovakia, newly admitted to the United Nations

---

1   The second seminar was held in 1985 in Budapest.
2   Géza Herczegh, *Development of International Humanitarian Law*, Akadémiai, Budapest 1984, 240 p.

on 19 January 1993. The Special Agreement was signed on 7 April 1993 in Brussels. It was subject to ratification which was to be completed within a short period of time.[3] Hungary and Slovakia were on their way to The Hague, where the 15 Members of the Court would have to adjudicate their dispute. However, on 14 January 1993, Judge Manfred Lachs from Poland passed away, after almost 26 years on the ICJ, then the longest serving judge.[4] The vacancy was to be filled by election, which the Security Council set for 10 May 1993 in accordance with Article 14 of the Statue of the ICJ. The newly elected Member of the Court was to complete the very short remainder of the late Judge Lachs's term of office which was to expire on 5 February 1994. The seat was traditionally considered as belonging to the Eastern European Group, although seats in the Court are not formally distributed between the UN regional groups. Judge Lachs's predecessor was another distinguished Polish lawyer, Professor Bohdan Winiarski, who served on the Court from its inception on 6 February 1946 for twenty-one years until 5 February 1967, when he retired.

Two candidates were nominated for election: Professor Géza Herczegh, then Vice-President of the Constitutional Court of Hungary, and Professor Krzysztof Skubiszewski, then since 1989 the first non-communist Foreign Minister of Poland after World War II. It was not easy to predict the outcome of the election. Certainly, Foreign Minister Professor Skubiszewski was much better known internationally, in particular in the UN.[5] On the other hand, Hungary was at that time a non-permanent Member of the Security Council and was represented by a highly respected top diplomat, Ambassador André Erdős. Judges of the Court are elected by the General Assembly and the Security Council, both main organs of the UN voting concurrently. A candidate who obtains an absolute majority of votes in both organs is declared elected.[6] I followed the forthcoming election with a partic-ular interest knowing that within a couple of months the dispute between Hungary and Slovakia should be submitted to the Court. Saturday, 8 May, just two days prior to the election, I met by chance the young Polish Ambassador, Dr. Zbigniew Włosowicz in Central Park on his roller skates. He informed me that he had received instructions from Minister Skubiszewski to withdraw his candidature for election to the Court. I was caught by surprise. Zbigniew explained to me that Professor Skubiszewski had been asked by President Wałęsa to stay on as Foreign Minster as he was considered to be a pillar, having served as Foreign Minister under four Prime Ministers, in the rather shaky Government

---

3   The instruments of ratification were exchanged on 28 June 1993 and the Special Agreement was notified jointly by Hungary and Slovakia to the Registrar of the ICJ on 2 July 1993, thus instituting the proceedings before the Court.

4   Subsequently, his record was surpassed by Judge Shigeru Oda from Japan who served three full terms, between 6 February 1976 and 5 February 2003. He retired from the Bench the same day as Judge Herczegh.

5   Professor Skubiszewski was nominated for election by eight national groups in the Permanent Court of Arbitration in accordance with Article 4(1), of the Statute of the ICJ. Professor Herczegh received four nominations.

6   Article 10(1) of the Statute of the ICJ.

of Prime Minister Hanna Suchocka. A month later, in June 1993, the Polish Parliament passed a vote of no-confidence by a majority of one vote. The Government fell. Wałęsa dissolved the Parliament and new elections were held. The Socialists came back to power and formed a coalition Government with the agrarian Polish People's Party. Professor Skubiszewski was not re-appointed as Foreign Minister.

Professor Herczegh remained, following the withdrawal of Minister Skubiszewski's candidature, the only candidate and on 10 May 1993 he was elected to the Court, having received all 15 votes in the Security Council and 129 votes in the General Assembly.[7] He assumed office immediately upon his election. I faced the question of how to report the outcome back to Bratislava. I decided to keep it low key. I sent a report only to the UN Department and the International Law Department of Slovakia's Foreign Ministry. I was afraid that it would be difficult to explain to politicians that we should complete the ratification procedure of the Special Agreement and submit the dispute with Hungary jointly to the Court, whose Members now included a Hungarian national. I was not sure that they would be persuaded that Slovakia was entitled, under Article 31(2) of the Statute of the ICJ, to appoint a Judge *ad hoc*.[8] Nor could they have been reassured by the fact that Judge Herczegh was born in Southeastern Slovakia, then in 1928 part of Czechoslovakia, in a small town that the Hungarian minority living there (in fact constituting the majority of its citizens) calls Nagykapos, while Slovaks call it Veľké Kapušany. Although he moved with his mother, when he was around four, to Southern Hungary, the fact remains that he was the first ever Judge of the ICJ born in Slovakia.[9]

Following his election, Judge Herczegh had to move to The Hague quickly, where he was welcomed by Sir Robert Jennings, the then President of the Court. He started on 14 June 1993 and sat on the Bench for a month of hearings in the *Territorial Dispute* case between Chad and Libya.[10] The judgment, the first one in which Judge Herczegh participated, was almost unanimous; only Judge *ad hoc* Sette-Camara, appointed by Libya, dissented. When he came to the Court, Judge Herczegh was not able to enjoy a proper judicial vacation in summer 1993. A few days after the hearings in the *Territorial Dispute* case were closed, the Court received, on 27 July 1993, the second request of Bosnia and Herzegovina for the indication of provisional measures in the *Genocide* case. The Court was reconvened for hearings on 25 and 26 August and issued a new Order on provisional measures on

---

7   See UN documents A/47/PV.103 and S/PV.3209.

8   Slovakia availed itself of this right and appointed in 1994 as Judge *ad hoc* Professor Skubiszewski who in the meantime had become President of the Iran-United States Claims Tribunal, based in The Hague.

9   In 2000 he was joined on the Court by Professor Thomas Buergenthal, a US national, who was born in 1934 in Ľubochňa, which is located in Slovakia at the foot of the Veľké Fatra Mountains.

10   *Territorial Dispute* (Libyan Arab Jamahiriya/Chad), Judgment of 3 February 1994, 1994 ICJ Reports 6, para. 16. The hearings were held between 14 June and 14 July 1993.

13 September 1993.[11] The very first procedural Order in which he was involved was a simple one, time-limits for filing a reply and a rejoinder in the *Certain Phosphate Lands in Nauru* case.[12]

8.4   JUDGE HERCZEGH'S RE-ELECTION TO THE INTERNATIONAL COURT OF JUSTICE

Hardly elected, Judge Herczegh had to be nominated for re-election as his mandate was to expire on 5 February 1994. The election was scheduled for 10 November 1993. This time Judge Herczegh faced competition for the so-called Eastern European seat. Three other candidates from Central and Eastern Europe were nominated: Professor Skubiszewski from Poland, who was no longer Foreign Minister, Professor Volodymyr Vassylenko from Ukraine and Professor Alexander Yankov from Bulgaria. Géza Herczegh was elected by the Security Council already in the first ballot, having received 13 votes. In the General Assembly, he was from the start of voting leading among these four candidates with 76 votes, but he received the required absolute majority only in the third ballot when 111 states voted for him.[13]

8.5   SITE VISIT BY THE COURT IN SLOVAKIA AND HUNGARY

My final encounter with him came during the *Gabčíkovo-Nagymaros Project* case. While during the hearings the Judges keep their distance from agents, counsel and advocates,[14] in the *Gabčíkovo-Nagymaros Project* case, the situation was rather different. On 16 June 1995, a few days before filing a reply in the case, which was due by 20 June, I sent as Agent of Slovakia a letter to the President of the Court (Judge Bedjaoui at that moment) asking the Court

> "to be so good as to implement its powers under Article 66 of the Rules of Court and to decide to visit the locality to which the case concerning the *Gabčíkovo-*

---

11   *Application of the Convention on the Prevention and Punishment of the Crime of Genocide* (Bosnia and Herzegovina v. Yugoslavia (Serbia and Montenegro)), Provisional Measures, Order of 13 September 1993, 1993 ICJ Reports, p. 325. The first Order on Provisional Measures in this case was issued by the Court on 8 April 1993, *see* 1993 ICJ Reports, p. 3, in which, of course, Géza Herczegh did not participate, as he was not yet a Member of the Court.

12   *Certain Phosphate Lands in Nauru (Nauru v. Australia)*, Order of 25 June 1993, 1993 ICJ Reports, p. 316.

13   See UN documents A/48/PV.51, A/48/PV.52, A/48/PV.53 and S/PV.3309.

14   The only occasion for a short social conversation is at the reception the Court offers to the Parties during the hearings on the merits.

Nagymaros Project relates, and there to exercise its functions with regard to the obtaining of evidence."

The meeting with the President of the Court was scheduled for 30 June 1995. The Court, therefore, invited the Agent of Hungary to offer any comments his Government might wish to make. Dr. Szénási, in his letter of 28 June 1995, informed the Court that if the Court

"should decide that a visit to the various areas affected by the Project (or, more precisely, affected by variant C) would be useful, Hungary would be pleased to co-operate in organizing such a visit."

The Court decided that such a visit may facilitate its task in the case at hand and, having received the Protocol and Agreed Minutes signed by the Parties, outlining the program, dates and details of the visit, adopted an Order for that purpose.[15] The visit took place between 1 and 4 April 1997: two days in Slovakia, two days in Hungary. It provided an opportunity to the Judges not only to see the main structures of the Gabčíkovo part of the Project and the areas along the Danube where the installations were planned under the 1977 Treaty between Hungary and Czechoslovakia on the joint construction and operation of the Gabčíkovo-Nagymaros System of Locks, but also an opportunity for agents of both Parties and two counsel of each Party, accompanying the Members of the Court, to engage in a little bit less formal conversation with the Judges. With protective helmets we walked together in the hydropower station at Gabčíkovo and we inspected the dyke at Čunovo. We had lunch together in Gabčíkovo and in the evening in Bratislava, Judges could have chosen either to go the Slovak National Theatre for a performance of Tchaikovsky's Eugene Onegin or to a typical Slovak restaurant on Koliba Hill with an open fireplace and live gypsy music. After two days in Slovakia we travelled by two buses to Hungary. This was, however, in the pre-Schengen era. We were stopped at the boundary and were not allowed to continue. The 'problem' was that the Vice-President of the Court, Judge Weeramantry from Sri Lanka, was travelling with his Sri Lankan passport and the Hungarian border police did not wish to allow him to enter Hungary despite the fact that he was travelling on an official mission with the principal judicial organ of the UN. Ambassador Szénási

---

15 *Gabčíkovo-Nagymaros Project* (Hungary/Slovakia), Order of 5 February 1997, 1997 ICJ Reports, p. 3. For more about the site visit, *see* Mohammed Bedjaoui, 'La descente sur les lieux dans la pratique de la Cour internationale et de sa devancière', *in* Gerhard Hafner *et al.* (eds.), *Liber Amicorum of Professor Ignaz Seidl-Hohenveldern*, Kluwer, The Hague, 1998, pp. 1-23; Peter Tomka & Samuel S. Wordsworth, 'The First Site Visit of the International Court of Justice in the Fulfilment of its Judicial Function', *American Journal of International Law*, Vol. 92, Issue 1, 1998, pp. 133-140; Frances Meadows, 'The First Site Visit by the International Court of Justice', *Leiden Journal of International Law*, Vol. 11, Issue 3, 1998, pp. 603-608.

spent more than one hour on the telephone with Budapest, his blood pressure visibly going up. Finally, somebody in Budapest ordered the border police in Rajka to allow the Court to enter Hungary. This, of course, delayed the whole program for the third day of the "site inspection". The accompanying spouses went to see a monastery in Pannonhalma, while Judges, having been re-seated into several smaller minibuses, went to see the branches of the Danube river and inundation polders. They had also an opportunity to taste local Hungarian cuisine in a small restaurant, Platán Borozó in Dunaremete near Mosonmag-yaróvár. We stayed overnight in a hilltop hotel in Visegrád, having the opportunity to admire in the morning the scenery of the area. The Court and the accompanying persons then continued to Budapest. Judge Herczegh was quietly observing the places we had visited. When we entered Budapest, Professor Alexandre-Charles (Károly) Kiss, who studied in Budapest, but then emigrated to France, acted as a sort of 'tour guide', pointing to different historical and cultural monuments. He was visibly emotionally moved when, as we were passing along St. Stephen's Basilica, he talked about the first King of Hungary, Stephen I, and the holy relic of his right-hand displayed in the Basilica. Later that afternoon, Prime Minister Gyula Horn offered a reception in honor of the Court in the majestic Parliament Building, clearly to reciprocate the reception hosted by the Slovak Prime Minister three days earlier in the Primate's Palace in Bratislava.

The case was not an easy one for Judge Herczegh. He disagreed with the majority of the findings of the Court and appended to the Judgment his only – rather long – 28-page dissenting opinion[16] in almost ten years of service in the Peace Palace. He voted seven times against the findings of the Court, once as a lone dissenter, and twice with the majority.

8.6   JUDICIAL WORK OF JUDGE HERCZEGH

Although he spoke both languages of the Court, Judge Herczegh wrote his confidential Notes[17] and occasional declarations and his only dissenting opinion attached to the Court's decisions in French, which he learned in the French Grammar School in Gödöllő.

---

16   *Gabčíkovo-Nagymaros Project* (Hungary/Slovakia), Judgment of 25 September 1997, 1997 ICJ Reports, pp. 176-203, Dissenting Opinion of Judge Herczegh.

17   Under Article 4 of the Resolution concerning the Internal Judicial Practice of the Court, adopted on 12 April 1976, each judge has to prepare a written note expressing his/her views on a case under deliberation indicating, in particular, his/her tentative views on the factual and legal issues involved in the case and his/her tentative conclusion as to the correct disposal of the case.

Herczegh joined the Court in the period when its docket started to grow, and its judicial activities intensified. He sat in the period of almost ten years, between 10 May 1993 and 5 February 2003 in 32 cases, 29 contentious matters and 3 advisory proceedings.[18]

In the Court, he was – as his colleague Judge (and later President) Higgins put it – "a voice of moderation", who approached cases "with a totally open mind" and sought "consensus where possible".[19] As she aptly characterized him: "He preferred the identification of common ground to the doctrinal battlefield."[20] He participated in the delivery of twenty judgments, three advisory opinions and eighteen orders on requests for the indication of provisional measures.[21]

This approach is reflected in the fact that he wrote separately rather sporadically. In addition to his already mentioned longer dissenting opinion in the *Gabčíkovo-Nagymaros Project*,[22] Judge Herczegh authored only five short declarations which in total do not exceed 9 pages.

For the first time, after having been in the Court for three years, he "spoke from the Bench" separately in the advisory opinion on *Legality of the Threat or Use of Nuclear Weapons*. This opinion, requested by the General Assembly of the UN in December 1994, was a challenging issue for the Court. Although the opinion is not particularly long, some forty pages, including seven pages describing the procedural history, it took almost eight months from the closing of the hearing for the Court to deliver its opinion. No doubt the Court was engaged in lengthy internal discussions. The key pronouncement that

> "the threat or use of nuclear weapons would generally be contrary to the rules
> of international law applicable in armed conflict, and in particular the principles
> and rules of humanitarian law"

---

18 *Legality of the Use by a State of Nuclear Weapons in Armed Conflict*, Advisory Opinion of 8 July 1996, 1996 ICJ Reports, p. 66; *Legality of the Threat or Use of Nuclear Weapons*, Advisory Opinion of 8 July 1996, 1996 ICJ Reports, p. 226 and *Difference Relating to Immunity from Legal Process of a Special Rapporteur of the Commission on Human Rights*, Advisory Opinion of 29 April 1999, 1999 ICJ Reports, p. 62.

19 Rosalyn Higgins, 'Géza Herczegh – Our Colleague and Friend at the International Court of Justice', in Péter Kovács (ed.), *International Law – A Quiet Strength / Le droit international, une force tranquille*, Pázmány Press, Budapest, 2011, pp. 21-22.

20 Id. p. 22.

21 Ten of these orders were rendered by the Court in the *Legality of Use of Force* cases brought by Yugoslavia (Serbia and Montenegro) against Belgium, Canada, France, Germany, Italy, the Netherlands, Portugal, Spain, United Kingdom and the United States.

22 For an analysis of this opinion *see* James Crawford, 'In dubio pro natura: The Dissent of Judge Herczegh', in Kovács 2011, pp. 251-269. Professor Crawford (as he then was) acted as lead counsel for Hungary in the *Gabčíkovo-Nagymaros Project* case.

was adopted only by the President's casting vote,[23] the Court being equally divided (seven to seven).[24] This conclusion was, however, qualified by the Court when it stated:

> "However, in view of the current state of international law, and of the elements of facts at its disposal, the Court cannot conclude definitively whether the threat or use of nuclear weapons would be lawful or unlawful in an extreme circumstance of self-defence, in which the very survival of a State would be at stake."[25]

Judge Herczegh supported the Court's conclusion. All fourteen Judges sitting in the case[26] attached to the Opinion either a declaration or a separate or dissenting opinion. Judge Herczegh penned a two-page declaration, the second most succinct; only Judge Shi from China was more economical in his style. Judge Herczegh touched on several points. He thought that since, according to Article 9 of the Statute of the Court, the principal legal systems of the world should be represented in the Court

> "[i]t is inevitable [...] that differences of theoretical approach will arise between the Members concerning the characteristic features of the system of international law [...], the presence or absence of gaps in this system, and the resolution of possible conflicts between its rules."[27]

In his view "[t]he diversity of these conceptions [of international law within the Court] prevented the Court from finding a more complete solution and therefore a more satisfactory result."[28] He was convinced that it was possible to formulate a more specific reply to the General Assembly's request, one less burdened with uncertainty and reticence. He argued that

> "[i]n the fields where certain acts are not totally and universally prohibited 'as such', the application of general principles of law makes it possible to regulate the behaviour of subjects of the international legal order, obliging or authorizing

---

23   This was the second occasion when the President had to exercise his power of using a casting vote, the first one occurred in 1966 in *South West Africa* cases, *see* 1966 ICJ Reports, p. 51, para. 100.

24   *Legality of the Threat or Use of Nuclear Weapons*, Advisory Opinion of 8 July 1996, 1996 ICJ Reports, p. 226, para. 105(2)E. Those voting in favor were: President Bedjaoui, Judges Ranjeva, Herczegh, Shi, Fleischhauer, Vereshchetin and Ferrari Bravo. Those voting against were: Vice-President Schwebel, Judges Oda, Guillaume, Shahabuddeen, Weeramantry, Koroma and Higgins.

25   Id., emphasis added.

26   The fifteenth seat had been vacant following the passing of Judge Andrés Aguilar Mawdsley from Venezuela on 24 October 1995, just six days before the opening of the hearing in the advisory proceedings.

27   *Legality of the Threat or Use of Nuclear Weapons*, Advisory Opinion of 8 July 1996, 1996 ICJ Reports, Declaration of Judge Herczegh, p. 275.

28   Id.

them, as the case may be, to act or to refrain from acting in one way or another."[29]

He was convinced that "[t]he fundamental principles of international humanitarian law [...] categorically and unequivocally prohibit the use of weapons of mass destruction, including nuclear weapons" and that "[i]nternational humanitarian law does not recognize any exceptions to these principles".[30] Next, he doubted the wisdom of the Court's dealing with the question of armed reprisals, as it did so only briefly, thus encouraging "hasty and unjustified interpretations."[31] He further pointed to the role of the General Assembly, under Article 13 of the UN Charter, to encourage progressive development of international law and its codification. He believed that

> "[t]he transformation, by means of codification, of the general principles of law and customary rules into treaty rules might remove some of the weaknesses inherent in customary law and could certainly help to put an end to the [controversies] which led up to the request for an opinion. [...] as to the legality or illegality of the threat or use of nuclear weapons, pending complete nuclear disarmament under strict and effective international control."[32]

It may be added that his appeal was followed by the General Assembly which convened in 2017 a negotiation which led, on 7 July 2017, to the adoption of the Treaty on the Prohibition of Nuclear Weapons. It was more of an exercise of progressive development of international law than its codification *stricto sensu*. One has, however, to note, that many States, including all States Members of NATO (except the Netherlands, which was the only country to vote against the adoption of the text of the Treaty[33]), decided not to participate in these negotiations. As long as NATO doctrine is based on nuclear deterrence, it is unlikely that the noble goal of nuclear disarmament supported by Judge Herczegh will be achieved any time soon.

In 1998, Judge Herczegh wrote two declarations in the two almost identical *Lockerbie* cases. In the case which involved Libya and the United Kingdom, he explained in his three-page declaration why he voted against certain parts of the *dispositif* of the Court's Judgment

---

29   Id., emphasis added. This was a retour for Judge Herczegh to the concept of general principles of law; he wrote many years earlier a monograph entitled *General Principles of Law and the International Legal Order*, Akadémiai, Budapest, 1969, 129 p.

30   Id., Declaration of Judge Herczegh.

31   Id.

32   Id. p. 276.

33   The text of the Treaty was adopted by 122 votes against one (the Netherlands) with one abstention (Singapore).

on preliminary objections. In paragraph 2, the Court rejected the United Kingdom's objection to admissibility on the grounds that adoption of Security Council resolutions 748 (1992) and 883 (1993) after the filing of the application rendered Libya's application without object.[34] The Court accordingly found that Libya's application was admissible.[35] The Court's reasoning was based on the proposition that events subsequent to the filing of the application were not relevant to admissibility because admissibility is to be assessed as of the date of filing.[36] Judge Herczegh considered this decision to be overly formalistic.[37] He recalled the Court's judgments in *Northern Cameroons* and *Nuclear Tests*, where the Court did dismiss applications as without object, and characterized the Court's decision in *Lockerbie* as "quite alien to [its] jurisprudence".[38]

The United Kingdom also asked the Court to dismiss Libya's application because, apart from admissibility, the intervening Security Council resolutions rendered Libya's application without object.[39] In paragraph 3 of the operative clause of its judgment, the Court declared that this objection did not have an exclusively preliminary character.[40] Disagreeing with this determination, Judge Herczegh drew a distinction between whether an objection affects the enjoyment of rights and the existence or content of the rights, considering the latter was not affected by the question of whether the rights and obligations of the parties were superseded by the Security Council resolutions rather than still governed by the Montreal Convention.[41] As deciding on the United Kingdom's objection would not require inquiry into the interpretation or application of the Montreal Convention, Judge Herczegh considered it to have a preliminary character.[42] Moreover, and consistently with his view on admissibility, he considered that the Court should have upheld the United Kingdom's objection.[43]

In his declaration in the *Lockerbie* case opposing Libya and the United States, Judge Herczegh referred the reader to the text of his declaration in the case against the United Kingdom.[44] This style in economy provided an example worthy to be followed by some

34   *Questions of Interpretation and Application of the 1971 Montreal Convention arising from the Aerial Incident at Lockerbie* (Libyan Arab Jamahiriya v. United Kingdom), Preliminary Objections, Judgment of 27 February 1998, 1998 ICJ Reports, p. 30, para. 53(2)(a).
35   Id. para. 52(2)(b).
36   Id. pp. 25-26, paras. 43-44.
37   Id. p. 52, Declaration of Judge Herczegh.
38   Id.
39   Id. para. 46.
40   Id. pp. 30-31, para. 52(3).
41   Id. pp. 52-53.
42   Id.
43   Id. p. 53.
44   *Questions of Interpretation and Application of the 1971 Montreal Convention arising from the Aerial Incident at Lockerbie* (Libyan Arab Jamahiriya v. United States of America), Preliminary Objections, Judgment of 27 February 1998, 1998 ICJ Reports, Declaration, p. 143.

Judges who write extensively on multiple occasions on the same issues. In these two cases, he was in fact a dissenter, as he would have dismissed these applications as being without object.

In 2001, Judge Herczegh wrote a one-page declaration in the *Maritime Delimitation and Territorial Questions between Qatar and Bahrain* case. He began by commenting on the difficulty of establishing the delimitation between the continental shelf and EEZ of the parties in view of the facts that relevant maritime features are much larger at low tide than at high tide and that the geographical maps available to the Court were accordingly inconsistent with each other.[45]

Second, Judge Herczegh emphasized the importance of the Court's determination that Bahrain was not entitled to apply the straight baselines method to the Hawar Islands, which were adjudged to belong to Bahrain and are located within a few kilometers of the Qatari west coast.[46] A consequence of this was that the waters around the Hawar Islands are the territorial, rather than internal, waters of Bahrain. Judge Herczegh cited approvingly the Court's specification in point 2(b) of the operative clause of the Judgment that Qatari vessels have a right of innocent passage through this territorial sea under customary international law.[47] This right enables Qatari vessels to navigate along the west coast of Qatar, as the Qatari territorial sea between Qatar and Hawar is too shallow to allow for navigation.[48] Judge Herczegh explained that these statements enabled him to vote in favor of paragraph 6 of the operative part of the judgement,[49] which established the single maritime boundary between the parties.[50]

In *Land and Maritime Boundary between Cameroon and Nigeria*, Judge Herczegh criticized the Court's description of the effect of Article 59 on the rights of Equatorial Guinea and Sao Tome and Principe.[51] In paragraph 238 of its judgment, the Court stated:

> "The Court considers that, in particular in the case of maritime delimitations where the maritime areas of several States are involved, the protection afforded by Article 59 of the Statute may not always be sufficient. In the present case, Article 59 may not sufficiently protect Equatorial Guinea or Sao Tome and

---

45   *Maritime Delimitation and Territorial Questions between Qatar and Bahrain* (Qatar v. Bahrain), Judgment of 16 March 2001, 2001 ICJ Reports, p. 216.
46   Id.
47   Id.
48   Id.
49   Id.
50   Id. p. 117, para. 252(6).
51   *Land and Maritime Boundary between Cameroon and Nigeria* (Cameroon v. Nigeria: Equatorial Guinea intervening), Judgment of 10 October 2002, 2002 ICJ Reports, p. 472.

Principe from the effects – even if only indirect – of a judgment affecting their legal rights."[52]

Judge Herczegh considered this criticism of Article 59 'misplaced'.[53] Rather, he viewed Article 59 as a necessary consequence of the foundation of the Court's jurisdiction on the consent of the parties.[54] The obligation of the Court not to affect the rights of the third states, he recognized, may occasionally pose problems for the Court.[55] This, in his view, explained the inclusion of Article 62 and the possibility of intervention by a third state which considers itself to have a legal interest that may be affected by the Court's decision.[56] He explained that it is for the Court to interpret and apply Article 59 in order to make the protection of third states' rights as effective as possible.[57] Accordingly, Judge Herczegh argued that the quoted texts was an unnecessary remark in the judgment.[58] This two-page declaration was his last piece written separately as Judge of the Court.

Judge Herczegh was a quiet and collegial man who was guided by the interests of the Court, not by promoting his own status. For him, a judgment of the Court was, as his colleague President Guillaume wrote, *"l'œuvre collective des membres de la Cour."*[59] He served on several drafting committees[60] entrusted with the preparation of draft judgments and opinions. As President Higgins notes "his reputation as a perfectionist as regards the accuracy of facts and the law, made him a natural choice."[61]

For his diligent work for almost ten years as Judge of the ICJ Géza Herczegh fully deserves a place in the history of international adjudication.

---

52   Id. p. 421, para. 238.
53   Id. p. 473.
54   Id. p. 472.
55   Id.
56   Id.
57   Id.
58   Id.
59   Gilbert Guillaume, 'Géza Herczegh – juge à la Cour internationale de Justice', in Kovács 2011, p. 17.
60   A drafting committee usually consists of three Members of the Court. They are elected by a secret ballot at the end of Article 5 deliberation. The President of the Court, if he is part of the majority, chairs *ex officio* the drafting committee. The composition of the committee remains confidential.
61   Higgins 2011, p. 22.

9   Languages and Linguistic Issues before the International Criminal Court

Péter Kovács[*]

Keywords

linguistic issues, ICC, language of criminal procedure, local languages, use of own language

Abstract

The present article deals with some of the language issues present before the International Criminal Court (ICC). These issues do not simply result from the challenges of translation to/from English and French but also from the fact that the English and French used before the ICC are specialist legal languages with centuries-old practice behind their well-established notions (*e.g.* 'no case to answer'). There are numerous other languages used by witnesses and victims with various backgrounds in the different cases and situations. They are mostly local, sometimes tribal languages often lacking the vocabulary necessary to describe complex legal issues, to deal with notions and phenomena of modern substantive or procedural law. It is equally important to note that there are always special local notions, which are impossible to translate with a single term, sometimes becoming a part of the English or French language of the procedure. Other languages, however, may bring with them their own special legal or historical-legal vocabulary, which must be reflected on in order to unpack its proper meaning. As such, language issues are omnipresent before the ICC, having also an impact on the budget of the Court. The efficient and accurate work of interpreters and translators is of outmost importance from the point of view of fair trial, rights of the accused but also from the perspective of access to information for victims, witnesses or local communities who are following the judicial procedure from home.

9.1   Introduction

Languages play a special role in all international organizations or entities formed inevitably by more than one state as they bring together people coming from different countries with different linguistic backgrounds, with the aim of working for a common cause. There are

---

[*]   Péter Kovács: professor of law, Pázmány Péter Catholic University, Budapest; judge at the International Criminal Court (2015-2024). The article was made in a personal capacity, the thoughts expressed here cannot be attributed to the ICC.

of course some monolingual organizations, in particular those where a common linguistic heritage is at the core of the will for cooperation. However, contemporary international organizations are typically multilingual especially when their ambition is to include as many members as possible.

International organizations incorporating international tribunals – particularly when these tribunals do not or do not only deal with interstate litigation but are vested with powers to adjudicate individuals' criminal charges – traditionally settle language issues (*e.g.* official languages, language parities in different bodies or main functions) using rules linked to the rights of the accused and other aspects of fair trial. Nevertheless, there are always issues which cannot be settled well in advance: questions, problems and challenges may emerge as a consequence of the particulars of a given situation or case.

Since my paper is much more centered on languages than law, I ask the readers' indulgence for the brief references on jurisprudence and at the same time, for the extensive references on information sheets published by the ICC, especially when I report on ongoing procedures. I tried to find open access and encyclopedia-type references on the different languages or special military terminology *etc.* that may be unknown to the reader, or with which they are not precisely known to the reader. Following a short presentation of the regulation of language issues in the Rome Statute of the ICC, some real problems, difficulties and challenges of linguistic nature will be examined.

9.2   LANGUAGE REGIME OF THE ROME STATUTE

As mentioned above, there are some typical language issues which should always be settled within a multilingual organization. The Rome Statute was no exception.

That's why beside the general rule on the six official languages (*i.e.* Arabic, Chinese, English, French, Russian and Spanish)[1] out of which two (English and French)[2] are the

---

1   Article 50(1) of the Rome Statute: "The official languages of the Court shall be Arabic, Chinese, English, French, Russian and Spanish. The judgements of the Court, as well as other decisions resolving fundamental issues before the Court, shall be published in the official languages. The Presidency shall, in accordance with the criteria established by the Rules of Procedure and Evidence, determine which decisions may be considered as resolving fundamental issues for the purposes of this paragraph."

2   Article 50(2) of the Rome Statute: "The working languages of the Court shall be English and French. The Rules of Procedure and Evidence shall determine the cases in which other official languages may be used as working languages." The Rules of Procedure and Evidence in its Rule 41 stipulates: "Working languages of the Court 1. For the purposes of article 50, paragraph 2, the Presidency shall authorize the use of an official language of the Court as a working language when: (a) That language is understood and spoken by the majority of those involved in a case before the Court and any of the participants in the proceedings so requests; or (b) The Prosecutor and the defence so request. 2. The Presidency may authorize the use of an official language of the Court as a working language if it considers that it would facilitate the efficiency of the proceedings." According to Rule 42 of the Rules of Procedure and Evidence: "The Court shall arrange

working languages of the Court, some special rules were inserted in articles dealing with the Assembly of States Parties.[3] Language criteria are mentioned in articles dealing with candidacy for the position of Judge,[4] Prosecutor and Deputy-Prosecutor,[5] Registrar and Deputy-Registrar.[6] Although the Rome Statute does not explicitly mention this requirement in respect of the staff, fluency in the working languages is definitely required.[7]

Fair trial related language rules show similarities with national criminal procedural law rules, *i.e.* provisions governing the rights of person under investigation[8] and the rights of the accused.[9] These rules complete the provision requiring the judges to determine the language(s) of the procedure.[10]

---

for the translation and interpretation services necessary to ensure the implementation of its obligations under the Statute and the Rules."

3   Article 112(10) of the Rome Statute: "The official and working languages of the Assembly shall be those of the General Assembly of the United Nations." These are (since 1983) the same six languages, *i.e.* contrary to the Court's working languages, Arabic, Chinese, English, French, Russian, and Spanish are legally on equal footing.

4   Article 36(3)(c) of the Rome Statute: "Every candidate for election to the Court shall have an excellent knowledge of and be fluent in at least one of the working languages of the Court."

5   Article 42(3) of the Rome Statute: "The Prosecutor and the Deputy Prosecutors shall be persons of high moral character, be highly competent in and have extensive practical experience in the prosecution or trial of criminal cases. They shall have an excellent knowledge of and be fluent in at least one of the working languages of the Court."

6   Article 43(3) of the Rome Statute: "The Registrar and the Deputy Registrar shall be persons of high moral character, be highly competent and have an excellent knowledge of and be fluent in at least one of the working languages of the Court."

7   Article 44 of the Rome Statute: "(1) The Prosecutor and the Registrar shall appoint such qualified staff as may be required to their respective offices. In the case of the Prosecutor, this shall include the appointment of investigators. (2) In the employment of staff, the Prosecutor and the Registrar shall ensure the highest standards of efficiency, competency and integrity, and shall have regard, *mutatis mutandis*, to the criteria set forth in article 36, paragraph 8." *Nota bene*: Article 36(8) deals however with different aspect of the equitable representation. But I think that there is no doubt that the words on "qualified", "efficiency", "competency" cover adequately the linguistic knowledge, even if the primacy of the English is manifest.

8   Article 55(1) of the Rome Statute: "In respect of an investigation under this Statute, a person: […] *(c)* Shall, if questioned in a language other than a language the person fully understands and speaks, have, free of any cost, the assistance of a competent interpreter and such translations as are necessary to meet the requirements of fairness;"

9   Article 67(1) of the Rome Statute: "In the determination of any charge, the accused shall be entitled to a public hearing, having regard to the provisions of this Statute, to a fair hearing conducted impartially, and to the following minimum guarantees, in full equality: *(a)* To be informed promptly and in detail of the nature, cause and content of the charge, in a language which the accused fully understands and speaks; […] *(f)* To have, free of any cost, the assistance of a competent interpreter and such translations as are necessary to meet the requirements of fairness, if any of the proceedings of or documents presented to the Court are not in a language which the accused fully understands and speaks; […]"

10   Article 64(3) of the Rome Statute: "Upon assignment of a case for trial in accordance with this Statute, the Trial Chamber assigned to deal with the case shall: […] *(b)* Determine the language or languages to be used at trial; and […]"

The third type of language rules is related to the cooperation between the ICC and the states and with special regard to the documents of judicial assistance.[11]

9.3 Language Issues in Practice

9.3.1 *English as Common Law English?*

Two of the official languages, *i.e.* English and French, which are also qualified as working languages, bring up now and then classical problems of interpretation in the same way as in any other fields of international law. As it is well known, the main part of the drafting of the Rome Statute was done in English.

Two of the most widely used commentaries[12] are in English, the third one is in French, with the English commentaries being more detailed. This also contributes to a more accentuated presence of English as compared to what was originally expected in Rome. Moreover, English means legal English *i.e.* the impact of common law terminology, sometimes in UK, sometimes in US terms. It is true that as to the Rome Statute and other norms, the use of "specific common law terminology [...] was, as in other parts of the ICC legal regime, deliberately avoided, in order not to prejudge the procedural approach to be taken."[13] Others claim, nevertheless, that depending on chambers, it is very well present in practice

> "although in cases against Mr. Bemba and Mr. Lubanga Trial Chambers preferred using neutral terms, in *The Prosecutor v. Katanga and Ngudjolo*, the ICC did formally adopt the traditional common law terminology."[14]

---

11 Article 87(2) of the Rome Statute: "Requests for cooperation and any documents supporting the request shall either be in or be accompanied by a translation into an official language of the requested State or one of the working languages of the Court, in accordance with the choice made by that State upon ratification, acceptance, approval or accession." Article 99(3) of the Rome Statute: "Replies from the requested State shall be transmitted in their original language and form." *Nota bene*: the title of the article refers to the so called "other forms of cooperation", *i.e.* other than arrest, provisional arrest, surrender, extradition.

12 Otto Triffterer *et al.* (eds.), *The Rome Statute of the International Criminal Court – A Commentary*, Nomos, 2016; Mark Klamberg (ed.), *Commentary on the Law of the International Criminal Court*, at www.casematrixnetwork.org/cmn-knowledge-hub/icc-commentary-clicc/; Julian Fernandez & Xavier Pacreau (eds.), *Statut de Rome de la Cour pénale internationale*, Pédone, 2012.

13 Ambos Kai, *Treatise on International Criminal Law: Procedure, Cooperation and Implementation*, Oxford University Press, 2016, p. 465.

14 Powers of the Prosecutor Before the Trial Chamber, at https://lawexplores.com/powers-of-the-prosecutor-before-the-trial-chamber/#Fn96.

It is clear that the text of the decisions prepared in English contain plenty of common law terms or formulas stemming from the judicial practice.[15] An example for this phenomenon would be the *'no case to answer' motion, which was accepted after certain hesitation as belonging unde*r the umbrella of the general principles of law mentioned as an element of the "applicable law".[16] While civil law also knows the legal concept of the prosecutor dropping the charges or the indictee's acquittal for lack of adequate and/or sufficient evidence necessary for a conviction beyond reasonable doubt, common law grants a legal possibility to the defence to "provoke" acquittal (or the discontinuation of the case) even during the presentation of the Prosecutor's case (*i.e.* before opening the defence's case) if the submitted evidence seems insufficient for a conviction.

Applied effectively in the case *The Prosecutor v. Ruto,*[17] but rejected in the case *The Prosecutor v. Bosco Ntaganda,* the concept of 'no case to answer' was explained by the Appeals Chamber in as follows:

> "the Court's legal texts do not expressly provide for a 'no case to answer' procedure. Moreover, the Appeals Chamber is not aware of any proposals made or discussions held during the drafting of the Statute or the Rules of Procedure and Evidence ("Rules") in relation to such a procedure. [...] Nevertheless, in the view of the Appeals Chamber, a 'no case to answer' procedure is not inherently incompatible with the legal framework of the Court. [...] A decision on whether or not to conduct a 'no case to answer' procedure is thus discretionary in nature and must be exercised on a case-by-case basis in a manner that ensures that the trial proceedings are fair and expeditious pursuant to article 64(2) and 64(3)(a) of the Statute."[18]

---

15   "Pre-trial brief"; "appeal brief"; "requested remedies"; "admissibility challenge"; "the request for a leave to appeal is granted"; "a good cause is shown"; "failed to raise any new factual grounds"; "it is not an appealable issue"; "it does not warrant an immediate solution"; "the submission failed to demonstrate the impact of alleged errors on [...]"; *etc.*

16   Article 21(1) of the Rome Statute: "The Court shall apply: *(a)* In the first place, this Statute, Elements of Crimes and its Rules of Procedure and Evidence; *(b)* In the second place, where appropriate, applicable treaties and the principles and rules of international law, including the established principles of the international law of armed conflict; *(c)* Failing that, general principles of law derived by the Court from national laws of legal systems of the world including, as appropriate, the national laws of States that would normally exercise jurisdiction over the crime, provided that those principles are not inconsistent with this Statute and with international law and internationally recognized norms and standards. [...]".

17   *The Prosecutor v. William Samoei Ruto and Joshua Arap Sang,* ICC-01/09-01/11, Questions and answers arising from the decision of no-case to answer in the case of *The Prosecutor v. Ruto and Sang,* at www.icc-cpi.int/iccdocs/PIDS/publications/EN-QandA-Ruto.pdf.

18   *The Prosecutor v. Bosco Ntaganda,* OA6 Judgment, ICC-01/04-02/06-2026, paras. 43-44.

This example of the presence of common law within the jurisprudence of the ICC, a topic researched in abundance by scholars[19] was merely cited to demonstrate that what is already a challenge for lawyers, *i.e.* to understand for legal concepts, is an even bigger challenge for interpreters. As Ludmila Stern puts it, "[t]he interpreter and translator must therefore find the means of overcoming the lack of lexical equivalents for legal practices that are articulated differently in other systems."[20] As Leigh Swigart notes,

> "[t]he need to accommodate both English and French speakers also raises some interesting linguistic phenomena. The mixing of elements in international criminal courts and tribunals from different legal systems and trial procedures has necessitated the creation of terms in working languages that did not previously exist."[21]

If harmonizing legal English and legal French seems difficult, the situation is even more complicated when small, local languages are involved, as we will see infra. Prieto Ramos rightly states that

> "at the ICC, the most challenging terminological difficulties arise precisely in the translation of less or non-standardized languages used by testifying witnesses to whom concepts such as 'victim' are unknown."[22]

---

19   *See e.g.* Gilbert Bitti, 'Two Bones of Contention Between Civil Law and Common Law. The Record of the Proceedings and the Treatment of Concursus Delictorum', *in* Horst Fischer *et al.* (eds.), *International and National Prosecution, BWV Berliner-Wissenschaft*, 2001, pp. 273-283; Robert Christensen, 'Getting to Peace by Reconciling Notions of Justice: The Importance of Considering Discrepancies between Civil and Common Legal Systems in the Formation of the International Criminal Court', *UCLA Journal of International Law and Foreign Affairs*, Vol. 6, Issue 2, 2001-2002, pp. 391-424; Colin B. Picker, 'International Law's Mixed Heritage: A Common/Civil Law Jurisdiction', *Vanderbilt Journal of Transnational Law*, Vol. 41, 2008, pp. 1083-1140; Salvador Guerrerdo Palomares, 'Common and Civil Law Traditions on Victims' Participation at the ICC', *International Journal of Procedural Law*, Vol. 4, Issue 2, 2014, pp. 217-235.
20   Ludmila Stern, 'Interpreting Legal Language at the International Criminal Tribunal for the Former Yugoslavia: Overcoming the Lack of Lexical Equivalents', *The Journal of Specialised Translation*, Issue 2, July 2004, p. 63.
21   Leigh Swigart, 'Linguistic and Cultural Diversity in International Criminal Justice: Toward Bridging the Divide', *University of the Pacific Law Review*, Vol. 48, Issue 2, 2016.
22   Fernando Prieto Ramos, 'International and Supranational Law in Translation: from Multilingual Lawmaking to Adjudication', *The Translator*, Vol. 20, Issue 3, 2014, p. 320.

9.3.2   Local Languages in the Ituri District of the Democratic Republic of Congo and the ICC

The latent conflict between Hema,[23] Lendu[24] and Ngiti[25] communities turned into a bloody civil war around 2000. Thomas Lubanga's conviction[26] for enlisting and using child soldiers and Germain Katanga's conviction[27] for his assistance in the massacre of the inhabitants of Bogoro village, as well as the trial against Bosco Ntaganda were rooted in these conflicts.[28]

The transcription of local names, war names and toponyms into English or French meant a minor challenge (*i.e.* whether the very similar but not identical forms cover the same person or two persons, different places) during the trial as well as during the reparation phase, but as always, the real difficulty was that sometimes the oral testimony of a witness during the trial was not as precise as, or even completely different from that registered years before, during the contacts established with them by the investigators or experts working on the reparations.[29] All in all, the concrete elements in a victim's narrative, recalling of names of commanders, localities of military engagement *etc.* played an important role in the assessment of the eligibility for reparation.[30] These elements had to be recorded in documents written by lawyers, national or international collaborators devoted to the task of fighting against impunity and for granting justice and reparation to victims. However, they were not necessarily trained to provide the proper transcription of an orally communicated geographical or personal name while putting into writing what the person providing testimony – without or with only a very rudimentary knowledge of

---

23   On the Hema language, *see* William Frawley, *International Encyclopedia of Linguistics, Volume 1*, Oxford University Press, 2003, p. 302.

24   On the Lendu language: Id. p. 302.

25   On the Ngiti language: Id. p. 304.

26   *See* www.icc-cpi.int/CaseInformationSheets/LubangaEng.pdf.

27   *See* www.icc-cpi.int/CaseInformationSheets/KatangaEng.pdf.

28   *See* www.icc-cpi.int/CaseInformationSheets/NtagandaEng.pdf.

29   *See* on that issue the summary of the defence's remarks (in para. 60 with a number of examples in footnotes) and the Trial Chamber II considerations (in para. 64) in the *Lubanga* reparation order. "60. [...] The Defence also points to contradictions and inconsistencies in the accounts of some potentially eligible victims regarding the circumstances of their enlistment, in particular to contradictions between participation forms and reparations forms or between reparations forms completed on different dates."; "64. [...] In that connection, it is of note that in *Katanga* the Chamber considered – as have other Chambers of this Court in relation to applications for participation – that the mere fact that an application for reparations contains slight discrepancies does not, on the face of it, cast doubt on its credibility.", at www.icc-cpi.int/Pages/record.aspx?docNo=ICC-01/04-01/06-3379-Red.

30   "64. The Chamber pays particular attention to the level of detail of the facts described, including the circumstances of enlistment, the positions held, and duties performed in the UPC/FPLC, the living conditions in the militia and the circumstances in which the victim left the UPC/FPLC. The Chamber also looks at references to relevant information, such as the activities connected to child-soldier status, the sites of recruitment, training, deployment (including battlefields) and demobilization, the names of superiors in the UPC/FPLC militia, and the organizations responsible for demobilization. [...]", at www.icc-cpi.int/Pages/record.aspx?docNo=ICC-01/04-01/06-3379-Red.

French – told them. Of course, interpreters helped facilitate communication in order to guarantee the highest possible precision in the documentation.

The other side of the coin is the assessment of the language skills of the person under trial. As I cited during the presentation of the legal framework, the person under arrest or under trial definitely enjoys linguistic assistance needed. (On the other hand, the choice between full or partial translation into working languages may be linked to the relevance of the item.[31]) The Court's practice may be considered to be in conformity with the standard set by international human rights' jurisprudence.[32] It is worth noting that in the Katanga trial – in the phase of deciding the applicable sentence – the Prosecutor submitted that the simultaneous interpretation into Lingala – granted on the indictee's demand – was not really necessary and this should be taken into consideration when assessing Katanga's cooperation with the Court.[33] However, apparently, the Court did not react to this submission.

9.3.3   Acholi and Other Traditional Languages of Northern Uganda before the ICC

One of the cases currently under trial –in which I am sitting as judge – is *The Prosecutor v. Dominic Ongwen*. The person charged – himself abducted as a child – is alleged to be one of the military leaders of the Lord's Resistance Army fighting in the Northern part of Uganda against government forces. At the time of writing this article, the evidentiary proceedings in this case are still ongoing.

In the regions concerned, a good part of the local population, especially those whose schooling was interrupted by armed conflict, abduction or as a result of their parents' poverty do not speak English (or at least no fluent English). Instead, they speak different

---

31   "9. Conversely, whilst the statutory instruments do not make it mandatory for the Prosecutor to provide translation of disclosed evidence into one of the working languages of the Court, the need for translation into a working language of the Court does indeed arise in respect of any portion of evidentiary item which is relevant to the nature, cause and content of the charges and upon which the Prosecutor intends to rely for the purposes of the confirmation hearing and will therefore include in her list of evidence. Those items will form the basis for the Chamber's determination on the charges brought by the Prosecutor and must therefore be submitted in a working language of the Court." *The Prosecutor v. Jean-Pierre Bemba Gombo, Aimé Kilolo Musamba, Jean-Jacques Mangenda Kabongo, Fidèle Babala Wandu and Narcisse Arido*, Decision on the "Defence request for an order requiring the translation of evidence", ICC-01/05-01/13-177, at www.icc-cpi.int/Pages/record.aspx?docNo=ICC-01/05-01/13-177.

32   *See* in detail in Triffterer (ed.) 2016, in comments made by William A. Schabas and Yvonne McDermott, pp. 1661 and 1672.

33   "The Prosecution denounced the behavior of the convicted person in that he insisted on *Lingala* interpretation throughout proceedings at both the preliminary and the trial stages, whereas, in due course, he chose to testify in French, showing perfect mastery of the French language.", at www.icc-cpi.int/CourtRecords/CR2015_19319.PDF.

local languages, like Acholi,[34] Luo[35] (some consider the first to be a dialect of the second), Lango,[36] Swahili[37] *etc.* Since Mr. Ongwen only fully understands and speaks Acholi, translation services had to be secured for him in this language. Acholi courtroom interpreters also translate the statements of many of the witnesses who have testified in the case.

The Prosecutor attributes great importance to the intercepted radio communications which have allegedly taken place between Joseph Kony, LRA leaders and the different commanders. Without making any comment on the authenticity or contents of these communications, it is noted that they have to be accurately translated into English in order to be understood by the Chamber. The speakers in these recordings may not be using standard language, noting that evidence has been received that LRA communications in Acholi were filled with regularly changing coded expressions and coded names in order to prevent the Ugandan army and police from understanding the communicated messages, orders and reports. Evidence has also been received on the work done by intelligence and radio experts of the Ugandan authorities to break these codes.

Such language services presuppose not only the establishment of a network of professional Ugandan Acholi interpreters and translators,[38] but also require sufficient time and resources required for providing high-quality simultaneous translation in a complex legal case where the Acholi language does not always have clear terms to convey legal notions used at the ICC. Some difficulties can be overcome, for example, by using explanations and paraphrases. The correct transposition of toponyms, tribal names and military aliases is also problematic. The difficulties or possible mistakes which occurred at the time statements were put into writing in English are corrected when the so-called real-time trial transcript is reworked into an 'edited transcript'. Parties may also request corrections to edited transcripts.[39]

Some local words have become widely used orally even in the English translation of the trial, such as *"lapwony"* (*i.e.* meaning literally "teacher" but witnesses explained that it is much rather used as 'comrade', referring to fellow LRA soldiers, adding this designation to their names or nicknames). Other examples include *"ting-ting"* (*i.e.* described as an abducted girl living and working in the household of the commandants), *"dog adaki"* (*i.e.* described as the guarded area surrounding the commanders' living quarters). The word *"kadogo"* (described by witnesses as referring to child soldiers) is used in Uganda and other

---

34 On the Acholi language, *see* Frawley 2003, p. 495.

35 On the Luo language: Id. p. 498.

36 On the Lango language: Id. p. 497-498.

37 On the Swahili language: Id. p. 181.

38 *See* on the methods of recruitment and training: Swigart 2016, p. 9.

39 Initial Directions on the Conduct of the Proceedings, 13 July 2016, ICC-02/04-01/15-497, para. 38, at www.legal-tools.org/doc/60d63f/.

African countries. Once their meaning is clarified and thoroughly understood, it is easier for participants of the trial to use these exact words instead of taking recourse to paraphrases or simplifying the meaning of the expression.

It is clear that even in testimonies rendered in Acholi, words belonging to the English military vocabulary (*e.g.* battalion, brigade, recoilless,[40] LMG[41]) or Russian military terms (*e.g.* PK,[42] AK,[43] RPG[44]) as absorbed in military English are recognizable, especially when reference is made to different weapons.

Even if the word "barracks" is often mentioned in the context of certain charged attacks,[45] the reader of this article should understand it in the local meaning *i.e.* as a quantity of small ground huts, surrounded by trenches and barbed wire with some observation posts, rather than dwellings of considerable size with large fortifications.

9.3.4   Arabic and Traditional Languages of Mali before the ICC

Ahmad Al Faqi Al Mahdi[46] was charged by the Prosecutor and convicted under a guilty plea by Trial Chamber VIII for the crime of destruction of cultural monuments committed in 2012 in Timbuktu. The Prosecutor also submitted different charges against Al Hassan Ag Abdoul Aziz Ag Mohamed Ag Mahmoud.[47] Both of them chose Arabic as the language in which they would like to be informed regarding the charges,[48] but some other languages, namely Tamasheq[49] or Songhay[50] and Bambara[51] also played an important role in the procedure.

---

40   *See* www.encyclopedia.com/social-sciences-and-law/political-science-and-government/military-affairs-nonnaval/recoilless-rifle.

41   *See* www.weaponslaw.org/weapons/light-machine-gun.

42   *See* https://modernfirearms.net/en/machineguns/russia-machineguns/pk-pks-pkm-pkms-eng/.

43   *See* www.warhistoryonline.com/guns/14-facts-ak-47.html.

44   *See* https://modernfirearms.net/en/grenade-launchers/russia-grenade-launchers/rpg-7-eng/.

45   Namely against the villages of Abok, Lukodi, Pajule and Odek.

46   *See* www.icc-cpi.int/CourtRecords/CR2016_07244.PDF. *See* the overview at www.icc-cpi.int/CaseInformationSheets/Al-MahdiEng.pdf.

47   *See* the overview at www.icc-cpi.int/CaseInformationSheets/al-hassanEng.pdf.

48   Decision on the Defence Request for an Arabic Translation of the Prosecution, *Application for the Issuance of a Warrant of Arrest*, ICC-01/12-01/18-42-tENG, at www.icc-cpi.int/CourtRecords/CR2018_04122.PDF, paras. 5, 9 and 13.

49   On the Tamasheq language, *see* Frawley 2003, p. 222.

50   On the Songhay language: Id. p. 110.

51   On the Bambara language: Id. p. 198.

The latter languages are used *inter alia* during consultations[52] with a good number of victims and to help them with their application for participation in the procedure[53] *etc.* Because many of the victims do not speak Arabic, a considerable number of witness statements were deposited in Tamasheq and Songhay. In order to render the apology formulated in Arabic by Mr. Al Faqi accessible to as many people as possible in Mali, versions in Bambara, Songhay and Tamasheq were also prepared and put on the homepage of the ICC.[54] As a result, people speaking Tamasheq, Songhay and Bambara had to be engaged[55] with all its direct consequences for the budget.[56]

As far as Arabic is concerned, it is to be noted that the transcription of the same Arabic first and family names and geographical names into English and French respectively often results in slightly different forms and not only in the form of "sh" in English and "ch" in French. Moreover, despite scholarly articles[57] written on this subject, when the transposition of a name is made *e.g.* by a local lawyer while typing up his client's testimony, it can happen that the transposition is not always *lege artis*.

And as always, the issues of names, surnames, patronyms *etc.* emerge, written sometimes according to Arabic (*e.g.* Mohamed ibn Hussayn) and elsewhere according to Tamasheq (as Mohamed Ag Hussayn) but referring to the same person when this can be established from the details of an individual's narrative.[58]

All this does not mean a major difficulty but certainly requires continuous attention on behalf of the legal staff of the ICC.

If there is such a thing as legal English, there certainly exists Arabic legal language too, which, moreover, is often intertwined with Islam. Because the introduction of *Sharia* in Timbuktu with such punishments like flogging (qualified by the Prosecutor as torture) or alleged forced marriages (understood as sexual slavery) played an important part already

---

52   Public redacted version of "Annex to the Registry's Joint Report on Outreach and Other Victim Related Issues", 27 July 2018, ICC-01/12-01/18-102-Conf-Exp-Anx, at www.icc-cpi.int/Pages/record.aspx? docNo=ICC-01/12-01/18-102-Anx-Red.

53   *See* www.icc-cpi.int/mali/al-hassan, www.icc-cpi.int/itemsDocuments/alHassan/2018-alHassanAppForm Ind_TAQ.pdf, www.icc-cpi.int/itemsDocuments/alHassan/2018-alHassanAppFormORG_TAQ.pdf, www.icc-cpi.int/itemsDocuments/alHassan/2018-alHassan-AppForm-Guidelines_TAQ.pdf, www.icc-cpi.int/itemsDocuments/alHassan/2018-alHassan-AppForm-Guidelines_Organizations_TAQ.pdf.

54   *See* www.icc-cpi.int/mali/al-mahdi.

55   On the recruitment aspects, *see* on the ICC's homepage under "Career Opportunities: Freelance Transcriber – Bambara, Fulfulde, Hassaniyya, Songhay or Tamasheq (18761)", at www.icc-cpi.int/jobs/pages/vacancies.aspx.

56   *See* para. 119. of the Proposed Program Budget for 2018 of the ICC, at https://asp.icc-cpi.int/icc-docs/asp_docs/ASP16/ICC-ASP-16-10-ENG.pdf.

57   Houda Saadane & Nasredine Semmar, 'Transcription des noms arabes en écriture latine', *Revue RIST*, Vol. 20, Issue 2, 2013, pp. 57-68.

58   These names are featured in the present article only as fictitious examples.

in the request for an arrest warrant[59] granted by the Pre-Trial Chamber,[60] one may assume that the Arabic concepts of criminal law, criminal procedural law and family law will play a certain role in the procedure. Moreover, these legal terms are often filled with notions and formulas of the *Quran*.

All these challenges can be managed and dealt with, but they require time, skills, continuous attention and knowledge, and all in all, do not make the job of legal officers working for the Prosecution or the Judiciary easier.

It is to be noted that the Defence asked also in the *Al Mahdi* and in the *Al Hassan* cases – based on Article 50(2) and (3) (pre-cited) of the Rome Statute – to use Arabic as well as a language in which oral submissions can be made by the legal counsel of the person charged. The request was granted in the first case,[61] but the Presidency dismissed it in the second, as improperly submitted, *i.e.* directly before the Presidency and not before the relevant chamber.[62]

---

59 Version publique expurgée de la "Requête urgente du Bureau du Procureur aux fins de délivrance d'un mandat d'arrêt et de demande d'arrestation provisoire à l'encontre de M. Al Hassan Ag Abdoul Aziz Ag Mohamed Ag Mahmoud", 20 mars 2018, ICC-01/12-01/18-1-Red, at www.icc-cpi.int/Pages/record.aspx?docNo=ICC-01/12-01/18-1-Red. (There is no English translation for this document.)

60 "60. The material submitted by the Prosecutor further shows that there was a defined policy to attack the civilian population. The policy was defined in that the armed groups wished to impose their authority and their new religious order. The policy followed a regular pattern in that it involved strict rules, prohibitions and punishments and was calculated to oppress anyone who failed to demonstrate the required religiosity, in particular women and girls. […]" (footnotes omitted). "70. The Prosecutor submits that there are reasonable grounds to believe that the members of the armed groups Ansar Dine and AQIM committed crimes against humanity of acts of torture. The Prosecutor refers to several methods of interrogation, physical violence and other brutal sanctions allegedly constituting cases of torture. The Prosecutor alleges that, in some cases, violations of the new rules by the population were referred to the Islamic court, which then ordered physical punishments, such as whipping in public." (footnotes omitted). "81. The Prosecutor submits that there are reasonable grounds to believe that women and girls in Timbuktu were forced to marry members of Ansar Dine and AQIM. The Prosecutor alleges that, although the families of the victims generally received a dowry in exchange, they were not free to object to the members' wishes and were either forced to submit or did so out of fear of retaliation. The Prosecutor alleges that the purpose of these marriages was to legitimize the rapes and sexual violence perpetrated against the victims by the members of the armed groups, and to integrate the members of the armed groups into the population. As noted above, the Prosecutor alleges that about forty cases of rape, sexual slavery and other sexual violence took place in the context of forced marriage." (footnotes omitted). Decision on the Prosecutor's Application for the Issuance of a Warrant of Arrest for Al Hassan Ag Abdoul Aziz Ag Mohamed Ag Mahmoud ICC-01/12-01/18-35-Red2-tENG, at www.icc-cpi.int/Pages/record.aspx?docNo=ICC-01/12-01/18-35-Red2-tENG.

61 *See* the reference in Defence request to authorize the use of Arabic as a working language, ICC-01/12-01/18-268 08-03-2019, at www.icc-cpi.int/CourtRecords/CR2019_01335.PDF, para. 7.

62 Decision on the admissibility of the "Defence request to authorize the use of Arabic as a working language", ICC-01/12-01/18-302 04-04-2019, at www.icc-cpi.int/CourtRecords/CR2019_01895.PDF, especially paras. 17-19.

9.4   By Way of Conclusion

The ICC has on its table other situations under investigation involving several other languages (*e.g.* Georgian, Russian and possibly[63] also Ossetian[64] in the so called Georgian situation[65]) and there are situations under preliminary-examination such as the Rohingyas case[66] involving a language[67] which is spoken exclusively by most of the victims *etc.* All these have their special difficulties, challenges, as well as legal and, last but not least, budgetary implications.

My ambition in the present contribution was not to give a comprehensive legal analysis but only to highlight some points which deserve a proper attention and may invite further research, similarly to research published on the language issues before the ICTY, ICTR or the STSL.[68]

It is worth studying the linguistic challenges that the ICC faces and these cannot be restricted only to the relationship of English and French in the Rome Statute and in the jurisprudence of the Court.

---

63   Due to South Ossetia's past since 1801 in Czarist Russia and then in the Soviet Union (at that time a so-called autonomous territory within the Georgian Soviet Socialist Republic), Russian can be considered a *lingua franca* for the inhabitants of this territory.

64   On the Ossetian language, *see* the *Worldmark Encyclopedia of Cultures and Daily Life*, Cengage Learning, 2009, at www.encyclopedia.com/humanities/encyclopedias-almanacs-transcripts-and-maps/ossetians.

65   *See* www.icc-cpi.int/georgia. On the recruitment aspects, *see* on the ICC's homepage under "Career Opportunities: Freelance Transcriber – Georgian, Ossetian or Russian (18759)", at www.icc-cpi.int/jobs/pages/vacancies.aspx.

66   *See* www.icc-cpi.int/rohingya-myanmar.

67   On the Rohingya language, *see* the Worldmark Encyclopedia 2009, www.encyclopedia.com/humanities/encyclopedias-almanacs-transcripts-and-maps/rohingyas.

68   Stern 2004, pp. 63-75; Swigart 2016, pp. 1-16, covering not only the International Criminal Tribunal for Yugoslavia (ICTY), but also the lessons learned from the practice of the International Criminal Tribunal for Rwanda (ICTR), the Special Tribunal for Sierra Leone (STSL) and the Extraordinary Chambers in the Courts of Cambodia (ECCC).

10   THE INTERNATIONAL TRADING SYSTEM AND MARKET DISTORTIONS

Revisiting the Need for Competition Rules within the WTO

*Franziska Sucker**

Keywords
cross-border business activities, developing countries, multilateral competition rules, trade and competition, WTO

Abstract
As a result of the interconnectedness of the global economy, cross-border activities of economic operators are soaring. Their business practices are not governed by multilateral rules, but merely, if at all, by regional or national laws. As a result, they are potentially subject to over- or under-enforcement and -regulation or to conflicting rules. The resultant legal uncertainties and, therefore, potential lack of discipline for practices facilitates the development of dominant positions and anticompetitive behavior. This advances market distortions to the detriment of diverse offerings and the competitiveness of small market players, especially in economically weak developed countries. Such unfavorable developments could be reduced by preventing market concentration and disciplining anticompetitive behavior. I argue that multilateral rules alone would ensure that cross-border activities of economic operators are subject to uniform rules, irrespective of which country's or region's market is affected; and thus, provide legal certainty for current gaps. Moreover, in spite of the resistance of numerous countries to include competition disciplines within the World Trade Organization (WTO), rules aimed at dismantling barriers to trade created by private economic operators are not only theoretically desirable but indispensable in the long term to avoid an erosion of the WTO system by effectively replacing state-created barriers. The increasing role of supply chains and the rising volatility of international commodity prices should give all, albeit particularly the economically weak developed countries, reason to pause and revisit an issue that has significant implications for the competitiveness of their economic operators.

---

*   Franziska Sucker: associate professor, University of the Witwatersrand, Johannesburg.

10.1 Introduction

As a result of globalization and technological revolution markets transcend countries. Increasingly interconnected, borderless and digitalized (global) markets tend to develop mass markets, increase the integration of enterprises and so produce goods and provide services readily accessible for consumers. While this does improve knowledge transfer and raises economic expectations, the ever diminishing distinction between goods or services in these markets poses a threat to the diversity of offers and, consequently, to small market players. Thus, the rise of cross-border activities of public and private economic operators such as coordination of behavior, international mergers and filling dominant positions gives reason to pause and revisit the relationship between competition and trade. More precisely, it raises the question of whether and to what extent the behavior of cross-border active operators is currently disciplined, including the effect thereof. For this purpose, I first demonstrate the effect of unrestricted competition for markets and market participants in general. Thereafter, I determine the rules applicable to cross-border activities of economic operators and assess the implications of the current legal situation for the competitiveness of small market players, in particular in economically weak developed countries. I then provide some thoughts on how to remedy the current legal situation.

10.2 Unrestricted Competition and Market Distortions

Both the economic relations between World Trade Organization (WTO) members and most of their national economies are based, in principle, on a capitalist system; a system characterized by private or corporate ownership of most of the means of production and service supply and their operation for profit, by investments determined by private decisions, and by prices, production, service supply and the distribution of goods and services primarily determined by competition in these markets.[1] Competition strives for a so-called market balance, that is, a balance between demand and supply for the optimal satisfaction of demand amongst consumers while ensuring the profit of suppliers. Such a win-win situation for consumers and suppliers, in other words for society, where a fair price is

---

1   In detail on the notion of capitalism, *see e.g.* Marina V. Rosser & Barkley J. Jr. Rosser, *Comparative Economics in a Transforming World Economy*, MIT Press, 2018, p. 7; Chris Jenks, *Core Sociological Dichotomies*, SAGE, London, 1998, p. 383; Andrew Zimbalist *et al.*, *Comparing Economic Systems: A Political-Economic Approach, Harcourt College Pub*, 1988, pp. 6-7. Various scholars convincingly argue that the use of the term market economy is a misapprehension (and ignorance) of reality, whereas capitalism would best describe the processes involved, namely using capital with the aim of making profit, whereby capital is efficient processes of production and constant advancement of technology (*e.g.* Joseph Schumpeter, *Capitalism, Socialism and Democracy*, Harper Perennial Modern Thought, 2008, p. 84. (first edition 1942); Wolfgang Streeck, *How will capitalism end?*, Juggernaut Books, New Delhi, 2017.

assumed to develop, emerges in case of a perfectly competitive market.[2] This theoretical (simplified)[3] model of a homogenous market is characterized by complete market transparency for fully informed commercial transactions and by unrestricted market access for all economic operators. It works on the assumption that there are no transaction costs and resources are available indefinitely.[4]

In reality though, these conditions are generally lacking, varying from market segment to market segment. Coupled with the supplier's pursuit of maximizing profits, which can only occur at the expense of competitors, at least in saturated markets, this results in a tendency for the development of dominant positions (*e.g.* monopolies, oligopolies).[5] Even though most competitors attempt to constantly increase their efficiency and production to offer the best possible range of goods and services at the best possible price,[6] usually only a few will outlast the competition. If no real competitors remain, it goes as far as eliminating competition. This is the paradox of unrestricted competition.

In addition to this tendency, without legal safeguards economic operators can abscond from competition through anticompetitive behavior, *i.e.* collusive practices between, or exclusionary practices by a single or few economic participant(s) (*e.g.* forming cartels, abusing dominant positions, boycotting, concluding exclusive and anticompetitive agreements such as anticompetitive mergers) to promote their interests. First, such practices can restrict imports and exports. This would erode the economic gains from reducing tariff and non-tariff barriers[7] and distort competition. Secondly, anticompetitive practices can prevent the efficient allocation of resources in a market, namely to provide the best range of choice and supply and the lowest price to consumers. Put differently, such practices jeopardize free pricing at the expense of consumers, more precisely at the expense of consumer welfare and the common good. This too, distorts competition. Consumers include economic operators that use products as inputs to, or services as enablers for, their own productive activities. Hence, anticompetitive behavior undermines the competitiveness

---

2   *See e.g.* John VC Nye, 'Standards of Living and Modern Economic Growth', *in The Concise Encyclopedia of Economics*, 2008, at www.econlib.org/library/Enc/StandardsofLivingandModernEconomicGrowth.html.
3   It facilitates the understanding and investigation of complex relationships (*e.g.* price formation).
4   A comprehensive definition in Phillip E. Areeda & Louis Kaplow, *Antitrust Analysis. Problems, Text, and Cases*, Aspen Publishers Inc, New York, 1997, p. 6, para. 107. *See also* Lawrence A. Sullivan & Warren S. Grimes, *The Law of Antitrust: An Integrated Handbook*, West Group, St Paul, 2000, p. 30. (competition is "ideal", if markets "comprise a large number of producers, none with a substantial market share, and each producing a fungible or undifferentiated product"); and W. Kip Viscusi *et al.*, *Economics of Regulation and Antitrust*, MIT Press, 2000, p. 2.
5   This observation goes as far back as 1776 (Adam Smith in *The Wealth of Nations*) and 1867 (Karl Marx in *Das Kapital*).
6   If they do not, consumers have the choice to buy elsewhere.
7   *E.g.* Pascal Lamy, *The Geneva Consensus. Making Trade Work for All*, Cambridge University Press, Cambridge, 2013, p. 132.

of these (often smaller) economic participants that are often found in economically weaker developed countries, in both export- and import-competing markets.

Both eliminated and distorted competition frustrates a market balance, the very aim of competition, essential to a dynamic and healthy market in a capitalist system: the system the economic (trade) relations between WTO members (and most of their national economies) are based on. In essence, this is the link between trade and competition.[8]

10.3   CROSS-BORDER ACTIVITIES AND MARKET DISTORTIONS

As a result of and the interconnectedness of the global economy, cross-border activities of economic operators are soaring: concentrations of businesses are no longer limited to specific territories,[9] anticompetitive agreements are concluded in increasingly globally active (international) cartels (*e.g.* vitamin cartel), and public and private economic operators are increasingly filling their dominant position in certain markets globally (*e.g.* Microsoft).[10] Such entrepreneurial activities can affect the competition, *i.e.* market balance in several states and could therefore be governed by the multilateral rules of the WTO, the primary forum for dealing with cross-border trade. Alternatively, these market behaviors may also be considered from the perspective of regional or national competition laws.

10.3.1   WTO Disciplines and Market Distortions

WTO agreements address state created barriers to international trade. More specifically, international trade law is not based on the idea of unconditional free trade but characterized by the recognition that state interventions in the national economic order may be necessary and are therefore generally permitted. Numerous WTO rules limit this power of creating barriers to international trade to prevent their potential abuse. Examples are the non-dis-

---

8   The direct connection between world trade and competition is also emphasized in the WTO Working Group on the Interaction between Trade and Competition Policy. Study on Issues Relating to a Possible Multilateral Framework on Competition Policy. WT/WGTCP/W/228, WTO, Geneva, 2003, pp. 9. *et seq.* On the link, *see* also Eleanor M. Fox, 'The WTO's First Antitrust Case – *Mexican* Telecom: A Sleeping Victory for Trade and Competition', *Journal of International Economic Law*, Vol. 9, Issue 2, 2006, pp. 271-292.

9   *E.g.* News Corporation (CEO and founder *Keith Rupert Murdoch*) has shares in book and newspaper publishers (*e.g.* in Australia, the UK and the US), in music production companies (*e.g.* MySpace Records), in rugby leagues (*e.g.* 50% of the Australian and New Zealand rugby league) and in film and television studios and internet companies (*e.g.* Fox News, The Wall Street Journal and Twentieth Century Fox).

10   The *Microsoft* case, for example, has been handled in parallel in the US, the EU and Japan. *See* in detail Jörg P. Terhechte, 'Das internationale Kartell- und Fusionskontrollverfahrensrecht zwischen Kooperation und Konvergenz', *Zeitschrift für ausländisches öffentliches Recht und Völkerrecht*, Vol. 68, Issue 3, 2018, pp. 689. *et seq.*, 700. *et seq.*

crimination obligations. They essentially aim at ensuring a level playing field, namely fair conditions of trade. This includes largely undistorted competition between products, services and IP-right holders from different member states and between foreign and domestic products, services and IP-right holders.[11] The latter presupposes market access. Market access is facilitated by the progressive dismantling of state-created barriers to trade through further reducing binding tariffs and trying to eliminate non-tariff barriers (NTBs) [*e.g.* quantitative restrictions,[12] technical barriers to trade (TBT)[13] and sanitary and phytosanitary (SPS) measures[14]].

Notably, numerous commercial practices of cross-border active economic operators also constitute barriers to international trade that distort competition amongst foreign, and between domestic and foreign products, services and IP-right holders (*e.g.* exploitation of dominant positions, coordination of behavior). Withal, the steady dismantling of state-created barriers to trade even increases their leeway, escalating the risk of their anticompetitive behavior with the described anti-competitive effects. Hence, state-created barriers to international trade have been, and may continue to effectively be, replaced with those created by cross-border active economic operators. This erodes the economic gains from tariff reductions and the removal of NTBs.[15] While this possibility has already been emphasized by the panel in the GATT Decision on Restrictive Business Practices back in 1960,[16] the WTO agreements hardly include any provision that aims at counteracting distortions of international trade and competition caused by cross-border active economic operators.[17] And this despite the fact that WTO members are guided by the desire "to

---

11   So too are the rules on trade remedies, *e.g.* on dumping (exporting below cost to gain market share) and export subsidies.

12   Article XI.1 of the WTO General Agreement on Tariffs and Trade (GATT).

13   *E.g.* Articles 2, 3 and 4 of the WTO Agreement on Technical Barriers to Trade (TBT).

14   *E.g.* Articles 2, 3 and 4 of the WTO Agreement on the Application of Sanitary and Phytosanitary Measures (SPS).

15   *See* also Jürgen Basedow, 'International Antitrust or Competition Law', *in* Rüdiger Wolfrum (ed.), *Encyclopedia of Public International Law*, Max Planck Institute for Comparative Public Law and International Law, September 2009, para 20.

16   GATT, Decision on Restrictive Business Practices: Arrangement for Consultation, *BISD* 9S/28, 1960, Recital (1).

17   *E.g.* Articles 8.2 and 40 of the WTO Agreement on Trade-Related Aspects of Intellectual Property Rights (TRIPS) (states may adopt measures to prevent abuses and adverse effects on trade), Article 10bis of the Paris Convention read with Article 2.1 of the TRIPS (states to *assure* nationals of all WTO members "effective protection against unfair competition"), Article VIII.2 of the WTO General Agreement on Trade in Services (GATS) (states shall adopt measures to ensure that monopolies adhere to non-discrimination principles) and Article IX GATS (shall enter into consultation) contain specific provisions on anti-competitive behavior. The trade remedies in the WTO Agreements on Subsidies and Countervailing Measures, on Anti- Dumping and on Safeguards merely allow for countervailing measures and do not directly counteract corporate pricing policy. *Japan – Measures Affecting Consumer Photographic Film and Paper*, WT/DS44, 31 March 1998, para. 10.49, private commercial restrictions were subject of the proceedings for the first time. The Panel noted that WTO rules only apply, if there is a satisfactory degree of state involvement. Mere tolerance of privately created trade barriers is by no means sufficient.

reduce distortions and impediments to international trade";[18] despite the very essence of the basic principles of the WTO[19] aspiring to create equal competitive conditions for products, services and IP-right holders;[20] despite undistorted competition (a market balance) being essential in a capitalist system, the system the economic relations between WTO members (and most of their national economies) are based on; and despite undistorted competition requiring legal safeguards.

10.3.2   National (and Regional) Disciplines and Market Distortions

Due to the absence of framework conditions for competition at international level, cross-border activities of economic operators are governed by national or regional competition rules. Their applicability can arise both from the territorial principle and, extraterritorially, from the impact principle.[21] Jurisdiction therefore, is not only given when entrepreneurial practices occur and are initiated in the rules' country of origin, but also when such practices are initiated in another country and merely affect competition in the rules' country of origin. Therefore, as an example, price bundling of globally active economic operators and mergers of two companies based in different countries can be investigated and assessed simultaneously by different competition authorities applying different competition rules based on varying legal and economic standards. The disparity of the more than 130 competition laws worldwide may lead to undesirable market distortions due to potential over- or under-enforcement and -regulation, and conflicts at either the substantive or procedural level.

Firstly, it is not regulated how an economic operator should conduct itself if its behavior is regulated or judged differently by the relevant competition laws. Without guarantee for a uniform application of law, there is no legal certainty;[22] a situation that facilitates market concentration and anticompetitive behavior.

Secondly, it is important to note that as long as the national or regional competition rules and their application are consistent with WTO obligations (that is, in principle, to not restrict market access and to apply all rules equally to foreign and domestic goods, services, operators and IP-right holders, subject to their commitments), a WTO member

---

18   Recital 1 of the Preamble to TRIPS.
19   *E.g.* the non-discrimination obligation.
20   *See e.g. Understanding the WTO*, WTO, Geneva, 2008, p. 12. ("The WTO […] is a system of rules dedicated to open, fair and undistorted competition.").
21   On externalities of one jurisdiction's regulatory acts on another's and the effect that behavior occurring in one jurisdiction can have elsewhere *see e.g.* Michael S. Gal, 'Regional Competition Law Agreements: An Important Step in International Antitrust', *University of Toronto Law Journal*, Vol. 60, Issue 2, 2010, p. 240.
22   See Terhechte's analysis using the example of international agency cooperation (Terhechte 2018, pp. 755. *et seq.*).

cannot successfully challenge the competition laws of another member as being restrictive to trade. This provides states with a very distinct and well-developed national, supranational or regional competition law (*e.g.* US and EU-members) with a wide scope to design rules that, for example, protect domestic industries in their territory. For WTO members with a rudimentary national or regional competition law (or without any), this possibility does not exist. Many economically weak developed countries cannot raise the necessary funds to introduce, implement and enforce effective national or regional competition rules. The disproportionately high implementation and enforcement costs in relation to the minimum standards to be guaranteed at national level under TRIPS reduce affordability even more,[23] leading to the aforementioned under-enforcement or -regulation. Therefore, in these markets the behavior of dominant economic operators is not disciplined, which enables them to consolidate their (dominant) position. As a result, other providers (and competitors) may be (further) displaced and their market entry impeded. This affects their competitiveness, generally restricts competition and may adversely affect the diversity of offers in the long term.

In order to avoid distortions, over- or under-enforcement and -regulation and conflicts of extraterritorial application, numerous states have concluded bilateral and regional agreements.[24] They improve and enhance cooperation between the various competition authorities and promote understanding of differences in the design of national and supranational competition rules and policies. At the same time, these agreements presuppose that the relevant rules protect the same interests and include comparable standards and levels of protection. While this applies to most developed countries, often the emerging and developing countries' standards still differ considerably. Hence, the latter concluded only a few bilateral or regional agreements both with developing countries and amongst themselves. This may be, however, slowly changing. African states, for example, are currently negotiating competition chapters within the African Continental Free Trade Area (AfCFTA) that entered into force on 30 May 2019[25] and within the Tripartite Free Trade

---

23   In detail Franziska Sucker, 'Why an Absent International Regulatory Framework for Competition and Strong Copyright Protection Harms Diversity of Expressions and What to Do About it', *in* Klaus Matthis & Avishalom Tor (eds.), *New Developments in Competition Law and Economics*, Vol. 7, Springer, 2019, p. 186. On the high administrative costs and the political pressure for economically weak developed countries to implement TRIPS, *see e.g.* Laurence R. Helfer, 'Regime Shifting: The TRIPs Agreement and New Dynamics of International Intellectual Property Lawmaking', *Yale Journal of International Law*, Vol. 29, Issue 1, 2004, p. 70.

24   On the rise of competition chapters in regional agreements, *see* Valerie Demedts 'Which Future for Competition in the Global Trade System: Competition Chapters in FTAs', *Journal of World Trade*, Vol. 49, Issue 3, 2015, pp. 407-436.

25   Agreement Establishing the African Continental Free Trade Area (adopted 21 March 2018, entered into force 30 May 2019) (AfCFTA).

Area (TFTA),[26] one of the three building blocks for the AfCFTA. An African regional competition law could close, or at least narrow, the gap that exists in 24 African countries without national competition laws and discipline the behavior of economic operators that affect the competition of markets within Africa (cross-African activities), thereby contributing to the reduction of market distortions among African countries.[27]

10.3.3   Concluding Observation

At multilateral level cross-border activities of economic operators are not disciplined. At national and regional level only those cross-border activities are disciplined (with legal certainty) that affect the competition of two or more markets within the territory of the relevant agreement. An entrepreneurial activity that affects the competition of two or more markets outside the relevant territory may be subject to two competition laws that conflict or differ, either in their application or due to their difference in over- or under-enforcement and regulation. The legal uncertainty in these cases, and thus the potential non-disciplining of the relevant entrepreneurial behavior, contributes to the development of market concentration and facilitates anticompetitive behavior. This strengthens oligopolies in their market positions, and insufficiently accounts for, and further displaces, small market players and market participants of economically weak developed countries.[28]

Companies think economically, act profit-oriented and try to take advantage of the current world trade system by essentially campaigning for a policy of maximum free trade without disciplining the behavior of economic operators to enable an unconstrained cross-border offering of goods and services while maximizing profits.[29] This should not be criti-

---

26 Agreement Establishing a Tripartite Free Trade Area Among the Common Market for Eastern and Southern Africa the East African Community and the Southern African Development Community (adopted 10 June 2015, not in force) (TFTA).

27 On the advantages and disadvantages of national and regional competition laws for developing countries Josef Drexl, 'Economic Integration and Competition Law in Developing Countries', in Josef Drexl et al. (eds.), *Competition Policy and Regional Integration in Developing Countries*, Edward Elgar, 2012, pp. 231. *et seq*; and Gary C. Hufbauer & Jisun Kim, 'International Competition Policy and the WTO', presented at a conference *One Year Later: The Antitrust Modernization Commission's Report and the Challenges that Await Antitrust*, New York, 11 April 2008, at www.piie.com/commentary/speeches-papers/international-competition-policy-and-wto.

28 *See* also Thomas Gibbons, 'The Impact of Regulatory Competition on Measures to Promote Pluralism and Cultural Diversity in the Audiovisual Sector', *Cambridge Yearbook of European Legal Studies*, Vol. 9, 2006/2007, pp. 239-259.

29 This is often coupled with the highest possible degree of IP-protection. In relation to the media industry, *see e.g.* Christopher M. Bruner, 'Culture, Sovereignty, and Hollywood: UNESCO and the Future of Trade in Cultural Products', *NYU Journal of International Law and Politics*, Vol. 40, Issue 2, 2008, pp. 351-436, citing at p. 414. footnote 270 *Bonnie JK Richardson* (who has been Vice President for Trade and Federal Affairs with the Motion Picture Association of America and chief US negotiator for the services market access negotiations during the Uruguay Round): "In terms of maximizing the value of their products and

cized. It is, however, necessary to question the legal situation, which permits unfavorable developments, for example economic profits at the expense of diversity of offers and of smaller market participants, especially those of developing countries.

10.4   WHAT TO DO ABOUT IT?

As illustrated above, markets that ensure economic efficiency and distributional equity do not work purely unaided by anything other than by market mechanisms themselves. Thus, some level of intervention is required.[30]

10.4.1   Reduction of Trade Barriers Created by Cross-Border Active Economic Operators

The described market distortions can be decreased by reducing barriers to international trade created by public and private cross-border active economic operators. This can be accomplished by doing on the international market what is done as a matter of course by most governments on their domestic market to achieve market balance: preventing practices such as international market concentration and disciplining potential anticompetitive behavior. This would reduce the possibility to abuse their position and thus contribute to achieving largely undistorted competition. Largely undistorted competition, an essential characteristic in the current economic (capitalist) system, would serve as a corrective to the principles of free trade and the continuously progressing liberalization. It would help break the oligopolistic structure of many industries (which often derives from exclusive rights). Decentralized structures would create incentives to offer a larger variety of products at prices consumers are ready to pay, countering thereby the potential displacement of other economic operators. Hence, competition law mechanisms can serve as an instrument

---

expanding the market for them, protectionist intellectual property law and liberalist international trade law are of a piece."

30   The need for multilateral competition rules is widely recognized (even amongst opponents of the inclusion in the WTO) see e.g. Joanna Shelton, 'Competition Policy: What Chance for International Rules?', *Wilton Park Conference: Global Trade Area*, 1998, at www.oecd.org/dataoecd/34/39/1919969.pdf; Friedl Weiss, 'From World Trade Law to World Competition Law', *Fordham International Law Journal*, Vol. 23, Issue 6, 1999, pp. 250-273; Andrew T. Guzman, 'International Antitrust and the WTO: The Lesson from Intellectual Property', *Virginia Journal of International Law*, Vol. 43, Issue 4, 2002, pp. 933-957. On pro and cons of world antitrust laws see e.g. Code Jürgen Basedow, *Weltkartellrecht. Ausgangslage und Ziele, Methoden und Grenzen der internationalen Vereinheitlichung des Rechts der Wettbewerbsbeschränkungen*, Mohr Siebeck, Tübingen, 1998; Karl Matthias Meessen, 'Das Für und Wider eines Weltkartellrechts', *Wirtschaft und Wettbewerb*, 2000/1, pp. 5-16; and David J. Gerber, 'Competition Law and the WTO: Rethinking the Relationship', *Journal of International Economic Law*, Vol. 10, Issue 3, 2007, pp. 707-727.

to create a more conducive environment for small market players and market participants of economically weak developed countries.

Only multilateral disciplines can ensure that cross-border activities of economic operators are subject to uniform rules, irrespective of which country's or region's market is affected and thus provide legal certainty for current gaps arising from conflicts between two competition laws or from over- or under-enforcement and -regulation. Therefore, I revisit the WTO's role in this regard.

10.4.2   Revisiting the WTO's Role

While the inclusion of competition issues as a corrective to free trade principles has been discussed among WTO members for quite some time,[31] the negotiation mandate restricts such endeavors, rendering their realization a distant prospect. It is, however, worth reflecting on the reasons for resistance and to highlight the benefits of multilateral competition rules.

10.4.2.1   Negotiation Mandate

Since the first Ministerial Conference in Singapore in 1996, competition has been on the WTO agenda, with the ministers agreeing to establish a special Working Group on Competition Policy to examine the relationship between trade and competition policy.[32] At the Ministerial Conference in Doha in 2001, the ministers "[r]ecognized the case for a multilateral framework to enhance the contribution of competition policy to international trade and development" and decided to start negotiations on multilateral competition rules in 2003, provided all members agree on its modalities.[33] This, however, never went beyond the stage of a proposal by the then European Communities, with both the US and developing countries rejecting multilateral competition rules in general.

The US "argued that world antitrust would mean lowering standards to the lowest common denominator".[34] In particular, it feared that states would try to create laws that protect domestic companies from more efficient competitors "rather than cultivate efficiency",[35] and therefore that multilateral rules would "no longer effectively protect compe-

---

31   Already Article 46 of the Havana Charter contains a catalogue of restrictive practices.
32   Working Group on the Interaction between Trade and Competition Policy (*see* Singapore Ministerial Declaration WT/MIN(96)/DEC, December 1996).
33   Doha Ministerial Declaration WT/MIN(01)/DEC/1, November 2001, paras. 23-25.
34   Eleanor M. Fox & Mor Bakhoum, *Making Markets Work for Africa. Markets, Development, and Competition law in Sub-Saharan Africa*, Oxford University Press, Oxford, 2018, p. 13.
35   Id.

tition".[36] Moreover, the WTO, so they argued, is an inappropriate forum for competition rules since it is run by trade officials who bargain and make concessions, whereas competition laws are based on pro-market rules.[37] Developing countries pointed to their limited experience with competition rules and feared that multilateral rules based on US or EU concepts would not be compatible with their current preferred investment screening techniques and industrial policies.[38]

> "They feared they were being short-changed by principles of efficiency (of multinationals) without equity; that they would lose their policy space; that they would be increasingly marginalized; that they would suffer a new economic colonialism."[39]

Developing countries too, stressed that the introduction of a comprehensive and meaningful competition agreement costs a lot of time and money.[40] Furthermore, for those countries without national competitions laws it was believed, the enforcement of multilateral standards cannot be effectively guaranteed and cause too high a cost. In addition, with the Doha Round underway they feared taking on more obligations, notwithstanding that their negotiating capacity was already largely or full deployed and could not be stretched to incorporate more issues.[41]

The Cancun Ministerial Conference of 2003 failed primarily due to the then EC and US not offering "sufficiently sizable cutbacks in their agricultural subsidies"[42] to developing countries; subsidies that are particularly harmful for their economic operators. With the intention to revive the negotiations, in July 2004 the WTO General Council decided to remove several items from the agenda, including competition, which

> "will not form part of the Work Program set out in that Declaration and therefore no work towards negotiations on any of these issues will take place within the WTO during the Doha Development Round."[43]

---

36   International Competition Policy Advisory Committee (ed.), *Final Report*, 2002, pp. 264. *et seq.*, at www.justice.gov/atr/icpac/finalreport.html.
37   Fox & Bakhoum 2018, p. 13.
38   Hufbauer & Kim 2008.
39   Fox & Bakhoum 2018, p. 13.
40   International Competition Policy Advisory Committee 2002, 267.
41   On the interests and perspective of developing countries in general, *see e.g.* Bernard Hoekman & Peter Holmes, 'Competition Policy, Developing Countries and the WTO', *Policy Research Working Paper World Bank 2211* (April 1999).
42   Fox & Bakhoum 2018, p. 15.
43   WTO General Council, Decision on the Doha Agenda Work Programme (July Package) WT/L/579, 1 August 2004, para. 1. lit. g.

Accordingly, competition is no longer covered by the WTO members' negotiating mandate. As a result, a serious discussion about a competition agreement within the WTO system can only be resume after the conclusion of the Doha Development Round.[44] To date, however, WTO members have not been able to resolve their fundamental conflict in relation to the so-called Singapore issues, most notably agricultural subsidies; a crucial issue for developing countries.[45]

10.4.2.2   Reflections on the Reasons for Resistance

(i) Developed countries. To begin with, at international level competition has never been 'effectively protected'. As illustrated, undistorted competition needs legal safeguards since the open world market facilitates world cartels and monopolistic practices across borders.[46] Hence, what the US might actually fear when stating that a multilateral competition agreement would "no longer effectively protect competition"[47] is not "that protectionist trade will compromise antitrust, but that free-market antitrust will endanger protectionist trade."[48]

Another consideration is that WTO members that were, in the past, quite satisfied with not having multilateral rules disciplining their cross-border active public and private economic operators – mostly economically strong developed members with sufficient funds for subsidies and a high proportion of both net exporters and dominant cross-border active operators – realize that their domestic economic operators are exposed to increasing anticompetitive behavior from operators of so-called emerging markets (*e.g.* China, Brazil, India).[49] This potential limitation of trading opportunities and competitiveness for their economic operators may be the reason why the US has recently shown more willingness to cooperate with the EU, an advocate of a multilateral competition agreement. In relation to key aspects, however, they favor different approaches and standards; each their own. More specifically, the US's main concern refers to cartels (efficiency for the consumer); that of the EU relates to abuse of dominance (equity for smaller market players).[50]

---

44   *See also* Josef Drexl, 'WTO und Kartellrecht. Zum Warum *und* Wie dieser Verbindung in Zeiten der Globalisierung', *Zeitschrift für Wettbewerbsrecht*, 2004, pp. 191. *et seq*. Somewhat optimistic Basedow 2009, para. 32: "The globalization of markets, which is evidenced and favored by world trade law, allows predicting further attempts at a substantive harmonization of principles of competition law in the foreseeable future."

45   *E.g.* Pierre Defraigne, 'The Doha Round Between a Narrow Escape and Freezing', *Studia Diplomatica*, Vol. LX, Issue 1, 2007, pp. 119-134; and 'Collapse in Cancun: The World Trade Agenda Gets Sidetracked', Knowledge@Wharton, University of Pennsylvania, 24 September 2003, https://knowledge.wharton.upenn.edu/article/collapse-in-cancun-the-world-trade-agenda-gets-sidetracked/.

46   *See also* Fox & Bakhoum 2018, p. 12.

47   International Competition Policy Advisory Committee 2002, pp. 264. *et seq.*

48   Eleanor M. Fox, 'International Antitrust and the Doha Dome', *Virginia Journal of International Law*, Vol. 43, Issue 4, 2003, pp. 911 and 931.

49   Id.

50   Fox & Bakhoum 2018, p. 13.

(ii) Developing countries. Meanwhile, the proliferation of national and regional competition laws in developing countries has allowed them to gain experience. As a result, they are now better prepared to deal with issues involved in a negotiation on competition. Moreover, their negotiation capacity is freed up due to the Doha Round negotiations being on hold. In any event, in the final declaration to the Doha Ministerial Conference the ministers requested the Director-General "to ensure that WTO technical assistance focuses, on a priority basis, on assisting developing countries [...] on increasing their capacity to participate more effectively in future multilateral trade negotiations".[51] This could include staff training on the economic effects of various competition disciplines in differently developed economies, assisting them in developing their own voice in relation to suitable competition disciplines.[52]

The concern around high implementation and enforcement costs could be met by putting multilateral competition rules under the supervision and enforcement structures of the WTO institutions,[53] provided that the Appellate Body and WTO dispute settlement system will recover from its current crisis and continue to be able to provide security and predictability to the multilateral trading system as their central element.[54] In so doing, economically weak developed members would not bear the brunt of implementation, as was, and still is, the case in relation to the TRIPS agreement (due to national minimum standard protection despite primarily foreign IP right holders benefitting[55]), but paid primarily by economically strong developed WTO members. The WTO budget derives from contributions paid by its members based on their share of international trade. National minimum standards following the TRIPS model would anyway be insufficient for dismantling trade barriers created by public and private economic operators since members are permitted to adopt higher levels of protection. Thus, cross-border activities could still be subject to different rules, resulting in legal uncertainty.

The fear of being marginalized by developed countries with a focus on efficiency without equity can be allayed by referring both to the fact that the EU's main concern also relates to equity for smaller market players and that, in general, the negotiating power of

---

51   Doha Ministerial Conference, Fourth Session, Implementation-Related Issues and Concerns. Decision of 14 November 2001, final provisions Doc WT/MIN(01)/17, 20 November 2001, para. 14. In particular, the Africa group advocated for such a request (*see* Communication from Kenya on Behalf of the Africa Group, Preparations for the 1999 Ministerial Conference. The Interaction between Trade and Competition Policy WTO-Doc WT/GC/W/300, 06 August 1999).

52   On the need of assistance, *see* Kim Them Do, 'Competition Law and Policy and Economic Development in Developing Countries', *Manchester Journal of International Economic Law*, Vol. 8, Issue 1, 2011, pp. 18-35.

53   Similar already Alan O. Sykes, 'Externalities in Open Economy Antitrust and Implications and Their Implications for International Competition Policy', *Harvard Journal of Law and Public Policy*, Vol. 23, Issue 1, 1999/2000, p. 95. (should be orientated at the DSB and perhaps include a new competition council).

54   Article 3.2 sentence 1 of the WTO Dispute Settlement Understanding.

55   Sucker 2019, p. 186.

states is much more balanced at the multilateral than at the bilateral level. For example, the US and the EU, both generally in a strong bargaining position, used the often complicated bilateral investment contracts to influence the design of the national copyright laws of economically weak developed countries.[56] They pressed for higher IP-protection than stipulated in TRIPS (TRIPS-Plus Standard) as a 'standard deal' for gaining access to third markets. High IP-standards are generally advantageous for their (dominant) economic operators, but rather disadvantageous for economically weak developed countries.[57] The latter often had little to counter this development in a negotiation in which they are seeking access to the US or EU market. At the multilateral level, negotiating parties with weak bargaining power can join forces with like-minded countries to pursue their interests with more leverage and weight than they would have in bilateral negotiations. That way, imbalances in bargaining power can at least be reduced, as can the WTO transparency obligations. Moreover, negotiations at multilateral level involve exchange of arguments and points of views in numerous debates that are well suited for all countries to understand the advantages and disadvantages of different arrangements. The rising role of supply chains and the increasing volatility of international commodity prices should give all, albeit in particular economically weak developed countries reason to pause and revisit an issue that has significant implications for the competitiveness of their economic operators: market distortions that their, primarily small market players are confronted with due to unrestricted competition in the global market.

(iii) Too diverse approaches to competition disciplines? Some members still argue that the various analytical competition concepts included in the, by now, more than 100 enacted national competition laws are too diverse for building consensus at the multilateral level. However, with a view to the preliminary work of the Working Group on the Interaction between Trade and Competition Policy[58] and various other draft documents, such as the Draft International Antitrust Code developed by a group of leading antitrust regulators,[59] among 'Western' economies a common perspective has emerged according to which restrictions on competition and market distortions are particularly harmful.[60] Moreover,

---

56   In more detail Peter Drahos, 'BITS and BIPS. Bilateralism in Intellectual Property', *The Journal of World Intellectual Property*, Vol. 4, Issue 6, 2001, pp. 791. *et seq.*, 806.

57   In detail Sucker 2019, 179-186.

58   On the work of the Working Group on the Interaction between Trade and Competition Policy, *e.g.* 'The Fundamental Principles of Competition Policy', WT/WGTCP/W/127, 7 June 1999; and, in general, at www.wto.org/english/tratop_e/comp_e/wgtcp_docs_e.htm. In the tradition of the EU, the working group emphasizes the direct relationship between trade and competition law (*see* Study on Issues Relating to a Possible Multilateral Framework on Competition Policy, 2003, pp. 9. *et seq.*).

59   On the Draft International Antitrust Code Basedow 1998, pp. 142. *et seq.* and Wolfgang Fikentscher & Josef Drexl, 'Der Draft International Antitrust Code', *Recht der Internationalen Wirtschaft*, 1994, pp. 93-99.

60   On the meaning of this common perspective, the consequences of globalization for state competition policy, the role of WTO law, and side effects, *see* Diane P. Wood, 'Antitrust at the Global Level', *University of Chicago Law Review*, Vol. 72, 2005, pp. 309-324; Basedow 2009, para. 17.

even though offering merely guidelines and recommendations, valuable capacity-building work has been done by the OECD Competition Committee and, very actively, by the UNCTAD Intergovernmental Group of Experts on Competition Law and Policy and the International Competition Network (ICN). The latter already consists of more than 130 competition authorities and numerous nongovernmental advisers devoted to building consensus and convergence, for example, on the treatment of cartels, merger standards, technical assistance, regulated industries, abuse of dominant position and the implementation of competition laws. Indeed, understanding and cooperation has increased, yet "predictably on Western terms".[61]

An inclusive building block for multilateral competition rules would require taking into account the legitimate interests of all groups of countries and, thus, the addition of a developing countries' perspective. Developing countries and regions are currently conducting conversations and testing collaborations of their own that have particular relevance for their context and their state of development (*e.g.* in the African Competition Forum, AfCFTA and TFTA). Thus, such a perspective could take shape in the near future.[62] In general, competition disciplines suitable for societies "ruled by few privileged families or firms or by autocrats",[63] with economies where markets do not work well, monopolies and state ownerships proliferate, barriers to market entry are high, and critical masses of people live near or below the poverty line, would have to seriously control the power of dominant operators and value equity for small market players.[64] Privileges hurt small market players. They reinforce a two-tier economy and constantly increase inequality gaps, with South Africa and five other Sub-Saharan African countries being the most unequal countries worldwide.[65]

It is likely to take a while until states agree on an inclusive common perspective about which restrictions on competition and market distortions are particularly harmful. Therefore, it may be worth reminding states of the following: As a matter of course, many governments adopted national competition laws to counter both the development of dominant positions and anticompetitive behavior. They are ultimately aimed at achieving largely undistorted competition, where fair prices can develop, maximizing benefits for

---

61   Fox & Bakhoum 2018, p. 16. In detail *see* Eleanor M. Fox, 'Linked-In: Antitrust and the Virtues of a Virtual Network', *International Law*, Vol. 43, 2009, pp. 151. *et seq.*

62   Gary C. Hufbauer & Jisun Kim, 'International Competition Policy and the WTO', *Antitrust Bulletin*, Vol. 54, Issue 2, 2009, pp. 327 and 334. (arguing that particularly bilateral and regional agreements allow developing countries to address their own "competition policy concerns").

63   Fox & Bakhoum 2018, p. 180.

64   Id. pp. xxi, xix, 180.

65   1. South Africa, 2. Namibia, 3. Botswana, 4. Zambia, 5. Central African Republic, 6. Lesotho and 7. Swaziland (World Bank most recent Gini index estimates).

all market participants; the maximum of welfare.[66] States that oppose competition disciplines at international level aimed at prohibiting the very same anticompetitive behavior that is illegal in their own jurisdiction, are hypocrites. As an example, almost all of the practices of multinational enterprises of which developing countries complained about in the 1970s "were then illegal per se under US antitrust law".[67] At the time, the US focus lay with economic democracy (*i.e.* to contain power and provide better conditions for the underdog), comparable to the EU's main concern today. Since the 1980s, the main US concern relates to efficiency (*i.e.* not to interfere with efficiency of large enterprises).[68]

10.5 CONCLUSION

Unrestricted competition facilitates market concentration and anticompetitive behavior. This can lead to eliminated or distorted competition which frustrates the market balance, the aim of competition, essential to a dynamic and healthy market in a capitalist system; the system the economic (trade) relations between WTO members (and most of their national economies) are based on. The absence of multilateral competition rules permits these most unfavorable developments to occur on the global market, for example, economic profits of various cross-border active economic operators at the expense of diversity of offers and smaller market participants, especially those of economically weak developed countries. While global market distortions are likely to remain in the international trading system, competition disciplines may internalize externalities (hold companies accountable for price-fixing, even foreign undertakings) and minimize disparities of legal rules among nationals and regions.

The impact of cross-border activities of private and public economic operators requires a holistic view of the global market, not merely an isolated assessment of successive regional or national markets.[69] Regional or bilateral agreements can discipline those cross-border activities with legal certainty that affect the competition of markets within their territory, but cannot replace multilateral disciplines for entrepreneurial activities that affect the competition of two or more markets outside their territorial scope. In spite of the hitherto

---

66 *See e.g.* Edward M. Graham & J. David Richardson, 'Issue Overview', *in* Edward M. Graham & J. David Richardson (eds.), *Global Competition Policy*, Columbia University Press, 1997, chapter 1, p. 3, who emphasize that worldwide national competition policies "commonly seek a blend of efficiency and fairness for domestic market"; and *Times-Picayune Publishing Co v. United States*, 345 U.S. 594, 1953 ("[b]asic to the faith that a free economy best promotes the public weal is that goods must stand the cold test of competition; that the public, acting through market's impersonal judgement, shall allocate the Nation's resources and thus direct the course its economic development will take."). On this, *see* Basedow 2009, para. 17.

67 Fox & Bakhoum 2018, p. 10.

68 Id. p. 11.

69 Id. p. 12.

expressed resistance to include competition disciplines within the WTO and the withdrawn negotiating mandate, rules aimed at dismantling barriers to international trade created by private or public economic operators are not only theoretically desirable but indispensable in the long term to avoid an erosion of the WTO system by effectively replacing state-created barriers.

The feasibility of the project depends on the strength and perseverance of progressive WTO members; that is, those who seriously pursue the objectives of the WTO proclaimed in the preamble and do not tolerate anticompetitive behavior of international economic operators whom they themselves consider unlawful at national level. Recital 5 of the preamble to the Marrakesh agreement states that WTO Members are "determined to uphold the fundamental principles [of the WTO Agreements] and to promote the achievement of its objectives." Achieving the goal of raising the common standard of living for all (not only for a few) requires a dynamic and healthy market underpinned by "inclusive, sustainable, economic growth, consistent with equity", for which a level playing field is as important as the reduction of tariffs and non-tariff barriers.[70] In fact, WTO members are guided by a desire "to reduce distortions and impediments to international trade",[71] with the very essence of WTO-rules being to create equally competitive conditions for products, services and IP-right holders. WTO members would then live up to their conviction that

> "there is need for positive efforts designed to ensure that developing countries, and especially the least developed amongst them, secure a share in the growth in international trade commensurate with the needs of their economic development",[72]

instead of protecting and subsidizing where it hurts them most.[73]

---

70   *See* also Lamy 2013, p. 132.
71   Recital 1 of the Preamble to the TRIPS.
72   Recital 2 of the Preamble to the Marrakesh Agreement.
73   On this, impressively, Martin Wolf, *Why Globalisation Works*, Yale University Press, 2004, pp. 212-218. ('hypocrisy of the rich').

11 CERTAIN FACTORS INFLUENCING COMPLIANCE WITH INTERNATIONAL HUMANITARIAN LAW

Réka Varga[*]

Keywords

implementation of international humanitarian law, compliance measures and mechanisms, enforcement of international humanitarian law, non-state actors, individual criminal responsibility

Abstract

There are various mechanisms within and outside the sphere of international humanitarian law (IHL) which contribute to a better application, respect and enforcement of its rules. The present study takes stock of specific factors or mechanisms that may have an effect on better respect. This analysis attempts to demonstrate that even though states could not agree on the setting up of a permanent mechanism to meet regularly and discuss IHL-related issues (the so-called Compliance process), there are certain instruments which could lead to similar result. The UN's role with respect to IHL is examined. The International Criminal Court (ICC) is also briefly analyzed from this perspective, bearing in mind the international politics within which it has to function. The International Humanitarian Fact-Finding Commission (IHFFC) that has successfully completed its first mandate is a string of hope if more frequently used. Soft law documents are filling a void caused by the fatigue of states in adopting new rules, at the same time they start to have a similarly binding effect as legally binding obligations. All these factors become especially interesting if we understand that most conflicts today are fought with the involvement of non-state armed groups who are not involved in law-making. This reality gives training, both within state and non-state armed forces a special significance. States should also make efforts to undertake enquiries in cases of serious violations of IHL, as well as through exercising jurisdiction to repress violations, be they their own nationals or not.

---

[*]   Réka Varga: associate professor, Pázmány Péter Catholic University, Budapest; Member of the International Humanitarian Fact-Finding Commission.

11.1 Introduction[1]

We are often struck by alarming accounts of international humanitarian law (IHL) being less and less complied with. Are we really living in a new era? Is compliance with IHL really worse than before? Is it not rather the issue that with the live streaming of conflicts, the spreading of social media and the CNN-effect we are in a position to follow conflicts more closely, even live, and obviously news will only reporting incidents of non-compliance? We often announce a new age of warfare upon the introduction of new technology. Our new technologies are no doubt novel in character, but so were the technologies introduced earlier. If we asked delegates on the field, we would probably be surprised by the variety of actors and often such actors' willingness to engage in a dialogue with each other. Today, we are witnessing terrible conflicts with a terrible toll on civilians, but, unfortunately, this is not necessarily new. This may lead us to think that our fight today for better compliance with IHL, for ensuring better enforcement of its rules is nothing new, and is in fact, a never-ending endeavor. The following article takes a broad look existing measures that enhance compliance with and enforcement of IHL, asking the question what other factors could be relevant to create an environment where IHL is better respected.

11.2 Relevant Enforcement and Compliance Measures and Mechanisms

In general, it can be said that enforcement is challenging in international law. As there is no global institutional framework for its ultimate enforcement, compliance with international law is largely left to the goodwill of states. While the basic principles of international law include the prohibition of the use of force and the *pacta sunt servanda* principle, if these were all respected, there would be very few armed conflicts in the first place. And even if such conflicts arose, there would be no violations of the law applicable in armed conflicts. Armed conflicts are typically situations where the rule of law suffers, the peaceful settlement of international disputes has clearly failed, and the warring parties are each other's worse enemies. To rely on the goodwill of states in such a situation seems paradox. Nevertheless, although there are numerous manifestations of violations, IHL is often, probably more often than we would think, complied with.

If it is true that international law generally lacks the teeth of effective enforcement, then this is all the more so for international humanitarian law. IHL treaties, especially the 1949 Geneva Conventions and their Additional Protocols adopted in 1977 tend to have

---

1 This article is based on a presentation delivered by the author at the Conference 'Seminar Humanitäres Völkerrecht und die Europäische Union – Aktuelle Entwicklungen während des österreichischen Ratsvorsitzes', organized by the Austrian Federal Ministry for Europe, Integration and Foreign Affairs, the Johannes Kepler University Linz, the University of Graz, and the Austrian Red Cross on 29 January 2019 in Linz.

much weaker enforcement/compliance provisions than other fields of international law.[2] In many instances, non-compliance with IHL was explained by the lack of reciprocity.[3] While inter-state relations are often based on reciprocity, this is not true for IHL obligations. Under international humanitarian law, parties' obligations remain unchanged irrespective of non-compliance by the other side. This is to ensure the protection of victims.

Moreover, one has to take into consideration the fact that non-state actors often play an equally big role in armed conflicts, consequently, they influence compliance/non-compliance with IHL. Therefore, traditional international law compliance mechanisms that are based on state-to-state relations (such as reporting, states meeting *etc.*) may not be appropriate in their case.

The Geneva Conventions and Additional Protocols include a few mechanisms aimed at facilitating compliance and enforcement. This includes the common Article 1, the grave breaches/war crimes regime, indirectly the command responsibility concept, the obligations to make legal advisers available to the armed forces, and mechanisms such as Article 36 of Additional Protocol I. There are also mechanisms that are foreseen in treaty law but, are rarely used. Parties to armed conflicts rarely make use of the special agreements under Article 3 of the Geneva Convention. The reality is that a state which considers the belligerent party to be a group of 'illegal' rebels is not inclined to enter negotiations with the adversary, since the latter could consider such a negotiation to be a manifestation of its recognition. Even though special agreements were not intended to affect the status of the parties,[4] there seems to be a general adversity towards the application of Article 3.[5] In summary, it seems there is no specific mechanism foreseen under international humanitarian law that would force or motivate states to comply with its rules.

The abovementioned mechanisms do not prescribe a regular meeting of state parties, regular reporting, let alone the establishment of treaty bodies aimed at monitoring the implementation of treaty rules. Recognizing this lacuna, the ICRC and the Swiss Government launched the 'Compliance initiative'[6] where states discussed the possibility of estab-

---

2   Yves Sandoz, 'How Does Law Protect in War?', *in Problems in the Implementation of International Law in General and International Humanitarian Law Specifically*, at https://casebook.icrc.org/law/implementation-mechanisms.

3   Daniel Munoz-Rojas & Jean-Jacques Frésard, *The Roots of Behaviour in War: Understanding and Preventing IHL Violations*, ICRC, Geneva, 2004, pp. 9 and 13.

4   Article 3 common to the 1949 Geneva Conventions: "The Parties to the conflict should further endeavor to bring into force, by means of special agreements, all or part of the other provisions of the present Convention. The application of the preceding provisions shall not affect the legal status of the Parties to the conflict."

5   Ben Clarke, 'Securing Compliance with International Humanitarian Law: The Promise and Limits of Contemporary Enforcement Mechanisms', *Journal of International Humanitarian Legal Studies*, Vol. 1, Issue 1, 2010, p. 215.

6   The facilitators received mandate from Resolution 1 on "Strengthening Legal Protection for Victims of Armed Conflicts" unanimously adopted by the 31st International Conference in 2011 and Resolution 2,

lishing a regular, voluntary forum for states where issues related to compliance with IHL could be discussed. However, notwithstanding numerous years of multilateral meetings and discussions, states failed to come to a common agreement on setting up such a mechanism.[7]

Although IHL treaties do not include such compliance mechanisms, bodies outside the IHL sphere have certain tools to promote better compliance with IHL. First and foremost, one has to mention the powers and the practice of the UN Security Council *vis-à-vis ius in bello* violations. Let us not forget that at the outset the UN was set up to maintain international peace and security, and not to ensure that armed conflicts are fought according to the rules. Still, while the Security Council remained silent on IHL matters for years,[8] it has demonstrated increased interest and activity with respect to IHL violations following the Cold War, and with the proliferation of non-international armed conflicts and their severe consequences for civilians.[9] Whereas the Security Council can only invoke Chapter VII when international peace and security is jeopardized, an argument can be made that serious and mass humanitarian law violations may pose a threat to international peace and security, hence the activation of Chapter VII. The Security Council regarded a situation where violations of international humanitarian law occur as a threat to international peace for the first time in its Resolutions setting up the two *ad hoc* Tribunals. These tribunals were established by Resolution 808 (1993)[10] with respect to former Yugoslavia, and later Resolution 995 (1994)[11] with respect to Rwanda. The Security Council then made a reference[12] to the possibility of systematic, flagrant and widespread violations being a

---

"Strengthening Compliance with International Humanitarian Law" unanimously adopted at the 32nd International Conference of the Red Cross and Red Crescent in 2015.

7   Helen Durham, *'Strengthening Compliance with IHL: Disappointment and Hope'*, December 14, 2018, Analysis/Generating Respect for IHL/Law and Conflict at https://blogs.icrc.org/law-and-policy/2018/12/14/strengthening-compliance-with-ihl-disappointment-and-hope/.

8   The first mention of international humanitarian law was made in the 1967 Resolution after the Six Days War in the Middle East. *See* Resolution 237 (1967), recommending for governments concerned to comply with the Geneva Conventions.

9   Marco Roscini, 'The United Nations Security Council and the Enforcement of International Humanitarian Law', *Israel Law Review*, Vol. 43, 2010, p. 331.

10 "Expressing once again its grave alarm at continuing reports of widespread violations of international humanitarian law occurring within the territory of the former Yugoslavia, including reports of mass killings and the continuance of the practice of 'ethnic cleansing', Determining that this situation constitutes a threat to international peace and security,"; *See* S/RES/808 (22 February 1993).

11 "Expressing once again its grave concern at the reports indicating that genocide and other systematic, widespread and flagrant violations of international humanitarian law have been committed in Rwanda, Determining that this situation continues to constitute a threat to international peace and security,"; *See* S/RES/955 (8 November 1994).

12 "Notes that the deliberate targeting of civilian populations or other protected persons and the committing of systematic, flagrant and widespread violations of international humanitarian and human rights law in situations of armed conflict may constitute a threat to international peace and security, and, in this regard, reaffirms its readiness to consider such situations and, where necessary, to adopt appropriate steps;" *See* OP 5, SC Res 1296, para. 5, UN Doc. S/RES/1296 (19 April 2000).

threat to international peace and security without mention of any specific armed conflict.[13] Also, there are interpretations of the Geneva Conventions' common Article 1 "respect and ensure respect" provision which assert that since this customary rule is a "general principle", it constitutes a legal ground for the Security Council to exercise its enforcement powers to ensure compliance "in all circumstances".[14]

Further examples for the UN's (softer) measures contributing to compliance with IHL are the biennial reports of the Secretary General on the status of the implementation of the 1977 Additional Protocols, prepared upon request of the UN General Assembly. The Secretary General requests states to provide, every two years on a voluntary basis, information on the status of implementation of the Additional Protocols. These voluntary national reports may be useful exercises for states to take stock of developments and lacunae in their implementing legislation or practice. These reports may also serve as a useful mirror on the state of implementation of IHL globally, although it should be mentioned that only 19 Member States submitted their national reports for the 2018 report.[15]

There are many primarily human rights bodies, most importantly the Human Rights Council that also address IHL issues. The Human Rights Council (HRC) was established to "address situations of violations of human rights" and "make recommendations thereon".[16] Even though it is clear that the mandate does not cover IHL, nor does it mention armed conflicts, the HRC examined IHL violations more than once. It also provided an extended understanding of human rights when it stated in its Resolution 9/9 (2008) that "conduct that violates international humanitarian law [...] may also constitute a gross violation of human rights."[17]

Whether examination of IHL violations by an essentially non-IHL body is good or bad for IHL can be examined from many angles. Those in favor argue that the HRC is only filling the gap where IHL treaties are silent on enforcement mechanisms, and this is still better than nothing. In addition, such commissions or inquiries are usually tasked to merely cover the documentation and investigation of serious violations, in order to ensure some kind of accountability for the future. From this perspective, so goes the argument, it is irrelevant whether these are IHL or human rights violations.[18] Those against claim that the experts sitting on HRC commissions and inquiries are for the most part not trained

---

13   Roscini 2010, pp. 334-335. *See* SC Res 808 at 2, UN Doc. S/RES/808 (22 February 1993).

14   Id. p. 340. *See* SC Res 808 at 2, UN Doc. S/RES/808 (22 February 1993).

15   *See* Report of the Secretary General A/73/277 (30 July 2018) and the subsequent GA Resolution A/RES/73/204 (9 January 2019).

16   GA Resolution A/RES/60/251 (3 April 2006), OP 3.

17   Human Rights Council Res. 9/9, Annual Reports of the HRC, 9th Session, 8-24 September 2008, A/HRC/RES/9/9 at 1 (18 September 2008).

18   Zsuzsanna Binczki, 'Summary of the Conference on "Victims or Armed Conflicts at the Juncture of International Humanitarian Law and Human Rights Law" (presentation by Luc Côté), *'Hungarian Yearbook of International Law and European Law'* Vol. 5, 2017, pp. 379-380.

in IHL, or are not even lawyers but diplomats.[19] Meanwhile, the HRC is being over-politicized, which is not for the benefit of IHL. A more observational standpoint claims that the correlation between IHL and human rights law has grown so strong[20] that it is impossible to reverse this trend.[21]

The establishment of the International Criminal Court (ICC) was clearly a huge step towards the enforcement of IHL. Many thought that the ICC could have an impact in two ways: directly through its own procedures, and indirectly through the inevitable effect it has on domestic legislation.

Many scholars and commentators were very satisfied with the Rome Statute having been drafted in a way that the UN has no or not too much influence over its jurisdiction or overall function. The Rome Statute foresees a role for the UN – most importantly from the point of view of the present article – in two ways: in referring cases to the ICC and in respect of the crime of aggression. In the first case, the UN's role is limited by its political possibilities to adopt a Security Council resolution on referral. Similarly, in the second case the determination of an act of aggression is highly politicized. Nonetheless, these roles do not appear to provide for the possibility that the UN intervenes in or influences the ICC's functioning too much. Marco Sassóli wrote in 2006:

> "Once the ICC Statute has been universally accepted and the ICC functions effectively without too much direct interference by the UN Security Council and its permanent members, this geographical limitation will be overcome. The very credibility of international justice depends on this: justice which is not the same for everyone is not justice."[22]

Today, we have come to understand that international politics and non-state parties have a larger influence over the ICC than we had anticipated. Campaigns against the ICC by certain states, either generally or linked to specific cases, are no doubt weakening the Court and making its space narrower. Even though the ICC is not, and shall not be dependent on politics, and while it is making tremendous efforts to navigate the given circumstances, the ICC does not operate in a political void.

In addition, although the withdrawal of some African states has fortunately not become a general tendency, one cannot avoid facing the legal question posed first and foremost by African states challenging the Rome Statute's non-recognition of head of state immunity and diplomatic immunity. The Rome Statute excludes the application of immunity of

---

19   Clarke 2010, p. 216.
20   Id. p. 218.
21   Id. p. 216.
22   Marco Sassòli, 'The Implementation of International Humanitarian Law: Current and Inherent Challenges', *Yearbook of International Humanitarian Law*, Vol. 10, 2007, pp. 45-73.

officials, including heads of states with respect to procedures in front of the Court, obliging States Parties to cooperate accordingly. This includes arresting persons enjoying immunity if they are wanted by the ICC. Several African states find this obligation to be in collision with customary and treaty international law obligations on diplomatic and head of state immunity. They claim that the rules on immunity enjoy precedence over the Rome Statute obligation. This question has become crucial for the states concerned and their ability to cooperate with the ICC. Thus, the ICC's efforts and effects are constrained both by its capability to deal with the magnitude of cases, and inevitably, by the politics surrounding it.

There are also arguments saying that the ICC's inability to exercise jurisdiction to deal with some of the most severe cases prompted bodies such as the Human Rights Council to increase their activities regarding IHL violations. It also led to the emergence of alternative bodies which serve the ultimate aim of promoting criminal accountability either on an international or national level. As an example of alternatives bodies, upon the initiative of Liechtenstein, the General Assembly adopted Resolution 71/248 on 21 December 2016 establishing the 'International, Impartial and Independent Mechanism'. It is to assist in the investigation and prosecution of persons responsible for the most serious crimes under International Law committed in the Syrian Arab Republic since March 2011 (IIIM). The IIIM was tasked to collect and document evidence of crimes committed in Syria, which can then be used in national or international criminal procedures. A similar mechanism was later established in connection with crimes committed in Myanmar: on September 28, 2018, the UN Human Rights Council passed a resolution that calls for an independent mechanism to collect and analyze evidence in regard to the serious international crimes committed in Myanmar against Rohingya Muslims and other minorities since 2011. The resolution foresees that the independent mechanism

> "prepare files in order to facilitate and expedite fair and independent criminal proceedings, in accordance with international law standards, in national, regional or international courts or tribunals that have or may in the future have jurisdiction over these crimes."

The resolution mentions "most serious international crimes" and "violations of international law",[23] which would include human rights and humanitarian law violations.

Last but not least, mention must be made of the International Humanitarian Fact-Finding Commission (IHFFC), established by Additional Protocol I of 1977. The IHFFC is tasked to "enquire into any facts alleged to be a grave breach as defined in the Conventions and this Protocol or other serious violation of the Conventions or of this Protocol and

---

23   Human Rights Council Resolution A/HRC/39/L.22 (28 September 2019), OP 22.

facilitate, through its good offices, the restoration of an attitude of respect for the Conventions and this Protocol."[24] The IHFFC has demonstrated its great value in inquiry during its first mandate received from the Organization for Security and Co-operation in Europe (OSCE) in 2017[25] to investigate an incident in Eastern Ukraine. The incident involved an OSCE car that drove over a landmine, the explosion resulted in the death of an OSCE paramedic and the injury of two other patrol members. The investigation revealed that the attack was most probably not directed against the OSCE,[26] possibly giving the OSCE a feeling of relative relief for not being a target, with an ability to carry out its important operations in the region. Because the IHFFC was established by Additional Protocol I of 1977, coming into force and effectively created in 1991, receiving its first mandate only in 2017, there were several analyses why its inquiry capability had not been used earlier. Many stressed that one reason the IHFFC had not been used was the complicated trigger mechanism foreseen under Article 90 of Additional Protocol I. The IHFFC nevertheless proved that its activity can easily be triggered by an organization and not a state through the 'good offices'[27] provision.[28] It also substantiated that it can contribute to the clarification of a situation and thus indirectly to fostering an attitude of respect for IHL. The IHFFC has also expressed its willingness to inquire into alleged violations of IHL in non-international armed conflicts, provided that all concerned parties agree.[29] In addition, one may argue that the setting up of *ad hoc* fact finding commissions by the Human Rights Council were meant to be a remedy for the earlier non-activation of the IHFFC. However, the existence of these *ad hoc* commissions may have also been the very causes of the inactivity of the IHFFC for long years.[30]

Summing up, it is probably fair to say that although IHL treaties are not especially strong on compliance and enforcement mechanisms, there are various other sources or procedures available through which compliance with IHL can be examined or supported.

---

24   Article 90(2)(c) of Protocol Additional to the Geneva Conventions of 12 August 1949, and relating to the Protection of Victims of International Armed Conflicts (Protocol I), 8 June 1977.

25   As a basic framework for the cooperation between the two organizations, the OSCE and IHFFC concluded a general Memorandum of Understanding, at www.ihffc.org/Files/en/pdf/osce-ihffc-memorandum-of-understand.pdf.

26   *See* the executive summary of the report following the investigation at www.osce.org/home/338361?download=true.

27   "*c)* The Commission shall be competent to: […] *(ii)* facilitate, through its good offices, the restoration of an attitude of respect for the Conventions and this Protocol." *See* Article 90, Protocol Additional to the Geneva Conventions of 12 August 1949, and relating to the Protection of Victims of International Armed Conflicts (Protocol I), 8 June 1977.

28   Réka Varga, *'Reinforcing Respect for the Additional Protocols: The 40th Anniversary as an Opportunity?'* at www.iihl.org/wp-content/uploads/2017/11/Varga-REV.pdf.

29   *See* www.icrc.org/en/doc/assets/files/other/fact_finding_commission.pdf.

30   Roscini 2010, p. 343.

11.3   EMERGENCE OF SOFT LAW DOCUMENTS AIMED AT PROMOTING COMPLIANCE WITH IHL

We are witnessing a decreased interest of states in law-making, and a greater appetite for soft law. Soft law documents in the realm of international law are generally understood as documents which have been adopted and agreed generally in the form of non-binding political declarations. However, these texts are not completely without legal significance:[31] although they normally indicate voluntary commitments by the signatories to respect its contents, due to many circumstances and

> "a number of enforcing soft mechanisms such as shaming, conformity, persua-
> sion, self-interest, opportunity, or fear are effective. From this perspective, soft
> or non-binding rules can be as coercive as binding rules and agreements. This
> is why it seems appropriate to refer to soft law also as 'non-binding coercions'
> [...]"[32]

and are thus often considered to be quasi-binding.

There are many soft law documents in IHL, such as the Safe Schools Declaration, the Montreux Document, the Guideline on Direct participation in hostilities or the Vancouver Principles. Some of these were prepared by States, some by international organizations or NGOs. Some can be endorsed by states, some cannot. All these documents are attempts at addressing questions of the interpretation of provision regarding contemporary conflicts, with the aim to come up with an answer acceptable to all states, or at least, to identify divergences of opinions or to provide some sort of guidelines for application. The relative reluctance of states towards international law-making may be regarded as missed oppor-tunity for the states, since the vacuum left by them is filled by NGOs, academics or tribunals interpreting the law,[33] eventually bringing these actors in a position to contribute to the formation of new customary law. States should probably resume their functions in legal interpretation and law-making, while academics, tribunals, NGOs also have their own role. Michael Schmitt argues that because states have withdrawn from the role of law-

---

31   Andrew T. Guzman & Timothy L. Meyer, 'International Soft Law', *Journal of Legal Analysis*, Vol. 2, Issue
      1, 2010, pp. 172-173.
32   Filipp M. Zerilli, 'The Rule of Soft Law: An Introduction', *Focaal – Journal of Global and Historical
      Anthropology*, Issue 56, 2010, pp. 5-6.
33   '*Is the Law of Armed Conflict in Crisis and How to Recommit to its Respect?*' comments by Michael N.
      Schmitt, 3 June 2016, ICRC at www.icrc.org/en/document/law-armed-conflict-crisis-and-how-recommit-
      its-respect.

making and interpretation, NGOs and academics shape the law in a way that states in the end may then reject.[34]

The legal and political nature of soft law documents has also become an increasingly interesting question. While basically it should be clear that soft law documents do not have a legally binding nature, there are some non-binding documents that may have achieved a quasi-binding character due to the will of the parties concluding it or due to pressure exerted over non-signatory states.

The IHL soft law documents mentioned above were undoubtedly adopted with the understanding that these do not have a binding effect. Many of these documents expressly state this.[35] Politically, however, there seems to be a tendency where such documents, even though intentionally put in a non-legally binding form with non-binding language, become politically *quasi* binding. This is a result of intensive, sometimes aggressive campaigning by states/NGOs/international organizations that have embraced the document and are often naming and shaming states that are not behaving the way the document prescribes.

Such effects of soft law documents may lead to several outcomes. If states are not expressing discontent with the document and follow practice akin to its contents, with all relevant conditions fulfilled, it may become customary law. From this perspective it makes no difference whether the soft law document can be or was endorsed by states or not, because it operates the same way: the 'rules' contained therein are referred to as those that should be followed or conduct that States should and do adhere to. It may also lead to a situation where the state may simply feel that due to political or diplomatic pressure it actually has to follow the document, even though at the time of signing or adoption everyone declared it to be non-binding, and its non-legally binding nature was probably one of the baits used to convince states to sign. This effect could equally work with documents that cannot be endorsed by states, if the document is often referred to as providing for the appropriate conduct in certain fields by a large number of actors and all the, more if political pressure is exerted to follow its contents.

Another layer of the same tendency is when there is mounting pressure on states that have not signed such documents. Those promoting the soft-law document often end up

---

34 Guzman & Meyer 2010, pp. 172-173.

35 "While reflecting the ICRC's views, the Interpretive Guidance is not and cannot be a text of a legally binding nature." *See* Interpretive Guidance on the Notion of Direct Participation in Hostilities under International Humanitarian Law, ICRC, May 2009, p. 10. at https://shop.icrc.org/guide-interpretatif-sur-la-notion-de-participation-directe-aux-hostilites-en-droit-international-humanitaire-2601.html. "We welcome the development of the Guidelines for protecting schools and universities from military use during armed conflict. The Guidelines are non-legally binding, voluntary guidelines that do not affect existing international law." *See* Safe Schools Declaration at www.protectingeducation.org/sites/default/files/docu-ments/safe_schools_declaration-final.pdf.

naming and shaming such states, what's more, signing these may appear in UN's,[36] NGO's[37] or other bodies' recommendations, or even requirements. In the end, sometimes these documents are treated the same way as if they were legally binding. Hence, documents non-binding at their inception have become a sort of must-do for states.

Whether soft law documents are contributing to better respect and compliance with IHL needs to be considered from different angles. On the one hand, specifically due to the fact that the need for interpretation does not necessarily mean that the law must be changed, and also considering states' unwillingness to make new law, the emergence of soft law documents, aimed at analyzing different interpretations, experiences and practices may be a welcome development. On the other hand, one must recognize the changing nature of such documents and be aware that they often, albeit not always, become more than simple recommendations, studies, interpretations. This may lead to a sense of fatigue by states towards soft law documents, and hence, a reluctance to adopt new ones.

11.4   HOPES AND OPPORTUNITIES

There are certain trends that give cause to optimism and opportunities that could be further explored.

Even though IHL is a part of international law, that is, a normative framework among states regulating their conduct in armed conflicts, the increasing role played by non-state armed actors in armed conflicts[38] is also considered as a topical feature.[39] There are authors who suggest that since non-state actors have not participated in the making of international law and have not consented to it, one cannot be surprised that non-state actors do not respect the law (even though they are also bound by it). Thus, it seems necessary to adopt IHL rules that are more suitable to contemporary conflicts.[40] This is an argument is based on a paradox. First, were we to develop new law, non-state actors would not participate in its formulation either. Second, many of the basic IHL rules are based on rules of human conscience shared by the entire international community Therefore, the argument that they have not consented to them seems unfounded. Third, were we to embrace this argu-

---

36   Report of the Secretary General on the protection of civilians in armed conflict, S/2017/414 (10 May 2017), para. 14.

37   *See* www.hrw.org/news/2018/06/19/opportunity-ukraine-endorse-safe-schools-declaration.

38   The number of parties to armed conflicts has exponentially increased in the past decades. In Libya, by the end of the conflict, 236 armed groups were registered, while in Syria 1000 armed groups have been counted in 2014. *See* Munoz-Rojas & Frésard 2004, p. 13.

39   *See* Varga 2017.

40   Thomas Previ Botchway & Abdul Hamid Kwarteng, 'Developing International Law in Challenging Times', *Journal of Politics and Law*, Vol. 11, Issue 3, 2018, p. 55.

ment, it would result in an endless debate on the adequacy of sometimes century-old rules. After all, the task of the lawyers is to apply existing rules.[41]

In 2017, 17 international and 38 non-international armed conflicts took place worldwide.[42] Non-state armed actors do not participate in diplomatic conferences, intergovernmental meetings, the Compliance process, and do not benefit from common training exercises. Hence, they don't have the same level of ownership of international humanitarian law as states do.[43] The ICRC and certain NGOs, such as Geneva Call, make efforts to provide training for or engaging in dialogue with non-state actors. Geneva Call often concludes Deeds of Commitment with them, where the non-state actor voluntarily undertakes to provide training in IHL or, comply with basic IHL rules. Such Deeds of Commitment, although non-binding in nature, often serve as catalysts for non-state actors to make efforts to comply with IHL.

Many thus claim that non-compliance with IHL can be led back first and foremost to non-international armed conflicts, and highlight the importance of involving non-state armed groups.[44] Non-state actors, which may not have a strict hierarchy and bureaucratic system similar to states, have a more difficult time enforcing rules within their group. Even though there are armed groups that are not interested in respecting IHL, or their aim is precisely to cause as much terror and loss as possible, other groups are more serious about compliance with IHL and about their public perception, in particular, if they want to receive international recognition.

As the ICRC's 'The Roots of Behaviour in War' study has shown, combatants' illegal actions are frequently down to a lack of specific orders not to violate the law.[45] While training provided for states' armed forces always includes IHL elements, this may not be true for trainings, if any, of non-state armed actors. At the same time, criminal responsibility is equally applied to individuals from state and non-state armed groups. This is why training/dissemination of IHL is equally important among armed groups, and while training itself may not necessarily have a direct effect on the correct application of IHL, it may have an indirect effect in helping prevent combatants enter into the cycle of violence.[46] Individual criminal responsibility is based on the individual's actions, while combatants submit to an authority and are psychologically shifting their focus from conforming to

---

41   Morgan Kelley, 'Challenges to Compliance with International Humanitarian Law in the Context of Contemporary Warfare', *Independent Study Project (ISP) Collection*, 2013, p. 29.

42   Annyssa Bellal (ed.), *The War Report. Armed Conflicts in 2017*, Geneva Academy of International Humanitarian Law and Human Rights, 2018, p. 29.

43   Id. p. 29.

44   Clarke 2010, p. 219.

45   Munoz-Rojas & Frésard 2004, p. 7.

46   Id. p. 11.

their own moral sense to satisfying their superiors.[47] This means they assess their own actions *vis-à-vis* the morale of the group, and not according to their own moral standards. Socialization within armed groups thus has a direct influence on how fighters behave. Socialization can go both ways: individuals can be socialized to commit violations, but also to demonstrate restraint.[48] This gives military training particular importance at all levels and makes us understand how important it is for commanders of non-state armed groups to understand the rules.

In light of new technologies, regular state armed forces also need a new approach to training. Understanding the specificities of remote-control technologies and the ability to carry out deadly attacks from thousands of kilometers away, trainers need to recognize this remoteness may have on decision-making. While studies have shown that humans find it difficult to kill their fellow human beings at close range,[49] following movements and monitoring the situation on the ground from a far-away computer, and then adopting the decision whether or not to attack is done in a completely different psychological setting. Therefore, a firm knowledge of the rules and an adequate psychological state of mind could also contribute to IHL-compliant behavior.

The position and importance of military legal advisers in the eyes of their commanders has also favorably changed. A couple of decades ago in many countries a military legal adviser was considered a necessary evil for the commander, someone who only puts obstacles in his way, without brining any benefits. Today (the Rome Statute greatly furthered this, not only by forcing states to voluntarily implement command responsibility provisions in their legislation, but also by making known that such concept exists, even though it had already existed in the 1977 Additional Protocol) legal advisers are often considered as useful contributors who can eventually help the commander prevent or avoid criminal responsibility. In addition, and equally important, they help avoid bad public relations. It has been recognized that IHL became an increasingly important factor in how military actions are considered by the public and the international community, and even big and powerful nations were forced to align their attitude to such expectations.

One serious demonstration by States to show they take IHL seriously would be to carry out genuine inquiries in case of alleged violations and make the results of such inquiries public.[50] Such voluntary inquiries would also be beneficial to close the credibility gap

---

47   Id. p. 7: "The disappearance of personal responsibility is by far the most serious consequence of submission to authority. Although, under these conditions, the individual commits acts which seem to violate the dictates of his conscience, it would be wrong to conclude that his moral sense has disappeared. The fact is that it has radically changed focus. The person concerned no longer makes value judgements about his actions. What concerns him now is to show himself worthy of what the authority expects of him."

48   Botchway & Kwarteng 2018, p. 25.

49   Munoz-Rojas & Frésard 2004, p. 10.

50   *'Is the Law of Armed Conflict in Crisis and How to Recommit to its Respect?'* comments by Marco Sassòli, 3 June 2016, ICRC at www.icrc.org/en/document/law-armed-conflict-crisis-and-how-recommit-its-respect.

between the alleged importance of IHL and inaction in the face of violations. We all remember the tragic attack at Kunduz hospital in Afghanistan in 2015. The US Air Force attacked a hospital operated by *Médecins Sans Frontières* (MSF) in Kunduz, resulting in the death of most of the patients and many of the medical staff.[51] Upon the MSF's call on the US to request an inquiry from the IHFFC, the US responded that it saw no need for the IHFFC to carry out fact-finding, since it can conduct its own inquiry.[52] The US did carry out its own inquiry amounting to a file of more than 3000 pages,[53] and made the executive summary public. Emphasizing that it is not common US policy to make the results of its inquiries public, it is significant here that the US government felt that the incident was so severe it had to act, make the findings public, and understand lessons learnt. The result was still criticized as unsatisfactory because no serious accountability measures were taken.[54] It may nevertheless be a noteworthy example where a state realized it had to adopt special measures to seem credible, to identify lessons learnt and to show the world it took IHL safeguards seriously.

It has become apparent that international criminal justice cannot be exhaustive, neither in including all the situations and cases due to political sensitivities, leaving entire conflicts or parties free of criminal accountability, nor in numbers: it is impossible to try all those responsible. A very positive effect of the International Criminal Tribunal for the Former Yugoslavia has been the 11bis procedures, through which a larger number of perpetrators could be tried in domestic courts, and through which domestic capabilities have strengthened. This strengthening of domestic capabilities has welcome long-term effects in that a number of judges, prosecutors, defense lawyers are trained in IHL and international criminal law and become familiar of the specificities of war crime trials. Handing over trials to domestic structures may also be a source of legitimacy for international or hybrid tribunals, since they need to garner recognition within the local population.[55] Recognizing that domestic trials may be one way out of impunity, it would be important to put more efforts into increasing domestic capabilities, giving domestic enforcement more teeth.

We need to believe in domestic trials and universal jurisdiction. It is probably easier to apply the more efficient, organized and cheaper domestic mechanisms, than to persuade sovereign states that a case should be submitted to the ICC, or that a new mechanism should be established. Exercising universal jurisdiction may have its political sensitivities,

---

51   *See* www.msf.org/kunduz-hospital-attack.
52   "Following the attack, we demanded an independent investigation by the International Humanitarian Fact-Finding Commission (IHFFC). In April 2016, the US military released its own investigative report. The request for an independent investigation has so far gone unanswered." Id.
53   *See* www.nytimes.com/2016/04/30/world/asia/afghanistan-doctors-without-borders-hospital-strike.html.
54   Only disciplinary measures have been adopted. *See* www.bbc.com/news/world-us-canada-36164595.
55   Juan Ernesto Mendez, 'Preventing, Implementing and Enforcing International Humanitarian Law', *Studies in Transnational Legal Policy*, Vol. 39, 2008, p. 97.

but it shall not be forgotten as a means to fight impunity. Enforcement should go hand in hand with prevention, dissemination, training, dialogue, and international processes. If we look at the disagreement among states to initiate proceedings before the ICC in the Syria case, and generally all the political attacks against the ICC, the only permanent international body available to try the most heinous cases, we realize that there is little global will to make use of this body. Even though alternative mechanisms are emerging, it is safe to say that international mechanisms alone will not be able to put an end to impunity and ensure better respect for IHL.

11.5   CONCLUSION

The Compliance mechanism was meant to provide, among others, a forum for discussion on the interpretation of law, its application and best practices. The inability of states to agree on a voluntary forum for regular discussions on IHL was seen by many as a sad and characteristic demonstration of the unwillingness of states to simply sit down and engage in structured discussions on IHL and their lack of interest in adopting procedures that would contribute to better respect of IHL.

The idea of the present article was triggered by the outcome of the Compliance process and attempted to demonstrate that the disagreement between states regarding the Compliance process does not necessarily mean that all is lost. While a regular meeting of states would have greatly contributed to a lively discussion on new challenges to the application of and compliance with IHL, there are many other mechanisms available that directly or indirectly contribute to compliance with IHL, both within the frameworks of IHL and beyond. It would be therefore important for states to map these mechanisms and to make better use of them.

The cornerstone of a successful application of IHL is that states and groups who are participating in conflicts understand the rules and enforce such rules within their own structures. Understanding the rules means that there is a general agreement on the contents, as well as on how to apply them in contemporary conflicts. Enforcing the rules means that there are internal structures available for enforcing them, both among and besides the armed actors. These require adequate and custom-built training, and an effective enforcement mechanism, as well as the will of states and armed groups to face their own failures and investigate them.

If we look at earlier projects, such as the Guidelines on direct participation in hostilities or the Montreux Document, even considering that not all states were happy with the outcome of such processes, we are already witnessing a huge amount of work, involving states, academics, practitioners and IGOs/NGOs from various geographic regions discussing specific IHL issues. Maybe states should continue with a step-by-step approach, with discussions centered around specific topics. We must also realize that even if such discussions result in heated arguments and disagreements, it is still a discussion on IHL. At the same time, we must not deceive ourselves. IHL violations will occur as long as armed conflicts exist. The best we can do is keep IHL on the agenda, and initiate procedures that assist in our common understanding of the rules, their application, and generally in raising awareness for IHL.

12 TO THE MARGIN OF THE THEORY OF A NEW TYPE OF WARFARE

Examining Certain Aspects of Cyber Warfare

Ádám Farkas – Roland Kelemen[*]

Keywords

new types of security challenges, cyberspace, cyber warfare, cyber attack, cyber defense

Abstract

In the second half of the 20th century, humanity went through an unprecedented technical and technological development. As a result, technological innovations emerged in the course of the last third of the century which have now become indispensable parts of everyday life, the whole society and even the state. Among them, we must mention the IT sector, which has effectively enabled global contacts and communication between people and organizations across different parts of the world through various tools, programs and networks. Moreover, it also facilitates and simplifies everyday tasks both in the private and the public sector. Cyberspace is a unique and complex phenomenon, since it can be described with physical and geographical concepts, but in addition, its virtual features also have extraordinary relevance. As a result of its remarkable expansion, fundamental areas such as sociology, geopolitics, security policy or warfare must also be reconsidered. This paper provides an overview of the new types of security challenges for the 21st century, most notably security risks related to the cyberspace. In addition, some aspects of cyber warfare, such as cyber intelligence, cyber attack and cyber defense are examined. Particular attention is given to the question whether a cyber attack in itself can reach the level of an armed attack, and if so, what means can be used by the State under attack in defense.

12.1 INTRODUCTION

Over the past decades, one of the most important novelties in the field of military technology and warfare was the appearance of cyber warfare and the cyber battlefield. At the same

---

*   Ádám Farkas: 1st Lieutenant of the Hungarian Defence Forces; associate professor, National University of Public Service, Budapest. Roland Kelemen: assistant lecturer, Széchenyi István University, Győr; assistant research fellow, National University of Public Service, Budapest.

time – endangering the very existence of the state – it poses perhaps the biggest security risk. Billions of civilians are present on this cyber battlefield – not unlike the traditional battlefields. But the scene is different, with hacktivists and terrorists engaging in partisan tactics hidden among civilians, as well as the administrative and military bodies of the state.

The weight of the security risk may be illustrated by the thoughts of Dennis C. Blair, Director of the National Intelligence (US), formulated in his senate report. Here, he highlights the real nature of the problem, namely the vastly increasing cyberspace – which is becoming uncontrollable – and the associated vulnerability of the fundamental social, economic, state and military infrastructures.[1] This line of thinking is further reinforced by James R. Clapper, who said that the constantly expanding cyber technology and the dependent governmental, commercial, military and social subdivisions are constantly exposed to the danger of cyber espionage or assault. In his words, these will cause a 'cyber Armageddon', but can nevertheless result in significant harms and costs to the economy and national security of the US and, must therefore be taken seriously.[2]

Based on the above, it is clear that the phenomena related to cyberspace are extremely significant, with the potential to have a relevant effect on the conventional space. Consequently, it is clearly necessary to develop legal, military and security concepts in this area as well. In this light, this study seeks to describe cyber warfare as security risk, to define and characterize cyberspace itself. Finally, it also investigates how the rules based on certain basic concepts of international law could be applied to the aspects of cyber warfare.

12.2   COMPLEX SECURITY – NEW TYPES OF CHALLENGES – THE CYBERSPACE AS A NEW BATTLEFIELD

The 21st century has brought a number of security changes that can either be symptoms or just phenomena of trends. International terrorism, international organized crime, hybrid warfare, or even attacks and threats from cyberspace are all included in these phenomena. It is worth considering these on a wider horizon, with the multidisciplinary approach offering a possible framework to analyze these phenomena. This framework is a complex[3]

---

1   Dennis C. Blair, *Annual Treat Assessment of the Intelligence Community for the Senate Select Committee on Intelligence*, 12 February 2009, p. 38.

2   James R. Clapper, *Statement for the Record Worldwide Threat Assessment of the US Intelligence Community Senate Armed Services Committee*, 26 February 2015, p. 1.

3   The question of complex security brought about the renewal of security-related sciences at the end of the twentieth century. In respect of security police, it can be said that "the bipolar world order and the security architecture of the Cold War began to change rapidly after the fall of the Berlin Wall. [...] In his study of 1991, Walt highlighted the following areas: At first, security studies have to pay more attention to the internal political affairs of each state, as it has been shown that there is a close connection between the

understanding of security and a broader interpretation of the security environment of our age. This broad understanding shows that we must adapt the legal aspects of defense against security challenges.[4]

Before the end of the twentieth century, the key element in the security approach was the preparation for war and maintaining a military power. However, this has changed irreversibly by the end of the twentieth and the beginning of the twenty-first century. No analysis focuses on military power without considering inner relations, positions emphasizing the international element and the avoidance of war can no longer be considered timely. The internal and external spheres, or with other words, law enforcement, military, national security and broadly conceived state defense come together in actions taken against new challenges. The increasingly comprehensive approach in the NATO also serves this purpose, just like the expansion of the regional defense cooperation with various non-classical military – *e.g.* anti-terrorist – elements. The new types of challenges are not only multifaceted but affect both the nation state and the international level at the same time, since they cannot be handled at nation state level only. The new challenges are prompting renewal in approach of the nation state as well as the different principles, institutions and tools of international law, for these are becoming ever more globalized.

Now our world has become truly globalized, as there is virtually not a square foot on Earth that is not a part of the world economy system, one way or another, and they all play a part in the power competition. Besides, with the explosive evolution of info-communication – in addition to some attempts and ambitions of restriction,– a complete information space has also emerged with the cyberspace: a secondary plane of existence in the information society. As a result, the emerging logic of the twentieth century's totality can be further enhanced by these. Of course, there may be a revolutionary scientific breakthrough in the future that will enhance our present situation, but with the changes that have already been made, all boundaries of influence (of tools for attack) can be effectively eliminated. This would mean that welfare infrastructures immediately become critical infrastructures, and our society is exposed to new threats. On the other hand, all the benefits of publicity and the world wide web would be accumulated in the hands of terrorists or those conducting

---

nature of the internal policy's institutional system and the foreign policy behavior of the states. Secondly, in terms of peace and cooperation between states, the role of international organizations ad regimes is inevitable. […]. Thirdly, the strengthening of the constructivist trend in the area of security studies also draw attention to the fact that ideas can influence foreign policy behavior. Fourthly, the close connection between economy and security is unquestionable […]." Ferenc Gazdag (ed.), *Biztonsági tanulmányok – Biztonságpolitika*, Zrínyi Miklós Nemzetvédelmi Egyetem, Budapest, 2011, p. 18.

4   About its emergence in scholarly thinking about national defense in Hungary, *see* Ádám Farkas, *Tévelygések fogságában? Tanulmányok az állam fegyveres védelmének egyes jogtani és államtani kérdéseiről, különös tekintettel Magyarország katonai védelmére*, Magyar Katonai és Hadijogi Társaság, Budapest, 2016; Ádám Farkas & Pál Kádár (eds.), *Magyarország katonai védelmének közjogi alapjai*, Zrínyi, Budapest, 2016; Szabolcs Till, *A honvédelmi alkotmányosság 30 éve Magyarországon 1988-2017*, Zrínyi, Budapest, 2017.

a hybrid war, allowing them to reach a new level of propaganda, as emphasized by numerous analyses on the Islamic State[5] as well as papers analyzing hybrid warfare operations in Ukraine.[6] These phenomena were further enhanced by the challenge of cyberspace as a factor capable of supporting the majority of the forms of illegitimate violence, but they are also significant in themselves.

The importance of this – namely the information world – cannot be overstated, since it has changed our worldview completely, affecting our everyday life, in addition, it is the framework for influencing entire societies or social groups. Numerous scholars have drawn attention to this, among others, Manuel Castells and Nico Stehr whose thoughts must be mentioned in connection with the relevance of knowledge and information acquisition and refinement shaping our world. For Manuel Castells speaks of nothing less than the world of knowledge. Recommending some rationality, but with proper weighting, he states that

"The problem is that the futurists have confused us by that things what they imagined about the internet-based world. The world is indeed based on the Internet; but because of this, geography, history and institutions are not disappearing; places will be preserved, but in networked form, just like people and companies, and some states still operate on the basis of bombing their enemies. But without information, you cannot know who, what and where to bomb [...]. So, the main thing is that communication and knowledge are higher value-creating activities, but no value can be separated from the material world. The information itself and the knowledge itself lie in it, and that is why and how

5   For the terrorist organization called the Islamic State and terrorism in a broader sense, *see* Loretta Napoleoni, *Terrorism and the Economy, How the War on Terror is Bankrupting the World*, Seven Stories Press, New York, 2010; Loretta Napoleoni, *Terror Incorporated, Tracing the Dollars Behind the Terror Networks*, Seven Stories Press, New York, 2005; Péter Tálas (ed.), *A terrorizmus anatómiája*, Zrínyi, Budapest, 2003; Péter Tálas (ed.), *A globális terrorizmus: Biztonsági kihívások és stratégiai válaszok*, Nemzeti Közszolgálati Egyetem, Budapest, 2013.

6   With regard to hybrid warfare and especially the Ukrainian crisis, *see* Heather A. Conley *et al.*, *The Kremlin Playbook. Understanding Russian Influence in Central and Eastern Europe. Center for Strategic and International Studies*, Chatham House, Washington, 2016; *Russia's 'New' Tools for Confronting the West. Continuity and Innovation in Moscow's Exercise of Power. Chatham House*, The Royal Institute of Foreign Affairs, London; Mikkel Vedby Rasmussen *et al.*, *The Ukraine Crisis and the End of the Post-Cold War European Order: Options for NATO and the EU*, Centre for Military Studies, University of Copenhagen, Copenhagen, 2014; Andrew Wilson, *The High Stakes of the Ukraine Crisis*, at www.currenthistory.com/Wilson_Current_History.pdf; Dmitri Trenin, *The Ukraine Crisis and the Resumption of Great-Power Rivalry*, Carnegie Moscow Center, Moscow, 2014; Péter Tálas, 'A jelenlegi ukrán válságról 2.0', *NKE Stratégiai Védelmi Kutatóközpont Elemzések*, Vol. 3, Issue 8, 2014; Péter Tálas, 'Folytatódó ukrán válság', *Nemzet és Biztonság*, Vol. 7, Issue 4, 2014, pp. 63-74.

the Internet is important; it connects the material reality with the processing of signs."[7]

Grasping the very essence of the issue, he also points out that the totality of cyberspace is in connection with material reality, so it obviously has a repercussion for the material world, whether it is propaganda goals, warfare recruiting to the new partisanship,[8] express cyber attacks or influencing order. Examining the relationship between knowledge and freedom, and more broadly, the relationship between knowledge and the modern state and society, Nico Stehr takes a clear position in his immersive work stating that

> "I would like to define knowledge as an ability to act (acting capacity) as a possibility to 'make something to move'. The ability to act (in opposition to – habitual – behavior) is not only about the possibility of creating something in the meaning of material-physical performance. [...] This making-something-to-move can also absolutely relate to the ability to create symbolic products, for example to create a hypothesis, organize the literature of a topic or defend a thesis against 'new facts'. [...] The direct power of knowledge is manifested only through the realization of the ability to act..."[9]

By doing so, however, it means a significant power capable of influencing social and dominant relationships, has a defining weight in the economy in supplying population, in guaranteeing safety and in nurturing the scientific sphere. Putting something in motion can also be actually applied to the creation of symbolic products, for example, formulating a hypothesis, sorting out the literature of a topic, or defending a thesis against 'new facts'.

Twentieth-century totality that had unfolded with world wars thus gained a new meaning at the beginning of the twenty-first century. Namely, the separation of serious security challenges from the state took place in the globalized, networked, and therefore

---

7   Manuel Castells, *A tudás világa*, Napvilág, Budapest, 2006, pp. 138-139.
8   Carl Schmitt, in his work on the Partisan theory, analyzed partisans, and essentially described all non-state actors who depart from the logic of classical inter-state conflicts to challenge international peace and security. While he showed that partisans were tied to states as a consequence of interstate conflicts, in his work he expected that there will be a time when partisans will be separated from the state. However, this question was not analyzed further by science as he was shunned due to his Nazi years. Schmitt's thoughts, however, have drawn the basic contours of most of today's challenges, which can be interpreted as a new partisan approach, irrespective of whether they include radicals, international terrorists, cyber criminals, cyber terrorists or even hybrid warlords. This question emerges in respect of most challenges. As Carl Schmitt said: "The modern partisan is neither legitimate nor does he expect pardon from the enemy. He turned away from the conventional hostility of the war encircled by the defamed defense institutions, and took his way to another territory, the territory of the real enemy, which is intensified with terror and counter-terror right to destruction." Carl Schmitt, *A politikai fogalma*, Osiris-Pallas Stúdió-Attraktor, Budapest, 2002, p. 31.
9   Nico Stehr, *A szabadság a tudás leánya*, Gondolat, Budapest, 2017, p. 21.

totalized world (including transport and information flow), meaning that a new threat horizon appeared, including cyber terrorism, Islamic terrorism and hybrid warfare. The challenges represented by non-state actors,[10] intertwined with the exposure of the economic, communicational and technical development and the exposure of the society coming from its addiction to infocommunication have fueled totality, and also confused military, law enforcement, national security and state administration boundaries of security challenges in the force field of complex security.

Thus, with the eve of the twenty-first century, total security challenges have emerged, which have no defining and unique attributes, but have complex characteristics related to many segments of security and also to the various sectors of the state's defense apparatus entrusted with upholding order. Another aspect is the escalating ability and the increasing mobility that can change the dominant character of security challenges within a short period time, including the system of tools needed to manage them. Thus, a domestic security challenge – be it the ISIS or the Ukrainian anti-government riot – can escalate within a short period of time into a conflict involving several states necessitating an armed and military approach (such as the nationalization aspiration of the ISIS in the case of Iraq and Syria, and the hybrid war in the case of Ukraine). This, following a relative resolution, requires co-operation, a comprehensive approach, namely civil-police-military-national security cooperation and even renewed international action.

This kind of transformation only intensifies when the evolution of the partisan –a group of phenomena caught under an umbrella concept – is coupled with changes in the world. As Márton Szabó writes:

> "Schmitt, however, describes the guerilla, the revolutionary and the terrorist as the three basic historical variants of the type in which the partisan develops from the role of the 'home's defensive primordial defender' into the character of the 'aggressive activist who tries to dominate the world'."[11]

He also underlined that

> "certainly terrorists signify the possibility of unregulated and uncontrolled violence; they represent the process of getting through the privatized struggle and the nature of the war that has been completely liberated from the obligations

---

10 *See* Erica Chenoweth & Adria Lawrence (eds.), *Rethinking Violence: States and Non-State Actors in Conflict*, MIT Press, Cambridge, 2010; Gábor Kajtár, *A nem állami szereplők elleni önvédelem a nemzetközi jogban*, ELTE Eötvös, Budapest, 2015; Gábor Sulyok, *A humanitárius intervenció elmélete és gyakorlata*, Gondolat, Budapest, 2004.
11 Márton Szabó, 'A politika fogalmának elmélyítése Carl Schmitt partizánelméletéről', *Világosság*, Vol. 44, Issue 7-8, 2003, p. 70.

of international law. So, the question is not how noble or insolent the idea is in light of which the terrorists are acting; but rather that they have a self-identity that makes the separation of armed struggles final, not even from the law and the state, but also from the civil society, as the terrorist occasionally kills even those whom he represents, what is more, he incorporates the suicide warrior into his system."[12]

Building on the thoughts of Márton Szabó, as a kind of thought experiment we could say that from the trope of total war the theory of total security challenges has been developed by now. This experiment was cemented by Carl Schmitt himself in his partisan theory, in the perspective and concepts of the final stage. Namely, he had foreseen the possibility that the partisan's interpretation framework must be independent from the state and its regular war, that is to say, as a non-state actor, he has to become an independent threat on the international stage.[13] However, this also means that the traditional role and the regulatory system of the states war can no longer provide an adequate interpretation framework for these challenges, which are not-only-state, or non-state challenges, but have international impacts. Based on the above, the total security challenges are the following: (i) they can generate and combine threats in all spheres of security; (ii) they use tools, achievements and rights for the benefit of the welfare society with the purpose of an attack; (iii) they can use significant living and inanimate resources to enhance the fight to an extreme; (iv) they blur the boundaries between the individual states and the acts must be treated by the tools of the government, police, military and national security; and (v) they are coupled with exceptional escalation factor.

In this scenario, the challenge of cyberspace should to be highlighted, for on the one hand, it may be an independent threat, and on the other hand, it will clearly be the part of the inter-state or state-driven conflicts of the twenty-first century, too. Cyberspace is now – in NATO's interpretation – a battlefield, so it is also necessary to map it in the regulatory system related to warfare, and at the same time shape the regulation of non-state cyber challenges and possibly the framework for action against them.

By now, the total war can be interpreted as the war being waged in surface, water, air and cyberspace that does not know the heartland-front line, nor does it know– or just with reservations – the civil-military confinement: It must therefore be interpreted as the final stage of hostility, and in a truly totalized world of complex security, it is to be complemented by total security challenges capable of breaking away from the total state. The only solution against these could be the re-thinking of protection and its adjustment to totality while

---

12   Id. p. 72.
13   *Cf.* Schmitt 2002, pp. 145-162.

also maintaining proper constitutional guarantees, and at the same time creating the opportunity for operational, rapid and effective action.

It is time to recognize that the total security challenges of our age have surpassed our nation-state defense solutions based on classical sharp delineations and our international legal instruments based on inter-stateness just like the total war surpassed the previous periods of armies' war in the twentieth century. As for the development of the state – according to the ideas of the good state and the good government – a comprehensive state reform, and strategic thinking with an aspiration for cost efficiency, in addition to the increase of efficiency are necessary. These require coordinated development and renewal is also necessary in the field of armed protection, including the reform of international legal instruments. This is not about radical change, but rather about the willingness to develop, since total security challenges require absolutely completely new type of task management. In fact, they did not strive for total rule. Just the opposite. The new types of security challenges are, in essence, combined with the earlier classical security challenges, and they even use these as tools. As such, the situation requires a new kind of approach and solutions in accordance with proven procedures, principles and tools. While all of the total security challenges build on every form of black economy, the commission of classical public law offenses, indications of various social tensions and conflicts, migration, the proliferation of weapons and organized crime, it cannot be excluded that they will try connect these with the proliferation of nuclear, chemical and biological arms and to the reinforcement of certain natural threats in order to have a social impact and ultimately, to carry out an attack.[14]

In this altered security force field it seems obvious that the challenges driven by states or non-state participants who are acting individually in major powers' buffer zones, as well as the cyber challenges which constitute individual challenges in many respects, and also support actions that endanger international peace and security in many respects are those, which require increased attention. Dealing with the former was inspired in many ways by increasing international terrorism since the 2000s, gaining new impetus by hybrid warfare. In the latter case, however, we believe that there are many fundamental questions to be clarified, investigated and explored, further underlined by the fact that cyberspace is now officially a battlefield in the thought system of the world's largest military alliance.

---

14   For more information on classic security challenges *see* Péter Deák, *Biztonságpolitikai kézikönyv*, Osiris, Budapest, 2007; Béla Galló, *A túlélés tudománya*, Helikon, Budapest, 2000.

12.3   A Draft Conceptual Overview of Cyberspace and Cyber Warfare

Cyberspace and its processes "radically change social, cultural, political, institutional and economic life."[15] This statement is absolutely right in that today's modern state apparatus, military, social network, economic life and people in their daily lives are 'managing' essential vital functions through cyberspace, changing their centuries-old dynamics. The social tensions of the traditional space – be they political, religious, ideological or criminological – also appear in this global internal cyberspace. Meanwhile, these tensions in these personalized global communities appear with increased intensity. The increasing social tension is also manifested in social movements, setting their own tools: globalizing technology and culture in opposition to the networking world. Thus, exploiting the opportunities offered by cyberspace, some terrorist organizations reinforce their transnational character and emerge as a new hybrid security problem and challenge.[16]

This security problem is compounded by the fact that certain economic and financial factors, as well as the institutions of nation-state and supranational communities are connected to the global cyberspace. Thus, the above-mentioned actors connected to cyberspace may also become a direct target of interstate conflicts, the conflicts themselves stemming from social tension.

Taking these circumstances into account, for the sake of the protection and safety of cyberspace, and as a corollary the traditional space, it is necessary that the armed defense systems of individual spaces, including their military-like bodies[17] – and researchers of this area – create their own cyberspace concepts, thereby helping the organizations to define their role and place in cyberspace processes. The need for this narrow interpretation of cyberspace is also confirmed by the fact that

> "anyone can put an end to life with information [...] because devices connected to Internet and telecommunication networks can lead to the same result as weapons do [...] the instrument, scale and social impact of destruction can be compared more likely to the legally-only judged consequences of wars or industrial and natural disasters."[18]

---

15   Martin Dodge & Rob Kitchin, *Mapping Cyberspace*, Routledge, London-New York, 2001, pp. 1-33.

16   *See* Sándor Magyar & László Simon, 'A terrorizmus és indirekt hadviselés az EU kibertérben', *Szakmai Szemle*, Vol. 15, Issue 4, 2017, pp. 57-68; László Simon & Sándor Magyar, 'A terrorizmus és indirekt hatása a kibertérben', *Nemzetbiztonsági Szemle*, Vol. 5, Issue 3, 2017, pp. 89-101.

17   On the concept of military-like bodies, *see* Ádám Farkas, 'A katonai büntetőjog és igazságszolgáltatás helye, szerepe, létjogosultsága az állam és társadalom rendszereiben', *Hadtudomány*, Vol. 22, Online issue, 2012, pp. 3-6.

18   László Simon, 'Az információ mint fegyver?', *Szakmai Szemle*, Vol. 14, Issue 1, 2016, pp. 34 and 41-42.

Recognizing this, NATO classified cyberspace as the fourth battlefield. In their work, Steve Winterfeld and Jason Andress said that in cyberspace, the battlefield includes networks, computers, hardware (this includes weapon systems with embedded computer chips), software (developed commercially and by the government), applications (like command and control systems), protocols, mobile devices and people that run them.[19] According to the definition by the US Department of Defense, cyberspace is

> "a global domain within the information environment consisting of the inter-dependent network of information technology infrastructures and resident data, including the Internet, telecommunications networks, computer systems, and embedded processors and controllers."[20]

Summarizing the concepts and features above, it may be concluded that this cyberspace is an ever-expanding entity, easily accessible to everyone but difficult to describe with conventional geographic space concepts. It has a real impact on the self-image of the individual and society, on social reflections and the global economy, and in this space, administrative and military-like organizations of the states appear as active players. Through this cyberspace, a massive amount of information flows through within a single minute. "It is clearly predictable that cyberspace systems are getting bigger, faster and more complex,"[21] but their vulnerability lies exactly in this complexity. Our traditional viewpoint on warfare was fundamentally revised when cyberspace appeared. As warfare changed, new equipment and warfare methods emerged, which cannot be considered as weapons based on their basic function, however many practical examples show that they may indeed be used as weapons (The case of Estonia in 2007, Stuxnet 2010). Operations carried out in cyberspace can be classified as information operations.

> "Information operations mean those coordinated activities which are capable of supporting decision makers via effects on opponents' information and telecommunications system in order to reach the aimed political and military objectives, besides they can also utilize and protect their own similar systems effectively."[22]

---

19   Steve Winterfeld & Jason Andress, *The Basics of Cyber Warfare Understanding the Fundamentals of Cyber Warfare in Theory and Practice*, Elsevier, Waltham, 2013, p. 22.
20   Joint Publication 1-02 Department of Defense Dictionary of Military and Associated Terms, at https://fas.org/irp/doddir/dod/jp1_02.pdf, p. 57.
21   Tibor Babos, '"Globális közös terek" a NATO-ban', *Nemzet és Biztonság*, Vol. 3, Issue 3, 2011, p. 42.
22   Zsolt Haig & István Várhegyi, 'A cybertér és a cyberhadviselés értelmezése', *Hadtudomány*, Vol. 18, Online issue, 2008, p. 2.

Information warfare became fully developed[23] around the time of the Gulf War.[24] The purpose of information operations is "to influence, disrupt, destroy or limit the decision making processes of enemies or potential opponents, and to protect our own decision making process."[25] In order to achieve these purposes, information operations are explicated in physical, informational and cognitive dimensions. During the realization of these dimensions

> "informational operations create harmony among pre-existing and those informational actions that were achieved through military means. Therefore, its components are made by these, supplemented by new features that appeared concurrently with IT innovation and their appearance on the battlefield (for example the appearance of computer networks on battlefields)."[26]

For these reasons the components of information operations generally are: *(i)* operational security, *(ii)* military deception, *(iii)* psychological operations, *(iv)* physical destruction, *(v)* electrical warfare, *(vi)* computer network operations.[27] So, as demonstrated above, one of these information operations is computer network operations, which is a subfield of cyber operations. Cyber operations can be further expanded to two more areas: electrical warfare and intelligence, but these can be interpreted as such inside a networked info-communications environment.[28] For this reason, in this study we will only consider computer network operations to be cyber operations – according to the broad social perspective – and we treat these two concepts as synonyms.

---

23   Some of its elements like intelligence or deception were already typical in the early wars of humanity.
24   Zsolt Haig, 'Az információs hadviselés kialakulása, katonai értelmezése', *Hadtudomány*, Vol. 21, Issue 1-2, 2011, p. 13.
25   Zsolt Haig *et al., Elektronikus hadviselés*, Nemzeti Közszolgálati és Tankönyv Kiadó, Budapest, 2014, p. 19.
26   Haig 2011, p. 18.
27   Haig *et al.* 2014, p. 18.
28   Id. p. 28.

Figure 12.1 **Warfare in the 21st Century (Based on the above-mentioned work of Haig et al. 2014; created by Roland Kelemen.)**

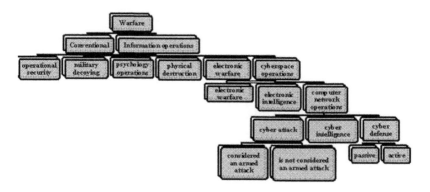

According to Zsolt Haig's definition, a computer network operation

"on the one hand is aimed at influencing, destroying or shutting down the opponent's networked IT system, on the other hand it is to maintain the operability of a similar, own system."[29]

Based on these, three areas can be separated: *(i)* cyber intelligence, *(ii)* cyber attack, *(iii)* cyber defense.

Figure 12.2 **Typology of Cyber Operations (Made by Roland Kelemen.)**

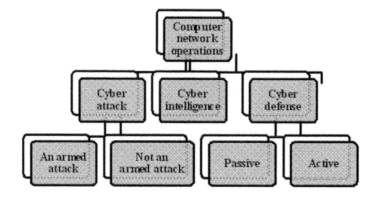

---

29 Zsolt Haig, 'Számítógép-hálózati hadviselés rendszere az információs műveletekben', *Bolyai Szemle*, Vol. 15, Issue 1, 2006, p. 60.

12.4   CYBER INTELLIGENCE/GATHERING OF CYBER INFORMATION – ESPIONAGE IN CYBERSPACE

The Hungarian cyber defense concept regards attack and intelligence as the same concept despite of their markedly different object and intensity. According to the concept's definition, a cyber attack can mean

> "an attack via cyber space aimed at interrupting, shutting down or destroying an information environment or infrastructure, or gaining its authority, destroying the integrity of data handled, or taking data out from under control."[30]

The concepts created by Zsolt Haig highlight the sharp difference between the two activities.

> "Computer network intelligence means penetration into the opponent's computer systems and networks via hardware or software, in order to access data and information that are stored in databases, and to use them for reconnaissance purposes. Computer network attack means penetration into the opponent's computer systems and networks via hardware or software, in order to destroy, modify or manipulate data that are stored in databases, or to make them inaccessible, or to make the whole system or network inaccessible. This attack can also mean physical damage, achieved by modifying or manipulating software."[31]

It is clear that while intelligence is nothing more than acquiring data and information required for an operational objective, the aim of an attack can be diverse from an operational perspective, because it can be directed at terminating the system or the disinformation of enemies, or to make those data inaccessible that would be necessary for the operation to make relevant decisions.

Based on our conventional military operational concepts, cyber intelligence[32] can mostly be considered spying. The handbook called Tallinn Manual – made by NATO experts (expert evidence) – also sharply separates intelligence and data acquisition from activities

---

30   Instruction of the Minister of Defense to the Publication of the Hungarian Army's Professional Concept of Cyber Defence 60/2013. (IX. 30.), Appendix 1, Section 2(7).

31   Haig 2006, pp. 60-61.

32   Such devices are the diversion of data transferred on Ethernet and Token Ring local networks by switching relays to promiscuity state, the devices aimed at cracking passwords, the L0phtCrack network monitoring program, the Server Message Block, and the Van Eck-Monitoring, which makes electromagnetic systems' electromagnetic signs perceivable (*e.g.* monitors).

deemed to be attacks, especially armed attacks.[33] According to the opinion of Katharina Ziolkowski, "spying alone is not against international law, so it is not an action that violates international law."[34] By contrast, Anikó Szalai states that "the first written international rights conventions of war (Hague Conventions 1899, 1907 and Geneva Conventions 1949, 1977) are actually not to prohibit spying, only the case when spies had been caught."[35] Furthermore, "international law does not contain almost any rules for spying, it is situated on the boarder of legality and illegality."[36]

> "The existing – uncertain – rules did not follow the technological innovations, and for example the Vienna Convention of 1961 about diplomatic relations can be interpreted to the current situation in spirit only."[37]

However, the responsibility of the spying country or individual can be established and the insulted country can take actions against it, but this action cannot be armed violence and only passive cyber defense tools can be used. Against such countries non-armed sanctions can be used only (political, economic, and diplomatic), meanwhile, punishment against individuals may be enforced.

12.5   CYBER ATTACK – CAN IT BE CLASSIFIED AS AN ARMED ATTACK?

Cyber attacks, as mentioned above, can satisfy a wide range of operational needs. Furthermore, in case of each attack, from the point of view of its legal assessment, the issue of intensity associated with the goal is extremely important, as well as the attributability to state(s).

Why is it important to examine these two criteria from legal point of view? To answer this, we have to go back to a *ius cogens* rule of international law, the absolute prohibition of violence. The absolute prohibition of violence covers not only war but all acts that are directed against the territorial integrity or political independence of another state, or manifests in any form of violence or threatening with violence are inconsistent with the

---

33   Michael N. Schmitt, *Tallinn Manual on International Law Applicable to Cyber Warfare*, Cambridge University Press, Cambridge, 2013, p. 55.

34   Katharina Ziolkowski, 'Peacetime Cyber Espionage – New Tendencies in Public International Law', *in* Katharina Ziolkowski (ed.), *Peacetime Regime for State Activities in Cyberspace International Law, International Relations and Diplomacy*, Tallinn, NATO CCD COE Publication, 2013, p. 456.

35   Anikó Szalai, *Kémkedés: nem tilos, mégsem szabad*, at http://drszalaianiko.hu/2013/11/22/kemkedes-nem-tilos-megsem-szabad/.

36   Szalai 2018.

37   Anikó Szalai, *Az 1979-es iráni forradalom éleslátása*, at http://drszalaianiko.hu/2013/11/04/az-1979-es-irani-forradalmarok-eleslatasa/.

purposes of the UN.[38] It follows from the definition of the term that the Charter prohibits all forms of armed violence irrespective of their weight, intensity and the nature of the weapon used.[39]

There are only two exceptions to the absolute prohibition of violence: the use of armed force upon the authorization of the UN Security Council and the exercise of the right to individual and collective self-defense. In the system of collective security, these binding decisions of the Security Council take precedence over the right to self-defense and its exercise. In addition, Article 39 authorizes the Security Council to introduce all the necessary measures in case of act of aggression. The Security Council is entitled to identify the act as an aggression, for which the Charter provides a wide margin of maneuver. This difficult concept is attempted to concretize by the UN General Assembly Resolution No. 3314, adopted in 1974. The decision defines the concept of aggression as follows:

> "the use of armed force by a State against the sovereignty, territorial integrity or political independence of another State, or in any other manner inconsistent with the Charter of the United Nations."[40]

The decision contains a list of the possible acts of aggression. It then states that this list is not exhaustive, and that the Security Council may also classify other acts as such. The significance of the decision is that it indicates the fact of that the intensity of armed violence is of relevance in international law, and that armed violence also can be committed indirectly. Finally, it reinforces the interstate nature of violence (here: aggression).

Another exception to the *ius cogens* rule of the absolute prohibition of violence is the right to self-defense, in respect of which the Charter declares that

> "[n]othing in the present charter shall impair the inherent right of individual or collective self-defense if an armed attack occurs against a member of the UN, until the Security Council has taken the measures necessary to maintain international peace and security."[41]

The basic condition for the exercise of the right to self-defense is armed attack, but the concept of the same is not defined by either the Charter or the subsequent documents, and therefore the classification of such an act in practice "is based on an extremely subjective

---

38   Article 2(4) of the UN Charter.
39   Orsolya Bartha, 'A fegyveres összeütközések fogalma, fajtái és elhatárolásuk', *in* Tamás Ádány *et al., A fegyveres összeütközések joga*, Zrínyi, Budapest, 2009, p. 20.
40   GA Res. 29/3314, The Definition of Aggression, Article 1.
41   Article 51 of the UN Charter.

decision; the same fact can be attributed to different classifications under the same law."[42] The subjective nature of the decision is reinforced by the fact that it is the resolution of the contested state that is relevant and there is no need for a decision adopted by the Security Council. Deeming this to be a condition would hollow out the essence of self-defense; even without this, the state can begin to use violence for self-defense purposes.

Armed attack is the only exception in the Charter where states or their communities have the option of using armed violence. "However, as the Charter does not include the definition of armed attack, there is nothing to exclude the possibility of using self-defense by analogy."[43] Armed attack must meet two conditions: *(i)* the act must have an extraordinary weight or intensity, and *(ii)* the act of the offending persons must be attributable to another state.

In determining the level of armed violence, the easiest way is to start from the concept of aggression, as both are a subset of violence. The ICJ declared that armed attack is the most serious case of violence.[44] "Because of this, only the most serious cases of aggression are classified as an armed attack."[45] So, these concepts are in a cause and effect relationship with each other. Another characteristic of an armed attack is that an attack must always be attributable to another state. So, armed attacks can only be committed by a state. It is obvious that if a state's regular troops commit an attack of a specific intensity, then in this case it will be classified as an armed attack. However, it is questionable whether the attack by individuals or their groups can be attributed to the state, and if so what level of relationship should this be? It is accepted that the acts of individuals and their groups can only be attributed to a state if they act under the instruction, guidance or control of the state. However, the level of control is not specified. In its judgment the ICJ in *Nicaragua* stated that an effective control was necessary,[46] while according to the international tribunal set up for investigating acts in violation of humanitarian rights in the former Yugoslavia declared that the overall control of the state is sufficient.[47] However, in the case of Bosnia and Herzegovina and Serbia and Montenegro the ICJ confirmed the principle of effective control, adding that the use of overall control as a criterion would significantly broaden the scope of the right to self-defense, which would be contrary to its original purpose.[48] In

---

42   Gábor Sulyok, 'Az egyéni vagy kollektív önvédelem joga az Észak-Atlanti Szerződés 5. cikkének tükrében', *Állam- és Jogtudomány*, Vol. 43, Issue 1-2, 2002, p. 108.
43   Gábor Sulyok, 'A terrorcselekmény elkövetéséhez használt polgári légi jármű lelövésének nemzetközi jogi és alkotmányjogi megítélése', *Fundamentum*, Vol. 9, Issue 3, 2005, p. 34.
44   *Military and Paramilitary Activities in and Against Nicaragua (Nicaragua v. United States)*, Judgement of 27 June 1986, ICJ Reports 1986, pp. 64-65, para. 191.
45   Gábor Kajtár, 'A terrorizmus elleni önvédelem a XXI. században', *Kül-Világ*, Vol. 8, Issue 1-2, 2011, p. 10.
46   *Military and Paramilitary Activities in and against Nicaragua (Nicaragua v. United States)*, Judgment of 27 June 1986, ICJ Reports 1986, pp. 64-65, para. 115.
47   *Prosecutor v. Dusko Tadic*, Judgment, Appeals Chamber, Case No. IT-94-1, 15 July 1999, para. 145.
48   *Application of the Convention on the Prevention and Punishment of the Crime of Genocide (Bosnia and Herzegovina v. Serbia and Montenegro)*, Summary of the Judgment of 26 February 2007, para 406.

the opinion of the International Law Commission, the desired level of control should be assessed on a case-by-case basis. "So, determining the responsibility of the state requires the precise knowledge of the details of the preparation."[49] In the light of the above, we must consider the following question: can cyber attacks be classified as armed attacks?

A cyber attack can be of several types; there are attacks which are aimed at disabling communication or making data or information inaccessible, while another group of attacks is destined for destruction; destruction of the system itself or the infrastructure controlled and managed by the system. "A cyber attack which is only intended to cause damage can be sophisticated or primitive, depending on the capacity of the attacker and the target of the attack."[50]

> "Hence, in the arsenal of warfare the instruments and methods of attack appeared in cyberspace – in the world of computer networks. At the same time, not only large, regular armies are capable of using these but also small countries which are much poorer in armaments and financial resources, or groups and cells that are driven by political goals or even terrorist organizations,"[51]

as well as some well-trained and well-equipped individuals. It is therefore necessary to examine whether the state has the right to self-defense in the case of an attack in cyberspace, and when can the attack be considered an armed attack? A cyber attack in itself is not necessarily sufficient to put a state in a position of self-defense because the intensity of the attack is one of the decisive factors. As we indicated above, there is no widely accepted concept of armed attack, but we can agree with the approach that attacks endangering the life of a large number of people or putting an end to their life, or those attacks that cause significant damage to the infrastructure can be considered armed attacks.[52]

Therefore, cyber attacks whose result reaches this intensity must be considered an armed attack. It is to be noted that according to the editors of the Tallinn Manual, cyber attacks should be compared to the use of radioactive, biological and chemical weapons,[53] which means that the authors are of the view that existing rules of international law must be applied by analogy.

In cyberspace, an attack leading to such a result could be an attack on a nuclear power plant or nuclear reactor, and there were several examples for this: the Blaster worm in 2003 and the Stuxnet virus in 2010. The Blaster worm caused a power outage in the US and in

---

49   Sulyok 2005, p. 35.
50   Ákos Orbók, *A kibertér, mint hadszíntér*, at www.biztonsagpolitika.hu/documents/1375084295_Orbok_ Akos_A_kiberter_mint_hadszinter - biztonsagpolitika.hu.pdf.
51   Haig 2006, p. 66.
52   Schmitt 2013, p. 55.
53   Id. p. 54.

Canada on 14 August 2003; "since the critical alarm systems has failed, the employees of the FirstEnergy have not stopped the series of events, because they did not know what was happening."[54] In just over an hour, the Blaster crashed the main server computer that operated the full alarm function, so the workers did not realize that the system's functioning was in danger, or even that the system's conditions had changed. It was fortunate that the Blaster did not carry out any malicious destruction in the infected machines, but only consumed their resources. The Stuxnet virus did not mean a direct threat to the power plants; its targets were the Iranian uranium enrichment facilities which had been so effectively attacked by the virus that it set back the nuclear program of the Iranian state by several years.

"The possibility that there was a state behind the Stuxnet is underlined by the fact that the software itself was very complex and sophisticated, and during its activity it applied a targeted differentiation in the scope of the pre-selected controlling systems."[55]

That 2012 case is less known, when a malware virus was transmitted to a power plant management system in the US that accessed all vital networks; again, luckily, the purpose of the action was not an attack. These cases reveal that attacking power plants with cyber instruments is not an impossible business; in all of the above cases if destruction had been the primary goal, it would have been achieved. Obviously, a cyber attack causing the destruction of a nuclear power plant would be classified as an armed attack by all states, and the consequence of the attack would be the same as the nuclear weapons' effect (nuclear radiation).

Another type of cyber attack is when the impact it produces does not reach the threshold that would qualify them as an armed attack, but the consequences of the attack can already go beyond that extent and therefore, the original attack may be classified as such. Such an attack can be one that attacks a state's drinking water system or water purification system. The direct impact of this attack is that the infrastructure is not functioning properly, but its indirect impact is the contaminated drinking water, which can have serious consequences for the civilian population. Such an attack was committed against the drinking water system of Haifa.[56]

---

54   Bruce Schneier, *Schneier a biztonságról*, Budapest, HVG, 2010, p. 144.
55   Tamás Lattmann, 'A nemzetközi jog lehetséges szerepe az informatikai hadviselés területén', *in* Zsuzsanna Csapó (ed.), *Emlékkötet Herczegh Géza születésének 85. évfordulójára – A ius in bello fejlődése és mai* problémái, Pécs, Kódex Nyomda, 2013, p. 211.
56   Benedikt Pirker, 'Territorial Sovereignty and Integrity and the Challenges of Cyberspace', *in* Ziolkowski (ed.), 2013, p. 56.

Such an attack may result in the deaths of tens of thousands of civilians, or it can have millions of victims depending on the size of the network.[57] In case of an attack like this, an analogy can be drawn with biological or chemical attacks. As both tactics are forbidden by a large part of the international community in multilateral agreements,[58] such an attack can be classified as an armed attack even in case of a small number of victims.

Unlike previous cases, an attack purely conducted in cyberspace that paralyzes a state's communication network can be classified as an armed attack, but of course the appropriate intensity is also necessary. As a result of this type of attack simulated by the US, "the controlling system of the attacked country and its functioning collapsed within two to four days",[59] which resulted in the dissolution of public order. The attacked country sank into anarchy, and its social network collapsed. The outcome is exacerbated by the fact that the attack "leads to distrust towards their own software running systemized tools and causes serious insecurity by raising uncertainty and decreasing the sense of security."[60]

A similar attack was launched against Estonia in 2007 and Georgia in 2008, which were not sufficiently intensive and lengthy to achieve the results above, but they predicted the system of such attacks, including the paralyzing of governmental bodies, the complete paralysis of the banking network, the police and military communication and then the civilian communication system. It cannot be predicted that how much infrastructural and humanitarian damage such an attack would cause beyond the economic and political consequences. There is also the possibility that in the event of such an attack the attacked state would not be able to exercise its right to self-defense.

According to the facts outlined above, it is clear that certain cyber attacks may be classified as armed attacks based on their intensity, but for this to hold water, it is necessary to examine the other criterion, whether it can be attributed to a state or not.

In the case of cyber attacks where a state body conducts the attack, if it reaches the required intensity, we can clearly talk about an armed attack. However, it is also necessary to investigate that scope of cases when individuals or groups of individuals commit attacks. Any of the three above mentioned elements, that is, guidance, instruction or control will mean that it can be attributed to the state. In the context of control, we can only imagine effective control in the case of the cyber attacks, since the application of the theory of overall control would, on the one hand, greatly extend the scope of attributability, and

57   Other circular infrastructures, such as natural gas network can be mentioned in this regard.
58   Convention of 1971 on the Prohibition and Destruction of the Development, Production and Storage of Bacteriological (Biological) and Toxin Weapons (158 states parties); Convention of 1993 on the Prohibition of the Development, Production, Stockpiling and Use of Chemical Weapons, signed in Paris on 13 January 1993 (184 states involved).
59   Zsolt Haig & László Kovács, 'Fenyegetések a cybertérből', *Nemzet és Biztonság*, Vol. 1, Issue 5, 2008, p. 67.
60   Lattmann 2013, p. 212.

beyond that it would obviously result in a restriction on the freedom of the internet, pre-supposing a much stricter state control.

It is necessary to examine what cases may fall within the scope of effective control. Since there is no international practice in this field, it is worth using analogy again and examining the practice regarding terrorist organizations. In Gábor Kardos' opinion, there is effective control in case of terrorist organizations, if the state provides resources, endures training bases or provides shelter for members of such organizations.[61] These criteria can also be applied to offenders of cyber attacks or their groups, with the addition that the provision of recruitment would also result in attributability. However, this scope of cases is questionable when the state 'only' knew about the activity, but has not done anything, or was not able to do anything. In relation to a similar case, Tamás Lattmann and Boldizsár Nagy noted that

> "the targeted state can act with violence if the territorial state is unable to control the attackers on its territory, and the international community (Security Council, in the form of coercive measures) does not act. Then defense is legiti-mate if it is proportionate and its implementation is in accordance with the rules of warfare."[62]

This category of cases also makes cyber attacks attributable. This is confirmed by the fact that

> "according to the current practice of states, rules on the use of violence and the right to self-defense are evolving in parallel in order to prevent the dangers arising with the use of violence."[63]

For this reason, it is necessary to take into account the mandatory standards of international law in the exercise of the right to self-defense, in particular the international rules of humanitarian law. In case of an armed attack, not only the right to self-defense, but also the humanitarian law will apply, including the "the *sic utere tuo* principle, the obligation of the states to prevent malicious computer activities that may harm the right of states."[64]

61 Gábor Kardos, 'Vannak-e jogai a terroristáknak?', *in* Péter Tálas (ed.), *Válaszok a terrorizmusra II. A politikai marketing csapdájában*, Mágustudió, Budapest, 2006, p. 89.
62 Tamás Lattmann & Boldizsár Nagy, 'Támadható-e Bejrút vagy Tel-Aviv?', *Élet és Irodalom*, Vol. 50, Issue 33, 2006, p. 2.
63 Zachary Newland, 'Collusion and Confusion: Evaluating the Right of Self-defense Against Private Actors', *Stellar*, 2009, at www.okcu.edu/uploads/arts-and-sciences/english/docs/stellar2009.pdf.
64 Katharina Ziolkowski, 'General principles of International Law as Applicable in Cyberspace', *in* Ziolkowski (ed.), 2013, p. 185.

In this category of cases, it is necessary to point out emphatically that attributability can only be confirmed solely and exclusively on the basis of the assessment of all circumstances of the case.

12.6   Cyber Defense, or Self-Defense in the Scope of Cyber Attacks

The normative concept of cyber defense is provided by the cyber defense concept of the Hungarian Defense Forces, according to which cyber defense is

> "the use of security measures designed to create cyber security against intentional impacts aimed to the designated critical infrastructural elements that can cause service interruption, termination or limitation, or unauthorized data handling, coming through a network or appearing in any other form. The most important tasks of defense are prevention, detection, analysis, evaluation, reaction, recovery and service improvement."[65]

The tools of defense can be divided into two main categories; passive and active protection.

> "Passive defense tools and methods can be firewalls, antivirus software, access control, intrusion detection and adaptive response tools. The following can be classified as active defense methods: pre-emptive attacks, counter attacks and active deception."[66]

From the viewpoint of cyber defense's legal assessment, the cases of cyber intelligence and cyber attacks conducted by a state must be separated from attacks and intelligence conducted by individuals and their groups, including terrorist organizations. State rules are defined by the principles of international law and the rules on the law of war, while the framework of actions to be taken against individuals and terrorist organizations are mainly set out by internal law rules, which must comply with guarantees laid down in universal and regional documents of fundamental rights.

In the case of states, passive defense tools can be used even in the case of cyber intelligence, and also in the case of both armed and non-armed attacks. However, active cyber defense tools can only be used legally in case of an armed attack and even then, only under specific conditions. The set of conditions are basic, *i.e.* the active cyber defense must be

---

65   Instruction of the Minister of Defence to the Publication of the Hungarian Army's Professional Concept of Cyber Defence No. 60/2013. (IX. 30.), Appendix 1, Section 2(9).
66   Haig 2006, p. 68.

necessary and proportionate, and it must comply with international law's current rules. The exercise of the right to self-defense can only serve to deflect and reflect the attack;

> "therefore, the use of armed violence should not be retaliatory, punitive or generally preventive of any future attacks. These are classified as self-help with the use of unlawful armed violence, or as unlawful armed repression."[67]

The principle of proportionality means that the violence used by applying the right to self-defense must be adapted to the extent of the armed attack in question.

The current rules of international law on self-defense deny the use of preventive defense tools or the use of pre-emptive attacks, so under no circumstances can pre-emptive attack-type cyber defense procedures be used, on the other hand, active cyber defense tools can only be used in the case of an armed attack and only until measures of the Security Council are implemented.

Figure 12.3   Typology of Cyber Operations (Made by Roland Kelemen.)

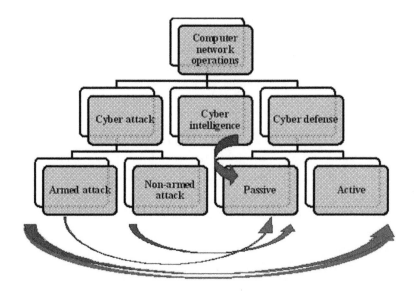

In the case of individuals, personnel actively involved in the attack and intelligence have to be separated from passive persons who provide resources. This separation also appears in the Tallinn Manual, which divides the individuals involved in the attack into active

---

67   Kajtár, 2011, p. 14.

offenders who demonstrate intentional attitude and into passive, careless offenders. In the case of the former, it declares that the civilian person loses his protection and becomes subject to attacks by IT and other lawful methods. These other legitimate methods have not been defined, however, since in this case too, the exercise of the right to self-defense can only be proportionate and reasonable, it is obvious that the use of these tools can only achieve the degree of contribution to the result. Otherwise a person may be eliminated who concedes the resources of his machine to complete the operation, alongside with hundreds, thousands or even hundreds of thousands of other users.

The Manual does not refer to any possible actions against passive offenders; this silence indicates that the attacked state is not authorized to take action against them. In our view in the case of exercising self-defense, cyberspace actions solely aimed at self-defense can be carried out against passive offenders to the necessary and proportionate extent, if this is indispensable to overcome the danger, but the responsibility of the passive participant cannot be determined for the armed attack.

The issue of pre-emptive cyber defense arises in case of both the active and passive circle of persons. Here, in the absence of international rules, in order to protect itself and its citizens, the state is able to prevent these actions – whether committed or not, but being at least in the preparatory or experimental phase – by possible pre-emptive defense tools to the extent necessary and proportionate. An example would be to prevent the activation of huge zombie networks or cyber attacks prepared against critical infrastructure. However, it is also necessary to emphasize the criterion of proportionality and necessity here, and the restriction of fundamental rights can only take place in accordance with the law.

12.7   Conclusion

The appearance of cyberspace and its worldwide nature made it possible for human society to become truly global and the existence of interactions that transcend continents and oceans within a fraction of the moment. This cyberspace is an ever-expanding entity that is difficult to describe with conventional geographic terms, and it has a significant impact on the life of individuals and the society and the relationships at large. Active players of this space are states that also claim a legitimate monopoly of policing this medium.

As a result, in line with conventional space, the state's administrative and militaristic bodies also appear in cyberspace, creating a new type of warfare in the twenty-first century; this is a specific type of information warfare, namely, computer network operations. Within this operation type, the triad of cyber intelligence, cyber attack and cyber defense can be distinguished, each of which can be identified by one single move of conventional warfare. Based on this, the exact rules of warfare applicable in this space to such acts are yet to be created. Building on analogy can be the way forward, taking into due consideration the non-standard nature of cyberspace, which requires a precise, appropriate regulation.

13 E PLURIBUS UNUM? RACIAL INJUSTICE IN THE US AND THE INTERNATIONAL RESPONSE

Thamil Venthan Ananthavinavagan[*]

Keywords

UN human rights machinery, prohibition of discrimination, segregation in the US, racial discrimination, UN Human Rights Council

Abstract

The UN issued a scathing report in 2016 stating that "[I]n particular, the legacy of colonial history, enslavement, racial subordination and segregation, racial terrorism and racial inequality in the US remains a serious challenge." After international slave trade, abolition of slavery, Jim Crow laws, civil rights struggle, ongoing systemic police brutality against African Americans and a prison machinery with a high prison rate with African Americans inmates the question remains: has racial discrimination ever ended in the US? The rising strength of a white supremacist movement poses another significant threat to the national cohesion of different communities in the US. Moreover, it reveals the dormant white nationalism that has awakened in light of policies and rhetoric animated and nourished by leading politicians in the country. To this end, this paper will investigate the following question: what is the impact of the colonial past on the US and how did the UN respond to this past? Finally, what will be the role of the UN to enhance the US human rights infrastructure for African Americans and ameliorate their situation in light of rising white supremacism?

13.1 INTRODUCTION

In 2016 the Working Group of Experts on People of African Descent (Working Group) visited the US, one of the many special procedures under the auspices of the UN Human Rights Council, in order to assess the treatment and situation of people with African Descent in the country. With their report, the Working Group concluded that

---

[*]   Thamil Venthan Ananthavinavagan: lecturer, Griffith College, Dublin.

"Contemporary police killings and the trauma that they create are reminiscent of the past racial terror of lynching. Impunity for State violence has resulted in the current human rights crisis and must be addressed as a matter of urgency."[1]

The current atmosphere in the US reveals a quite blunt manifestation of a deeply divided and troubled society, a society that is haunted by its past and offers a bare view of the remnants of slavery that preoccupies the public discourse and society's consciousness. The philosopher Frantz Fanon wrote that

"In divided societies, a behavior can be observed characterized by a predominant nervous tension leading quite quickly to exhaustion. Among American Blacks, control of the self is permanent and at all levels, emotional, affective [...] This division, which is called the color bar, is a rigid thing, its ongoing presence has something nagging about it."[2]

Slavery is over, but the roots of exploitation are still encoded into DNA of the US, revealing dark and twisted memories. The election of Barack Obama did not usher in an era of post-racial justice. On the contrary, it laid bare the unaddressed blood-soaked agonies of the past. In 2018, it seems that the US has never transitioned into a post-racial society as it is divided as ever before. What is, now, the role of the UN human rights machinery to address the past, to provide remedy to human rights violations and to help towards a post-racialized society? The study is relevant and timely, as it inquires the impact of the engagement with the UN, if any, while elaborating upon the potential of the international human rights machinery in light of rising white supremacy in the US. Charleston, Charlottesville and now El Paso are painful evidence of the dormant white supremacist movement that has found encouragement in the public debate.[3] Moreover, the killings of Trayvon Martin, Michael Brown, Eric Garner, Sara Bland and many others sparked a debate on radicalized police violence and the lack of accountability. This, in turn led to decrease in the trust in the police among African Americans[4] and the rise of the Black Lives Matter Movement.[5]

---

1   UNGA, *Report of the Working Group of Experts on People of African Descent on its Mission to the United States of America*, A/HRC/33/61/Add.2, para. 68.

2   Frantz Fanon, *Alienation and Freedom*, Bloomsbury Publishing, 2015, p. 524.

3   Vera Bergengruen & W. J. Hennigan, 'We Are Being Eaten from Within. Why America Is Losing the Battle Against White Nationalist Terrorism', at time.com/5647304/white-nationalist-terrorism-united-states/.

4   Pew Research Centre, 'Deep Racial, Partisan Divisions in Americans' Views of Police Officers', at www.pewresearch.org/fact-tank/2017/09/15/deep-racial-partisan-divisions-in-americans-views-of-police-officers/.

5   *See* also Garrett Chas, 'The Early History of the Black Lives Matter Movement, and the Implications Thereof', *Nevada Law Journal*, Vol. 18, Issue 3, 2018, pp. 1091-1112.

As the Anti-Defamation League noted, from 2009 through 2018, the far right has been responsible for 73% of domestic extremist-related fatalities.[6] The paper provides an overview and analysis of the colonial past, the slave trade and racial laws and policies, and examines the role of the UN human rights machinery. The article also analyzes a selected interaction between the UN human rights machinery and the US and discusses the current race issue in the US. Finally, the article engages with the majoritarian resistance coming from the US to take heed of recommendations issued by the UN.

13.2   THE IMPACT OF SLAVE TRADE, JIM CROW AND THE RISE OF WHITE SUPREMACY

Slavery was introduced in the territories that today represent the US in the 16th century, much later than in Spanish South America and Brazil. The scope was to replace European and African indentured servants as the main source of plantation labor, at the time mostly employed for the cultivation of rice and tobacco. Between 1675 and 1695 the import expanded rapidly.[7] As the British Archives reveal

> "Portugal and Britain were the two most 'successful' slave-trading countries accounting for about 70% of all Africans transported to the Americas. Britain was the most dominant between 1640 and 1807 when the British slave trade was abolished. It is estimated that Britain transported 3.1 million Africans (of whom 2.7 million arrived) to the British colonies in the Caribbean, North and South America and to other countries. The early African companies developed English trade and trade routes in the 16th and 17th centuries, but it was not until the opening up of Africa and the slave trade to all English merchants in 1698 that Britain began to become dominant."[8]

Slavery's diffusion escalated throughout the next centuries, with an estimated 645,000 slaves brought in mostly from Africa. Initially slaves were forcibly settled in the coastal southern colonies, while between the American Revolution and the American Civil War most were relocated in the inland regions. By the 1860 census the slave population of the US amounted to four million, *i.e.* about 13% of the population, and was distributed within 15 slave states, mostly belonging to the south. The American Civil War led to the abolition

---

6   ADL, *'Murder and Extremism in the United States in 2018'*, at www.adl.org/media/12480/download.
7   Graziella Bertocchi, 'The Legacies of Slavery in and out of Africa', *IZA Journal of Development and Migration*, Vol. 5, 2016, pp. 13-14.
8   *The National Archive, Britain and the Slave Trade*, at www.nationalarchives.gov.uk/slavery/pdf/britain-and-the-trade.pdf.

of slavery in 1865.[9] British colonialism, in the end, did not use slavery for the creation of a colonial state on the back of cheap labor, but it created the conditions of white supremacy.[10] British colonialism has not designed slave trade – it was white British colonialism that was designed by and benefitted from slave trade. The wealth of the British Empire was built upon the racism and white supremacy – the seeds that flourish in the contemporary society of the US.

The evolving Jim Crow law, subsequently, was a racial segregation system, which operated mostly in southern and border states, between 1877 and the mid-1960s. Jim Crow was more than a series of strict anti-black laws: it was a way of life. Under Jim Crow, African Americans were given the status of second-class citizens.[11] Jim Crow helped to make anti-black racism appear right. Many Christian ministers taught that whites were the Chosen people, blacks were cursed to be servants, and God supported racial segregation. Many scientists and teachers at every educational level, supported the belief that blacks were intellectually and culturally inferior to whites. Pro-segregation politicians gave persuasive speeches on the great danger of integration: the destruction of the purity of the white race. Newspaper and magazine writers routinely referred to blacks as niggers, coons, and darkies; and worse, their articles reinforced anti-black images and ideas.[12] Two incidents in US history marked a change in race relations, namely *Brown v. Board of Education* and the brutal killing of Emmett Till.[13] In a climate of internationalization of the race issue, the world took more and more notice of the struggle of African Americans, with the forum of the UN.[14] As it is written,

---

9   *See* also Ira Berlin, *Generations of Captivity: A History of African American Slaves*, Harvard University Press, 2003.

10   David Olusoga, 'The Roots of European Racism Lie in the Slave Trade, Colonialism – and Edward Long', at www.theguardian.com/commentisfree/2015/sep/08/european-racism-africa-slavery.

11   Aldon D. Morris, 'A Retrospective on the Civil Rights Movement: Political and Intellectual Landmarks', *Annual Review of Sociology*, Vol. 25, 1999, pp. 517-539.

12   Ta-Nehesi Coates, '*The Case for Reparations*', at www.theatlantic.com/magazine/archive/2014/06/the-case-for-reparations/361631/. Aldon Morris explains further that the Jim Crow regime was a major characteristic of American society in 1950 and had been so for over seven decades. Following slavery, this became the new form of white domination, which insured that Blacks would remain oppressed well into the twentieth century. Racial segregation was the linchpin of Jim Crow, for it was an arrangement that set Blacks off from the rest of humanity and labeled them as an inferior race. Elsewhere I characterized Jim Crow as a tripartite system of domination, because it was designed to control Blacks politically and socially, and to exploit them economically. In the South, Blacks were controlled politically because their disenfranchisement barred them from participating in the political process. As a result, their constitutional rights were violated because they could not serve as judges nor participate as jurors. Id.

13   Id.

14   Jacqelyn Dowd Hall, 'The Long Civil Rights Movement and the Political Uses of the Past', *The Journal of American History*, Vol. 91, Issue 4, 2005, pp. 1249-1250.

"on balance, historians have emphasized the effectiveness of this strategy and viewed the movement's successes in the 1950s as 'at least in part a product of the Cold War.' Seen through the optic of the long civil rights movement, however, civil rights look less like a product of the Cold War and more like a casualty. That is so because antifascism and anticolonialism had already internationalized the race issue and, by linking the fate of African Americans to that of oppressed people everywhere, had given their cause a transcendent meaning."[15]

The Civil Rights Movement, indisputably, had a decisive impact on the enhancement of the status of African Americans, with a wide range of successes to present: the Civil Rights Act, Voting Rights Act and the Fair Housing Act are the few milestones among the many which can be contributed to the constant pressure exerted by the Civil Rights Movement.[16] Nonetheless, it is Antony Anghie who points out that

"slavery was crucial to the making of the U.S. and, more broadly, the modern world. And yet, international law's attempts to deal with that past and its aftermath seem inadequate and inapposite, whatever the progress that has been made in abolishing slavery. The experience of slavery offers us an epistemology, a framework for imagining a different world and a lens from which to continue to think of how oppression operates in the world."[17]

To this end, what is the role of the UN to rectify the ills of British colonialism inflicted upon the US that is still pertinent in its modus operandi?

13.3   The Role of the UN Human Rights Machinery and the US

The UN human rights machinery consists of two strands, the charter-based and treaty-based bodies.[18] The US has signed nine human rights treaties, while ratifying five of them. It has accepted the inquiry procedure to one treaty, namely the inquiry procedure under

---

15   Id.

16   Douglas S. Massey, 'The Past & Future of American Civil Rights', *Daedalus – the Journal of the American Academy of Arts & Sciences*, Vol. 140, Issue 2, 2011, p. 42.

17   Antony Anghie, 'Slavery and International Law: The Jurisprudence of Henry Richardson', *Temple International Law and Comparative Law Journal*, Vol. 31, Issue 1, 2017, p. 23.

18   Sir Nigel Rodley, 'United Nations Human Rights Treaty Bodies and Special Procedures of the Commission on Human Rights: Complementarity or Competition?', *Human Rights Quarterly*, Vol. 25, Issue 4, 2003, p. 883.

the Convention against Torture.[19] The focus of treaty bodies is to monitor the compliance of state parties to the human rights treaties and provide guidance and interpretation of international human rights standards.[20] In particular, the US has signed the Convention on the Elimination of All Form of Racial Discrimination on 28 September 1966, yet they had ratified this Convention only on 21 October 1994. One of the most important articles and an international standard to tackle racial discrimination is Article 2 of the Convention.[21]

The second strand is the charter-based body, *i.e.* the UN Human Rights Council (succeeding the UN Human Rights Commission) which was created in 2006. At its inception in 2006, the Bush administration refused to join the UN Human Rights Council due to various reservations the administration had towards this new body.[22] The UN Human Rights Council offers a wide array of human rights tools, – *inter alia* – the Universal Periodic Review, Special Sessions, Complaint Procedure and Special Procedures.

The latter mechanism will be subject to further investigation in this article. To this end, the UN Human Rights Council is entrusted to promote and protect human rights globally with its wide spectrum of human rights tools.[23] The US joined the UN Human Rights Council under the Obama administration and was elected three times to it.[24] In June of 2018 the Trump administration decided to leave the UN Human Rights Council.[25]

Meanwhile, the Office of the High Commissioner for Human Rights (OHCHR) has streamlined activities for the promotion of human rights.[26] Promotional activities are weaved through all parts of the UN human rights machinery, charter- and treaty-based bodies alike. Fact-finding, information sharing, cooperation, constructive dialogue, technical assistance, capacity building, peer support and review, can be effective tools in promoting human rights within states.[27] The problem, of course, is the human-rights protection

---

19   Ratification status for the US at http://tbinternet.ohchr.org/_layouts/TreatyBodyExternal/Treaty.aspx?CountryID=187&Lang=EN.
20   Rodley 2003, p. 888.
21   International Convention on the Elimination of All Forms of Racial Discrimination (ICERD), adopted and opened for signature and ratification by General Assembly Resolution 2106 (XX) of 21 December 1965 entry into force 4 January 1969.
22   *See* also Rosa Freedman, 'The United States and the United Nations Human Rights Council: An Early Assessment', *St. Thomas Law Review*, Vol. 23, Issue 1, 2010, pp. 89-128.
23   UNGA Resolution 60/251 paved the way for the creation of the UN Human Rights Council. UNGA, A/RES/60/251.
24   See the list of past members of the Human Rights Council at www.ohchr.org/EN/HRBodies/HRC/Pages/Past-Members.aspx.
25   *See* also 'The Art of the Empty Gesture: America's Spat with the UN Human Rights Council', *The Economist*, Vol. 414, 2018; *The United States and the Human Rights Council – A Tumultuous Relationship?*, Heinrich-Boell-Stiftung North America, at www.us.boell.org/2017/09/13/united-states-and-human-rights-council-tumultuous-relationship.
26   UNGA Resolution, A/RES/48/141.
27   Henry J. Steiner, 'International Protection of Human Rights', *in* Malcolm D. Evans (ed.), *International Law*, Oxford University Press, 2018, p. 797.

mandate. Developing and promoting human rights are aimed at the medium- to long-term. They require dialogue, cooperation and constructive engagement. Protecting human rights focuses on the short-term. States are far less willing to engage with protection activities because they impact upon the immediate situation within a country.[28] And a key weakness of UN human rights bodies is that, while they are set up for dialogue and engagement, they lack the teeth to effectively protect rights where a state is not willing to cooperate. Unlike the UN Security Council, human rights bodies do not have enforcement powers. Unlike international financial institutions, the UN human rights machinery does not have any leverage over states that fail to comply with their obligations. That is one main flaw in the system, and one that cannot easily be resolved. Ever since its establishment, the UN has attempted to rectify past ills to a certain extent, especially it tried to overcome the persistent ills created by colonialism and create favorable conditions for all human beings regardless of race, gender and creed. In this context it is necessary to highlight one passage of the Declaration on Race and Racial Prejudice, adopted and proclaimed by the General Conference of the UNESCO at its twentieth session, on 27 November 1978, which highlights that the member states are

> "mindful of the process of decolonization and other historical changes which have led most of the peoples formerly under foreign rule to recover their sovereignty, making the international community a universal and diversified whole and creating new opportunities of eradicating the scourge of racism and of putting an end to its odious manifestations in all aspects of social and political life, both nationally and internationally."[29]

It was Malcolm X who saw the potential force of rigorous human rights engagement and the international forum to advance the African American issue. In particular, his strategy was to dismantle the African perception of Black Americans as US citizens, while creating an identity of African Americans who are subjected to racial oppression and who are colonized by white people.[30] Malcolm X enunciated at a founding rally of an organization he wanted to create that it was essential to internationalize the raise issue by

---

28   Kirssa Cline Ryckman, 'Ratification as Accommodation? Domestic Dissent and Human Rights Treaties', *Journal of Peace Research*, Vol. 53, Issue 4, 2016, p. 583.

29   Declaration on Race and Racial Prejudice, Adopted and proclaimed by the General Conference of the United Nations Educational, Scientific and Cultural Organization at its twentieth session, on 27 November 1978, at www.ohchr.org/EN/ProfessionalInterest/Pages/RaceAndRacialPrejudice.aspx.

30   William W. Sales Jr., *From Civil Rights to Black Liberation: Malcolm X and Unity*, South End Press, 1999, p. 101.

"taking advantage of the Universal Declaration of Human Rights, the United Nations Charter on Human Rights, and on that ground bring it into the UN before a world body wherein we can indict Uncle Sam for the continued criminal injustices that our people experience in this government."[31]

This article does not warrant a lengthy discussion surrounding the UN human rights machinery at large and a discussion of the historical evolution from the UN Human Rights Commission to the UN Human Rights Council. The article will however, focus on two more recent engagements of the UN human rights machinery with the US: interactions with the Committee on the Elimination of All Forms of Racial Discrimination in 2014 and the visit of the Working Group to the US in 2016, its subsequent outcome and its potential impact of these engagements against the background of the past and in light of current developments.

13.4 THE ENGAGEMENT WITH THE INTERNATIONAL HUMAN RIGHTS MACHINERY

13.4.1 *The Appearance before the Committee on the Elimination of All Forms of Racial Discrimination*

Ever since the US ratified the Convention on the Elimination of All Forms of Racial Discrimination in 1994, it has submitted its state reports only on three occasions: 2001, 2008 and 2014. Long had been resistance in the US to adhere to international human rights standards – as Bradley points out,

"some conservatives in the United States, especially in the South, were concerned that the national government would use international human rights law to achieve civil rights reform that was otherwise beyond the scope of either Congress's authority or what the Constitution mandated."[32]

During an appearance during the Obama era, the state delegation pointed out to the protections in place in the US to safeguard aforementioned Article 2 of the Convention. To this end, the state delegation stated *inter alia* that

---

31 Malcolm X, 'The Founding Rally of the OAAU, 28 June 1969', *in By Any Means Necessary, Speeches, Interviews and A Letter by Malcolm X*, Pathfinder Press, 1970, p. 59.
32 Curtis A. Bradley, 'The United States and Human Rights Treaties: Race Relations, the Cold War, and Constitutionalism', *Chinese Journal of International Law*, Vol. 9, 2010, p. 325.

"racial discrimination by the government is prohibited at all levels. Prohibitions cover all public authorities and institutions as well as private organizations, institutions, and employers under many circumstances. For a description of the general legal framework and policies addressing racial discrimination, see paragraphs 142-175 of the common core document.

18. Recent laws relating to discrimination, including discrimination based on race, color, and national origin, or minority groups, include: *(i)* The Lilly Ledbetter Fair Pay Act, signed by President Obama in 2009, provides that the statute of limitations for bringing a wage discrimination claim, including claims; *(ii)* alleging wage discrimination based on race or national origin, runs from the time an individual is 'affected by application of a discriminatory compensation decision including each time wages, benefits, or other compensation is paid.' The law overrides a Supreme Court decision in *Ledbetter v. Goodyear Tire & Rubber Co.*, 500 U.S. 618 (2007). […]"

Rebuking this, however, Racial Justice Now! stated that

"42. The United States has violated Article 2-1(a)19, 2-1(b)20, 2-1(d)21 by not eliminating all forms of racial discrimination. The Court of the United States interpretation of Title VI of the Civil Rights Act of 1964 is that it forbids intentional discrimination. The law permits all other forms of discrimination including negligent discrimination. There is nothing on in the constitution that explicit limits discrimination law to intentional. Since most discrimination is based non-intentional conduct, the law permits most discrimination.

43. Furthermore, United States has blocked direct access to the court for disparate impact discrimination. In 2001, in *Alexander v. Sandoval*, the Supreme Court held that individuals could not sue for disparate impact discrimination because it was a right of action created through regulation. The Court held that the only recourse was to file a complaint with the appropriate government regulation. This could have been remedied by the passage of a law granting direct access to the courts. However, in the 13 years since that decision there has been no attempt to solve this problem by any president or the congress. This is devastating since most discrimination is disparate impact or negligent discrimination based on implicit bias rather than intent. Thus, the United States

has allowed a law to stand that perpetuates racial discrimination rather than eliminate it."[33]

Echoing this, the Committee noted in its concluding observation that

> "it thus reiterates its previous concern that the definition of racial discrimination used in federal and state legislation, as well as in court practice, is not in line with article 1, paragraph 1, of the Convention on the Elimination of All Forms of Racial Discrimination, which requires States parties to prohibit and eliminate racial discrimination in all its forms, including practices and legislation that may not be discriminatory in purpose, but are discriminatory in effect (para. 10). The Committee expresses further concern at the lack of progress in withdrawing or narrowing the scope of the reservation to Article 2 of the Convention and in prohibiting all forms of discriminatory acts perpetrated by private individuals, groups or organizations (para. 11) (Arts. 1(1), 2 and 6)."[34]

What becomes evident is that, while the US has enacted different laws to ameliorate the state of African Americans (and other minorities) this has rarely translated into feasible results. On the contrary, the heritage of white colonialism became an impeding grain in the state apparatus. Following this, the article will amplify the most recent human rights engagement on race issues, namely the visit of the UN Working Group of Experts on People of African Descent to the US in 2016.

13.4.2   The Visit of the UN Working Group of Experts on People of African Descent to the US

The Working Group was established in 2002 by the Commission on Human Rights with its Resolution 2002/68, one of the many Special Procedures under the UN Human Rights Council.[35] The creation of this Special Procedure was triggered by the World Conference against Racism, Racial Discrimination, Xenophobia and Related Intolerance, held in Durban, South Africa in 2001. When it adopted the Durban Declaration and Program of Action, it requested the Commission on Human Rights

---

33   Response to the Periodic Report of the United States of June 12, 2013, accompanied by the Common Core Document and Annex submitted on December 30, 2011, to the UN Committee on the Elimination of Racial Discrimination, submitted by Racial Justice Now!

34   Concluding Observations, CERD/C/USA/CO/7-9, p. 2.

35   OHCHR, E/CN/4/RES/2002/68.

"to consider establishing a working group or other mechanism of the United Nations to study the problems of racial discrimination faced by people of African descent living in the African Diaspora and make proposals for the elimination of racial discrimination against people of African descent."[36]

The Working Group's mandate, as established under the aforementioned resolution was renewed by five more resolutions.[37] In 2008, the UN Human Rights Council entrusted the Working Group

"*(a)* To study the problems of racial discrimination faced by people of African descent living in the diaspora and, to that end, gather all relevant information from Governments, non-governmental organizations and other relevant sources, including through the holding of public meetings with them; [...]

(e) To address all the issues concerning the well-being of Africans and people of African descent contained in the Durban Declaration and Program of Action;

(f) To elaborate short-, medium- and long-term proposals for the elimination of racial discrimination against people of African descent, bearing in mind the need for close collaboration with international and development institutions and the specialized agencies of the United Nations system to promote the human rights of people of African descent [...]"[38]

At the invitation of the Government of the US, the Working Group of Experts undertook a visit to the country from 19 to 29 January 2016. The members of the delegation were Mireille Fanon Mendès-France, Sabelo Gumedze and Ricardo Sunga III.[39] On this opportunity, the Working Group visited Washington, D.C.; Baltimore, Maryland; Jackson, Mississippi; Chicago, Illinois; and New York City. The Working Group met with representatives of several government departments and offices.[40] They also met hundreds of African Americans from communities with a large population of people of African descent living in the suburbs, as well as with lawyers, academics and representatives of non-governmental organizations.[41] The Working Group was, however, not given access, contrary to the terms of reference for special procedure mandate holders, to the Mississippi State Penitentiary

---

36   World Conference against Racism, Racial Discrimination, Xenophobia and Related Intolerance, Section II. Victims of Racism, Racial Discrimination, Xenophobia and Related Intolerance, p. 23.

37   For more information *see* CHR 2003/30, 2008/HRC/RES/9/14, 2011/HRC/RES/18/28, 2014/HRC/RES/27/25 and A/HRC/RES/36/23.

38   UNGA, 2008/HRC/RES/9/14, paras. a-f.

39   UNGA, *Report of the Working Group of Experts on People of African Descent on its mission to the United States of America*, A/HRC/33/61/Add.2, para. 1.

40   Id. para. 2.

41   Id. para. 3.

(Parchman Farm).[42] Concluding this visit, the Working Group issued its report to the international human rights community by presenting it to the UN Human Rights Council at its 33rd Session between 13 and 30 of September 2016.[43] The Working Group, not only describes the situation, highlights good practices, identifies the main challenges, but also makes concrete recommendations. This is, evidently, an important aspect of the Special Procedures: they provide an impartial and unbiased view of an independent expert view on human rights issues, offering an important venue also for lawyers to lodge urgent appeals and engage directly during on-site visits to increase the international attention of domestic cases.[44]

When issuing the report after its visit to the US, the Working Group acknowledged that experiencing racially motivated discrimination is routine for African Americans and it hinders their effective enjoyment of economic, social and cultural rights.[45] The fact is that a particularly heavy share of the burden of current economic changes is borne by poor African Americans, which is not simply an artifact of the uncompetitive labor market position of many black workers and the civil rights revolution of the 1960s has by no means eradicated racial discrimination in American social and economic life.[46] For example, the Working Group, through authoritative interaction with governmental entities and non-governmental organizations, established that the racialized history has its reverberating impact on the contemporary human rights violations. By way of example, the Working Group ascertained that

"the cumulative impact of racially motivated discrimination faced by African Americans in the enjoyment of their rights to education, health, housing and employment, among other economic, social, cultural and environmental rights, has had serious consequences for their overall well-being. Racial discrimination continues to be systemic and rooted in an economic model that denies development to the poorest African American communities."[47]

Not only here, but the Working Group ascertained problematic issues such as, inter alia, 'racial steering' leading towards gentrification of neighborhoods, limited access to healthy

---

42   Id. para. 5.
43   UN Human Rights Council, at www.ohchr.org/EN/HRBodies/HRC/RegularSessions/Session33/Pages/33Reg-ularSession.aspx.
44   OHCHR, Urgent appeals, at www.ohchr.org/EN/Issues/Torture/SRTorture/Pages/Appeals.aspx; *A Guide for Engaging with UN Special Procedures Mandate Holders*, FLAC Ireland, at www.flac.ie/down-load/pdf/guide_for_engagement_with_un_special_procedures_mandate_holders.pdf.
45   UNGA, *Report of the Working Group of Experts on People of African Descent on its mission to the United States of America*, A/HRC/33/61/Add.2, para. 43.
46   Id. paras. 50-54.
47   Id. para. 43.

food and precarious employment of African Americans.[48] But in particular, the Working Group dedicated an extended examination and observation of the justice system, by pointing out at one point out that

> "killings of unarmed African Americans by the police is only the tip of the iceberg in what is a pervasive racial bias in the justice system. The Working Group heard testimonies that African Americans face a pattern of police practices which violate their human rights: they are disproportionately targeted for police surveillance, and experience and witness public harassment, excessive force and racial discrimination."[49]

International standards offer a yardstick, a clear indication of what needs to be achieved to improve human rights in the US. It was Malcolm X who had enunciated that by referring to human rights (rather than invoking civil rights), Black Americans were in a position to internationalize their movement and take their grievances beyond the domestic jurisdiction of the US.

> "All the nations that signed the charter of the UN came up with the Declaration of Human Rights and anyone who classifies his grievances under the label of 'human rights' violations, those grievances can then be brought into the United Nations and be discussed by people all over the world. For as long as you call it 'civil rights' your only allies can be the people in the next community, many of whom are responsible for your grievance. But when you call it 'human rights' it becomes international. And then you can take your troubles to the World Court. You can take them before the world. And anybody anywhere on this earth can become your all."[50]

The Special Procedure mandates, to this end, to provide a "microcosm for the issue of rights proliferation."[51] The key aspect for them is to have some effect and provide guidance in a short time frame.[52] For this purpose, the Working Group concluded their visit with

---

48   Id. paras. 49, 51 and 55.
49   Id. para. 24.
50   Malcolm X, *Not Just An American Problem, But A World Problem*, Address delivered in the Corn Hill Methodist Church, Rochester, New York, 16 February 1965, at www.nationalhumanitiescenter.org/pds/maai3/community/text10/malcolmxworldproblem.pdf.
51   Rosa Freedman & Jacob Mchangama, 'Expanding or Diluting Human Rights? The Proliferation of United Nations Special Procedures Mandate', *Human Rights Quarterly*, Vol. 38, 2016, p. 192.
52   Rodley 2003, p. 907.

observing best practices and effective measures in the US,[53] but also offering key recommendations to the US to remedy the domestic human rights violations. A comprehensive reproduction of the recommendations will not be possible here. Among the many important aspects that were stressed, and recommendations were issued upon, however, was the need for transitional justice.[54] One recommendation is of worthy consideration

> "Community policing strategies should be developed to give the community control of the police that are there to protect and serve them. The Working Group recommends that communities establish boards that would elect police officers they want playing this important role."[55]

All in all, by being and "grounding themselves in situations of mural urgency, rapporteurs hold the potential to operationalize abstract human rights norms in specific domestic contexts, giving those norms practical meaning."[56] As it was illustrated, Special Procedures translate universal principles into localized solutions for change, while also having reverberating effect on the international plane.[57] Finally, visits of the Special Procedures, such as the examined one, make a unique contribution to the international human rights system, identify the crises and provide valuable international expertise to find solution to encounter them.

13.5 CURRENT CLIMATE ON RACE IN THE US

Race as a prescriptive schema, as established by early Europeans in the US, was reproduced and reinforced in the institutional and individual sphere. The question of race is also fueled and maintained by the current administration.[58] The former US Supreme Court Justice Thurgood Marshall made a nimble-witted assertion in his dissenting opinion in *Regents of University of California v. Bakke*:

---

53 For example, the Working Group welcomed the My Brother's Keeper and White House Initiative to narrow the educational gaps and increase African American livelihood chances, *see* UNGA, *Report of the Working Group of Experts on People of African Descent on its mission to the United States of America*, A/HRC/33/61/Add.2, para. 61.

54 Id. paras. 90-93.

55 Id. para. 108.

56 Joanna Naples-Mitchell, 'Perspectives of UN Special Rapporteurs on their Role: Inherent Tensions and Unique Contributions to Human Rights', *The International Journal of Human Rights*, Vol. 15, Issue 2, 2011, p. 243.

57 Id. p. 244.

58 Jesse Washington, *African-Americans See Painful Truths in Trump Victory*, at www.theundefeated.com/features/african-americans-see-painful-truths-in-trump-victory/.

"For several hundred years Negroes have been discriminated against, not as individuals, but rather solely because of the color of their skins. It is unnecessary in twentieth-century America to have individual Negroes demonstrate that they have been victims of racial discrimination; the racism of our society has been so pervasive that none, regardless of wealth or position, has managed to escape its impact. It is not merely the history of slavery alone but also that a whole people were marked as inferior by the law. And that mark has endured."[59]

Two distinct moments in history were missed to remedy the mark of racial injustice: first, the Reconstruction period following the Civil War and, second, the Civil Rights Era.[60] Unsurprisingly, the Working Group had pointed out to impunity, lack of accountability and absence of dialogue which create an atmosphere of distrust and further entrench injustice towards African Americans.[61] With, according to a recent poll, a majority of the population saying that race relations have worsened under the current administration,[62] Connie M. Razza poignantly sums up "social exclusion is a set of decisions and actions" by the "economically and politically powerful" to

"[deploy] white supremacist and racist ideas to further concentrate their wealth and power. They have deputized others – including people who are not white – to enforce the social exclusion of black people through simple and seemingly individual acts, as well as through sweeping rules."[63]

13.6   Majoritarian Resistance in the US to International Human Rights Engagement

Kathleen Cleaver elucidates that leaders of the US have attempted to "minimize the international, broad concept of human rights that motivated us and turn it into something smaller and less threatening."[64] Usually, any government will not approve on the report

---

59   *Regents of the Univ. of Cal. v. Bakke*, 438 U.S. 265, 400 (1978), Marshall dissenting.

60   Desmond S. King & Jennifer M. Page, 'Towards Transitional Justice? Black Reparations and the End of Mass Incarceration', *Ethnic and Racial Studies*, Vol. 41, Issue 4, 2018, p. 741.

61   UNGA, *Report of the Working Group of Experts on People of African Descent on its mission to the United States of America*, A/HRC/33/61/Add.2, paras. 31, 46 and 47.

62   National Tracking Poll Politico, at www.politico.com/f/?id=00000165-16f9-d25f-abef-37fbe0ca0001.

63   Connie M. Razza, 'Social Exclusion: The Decisions and Dynamics that Drive Racism', *Demos*, May 2018, at www.demos.org/sites/default/files/publications/Social%20Exclusion.

64   Susie Day & Laura Whitehorn, 'Human Rights in the United States: The Unfinished Story of Political Prisoners and COINTELPRO', *New Political Science*, Vol. 23, Issue 2, 2001, p. 289.

in its entirety.[65] However, as Mertus stated, the US tends to place its own sovereignty above international human rights standards because it applies those norms in a selective and self-serving manner, both domestically and internationally.[66] Finally, as one commentator notes,

> "abroad the US defended human rights in helping defeat brutal dictatorships in the world wars and leading subsequently the free world. Yet no 'exceptionalism' is perfect. Today in the US far too much violence and shameful discrimination and social injustice remain."[67]

With the current administration in power, international human rights engagement becomes even more difficult. The far right is rising in an environment that is stimulated and maintained by white American exceptionalism. The advocates of the view hold the governmental power.[68]

13.7   CONCLUSION

Many community members, human rights activists, understand the impact and long-term consequences of trans-Atlantic slave trade, Jim Crow laws, lynchings, housing and labor market discrimination and police brutality, which figure in the contemporary discourse in the US. The international community, predominantly epitomized by the UN human rights machinery, can and must concentrate on decreasing the gravity and scope of racist practices, prevailing racial injustice and the extent to which their effects continue to this day. The UN offers solutions, ideas, innovations in a communitarian spirit where dialogue prevails, and engagement means support and understanding. The impetus provided by the human rights engagement must usher in follow-up efforts on the ground.

---

65   US Mission to Geneva, Dialogue with Working Group of Experts on People of African Descent: "[T]he United States has made great progress toward countering racial discrimination, xenophobia, and related forms of intolerance, but we acknowledge much remains to be done. Although we may not agree with all of its factual or legal conclusions, we thank the Working Group for its findings from its constructive visit.", at www.geneva.usmission.gov/2016/09/26/dialogue-with-working-group-of-experts-on-people-of-african-descent/.

66   Julie Mertus, *Bait and Switch: Human Rights and U.S. Foreign Policy*, Routledge, 2014, p. 33.

67   Donald McKale, *Opinion: American Exceptionalism Hijacked by Chauvinism*, at www.eu.greenvilleonline.com/story/opinion/2018/04/30/opinion-american-exceptionalism-hijacked-chauvinism/559128002/.

68   *See* also Serge Ricard, 'The Trump Phenomenon and the Racialization of American Politics', *Revue LISA/LISA e-journal*, Vol. 16, Issue 2, 2018.

These follow-up efforts, eventually, must translate into local organizing efforts.[69] Lawyers, activists, academics, community organizers *et al.* must be all involved in this endeavor so that international human rights engagement can make meaningful impact. The schism between internationalists and isolationists in the US over the UN's human rights intervention, is largely due to the suspicion over any alien intervention (a prevailing note that is prevalent in other countries as well), a reflex recalling memories of domestic challenge posed by civil rights groups, but in particular also with regards to a certain sense of self-indulged human rights superiority that exists in the US. Malcolm X wanted

> "the United Nations project as his monument-wanted said of him that he had renewed the link between black America and the mother continent and so had been able to bring the plight of his people before a tribunal of the nations of the world."[70]

The ideological basis for Malcolm X's UN project was premised upon the US' historical failure to guarantee civil rights to its citizens of color. In contrast to the US' questionable approach to civil rights, Malcolm X considered the UN Charter, the UDHR, and the Genocide Convention as an uncompromising resource for human rights.[71] Speaking with US Justice Thurgood Marshal, if the mark of racial injustice must vanish from the US, then engagement with the international community is needed more than ever before.

---

69   Justin Hansford & Meena Jagannath, 'Ferguson to Geneva: Using the Human Rights Framework to Push forward a Vision for Racial Justice in the United States after Ferguson', *Hastings Race and Poverty Law Journal*, Vol. 12, 2015, p. 154.

70   Peter Goldman, *The Life and Death of Malcolm X*, Harper & Row Publishers, 1973, p. 240.

71   Charles Lewis III Nier, 'Guilty as Charged: Malcolm X and His Vision of Racial Justice for African Americans Through Utilization of the United Nations International Human Rights Provisions and Institutions', *Penn State International Law Review*, Vol. 16, Issue 1, p. 189.

14 ECtHR Advisory Opinion and Response to Formal Requests Given by the Jurisconsult

*Tamás Tóth**

Keywords

ECtHR advisory opinion, Protocol No. 16 ECHR, Superior Courts Network, Article 47 ECHR, interaction between courts

Abstract

The aim of this article is to present the role of the Superior Courts Network (SCN) launched by the ECtHR in preparation of national request for an advisory opinion issued by the ECtHR. The actuality of the topic is given by Protocol No. 16 of the ECHR that entered into force on 1 August 2018 and the issuance of the first advisory opinion published on 10 April 2019. Hungary has not acceded to Protocol No. 16, so this option is currently not available for the Hungarian courts. Actually, there is another way to assist the domestic courts in understanding the principles of the ECtHR's case-law that are relevant to the case pending before them. This option is the so-called formal request for case-law information that could be submitted by a national court to the Directorate of Jurisconsult of the Registry of ECtHR with the help of SCN. Later, after acceding to Protocol No. 16, this channel of information could be helpful in preparation of request for advisory opinion.

14.1 Introduction

Advisory opinions are well-known legal instruments not only in domestic jurisprudence but also in international legal practice. Such opinions usually serve as guidance for natural or legal persons on a point of law. They are legally binding on the requester only if the relevant legal provision provides for this. Advisory opinions were issued by several international courts, such as the ICJ, the Permanent Court of International Justice, the Inter-American Court of Human Rights, the International Tribunal for the Law of the Sea, the

---

*   Tamás Tóth: chief counselor, Constitutional Court of Hungary; National Focal Point of the Superior Courts Network.

CJEU and the ECtHR too.[1] This article focuses on the practice of the ECtHR, where a certain type of advisory opinion was also known earlier.

14.2 The ECtHR's Advisory Opinions

14.2.1   Advisory Opinions under Article 47

Article 47 of the ECHR states that "the Court may, at the request of the Committee of Ministers, give advisory opinions on legal questions concerning the interpretation of the Convention and the Protocols thereto" (advisory opinion under Article 47). This type of advisory opinion – as to the conditions of submission and the procedure – significantly differs from the advisory opinion introduced by Protocol No. 16.

The Committee of Ministers is entitled to initiate advisory opinion under Article 47, while in case of Protocol No. 16 the requester is a domestic high court. The scope of the advisory opinion under Article 47 is limited, since essential parts of the Convention – *i.e.* the rights and freedoms – are excluded. It is not surprising that there have been only three requests for advisory opinion under Article 47, but one of them was not admissible.[2] The first request was rejected by an ECtHR decision (A47-2004-001) in 2004. The ECtHR gave its first advisory opinion under Article 47 (A47-2008-001) on the merits on 12 February 2008, and the second opinion (A47-2010-001) was issued on 22 January 2010.

14.2.1.1   First Request for an Advisory Opinion under Article 47 (A47-2004-001)

The first request for an advisory opinion under Article 47 was inadmissible. The Convention on Human Rights and Fundamental Freedoms of the Commonwealth of Independent States (the CIS Convention) was opened for signature on 26 May 1995 and came into force on 11 August 1998. In May 2001, the Parliamentary Assembly of the Council of Europe adopted Resolution 1249(2001) on the coexistence of the ECHR and the CIS Convention. It considered that the CIS Convention offers less protection than the ECHR, both with regard to the scope of its contents and the body enforcing it. According to Recommendation 1519(2001) adopted by the Parliamentary Assembly on the same date, the Chairman of the Committee of Ministers requested the ECtHR in a letter sent on 9 January 2002 and addressed to the President of the ECtHR to give an advisory opinion on the matter raised in Recommendation 1519(2001) of the Parliamentary Assembly concerning "the coexistence

---

1   Anthony Aust, 'Advisory Opinions', *Journal of International Dispute Settlement*, Vol. 1, Issue 1, 2010, pp. 123-151.
2   David Harris *et al., Law of the European Convention on Human Rights*, Oxford University Press, 2014, p. 135.

of the Convention on Human Rights and Fundamental Freedoms of the Commonwealth
of Independent States and the European Convention on Human Rights." The ECtHR
found that the request for an advisory opinion was related to a question which the Court
might have to consider in consequence of proceedings instituted in accordance with the
Convention, and, therefore, it did not have competence to give an advisory opinion on
the matter referred to it.

14.2.1.2   First Advisory Opinion on Merits (A47-2008-001)

The request for an opinion arose out of the correspondence between the Maltese authorities
and the Parliamentary Assembly concerning the composition of the Maltese list of candidates for the position of judge at the ECtHR. Article 21 of the ECHR regulates the criteria
for the office of judges. According to Article 22, the judges shall be elected by the Parliamentary Assembly from a list of three candidates nominated by the state parties. As it is
laid down by its Resolution 1366(2004) and Resolution 1426(2005), the Parliamentary
Assembly expects that at least one of the domestic nominees should be from the opposite
sex. In 2009, the candidature list put forward by the Maltese government was rejected on
three separate occasions because none of the candidates was a woman. By letter of 17 July
2007 to the President of the ECtHR, the Chairperson of the Committee of Ministers
requested the ECtHR, in accordance with Article 47 ECHR, to give an advisory opinion
on the questions set out below: *(i)* Can a list of candidates for the position of judge at the
ECtHR, which satisfies the criteria listed in Article 21 of the ECHR, be refused solely on
the basis of gender-related issues? *(ii)* Are Resolution 1366(2004) and Resolution 1426(2005)
in breach of the Assembly's responsibilities under Article 22 of the Convention to consider
a list, or a name on such list, on the basis of the criteria listed in Article 21 of the Convention?

The ECtHR decided that it had jurisdiction to answer the first question, and that it was
not necessary to answer the second. According to the reasoning of the ECtHR, where a
state party has taken all the necessary and appropriate steps with a view to ensuring that
the list contains a candidate of the under-represented sex, but without success, and especially
where it has followed the recommendations of the Parliamentary Assembly advocating an
open and transparent procedure involving a call for candidatures, the Parliamentary
Assembly may not reject the list in question on the sole ground that no such candidate is
featured on it.

14.2.1.3   Second Advisory Opinion on Merits (A47-2010-001)

The request for an opinion arose out of an exchange of letters between the Ukrainian
authorities and the Parliamentary Assembly on the composition of the list of candidates
for election as a judge of the ECtHR in respect of Ukraine. By letter of 15 July 2009 to the
President of the ECtHR, the Chairperson of the Committee of Ministers requested the

ECtHR, under Article 47 of the ECHR, to give an advisory opinion. The core issue of the questions was whether a state party is entitled to withdraw a previously submitted list of candidates for the position of judge in order to replace with a new list of three candidates and whether there was any time limit for it. The other aspect of the questions was whether the Parliamentary Assembly was obliged to consider the new list.

According to the ECtHR, the state parties may withdraw and replace a list of candidates for the position of judge at the ECtHR, but only on condition that they do so before the deadline set for submission of the list to the Parliamentary Assembly. After that date, the state parties are no longer entitled to withdraw their lists. If the withdrawal occurs before the time limit, the state party concerned may either replace any absent candidates or submit a new list of three candidates. If, however, the withdrawal occurs after that date, the state party concerned must be restricted to replacing any absent candidates.

14.2.2   Advisory Opinions under Protocol No. 16.

The idea of reforming the jurisdiction of advisory opinions has been discussed nearly from the very moment of its introduction. At the beginning of the reform of the ECtHR, the Group of Wise Persons was set up by the Third Council of Europe Summit in Warsaw in May 2005. The Committee of Ministers agreed on the members of the Group of Wise Persons and set the goal for them to draw up a comprehensive strategy to secure the long-term effectiveness of the Convention and its control mechanism. The Group of Wise Persons concluded that

> "it would be useful to introduce a system under which the national courts could apply to the Court for advisory opinions on legal questions relating to interpretation of the Convention and the protocols thereto, in order to foster dialogue between courts and enhance the Court's 'constitutional' role. Requests for an opinion, which would be submitted only by constitutional courts or courts of last instance, would always be optional and the opinions given by the Court would not be binding."[3]

This aim has, however, not materialized into legislative proposals until the Brighton Conference on the future of the ECtHR organized by the UK government in April 2012. The Brighton Declaration invited the Committee of Ministers to draft a new protocol

---

3   *Explanatory Report to Protocol No. 16*, at www.echr.coe.int/Documents/Protocol_16_explanatory_report_ENG.pdf, p. 1.

widening the ECtHR's power to render advisory opinions on request from state parties on the interpretation of the ECHR in the context of a specific case at domestic level.[4]

The new type of advisory opinion is regulated by Article 1 of Protocol No. 16 that summarizes the main features of this legal instrument.[5] According to this rule, the

> "[h]ighest courts and tribunals of a High Contracting Party may request the Court to give advisory opinions on questions of principle relating to the interpretation or application of the rights and freedoms defined in the Convention or the protocols thereto."

The requesting court or tribunal may seek an advisory opinion only in the context of a case pending before it.

Comparing the two instruments, we could find several important differences between the advisory opinion under Protocol No. 16 and the advisory opinion under Article 47. The main differences and similarities are summarized in Table 14.1.

	Advisory Opinion under Protocol No. 16	Advisory Opinion under Article 47
Requester	Designated domestic highest court	Committee of Ministers
Conditions of request	Concerning the interpretation and application of the ECHR and the Protocols	
	Question of principle relating to human rights and freedoms	Any question *except* for those relating to – human rights and freedoms – any such proceedings as instituted by the Committee of Ministers in accordance with the ECHR
	Pending domestic proceedings	
Competent forum	Grand Chamber	Grand Chamber

Protocol No. 16 has a dual purpose: the reinforcement of dialogue between ECtHR and the national judicial systems, and, on the other hand, the reduction of workload of ECtHR. Relating to the first aim – enhancing the dialogue between ECtHR and national courts –,

---

4   Kanstantsin Dzehtsiarou, 'Advisory Opinions: More Cases for the Already Overburdened Strasbourg Court', *Verfassungsblog*, No. 5, 2013, p. 31. at https://verfassungsblog.de/advisory-opinions-more-cases-for-the-already-overburdened-strasbourg-court/.

5   Protocol No. 16 was opened for signature on 2 October 2013. On 10 April 2019 – on day of issuance of the first Protocol No. 16 advisory opinion – there were 13 signatures followed by ratifications (Albania, Andorra, Armenia, Estonia, Finland, France, Georgia, Greece, Lithuania, the Netherlands, San Marino, Slovenia, Ukraine) and 9 signatures without ratifications (Belgium, Bosnia and Herzegovina, Italy, Luxembourg, Norway, Republic of Moldova, Romania, Slovak Republic, Turkey). The majority of the Council of Europe and those big countries that represent the majority of EU citizens have not acceded to Protocol No. 16, yet.

some sceptic views emerged at a relatively early stage of the debate. There are several questions to be answered, such as the guidelines of defining highest courts and tribunals, the relationship between individual application and advisory opinion requested in the same case, the appropriate stage at which to make a request for this opinion and procedural issues (anonymity, priority, costs, follow-up and publication of advisory opinion).[6] The most important problem could be that the ECtHR can only pronounce itself on a certain matter if all national remedies have been exhausted. During the often lengthy procedures, the ECtHR is not in a position to provide any guidance or to correct any faulty interpretation of the ECHR. Potentially, an advisory opinions procedure could enable the ECtHR to have a more direct impact on national judgments and could offer national courts a more concrete guidance at an earlier stage of the proceedings.[7]

The other main goal is the reduction of workload of the ECtHR. It is supposed to help hold domestic judicial decisions in accordance with the provisions of the Convention, so these cases will be remedied at national level. This aim is also doubtful according to some authors, because Protocol No. 16 will add even more cases to the already overburdened ECtHR. The Grand Chamber procedure is complex and long, and it does not normally deliver more than 20 judgments per year. The drafters of Protocol No. 16 argued that this procedure would not be adversarial, and it would take much less time that the procedure in any contentious cases. One can recall that, in the early days of the Court, its procedure in contentious cases was also not really adversarial, but it gradually became such. Moreover, the legitimacy of a procedure where one or both parties would not have an opportunity to present their arguments is questionable. So, one can suggest that even if the length of the advisory opinion procedure will not be as lengthy as a contentious case, it will be considerably burdensome, which can be detrimental taking into account the backlog of the Court.[8]

Later, some concerns and questions were answered by the Rules and the Guidelines issued by the ECtHR in connection with this type of advisory opinion. The procedure relating to advisory opinion according to Protocol No 16 is regulated in Chapter X of Rules of Court (Rules 91-95). Some important details are explained also in the Guidelines approved by the Plenary Court on 18 September 2017, *e.g.* such question was the schedule and timing for submitting the application (at an early stage of the procedure or not). The Guidelines says that "it is recommended that a request be lodged with the Court only after,

---

6 Open Society Justice Initiative, *Implementing ECtHR Protocol No 16 on Advisory Opinions*, at www.opensocietyfoundations.org/sites/default/files/briefing-echr-protocol-16-20160322.pdf, March 2016, pp. 16-18.
7 Janneke Gerards, 'Advisory Opinions, Preliminary Rulings and the New Protocol No. 16 to the European Convention of Human Rights. A Comparative and Critical Appraisal', *Maastricht Journal of European and Comparative Law*, Vol. 21, Issue 4, 2014, p. 638.
8 Dzehtsiarou 2013, p. 31.

in so far as relevant, the facts and legal issues, including issues Convention law, have been identified."[9]

However, the real answers will be given by the practice, but it seems that this procedure works despite of these concerns.

The ECtHR has delivered its first advisory opinion nine months after the Protocol entered into force (No. P16-2018-001). On 16 October 2018, the Court received a request for an advisory opinion from the French Court of Cassation. The Court of Cassation adjourned the proceedings until the Court would give its opinion. On 3 December 2018, the panel of the Grand Chamber accepted the request for an advisory opinion under Protocol No. 16, and on 4 December a Grand Chamber was constituted in accordance with Rule 24 § 2 (h) of the Rules of Court in order to consider it. The President of the Grand Chamber invited the parties to the domestic proceedings to submit written observations by 16 January 2019. The Grand Chamber delivered its opinion in writing on 10 April 2019.

During the procedure, the French Government submitted written observations under Article 3 of Protocol No. 16. The Commissioner for Human Rights of the Council of Europe did not avail herself of that right. Written observations were also received from the Governments of the United Kingdom, the Czech Republic and Ireland, the French Ombudsman's Office and the Centre of Interdisciplinary Gender Studies at the Department of Sociology and Social Research of the University of Trento, and from non-governmental organizations such as the AIRE Centre, the Helsinki Foundation for Human Rights, the ADF International, the International Coalition for the Abolition of Surrogate Motherhood, and the Association of Catholic Doctors of Bucharest, all of which had been given leave by the President to intervene (Article 3 of Protocol No. 16). The NGO Child Rights International Network, which had also been given leave to intervene, did not submit any observations. Then the copies of the observations received were transmitted to the Court of Cassation, which did not make any comments (Rule 94 § 5). After the close of the written procedure, the President of the Grand Chamber decided that no oral hearing should be held (Rule 94 § 6).[10]

As we can see, there were several interveners, so the issuance of such advisory opinion could be a result of a complicated process depending on the topic and it could be also time-consuming. The length of the proceedings before the Grand Chamber obviously varies depending on the case, the diligence of the parties in providing the Court with information and many other factors, such as the holding of a hearing or referral to the Grand Chamber

---

9   *Guidelines on the Implementation of the Advisory Opinion Procedure Introduced by Protocol No. 16 to the Convention*, para. 10. at www.echr.coe.int/Documents/Guidelines_P16_ENG.pdf.

10   *Advisory opinion concerning the recognition in domestic law of a legal parent-child relationship between a child born through a gestational surrogacy arrangement abroad and the intended mother requested by the French Court of Cassation*, No. P16-2018-001, 10 April 2019, paras. 5-8.

or not. So, this half-year duration of the Grand Chamber procedure in the case of the first advisory opinion under Protocol No. 16 was relatively short.

As to the merits of the advisory opinion we could find that the case concerned was very special. The main issue of the case was the possibility of recognition in domestic law of a legal parent-child relationship between a child born abroad through a gestational surrogacy arrangement and the intended mother, designated in the birth certificate legally established abroad as the 'legal mother', in a situation where the child was conceived using the eggs of a third-party donor and where the legal parent-child relationship with the intended father has been recognized in domestic law.

According to the opinion of the Grand Chamber in this situation the child's right to respect for private life within the meaning of Article 8 of the ECHR requires that domestic law provides a possibility of recognition of a legal parent-child relationship with the intended mother, designated in the birth certificate legally established abroad as the legal mother. The child's right to respect for private life does not require such recognition to take the form of entry in the register of births, marriages and deaths of the details of the birth certificate legally established abroad; another means, such as adoption of the child by the intended mother, may be used.[11] The first advisory opinion under Protocol No. 16 emphasizes that

> "[t]he aim of the procedure is not to transfer the dispute to the Court, but rather to give the requesting court or tribunal guidance on Convention issues when determining the case before it [...]. The Court has no jurisdiction either to assess the facts of a case or to evaluate the merits of the parties' views on the interpretation of domestic law in the light of Convention law, or to rule on the outcome of the proceedings. Its role is limited to furnishing an opinion in relation to the questions submitted to it. It is for the requesting court or tribunal to resolve the issues raised by the case and to draw, as appropriate, the conclusions which flow from the opinion delivered by the Court for the provisions of national law invoked in the case and for the outcome of the case."[12]

In order to make the advisory opinion under Protocol No. 16 useful and applicable for the domestic court, the requester has to prepare the request thoroughly. According to the Guidelines the request for this advisory opinion must contain not only the questions on which the domestic court concerned seeks the guidance of the ECtHR, but several additional elements, among them the relevant ECHR issues, in particular the rights or freedoms at stake. The case on which the first advisory opinion under Protocol No. 16 was based was

---

11   Id. paras. 1-2.
12   Id. para. 25.

the *Mennesson v. France* case,[13] so the relevant case-law could be determined relatively easily. However, there may be issues in which respect it is not easy to determine the relevant case-law. In this preparation work, the Superior Courts Network and the national request to the Directorate of Jurisconsult of the Registry of ECtHR (Jurisconsult) could help the domestic courts.

14.3   Preliminary Ruling Procedure and Advisory Opinion under Protocol No. 16

Preliminary ruling procedure provided for in Article 19(3)(b) TEU and Article 267 TFEU is designed to ensure the uniform interpretation and application of law within the EU. It offers the courts and tribunals of the EU Member States a means of bringing questions concerning the interpretation of EU law or the validity of acts adopted by the institutions, bodies, offices or agencies of the EU before the CJEU for a preliminary ruling.

The two types of interpretation procedure for EU Member States might cause a potential problem when a domestic highest court finds itself dealing with a matter of an EU law that could violate some provisions of the ECHR.[14] Article 52(3) of the EU Charter of Fundamental Rights and Article 6(3) of the TEU ensure the same level of protection of human rights provided by the ECHR, and the CJEU has frequently based its judgments on principles coming from the ECHR and used the ECtHR's case-law. On the other hand,

---

13   *Mennesson v. France*, No. 65192/11, 26 June 2014. The case concerned the refusal by the French authorities to grant legal recognition in France to parent-child relationships that had been legally established in the US between children born through a surrogacy agreement and their intended parents. While the Court did not find a violation of the right to respect for family life of children and intended parents, it did find a violation of the right to respect for private life of the children because their right to identity was affected as a result of the non-recognition, in particular as one of the intended parents was also the biological parent. The case-law of the Court of Cassation evolved in the wake of the *Mennesson* judgment. Registration of the details of the birth certificate of a child born through surrogacy abroad is now possible in so far as the certificate designates the intended father as the child's father where he is the biological father. It continues to be impossible with regard to the intended mother. Where the intended mother is married to the father, however, she now has the option of adopting the child if the statutory conditions are met and the adoption is in the child's interests; this results in the creation of a legal mother-child relationship. French law also facilitates adoption by one spouse of the other spouse's child. In a decision of 16 February 2018 the French Civil Judgments Review Court granted a request for re-examination of the appeal on points of law submitted on 15 May 2017 by Mr. and Mrs. Mennesson, acting as the legal representatives of their two minor children, against the Paris Court of Appeal judgment of 18 March 2010 annulling the entry in the French register of births, marriages and deaths of the details of the children's US birth certificates. The Court of Cassation's request for an advisory opinion from the Court was made in the context of re-examination of that appeal.

14   Giovanni Zampetti, 'The Recent Challenges for the European System of Fundamental Rights: Protocol No. 16 to the ECHR and its Role Facing Constitutional and European Union Level of Protection', *Discussion Paper No 2/18*, Europa-Kolleg Hamburg, Institute for European Integration, at http://www.europa-kolleg-hamburg.de, pp. 14-17.

the ECtHR shaped the presumption of equivalent protection or Bosphorus-presumption. This presumption means that the state party concerned could not infringe the provisions of the ECHR by fulfilling the EU obligation itself, because the EU ensures the same level of human rights' protection. However, this presumption has two preconditions: *(i)* the national authorities have no margin of maneuver during the application of EU law, and *(ii)* they deploy the full potential of the supervisory mechanism provided by the EU law. In that case the ECtHR does not exercise its power of review, except the protection of fundamental rights is manifestly deficient.[15] The main features of these legal means are compared in Table 14.2.

	Request for Advisory Opinion under Protocol No. 16	Request for Preliminary Ruling Proceedings
Requester	Designated highest court	Any domestic court
Issues	Question of principle of ECHR	Interpretation or validity of EU law
Domestic case	Pending before the requesting court	Pending before the requesting court
Binding force	Not binding opinion	Binding decision
Competent forum	ECtHR Grand Chamber	CJEU

At first glance, it seems that these principles could solve the problem of different interpretations. However, there are some uncertainty factors. The most important of them is that these types of interpretation could be applicable when the domestic procedure is still in progress. So, the central question for the highest court could be the appropriate order of these procedures.

If EU law must be applicable in the case, the right order must be to request for preliminary ruling first, but, in that case, there is also an important uncertainty factor. According to the *CILFIT* case and the *Da Costa* judgment, the domestic court may take into consideration the necessity of request for preliminary ruling. If the court considers that the EU provision is clear, it does not need to be interpreted in the meaning of doctrine of *acte éclairé* (*clara non sunt interpretanda*).[16] This margin of appreciation or circumvention of the obligatory submission of request could result some differences in domestic interpretation of the same EU provision and this situation could cause uncertainty in the interpretation of ECHR provision connecting to it.

If there is no questionable EU provision or there is no EU provision that needs to be interpreted at all, only the necessity of request for advisory opinion under Protocol 16 could be emerged. However, it could be also problematic. This advisory opinion is not binding either for domestic courts or the ECtHR. Applying the jurisprudence originated

---

15   *Bosphorus Hava Yollari Turizm ve Ticaret Anonim Sirketi v. Ireland*, [GC], No. 45036/98, 30 June 2005.
16   Blutman László, *Az Európai Unió joga a gyakorlatban*, HVG-ORAC, Budapest, 2013, pp. 439-440.

from the *Bosphorus* case, it means that, after the final domestic decision, the ECtHR could supervise the deliberation or assessment of the domestic court including its interpretation of EU provision and regarding to the advisory opinion under Protocol No. 16, too. There is a possibility that the ECtHR could supervise its former opinion with a view to the specific circumstances of the case. It is not surprising that the domestic court could call into question the usefulness of advisory opinion under Protocol No. 16. This could be a reason of reluctance of accession to it.

14.4   The Role of the Superior Courts Network

In his address at the Solemn Hearing during the opening of the Court's Judicial Year in January 2015, President Spielmann underlined the importance he attached to Protocol No. 16, the protocol of dialogue with the highest courts of the Contracting States. Even before its entry into force, reinforcing this dialogue was one of his priorities which explained why the President wished to set up an information exchange network which would enable superior courts to have a point of contact within the Court through which case-law information could be provided to them, under the supervision of the Jurisconsult.[17] The SCN is a new form of mutual exchange of respective research resources between courts. According to the Charter of SCN,

> "[t]he Network shall be set up with a view to ensuring the effective exchange of information, between the European Court and the national courts belonging to the Network, on the case-law of the European Court, Convention law and practice and the domestic law of States whose superior courts are members of the Network."[18]

On 10 April 2019 – at the time of issuance of the first advisory opinion –, the Network had 74 courts from 36 state parties. The number of SCN members is increasing continuously. Each member court must designate a person who will contact the SCN as a focal point. The so-called Focal Points are, both in the Registry of ECtHR and in the national superior courts, through whom SCN day-to-day exchanges are conducted. Hungary has two high court members at the SCN, such as the Curia of Hungary and the Constitutional Court of Hungary, so there are two national focal points. Every year, the Registry of ECtHR

---

17   *Introduction to the Superior Court Network,* at www.echr.coe.int/Documents/SCN_Introduction_Network_June2018_ENG.pdf.
18   *Cooperation Charter of the Superior Courts Network*, para. 1. at www.echr.coe.int/Documents/SCN_Charter_ENG.pdf.

organizes an annual forum for the national contact points in order to discuss together the functioning and future of the SCN.

The ECtHR has developed a dedicated website to facilitate the exchanges with member courts, access to which is restricted to the ECtHR and superior court members (the SCN Intranet). Within this space, the member superior courts have privileged access to material not in the public domain such as the Jurisconsult's analytical notes on new decisions and judgments, a weekly selection of notable decisions and judgments by the Jurisconsult as well as research reports on a range of ECHR subjects drafted under the supervision of the Jurisconsult. Beyond such regular exchanges, the member courts can also ask specific questions on ECHR case-law, responses to which are provided by the Jurisconsult (*e.g.* in the form of short research items). These replies are the Jurisconsult's sole responsibility and are not binding on the ECtHR in its judicial activity.[19]

	Request under Protocol No. 16	**Formal request in SCN**
Requester	Designated highest courts	Any domestic court assisted by focal points
Issues	Question of principle	Question relating to existing case-law
Responder	Grand Chamber	Jurisconsult
Domestic case	The case is pending before the domestic court; request must refer to it.	It should not refer to the pending domestic case to which it relates.
Output	Advisory opinion (judicial interpretation)	Short research item (a list of cases with short comments)

The second annual forum discussed the question of formal requests addressed to the Jurisconsult. The report on Second Annual Focal Point Forum contains that any questions on the ECtHR's case-law might require some preliminary work on the wording to ensure that the most specific response would be obtained. Courts which had already made formal requests expressed their satisfaction with the added value of the answers received, which at least allowed them to verify whether their own research was complete. In addition, the selective and structured nature of the case-law lists prepared by way of reply often helped to identify the ECHR issues better. Expectations as to a more analytical type of answer could not be satisfied since such an approach would render the answer tantamount to an interpretation or opinion, thus falling outside the Network's objective of information exchange. Nevertheless, the process of dialogue between the requesting court and the ECtHR, in the formulation of the questions, helped to fine-tune and adjust the result of that exchange.[20] The Third Annual Focal Point Forum was held on 6-7 June 2019, and the

---

19 Id.
20 *Report – Focal Points Forum of the Superior Courts Network, 8 June 2018*, at www.echr.coe.int/Documents/SCN_Forum_Report_2018_ENG.PDF, para. II/C.

SCN launched a new platform of the so called Knowledge Sharing. This new platform makes it possible to access to more different databases (guidebooks, short research items, reports *etc.*) managed by the SCN.

14.5   Conclusions

As we can see, the response for the formal request provided by Jurisconsult in the framework of SCN has its limitations compared to the advisory opinion. The formal request should not refer to the pending domestic case to which it relates, it is not a judicial interpretation of case-law, only a list with some explanations but it is not an analysis. So, it is desirable that the requesting court prepares and attaches its own research made by the help of HUDOC and the Jurisconsult could update and complete this research.

The conclusion of this article is that the new type of advisory opinion is an adequate solution to solve a well-defined, new issue of ECtHR case-law emerged in connection with a domestic, pending case and an opportunity for the domestic courts without any legal risk, so the accession to Protocol No. 16 and its ratification would be useful and fruitful for Hungary. Hoping that, after the entry into force of Protocol No. 16 in Hungary, the highest domestic courts will use this opportunity properly. In the professional preparation work of the request for advisory opinion under Protocol No. 16, the courts could be helped by the SCN and its knowledge sharing methods, such as the coöperation with Jurisconsult from the aspect of determination of the relevant ECtHR case-law.

15 THE EUROPEAN CHARTER FOR REGIONAL OR MINORITY LANGUAGES

Specific Features and Problems of Application

Gábor Kardos[*]

Keywords
European Charter for Regional or Minority Languages, protection of minority languages, protection of regional languages, supervisory regime

Abstract
As was the case after the Great War, World War II was followed by the setting up of international legal regimes to protect national (national, ethnic, linguistic, and religious) minorities in Europe. The emerging ideas of universalism and European unity were to prevent the aftermath of World War I, a conflict which erupted as a result of Western focusing the system of European minority protection on Central and Eastern Europe. The European Charter for Regional or Minority Languages protects minority languages, without granting minority rights. It provides an *á la Carte* system of obligations, with a supervisory system hinged on government reports. The Charter was intended to be a 'high politics' treaty. Nevertheless, with the protection of the minority linguistic heritage and the indirect provision of minority linguistic rights, it meant a first step towards bringing an end to the 19th century processes linguistic homogenization of the budding nation-states. As such, its implementation is highly political. The minority languages protected by the Charter are strongly varied in nature. If we add this factor to the *á la Carte* system of obligations, the sheer complexity of the system prevents evaluations of the Committee of Experts from being as consistent as they should be. An important contribution of the soft supervisory mechanism is that it at least puts some problematic issues on the agenda, however, experience has shown that the transposition of treaty obligations into national law is always a simpler task than creating the substantive conditions for the actual use of minority languages.

---

[*]   Gábor Kardos: professor of law, ELTE Law School, Budapest; Member of the Committee of Experts of the European Charter for Regional or Minority Languages. The views exhibited in the article do not or (do not necessarily) reflect the opinion of the body.

15.1 MINORITY PROTECTION IN EUROPE: GEOPOLITICS AND ZEITGEIST

Following the end of both World War I and the Cold War, international legal regimes were established to protect national (national, ethnic, linguistic, and religious) minorities in Europe. The historical circumstances of the times were different, of course, yet in both cases, geopolitical and *Zeitgeist* related reasons were the triggers for the emergence of international legal regimes. Perhaps the most important difference was that while World War I was followed by a large-scale territorial reorganization between states, after the Cold War, it was 'only' federations that broke down in Central and Eastern Europe, strictly within the confines of *uti possidetis*. Nevertheless, it is worth clarifying some similarities and differences between the legal regimes of these two periods.

Following World War I, the peace treaties gave rise to states comprising several different minorities, the boundaries of which had been arbitrarily redrawn in light of power considerations. Minorities were guaranteed protection under aegis of the League of Nations to achieve the desired stability. At the same time, however, the other goal was to pave for a possible, albeit not so painful assimilation of those groups.[1] In this vein, treaties were concluded between the Great Powers and the newly established or territorially enlarged Central and Eastern European states which guaranteed minority rights and limited the sovereignty of the latter states. In contrast with the peace treaties signed with the states losing World War I, such restrictions had to be justified. The justification was laid down in the Clemenceau doctrine. In a letter to the Prime Minister of Poland, French Prime Minister Clemenceau explained that, according to European public law, there was nothing new about the fact that when a new state is born or where an existing state has grown in territory, the major powers require binding international commitments in the form of an international treaty on certain principles of governance.[2]

As a result of World War I, a new era dawned in the history of international law, which in many respects constituted a break with the state-centered positivism that preceded the Great War. Four traits characterized this modernist concept: the criticism of the sovereign state as the only source of power; openness to the legitimacy of national sentiment; belief in a wide range legal procedural techniques and decision-making procedures for dealing with international conflicts; and piecing together entities hitherto unthinkable in the traditional international approach: states, nations, peoples and individuals. In the international law career of the people, the nation, the minority, the *Zeitgeist* as well as the emergence of

---

1   Patrick Thornyberry, *International Law and the Rights of Minorities*, Clarendon Press, Oxford, 1991, p. 49.
2   Péter Kovács, 'The Protection of Minorities Under the Auspices of the League of Nations', *in* Dinah Shelton (ed.), *The Oxford Handbook of International Human Rights Law*, Oxford University Press, 2013, p. 327.

the concept of 'people' in the social sciences or in the arts, may have played a role. An example would be the ethnography research or the music of Béla Bartók.[3]

As far as post-Cold War geopolitical considerations were concerned, the severe escalation of the tension between the majority population and minorities in certain Central and Eastern European states, in the immediate neighborhood of Western Europe, threatened the international order. The consolidated operation of a state can easily be affected by humanitarian threats, gross violations of fundamental rights on a large scale, or ethnic conflicts in neighboring or nearby states, leading to mass influxes of refugees and tensions between governments. All this was vividly illustrated by the Yugoslav crisis. These threats raised the question of how and to what extent international institutions should participate in the resolution of inter-ethnic conflicts, and what the winners of the Cold War were to do with Eastern Europe.[4] Not unlike the post-World War I period, stability in Central and Eastern Europe was once again at stake. The difference is that in our days besides the stability of borders, the prospect of cross-border humanitarian threats was equally important in the eyes of the 'peace-makers'. The idea that countries of Central and Eastern Europe are in permanent conflict with each other was decisive in shaping the Western political approach to the region. The prospect of NATO and EU accession eased tensions between Eastern and Central European states. It is not an overstatement to say that it was the Central and Eastern European ethnic conflicts that led to the development of contemporary European instruments for minority protection. As Will Kymlicka underlined, a

"rapid consensus developed amongst all the major European organizations that the best approach to influencing the treatment of national minorities in post-communist countries was to establish minimum norms and standards, along with international mechanisms to monitor a country's compliance with them."[5]

Thus, the Framework Convention for the Protection of National Minorities and the European Charter for Regional or Minority Languages were adopted in the Council of Europe. The idea that it was the Central and Eastern European ethnic conflicts that led to the adoption of the above mentioned international treaties is well illustrated by the fact

---

3   See Nathaniel Berman, 'Modernism, Nationalism, and the Rhetoric of Reconstruction', *Yale Journal of Law and Humanities*, Vol. 4, Issue 2, 1992, pp. 351-380.

4   Rainer Hoffmann, who used to be the chairman of the Advisory Committee of the Framework Convention looked back and concluded that everybody in the Committee and the Secretariat was convinced that what happened in the Yugoslav war cannot repeat itself. *See 20 Years of Dealing with Diversity. Is the Framework Convention at a Cross-Road?* European Center for Minority Issues, Flensburg, 2018, p. 22.

5   Will Kymlicka, *Multicultural Odysseys: Navigating the New International Politics of Diversity*, Oxford University Press, Oxford, 2007, p. 197.

that the 20th anniversary of the entry into force of those treaties did not prove to be an occasion for revising their provisions or at least concluding some additional protocols. The moment of upheaval had passed, and the protection of autochthonous minorities is now overshadowed by attempts to solve other humanitarian issues, such as the challenges of coping with the influx of immigrants and refugees arriving from outside of Europe.

Although the end of the Cold War did not see the wake of a new period of international law, it nevertheless boosted human rights protection and aspirations for European unity. The ideas of human rights universalism and European unity precluded the repeating of events following World War I when Western powers narrowed the system of the European minority protection to Central and Eastern Europe within the League of Nations.[6] The decisive factor, however, was that the protection of minority rights was recognized as an integral part of the international law regime for the protection of human rights. This link was established by Article 1 of the Framework Convention for the Protection of National Minorities. According to this Article, minority rights are covered by the international protection of human rights, consequently they are not the exclusive competence of sovereign states, and this conveys the message that, affording minority rights cannot be made conditional upon a declaration of loyalty to the state.

15.2   The Charter in a Nutshell

The Charter protects languages that are traditionally present in specific areas, yet it also stipulates that languages that do not have a clear territorial base should also be protected.[7] The objects of protection are the languages of minorities, excluding their local variations. Since the Charter is based on the concept of protecting the European cultural heritage, the languages of immigrant communities are not covered by the protection guaranteed under the Charter. If a regional or minority language is an official language, it will only be protected in case the State Party voluntarily undertakes to do so.[8]

The Charter offers both lower and higher levels of protection. The objectives and principles set out in Part II must be applied to all regional or minority languages. Goals

---

6   Julie Ringelheim, 'Minority Rights in a Time of Multiculturalism – The Evolving Scope of the Framework Convention on the Protection on National Minorities', *Human Rights Law Review*, Vol. 10, Issue 1, 2010, p. 107.

7   *See* Jean-Marie Woehrling, *The European Charter for Regional or Minority Languages. A Critical Commentary*, Council of Europe Publishing, Strasbourg, 2005; Alba Nogueira López *et al.* (eds.), *Shaping Language Rights, Commentary on the European Charter for Regional or Minority Languages in Light of the Committee of Experts' Evaluation*, Council of Europe Publishing, Strasbourg, 2012.

8   However, an official language in a minority position should automatically have at least the lower level of protection, since, despite being recognized as official, its position is basically determined by its minority position.

and principles include the recognition of minority language use as a manifestation of cultural wealth, respect for the geographical boundaries of the minority language, and ensuring that new administrative units do not impede the use of a minority language. They further include the teaching and learning of minority languages at all levels, as well as the promotion and encouragement of minority language use in public and private life, in oral and written form.

Part III covers the following areas: education, court procedures, public administration, media, and culture, economic and social life, and cross-border relationships. Part III provides for a higher level of protection, according to which State Party may designate certain minority languages for this purpose. The Charter allows State Parties to choose from various commitments of different degrees of protection for selected languages in each area of language use. A minimum of 35 paragraphs must be selected, with at least 3 paragraphs from the field of education and culture, and at least one from the other fields. It is not mandatory to undertake any obligations regarding cross-border relationships. The scope of ratification can be extended.

The government reports compiled on the implementation of the Charter are examined by a Committee of Experts, which draws up a report and draft recommendations. Based on the report and the draft recommendations of the Committee of Experts, the Committee of Ministers of the Council of Europe draws up recommendations. Unlikely the Advisory Committee of the Framework Convention, the Committee of Experts consisting of independent experts can clearly state – even on delicate issues – their opinion on the compliance of State Parties in their evaluation report. An example is that the Advisory Committee

> "finds it important that the authorities favor a flexible approach to the application of the 20% threshold, taking into account the specific local situation, notably the actual needs and demands of persons belonging to national minorities."[9]

In the same case, the Committee of Experts expressly invited Slovakia to revise the 20% population threshold for the use of minority languages in court procedures and public administration.[10] In summary, the Charter protects minority languages and not minority rights, provides an *á la Carte* system of obligations and its supervision is based on government reports.

---

9   Third Opinion on the Slovak Republic, ACFC/OP/III(2010)004, p. 8.
10   Application of the Charter in the Slovak Republic (2nd monitoring cycle), ECRML, 2009, p. 8.

15.3 Changes in International Law, Language Conservation and Politics

International law preceding 1914 was referred to as 'titanic law'.[11] According to this metaphor, this law was created by powerful entities, towering over the individuals, regulating relationships between them. These titans lived in their own caves, not caring much about the world, slaughtering those who violated the boundaries of their territory. International law was limited to regulating contacts between states, such as diplomatic and consular relations, or war and warfare.

Due to the tremendous changes to its structure which took place in the 20th century, today international law is not simply the regulator of the interstate arena. In recent decades, international law has gone far beyond mitigating interstate confrontation and delimiting competencies of sovereign entities by addressing issues stemming from the complex interdependency of states, the protection of common values, including cultural values. Rules coordinating domestic laws, are incorporated into the internal legal systems of the states.[12] More and more issues earlier covered exclusively by internal law have become areas of international law. The rights, interests and well-being of individuals and communities have become a priority; the protection of cultural heritage being an obvious example. The protection of cultural heritage emerged as a special area of international law.

The protection of cultural heritage at the universal level began in the framework of the UNESCO with the establishment of international rules for the preservation of tangible cultural and natural heritage. Finally, the regime included also intangible values, covering *e.g.* language.[13] In the context of the Council of Europe, Article 2 of the European Cultural Convention required State Parties to encourage and support their own citizens to learn other European languages. The Preamble to the European Charter for Regional or Minority Languages stated:

> "[c]onsidering that the protection of the historical, regional or minority languages of Europe, some of which are in danger of eventual extinction, contributes to the maintenance and development of Europe's cultural wealth and traditions;"

---

11   The term was introduced by Giambattista Vico. *See* Antonio Cassese, *Terrorism, Politics and Law. The Achille Lauro Affair*, Polity Press, Cambridge, 1989, p. 145.

12   As David Kennedy observed: "Specialists in every field – family law, antitrust, intellectual property, civil procedure, criminal law, banking and commercial law – have all come to see their subject in international or comparative structure." David Kennedy, 'The Mistery of Global Governance', *in* Jeffrey L. Dunoff & Joel P. Trachtman (eds.), *Ruling the World? Constitutionalism, International Law and Global Governance*, Cambridge University Press, Cambridge, 2009, p. 39.

13   *See* the 1972 Convention Concerning the Protection of the World Cultural and Natural Heritage.

This statement is a clear manifestation of the conservationist ideology dominating of the protection of both the environment and cultural heritage in international law.[14] The declared purpose of the Charter is to remove minority language protection from the highly politicized world of minority rights, thereby making it more acceptable to certain European states. However, this benevolent effort is doomed to fail. Language issues are highly political even if they are disguised as cultural heritage protection. States and state languages emerge hand in hand, suffice to consider the evolution of the Bosnian and Montenegrin languages. Some fear that the recognition of the Silesian language would lead to autonomy claims in Poland. There is nothing more political than the perceived threat to the integrity of the state and the fear of the other.

It is reasonable to say that the Charter definitely forms a part of the 'Law of Minorities'.[15] Its main aim – the protection of minority linguistic heritage and indirectly, affording minority language rights – classifies it as belonging to minority law. It introduces the political concept of multilingual citizenship, an understanding of citizenship that takes linguistic equality seriously.[16] The Charter can also be interpreted as a text describing the ideal type of state minority language policy, while at the same time, it is also a tool for assessing minority language policies.[17] All of the above leads us to the further conclusion that perhaps even beyond the original intentions of founding fathers, the Charter is in effect regulator of the complex area of 'diversity management'.[18] According to a more modest assessment, the Charter is "a plea for tolerance."[19] This is undoubtedly true, especially when we consider that the concept of tolerance is complementary to the concept of human rights, of which minority rights, including language rights, are an integral part. At the same time, the Charter foresees much stronger obligations for States Parties than to merely tolerate minority language use: they are to protect and promote minority languages. At a higher level of abstraction, this means that the 19th century nation-state model of linguistic homogenization should finally be overcome through a series of positive steps.

---

14   Robert Dunbar speaks about ecological attitude. Robert Dunbar, 'Minority Language Rights in International Law', *International and Comparative Law Quarterly*, Vol. 50, January 2001, p. 94.

15   Péter Kovács laments in the title of his book, rights of minorities or law of minorities? Péter Kovács, *International Law and Minority Protection: Rights of Minorities or Law of Minorities?* Akadémiai, Budapest, 2000.

16   R. Gwynned Parry, 'History, Human Rights and Multilingual Citizenship: Conceptualising the European Charter for Regional or Minority Languages', *Northern Ireland Legal Quarterly*, Vol. 61, Issue 4, 2010, p. 329.

17   *See* Francois Grin, *Language Policy Evaluation and the European Charter for Regional or Minority Languages*, Houndmiles, Basingstoke, Palgrave Macmillan, 2003.

18   Stefan Oeter, 'Conventions on Protection of National Minorities', *in* Stefanie Schmahl & Martin Breuer (eds.), *The Council of Europe. Its Law and Policies*, Oxford University Press, Oxford, 2017, p. 545.

19   *See* Camiel Hamans, 'The Charter: A Plea for Tolerance', *Scripta Neophilologica Posnaniensia*, Tomus XVIII, 2018, pp. 165-189.

In any case, the Charter was not intended to be a 'high politics' treaty, a treaty directly touching upon the delicate questions of sovereignty, such as security, military cooperation, state succession, membership in the EU, or even minority rights. This is not only evidenced by the cultural heritage context, but also by the fact that the Charter has less political weight than the Framework Convention in the Council of Europe. It is clear from the chronically understaffed nature of the Secretariat of the Charter, or from the fact that the Charter still does not have provision to elaborate Thematic Commentaries. Moreover, in contrast with the Framework Convention, the European Commission did not expect candidate countries to ratify the Charter as a precondition to membership in the EU. This was presumably down to the Baltic States: the European Commission respected their special sensitivity *vis-à-vis* the Russian language. However, in the case of Serbia, the implementation of the Charter is also under review in the accession negotiations.

The political nature of the Charter is well illustrated by the fact that there are fierce political debates in the Committee of Ministers over the draft recommendations forwarded by the Committee of Experts as the essence of their supervisory work. It is problematic for the Council of Europe Committee of Ministers to allow all member states to participate in the debate on the draft recommendations. In some cases, this may open up a new front in the political conflict between two member states, such as Ukraine and Russia, the former being a party to the treaty, the latter not.

The Charter strives towards balancing majority and minority interest, state resources and institutional needs in the context of minority language protection, in the *á a Carte* system geared towards the widest possible ratification. The latter, namely, that the Charter leaves the initiative completely to states has been the subject of criticism.[20] The Charter indeed follows the example of the European Social Charter giving State Parties the right to choose obligations from Part III of the Charter, so that commitments may be adapted to the different situations of minority languages. Unfortunately however, the text of the Charter did not state that State Parties should select commitments according to the objective situation of minority languages, but at least the Explanatory Report does so.[21] (The objectives and principles set out in Part II should be applied to all regional or minority languages.) The Explanatory Report also states that the exclusion of a minority language from the scope of Article III. Part II of the Charter may not be applied in a manner contrary to the spirit, objectives and principles of the Charter.[22]

By choosing minimum standards under Part III State Parties simply consolidated the level of protection that has already existed.[23] According to another opinion in most cases,

---

20   Tove H. Malloy, *National Minority Rights in Europe*, Oxford University Press, Oxford, 2005, p. 219.
21   Explanatory Report, para. 43.
22   Id. para. 42.
23   Gaetano Pentassuglia, *Minorities in International Law*, Council of Europe Publishing, Strasbourg, 2002, p. 130.

the existing level of protection only served as a starting point for the drafting of the ratification document, mainly due to the involvement of minority language organizations. The inclusion of such normative ambitions in the ratification processes may have given the impression that far-reaching reform processes were taking place in the ambit of minority language policies. At the same time, the ratification also drew attention to certain neglected minority languages, such as the Kven language in Norway or Limburg in the Netherlands.[24]

One criticism voiced in respect of the Charter, was that its standard-setting role hampered the emergence of genuine minority language rights.[25] This position, however, does not take into consideration that the objective standards set by the Charter[26] may lead to enforceable rights. Moreover, if we consider that only Article 3 of the Framework Convention for the Protection of National Minorities contains a subjective right – the right to identity – then, given the cultural heritage scope of the Charter, this criticism seems unfair.

15.4   Features and Problems of Supervising Implementation

The supervisory mechanism over the implementation of the Charter is based solely on government reporting. This is down to the fact that minority language rights were integrated into cultural heritage protection, since individual complaints would an expression of subjective language rights. A more efficient form of supervision would include individual complaints as well. As of yet, however, the Charter does not contain rights, only state obligations. Meanwhile, if we look closely for example at the text of the UN Rights of the Child Convention, it also basically only refers to state obligations, and it has an optional complaint procedure. Even the UN International Covenant on Economic, Social and Cultural Rights has been supplemented by such a protocol.[27]

If we consider international law not only as a set of norms but also as law in practice, great importance must be attached to the activities of bodies set up to monitor implementation, even if they are not judicial in nature and are not empowered to provide mandatory interpretation.

The Committee of Experts consisting of independent experts' reviews government reports, in addition, it receives shadow reports which help in the evaluation process. This can be easily justified in light of the fact that the minority languages protected by the

---

24   Sterfan Oeter, 'Council of Europe – The European Charter for Regional or Minority Languages', *in* Daniel Thürer (ed.), *International Protection of Minorities – Challenges in Practice and Doctrine*, Schulthess, Zurich, 2014, pp. 63-64.

25   Malloy 2005, p. 218.

26   Pentassuglia 2002, pp. 130-131.

27   Gábor Kardos, 'The European Charter for Regional or Minority Languages: Some of its Characteristics and the Future of the Supervisory Mechanism', *Gdanskie Studia Prawnicze*, Issue 2, 2019, p. 270.

Charter are very varied as regards the number of their speakers, the geographical concentration of users, their language consciousness, the development of their educational and cultural infrastructure, their degree of recognition and protection. Even the level of activity of minority NGOs in bringing certain issues to the Committee of Experts' attention can vary greatly from state to state.

Commitments under Part III cannot be properly evaluated without a sound knowledge of the sociolinguistic position of the minority language[28] and of the legal system of the state in question. In addition, public authorities, misunderstanding the substance of certain obligations, opt for an unsuitable commitment,[29] or, alternatively, choose randomly to avoid criticism.[30] A consequence of this complexity is that the evaluations of the Committee of Experts are not always as consistent as they should be. Moreover, recent changes to the format of the reports of the Committee of Experts do not necessarily pave the way towards improvement.[31]

The report-based supervisory system has three key players: public authorities, the Committee of Experts and the minority language community. Article 16(2) of the Charter explicitly authorizes the Committee of Experts to use information provided by civil society groups when evaluating government reports, giving the state the opportunity to respond. The Working Group of the Expert Committee always visits the state party in question and always meets with representatives of minority language organizations first. Moreover, after the adoption of the report, it may be the case that the member responsible for the Committee of Experts' evaluation report is involved in the deliberations of government bodies and minority organizations, discussing what follows from the recommendations made by the Committee of Ministers of the Council of Europe. Optimally, there is an ongoing 'trialogue' between the stakeholders to ensure better compliance with the Charter.

Perhaps the most important part of the Committee of Experts' evaluation work is that where the language of the commitment allows, it insists on putting it into actual practice and is not satisfied with the mere fact that only the law in books is in line with the Charter. This approach leads the Committee of Experts to pay close attention to monitoring the

---

28   Robert Dunbar points out that the Committee of Experts gives considerable attention to sociolinguistic questions. Robert Dunbar, 'Definitely interpreting the European Charter for Regional or Minority Languages: The Legal Challenges', in *The European Charter for Regional or Minority Languages: Legal Challenges and Opportunities (Regional or Minority Languages No. 5.)*, Council of Europe Publishing, Strasbourg, 2008, p. 60.

29   As it happened in conjunction with Article 11, mixing up public and private media.

30   Oeter 2014, p. 72.

31   Evaluation charts have recently been introduced in the reports of the Committee of Experts. The charts feature arrows indicating the direction of change in compliance, upward or downward. Although short explanations are provided, delicate investigation is needed to clarify whether there have been real changes on the ground, or whether the same facts were simply reevaluated.

infrastructural prerequisites of minority language use. In fact, this is a persistent element of the 'case law' of the Committee of Experts.

The self-image of the State Parties differs in respect of the international legal obligations undertaken. As an observer underlines, some states are more sensitive to criticism and are proud of what they are trying to achieve, such as Norway. Others are less sensitive, but more hypocritical. Most of the states are located between the two extremes. The ambitious reforms announced as a result of some recommendations are often accompanied by passionate resistance to other issues.[32] Experience has shown that transforming internal law is always a simpler task than creating the substantive-technical conditions for the actual use of minority languages.[33] Repeating certain recommendations on the same subject over and over will sometimes yield important results. The situation may be different where the recommendation is affected by a sharply disputed domestic issue, yet even where this is the case, the opposition may exploit the recommendation to criticize the government.

A serious problem of the supervisory regime is that the Committee of Experts has a very limited scope of action between two rounds of reporting. The most they can do is write a letter asking for information and/or draw attention to the state's obligation under the Charter.

As is generally the case with international treaties maintaining a review procedure ending with recommendations, it can be said that on the one hand, the soft mechanism at least puts some problematic issues on the agenda but on the other, it weakens the international liability resulting from non-enforcement. The essence of state responsibility under international law is accountability.[34] For this, however, it is necessary to establish the international infringement in an authentic way, including the legal consequences of state liability. Where this is missing state liability is watered down. What remains is a soft responsibility to take the recommendations seriously.

---

32   Oeter 2017, p. 569.
33   That is the main message of the 'case-law' under the Charter.
34   James Crawford & Jeremy Watkins, 'International Responsibility', *in* Samantha Besson & John Tasioulas (eds.), *The Philosophy of International Law*, Oxford University Press, Oxford, 2010, p. 283.

PART III
DEVELOPMENTS IN EUROPEAN LAW

16   Snapshot of the EU Soft Law Research Landscape

Main Issues and Challenges

Petra Lea Láncos*

Keywords

soft law, normativity, bindingness, directive-like recommendations, hybridity

Abstract

Inspired by research into international soft law norms, the last two decades have seen an intensified investigation of the non-binding measures of the EU. With the proliferation of such norms at EU level, attempts at a taxonomy of EU soft law have been undertaken. The present paper tries to map the current status of EU soft law research, highlighting possible directions for future research.

16.1   Introduction

The body of EU soft law is vast and hard to pin down. It is an amorphous, ever-growing class of norms, with fuzzy borders, existing in close connection with hard law measures.[1] While seemingly unobtrusive, EU soft law norms should not be underestimated: they may be 'harder' than expected. Accordingly, legal scholars have long discovered the field of EU soft law research,[2] focusing in particular, on non-binding acts burgeoning in certain policy

---

*   Petra Lea Láncos: researcher, Deutsches Forschungsinstitut für öffentliche Verwaltung, Speyer; associate professor, Pázmány Péter Catholic University, Budapest.

1   David M. Trubek *et al.* "Soft Law,' 'Hard Law,' and European Integration: Toward a Theory of Hybridity', *University of Wisconsin Legal Studies*, Research Paper No. 1002, 2005, p. 4.

2   *See* in particular Gustaaf M. Borchardt & Karel C. Wellens, 'Soft Law in European Community Law', *European Law Review*, Vol. 14, 1989, pp. 267-321; Linda Senden, *Soft law in European Community Law*, Hart, 2004; Linda Senden, 'Soft Law and its Implications for Institutional Balance in the EC', *Utrecht Law Review*, Vol. 1, Issue 2, 2005, pp. 79-99; Jürgen Schwarze, 'Soft law im Recht der Europäischen Union', *Europarecht*, Vol. 1, Issue 1, pp. 3-18; Anne Peters, 'Soft Law as a New Mode of Governance', *in* Udo Diedrichs *et al.* (eds.), *The Dynamics of Change in EU Governance*, Edward Elgar, 2011, pp. 21-51; Fabien Terpan, 'Soft Law in the European Union – The Changing Nature of EU Law', *European Law Journal*, Vol. 21, Issue 1, 2015, pp. 68-96; Oana Ştefan, 'Soft Law and the Enforcement of EU Law', *in* András Jakab & Dimitry Kochenov, *The Enforcement of EU Law and Values: Ensuring MS's Compliance*, Oxford University Press, 2017, pp. 200-217.

fields, such as competition law, state aid and fiscal policy, or innovative new governance mechanisms, such as the Open Method of Coordination. Meanwhile, the use of soft law in other areas (*e.g.* media law, agricultural land law *etc.*) has yet to be charted. The study of EU soft law continues to be an intriguing subject, giving rise to, it seems just as many questions as answers.

In the following, based on the survey of the relevant scholarly literature and CJEU case-law, I attempt to briefly summarize the chief areas and the main challenges of soft law research. I depart from an analysis of scholarly attempts to draw a distinction between hard law and soft law and proceed with the classification of the different types of soft law sources. I recount the possible reasons for the legislator to take recourse to soft law, explore the normativity of these acts and their role in shaping national jurisprudence. Finally, I also formulate some suggestions for future research.

16.2 Overcoming the Illusion of the Great Divide: 'Hybridity' and the 'Spectrum of Normativity'

It is worth noting, that neither the founding treaties, nor soft measures themselves or the relevant judgments of the CJEU speak of 'soft law', in fact, it is a term that is hardly ever employed in EU documents.[3] Nevertheless, it is clear that there is a group of norms that stands in stark contrast with binding measures of EU law, with the aim of affecting change through persuasion, cooperation or good practices. While the difference between the two classes of norms clearly exists, the exact markers of the soft/hard law divide are difficult to determine. As Terpan stresses,

> "the difficulty with soft law is the very fluidity of the notion. Paradoxically, soft law is an oft-used concept, which is still given very different meanings as no consensus has emerged in scholarship."[4]

Seeking to grasp the concept of soft law, Trubek *et al.* observe that it is

---

3   Vassilios Christianos, 'Effectiveness and Efficiency Through the Court of Justice of the EU', *in* Julia Iliopoulos-Strangas & Jean-François Flauss(†) (eds.), *Das soft law der europäischen Organisationen – The Soft Law of European Organisations – La soft law des organisations européennes*, Societas Iuris Publici Europaei (Sipe), Nomos, 2012, p. 327.
4   Terpan 2013, p. 5.

"a very general term, and has been used to refer to a variety of processes. The only common thread among these processes is that while all have normative content they are not formally binding."[5]

Perhaps the most widely accepted and cited definition of soft law is that developed by Snyder, who describes them as

"rules of conduct that are laid down in instruments which have not been attributed legally binding force as such, but nevertheless may have certain – indirect – legal effects, and that are aimed at and may produce practical effects."[6]

Yet with the proliferation of EU measures, drawing the line between binding and non-binding norms becomes an ever so challenging endeavor, since it is grounded in an assumed binarity inherent in the distinction between 'hard law' and 'soft law'.[7] In fact, this binary approach is criticized insightfully by Armstrong:

"if expressed simply as a dichotomy, then it is obvious that the hard/soft law distinction is highly reductive as a means of accommodating pluralization of governance forms. Indeed, it tends to treat any departure from an archetypal 'hard law' position as the beginning of soft law making the soft law characteri-zation analytically all-encompassing."[8]

Several authors have pleaded for a more holistic view of norms, abandoning the traditional quest for separating soft law and hard law.

One way of overcoming the problematic binary approach to the soft/hard law conun-drum is the practical approach of 'hybridity' as employed by the CJEU: acknowledging the close and interdependent nature of relevant binding and non-binding rules by applying

---

5   Trubek *et al.* 2005, p. 1.
6   Francis Snyder, 'The Effectiveness of European Community Law: Institutions, Processes, Tools and Tech-niques', *The Modern Law Review*, Vol. 56, Issue 1, 1993, p. 32; *see* also Linda Senden, 'Soft Law, Self-Regu-lation and Co-Regulation in European Law: Where Do They Meet?', *Electronic Journal of Comparative Law*, Vol. 9, Issue 1, 2005, p. 22; Linda Senden, *Soft Law in European Community Law*, Hart Publishing, 2004, p. 112.
7   Thomas M. J. Möllers, 'Sources of Law in European Securities Regulation – Effective Regulation, Soft Law and Legal Taxonomy from Lamfalussy to de Larosiere', *European Business Organization Law Review*, Vol. 11, Issue 3, 2010, p. 388.
8   Kenneth A. Armstrong, 'The Character of EU Law and Governance: From 'Community Method' to New Modes of Governance', *Current Legal Problems*, Vol. 64, Issue 1, 2011, p. 206.

them with due consideration to each other.[9] Hybridity is thus an approach which shifts the focus from differentiating between soft law and hard law, by acknowledging the reality that several policy fields are operated through a mesh of binding and non-binding rules, mutually supplementing, clarifying, detailing the requirements laid down.[10]

While hybridity may divert the attention from the differences between soft law and hard law, it is nevertheless an issue of application, and does little to integrate hard law and soft law on a conceptual level. Instead, this is achieved by efforts attempting to describe normativity as a spectrum, ranging from "non-legal positions to legally binding and judicially controlled commitments."[11]

Terpan attempts to navigate this spectrum by identifying soft and/or hard elements of a norm along the lines of source, content and enforcement, proposing that the category of hard law is conditional upon the 'hardness' both content and enforcement.[12] Terpan explains that the spectrum approach helps locate soft law between non-law and enforceable commitments, while also highlighting processes of transformation into hard and soft law, respectively.[13] These insights fit well with Peters' observation that

> "law can have a variety of legal impacts and effects, direct and indirect ones, stronger and weaker ones. To accept graduated normativity means to assume that law can be harder or softer, and that there is a continuum between hard and soft (and possibly other qualities of the law)."[14]

However, Peters further develops this approach with Pagotto, abandoning the idea of a strict division between hard law and soft law, submitting that "soft law is in the penumbra of law. [...] [T]here is no bright line between hard and soft law. Legal texts can be harder or softer."[15]

They contend, that a 'prototype theory' of soft law is most workable: while a "fixed set of necessary and sufficient conditions" of soft law cannot be determined, in practice,

---

9   Tamara Hervey, 'Adjudicating in the Shadow of the Informal Settlement? The Court of Justice of the European Union, 'New Governance' and Social Welfare', *Current Legal Problems*, Vol. 63, Issue 1, 2010, p. 146.
10   Trubek *et al.* 2005, p. 33.
11   Terpan 2013, p. 2.
12   Id. p. 9. These 'distinguishing paramaters' are what Peters and Pagotto refer to the "intention to be legally bound" and the 'sanction potential' of norms. *See* Anne Peters & Isabella Pagotto, *Soft Law as a New Mode of Governance: A Legal Perspective*, New Modes of Governance Project, Project No. CIT1-CT-2004-506392, 2006, p. 10.
13   Terpan 2013, p. 2.
14   Anne Peters, 'Typology, Utility and Legitimacy of European Soft Law', *in* Astrid Epiney *et al.* (eds.), *Die Herausforderung von Grenzen. Festschrift für Roland Bieber*, Nomos, Baden-Baden, 2007, p. 410.
15   Peters & Pagotto 2006, p. 12.

lawyers will be able to identify soft law with the premise 'I know it when I see it', accepting that the boundaries between the concepts of soft law and hard law will remain blurry.[16]

Apparently, all-encompassing definitions and approaches seeking to capture the common denominator of the vast array of phenomena characteristic of soft law will only yield a bland concept and will invariably disappoint.[17] Hence, efforts to categorize and describe the different types of soft law measures to come closer to the precise forms in which soft law manifests itself, have also taken off.

16.3   THE CATEGORIZATION CONUNDRUM: ATTEMPTS TO CLASSIFY EU SOFT LAW MEASURES

Soft law measures are so varied and diverse in their form and nature that their classification is already a challenge. In fact, these sources may be categorized along various different lines.

16.3.1   Formal and Informal Soft Law Measures

Perhaps the most obvious differentia specifica is whether the given soft law measure is Treaty-based or not. Namely, beyond the restricted category of soft law acts foreseen in the Treaty [Article 288 TFEU (ex-Article 249 EC)],[18] that is, opinions and recommendations (formal measures), a burgeoning of non-Treaty based measures including guidelines,[19] communications, notices, green papers and white papers, comfort letters *etc.* (informal measures) may be discerned. The rise of informal measures is explained by Senden and Prechal as follows:

---

16   Id.
17   Peters and Pagotto are acutely aware of the problems with both the binary and the spectrum-based view, stressing: "The first danger is that of black-and-white painting, of construing dichotomies, in short: the danger of over-simplification. The contrary danger is that of losing oneself in endless subtle distinctions and overly fine shades and graduations. Overs-simplification and dichotomic arguing may prevent lawyers from adequately capturing the much more complex reality and may thereby contribute to unsound legal analysis and unfair results. Over-subtleties, on the other hand, may hinder the formulation of general concepts, leads lawyers to produce single-case solutions and forecloses generalizable and workable legal constructs." Id. p. 7.
18   Article 288 (ex-Article 249 TEC): "To exercise the Union's competences, the institutions shall adopt regulations, directives, decisions, recommendation and opinions. [...] Recommendation and opinions shall have no binding force."
19   'Akte sui generis', Gunnar Pampel, 'Europäisches Wettbewerbsrecht. Rechtsnatur und Rechtswirkungen von Mitteilungen der Kommission im europäischen Wettbewerbsrecht', *Europäische Zeitschrift für Wirtschaftsrecht*, Vol. 16, Issue 1, 2005, pp. 11-12.

"[T]he instruments listed in Article 249 EC may be particularly inappropriate or disproportionate for the adoption of certain measures. [...] It would seem that, even from the very beginning, the practice has made it clear that there is a need and desire for instruments other than those listed in Article 249 EC. However, the range of instruments, as provided for in this Article, has never been adapted to the changed circumstances and to the new needs resulting from the expanded sphere of Community action."[20]

This has consequences for the adoption of such measures: while the Treaty stipulates rules for the adoption of formal soft law (*e.g.* Article 292 TFEU), informal acts are captured under more general legal bases empowering Union institutions to take appropriate measures (*e.g.* Article 108 TFEU) or are left completely unregulated.

16.3.2   Differentiation by Source

EU soft law measures may be categorized on the basis of their source, resulting in a distinction between measures adopted by Union institutions or bodies (ranging from formal, Treaty-based acts to informal measures adopted by EU agencies, documents issued jointly by Member States (*e.g.* Charter of Fundamental Rights),[21] self-regulation and co-regulation instruments of stakeholders [*e.g.* European Advertising Standards Alliance (ESEA) self-regulatory body's work],[22] cooperation-based soft mechanisms operated by Member States and the institutions (*e.g.* OMC).[23]

16.3.3   Distinction by Function

Several authors distinguish between soft law instruments based on their function: accordingly, measures may serve preparatory and informative nature (pre-law), interpretative and decisional (law-plus), steering (para-law) functions.[24]

---

20   Linda Senden & Sacha Prechal, 'Differentiation in and Through Community Soft Law', *in* Bruno de Witte *et al.* (eds.), *The Many Faces of Differentiation in EU Law*, Intersentia 2001, p. 186. *See* also Terpan 2013, pp. 19-26; Håkon A. Cosma & Richard Whish, 'Soft Law in the Field of EU Competition Policy', *European Business Law Review*, Vol. 14, Issue 1, 2013, p. 46.
21   Peters & Pagotto 2016, p. 18.
22   Senden traces back the origins of the self- and co-regulatory efforts on Community level to the White Paper for the Internal Market and the SEA, where "reflections on the existing body of European legislation and new legislation to be adopted and the burden it imposes on national authorities and companies have led to deregulatory and self-regulatory tendencies also at the EC level." Senden 2005, p. 4.
23   Peters & Pagotto 2016, pp. 17-23.
24   *See* in detail Senden 2004, p. 457. *et seq*; Peters & Pagotto 2016, p. 23.

i.   The pre-law function may be understood as the preparatory role of soft law norms. In this understanding, soft law precedes hard law with the potential of achieving convergence of Member State laws and enabling also the gathering of data on the effect of national legislation implementing such soft law. Lack of transposition or information gleaned from the impact assessment made possible by such preparatory norms may constitute the grounds for (and as such, the first step towards) the adoption of hard law in the very same field (*e.g.* the General Data Protection Regulation, informed by a number of working group recommendations, opinion *etc.*).[25] Peters and Pagotto refer to this as *'ultra vires'* soft law, since it "pave[s] the way to a formal extension of the competences of the organization which will be effected by a revision of the founding treaty."[26] But the informative function of soft law is also important: it represents the implicit consensus of institutions (*e.g.* declarations, gentleman's agreements *etc.*) or the reading of a single institution (*e.g.* opinion) on a given subject.[27]

ii. The law-plus function of soft law harks back to the empirical evidence of hybridity: "soft law and hard law increasingly intermesh and add up to more or less coherent normative regimes", with soft law providing an orienting, interpretative function to promote compliance (*e.g.* notices, guidelines, recommendations *etc.*).[28]

iii. The para-law role of soft law is to provide a meaningful alternative to hard law, with a steering function even in situations where the adoption of hard law instruments is impossible or unfeasible.[29] To distinguish between instances of hybridity and the para-law function of soft law, as a rule of thumb we may consider the proliferation of soft law in the policy field under scrutiny. In fact, where the proliferation of soft law norms is considered to be low (*e.g.* consumer protection, development policy) soft law much rather serves to supplement hard law regulation. Meanwhile, soft law appears as an alternative to hard law in areas (*e.g.* fiscal policy, economic governance, education and culture *etc.*) dominated by new modes of soft governance[30] for lack of supranational competence or the political will to harmonize.

While these efforts at taxonomy are sufficiently broad, they help bring the observer closer to understanding the specific nature and purpose of the different forms of soft law. However, the diversity inherent in the category of soft norms not only renders the concep-

---

25 Ulrika Mörth, *Soft Law and New Modes of EU Governance – A Democratic Problem?*, Paper presented in Darmstadt, November 2005, pp. 16. *et seq.*
26 Peters & Pagotto 2016, p. 23.
27 Id.
28 Id.
29 Id. pp. 23-24.
30 Terpan 2013, p. 31.

tualization of soft law problematic, but also excludes the formulation of sweeping notions regarding the practical effects and bindingness of these measures.

16.4 How Binding Are Non-Binding Measures of the EU?

As the CJEU pointed out in the landmark case *Grimaldi*, the fact that soft measures are not intended to produce binding effects, does not mean that they have absolutely no legal effect.[31] In fact, non-binding norms may well have 'practical effects', reflecting "the degree to which rules are actually implemented domestically or to which states comply with them."[32] Meanwhile, bindingness indicates the obligation of national courts, legislators and authorities associated with the interpretation, application or transposition of EU soft law.[33] To complicate matters, in line with the spectrum approach there is a discernible graduation of normativity within the realm of soft law measures. This results in a spectrum of Member States obligations ranging from room for a total disregard for certain soft instruments, to the obligation of due consideration or even the binding implementation of provisions laid down in European soft law measures.

16.4.1 'Harmonizing' Soft Law – Duty to Consider

Formal recommendations are measures proposing different actions to be taken by the Member States, effectively seeking to harmonize national law on a non-binding basis. Based on the *Grimaldi* case-law of the CJEU national courts are bound to take recommendations (*i.e.* formal soft law) into consideration in order to decide disputes submitted to them.[34] The breadth of the obligation was not detailed by the Court, yet commentators were quick to declare that it could not amount to an obligation of consistent interpretation.[35] In fact, nowhere does the CJEU require the national court (or any other Member State

---

31 Judgment of 13 December 1989, *Case C-322/88, Salvatore Grimaldi v. Fonds des maladies professionnelles (Grimaldi)*, ECLI:EU:C:1989:646, paras. 16 and 18.
32 Kenneth W. Abbott *et al.* 'The Concept of Legalization', *International Organization*, Vol. 54, 2000, p. 18.
33 Petra Lea Láncos, 'A Hard Core Under the Soft Shell: How Binding Is Union Soft Law for Member States?', *European Public Law*, Vol. 24, Issue 4, 2018, pp. 755-784.
34 *Case C-322/88, Grimaldi*, para. 18.
35 Senden 2004, p. 473. "It was argued that the reading of this judgment should be less strict, and that national courts would be required to take soft law into consideration only when it helps to clarify the meaning of Community or national law." Ştefan 2017, p. 213; *see also* Albrecht von Graevenitz, 'Mitteilungen, Leitlinien, Stellungnahmen – Soft law der EU mit Lenkungswirkung' *Europäische Zeitschrift für Wirtschaftsrecht*, Vol. 24, Issue 5, 2013, pp. 169 and 173. By contrast, Christianos argues that there is a duty of consistent interpretation, *see* Christianos 2012, p. 327.

authority or body)[36] to the full extent of its discretion, to interpret national law in accordance with Community (soft) law. Instead, it seems to foresee "a duty of effort",[37] that is, the consideration of recommendations to a minimum standard where "only non-consideration is disallowed."[38]

The CJEU seems to foresee a similar obligation in respect of certain informal soft law measures, such as leniency programs under competition law, which are also designed to indirectly harmonize national laws, with no consent on the side of the Member State. In this case the principles of sincere cooperation and effectiveness require, that Member States promote all interests and rights guaranteed under European law through balancing the same on a case-by-case basis. As a result, a duty of the national court or authority very similar to the one expressed in *Grimaldi* arises: the duty to weigh interests.[39]

16.4.2   'True' Soft Law – No Duty Whatsoever

Within the varied category of EU soft law there is actually a sub-group of norms that is truly non-binding and without any practical effects: these are the so-called informative informal measures.[40] This sub-group includes *de minimis* notices and communications which only bind the Commission adopting them,[41] for reasons of legitimate expectations; 'comfort letters' of individual application, which are not even binding upon the issuing

---

36   As far as the addressees are concerned, as Sarmiento points out, although the CJEU referred to the obligations of national courts to take such measures into consideration, "nothing stops it from being extended to national administrations as well," framing the obligation of consideration to be of a more general scope. This may be due to the fact that while Member States are generally bound by the same obligations under EU law, there is great diversity among them with respect to the distribution of competencies between the judiciary and administrative bodies. The principle of loyalty should therefore require that national bodies be bound by the same obligations of interpretation and application of EU law, no matter their status as court or administrative authority – Daniel Sarmiento, 'European Soft Law and National Authorities: Incorporation, Enforcement and Interference', *in* Iliopoulos-Strangas & Flauss 2012, p. 267; *Cf.* Judgment of 20 January 2016, *Case C-428/14, DHL Express (Italy) Srl and DHL Global Forwarding (Italy) SpA v. Autorità Garante della Concorrenza e del mercato (DHL)*, ECLI:EU:C:2016:27, para. 41.

37   Senden 2004, p. 474.

38   Kai Krieger, *Die gemeinschaftsrechtskonforme Auslegung des deutschen Rechts*, Lit Verlag 2005, p. 97.

39   *Judgment of 14 June 2011, Case C-360/09, Pfleiderer AG v. Bundeskartellamt (Pfleiderer)*, ECLI:EU:C:2011:389.

40   Senden & Prechal 2001, p. 188; Cosma & Whish 2013, pp. 47-48.

41   *Judgment of 13 December 2012, Case C-226/11, Expedia Inc. v. Autorité de la concurrence and Others (Expedia)*, ECLI:EU:C:2012:795. Senden and Prechal classify de minimis notices as decisional instruments, which "indicate in what way a Community institution will apply Community law provision in individual cases where the institution has discretion. In other words, the decisional instruments are instruments structuring the use of discretionary powers, both for the civil servants within the institutions and for the outside world, which can, on this basis, anticipate the application of Community law in concrete cases." Senden & Prechal 2001, p. 190; Judgment of 19 July 2016, *Case C-526/14, Tadej Kotnik and Others v. Državni zbor Republike Slovenije (Kotnik and Others)*, ECLI:EU:C:2016:570.

PETRA LEA LÁNCOS

Commission;[42] and leniency notices, which in no way change the fact that national procedural autonomy prevails.[43]

From the perspective of the Member States these measures foresee no obligations in substance and the element of consent to be bound is also lacking. This explains the fact that such measures confer no duties whatsoever on the Member States.[44] It is worth noting, that the CJEU additionally recalled the fact that these measures had only been printed in the 'C' series of the Official Journal for information purposes.[45] The CJEU understood this as a further indication of the soft law nature of the acts.

16.4.3   Hardening Soft Law – Fully Binding

Soft law adopted as an appropriate measure foreseen in the Treaty and developed in cooperation between the Commission and the Member States may become binding through the participation and consent of the Member States.

For example, so-called Commission disciplines in the field of state aid policy are elaborated in agreement with the Member States,[46] and as a consequence, they have binding

---

42   *Judgment of 10 July 1980, Case C-37/79, Anne Marty SA v. Estée Lauder SA. (Anne Marty v Lauder)*, ECLI:EU:C:1980:190; Judgment of 10 July 1980, *Joined Cases 253/78 and 3/79, Procureur de la République and Others v. Bruno Giry and Guerlain SA and Others (Giry and Guerlain)*, ECLI:EU:C:1980:188.

43   *Case C-428/14, DHL.* DHL had summited a leniency application to the European Commission for immunity from fines concerning cartel infringements in the international freight sector, while also providing some information on infringements in the Italian road freight forwarding business, from which the Commission decided only to pursue infringements related to international air freight forwarding services. At the same time, the Commission left it up to national competition authorities to pursue infringements concerning maritime and road freight services (para. 17.). Although DHL submitted a summary application for immunity under the Italian national leniency program, Schenker was considered to be the first company to have applied for and therefore granted immunity from fines in Italy for the cartel in the road freight forwarding sector (paras. 18-20 and 23-24.). DHL sought the annulment of the AGCM's decision and on appeal the *Consiglio di Stato* (Council of State) turned to the CJEU for a preliminary ruling, asking, among others, whether instruments adopted in the context of the European Competition Network are binding upon national competition authorities.

44   Geiger claims that such Commission communications and guidelines are 'factually binding', the principle of loyalty would deter national courts and authorities to depart from such measures for fear of an impending infringement procedure. This approach has not been confirmed by the CJEU. Andreas Geiger, 'Die neuen Leitlinien der EG-Kommission zur Anwendbarkeit von Art. 81 EG auf Vereinbarungen über horizontale Zusammenarbeit', *Europäische Zeitschrift für Wirtschaftsrecht*, Vol. 11, Issue 11, 2000, p. 325.

45   *Case C-428/14, DHL*, paras. 32-35. and 42; Judgment of 1 July 2010, *Case C-99/09, Polska Telefonia Cyfrowa sp. z o.o. v. Prezes Urzędu Komunikacji Elektronicznej (Polska Telefonia)*, ECLI:EU:C:2010:395, para. 35; *Case C-226/11, Expedia*, paras. 24 and 29-30.

46   Judgment of 24 March 1993, *Case C-313/90, Comité International de la Rayonne et des Fibres Synthétiques and Others v. Commission of the European Communities (CIRFS)*, ECLI:EU:C:1993:111, paras. 1 and 3. The International Rayon and Synthetic Fibers Committee (CIRFS) sought the annulment of the Commission's decision stating that there was no obligation for the prior notification of state aid granted to Allied Signal by the French government. In its action, CIRFS referred to a letter sent by the Commission on 19 July 1977 to the Member States headed 'Aid to the synthetic fiber industry', which read that due to the excess capacity

effect.[47] Accordingly, in the CIRFS case, a Commission discipline otherwise classified as an informal soft law measure, was found to be fully binding, both upon the issuing institution and the addressee Member States. Hence, not only the Commission, but the Member States implementing the discipline were held to be fully liable for breaching the principles of equal treatment and legitimate expectations.

In *IJssel-Vliet*[48] the CJEU held that appropriate measures[49] of the Commission, the so-called guidelines on national aid schemes were binding. According to the CJEU, the elaboration of such guidelines involved "an obligation of regular, periodic cooperation on the part of the Commission and the Member States",[50] where national observations were taken into account.[51] This periodic cooperation seems to amount to Member State consent in the understanding of the CJEU, giving rise to the bindingness of this otherwise soft measure. In this respect, it is worth mentioning that "the general duty of sincere cooperation as established in Article 10 EC does not provide sufficient ground for the recognition of legally binding force of 'agreed' acts",[52] and Member States are under no obligation to

---

of the synthetic fiber industry in the EEC, Member States should desist from granting aid to the industry, and should notify the Commission beforehand of any aid Member States proposed granting to the sector. The discipline laid down in the letter was agreed to by all Member States. In its 1978 memorandum, the Commission defined the scope of the discipline as one that 'covered acrylic, polyester and polyamide fibers for textile or industrial use', while it continued to extend the temporal scope of the discipline every two years. When CIRFS and AKZO (a party that later withdrew from the proceedings) learned that the French government decided to award the manufacturer Allied Signal a regional planning grant for setting up a factory for the production of polyester fibers for industrial application to supply tire manufacturers, they wrote to the Commission and the Commission's Vice-President, Sir Leon Brittan respectively, to request their intervention with French authorities and ask for any comments. Both the Commission and the Vice-President of the Commission sent their replies, on the one hand explaining that the grant was awarded before the discipline was broadened to cover industrial fibers and therefore no obligation to give prior notification of the grant to the Commission existed, while Sir Leon Brittan noted that although the discipline was generally worded, the Commission interpreted it in a narrow sense as applying only to textile fibers.

47   *Case C-313/90, CIRFS*, summary of judgment, para. 4.
48   The judgment was rendered upon the reference for a preliminary ruling submitted by the Dutch Council of State in relation to an action brought by the Dutch company IJssel-Vliet contesting the refusal of its application by the Minister for Economic Affairs of the Netherlands for a subsidy for the construction of a fishing vessel. The Minister for Economic Affairs rejected the application since it failed to comply with the Netherlands national aid scheme approved by the Commission and based on the Guidelines of the Commission on the application of aid schemes and the 1987 multiannual guidance program for the fishing fleet, which did not authorize the grant of national aids for the construction of fishing vessels intended for the Community fleet. Judgment of 15 October 1996, *Case C-311/94, IJssel-Vliet Combinatie BV v. Minister van Economische Zaken (IJssel-Vliet)*, ECLI:EU:C:1996:383, paras. 1-2, 13-15, 17 and 20.
49   "Apparently, the Court is of the opinion that aid codes, disciplines and the like which the Commission adopts on the basis of this provision constitute such 'appropriate measures'. In particular, these rules must have been adopted on the basis of Article 93(1), providing for a specific duty of cooperation between the Commission and the Member States." Senden 2004, p. 279.
50   *Case C-311/94, IJssel-Vliet*, para. 36. See also Ştefan 2016, p. 11. *But cf.* Judgment of 22 October 1996, *Case T-330/94, Salt Union Ltd v. Commission of the European Communities (Salt Union)*, ECLI:EU:T:1996:154.
51   *Case C-311/94, IJssel-Vliet*, paras. 37-39.
52   Senden 2004, p. 465.

agree to such measures of the Commission, "only if they choose to do so, are they bound by them."[53] However, when they do, the substance of the measure and Member State consent has a transformative effect on informal measures which would otherwise be destined to qualify as soft law. In fact, such informal have 'hardened' to become fully mandatory and we are actually faced with a misfit between the choice of a soft legal instrument and the true legislative intent of producing binding effects.

16.5 DLRs: A Spectrum between Recommendations and Directives?

As indicated above, soft law acts may be in fact be binding "despite [their] soft outward appearance", for example, "on the basis of their substance or as a result of an agreement between the author of an act and its addressees."[54] In such cases there is "an intention of binding force and what is at issue then is not true soft law, but hard law in the clothing of a soft law instrument."[55] The CJEU has devised a test for determining whether the measure under scrutiny is in fact hard law,[56] foreseeing an assessment of the content, context, wording and intention of the measure to ascertain whether it is designed to produce legal effects as a binding measure.

In the most recent attempt to reveal that a recommendation was in fact a hidden directive, Belgium sought the annulment of the Commission's recommendation on the organization of gambling.[57] The measure is what I have termed a directive-like recommendation (DLR): a specific version of Commission recommendations carrying a clause on implementation, deadlines and Member State reporting, highly reminiscent of directives.[58] Although it was adopted in the seemingly unthreatening form of a soft law measure, the Belgian government understood the gambling recommendation as a move to circumvent the Council, where the Commission would have otherwise expected some push-back. Belgium also feared that the Recommendation would constitute a first step in the process of harmonizing gambling regulation across Europe.

Belgium filed its action for annulment of the Recommendation in October 2014 at the General Court. Among others, Belgium pleaded the recommendation is in fact a binding measure in disguise, giving rise to obligations on the side of the Member States. The Commission maintained throughout that the recommendation has no binding force, and

---

53   Id. p. 279.
54   Senden 2004, p. 289. For an opposing view, *cf.* Peters 2007, pp. 411-412.
55   Senden 2004, pp. 462-463; *see* the cases *CIRFS, IJssel-Vliet* and *Germany v. Commission* below.
56   *Case C-322/88, Grimaldi*, paras. 14-16.
57   Commission Recommendation 2014/478/EU of 14 July 2014 on principles for the protection of consumers and players of online gambling services and for the prevention of minors from gambling online.
58   Commission Recommendation 2014/478/EU, Section XII.

being a measure with no legal effect, it cannot be challenged. While the General Court confirmed, that in line with the *Grimaldi* case-law "the mere fact that the contested recommendation is formally designated as a recommendation [...] cannot automatically rule out its classification as a challengeable act"[59] it underlined that the measure in question was "worded mainly in non-mandatory terms."[60] Following a comparison of the French, Danish, German, Estonian, Spanish, Italian, Dutch, Polish, Swedish and English language versions of the recommendation, it came to the conclusion that the measure was clearly not meant to be binding.[61]

Turning to the content, context and intention of the Recommendation, the General Court recalled that heed must be paid to the "purpose and general scheme of the rules of which it forms part."[62] In fact, several provisions of the Recommendation clarify, that the measure is not meant to interfere with national regulatory prerogatives in the area of gambling, recalling that in the absence of harmonization, Member States are free to design their own policies for the organization of gambling and the protection of consumers.[63] The General Court specifically elaborated on the special directive-like Section of the measure, noting that "despite the binding wording of [the relevant paragraphs] of the recommendation in certain language versions, the recommendation does not impose any obligation" on the Member States to effectively apply the principles set out in the act.[64] Hence, the General Court concluded that since the Recommendation "does not have and is not intended to have binding legal effects", it cannot be challenged in an action for annulment, and dismissed the action as inadmissible.[65] Belgium then appealed to the Court, only to have the General Court's order confirmed.

Since DLRs are considered to be non-binding and share the same fate as any other recommendation, there is no spectrum between recommendations and directives. Since the CJEU considers them to be simple recommendations, they do not seem to have any added value. Therefore, the question arises, why does the Commission regularly take recourse to this specific type of measure in various policy-fields? Is it a strategy to achieve directive-like effects through the compliance-pull of soft law while side-stepping the co-legislators?

---

59   Order of the General Court (Second Chamber) of 27 October 2015, *Case T-721/14, Kingdom of Belgium v. European Commission*, ECLI:EU:T:2015:829, para. 20.
60   Id.
61   Id. para. 72.
62   Id. para. 28.
63   Id. paras. 29-31.
64   Id. paras. 33-35.
65   Id. para. 37.

16.6 GOING SOFT: STRATEGIES FOR ADOPTING NON-BINDING NORMS

As Guzman and Meyer note, "the central mystery of soft law is the fact that states opt for something more than a complete absence of commitment, but something less than full-blown [...] law."[66] Why then, will the Commission or the co-legislators opt for the regulatory form of soft law? Scholarly literature has suggested several reasons for the choice of soft measures: accommodating the hard realities of policy assignment, institutional constraints and the need for inclusive, fast and flexible decision-making.

Adopting soft law may actually be a foregone conclusion and mandated by the Treaty legal basis itself, for example in the case of education policy measures enacted under Article 165(4) TFEU.[67] This reflects certain prior constitutional choices of the masters of the treaties, that is, the Member States, as enshrined in the distribution of competences.[68] In a Union "(still) marked by diversity in demands and national preferences, plus the (still) low mobility of families" hard law will be the exception, applied to policies "that have a clear supranational nature."[69] Only in areas of a 'clear supranational nature' where strong convergence is foreseen will the Union hold exclusive competences and/or the powers to enact hard law, for the harmonization or unification of national laws.

Based on the above, the burgeoning of soft law in policy fields pertaining to the exclusive competence of the EU may come as a surprise. Yet the high number of soft norm in the area of *e.g.* customs may be explained by the regulator's quest for greater flexibility: the level of detail necessary in this area, the need for rapid amendments and the imperative of taking "the latest developments of technology, safety and security" into account all call for the employment of soft measures.[70] Meanwhile, the desire to evade structural constraints such as tedious and lengthy legislative procedures producing hard law, will also prompt decision-makers to find more flexible solutions with the help of soft law. Finally, the Commission may resort to soft tools out of

> "a necessity, because of lacking legislative powers of the EU or because the Union legislator does not manage to adopt legislation or only to a (too) limited

---

66 Andrew T. Guzman & Timothy L. Meyer, 'Explaining Soft law' *Berkeley Program in Law and Economics, Working Paper Series*, 2009, p. 10.

67 *See* Senden 2005, pp. 91 and 93; Petra Lea Láncos, 'Soft Structure vs. Soft Measure: Fleshing Out the Tension in EU Education Policy', *Legal Issues of Economic Integration*, Vol. 45, Issue 3, 2018, pp. 258. *et seq.*

68 *Cf.* Agustín José Menéndez, 'A Proportionate Constitution? Economic Freedoms, Substantive Constitutional Choices and Dérapages in European Union Law', *in* Edoardo Chiti *et al.* (eds.), *The European Rescue of the European Union? The Existential Crisis of the European Political Project*, Oslo, 2012, p. 80.

69 Rui Henrique Alves & Oscar Afonso, 'Fiscal Federalism in the European Union: How Far Are We?', *in* Jesús Ferreiro *et al.* (eds.), *Fiscal Policy in the European Union*, Palgrave Macmillan, 2008, p. 9.

70 Láncos 2018, p. 268.

extent as a result of the applicability of the unanimity requirement and national sovereignty objections."

An example would be the DLR discussed above: the Commission recommendation on the organization of gambling, a measure adopted in the form of soft law, due to the tension between the push for legislation coming from the European Parliament and the lack of Council support on this issue. Often, the informality of soft mechanisms will "prove to be the only way forward with a view to realizing certain transnational socio-economic goals that cannot be addressed otherwise."[71]

16.7   Summary and Suggestion for Further Research

This short overview of the notion, classification and normativity of soft law measures in general and EU soft law in particular sheds light on the relative imprecision characteristic of legal concepts. Soft law may be employed by the EU legislator for a plethora of reasons and the manifold soft instruments and mechanisms will give rise to very different obligations on the side of the Member States as elaborated in the relevant jurisprudence of the CJEU. This complex system of soft norms supplementing, substituting and interpreting hard law is so diverse, one could say each Union policy field has its own selection of preferred soft instruments and the strategies for adopting them.

Meanwhile, research into Union soft law seems to completely disregard the national implementation of the same, or the lack thereof. Even the Commission seems only to focus on the national implementation certain types of soft measures, in particular DLRs. The Commission's collection of soft law implementation data is therefore unsystematic and is restricted in focus: which soft provisions had been implemented through national legislation and to what extent. What we are missing is the mapping of systems and procedures at national level governing soft law implementation and the considerations of Member State legislators guiding the decision on whether or not to implement. This data could be used as a starting point for determining indicators for the effectiveness of EU soft law and its contribution to the convergence of Member States' law.

---

71   Linda Senden & A. (Ton) van den Brink, 'Checks and Balances of Rule-Making', *European Parliament Policy Department C – Citizens' Rights and Constitutional Affairs*, 2012, pp. 13-14.

17 FROM KÁSLER TO DUNAI

A Brief Overview of Recent Decisions of the CJEU in Hungarian Cases Concerning Unfair Terms in Consumer Contracts

*Miklós Zoltán Fehér**

Keywords

preliminary ruling, consumer protection, unfair terms, Directive 93/13/EEC, consumer loan contract

Abstract

The CJEU was recently called upon to interpret Council Directive 93/13/EEC on unfair terms in consumer contracts in relation to consumer loan contracts denominated in a foreign currency and in relation to the legislation adopted by the Hungarian Parliament in 2014 concerning such contracts in several Hungarian preliminary ruling procedures. The decisions of the CJEU, starting with the judgment rendered in case *C-26/13, Kásler and Káslerné Rábai,* have not only contributed to the ever-evolving case-law relating to Directive 93/13/EEC but also provided national jurisdictions with useful guidance on the interpretation and application of the Directive in the specific area of consumer loan con-tracts concluded in a foreign currency, an area of prolific litigation before Hungarian courts in recent years. The CJEU also evaluated the Hungarian legislation adopted in 2014 to deal with certain issues relating to such contracts and seemed to approve of its conformity with Directive 93/13/EEC in a series of decisions up until the judgment made in case *C-117/18, Dunai.* In that judgment, however, the findings of the CJEU may have been based on a misinterpretation of the content of national legislation, leading to a perhaps erroneous conclusion and most certainly prompting a re-emergence of controversies before national courts.

17.1 INTRODUCTION

Hungarian judges have been very active in requesting preliminary rulings from the CJEU since the accession of Hungary to the EU in 2004. This is also illustrated by the fact that

---

* Miklós Zoltán Fehér: Head of Department at the Hungarian Ministry of Justice, Agent of the Hungarian Government before the CJEU. The views and opinions expressed in this article are those of the author.

the first request for a preliminary ruling to arrive from one of the new Member States in 2004 was from the Szombathely District Court *(Szombathelyi Városi Bíróság)* in *Ynos*,[1] relating to the interpretation of Directive 93/13/EEC on unfair terms in consumer contracts.[2] As of 1 May 2019, 195 preliminary ruling procedures have been initiated by Hungarian courts in the most diverse subjects including taxation, consumer protection, the four freedoms, competition policy, public procurement, private international law *etc.* This impressing number, which places Hungary in the front-ranks regarding the number of preliminary ruling references relative to the size of the country, demonstrates an awareness on behalf of the Hungarian judicature in relation to EU law as well as a genuine trust in the CJEU to resolve questions regarding the interpretation of EU law that are crucial to national judicial proceedings.

It is not surprising therefore that in recent years Hungarian courts have repeatedly sought the interpretation of Directive 93/13/EEC on unfair terms in consumer contracts in relation to loan contracts denominated in a foreign currency that have become a source of bitter litigation before these courts. Most of the 22 Hungarian preliminary ruling procedures relating to Directive 93/13/EEC[3] had been initiated in connection with such (mortgage) loan contracts and several of them directly referred to a new series of laws adopted by the Hungarian Parliament in 2014 to address certain issues surrounding such loan contracts and the unfair terms they contained.

The origins of the problem may be traced back to the 2000s when a considerable part of mortgage and other loans in Hungary had been taken out in euro, Swiss franc or Japanese yen, given the difference in the interest rates of these currencies and the Hungarian forint. The economic crisis of 2008 has had a negative impact on the exchange rate of the Hun-

---

1   Judgment of 10 January 2016, *Case C-302/04, Ynos kft v. János Varga*, ECLI:EU:C:2006:9.
2   Council Directive 93/13/EEC of 5 April 1993 on unfair terms in consumer contracts.
3   The Hungarian cases relating to Directive 93/13/EEC are: *Case C-302/04, Ynos kft v. János Varga*; Judgment of 9 November 2010, *Case C-137/08, VB Pénzügyi Lízing*, ECLI:EU:C:2010:659; Judgment of 4 June 2009, *Case C-243/08, Pannon GSM*, ECLI:EU:C:2009:350; Judgment of 26 April 2012, *Case C-472/10, Invitel*, ECLI:EU:C:2012:242; Judgment of 30 May 2013, *Case C-397/11, Jőrös*, ECLI:EU:C:2013:340; Judgment of 21 February 2013, *Case C-472/11, Banif Plus Bank*, ECLI:EU:C:2013:88; Judgment of 30 April 2014, *Case C-26/13, Kásler and Káslerné Rábai*, ECLI:EU:C:2014:282; Order of 3 April 2014, *Case C-342/13, Sebestyén*, ECLI:EU:C:2014:1857; Judgment of 12 February 2015, *Case C-567/13, Baczó and Vizsnyiczai*, ECLI:EU:C:2015:88; Judgment of 1 October 2015, *Case C-32/14, ERSTE Bank Hungary*, ECLI:EU:C:2015:637; Judgment of 3 December 2015, *Case C-312/14, Banif Plus Bank*, ECLI:EU:C:2015:794; Judgment of 31 May 2018, *Case C-483/16, Sziber*, ECLI:EU:C:2018:367; Judgment of 20 September 2018, *Case C-51/17, OTP Bank and OTP Faktoring*, ECLI:EU:C:2018:750; Judgment of 14 March 2019, *Case C-118/17, Dunai*, ECLI:EU:C:2019:207; Order of 22 February 2018, *Case C-126/17, ERSTE Bank Hungary*, ECLI:EU:C:2018:107; Order of 21 November 2017, *Case C-232/17, VE*, ECLI:EU:C:2017:907; Order of 21 November 2017, *Case C-259/17, Rózsavölgyi*, ECLI:EU:C:2017:905; Order of 8 November 2018, *Case C-227/18, VE*, ECLI:EU:C:2018:891. Still pending before the CJEU at the time of the submission of the manuscript were *Case C-38/17, GT; Case C-621/17, Kiss and CIB Bank; Case C-511/17, Lintner;* and *Case C-34/18, Lovasné Tóth.*

garian forint in relation to these currencies, which in turn resulted in a considerable rise in the amount of the monthly instalments for many debtors, given the fact that the instalments were determined in the foreign currency of the contract. Thousands of consumers challenged the loan contracts claiming that the contracts were void, referring *inter alia* to unfair terms they allegedly contained. The Hungarian courts were thus called upon to interpret and apply the Hungarian legal provisions transposing Directive 93/13/EEC.[4]

17.2   THE KÁSLER JUDGMENT[5]

In 2013 the Curia of Hungary *(Kúria)* requested a preliminary ruling from the CJEU seeking the interpretation of Directive 93/13/EEC. In particular, it requested the interpretation of one of the controversial terms that most of the consumer loan contracts denominated in foreign currency contained: the contractual term that allowed the lender to calculate the amount of the monthly repayment instalments owed by the consumer in accordance with the selling rate of exchange of the foreign currency it applied. Before this contractual term could be assessed, however, it had to be clarified whether the term in question defined 'the main subject matter of the contract' which, pursuant to Article 4(2) of Directive 93/13/EEC, may not be subject to an assessment of unfairness in so far as it was drawn up in plain intelligible language.

On request of the Curia of Hungary, the CJEU found that the national court may find such a term to constitute the 'main subject-matter of a contract' only in so far as it was found, having regard to the nature, general scheme and stipulations of the contract and its legal and factual context, that that term laid down an essential obligation of that agreement which, as such characterized it. The CJEU has excluded that the contractual term in question constituted 'remuneration' the adequacy of which could not be the subject of an examination as regards unfairness under Article 4(2) of Directive 93/13/EEC.

The CJEU went on to interpret the requirement of transparency of contractual terms laid down by Directive 93/13/EEC as requiring not only that the relevant term be grammatically intelligible to the consumer, but also that the contract set out transparently the specific functioning of the mechanism of conversion for the foreign currency and the

---

4   For a more detailed background of the issue of loan contracts concluded in a foreign currency in Hungary, *see* Judit Fazekas, 'The Consumer Credit Crisis and Unfair Contract Terms Regulation – Before and After Kásler', *Journal of European Consumer and Market Law*, Vol. 6, Issue 3, 2017, pp. 99-106. More generally on the subject of EU consumer law *see* Christian Twigg-Flesner (ed.), *Research Handbook on EU Consumer and Contract Law*, Edward Elgar Publishing, 2016.

5   *See* Case C-26/13, *Kásler and Káslerné Rábai*. For a detailed analysis of the judgment, *see* Rita Sik-Simon, 'Missbräuchliche Klauseln in Fremdwährungskreditverträgen – Klauselersatz durch dispositive nationale Vorschriften, EuGH Rs C-26/13 (Kásler) und Kúria 2/2014. PJE határozata', *Journal of European Consumer and Market Law*, Vol. 3, Issue 4, 2014, pp. 256-261.

relationship between that mechanism and that provided for by other contractual terms relating to the advance of the loan, so that that consumer is in a position to evaluate, on the basis of clear, intelligible criteria, the economic consequences for him which derive from it. This formula established by the CJEU relating to the requirement of transparency of contractual terms and that they should be intelligible to the consumer has appeared in several judgments since *Kásler and Káslerné Rábai.*[6]

Finally, the CJEU answered the question of the Curia of Hungary relating to the possible substitution of an unfair term with a national legal provision in the affirmative by stating that Article 6(1) of Directive 93/13/EEC does not preclude a rule of national law enabling the national court to remedy the invalidity of an unfair term by substituting it with a supplementary provision of national law.

17.3 FOLLOW-UP OF THE KÁSLER JUDGMENT

Following the CJEU's judgment in *Kásler and Káslerné Rábai,* the Curia of Hungary adopted a so-called uniformity decision. Decision No. 2/2014 PJE[7] sought to give guidance to lower courts and ensure a uniform application of the law in cases relating to consumer loan contracts denominated in foreign currency. In the decision the Curia of Hungary concluded that the contractual term considered in *Kásler and Káslerné Rábai* was unfair because the financial institution did not provide any direct service to the consumer, and therefore it constituted an unjustified cost for the consumer. According to the Curia of Hungary, these terms were also unfair because the economic reasons for their application were not clear, not intelligible and not transparent to the consumer. The Curia of Hungary decided that the buying and selling rates applied in foreign exchange loan contracts as rates of conversion were to be replaced by the official foreign exchange rate of the Hungarian National Bank (the central bank of Hungary) until mandatory provisions of law enter into force.

In Decision No. 2/2014 PJE the Curia of Hungary also considered another term frequently applied in loan contracts, namely contractual clauses allowing for the unilateral amendment of a contract. These terms were, according to the Curia of Hungary, only fair if they complied with the principles previously determined by the Curia of Hungary. That is the principle of clear and intelligible drafting, the principle of specific definition, the principle of objectivity, the principle of effectivity and proportionality, the principle of transparency, the principle of terminability, and the principle of symmetry.

---

6   *See* in particular in relation to loan contracts concluded in a foreign currency, Judgment of 20 September 2017, *Case C-186/16, Andriciuc and Others,* ECLI:EU:C:2017:703.
7   Hungarian Official Gazette *(Magyar Közlöny),* 2014/91, p. 10975.

Perhaps the most controversial part of the decision of the Curia of Hungary at the time concerned the contractual term that allocated the risk of the exchange rate of the currency in which the contract was concluded entirely to the consumer. To the disappointment of many consumers who have concluded such contracts, and who anticipated that these contractual terms would be found to be unfair and, as a consequence, void, the Curia of Hungary found that such terms form part of the main subject-matter of the contract, and are, therefore, as the main rule, exempt from assessment from the perspective of unfairness. The unfairness of such a clause may be assessed and established only if its content, *i.e.* the text of the contract and the information provided by the financial institution, was not clear and intelligible to the average consumer, who was reasonably well-informed, reasonably observant and circumspect when the contract was concluded. If there was a reason for the consumer to believe that the risk of exchange was not real or that it only entailed a limited burden, the contractual clause regarding the risk of exchange was unfair, resulting in the invalidity of the contract in part or in full.

In 2014 the Hungarian government proposed a series of legislation to Parliament with a view to implement the CJEU's judgment in *Kásler and Káslerné Rábai* and Decision No. 2/2014 PJE of the Curia of Hungary. The three laws subsequently adopted[8] have, *inter alia*, declared the contractual terms relating to the application of different exchange rates for the advancement and the repayment of the loan, considered in *Kásler and Káslerné Rábai* earlier, to be unfair. Another term previously dealt with by the Curia of Hungary, the contractual clauses allowing for a unilateral amendment of the contract were presumed to be unfair, with the possibility for the financial institutions applying such terms to demonstrate in court proceedings that they satisfied the conditions reiterated by the Curia of Hungary in Decision No. 2/2014 PJE. The new legislation provided for the settlement of accounts to be conducted by the lenders having regard to the consequences of the unfair nature of the two terms in question. It also set out a series of procedural rules relating to ongoing court procedures, including those where consumers decided to proceed with their case after the unfair terms in questions were removed from their contract and after the settlement of accounts had taken place. The Hungarian legislator also prescribed a mandatory transformation of contracts. These were to be denominated in Hungarian forints, to exclude any future escalation of consumer burdens in relation to the change in the exchange rate of the foreign currency in which the contract was originally concluded.

---

8   Act XXXVIII of 2014 regulating specific matters relating to the decision of the Curia of Hungary to safeguard the uniformity of the law concerning loan contracts concluded by financial institutions with consumers; Act XL of 2014 on the rules relating to the settlement of accounts referred to by Act XXXVIII of 2014, regulating specific matters relating to the decision of the Curia of Hungary to safeguard the uniformity of the law concerning loan contracts concluded by financial institutions with consumers, and other provisions and Act LXXVII of 2014 regulating various matters relating to the amendment of the currency of denomination of consumer loan contracts and to the rules governing interest.

17.4   THE SZIBER JUDGMENT[9]

The conformity with Directive 93/13/EEC of some of the procedural provisions set out by the new legislation was raised by the Budapest Regional Court *(Fővárosi Törvényszék)* in *Sziber*. The national court wanted to ascertain in particular whether Directive 93/13/EEC precluded the provisions of the new legislation that required the applicant to regularize his application by stating the legal consequences sought in the event of a finding that the loan agreement or part of it was invalid and to complete the settlement of accounts by specifying the amounts considered to have been paid on the basis of unfair terms other than those already taken into account in that settlement. The referring court also inquired on the conformity with Directive 93/13/EEC of Hungarian legislative provisions that excluded the consumer from requesting the application of *restitutio in integrum* as the legal consequence of the contract's invalidity.

The provisions in question were intended by the Hungarian legislator to ensure a more effective resolution of court proceedings in cases where consumers relied on the unfairness of contractual terms other than the ones already deemed unfair by the legislation on the basis of Decision No. 2/2014 PJE. In particular, the applicants were required to state the legal consequence they sought in order to avoid an incomplete ruling, *i.e.* a ruling declaring the contract or the contractual term void without determining the legal consequence applied, otherwise permitted by generally applicable rules of the Hungarian Civil Code. Experience had shown that this possibility was frequently employed by debtors, resulting merely in the prolongation of litigation, as the final resolution of the dispute usually required further court proceedings. The legal consequences that the consumers were required by the legislation to choose from were those established by earlier case-law relating to such contracts as the only possible legal consequences among those provided for by the general rules of the Hungarian Civil Code. By excluding the possibility of *restitutio in integrum,* the legislation had taken note of the particular nature of loan contracts, where provisions already rendered by the parties under the contract cannot be made undone and therefore the original situation of the parties may not be fully restored as if the contract had never existed.[10]

In its judgment the CJEU found that Article 7 of Directive 93/13/EEC did not preclude, in principle, national legislation which lays down specific procedural requirements, such as those referred to by the national court, provided that a finding that terms in such an agreement were unfair would restore the legal and factual situation that the consumer would have been in had those unfair terms not existed. In particular, the CJEU reiterated that the imposition of additional procedural requirements on consumers deriving rights

---

9   *Case C-483/16, Sziber.*
10   *See* more on the question of irreversibility of loan contract below.

from EU law does not, in itself, mean that those procedural requirements are less favorable and thus violate the principle of equivalence.

The CJEU acknowledged that the aim of the legislation in question was to shorten and simplify the procedures before the national courts, with due consideration to the large number of consumer loan contracts denominated in foreign currency that included the two contractual terms in question. It added that, in similar cases which did not involve rights derived from EU law, a finding of invalidity of one or more unfair terms may not be sufficient to resolve the dispute definitively, a second procedure being necessary to determine the legal consequences of the total or partial invalidity of the contract. As regards the obligation of the consumer to specify the amount considered to be unduly paid, the CJEU found that it did not appear to be less favorable than the rules applicable to similar actions based on national law. This is because this obligation only applied where the consumer relied on the invalidity of allegedly unfair terms other than the two terms covered by the legislation and it may be considered to be merely a specific expression of the general rule applicable to civil procedural law, in accordance with which an application must be specific and quantified.

The CJEU went on to consider the provisions in question from the perspective of the principle of effective judicial protection. The CJEU recalled that the fact that a particular procedure sets out certain procedural requirements that the consumer must respect in order to assert his rights did not mean that he did not enjoy effective judicial protection. According to the CJEU, although it was true that the procedural rules in question required an additional effort from the consumer, they were aimed at addressing an exceptional situation and pursued a general interest in the proper administration of justice, and were therefore likely to prevail over private interests, provided that they did not go beyond what was necessary to achieve their objective. As regards the provision that precluded the consumer from requesting the court to order the restoration of the situation prior to the conclusion of the loan contract, or *in integrum restitutio*, the CJEU held that it was for the referring court to ascertain whether it may be considered that a finding that terms of the contract were unfair would restore the legal and factual situation that the consumer would have been in had those unfair terms not existed, including a right to restitution of advantages wrongfully obtained by the lenders on the basis of those unfair terms.

17.5   THE OTP BANK AND OTP FAKTORING JUDGMENT[11]

The next series of questions to be raised in a preliminary ruling procedure related to whether the legislation of 2014 excluded the examination under Directive 93/13/EEC of

---

11   *Case C-51/17, OTP Bank and OTP Faktoring.*

the terms that were replaced as a result of the legislation, since these terms were, according to the referring court, the Budapest Regional Court of Appeal *(Fővárosi Ítélőtábla)*, no longer 'contractual terms which have not been individually negotiated' within the meaning of the Directive. Even if those terms would be classified as 'contractual terms', according to the referring court, the term relating to the exchange rate risk that the consumer ran in relation to the currency of the contract could fall within the exclusion laid down by Article 1(2) of Directive 93/13/EEC. This is because it may constitute a contractual term which 'reflects mandatory statutory or regulatory provisions' within the meaning of that provision and would therefore not be subject to the provisions of the Directive. Subsequent questions addressed the assessment of the terms under the Directive and whether it would be permissible to take account of any other unfair terms, as they appeared in the contract at the time of its conclusion, even though they were annulled and, where necessary, replaced pursuant to provisions of national law. The referring court also sought clarification on the CJEU's case-law relating to the identification of unfair terms by the national court of its own motion.

The CJEU found, first, that the concept of 'term which has not been individually negotiated' in Article 3(1) of Directive 93/13/EEC covered contractual terms amended by a national statutory provision adopted after the conclusion of a contract with a consumer, for the purpose of removing a term from that contract which was null and void. On the other hand, Article 1(2) excluded from the scope of Directive 93/13/EEC terms which reflected mandatory provisions of national law that were inserted after the conclusion of a loan contract, with the intention of removing a term from the contract which was void, by imposing an exchange rate set by the National Bank.

The CJEU, however, found that a term relating to the foreign exchange risk was not excluded from the scope of the Directive. The CJEU recalled that Article 1(2) of Directive 93/13/EEC must be construed narrowly and therefore the fact that some terms which reflect statutory provisions fall outside the scope of the Directive does not mean that the validity of other terms, which were included in the same contract and were not covered by statutory provisions, may not be assessed by the national court in light of the Directive. The CJEU acknowledged that the Hungarian legislation in question was not intended to address in full the issue of foreign exchange risk in respect of the period between the time when the loan contract was concluded and its conversion into Hungarian forints. Thus, the contractual terms which addressed the issue of foreign exchange risk and which were not covered by statutory amendments fell within the scope of Article 4(2) of Directive 93/13/EEC and could be assessed in light of the requirement of being drafted in plain intelligible language.

As far as the requirement for a contractual term to be drafted in plain intelligible language is concerned, the CJEU reiterated the formula established in *Kásler and Káslerné Rábai* and in *Andriciuc and Others*, requiring financial institutions to provide borrowers with adequate information to enable them to make well-informed and prudent decisions. The term relating to foreign exchange risk must be understood by the consumer both at the formal and grammatical level and also in terms of its actual effects, so that the average consumer, who is reasonably well informed and reasonably observant and circumspect, would not only be aware of the possibility of a depreciation of the national currency in relation to the foreign currency in which the loan was denominated, but would also be able to assess the potentially significant economic consequences of such a term in respect of his financial obligations.

As far as the questions concerning the scope of assessment by the national court are concerned, the CJEU found that the plainness and intelligibility of contractual terms must be assessed by referring, at the time of conclusion of the contract, to all circumstances surrounding the conclusion of the contract and to all the other terms of the contract, notwithstanding that some of those terms have been declared or were presumed to be unfair and, accordingly, annulled at a later point in time by the national legislature. Based on earlier case-law, the CJEU reaffirmed that Articles 6(1) and 7(1) of Directive 93/13/EEC must be interpreted as meaning that it is for the national court to identify of its own motion, in the place of the consumer in his capacity as an applicant, any unfairness of a contractual term, provided that it has available to it the legal and factual elements necessary for that task.

17.6   THE DUNAI JUDGMENT [12]

Already addressed some extent in *Sziber*, the question whether the Hungarian legislation of 2014 ensured that when a court finds a contractual term to be unfair the consumer should be placed in a legal and factual situation in which the consumer would have been in had the unfair term never existed, was brought before the CJEU once again in *Dunai*. The referring court, the Buda Central District Court *(Budai Központi Kerületi Bíróság)* has, in its reference for a preliminary ruling, interpreted the Hungarian legislation as pre-cluding the national court from finding that the loan contract denominated in a foreign currency is invalid since legislation voided the term concerning the difference between the buying rate and the selling rate of the currency concerned. This meant that the contract remained valid and, consequently, the consumer was obliged to bear the financial cost resulting from the exchange risk of the foreign currency. The national court had asked for the interpretation of the judgment in *Kásler and Káslerné Rábai* as regards the possibility of national courts to remedy the invalidity of the contract where the continuation of the contract was contrary to the economic interests of the consumer. The referring court also

12   *Case C-118/17, Dunai.*

challenged the possibility of Member State legislators to adopt legislation modifying consumer contracts, such as the Hungarian legislation of 2014. It also challenged the possibility of the highest court of a Member State to adopt decisions to orient lower courts and ensure the uniform application of the law, as the Curia of Hungary had done in Decision No. 2/2014 PJE.

The CJEU understood the questions relating to the substance of the legislation as referring to the possibility of the consumer to rely on the unfair nature of the term regulating the exchange rate risk. The CJEU first reiterated its judgment in *OTP Bank and OTP Faktoring*, in which it had held that the terms included in consumer contracts as a result of such legislation reflected statutory provisions, and as such were excluded from the scope of Directive 93/13/EEC in accordance with Article 1(2) of the Directive. The CJEU went on to find that the questions referred did not relate to terms included by legislation in the loan contracts, but to the impact of that legislation on protection guarantees resulting from Article 6(1) of Directive 93/13/EEC.

The CJEU noted that by addressing the problems of contractual terms governing the exchange difference, by amending those terms through legislation and by upholding, at the same time, the validity of loan contracts, the Hungarian legislation fulfilled the objective pursued by Directive 93/13/EEC to restore the balance between the parties, whilst maintaining, as far as possible, the validity of the entirety of the contract. The Hungarian legislation was found to be in compliance with Directive 93/13/EEC as far as the term relating to the exchange difference was concerned, in the case of which the legislation allowed the restoration of the legal and factual situation that consumers would have been in if those unfair terms had not existed. However, the CJEU found that legislation governing the term relating to the exchange rate risk seemed to preclude that outcome and was therefore in violation of the requirements of the Directive. This was because, in the opinion of the CJEU and based on the information submitted to it by the referring national court, Hungarian legislation seemed to imply that when consumers invoked the unfair nature of the term relating to the exchange rate risk, they also had to request that the court declare the contract to be valid until the date of the decision. Therefore, according to the CJEU, this legislation was capable of preventing consumers from being unbound by the unfair terms and the contract from being cancelled in its entirety if it could not continue to exist without that contractual term.

The CJEU also noted that, whereas in *Kásler and Káslerné Rábai* it had ruled that a national court may substitute an unfair contractual term with supplementary provision of domestic law in order to ensure the continued existence of the contract, that possibility was limited to cases in which the cancellation of the contract in its entirety would expose the consumer to particularly unfavorable consequences. The CJEU found that in the main proceedings, based on the information provided by the national court, the continuation of the contract would be contrary to the interests of the consumer and, therefore, the substitution pursuant to *Kásler and Káslerné Rábai* did not appear to be applicable in the present case.

As regards the uniformity decisions adopted by the Curia of Hungary, the CJEU found that Directive 93/13/EEC, read in the light of Article 47 of the EU Charter of Fundamental Rights, did not preclude the adoption of such decisions, in so far as they did not prevent lower courts from ensuring the full effect of the provisions of Directive 93/13/EEC and from offering consumers an effective remedy for the protection of the rights that they can derive therefrom, or from referring a question for a preliminary ruling to the CJEU in that regard.

17.7   A Brief Comment on the Dunai Judgment

The judgment in *Dunai* was the first judgment in relation to the Hungarian legislation of 2014 on consumer loan contracts concluded in foreign currency more or less explicitly declaring that the legislation had failed to comply with Directive 93/13/EEC. Although the CJEU has been careful to emphasize at every step of the way that it based its assumptions on the information provided by the national court in the reference for a preliminary ruling and that the national court had to verify whether, in fact, the legislation had the effects attributed to it by the CJEU, the judgment has been quickly interpreted in Hungary as a categorical declaration of the incompatibility of the relevant legislative provisions with Directive 93/13/EEC.[13]

Within a few days of the delivery of the judgment in *Dunai*, on 18 March 2019, the Curia of Hungary issued a statement dealing with the judgment.[14] The Curia of Hungary stated that it was of the view that the Hungarian legislation in question did not have the effect of excluding the cancellation of the loan contract based on the unfair nature of the term relating to the exchange rate risk, which would result in the consumer being relieved of the burden of the exchange rate risk. In the opinion of the Curia of Hungary, while it was true that the legislation had prescribed that the consequences of the invalidity of the contract were the 'declaration of validity or effectiveness of the contract up to the time of adoption of the [court's] decision', these legal consequences resulted in relieving the consumer from the exchange rate risk with retroactive effect as of the conclusion of the contract, if it was to be found that the term relating to the exchange rate risk was unfair due to the

---

13   This may probably also be due in part to the press release of the CJEU relating to the judgment, the 'headline' of which read: "The Hungarian legislation excluding the retroactive cancellation of a loan contract denominated in a foreign currency which includes an unfair term relating to the exchange-rate risk is contrary to EU law", at https://curia.europa.eu/jcms/upload/docs/application/pdf/2019-03/cp190028en.pdf.

14   *See* https://kuria-birosag.hu/hu/sajto/kuria-kozlemenye-az-europai-unio-birosaganak-dunai-ugyben-hozott-hatarozatarol.

breach of the obligation of providing the consumer with adequate information in accordance with Decision No. 2/2014 PJE and the CJEU's judgment in *OTP Bank and OTP Faktoring*. The Curia of Hungary also stated that the legal consequences of the invalidity of unfair terms relating to the exchange rate risk would be further discussed in future meetings of the consultative body previously set up by the president of the Curia of Hungary for the purpose of analyzing the case-law relating to the loan contracts concluded in a foreign currency.

Although the Curia of Hungary has omitted to expressly address the possible reasons for the obvious contradiction between its position and the CJEU's judgment in *Dunai*, it may be concluded that the latter may have been based on a misinterpretation of the precise content of the national legislation, leading to an erroneous conclusion.[15] In fact, the legal consequence of invalidity of a contract known in Hungarian civil law as 'declaration of effectiveness of the contract up to the time of adoption of the [court's] decision', prescribed in the legislation of 2014 as one of the legal consequences that the consumer had to request, can easily be misread as precluding the national court from drawing the consequences of invalidity of the whole contract with *ex tunc* effect. Meanwhile in reality it is merely a legal instrument to address situations where *restitutio in integrum* is not possible, as for example, one could argue, in the case of loan contracts.[16]

While the finding of the invalidity of the whole contract entails that it is null and void from the time of its conclusion by the parties, certain types of contracts cannot be fully reversed, as the services already rendered by the parties under the contract cannot be made undone. Therefore, in such cases, when the contract is declared invalid by a court, the latter has to rule on these services already rendered by the parties. The 'declaration of effectiveness of the contract up to the time of adoption of the [court's] decision' is the legal concept in Hungarian law that enables the court to rule on such services by filling the void that the declaration of invalidity has left. This does not, however, mean that the consequences of invalidity are in any way restricted or that the term found to be unfair by the court continues to exert an effect between the time of the conclusion of the contract and the judgment declaring its invalidity. On the contrary, should a court declare a consumer

---

15 It must be emphasised once again that the CJEU has presumably based its reading of national law on the information it received from the referring court and on the case file, including a translation of the legal provisions in question, which may have contributed to a misunderstanding of its content. It may also be pointed out, however, that the CJEU decided to proceed without holding a hearing in the case, which might have proved useful in clarifying the precise meaning of the national legislation, particularly because the reference for a preliminary ruling did not address the issue with sufficient clarity.

16 The question of the legal consequences of the invalidity of loan contracts has been addressed by an expert group analyzing the case-law set up by the Curia of Hungary in March 2014, where the majority opinion opted for the impossibility of *restitutio in integrum* in case of the invalidity of loan contracts, while a strong minority supported the contrary opinion, at https://kuria-birosag.hu/sites/default/files/joggyak/ossze-foglalo_velemeny_i.pdf.

loan contract null and void *ab initio* as a consequence of the unfair nature of a term that constituted the main subject-matter of the contract and without which the contract may not continue to exist, it must settle the accounts between the parties and rule on the services rendered without offset, having full regard to the fact that the unfair term was not binding upon the consumer. Therefore, in such cases the court first finds that the contract is invalid, resulting in the consumer being unbound by the unfair term and then proceeds to settle the outstanding claims between the parties based on the factual circumstance that the contract had nevertheless deployed certain effects until the declaration of its invalidity. It seems, therefore, that if the above interpretation of the national legal concept is correct, the premise of the judgment in *Dunai* as to the effects of the legislation is mistaken, and the legal provisions may pass the test of conformity with Directive 93/13/EEC after all.

It should also be noted that the CJEU has made an important point in the judgment as to the relevance of the consumer's economic interests in deciding on the eventual cancellation or continuation of the contract. Unfortunately, the question was addressed only in a brief two paragraphs of the judgment,[17] which is in stark contrast with the opinion of Advocate General Wahl,[18] who devoted 24 paragraphs to this question, coming to an entirely different conclusion. Considering that the consequences to be attached to the economic interest of the consumer was one of the questions explicitly raised by the referring court, it is all the more surprising that the CJEU merely declared that the possibility of the national court to substitute a supplementary provision of domestic law for an unfair contractual term in order to ensure the continued existence of the contract is limited to cases where the cancellation of the contract would be unfavorable to the consumer. This seems to be an important distinction as compared to earlier judgments, where the CJEU seemed to confirm that the continued existence, if legally possible, of the contract was the solution preferred by Directive 93/13/EEC,[19] and that the national court cannot base its decision to annul the contract solely on a possible advantage for one of the parties.[20] Apart from the novelty of the approach it is also noteworthy that here again, the CJEU has fully relied on the information provided by the referring court to find that in the main proceedings the continuing existence of the contract seemed to be contrary to the interest of the consumer and therefore, the substitution of a supplementary provision of domestic law 'did not seem to be applicable'.

---

17   *Case C-118/17, Dunai,* paras. 54-55.
18   Opinion of Advocate General Nils Wahl delivered on 15 November 2018, ECLI:EU:C:2018:921.
19   *See e.g. Case C-51/17, OTP Bank and OTP Faktoring,* para. 60.
20   Judgment of 15 March 2012, *Case C-453/10, Pereničová and Perenič,* ECLI:EU:C:2012:144, paras. 31-33.

17.8   Conclusions

Several conclusions may be drawn from this brief overview of recent decisions rendered in Hungarian preliminary ruling procedures relating to consumer loan contracts concluded in foreign currencies. First, it seems clear that several national courts were not satisfied with the solutions adopted by the Curia of Hungary and later on by the national legislator to the problems relating to these contracts. They have therefore challenged certain elements of the case-law of the Curia of Hungary and the Hungarian legislation adopted in 2014 with regard to Directive 93/13/EEC. It follows that the CJEU had to verify the conformity of a juxtaposition of contractual terms, national case-law and several layers of national legal provisions with the Directive. These national provisions were, and continue to be, disputed before the courts and also by the courts themselves. It may also be concluded that the untangling of the meaning of national legal provisions and in particular those of national civil law concepts in light of Directive 93/13/EEC remains a difficult task where the CJEU shall not neglect to take into account the complexity of issues raised and should preferably rely on multiple sources of information relating to the exact content of national legislation brought before it by the national courts. As for the national courts, it should be reiterated that in the context of the judicial dialogue under the Article 234 TFEU procedure they have the responsibility to provide the CJEU with reliable and clear information relating to the national legal provisions that they intend to apply or, as the case may be, set aside in the light of the interpretation of EU law sought by a reference for a preliminary ruling.

18 LEGAL CHALLENGES OF THE RETENTION OF WORKER STATUS AS REFLECTED IN RECENT CASE-LAW OF THE CJEU

Laura Gyeney*

Keywords

free movement of workers, EU citizens, right to move and reside freely, retention of EU worker status, equal treatment, welfare benefits

Abstract

In recent years, a growing number of cases related to the retention of worker status have emerged in CJEU jurisprudence with reference to welfare benefits, requiring a much deeper analysis of the field treated earlier as peripheral. Such an analysis seems especially justified in light of the current political and legal discourse concerning the issue of free movement, focusing on the question of equal treatment in the field of welfare assistance for mobile citizens. The purpose of this study is to present and put into context the relevant case-law of recent years by analyzing the judgments of the CJEU in two cases that are benchmarks in this field: the *Tarola* and *Saint Prix* cases. Both cases highlight the key role that economically active status continues to play in integration law. These judgments also shed light on the challenges arising from the difficulties in distinguishing between the economically active and inactive EU citizen statuses. This issue emerged as an increasingly grave problem in the field of law of free movement, posing a serious dilemma for law enforcement.

18.1 INTRODUCTION

In legal literature the issue of the retention of worker status[1] is generally discussed only peripherally, within the framework of the general presentation of the field of free movement of persons, as an inherent but marginal slice of it.[2] This is not surprising, for in the history

---

* Laura Gyeney: associate professor, Pázmány Péter Catholic University, Budapest.

1 The retention of worker status refers to the legal statuses defined under Article 7(3) of Free Movement Directive, meaning all economically active statuses including the self-employed status. Where the differentiation between the two statuses has relevance, this is obviously indicated.

2 *Cf. e.g.* Éva Gellér Lukács, *Munkavállalás az Európai Unióban*, KJK Kerszöv, Budapest, 2004.

of integration the number of court cases in this field can be regarded marginal on the whole.[3] In recent years, a growing number of cases in relation to welfare benefits emerged in the jurisprudence of the CJEU however, requiring a much deeper analysis of the field treated earlier as peripheral. Such an analysis seems especially justified in light of the current political and legal discourse concerning the issue of free movement, focusing on the question of equal treatment in the field of welfare benefits for mobile EU citizens.

The purpose of this study is to present and put into context the relevant case-law of recent years by analyzing the judgments of the CJEU in two cases that are benchmarks in this field: the *Tarola*[4] and *Saint Prix* cases.[5] Both cases focus on *de facto* unemployed persons who had drifted to the periphery of worker status having lost their earlier worker or self-employed status. However, following from Article 45 TFEU or by virtue of the rules laid down in secondary legislation, *i.e.* Directive 2004/38/EC[6] (Free Movement Directive) could retain their status and the broad entitlements stemming from it.

In the *Tarola* case it is remarkable how, in relation to examining the legal status of a mobile EU citizen who had pursued just a few weeks' gainful activity he was forced to terminate, the Court blended its very marked case-law attitude towards economically active citizens, with the case-law governing economically inactive citizens reflecting a much more considerate approach due to a change of trend in the past few years.[7] What is more, the ruling adds a new hue to the spectrum of welfare benefit issues arising in the context of free movement.[8]

The significance of the *Saint Prix* case, on the other hand, lies in the fact that it provided an exceptional opportunity for the Court to evaluate the special situation of pregnancy and childbirth in the context of free movement. What is more, it was called upon to

---

3   Sandra Mantu, *Analytical Note – Retention of EU worker status – Article 7(3)(b) of Directive 2004/38*, European Network on Free Movement of Workers, 2013, p. 12.

4   Judgment of 11 April 2019, *Case C-483/17, Neculai Tarola v. Minister for Social Protection (Tarola)*, ECLI:EU:C:2019:309.

5   Judgment of 19 June 2014, *Case C-507/12, Jessy Saint Prix v. Secretary of State for Work and Pensions (Saint Prix)*, ECLI:EU:C:2014:2007.

6   Directive 2004/38/EC of the European Parliament and of the Council of 29 April 2004 on the right of citizens of the Union and their family members to move and reside freely within the territory of Member States amending Regulation (EEC) No 1612/68 and repealing Directives 64/221/EEC, 68/360/EEC, 72/194/EEC, 73/148/EEC, 75/34/EEC, 75/35/EEC, 90/364/EEC, 90/365/EEC and 93/96/EEC.

7   Opinions in legal literature vary as regards the question whether this was a genuine change in the Court's approach. There is no doubt however, that in its recent judgments on economically inactive citizens the Court has increasingly insisted on the literal interpretation of the Free Movement Directive. For more details *cf.* Herwig Verschueren, 'Preventing Benefit Tourism in the EU. A Narrow or Broad Interpretation of the Possibilities Offered by the ECJ in Dano?', *Common Market Law Review*, Vol. 52, Issue 2, 2015, pp. 363-390; Daniel Thym, *Questioning EU Citizenship. Judges and the Limits of Free Movement and Solidarity in the EU*, Hart Publishing, Oxford, 2017.

8   Francesca Strumia, *Unemployment, Residence Rights, Social Benefits at Three Crossroads in the Tarola Ruling*, at http://eulawanalysis.blogspot.com/2019/04/unemployment-residence-rights-social.html.

interpret this special case of retaining worker status in the light of the CJEU case-law on gender discrimination.[9] Although the Court did not fully exploit this opportunity, as an important contribution of the case it made the declaration of theoretical significance that the list in the Directive in force laying down the conditions for retaining worker status was not of an exhaustive nature. As such, the CJEU underlined the fundamental role of primary law in defining and enforcing the scope of employee rights.[10]

In what follows I shall first outline the relevant legislative background, focusing chiefly on secondary legislation governing the retaining of worker status, mentioning in general the legislative uncertainties that may cause problems of interpretation in this field. Next, I outline the relevant case-law in the recent years, especially the *Tarola* and *Saint Prix* cases, which are excellent examples for the existing lacunae in the legislation on retaining worker/self-employed status. By providing interpretative explanations and some criticism for the above judgments I attempt to throw light, beyond the shortcomings in the actual wording of the legislation, on systemic problems as well. Thus, also on the challenges arising from the difficulties in distinguishing between the economically active and inactive EU citizen statuses, which have emerged as increasingly grave problems in the field of law of free movement, posing a serious dilemma for law enforcement. Finally, in light of these future challenges I evaluate the judgments of the Court chosen for this analysis.

18.2   A SHORT OVERVIEW OF THE EFFECTIVE LEGISLATION GOVERNING THE RETENTION OF WORKER STATUS

While there are no express primary law rules on the retention of worker or self-employed status,[11] the relevant rules may be found in the secondary legislation of the EU.[12] Article 7 of the Free Movement Directive lays down EU citizens' right of residence in the territory of Member States exceeding three months, setting out the conditions thereof. The novelty of the Directive is that it seeks to replace the former sectoral approach by setting out the conditions of residence for all EU citizens and their family members in a single legal act. However, the former fragmented approach – as a kind of political compromise - continues to exist in the sense that the right of residence and the conditions thereof are adjusted to the performance of an objective recognized by EU legislation, *e.g.* work. The rationale

---

9   Samantha Currie, 'Pregnancy-Related Employment Breaks, the Gender Dynamics of Free Movement Law and Curtailed Citizenship', *Common Market Law Review*, Vol. 53, Issue 2, 2016, p. 544.

10   Eleanor Spaventa, *The Impact of Articles 12, 18, 39 and 43 of the EC Treaty on the Coordination of Social Security Systems in 50 Years of Social Security Coordination: Past – Present – Future*, European Commission, Luxembourg, 2010, p. 121.

11   Article 45 TFEU referring to employees and Article 49 TFEU referring to self-employed persons do not have any express provisions on this issue.

12   Mantu 2013, p. 5.

lying behind this is the twofold aim of the Directive, which is to guarantee a wide range residence rights on the one hand, and to protect member states' welfare assistance systems on the other. Thus, while EU workers or self-employed persons as economically active persons have no other conditions to meet in order to make residence lawful, students or self-sufficient (*i.e.* economically inactive) persons are required to have comprehensive sickness insurance cover and sufficient financial resources for residence, thereby ensuring that they will not become an unreasonable burden for the welfare system of the host Member State. Within the framework of Article 7 guaranteeing the right of residence in general, Article 7(3) explicitly regulates the issue of retaining the worker and the self-employed status, as well as the right of residence following from the former.

The Directive introduces a system of gradation in respect of the existence and conditions of the right of residence. In addition, it establishes a stepwise system as regards the retention of worker and self-employed status, based on two guiding principles: the reasons for the person's inactivity and the initial duration of work. These two organizational principles establish a hierarchical system, by virtue of which persons who have temporarily become unable to work as a result of an illness or accident, [Article 7(3)(a)], embark on vocational training [Article 7(3)(d)][13] or are in duly recorded involuntary unemployment after having been employed for more than one year [Article 7(3)(b)] shall retain worker status without time limitation. By contrast, the status of worker can be retained with time limitation, thus for a period of time guaranteed by the Member State concerned which shall be no less than six months, in cases laid down under Article 7(3)(c).

This latter provision, which was the subject of interpretation in the *Tarola* case was formulated in a somewhat complicated way.[14] Namely, it included two different scenarios simultaneously, which were only clearly distinguished by the judgment.[15] The regulation stipulates that an EU citizen who "is in duly recorded involuntary unemployment after completing a fixed-term employment contract of less than a year"[16] or "has become

---

13   In the case of vocational training it is a strict condition of retaining legal status that training be related to the previous occupation, with the exception of the case of becoming involuntarily unemployed. *See* Judgment of 7 June 1988, *Case C-39/86, Sylvie Lair v. Universität Hannover*, ECLI:EU:C:1988:322, para. 37; Judgment of 6 November 2003, *Case C-413/01, Franca Ninni-Orasche v. Bundesminister für Wissenschaft, Verkehr und Kunst*, ECLI:EU:C:2003:600, para. 14.

14   Steve Peers, *Pregnant Workers' and EU Citizens' Free Movement Rights*, at http://eulawanalysis.blogspot.com/2014/06/pregnant-workers-and-eu-citizens-free.html.

15   Before the Court judgment concerned there was even uncertainty as to whether the provision in fact referred to two distinguishable scopes of cases. The Court maintained that the use of the conjunction 'or' clearly indicated that the legislator had this intention. *Case C-483/17, Tarola*, para. 30.

16   It was on the basis of this first clause that the Court decided in the recently delivered *Alimanovic* judgment that migrant citizens who had just worked for 11 months were entitled to retain this status for six months only, after which they qualified as jobseekers. Judgment of 15 September 2015, *Case C-67/14, Jobcenter Berlin Neukölln v. Nazifa Alimanovic and Others*, ECLI:EU:C:2015:597. For a detailed analysis *see* Dion Kramer, *Had They Only Worked One Month Longer! An Analysis of the Alimanovic Case*, at https://euro-

involuntarily unemployed during the first twelve months" shall also retain their worker status provided they have been registered as jobseekers with the relevant employment office.

The provisions of Article 7(3) clearly reflect the legislators' intention to protect those who are temporarily unable to work or are unemployed. This includes those who did not quit the labor market voluntarily but were forced to do so for some reason such as an illness, accident or the fact that there are no vacancies on the labor market. The temporary nature of the protection is emphasized by the wording of the regulation itself in the case of persons unable to work as a result of an illness or accident [Article 7(3)(a)]. Meanwhile in the case of persons who have become unemployed [Article 7(3)(b) and (c)] it is apparent from the legislative requirement according to which the former must be registered with the employment office, clearly with the purpose that, with time, they should return to the labor market.

At the same time, the above provisions leave several questions open, including first of all whether the above list of the Directive is of an exhaustive nature as regards the conditions of retaining the worker status or can be further extended through case-law based on the provisions of primary legislation. It must also be clarified whether the above provisions also govern those who are self-employed. While Article 7(3) is about retaining the worker and the self-employed status in general, at several points later on the text mentions only 'worker status' expressly[17] or operates with the expression 'employment'.[18] Finally, in relation to the legal institution of worker status for the sake of completeness it should be mentioned that if the person in question is unable to retain their worker status, their situation becomes uncertain in view of the fact that he/she already qualifies as a jobseeker. Although the scope of Article 45 TFEU does cover jobseekers, their right of residence and especially their right to equal treatment as regards social benefits are much more restricted than of those who retain their worker status.[19]

Although the CJEU judgments to be outlined below provide an answer to the above problems arising from the shortcomings of the provision's wording, at the same time, as will be demonstrated below, they raise further and far more serious questions. These questions concern the outstanding role of worker status in EU legislation and in general

---

peanlawblog.eu/2015/09/29/had-they-only-worked-one-month-longer-an-analysis-of-the-alimanovic-case-2015-c-6714/.

17   "In this case, the status of worker shall be retained for no less than six months". *Cf.* Article 7(3) of the Directive.

18   "He/she is in duly recorded involuntary unemployment after having been employed for more than one year [...]". *Cf.* Id. Article 7(3)(b).

19   In compliance with Article 14(4)(b) of the Directive, EU citizens and their family members may not be expelled for as long as EU citizens can provide evidence that they are continuing to seek employment and that they have a genuine chance of being engaged. However, Article 24(2) provides that in this period the host Member State shall not be obliged to confer to them entitlement to social assistance.

the sustainability of the fragmented system of the law governing the free movement of persons, which survives in the Directive. As Dion Kramer's metaphor perfectly illustrates, "economic activity has been the Holy Grail of free movement of persons since the start of the European integration project" and continues to be even today.[20] The marked distinction in EU law between economically active and inactive persons[21] in parallel with the transformation of the world of employment and the expansion of the welfare state has increasingly brought about difficult-to-manage circumstances, which is well reflected by the judgments of the Court in the *Tarola* and *Saint Prix* cases, analyzed below.

18.3   THE TAROLA CASE

18.3.1   *Statement of Facts and the Questions Referred for Preliminary Ruling*

In its *Tarola* judgment, the Court interpreted in response to the request for preliminary ruling by the Court of Appeal of Ireland, Article 7(3)(c) of Free Movement Directive. What is special about the case in question is that it lies at the intersection of legislations on the economic freedom of free movement of workers and the free movement of EU citizens.

According to the statement of facts, the Romanian citizen Mr. Tarola pursued gainful activity for periods of several weeks, alternately as an employee or as a self-employed person in Ireland. In 2013 and 2014 he applied for jobseeker's allowance and supplementary welfare allowance, which the competent authorities denied with reference to the lack of a habitual residence in Ireland, in view of the fact that his employment in Ireland was not long enough and he was unable to produce evidence proving he had sufficient resources to sustain himself. Mr. Tarola appealed to the High Court with reference to Article 7(3)(c) of the Free Movement Directive providing for the retention of worker status, by virtue of which, he claimed he was entitled to reside in the Member State concerned for six months following his employment of merely two weeks in July 2014. The High Court ruled that the above provision applied only to persons who were on fixed-term employment contracts of less than a year. However, the period of two weeks of work Mr. Tarola reported to have completed – in construction – did not meet this requirement.[22]

---

20   Dion Kramer, *A Right to Reside for the Unemployed Self-Employed: The Case Gusa*, at https://europeanlaw-blog.eu/tag/gusa-case/.

21   A question organically related to this is whether the EU citizenry are able to fulfil their role, or the EU is becoming increasingly distanced from a solidarity community. Although these questions have serious significance, discussing them would go beyond the framework of this study.

22   The referring court itself noted that the terms of casual work contracts were not specified in advance; these depended on labor market conditions in the construction industry.

The case finally reached the Court of Appeal, which referred the following questions to the CJEU for preliminary ruling. Does a citizen exercising free movement who before his involuntary unemployment worked for a two-week period – otherwise than on a fixed-term contract – thereby retain the status of worker for the purposes of Article 7(3)(c) of the Directive, such as would entitle him to receive social assistance payments or – as the case may be – social insurance benefits on the same basis as if he were a resident citizen of the host State?

18.3.2   The Judgment in the Tarola Case

Thus the first question the Court had to answer was whether fixed-term employment of merely two weeks in a framework other than a fixed-term contract was appropriate grounds for retaining worker status under the Directive, and as a corollary, lawful residence in the territory of the Member State in question.

Article 7(3)(c) provides that an EU citizen who "is in duly registered involuntary unemployment after completing a fixed-term employment contract of less than a year" or "has become involuntarily unemployed during the first twelve months" shall retain the worker status for a period of time to be specified by the Member State, but for no less than six months, provided that he has been registered as a jobseeker with the relevant employment office.

The Court found it important to point out first of all that the purpose of the Free Movement Directive was to facilitate the exercise of EU citizens' right to move and reside freely, which right was granted by virtue of Article 7(1)(a) to EU citizens pursuing gainful activity in the territory of another Member State for a period longer than three months.[23] As regards retaining the right of this worker status it noted that "the referring court – which has not questioned the Court in this regard, considers that [...]"[24] Mr. Tarola has the status of worker on account of the activity that he pursued in the host Member State for a period of two weeks.

After establishing the retention of worker status, the Court proceeded to examine the provision of the Directive on the retention of worker status with the tools of legal interpretation, i.e. Article 7(3)(c).

---

23   In this respect the Court cited two judgments with a rather broad scope, i.e. its earlier judgments in the Metock and Coman cases where the CJEU declared the right of residence of EU citizens' third-country national spouses, what is more, irrespective of the circumstances of concluding the marriage or of the fact whether the host country acknowledged same-sex marriage.

24   Case C-483/17, Tarola, para. 25.

Similarly to the opinion of the Advocate General, the Court first of all pointed out that the two clauses referred to two distinct situations.[25] Furthermore, it was clear from the documents that Mr. Tarola was not employed in the host state during the period concerned, within the framework of a fixed-term work contract, so that he was not covered by the first situation. The question that essentially remained was whether he was covered by the second situation.

The problem was that while the first situation was formulated quite clearly, the second was worded rather vaguely. It only said to cover persons who "became involuntarily unemployed in the first twelve months", not clarifying either within the framework of what contract or type of activity the persons in question actually became involuntarily unemployed, or[26] whether the twelve months referred to therein referred to the period of residence spent by the worker concerned in the host state or in the employment itself. With reference to the opinion of the Advocate General[27] the Court concluded that it was impossible to establish from the wording of the provision in question whether Mr. Tarola was covered by the second situation.[28] Thus the Court gleaned the above interpretation of the wording of the regulation from the context of the provision, the purpose of the Directive and the origin of the Directive.[29]

As regards the context of the provision in question the Court noted[30] that the provision under discussion was to be interpreted in conjunction with Article 7(1)(a) guaranteeing the right of residence to EU citizens pursuing a gainful activity beyond three months. Thus the right to retain the earlier legal status is granted to all EU citizens who pursued gainful activity in the host Member State, either as a worker or as a self-employed person. In order to underpin its statement of grounds, the Court cited[31] the substance of the earlier *Gusa* judgment,[32] in which the CJEU established with reference to a Romanian plasterer active

---

25 Id. para. 30.
26 "That provision does not specify whether it applies to employed or self-employed persons or to both categories of worker, or whether it concerns fixed-term contracts for more than a year, contracts of indefinite duration or any type of contract or activity [...]", Id. para. 35.
27 *Case C-483/17, Tarola*, Opinion of the Advocate General, para. 30.
28 *Case C-483/17, Tarola*, para. 34.
29 Id. para. 37.
30 At the same time, it certainly stipulated the double requirement of the efficient enforcement of the Directive and the prohibition of a restrictive interpretation. Id. para. 38.
31 Id. para. 39.
32 Judgment of 20 December 2017, *Case C-442/16, Florea Gusa v. Minister for Social Protection and Others*, ECLI:EU:C:2017:1004, paras. 37 and 38. Gusa pursued self-employed activity as a Romanian national in Ireland for several years, but he ceased working due to the absence of work later on. He applied for social assistance, which he was refused on the grounds that he no longer pursued a gainful activity; what's more, Article 7(3)(b) of Free Movement Directive was not applicable in his case because only persons who had earlier had a worker's status could retain it. The question was whether the provision of the Directive according to which the person in question "was employed for more than a year" excluded self-employed persons from the scope of beneficiaries. The Court found that although Article 7 of the Directive setting

in the Irish construction industry as a self-employed person for several years that the retention of the legal status regulated by Article 7(3) was independent of the nature of the economic activity.[33] The CJEU considered it important to mention[34] its earlier *Prefeta* judgment,[35] according to which the opportunity of an EU citizen temporarily ceasing to practice their activity as a worker or self-employed person to retain the legal status was based on the precondition that the citizen concerned was willing and able to return to the labor market of the host country within a reasonable period.

The Court added moreover that Article 7 introduced gradation with regard to the duration of the residence right granted to all citizens in the host Member State. This stepwise system followed from Article 7(3) itself with respect to the retention of the right of residence for temporarily inactive workers and self-employed persons. By virtue of this stepwise system EU citizens who pursued work or self-employed activity in the host state for less than one year are entitled to keep their worker status for six months only.[36] This is the case if the worker's activity ceases when the fixed-term work contract for less than one year terminates, as is stipulated by the first scenario of the relevant provision, and this is the situation also in the case of the second scenario when, irrespective of their intention, the worker is forced to cease activity before one year is completed irrespective of the type of contract concluded or the nature of the activity performed.[37]

According to the Court such an interpretation is consistent with the principal aim pursued by the Free Movement Directive, to strengthen the right of free movement and residence of all EU citizens and within its scope, the granting of the right of residence to

---

the conditions of residence beyond three months made a distinction between economically active and inactive persons, it applied no further distinctions within the first group. An interpretation contrary to the above would not be in line with the objectives of the Directive, which was expressly meant to surpass the previous sector-by-sector approach. Finally, such an interpretation would introduce unjustified differentiation in the treatment of the two categories. This latter approach by the Court is especially welcome in light of earlier case-law where such rigid differentiation was kept in several cases. *See e.g.* Judgment of 6 2012, *Case C-147/11, Secretary of State for Work and Pensions v. Lucja Czop and Margita Punakova,* ECLI:EU:C:2012:538.

33   *Case C-442/16, Gusa,* paras. 35-38.
34   *Case C-483/17, Tarola,* para. 40.
35   Judgment of 13 September 2018, *Case C-618/16, Rafal Prefeta v. Secretary of State for Work and Pensions,* ECLI:EU:C:2018:719, para. 37.
36   *Case C-483/17, Tarola,* paras. 43-45.
37   Id. paras. 47-48. At this point it is worth mentioning the Advocate General's reasoning with regard to the context of the provision in question. The Advocate General opines, while Article 7(3)(b) lays the emphasis on the initial duration of beyond one year, irrespective of the activity performed or the type of contract, Article 7(3)(c) emphasizes the initial duration of less than one year while establishing a second distinction, too, according to whether or not the EU citizen could predict the precise duration of their contract or activity. The second scenario – at least in the opinion of the Advocate General – settles the situation of the citizens who, contrary to their expectations or at least without a chance to predict the actual term of their activity, became involuntarily unemployed in the first twelve months of their employment. *Case C-483/17, Tarola,* Opinion of the Advocate General, para. 35.

persons who "have ceased their occupational activity because of an absence of work due to circumstances beyond their control".[38] The Court found moreover that this solution was in line with the other important objective of the Directive, *i.e.* the protection of the welfare system of Member States. According to the provisions of the Directive the retention of the status presupposes that the citizen concerned actually held the status of worker earlier, has registered as a jobseeker, *i.e.* actually has the intention to return to the labor market and finally, it is sufficient guarantee that the retention of the status can be restricted to six months by the host state.[39] In order to confirm the above the Court noted that the preparatory materials for the Directive[40] already reflected the legislator's intention to extend by way of the second clause the right of retention to persons in involuntary unemployment after having worked for less than a year otherwise than under a fixed-term employment contract.[41]

After establishing that a person who had worked for merely two weeks otherwise than under a fixed-term employment contract and became involuntarily unemployed afterwards could retain the legal status there was nothing left for the Court but to declare the principle many times confirmed in earlier case-law,[42] namely, that a citizen lawfully residing in the territory of a host Member State was entitled to the requirement of equal treatment laid down under Article 24(1) of the Directive.[43]

Following the opinion of the Advocate General the Court drew its final conclusion stating where national law excludes persons who have performed gainful activity only for a short period of time from the entitlement to social benefits that exclusion applies the same way to workers from other Member States. The judgment in this case, *i.e.* whether Mr. Tarola was entitled to receive the requested social benefits based on national law and

---

38 *Case C-483/17, Tarola*, para. 49.
39 Id. para. 52. The contents of this paragraph are partly in accordance with the substance of the Advocate General's opinion in which the latter examines if it is possible to set a minimum duration of gainful activity as a requirement for the retention of the worker status. In relation to this he concludes that the provision of the directive prescribing equal treatment does not necessarily involve guaranteeing entitlement to jobseeker's allowance. It also allows for avoiding misuse to require that unemployment should happen involuntarily and that the person concerned should be registered. On the whole he opines with regard to the Member State's making the retention of the worker status subject to working in an employed capacity for a minimum period of time beyond what is set in the directive would be such as to introduce an additional requirement not provided for by the EU legislature, which would certainly violate the requirement of legal certainty.
40 This is confirmed by the Amended proposal for a Directive of the European Parliament and the Council on the right of citizens of the Union and their family members to move and reside freely within the territory of Member States [COM(2003) 199 final] and Common Position (EC) 6/2004 of 5 December 2003.
41 *Case C-483/17, Tarola*, para. 53.
42 It was in the *Martinez Sala* case where the Court laid down the principle that has continued to be decisive for the development of integration law.
43 *Case C-483/17, Tarola*, para. 55.

considering the requirement of equal treatment, was ultimately referred back by the CJEU to the competence of the national court.[44]

It is clear from the above, that the Court skillfully blended its marked case-law referring to economically active citizens with its much stricter approach towards economically inactive EU citizens, thereby complying with the requirements following from the twofold objective of the Directive.

18.4   The Saint Prix Case

18.4.1   Statement of Facts and the Questions Referred for Preliminary Ruling

A French lady called Ms. Saint Prix arrived in the United Kingdom in 2006 to start a teaching career. For one year she worked as a teaching assistant, after which she enrolled at the University of London with the aim to obtain a teacher qualification certificate. As Steve Peers somewhat ironically noted, in the course of that she acquired much more knowledge than she had ever assumed, at least as far as EU and English law are concerned.[45] In the meantime she became pregnant and quitting her studies, in the hope of getting a teacher's position at a secondary school, she registered with an employment agency. As no secondary school work was available, she worked at nursery schools as a replacement teacher. Finally, when she was nearly six months pregnant, she stopped that work on the grounds that it had become too strenuous for her.[46] Eleven weeks before her expected date of confinement she made a claim for income support, but the claim was refused by authorities on the grounds that she no longer qualified as a worker and thereby lost her right of residence in the United Kingdom. Eleven weeks are relevant in this respect because under British law at that stage of pregnancy British citizen mothers become entitled to the income support in question without having to prove that they work or are looking for a job.

Three months after the premature birth of her child, Saint Prix resumed work. She brought an appeal against the rejecting judgment, which was upheld by the First Tier Tribunal but rejected by the Upper Tribunal. Finally, she appealed to the Supreme Court, which requested a preliminary ruling from the CJEU. The question was essentially whether Article 45 TFEU guaranteeing the free movement of workers and Article 7 of the Free Movement Directive granting the right of residence beyond three months were to be interpreted as meaning that a woman who gave up work or seeking work because of the

---

44   Id. paras. 56-57.
45   Peers 2014.
46   Although for a few days she looked for work that was more suited to her pregnancy, without success.

physical constraints of the late stages of pregnancy and the aftermath of childbirth retained the status of worker within the meaning of those Articles.

18.4.2   The Judgment in the Saint Prix Case

The main track followed by the Court in the case was essentially to determine by virtue of what provisions of EU legislation Saint Prix could retain her worker status and following from that, the various benefits.

The CJEU stipulated at the outset that Article 7(3) governing the retention of worker status did not expressly envisage the case of a woman who was in a particular situation because of the constraints of the late stages of pregnancy and the aftermath of childbirth.[47] The Directive itself does not say at all whether the above list can be added to. In no way did this fact stop the Court, however, from repeatedly insisting in its judgments that the EU concept of worker was a matter of primary law. As secondary legislation may not, in itself, restrict the scope of worker under TFEU, it shall be interpreted broadly in every case.[48] At the same time the Court considered it necessary to note that Saint Prix could not be considered a person temporarily unable to work by virtue of Article 7(3)(a) of the Directive.[49] This is because the case-law developed in relation to the Directive referring to discrimination on the grounds of sex[50] foresaw that pregnancy had to be clearly distinguished from illness in that pregnancy was not in any way comparable with a pathological condition. As regards Saint Prix's worker status, following the above extensive interpretation the Court concluded that the physical constraints associated with pregnancy and childbirth, which required a woman to a give up work for a period needed to regain physical strength, were not of a nature in principle that they could deprive this person of the 'status of worker' within the meaning of Article 45 TFEU.[51]

Following the Advocate General's opinion, the CJEU used a surprising analogy when drawing a parallel between the *Saint Prix* and the *Orfanopoulous*[52] cases. In the latter case it was established that a person spending his/her sentence was still under the scope of Article 45 TFEU provided that after his/her release he/she would ensure employment within reasonable time. Thus, the Court maintained that the circumstance that Saint Prix had not been present at the labor market of the host state for a few months did not mean

---

47   *Case C-507/12, Saint Prix*, para. 27.
48   Id. paras. 31-37.
49   Id. paras. 29-30.
50   *See* the *Webb* case, cited by the Court directly. Judgment of 14 July 1994, *Case C-32/93, Carole Louise Webb v. EMO Air Cargo (UK) Ltd. (Webb)*, ECLI:EU:C:1994:300.
51   *Case C-507/12, Saint Prix*, paras. 39-40.
52   Judgment of 24 April 2004, *Joined Cases C-482/01 and C-493/01, Georgios Orfanopoulos and Others and Raffaele Oliveri v. Land Baden-Württemberg*, ECLI:EU:C:2004:262.

that she had ceased to hold that legal status, provided that she would return to work or find a job within reasonable time after confinement.[53] This, too, reflects the tenet often mentioned by the Court that the retention of legal status was not without limitations by far. But what can be considered reasonable time as far as returning to work is concerned?

In order to determine whether the period that has elapsed between childbirth and taking up work again may be regarded as reasonable, according to the CJEU, the national court concerned should take account of all the specific circumstances of the case as well as the applicable national rules on the duration of maternity leave, in accordance with the provisions of the directive[54] on pregnant women.[55] The directive itself prescribes a leave of at least 14 weeks, requiring that at least two weeks from this should be allocated before confinement. At this point it should be noted that the Court did not mention the requirement of compliance with national law as regards the period of leave prior to childbirth.

The Court finally found it necessary to support its above argumentation with a reference, on the one hand, to the deterrent effect doctrine. According to this doctrine, an EU citizen would be deterred from exercising her free movement right in the event of her pregnancy and her being absent from the labor market she would risk losing her worker status in the host state.[56] On the other hand they emphasized that EU legislation on free movement granted special protection to women in the event of maternity, in relation to the right of permanent residence.[57] In this respect they concluded that if an absence for an important event such as pregnancy or childbirth did not affect the continuity of residence required for granting the permanent residence status, these circumstances could not, *a fortiori*, result in losing worker status.[58]

Based on the above, the CJEU's argumentation was centered on the worker status of Ms. Saint Prix following from Article 45 TFEU, essentially disregarding the secondary legislation on the retention of worker status or the treaty provision on the free movement of EU citizens (Article 21 TFEU). At this point, however, there is a significant discrepancy between the Advocate General's opinion and the ruling of the Court. The former makes a long-winded argument in his opinion about the consequences it may have if a migrant EU citizen in the situation of Ms. Saint Prix is not allowed to retain her worker status. In

---

53   *Case C-507/12, Saint Prix*, para. 41.
54   Council Directive 92/85/EEC of 19 October 1992 on the introduction of measures to encourage improvements in the safety and health at work of pregnant workers and workers who have recently given birth or are breastfeeding.
55   *Case C-507/12, Saint Prix*, para. 42.
56   Id. para. 44.
57   By virtue of Article 16(3) of the Directive continuity of residence shall not be affected by absence of a maximum of twelve consecutive months for important reasons such as pregnancy or childbirth.
58   *Case C-507/12, Saint Prix*, para. 46.

this respect the Advocate General refers to the fundamental nature of EU citizen status and the rights following from it.[59]

18.5 Comments on the Tarola and Saint Prix Cases

There is no doubt that in both cases the Court met its task of interpretation when filling the regulatory gaps in secondary legislation. It met its task when declaring in the *Saint Prix* judgment that further conditions could be added to the Directive's list stipulating the grounds for the retention of the legal status, following from primary legislation. It also clarified in relation to the *Tarola* case – and confirming the conclusions of the *Gusa* case – that the provisions of the Directive for the retention of the worker status were independent of the nature of economic activity or the type of contract serving as the basis of gainful activity.

Beyond resolving the interpretation problems following from the wording of the regulation or its shortcomings, the two law cases gave the Court an opportunity to interpret the legislation on free movement in the light of the case-law on gender discrimination (*Saint Prix* case), adding a new hue to this area, as well as to respond to the increasingly pressing issues in the area of free movement, namely to the challenges arising from difficulties in the distinction between the economically active and inactive EU citizen statuses (*Saint Prix* and *Tarola* case).

As regards the first issue, the fact that the appellant of the main proceeding was pregnant clearly played a role in the outcome of the Saint Prix case since this special condition otherwise enjoys broad protection in EU legislation.[60] In integration legislation, facilitating and encouraging the equal treatment of women – and within that category of expectant and young mothers – at the labor market has a long history. In light of this it is surprising that, contrary to the Advocate General's opinion, the Court only alluded to the provisions of the Charter of Fundamental Rights and EU regulations on gender discrimination and expectancy in general.[61] What is more, even earlier CJEU case-law related to expectancy

---

59   The Advocate General, emphasizing the fundamental nature of EU citizenship in the CJEU case-law, declared that an EU citizen who did not enjoy the right of residence in the host member state under what is now Article 45 TFEU, may nonetheless, simply as a result of EU citizenship, enjoy it by direct application of what is now Article 21(1) TFEU. *See Case C-507/12, Saint Prix*, Opinion of the Advocate General, para. 45.

60   Peers 2014.

61   As Currie puts it: "Substantive equality, previously said by the CJEU to be the basis of the pregnancy rights contained in the Pregnancy Directive, receives no attention." What is more, there is no clear declaration that pregnancy and childbirth – necessitating a break in employment – should not result in a woman, effectively, being treated in a disadvantageous way. Currie 2015, p. 554.

and discrimination[62] is solely mentioned in the context of the relationship between illness and expectancy (or the lack thereof).[63]

The central core of the Court's argument is the free movement of workers and within that the EU concept of worker under Article 45 TFEU. The Court does not even mention alternatives to the retention of worker status as regards ensuring the right of residence and related social rights of mobile EU citizens. Namely, they do not discuss the issue that for want of retention of worker status EU citizens are entitled to residence in the host state by the direct application of Article 21(1) TFEU,[64] *i.e.* simply arising from this fundamental status.[65] Although the questions asked by the referring court do not make any reference to this, Currie's question whether the Court would have made a similarly generous ruling if the questions had directly referred to the right of residence granted by Article 21 TFEU was absolutely justified.[66] The answer is clearly no, especially considering the case-law on economically inactive citizens, in relation to which the Court, contrary to its marked case-law on citizens performing a gainful activity, represents a much more cautious and moderate approach.

While, however, it is true in the case of Ms. Saint Prix that during her stay in the host country she assumingly paid more into the state finances than she received therefrom, this was by far not the case in the case of *Tarola*, who applied for a benefit with reference to merely a few weeks' gainful activity, *de facto* swelling the ranks of economically inactive citizens. The Court apparently ignoring this circumstance, provided social protection for mobile EU citizens following a well-trodden path of EU worker status.[67] Thus, after Mr. Tarola's 'actual' quality of worker was confirmed by the CJEU on the basis of the referring court's motion, the Court almost automatically proceeded[68] to the broad interpretation of

---

62 *Case C-32/93, Webb.*

63 Thus, no reference is made among others to *C-177/88, Dekker*, ECLI:EU:C:1990:383, or *C-207/98, Mahlburg*, ECLI:EU:C:2000:64.

64 Article 21(1) TFEU: "Every citizen of the Union shall have the right to move and reside freely within the territory of the Member States, subject to the limitations and conditions laid down in the Treaties and by measures adopted to give them effect."

65 According to the Advocate General's argumentation it is a fact that secondary legislation sets conditions for exercising this right, among others the condition of sufficient financial resources. At the same time, these conditions should in every case be applied by respecting the principle of proportionality. And from the fact that some expectant woman applies for a benefit-like income support it does not automatically follow that she no longer has sufficient resources for residence in the host country. As the Advocate General points out, the subsistence problems arising in the *Saint Prix* case were of a temporary nature, the expectant lady applied for social assistance only for a temporary period, which happened to coincide with the regular maternity leave granted to UK citizens. *Case C-507/12, Saint Prix*, Opinion of the Advocate General, paras. 49-52.

66 Currie 2015.

67 Peers 2014.

68 For the sake of completeness, it is necessary to note, however, that, beyond the implementation of individual rights, the Court already at this point mentioned the emphatic nature of removing the burden from the social assistance system. In this respect the Court found that Article 7(3) offers sufficient guarantee as on

the provision of the Directive on the retention of worker status. This of course, is less than surprising in the light of the generous CJEU case-law concerning persons pursuing gainful activity.

The Court's much more cautious approach towards economically inactive EU citizens is, at the same time, also apparent from the final conclusion of the judgment in question in that it does not automatically put an equation mark between equal rights following from lawful residence and actual entitlement to social benefits. By virtue of the *Tarola* judgment the retention of worker status and, as the Court asserts, the retention of the right of residence inevitably related to the former,[69] do not mean automatic access to the social provisions of the host state. Retention only means that the assessment of Tarola's application by the authorities must in every case take place under the conditions of the host state applicable to its own citizens. The Court thereby offers the guarantee to Member States that they will continue to enjoy a high degree of latitude in establishing their own system of social provisions. If these do not wish to provide assistance to those who work little or show little activity in the labor market in general, they continue to be able to do so in their national legal order.

The Court's gesture towards Member States properly reflects the intention of the former to follow a well-balanced practice with respect to the double objective of the Free Movement Directive:[70] to strengthen EU citizens' right to free movement and residence on the one hand and to safeguard the welfare system of host states on the other.[71] The conflict of the two above objectives, as is also apparent from the *Tarola* case – are deeply woven into the legislation on welfare benefits arising in the area of free movement.

In light of the above it can be said that the Court maneuvered skillfully in the case in question when, by applying the legislation on workers, essentially not moving from its comfort zone[72] it guaranteed social protection for mobile EU citizens. It certainly did so only with a theoretical nature since, as I mentioned above, the CJEU ultimately left it to the court of the Member State to give the ultimate answer with respect to the actual invocability of welfare benefits.

According to certain opinions the substance of the *Saint Prix* judgment, too, provided support to the mobile expectant mother only at a theoretical level in that the Court set the

the one hand it requires return to the labor market and on the other hand it limits the invocability of these rights in time.
69 *Case C-483/17, Tarola*, para. 55.
70 With reference to the hybrid nature of the case the Court lays down these two objectives with reference to workers and inactive citizens in separate paragraphs. *Case C-483/17, Tarola*, paras. 49-50.
71 The Court's approach applied in relation to the *Tarola* case, thus considering the double objective thereof, seems to follow the Court's 'Dano' stance in the case-law with reference to economically inactive persons represented in recent times, more restrictive than the former jurisprudence, in contrast to its case-law after the *Trojani* judgment.
72 Peers 2014.

318

return to employment within a reasonable time as a strict requirement for the retention of worker status.[73] Thus if return to employment is not performed within reasonable time, the young mother shall be considered a jobseeker, with much more restricted entitlements, as mentioned in the introduction. The question what qualifies as reasonable was further- more referred by CJEU to the competence of the national court, raising several further questions. What if the young mother is unable to go back to work because her workplace has closed in the meantime, or she is unable to find suitable work because of her changed family circumstances?[74] The situation is made even more complicated if an ill or special needs child must be looked after, with whom early return to work is impossible or very difficult to organize. This, in turn, leads us to the delicate issue how to relate to home care and to unpaid work in general. In its case-law up until today, the Court has consistently refused to include unpaid home care work under the scope of economic freedom.[75] Although Ms. Saint Prix can be considered fortunate as she easily found a job, a situation may arise when, after completing maternity leave the young mother is unable to find work despite utmost efforts.[76] In this case she enjoys protection according to EU legislation only from expulsion.

Considering the range and scope of entitlements of EU citizens it is not at all irrelevant if a mobile citizen qualifies as an economically active citizen and within that concept, as a worker, a self-employed or an economically inactive citizen. Sometimes there is a very narrow margin between these statuses and making a distinction involves a considerable burden for law enforcers. It is this issue that will be considered in brief, below.

18.6   DIFFICULTIES IN DISTINGUISHING THE CATEGORIES OF FREE MOVERS

As regards the group of economically active persons, making a distinction between the worker and self-employed status and thereby establishing the governing legal framework may involve great difficulties in future, in view of the fact that the concept of work is

---

73   Currie 2015.

74   It is not clear, either if in such cases the benefits already paid are to be paid back.

75   Judgment of 7 November 1996, *Case C-77/95, Bruna-Alessandra Züchner v. Handelskrankenkasse (Ersatzkasse) Bremen*, ECLI:EU:C:1996:425; Judgment of 21 July 2011, *C-325/09, Secretary of State for Work and Pensions v. Maria Dias*, ECLI:EU:C:1992:327. In the *Dias* case, a mother caring for her child stopped working. The Advocate General opined that the two issues had to be treated separately because in the former the mother's absence from work went beyond the period when she did not return to work because of the illness. *Case C-325/09, Dias*, Opinion of the Advocate General, para. 24. According to Currie, this is indicative of the fact that there is no intention to consider opportunities for expectant and young mothers' flexible return to the labor market in future, either. Currie 2016, p. 560.

76   Steve Peers opines, on the other hand, that in this case the consideration of individual circumstances can help. *Cf.* Peers, 2014.

undergoing a considerable transformation.[77] The digital world has reshuffled the world of labor, too, which is well illustrated by a new phenomenon in the labor market called the 'gig economy', the essence of which is that private persons may apply for short-term occasional work through online platforms or applications.[78] In the *Gusa* and *Tarola* cases discussed this posed no problems as the Court established that from the point of view of retention of legal status it was totally irrelevant what kind of economic activity the person in question used to perform. This is certainly not so in every case as in other areas of free movement the fragmented approach has survived, *i.e.* if a specific regulation governs only certain groups of economically active citizens, *e.g.* workers, the Court will obviously not expand the rights laid down therein to self-employed persons. A good example for this is the *Czop* case[79] where the Court established with reference to Regulation (EEC) of the Council 1612/68 on freedom of movement for workers within the Community[80] that it could be applicable to workers only, *i.e.* it did not grant a right of residence to persons providing parental care for self-employed citizens' children.

A problem much more serious than the above could be making a distinction between economically active and inactive statuses. While in the *Tarola* case the referring forum decided on the retention of worker status, in the *Saint Prix* case this was confirmed by the Luxembourg forum itself. From the justification of the *Tarola* judgment it is clear, however, that although the CJEU accepts the decision of the referring forum, it very much has its own stance, too.[81] This is exemplified by the earlier *Kempf* case, although somewhat surprisingly but, in view of the division of labor between the courts it did consider the decision of the referring forum.[82] Here, it found that the work performance of a teacher teaching

---

77 Niamh Nic Shuibhne, 'Reconnecting Free Movement of Workers and Equal Treatment in an Unequal Europe', *European Law Review*, Vol. 43, Issue 4, 2018, p. 502.

78 As such type of employment has been spreading, a question has arisen with regard to the labor law status of private persons employed in the 'gig economy' in several EU countries including the United Kingdom and France. Namely if *e.g.* private persons who work as drivers for Uber qualify as employees of the companies or as customers using the platform? The British court found that they belonged to the former category, as a consequence of which they were covered by some work law regulations. Thus, they were entitled to minimum salary, paid leave and rest periods. *See Uber BV v. Aslam [2018]*, England and Wales Court of Appeal, Civ. 2748.

79 *Case C-147/11, Czop.*

80 Regulation (EEC) No 1612/68 of the Council of 15 October 1968 on freedom of movement for workers within the Community. This regulation has since then been repealed by Regulation No 492/2011/EU of the European Parliament and the Council of 5 April 2011 on freedom of movement for workers.

81 "In the present case it is clear from the order for reference that the referring court, which has not questioned the Court in this regard, considers that the appellant in the main proceedings has the status of worker within the meaning of the latter provision, on account of the activity he pursued in the host Member State for a period of two weeks." *Case C-483/17, Tarola*, para. 25.

82 "According to the division of jurisdiction between national courts and the Court of Justice in connection with references for a preliminary ruling, it is for national courts to establish and to evaluate the facts of the case. The question submitted for a preliminary ruling must therefore be examined in the light of the

12 hours a week could not be considered marginal or ancillary even if their salary had to be supplemented from welfare assistance.[83] Thus, according to the case-law of the Court, the EU concept of worker may cover those working part-time, even if their earnings are scarce for subsistence but their activity does reach a certain threshold. As regards what that threshold means, no specific guidance has been given, but it can be gleaned from the case-law that work performance of one or two days per week may lay the basis for such legal status.[84] The *Tarola* case is a further addition in this respect since in this case the retention of worker status was confirmed based on work performance of merely two weeks. The broad application of the concept of EU worker status may, however, even lead to seemingly arbitrary decisions. As is well known people pursuing gainful activities have enjoyed widespread entitlements from the outset of integration already; including comprehensive equal treatment in the area of welfare assistance. The question therefore arises if the legislative intent at the beginning of integration extended to covering financing workers' subsistence from public funds.

The answer is probably 'no', considering that the economic freedom of free movement of persons was based on the assumption that the latter enjoyed free movement (and extensive related social entitlements) because they contributed to the host country's economy, *i.e.* were able to sustain themselves. The Free Movement Directive, too, reflected the above political consensus in that albeit it granted the right of free movement to all EU citizens, it did so only under the conditions and with the restrictions included in secondary legislation. Accordingly, the right of free movement and residence is granted to economically active citizens as net contributors whose migration, at least at the theoretical level, poses no burden on the welfare system of the host country. This right is furthermore granted to jobseekers as well as they are close to that status and finally it is enjoyed by self-sufficient persons who are able to sustain themselves. Dependents are not granted the right of residence in other Member States, at least not in their own right.

Thus, although the Directive lays down the theoretical framework, some Member States tend to view persons exercising free movement – irrespective of whether they are inactive persons or workers – increasingly as sources of danger. The question of welfare benefits

---

assessment made by the Raad van State." Judgment of 3 June 1986, *Case C-139/85, R. H. Kempf v. Staatssecretaris van Justitie*, ECLI:EU:C:1986:223, para.12.

83   "[...] The fact that the worker's earnings do not cover all his needs cannot preclude him from being a member of the working population and that employment which yields an income lower than the minimum required for subsistence or normally does not exceed even 10 hours a week does not prevent the person in such employment from being regarded as a worker within the meaning of Article 39 EC." Judgment of 4 February 2010, *Case C-14/09, Hava Genc v. Land Berlin*, ECLI:EU:C:2010:57, para. 25. "Those supplementary means of subsistence can be drawn from the public funds." *Case C-139/85, Kempf*, para. 14.

84   Judgment 3 of July 1986, *Case C-66/85, Deborah Lawrie-Blum v. Land Baden-Württemberg*, ECLI:EU:C:1986:223, para. 21; Judgment 21 of February, *Case C-46/12, L. N. v. Styrelsen for Videregående Uddannelser og Uddannelsesstøtte*, ECLI:EU:C:2013:97, para. 41.

became "one of the hottest political topics in the public debate prior to the Brexit referendum".[85] But it is not only the British who are skeptical. The German and Austrian governments also promised to reduce incentives for migration and to take steps towards reducing benefits by adopting more restrictive laws. This is well illustrated by the fact that the new Austrian government already cut family benefits for workers whose children live abroad.[86] This shows that not even the situation of workers seemingly enjoying a secure position should be taken for granted.[87] At this point it is worth briefly examining the main reasons underlying Member States' criticism of the institution of free movement.

While in the case of economically inactive citizens already the dubious wording of the regulation poses a challenge,[88] the main problem in the case of economically active citizens is that in this area law seems to break away from the above political compromise that serves as the basis of integration. There are several reasons for this, primarily including changes ongoing in society, *i.e.* transformation in the world of labor on the one hand and in parallel with that the excessive expansion of the welfare state by overtaking responsibilities from market players.[89] In western societies namely part-time employment has become increasingly frequent what is more, special in-work benefits related to low-paid jobs have become increasingly general. It is exactly these benefits that raise concern with *e.g.* the British.[90]

While the actual number of active migrants and the volume of welfare benefits they use may be subject to dispute, it is a fact that in fields where wages are low and the costs of living are high, even economically active citizens can be a serious burden for the state, thus, the substance of the *Kempf* judgment may have graver consequences than one could ever have expected. The assumption that the original idea of free movement and the automatic awarding of the right of residence are based on, *i.e.* that economically active

---

85   Daniel Thym, 'The Judicial Deconstruction of Union Citizenship', *in* Daniel Thym (ed.), *Questioning EU Citizenship. Judges and the Limits of Free Movement and Solidarity in the EU*, Hart Publishing, Oxford, 2017, p. 2.

86   A government decision that would mostly affect employees from Central European countries such as Poland, Slovakia and Hungary. The Commission has already initiated infringement proceedings with reference to new regulations, by virtue of which the family allowances and tax benefits of EU citizens working in Austria shall undergo indexation if their children live abroad.

87   Shuibhne 2018, p. 478.

88   It is beyond the purpose of this study to analyze the legislation on economically inactive citizens, yet it is worth mentioning that immature concepts, legal gaps, dubious passages generate legal uncertainty and render the enforcement of rights difficult in this area. "Making the right to social assistance dependent on lawful residence, while lawful residence is in turn dependent upon the degree of use of social assistance creates a confused and confusing circularity in the law." Gareth Davies, 'Migrant Union Citizens and Social Assistance: Trying to be Reasonable about Self-Sufficiency', *Research Paper in Law*, Issue 2, 2016, p. 4.

89   This phenomenon gives grounds for concern also from the point of view of competition law because the governments of Member States may indirectly support whole branches through benefits related to certain low-salary jobs.

90   Considering that housing costs are extremely high in the United Kingdom and especially London, the government supplements the earnings of low-paid workers with various social benefits required for subsistence.

migrants are at the same time self-sufficient, is no longer the case in several Member States today. In fact, a considerable proportion of the workforce can claim and does claim housing support, various health services, tax benefits and other income supports.

According to some views the fact that worker status has become the ace with respect to the right of residence and related welfare rights may even reverse the original idea as, in extreme cases, this legal status may be the key to access services provided by the welfare state.[91] Clearly in the vast majority of the cases – as illustrated by the *Saint Prix* and the *Tarola* cases – this is not the case. We have to see at the same time that, while at the outset of integration the *Kempf* case was the exception, by now, application for in work benefits has become widespread. Coupled with populist political communication this may easily generate tension, as it did in the area of free movement. What could be the solution in this case?

In the context of Brexit, the idea of amending Regulation (EU) No 492/2011 arose, which the Commission proposed for the case that the British voted for EU membership.[92] Through the application of a protection mechanism, the proposal would have given a solution to concerns raised by the United Kingdom arising as a result of an exceptional influx of workers from other EU Member States over the last few years.[93] It would have allowed the United Kingdom to restrict access to work-related benefits for migrant workers in exceptional situations in the first four years of their residence. This restriction would have been gradual, proportionate in time to the labor market participation, *i.e.* the lawful stay of the workers concerned.[94]

At the same time, this ruling from 2016 did not arouse much enthusiasm in legal literature; Shuibhne for instance went so far as calling it a "double attack" against the basis of the EU. In his view, it both violated the institution of free movement and the principle of

91   Davies 2016, p. 5, Éva Gellérné Lukács *et al.*, 'Szabad mozgás az Európai Unióban a Brexit tükrében', *in* Ilona Pajtókné Tari & Antal Tóth (eds.), *Magyar Földrajzi Napok 2016*, Eger, 2016, 11 p.
92   Draft Declaration of the European Commission on the Safeguard Mechanism referred to in paragraph 2(b) of Section D of the Decision of the Heads of State or Government, meeting within the European Council, concerning a new settlement for the United Kingdom within the European Union. EUCO 9/16, at www.consilium.europa.eu/media/24423/declaration-cion-safeguard-mechanismen16.pdf.
93   The other proposal would have targeted the abovementioned indexation of the family allowances.
94   This solution would essentially introduce a system based on the principle of proportionality, similar to that of economically inactive citizens, where the duration of time spent in the host state and the requirement of social integration would appear with growing emphasis. *Cf.* Judgment of 11 November 2014, *Case C-333/13, Elisabeta Dano, Florin Dano v. Jobcenter Leipzig*, ECLI:EU:C:2014:2358. This concept could, at the same time, be questioned in the light of the higher moral quality of the employer status. Certainly, the question, too, arises what the outstanding nature of this status is based on if the worker is unable to sustain themselves. According to some views, the fetishizing of gainful activity involves the danger of underestimating other, socially useful and important activities. These questions, however, lead far beyond the scope of this study.

equal treatment granted to workers.[95] It was for this reason that Davies made an alternative proposal according to which the equal treatment enjoyed in the field of welfare benefits could be retained, in that case, however, the worker status itself would depend on a certain salary threshold.[96] This proposal would, however, lead too far, to the issue of the harmonization of the EU concept of worker, which is beyond the scope of this study.

18.7 Conclusion

In its latest case-law related to the retention of worker status the Court undoubtedly performed duty of interpretation by filling the gaps in secondary legislation, turning it into a coherent system. The analyzed cases, however, go far beyond the semantic questions of the retention of worker status considering that they created an opportunity for the Court to examine the legislation concerned in a broader context and as a corollary, to reconsider the slippery slope area of the free movement of persons. This would have been especially desirable in light of the criticism that the Court and law enforcers have had to face in recent years, centering on the broad interpretation of the worker status, which lead to seemingly arbitrary decisions. This criticism is not completely unfounded in that the societal changes that have taken place since the outset of integration, including the transformation of the world of labor and the excessive expansion of the welfare state seem to undermine the political compromise that serves as the basis of the integration. This compromise entailed that economically active persons are self-sufficient and thus do not pose any burden for the host state.

The outstanding role of the economically active status in integration law is well illustrated by the fact that in both cases analyzed above the argumentation of the Court focused on the worker status. As we have seen, in its *Tarola* judgment the CJEU wished to guarantee the social protection of EU citizens following the well-trodden path of extensive worker rights. While doing so, however, the Court continued to keep in mind the twofold objective of the free movement Directive, *i.e.* beyond granting extensive free movement and residence rights, the requirement of protecting the welfare system of the Member State. Thereby it clearly indicated that it wished to assume a more emphatic role than before in balancing the competing interests in the sphere of free movement.

In the *Saint Prix* judgment of the Court the argumentation was similarly built on the central element of worker status. At the same time, in this case, too, it considered the enforcement of the interests related to the protection of the welfare system of the Member

---

95   Respecting equal treatment does in fact belong to the fundamental values of the EU (Article 2 TFEU). *See* Shuibhne 2018, p. 478.
96   Davies 2016, p. 24.

State when leaving it up to the national forum to decide at which time they considered reasonable for the retention of the worker status for the young mother to resume work. All these reflect that the Court is absolutely aware of the pervasive implementation problems in the sphere of free movement but, however pressing these issues may be, it obviously does not wish to take over the role of the legislator.

19 THE EUROPEAN INVESTMENT BANK

An EU Institution Facing Challenges and Providing Real European Added Value

*Zsolt Halász**

Keywords

European Investment Bank, status and role of development banks, Green Bonds, European Fund for Strategic Investments (EFSI), InvestEU

Abstract

Multilateral banks play an important role in financing larger investment projects within the EU and in most parts of the world. These institutions are less known than that commercial banks, even though many of these institutions – and in particular, the European Investment Bank – have provided a truly remarkable volume of financial support for the countries where they operate, including EU Member States. This paper introduces the largest of the multilateral financial institutions: the European Investment Bank. It elaborates on the specific regulatory framework applicable to its structure and operation as well as a number of special characteristics affecting this institution exhibiting a unique dual nature: a multilateral bank and an EU institution. This paper examines the complexity of the EIB's operation, in particular, the impact of external circumstances such as EU enlargements of the past and the Brexit issue in the present. Beyond these specific questions, generic issues relating to its operations, governance, the applicable specific prudential requirements and the non-supervised nature of multilateral financial institutions are analyzed as well. This paper also reflects on the EIB's unimpeachable role in financing the EU economy and on its pioneering role in bringing non-financial considerations, such as environmental protection into the implementation of financial operations.

19.1 INTRODUCTION

Multilateral financial institutions play an undeniable and rather significant role in a wide range of investment projects while providing a financial contribution to the different

---

*   Zsolt Halász: associate professor, Pázmány Péter Catholic University, Budapest. The author is grateful to the former EIB vice-president Mr. László Baranyay for his valuable inputs and his availability for several interviews on the topic.

economies of Europe and the world. Compared to commercial banks, the function and operation of these institutions is less conspicuous, even if the volume of financing provided by them can be regarded as considerable.[1] In this paper I intend to analyze the function and operation of the European Investment Bank (EIB) – which is the largest among the multilateral financial institutions –, and beyond the assessment of its formal regulation, I elaborate on its specific characteristics and the circumstances affecting it.

In Europe altogether four significant multilateral financial institutions provided financial contribution to investment projects in the past, and three of them are still present on the continent: *(i)* the World Bank (International Bank for Reconstruction and Development – IBRD) group, *(ii)* the European Bank for Reconstruction and Development (EBRD), *(iii)* the Council of Europe Development Bank (CEB), and *(iv)* the EIB – together with its subsidiary, the European Investment Fund (EIF). Although three of the aforementioned four institutions are named 'European', only one of them, namely the EIB can be considered an institution of the EU. The EIB is owned by the EU Member States and operates worldwide (with very few exemptions such as the US, Japan, North Korea) with an emphasis on the financing of EU economies. This paper aims to describe and analyze how the EIB's organization can serve and support the performance of financial activities within and beyond the framework of the applicable status regulation.

19.2 BASIC FEATURES OF THE EUROPEAN INVESTMENT BANK'S OPERATION

The EIB started its operation on 1 January 1958 with a paid-in capital of EUR 100 million current value contributed by the founding Member States. This resulted in EUR 250 million (current value) of activities value (total assets and guarantees) by the end of that very same year.[2] The last paid-in capital increase took place in 2014 with EUR 10 billion, with the paid-in capital reaching EUR 21.6 billion. In essence, this capital increase made it possible to achieve a peak level of the EIB's overall activities by the end of 2017 at EUR 549.2 billion. The level of the Bank's own funds at the end of 2017 stood at EUR 69 billion. The yearly financial surplus from the Bank's activities increases the level of own funds year by year.[3]

The EIB is not a profit-oriented institution, however, its operational surplus within the last three years until 2017 exceeded EUR 2.5 billion. The EIB does not pay dividends,

1   Nick Robinson, 'The European Investment Bank: The EU's Neglected Institution', *Journal of Common Market Studies*, Vol. 47, Issue 3, 2009, pp. 651-673.
2   *European Investment Bank Annual Report 1958*, at www.eib.org/attachments/general/reports/ar1958en.pdf. On the history of EIB *see* Lucia Coppolaro, 'Setting up the Financing Institution of the European Economic Community: The Creation of the European Investment Bank (1955-1957)', *Journal of European Integration History*, Vol. 15, Issue 2, 2009, pp. 87-104.
3   Data from *EIB Financial Report 2017*, at www.eib.org/attachments/general/reports/fr2017en.pdf.

therefore it was able to increase its own funds and risk-taking capacity, while also continuously complying with the best banking risk management practices and all applicable elements of the Basel capital adequacy requirements. Although the EIB is not a profit-oriented bank, it does not mean it would operate at a financial loss. However, it does not aim to maximize its profit to pay dividends. The business model of the Bank is to use its best AAA credit rating to get cheap and long-term financing from the capital markets, which it passes on to its counterparts. On this basis the most important international credit rating agencies maintained the bank's best rating level with a stable outlook over the past years. The business model of the bank – passing over financial advantages to its counterparts, relying on the high level of capital adequacy ratio (28.5% at the end of 2017) on the one hand and cheap and long-term fundraising on the other – has proven to be successful.

Although all EU Member States are owners of the Bank, their shares in the capital are not equal. The four biggest shareholders (Germany, France, Italy and at present the United Kingdom) hold 16.1% each, while others hold minor stakes in the ownership structure. *E.g.* Austria 2.2, Belgium 4.6%, the Czech Republic 0.76%, Hungary 0.72%, Poland 2.0%, Spain has 10%. These reflect the economic weight of the Member States at the time of their accession to the EU. These proportions, however, should be reviewed in the light of the economic changes that have taken place since 2004.

The volume of the EIB's activity is rather significant, however, it is not necessarily widely known and recognized in the Member States. At the end of 2017 the overall exposure of the Bank stood at EUR 567.7 billion, of which EUR 504 billion were earmarked for projects within the EU. During its 60 years' history the EIB as a policy driven bank has contributed to the settlement of several significant political issues.[4] At the time of its foundation, it served the unification of the developed part of Europe. It helped avoid further devastating wars, it facilitated reconstruction and fast recovery after World War II and later supported the enlargements of the European Communities. The Bank also helped prevent economic crises and mitigate their effects, and during the change of political regimes (in Greece, Portugal, Spain, and the former socialist countries of Europe) it helped the economic restructuring.

After the last financial crisis started in 2008, the EIB assumed a significant role in reopening frozen financial markets and later in stimulating sluggish investments. Besides its direct financial tools, the EIB took the lead in several mediatory tasks and initiatives serving the public interest. Historically, but even now the Bank's role in the theoretical and practical support for the environment policy, awareness-raising for climate change issues and dissemination of financial tools serving these is especially important. The EIB not only advocated for and publicized climate-action but also took lead in implementing

---

4   Patrick Honohan 'The Public Policy Role of the European Investment Bank within the EU', *Journal of Common Market Studies*, Vol. 33, Issue 3, 1995, pp. 315-330.

conventions on climate protection, acting as an innovator *e.g.* by issuing so-called Green Bonds.[5] The development and introduction of innovative banking products served and serves the common political vision to reduce Europe's technological disadvantage *vis-á-vis* the US and the large economies of the Far East. The most recent innovative product is the European Fund for Strategic Investments (EFSI) which will be examined later in this paper.

According to the Statute of the EIB the Bank shall grant financing, in particular in the form of loans and guarantees to its members or to private or public undertakings for investments to be carried out in the territories of Member States, to the extent that funds are not available from other sources on reasonable terms.[6] The primary role of the EIB is therefore to cover market financing gaps where commercial banks are not able or for some reason unwilling to take on the role of financer. Such cases are in particular investment projects where, in addition to the amount of funding required, the duration (expected maturity) exceeds the possibilities of commercial bank financing. These cases include the financing of investment projects at the time of financial and economic crises. In certain cases, the Bank may grant loans or provide other financial means for investments to be carried out, in whole or in part, outside the territories of the Member States. When granting a loan to an undertaking or to a body other than a Member State, the Bank shall make the loan conditional either on a guarantee from the Member State in whose territory the investment will be carried out, or other adequate guarantees regarding the financial means of the debtor. Such other adequate securities may be a guarantee from the EU budget[7] for financing investments in third countries or a guarantee for European Fund for Strategic Investments.[8]

The EIB's specific situation and the targeted nature of its activities are also reflected in the need for preliminary approval by the European Commission as well as the non-objection opinion of the Member State concerned for each financing operation.

---

5   *EIB Climate Awareness Bonds Factsheet*, at www.eib.org/attachments/fi/2018-cab-factsheet-v7.pdf.

6   Protocol on the Statute of the European Investment Bank, Article 16.

7   Decision No 466/2014/EU of the European Parliament and of the Council of 16 April 2014 granting an EU guarantee to the European Investment Bank against losses under financing operations supporting investment projects outside the Union.

8   Regulation (EU) No 2015/1017 of the European Parliament and of the Council of 25 June 2015 on the European Fund for Strategic Investments, the European Investment Advisory Hub and the European Investment Project Portal and amending Regulations No 1291/2013 and No 1316/2013.

19.3   THE INSTITUTIONAL STATUS OF THE EIB

The European Investment Bank – celebrating its 60th anniversary last year – is a fully-fledged EU institution. The Bank was established by the Treaty of Rome in 1958.[9] The EIB was set up at the same time as the EEC and the EU's core institutions (Commission, Council, Parliament, Court of Justice) as a part of the EU institutional system, sooner than the European Court of Auditors, the Ombudsman or the European Central Bank. Although the TEU does not mention the Bank among the institutions of the EU, it has clearly been placed in the institutional chapter of TFEU and in the Protocols No. 5, 6 and 7 attached thereto. The amendments to the Treaties did not fundamentally affect the rules governing the EIB's status, so one can still find these rules in Articles 308-309 TFEU. Similarly to other EU institutions (*e.g.* the CJEU or the ECB), the Statute of the EIB (Statute) containing the fundamental rules of its operation are also incorporated into the TFEU.[10] As an EU institution, the Bank has the same privileges and immunities as all other EU institutions,[11] its existence and legal personality derives from the Treaty itself.[12]

Multilateral development banks are set up in a special framework compared to commercial banks. Their founders are exclusively states (and in exceptional cases international organizations such as the EU and the EIB in respect of the EBRD), which established these institutions by way of an international treaty, determining the basic rules of their operation in their founding treaties: their statutes. This is not different in case of the EIB, in addition to the special circumstance that the international treaty establishing the Bank – the Treaty of Rome – was not exclusively (and not primarily) concerned with the establishment of the Bank, but of many other well-known rules and institutions of the EEC.

In the case of the EIB, Article 1 of the Statute – an international treaty – annexed to the TFEU, provides that "the Bank shall perform its functions and carry on its activities in accordance with the provisions of the Treaties and of this Statute", *i.e.* not on the basis of other EU and national banking regulations. However, this does not mean that the EIB could operate without taking into account prudential requirements. The Statute itself lays down certain basic requirements, such as: *(i)* the requirement of co-financing [Article 16(2)], *(ii)* the highest level of aggregate amount outstanding at any time of loans and guarantees granted by the Bank. [It shall not exceed 250% of its subscribed capital, reserves, non-allocated provisions and profit and loss account surplus – Article 16(5)], *(iii)* the

---

9   *Cf.* Articles 266-267 EC Treaty, Articles 308-309 TFEU. As regards the development of EIB's institutional status and its institutional connections *see* Sheila Lewenhak, *The Role of the European Investment Bank*, Routledge, London, 2012, pp. 1-14 and 67-80.

10   Protocol No. 5 attached to TFEU on the Statute of the European Investment Bank.

11   Protocol No. 7 attached to TFEU on the privileges and immunities of the European Union.

12   *Cf.* Judgment of 3 March 1988, *Case C-85/86 Commission v. European Investment Bank*, ECLI:EU:C:1988:110, para. 24.

requirement of sufficient coverage for expenses, risks, guarantees, as well as the prohibition on interest rate reduction (Article 17), *(iv)* the principle of rational financing [Article 18(1)], and *(v)* the prohibition on taking equity participation [Article 18(2)].

However, these general rules may be regarded as general principles of operation, and a specific prudential regulation for the EIB like the generic CRD/CRR[13] applicable to commercial banks does not exist. Although the Bank's Audit Committee is responsible for verifying, in accordance with Article 12 of the Statute, that the activities of the Bank are in conformity with best banking practices (BBPs), the benchmark is merely a Board of Governors Decision on the application of best banking practices and not a form of external legal regulation.[14] These best practices cover the following areas: prudential requirements, limits, internal organization, control mechanisms, risk taking, reporting, business conduct. Although the EIB's most recent reports refer to the application of best banking practices, the Bank itself highlights the fact that the BBPs can only be used to the extent that they do not conflict with the core legal framework applicable to the EIB.[15]

Article 309 TFEU clearly states that the Bank's primary task is to contribute to the balanced and even development of the internal market in the EU interest without profit-making requirements. This contribution means funding projects in less developed regions on the one hand and financing businesses if they cannot be fully financed by the various instruments available in certain Member States on the other. Thirdly, it provides funding for projects that are in the common interest of several Member States and are so large in extent or are of such nature that they cannot be fully financed by the various means available in the Member States concerned.

The owners of the EIB are EU Member States, who have established the Bank as parties to the Treaty of Rome and who are currently contracting parties of the TFEU. Only Member States can become owners of the Bank. Since the basic rules of the Bank's operation are laid down in the Statute, which forms part of the TFEU, it can only be amended by the Member States unanimously. However, this follows a special procedure in the Council: it can be launched either upon request of the Bank or, on the basis of a special legislative procedure on a proposal from the Commission.[16]

The Statute determines the Bank's capital and the share of each Member State in the capital subscribed. Similarly to other multilateral development banks, the EIB's subscribed

---

13   Directive 2013/36/EU of the European Parliament and of the Council on access to the activity of credit institutions and the prudential supervision of credit institutions and investment firms; Regulation (EU) No 575/2013 of the European Parliament and of the Council on prudential requirements for credit institutions and investment firms.

14   *Cf.* Best Banking Practice Guiding Principles of the European Investment Bank, at www.eib.org/attachments/general/best_banking_practice_guiding_principles_en.pdf.

15   EIB Group Corporate Governance Report 2017, p. 10, at www.eib.org/attachments/general/reports/eib_group_corporate_governance_report_2017_en.pdf.

16   Article 308 TFEU.

capital is not paid in entirely. The subscribed capital shall be paid in by Member States according to the ratio set out in the Statute, however the owners must be ready to make the unpaid capital available to the Bank, upon request of the Board of Directors, in other words, without further decision by the owners. At the same time, a formal capital increase requires a unanimous decision of the owners (Member States) represented by the Governors within the Board of Governors.

What the regulation is not prepared for are steps taken in reverse, *e.g.* a possible decrease or withdrawal of capital, either with or without a reduction in the number of owners. The United Kingdom's forthcoming exit from the EU also creates a special legal, regulatory and economic situation to which the currently applicable legal framework is unable to give effective answers. In case of an unregulated Brexit, the Bank would be thrust into a very serious legal and economic situation – not only due to the impending uncertainties in relation to its capital structure.

19.4   The Institutional Structure of the EIB

The Bank is governed and managed by the Board of Governors, the Board of Directors and the Management Committee. The competences of the governing bodies are laid down in the Statute, however the differences between the applicable rules and the operative practice of the Board of Directors and the Management Committee raise certain questions.

19.4.1   The Board of Governors

The Board of Governors consists of the designated ministers of the Member States (normally the finance ministers), exercising owners' rights especially in the field of *(i)* capital increase (requires unanimous decision); *(ii)* deciding the paid-in ratio of the subscribed capital (requires unanimous decision); *(iii)* laying down general directives for the credit policy of the Bank, the supervision of their implementation and their interpretation; *(iv)* appointment, discharge and compulsory retirement of the members of the Board of Directors, the Audit Committee and the Management Committee (requires qualified majority); *(v)* approval of the annual balance sheet, profit and loss account, as well as the annual report of the Board of Directors; *(vi)* decisions concerning the suspension of the operations of the Bank and liquidation (requires unanimous decision), the appointment of liquidators; and *(vii)* decision on establishing subsidiaries, approval of their respective statutes (requires unanimous decision). The decisions of the Board of Governors are usually taken by simple majority of its members. This majority must represent at least 50% of the subscribed capital. Qualified majority requires 18 votes in favor and 68% of the subscribed capital.

19.4.2   The Board of Directors

The Board of Directors is the main decision-making body of the Bank both in the field of loans and other financing transactions, as well as fundraising operations. The Board of Directors consists of 29 directors, 19 alternate directors and 6 non-voting experts. The Chairman of the Board of Directors is the President of the Bank (who has no voting rights). Each Member State and the Commission may nominate one Director. Two Deputies can be nominated by Germany, France, Italy and the United Kingdom each, and one Deputy per Country Groups set out in the Statute. Directors and alternates are appointed by the Governing Council, while the expert members of the Board of Directors are elected by the Board of Directors for a period of five years. In the course of EU enlargements, the Board of Directors was supplemented by the deputy directors of member countries holding larger shares, as well as the deputy directors rotated between smaller Member States according to a specific order established by the country group or constituency agreements.

It is worth noting, however, that the legal status of the country group agreements (constituency agreements) is not exactly regulated and does not comply with the applicable provisions of the Treaty (or the Statute). The Czech Republic, Hungary, and Poland are members of the largest constituency by virtue of the number of its members: the constituency has nine member countries, which is almost 1/3 of the Member States.[17] The constituency agreement was adopted by the Member States concerned in 2006 and slightly modified in 2016, in respect of the rotation of the Vice-President' nomination, and the nomination of the Audit Committee and the Deputy Directors.

From a practical point of view, the constituency system seemed a good solution to the management and control claims of the Member States during the continuous enlargements of the EU. Today, however, a review of the organizing principles has become overdue due to changes in the political and economic situation of the different Member States.

Some consequences of Brexit would also justify a comprehensive reform. The most important issue is, however, that these agreements have not been incorporated into the legal documents applicable to the Bank's operation, nor do these legal texts refer to them. In some cases, they serve as a reference and are respected by the Member States, but the Bank itself is in no way bound by them. It is quoted as a reference not only in informal and background consultations, but even during the appointment processes of Management Committee or Audit Committee members, but there is no trace of such a rule in the Statute. This system also includes a number of elements that are disadvantageous for new Member States (which are almost all – except for Romania – members of the constituency consisting of nine Member States), such as the frequent switching of vice-presidents or the disproportionate representation in individual committees and working groups of the Board of

---

17   Further members of these constituency are Bulgaria, Croatia, Cyprus, Malta, Slovakia, Slovenia.

Directors. Where one Member State has independent representation in each position, while others are be consulted through representatives of eight other Member States, who must jointly develop the position to be represented, there is a serious and grave disadvantage in advocacy.

The primary task of the Board of Directors is to ensure that the Bank runs properly and to manage it in accordance with applicable legal provisions in force and with the general directives laid down by the Board of Governors. The main competences of the Board of Directors are: *(i)* approval of financing and fundraising transactions; *(ii)* decision on payment of subscribed but not paid-in capital (to the necessary extent); *(iii)* approval of general, theoretical issues relating to the operation of the Bank; *(iv)* approval of the business plan (Corporate Operational Plan); and *(v)* approval of the annual accounts and reports and their submission to the Governing Council (and also their publication upon approval).

The Board of Directors makes the majority of its decisions on the basis of a proposal from the Management Committee. Each Director has one vote, which may be transferred firstly to the Deputy Director nominated by the Member State (or group of Member States to which the Member State belongs) or to another Director. In such a case, a Director may have up to two votes. This rule makes the role and existence of the alternate directors at least questionable.

A simple majority requires at least one third of the members representing a minimum of 50% of the subscribed capital. Qualified majority requires at least 18 votes in favor, representing a minimum of 68% of the subscribed capital. The quorum of the Board of Directors is at least 18 members with voting rights. Although not mandatory, the Board of Directors strives for unanimous decision-making.

The Management Committee is responsible for implementing decisions of the Board of Directors (see below). In practice, however, there is a certain degree of irregularity in the selection of projects approved, but not yet contracted by the Board of Directors, as the Board decision is not followed by automatic contracting. The actual date of conclusion of the contract is determined by the internal management and/or the Management Committee and the Bank. While the Board of Directors has the ultimate responsibility for financing transactions, it does not have a real influence on the implementation of its decision.

The Board of Directors may, by a qualified majority, delegate certain tasks to the Management Committee. Such delegation can be the approval of specific financing transactions based on an approved framework. The general requirements governing delegation of powers must be applied in respect of the powers delegated by the Board of Directors, as set forth in the *Meroni* case.[18]

---

18   Judgment of 13 June 1958, *Case C-9/56, Meroni & Co., Industrie Metallurgiche, SpA v. High Authority*, ECLI:EU:C:1958:7.

According to the Statute of the Bank,[19] members of the Board of Directors are selected from persons whose independence and suitability are beyond doubt; the members are solely responsible to the Bank. However, the condition concerning the independence of members and their sole responsibility towards the Bank raises certain questions from a practical point of view. The overwhelming majority of board members hold a position in their respective government and this duality can at least give rise to doubts regarding the actual independence of members.

19.4.3   The Management Committee

The Management Committee is responsible for the daily management of the Bank under the authority of the President and under the supervision of the Board of Directors. Members of the Management Committee are the President and the eight Vice-Presidents appointed for a six-year term by the Board of Governors upon the proposal of the Board of Directors. The Management Committee ensures the preparation and subsequent implementation of the Board of Directors' decisions for funding and financing operations. In case of urgency, it may take immediate measures while simultaneously informing the Board of Directors. Rules governing the organization and operation of the Bank are adopted by the Management Committee. The Management Committee is a corporate decision-making body whose members are equal and not subordinated to the President of the Bank. The President has very few own competences: *(i)* they chair the meetings of the Board of Directors and the Management Committee; *(ii)* exercise powers of appointment and dismissal at the Bank's work organization; *(iii)* represent the Bank in legal and other matters (transferable competence); and *(iv)* make proposals for the expert members of the Board of Directors.

The Management Committee makes its decisions by a simple majority of its members present. In addition to formal meetings, the President and vice-presidents are also frequently consulted on a number of banking issues. The result of these discussions is normally unanimity, apart from some rare exceptions. Within the purview of the President's special powers mentioned above, it is up to his own habits and leadership culture to consider proposals and opinions of the Vice-Presidents on matters where the President has the right to decide. The current and former members of the Management Committee have not yet made public their views on this experience.

The selection of the members of the Management Committee is based in part on formal regulation and partly on customary law. Although the number of members is determined by the Bank's Statute, there is no formal rule concerning the privileges of the four largest shareholders who have always nominated a member to the Management Committee, while

---

19   Article 9 of the Statute.

other Member States are only entitled to nominate members by country groups (constituencies) on a rotational basis. These country groups (constituencies) are: *(i)* Spain, Portugal; *(ii)* Belgium, Netherlands, Luxembourg; *(iii)* Ireland, Denmark, Greece, Romania; *(iv)* Austria, Sweden, Finland, Estonia, Latvia, Lithuania; and *(v)* Bulgaria, Czech Republic, Cyprus, Croatia, Hungary, Malta, Poland, Slovakia, Slovenia.

While the term of office of the Management Committee's members is officially six years, in case of members (vice-president) of larger constituencies it often happens that they resign after three or four years of service on the basis of an internal agreement, surrendering the position to the candidate of the next nominating Member State within the constituency. This resignation is formally always voluntary, but strongly expected, and this practice contravenes the provisions of the Statute and TFEU. This practice also has the consequence that some members of the Management Committee are basically not in a position to perform as efficiently as those who can complete their six-year mandate, which has an overall detrimental effect on the Bank's operational efficiency.

The example of vice-presidents nominated by the constituency composed of nine Member States that joined the EU in and after 2004 clearly illustrates the disadvantages of the country group system as detailed above. Since 2004, Czech, Hungarian, Polish, Slovenian, and Slovak vice-presidents from this country group have been nominated. All were appointed for a six-year term and resigned after three years. There were five vice-presidents in 15 years, while the vice-resident nominated by Italy for example has served two full terms and the President from Germany has also been reappointed in 2018 for a second six-year term. This situation clearly shows that the opportunities and gravitas of the different Management Committee members are not comparable.

There is a further weakness concerning the succession of Management Committee membership. While members may be reappointed, if a member's term of office expires without immediate reappointment or the appointment of a new member, the position remains vacant.[20] This situation could be remedied by a solution employed in EU institutional rules – *e.g.* for members of the CJEU or the Court of Auditors – whereby the member's term of office is automatically extended until the successor is appointed.

19.4.4   The Audit Committee

The proper operation of the Bank is supervised by the Audit Committee composed of six members who are appointed by the Board of Governors for a six-year term (non-renewable); one new member is appointed yearly. The nomination and replacement of members raises similar issues to those of Management Committee members, and the substantial difference

---

20   In May 2019 there were two seats vacant in the Management Committee.

between regulation and practice also raises important operational and transparency issues here. The core task of the Audit Committee is the same as that of the supervisory board in company law. The Committee is responsible for certifying to the Board of Governors that the information contained in the annual report gives a true, reliable and fair view of the financial position of the Bank, that the Bank has performed its activities properly and that its activities are in accordance with the provisions of the Statute and the Rules of Procedure. The adoption of this statement by the Audit Committee requires unanimity.

According to the Statute, the Audit Committee also supervises whether the Bank's activities are in line with best banking practices. In terms of definition, it is important to emphasize that prudential banking requirements are found in EU prudential rules (especially in the CRD Directive and the CRR Regulation), but these legislative acts are not applicable to the EIB and other multilateral banks. The concept, elements and requirements of the best banking practices do not take the form of formal legislation. Instead, they can be found in the guidelines and other industry standards of the European Banking Authority. These guidelines and standards are however of a general nature and as such they can serve as a benchmark for commercial banks. The EIB, like other multilateral development banks, differs from commercial banks in many aspects, as such it can apply the requirements of best banking practices with certain restrictions only.[21]

The Audit Committee has recourse to the external auditor(s) it has designated. A special feature of the rules applicable to EIB auditors is that they are not mentioned in the external rules (TFEU, Statute of the EIB). Only the internal rules, namely the Rules of Procedure refer to them, to their designation, laconically foreseeing that the Audit Committee designates external auditors (after consulting the Management Committee).[22] No further guidance or rules may be found in the Rules of Procedure on further details of the selection procedure (*e.g.* details of the selection process, time of assignment and its possible extension, other possible or excluded tasks). In fact, the current auditor selected in 2008 is still in charge of the Bank's audit duties, which is in line with the relevant EU legislation.[23] At the same time, it may also be stated that his mandate has been significantly longer than the non-renewable term of office of Audit Committee members.

---

21 The EIB has published the applicable BBP rules in a document on the Bank Best Banking Practice Guiding Principles of the European Investment Bank in October 2018, at www.eib.org/attachments/general/best_banking_practice_guiding_principles_en.pdf.
22 Article 26(2) of the Rules of Procedure of the EIB.
23 According to Article 17 of Regulation 537/2014 of the European Parliament and of the Council on specific requirements regarding statutory audit of public-interest entities the maximum duration of the appointment of a statutory auditor is 10 years and in case public tendering in selection process 20 years. Certain Member States like Hungary apply significantly stricter rules for the maximum duration of appointment.

19.5   THE EIB's OPERATIONS AND THE INCORPORATION OF ENVIRONMENTAL CONSIDERATIONS

In general, the EIB offers loans, guarantees and other specific financing products for its counterparts in the field of innovation, infrastructure, energy, social and environmental investments, SME-finance *etc.* The recipients of EIB's loans and other financial instruments are *(i)* the EU Member States, and in certain cases also non-Member States; *(ii)* enterprises, public and private undertakings or bodies directly (above EUR 25 million financing volume, *e.g.* public sector or corporate loans, project financing); and *(iii)* enterprises, public and private undertakings or bodies indirectly via financial intermediaries (under EUR 25 million financing volume).

The financing provided by the EIB must be always additional and should not exceed 50% of the investment costs. However, in exceptional cases (*e.g.* projects concerning renewable energy infrastructure, energy efficiency, migration or projects following natural disasters) the EIB may finance a higher share of the investment costs. In addition to traditional financing operations, the EIB offers further ancillary services. Its activity is often described by three words: lending, blending and advising. Blending means that the EIB's refundable financing is blended with other sources such as EU grants (non-refundable funds), guarantees, structured financing *etc.* Providing financing is only one step towards a successful project. They also need to be properly managed. As there is a significant need for assistance in project management, the EIB provides advisory services on both project administration and project management to help investments.

Multilateral development banks such as the EIB play a key role in boosting climate related or climate conscious financial products. In the past years the Bank has reached an annual lending level exceeding 25% of its own total resource dedicated to climate action and it aims to increase the share of climate action financing from 25% to 35% of its total lending outside the EU. In its Corporate Operational Plan the Bank made a commitment to maintain these volumes.[24]

Climate action financing is not only a fashionable buzzword, it has legal relevance too. In case of the EIB, a prerequisite of any financing operation is the Environmental and Social Assessment to be prepared and attached to the operation documentation. It is for determinant the acceptability of all EIB-financed projects to ensure the protection and improvement of the environment and the application of appropriate social safeguards in line with the EIB Statement of Environment and Social Principles and Standards.[25]

---

24   EIB Corporate Operational Plan for 2019, at www.eib.org/attachments/strategies/operational_plan_2019_en.pdf.

25   *See* www.eib.org/attachments/strategies/eib_statement_esps_en.pdf.

In case of all projects the EIB aims to verify compliance with both national and EU environmental law, including the Environmental Impact Assessment (EIA) Directive[26] and the nature conservation directives.[27] Beyond EU legislation, all EIB-financed projects must comply with national environmental law, including international conventions ratified by the host country. Where EU standards are stricter than national standards the higher EU standards must be fulfilled.

Besides the general financial products, the EIB also has specific instruments for environment/climate related financial purposes: the Natural Capital Financing Facility (NCFF) and the Private Finance for Energy Efficiency (PF4EE). The NCFF is a financial instrument that supports projects delivering on biodiversity and climate adaptation through tailored loans and investments. The NCFF is a loan (amounting to up to EUR 15 million) backed by an EU guarantee. It contains a technical assistance facility that can provide each project with a grant – financed by the EU's LIFE program – of up to a maximum of EUR 1 million for project preparation, implementation and monitoring. The PF4EE is a joint operation of the EIB and the European Commission. It consists of energy efficiency loans financed by the EIB and credit risk protection (guarantee) and expert support services (technical assistance) funded by the EU's Life program.

From a funding perspective, for its own financing, the lending activities are mainly funded via bond issuance in international capital markets. The EIB issues a very wide range of debt products, in terms of size, currency, maturity and structure. The Bank offers large benchmark/reference bonds, public bonds, and private placements (typically in smaller size). The EIB issues Green Bonds, officially called Climate Awareness Bonds (CAB), whose proceeds are dedicated to climate action projects. Green Bonds generate accountability of project disbursements, which explains policy makers' increasing attention to this segment. The first Green Bonds were issued by the EIB in 2007, and then by the World Bank in 2008. Later on, others have followed suit: multilateral financial institutions and sovereigns such as the State of California, Sweden or Poland. The concept of Green Bonds is not a legal category. Nevertheless, Green Bond issuers have developed the Green Bond Principles (GBPs). Issuance aligned to the GBPs should provide an investment opportunity with transparent green credentials. The GBPs are voluntary process guidelines that recommend transparency and disclosure, while promoting integrity in the development of the Green Bond market by clarifying the approach for issuing the Green Bond. The GBPs are intended for broad use by market players. According to the GBPs, eligible Green Project categories include: renewable energy, energy efficiency, pollution prevention and control, environ-

---

26   Directive 2011/92/EU of the European Parliament and of the Council of 13 December 2011 on the assessment of the effects of certain public and private projects on the environment.

27   Council Directive 92/43/EEC of 21 May 1992 on the conservation of natural habitats and of wild fauna and flora (Habitats Directive) and Directive 2009/147/EC of the European Parliament and of the Council of 30 November 2009 on the conservation of wild birds (Birds Directive).

mentally sustainable management of living natural resources and land use, terrestrial and aquatic biodiversity conservation, clean transportation, sustainable water and wastewater management, climate change adaptation, eco-efficient and/or circular economy adapted products, production technologies and processes, green buildings.[28] EIB-issued Green Bonds currently focus on renewable energy and energy efficiency. For the sake of transparency, the EIB annually publishes its Report on climate finance, which gives – among others – detailed information on the utilization of funding deriving from Green Bonds.

19.6   The European Fund for Strategic Investments and the EIB

The European Fund for Strategic Investments (EFSI) has particular importance in the financial activities of the Bank and the EU. The EFSI backed by an EU guarantee makes the expansion of the EIB's activities and risk-taking capacity possible. The European Strategic Investment Fund was set up by the European Commission and the EIB during autumn of 2014 to find a solution to halt the decline in investment volume within the EU and reverse the process.[29] The EFSI is not a traditional fund but a contractual cooperation between the Commission and the Bank. The Bank originally contributed EUR 5 billion of its own funds and the Commission (EU budget) provided a portfolio guarantee of EUR 16 billion to EFSI. This guarantee allows the Bank to finance riskier (obviously non-speculative) projects than it was able to finance earlier, (which were not eligible for financing due to lower risk limits). The original target level of investments was EUR 315 billion by 2018. Since the target was reached in time, the Commission and the EIB decided to extend the cooperation to achieve a level of EUR 500 billion investments by 2020. In order to be able to continue the operations under EFSI, both the EIB and the Commission increased their contribution (to EUR 7.5 billion and EUR 26 billion respectively), amounting to a total of EUR 33.5 billion.[30] The EFSI is an excellent example for the Bank's policy-driven, but also bank-type operation, and its results illustrate the different situations and opportunities within the Member States. The initiative was established by the European Commission (in 2014) which recognized that the post-crisis economic recapture was slow and uneven,

---

28   International Capital Market Association: Green Bond Principles (GBP), at www.icmagroup.org/assets/documents/Regulatory/Green-Bonds/June-2018/Green-Bond-Principles---June-2018-140618-WEB.pdf.

29   *An Investment Plan for Europe*, COM(2014) 903 final, 26 November 2014.

30   Regulation (EU) 2015/1017 of the European Parliament and of the Council on the European Fund for Strategic Investments, the European Investment Advisory Hub and the European Investment Project Portal (EFSI Regulation).

and that there were backlogs in EU competitiveness and limits to the financial capacities of the EU budget.[31]

The EU budget guarantee supports the Bank's stability. Meanwhile, new products and methods facilitate leverage and are a source of real economic impact, they promote volume of mobilized investment and, of course, its qualitative and quantitative results. Thus, by the end of July 2018, the investment volume mobilized exceeded the planned EUR 315 billion, reaching EUR 330 billion. This achievement has contributed to the stabilization the EU economy. Starting with 2018 the scope of eligible projects was extended and there is also the possibility of financing projects in the field of agriculture, forestry and general projects for strengthening cohesion.

The EFSI Regulation empowers the EIB to execute financing operations, but it sets up a specific organizational and procedural system for implementation. The Steering Board is responsible for the strategic orientation of the EFSI, defining operational rules and procedures, laying down rules on operations with investment platforms and national development banks or institutions, as well as defining the risk profile of EFSI. The Board has five members: three members from the Commission, one from the EIB and one non-voting expert member from the European Parliament.

The Investment Committee is the main decision-making body, it decides whether to grant an EU guarantee for a proposed transaction. This Committee is a body fully independent from the EIB, and its members cannot request or accept instructions from the EIB, or from any other EU institution, Member State or other public or private bodies. The Investment Committee consists of eight independent experts and the Managing Director. Its members are appointed by the Steering Committee on the basis of an open selection procedure for a single renewable term of three years.

The chief executive of the EFSI is the Managing Director, who is responsible for the day-to-day management of the EFSI and for the preparation of Investment Committee meetings. The Managing Director reports on the activities of the EFSI to the Steering Board on a quarterly basis. The Managing Director and the Deputy Managing Director are selected in a very complex procedure. At the start of the selection procedure, the Steering Board, following an open procedure conducted by the EIB, selects a candidate for the position. The candidate is heard by the European Parliament and appointed by the President of the EIB for a fixed term of three years (renewable once). In general, this procedure is much more complicated than the selection procedure of the EIB President.

---

31   *Cf.* Daniel Mertens & Matthias Thiemann, 'Building a Hidden Investment State? The European Investment Bank, National Development Banks and European Economic Governance', *Journal of European Public Policy*, Vol. 26, Issue 1, 2019, pp. 23-43.

In June 2018 the European Commission tabled its proposal on the financial instruments for boosting investments in the EU between 2021-27, the so-called InvestEU program.[32] In its proposal and the accompanying evaluation, the Commission considered the EFSI implemented by the EIB a success. The Commission designed the new program on the basis of the EFSI. However, there is a substantial difference between the EFSI and the InvestEU proposal. Within the framework of InvestEU the EIB – who delivered the success of the EFSI – would not be the sole beneficiary of the EU guarantee entrusted by the execution of the program, but also other multilateral financial institutions (World Bank, EBRD, CEB *etc.*), and Member State promotional institutions would also be invited. According to the Commission's statement opening up the possibility to other institutions to benefit from the EU guarantee is driven by the consideration that there are other experienced potential financial partners in the EU, that have specific expertise, knowledge of their local market *etc.* However, the EIB Group will remain the Commission's main financial partner in this program. One can easily recognize that these circumstances are not new, the multilateral and national promotional institutions existed already at the time of the launching of the EFSI. By contrast, it is hard to understand why the Commission intends to take – at least partially – the implementation out of the EIB's hands, especially after acknowledging it had done a great job.

19.7   THE IMPACTS OF BREXIT ON THE EIB

Brexit – as a political decision – may have, albeit different in nature, but serious and disadvantageous direct and indirect consequences for the Bank. Brexit shall bring about not only a major change in the Bank's ownership structure, but it also prompts a substantial amendment of the decision-making, management and internal regulatory system of the Bank. As a result of the United Kingdom's exit, the Bank's capital position must be settled and increased. All this should be implemented in a well-regulated, transparent, understandable, measurable, predictable way for markets, credit rating agencies, customers and members, in a way that does not reduce the trust in the Bank and maintains the Bank's business activity, problem solving ability, and provides a stable framework for future operations.

A significant part of these tasks had to be completed before the originally set date of Brexit (29 March 2019). Transformations change ownership ratios, strengthen or somewhat reduce the positions of the largest members, and change the decision-making proportions

---

32   *Proposal for a Regulation of the European Parliament and of the Council establishing the InvestEU Program,* COM(2018) 439 final.

within the Board of Directors. The composition and role of the Management Committee may also change. Until May 2019 these decisions have not yet been taken.

The UK's share of the EIB's capital is 16.11%, amounting EUR 3,5 million paid-in capital, EUR 35.7 million callable capital, a total of EUB 39.2 million subscribed capital by the UK. The most important step is to preserve the pre-Brexit level of subscribed capital, which would does not increase the paid-in capital by Member States. Further questions relate to the potential repayment of the paid-in capital to the UK, its impact on the capital adequacy ratio and other ratios of the EIB. On the lending side, the UK represents 8% of the overall exposure of the Bank. Should there be no agreement on withdrawal, there will be no guarantee for the continuation of the protections and privileges of the EIB and its assets in the UK, and the EIB's further activities in the UK must be terminated as well.[33]

On the other hand, Brexit also creates opportunities. One of them is to modify the composition and role of the constituencies (Member State groups), taking into account the increased economic gravitas of the younger Member States (which has been recognized in the Commission's legislative proposals for the next Multiannual Finance Framework). All these issues are currently in the discussion and decision-making phase. Neither before the original Brexit deadline, nor in May 2019 was there an adopted Agreement on withdrawal. From the Bank's side, there were no published internal steps or decisions of generic nature to prepare the Bank properly for such an unprecedented situation, when the number of its owners decrease.

Whatever happens, uncertainty will lead to the worst situation. It causes complicated governance issues, delays capital replacement, which has – through formal arrears and decreasing market reputation – consequences for both the Bank's own funding and its active financial operations. The longer it takes, the harder it impacts the Bank and indirectly, the European economy has to suffer.

19.8 Conclusions

In this short study, I have not only aimed to give a simple description of the organizational operation of the world's largest multilateral financial institution, but also tried to present the background, deficiencies and open issues of its operation. I have demonstrated, that the Bank's proactive operation is increasing, and the renewal in both organizational and personal terms is not only a continuous endeavor, but also a practice, however complex, slow and somewhat unbalanced. In recent years, the presentation of the Bank's activities to the general public has greatly improved, and it is much better understood how the Bank's

---

33 Source of the figures is EIB Investor Presentation, at www.eib.org/attachments/fi/eib-investor-presentation.pdf.

operations affect the everyday life and living standards of European citizens. One can clearly see, that the Bank is sensitive not only towards financial risks and the impact of its operations, but also towards their social and environmental consequences. Clear signs of this sensibility are the compulsory Environmental and Social Assessment which must be prepared and attached to the operation documentation and the issuance of Green Bonds on the funding side.

Based on the assessment above, I consider the issues experienced in relation to the governing bodies of the bank, including the Board of Directors and the Management Committee, to be of particular importance, the effects of which clearly evolve into the daily management of the Bank. The relationship between the status of deputy directors and members of the Board of Directors is unjustified, while the current structure of the country group (constituency) system must also be reviewed. These may be the hardest nuts to crack within the Bank's operation. It would result in not only a formal rearrangement of the respective bodies, but also a substantial change in the influence of the Member States on decision-making within the Bank.

An important measure would be the reform of the relevant institutional rules, and as a first step, the reform of the selection of the external auditor and the precise definition of their tasks. Furthermore, the selection of the EFSI's Managing Director should also be reconsidered, since the selection procedure is even more complex than that of the President of the Bank, notwithstanding the fact that the Managing Director has no special decision-making competences. The Bank should be much more prepared for external challenges, as the recent Brexit conundrum shows. Right now, the Bank is incapable of properly tackling a partial decrease of its capital following the exit of one of its main owners. The Bank must be prepared for such situation, both internally and in respect of the applicable regulatory environment.

What is missing is regulatory support from the EU, more precisely, the Commission. A great many decision makers failed to realize even after 60 years, that the EU has a truly capable financial institution – currently the largest in the World – which would deserve more support and recognition. This is in the common European interest. Further questions are raised by the lack of prudential regulation of the Bank's operations (not only in the case of the EIB, but also in case of all other multilateral institutions), and more specifically, the substitution of regulation by reference to best banking practices. The EIB and similar institutions are comparable in size with important systemic commercial banks, which in contrast with the multilaterals, seem to be rather over-regulated and supervised.

20   Towards a Conceptualization of the Notion of Solidarity in the Legal Framework of the EU

András Pünkösty[*]

Keywords

Concept of solidarity, principle of solidarity in EU law, theory of EU law, solidarity as a value concept

Abstract

This article carries out an in-depth analysis of the complex meaning of solidarity within the EU legal framework. Solidarity is a multi-layered concept that serving as the basis for different policy-making choices of highly variable material substance, contributing significantly to the judgments of the CJEU. The point of departure in the analysis are references made to the notion of solidarity in the Founding Treaties. An important layer of its meaning derives from solidarity considered as a 'value'. Important references are made to solidarity as a 'principle' or 'spirit' and there are additional layers of its meaning in the Treaties. In secondary legislation and the institutions' communications, solidarity serves mainly as a basis for socially orientated policymaking. Following the analysis of the meaning of solidarity, I consider the notion of 'solidarity *acquis*' elaborated by Malcolm Ross that suggests that solidarity is one of the most effective tools in maintaining the consistency of the EU legal framework. Finally, the paper focuses on the case-law of the CJEU to conceptualize core legal implications of solidarity in order to establish whether solidarity may be recognized as a general principle of EU law.

---

[*]   András Pünkösty: senior lecturer, Pázmány Péter Catholic University, Budapest.

20.1 RETHINKING THE MEANING OF SOLIDARITY AND THE IMPORTANCE OF THE CONCEPT

There has been an extensive literature written on the concept and the precise meaning of solidarity[1] and its place within EU legal system[2] by scholars in recent years. Yet a common understanding regarding the precise meaning of solidarity has not emerged. The importance of solidarity as a point of reference increased following the adoption of the TEU and the legally binding force of the EU Charter of Fundamental Rights. The principle of solidarity is a point of reference not just in EU legislation, but also in the policy-making processes of the Union. What's more, the CJEU extensively refers to the concept in its case-law. Thus, while recognizing the increasing importance of the solidarity in the legal order of the EU, it is not clear how we are to define its precise meaning. While investigating the inherent meaning of solidarity, the question may raise whether it is, after all, a legal concept that shapes the case-law of the CJEU and the EU's constitutional framework or is it merely used as a reference for contradictory policy- and decision-making. This paper aims to examine the place of solidarity within the legal framework of the EU with an outlook on the possible dimensions of the concept.

20.2 THE POSSIBLE INTERPRETATIVE FRAMEWORK OF THE NOTION OF SOLIDARITY

20.2.1 Solidarity as a Value Concept

In the Founding Treaties there are altogether 17 references made to the notion of solidarity, in addition, Title IV of the Charter of Fundamental Rights is called 'Solidarity'.[3] As far as the Treaties are concerned, there is no crystal clear, homogeneous meaning attached to the notion of solidarity. Instead, several references are made to the notion within a broad spectrum regarding both its quality and direction. Among these references, the most explicit are those which designate solidarity as a value.[4] The values of the EU are listed in Article 2 TEU. Those values overlap with the principles of the EU, as they were referred

---

1   For a prominent theoretical analysis, *see* Andrea Sangiovanni, 'Solidarity in the European Union', *Oxford Journal of Legal Studies*, Vol. 33, Issue 2, 2013, pp. 213-241.
2   Ester di Napoli & Deborah Russo, 'Solidarity in the European Union in Times of Crisis: Towards "European Solidarity"?', *in* Veronica Federico & Christian Lahusen (eds.), *Solidarity as a Public Virtue?*, Nomos, 2018, pp. 195-248.
3   *See* Articles 27-38.
4   Article 2 and Article 3(5) TEU, and the Preamble of the EU Charter of Fundamental Rights.

to before the last Treaty amendment.[5] These prominent notions are now called 'values'. The wording of the second sentence of Article 2 TEU, however, differentiates somewhat between the values on which the Union is founded and the values that are common in the Member States' societies, such as – among others – 'solidarity'. Nevertheless, this latter group should not be distinguished from the values of the EU, but should rather be treated equally, since those values are already manifested in the Member States' societies.[6] In addition, the Lisbon Treaty included the 'solidarity clause'[7] into the Founding Treaties.

The values of the EU are stipulated *expressis verbis* in the first sentence of Article 2 TEU, such as the respect of human dignity, freedom, democracy, equality, the rule of law, respect of human rights, including rights of persons belonging to minorities. The societies of the Member States are shaped by the values of pluralism, non-discrimination, tolerance, justice, solidarity and equality between women and men. With this wording, the Treaty puts these values into the context of Member States' societal structures. Article 3 TEU recognizes the dynamics of Union values[8] and declares that the aim of the EU is, among others, to foster the values of the EU. To make further distinctions between the values and features of Member States' societies seems unnecessary for several reasons. Both the notions of EU values and the features of Member States' societies are considered to bear value-content and are to be maintained within the EU, both at the Union and the Member State level. Based on the wording of the Treaties as such[9] and the possible intent of its signatories, namely that of the Member States, Article 3(1) TEU shall be understood in a way that all values listed in Article 2 TEU are to be fostered without distinction and, consequently, solidarity is to be considered as a value.

The legal scope of Articles 2 and 3 TEU is uncertain however, and some claim that the values of the EU are to be understood as program-orientated constitutional aims only[10] or that they are chiefly subject to political interpretation.[11] Armin von Bogdandy claims that the rephrasing of the principles to values of the EU is somewhat problematic, since

---

5 Article 6(1) TEU: "The Union is founded on the *principles* of liberty, democracy, respect for human rights and fundamental freedoms, and the rule of law, principles which are common to the Member States." (emphasis added).

6 Christoph Vedder & Wolff Heinschel von Heinegg (eds.), *Europäisches Unionsrecht Nomos Kommentar*, Baden-Baden, Nomos, 2012, p. 49.

7 Article 222(1) TEU: "The Union and its Member States shall act jointly in a *spirit of solidarity* if a Member State is the object of a terrorist attack or the victim of a natural or man-made disaster." (emphasis added).

8 Article 3(1) TEU: "The Union's aim is to promote peace, its values and the well-being of its peoples."

9 The wording of the Treaty with regard to the general provisions of external action does not distinguish between values and principles, but equally uses the term of 'principles' in Article 21(1).

10 András Osztovits (ed.), *Az Európai Unióról és az Európai Unió működéséről szóló Szerződés magyarázata* 1. Complex, Budapest, 2011.

11 András Jakab, 'Application of the EU Charter by National Courts in Purely Domestic Cases', *in* András Jakab & Dimitry Kochenov (eds.), *The Enforcement of EU Law and Values: Ensuring Member States' Compliance*, Oxford University Press, at https://papers.ssrn.com/sol3/papers.cfm?abstract_id=2512865.

this presupposes a certain ethical interpretation stance from the citizens and, according to von Bogdandy, a normative foundation of the EU should be established on a more palpable notion other than any kind of sociological or philosophical presumption. Von Bogdandy points out that, in a dogmatically well-founded legal framework, legal and ethical claims should be distinguished; this follows from the principle of liberty. At the same time, he adds that any discourse on the values may lead to a paternalistic approach.[12] Koen Lenaerts and Piet Van Nuffel take a somewhat more permissive position, since they claim that the usage of the designation values is a definite advancement.[13] Andrew T. Williams suggests that the designation of values of the EU in the Founding Treaties is a stabilizing step on the way to integration itself. Williams attaches paramount importance to the value-based approach that could lead to a more just institutional framework of the EU if the philosophical substance of values were formulated at a constitutional level.[14]

20.2.2   Solidarity as a Legal Principle

In the Founding treaties, several references were made to solidarity as a 'principle', or to the 'spirit' of solidarity.[15] The question arises whether solidarity should be considered a general idea or a legal principle that shapes the legal framework of the EU. According to Malcom Ross, solidarity is not just an incidental reference among the other principles that underpins the operation of the EU, but a transformative constitutional concept given its inherent methodological dimension.[16] Ross claims that the duty of the sincere cooperation elaborated by the Court is based on the conceptual framework of solidarity. Accordingly, solidarity is a cross-cutting principle, binding the institutions in the former pillar system[17] and providing an example for the conduct to be followed in the legal relationship between the Member States.[18] According to Ross, solidarity is a fundamental value and a tool for the reconciliation of diverse legal regimes whereby emerging conflicts and differences may remain sustainable within the legal establishment. Thus, solidarity is a cooperative, social

---

12   Armin von Bogdandy & Jürgen Bast (eds.), *Principles of European Constitutional Law*, Hart Publishing, Oxford, 2011, p. 20.
13   Koen Lenaerts & Piet Van Nuffel (eds.), *European Union Law*, Sweet and Maxwell, London, 2011, p. 107.
14   Andrew T. Williams, 'Promoting Justice after Lisbon: Groundwork for a New Philosophy of EU Law', *Oxford Journal of Legal Studies*, Vol. 30, Issue 4, 2010, pp. 663-693.
15   Article 21(1) TEU: "principle"; Article 31(1) TEU: "spirit of mutual solidarity"; Article 80 TFEU: "principle"; Article 122(1) TFEU: "spirit of solidarity"; Article 194(1) TFEU: "spirit of solidarity"; Article 222 TFEU: "spirit of solidarity".
16   Malcom Ross, 'Solidarity – A New Constitutional Paradigm for the EU?', *in* Malcom Ross & Youri Borgmann Prebil (eds.), *Promoting Solidarity in the European Union*, Oxford University Press, Oxford, 2010, p. 42.
17   Judgment of 16 June 2005, *Case C-105/03, Criminal proceedings against Maria Pupino*, ECLI:EU:C:2005:386, para. 41.
18   Ross 2010, p. 42.

concept, and Ross sees its role as a more credible and capable tool for maintaining the reconciliation of regimes than the doctrine of supremacy or the harmonization of laws.[19]

Von Bogdandy understands solidarity as a classic principle of European constitutionalism. Driven by solidarity, the Community polity fosters cohesion between its citizens and organizes mutual cooperation between them on a higher level.[20] Von Bogdandy claims that solidarity should be construed with respect to the EU as an interpretive framework that facilitates the development of the EU from a form of international cooperation to a federal entity. Von Bogdandy underlines the importance of solidarity with respect to its crucial role in the Charter of Fundamental Rights and the area of CFSP. Based on these, solidarity is a key concept of the EU that, on the one hand, contributes to distinguishing it from other international organizations and, on the other hand, it emphasizes the social commitment of Europe in contrast with the US.[21] Similarly to the above conveyed ideas, Koen Lenaerts and Piet Van Nuffel understand the requirement of sincere cooperation between EU institutions as a form of solidarity that differs qualitatively from Member States' obligations under international law in general where they have to transpose international agreements into their domestic law only *bona fide*.[22]

The 'principles' of EU law have extensive literature, however, for the purpose of this paper, some distinctions may be useful. The general principles of EU law are elucidated by the CJEU in its case-law on the interpretation of EU law and, are sources of the EU law themselves. The founding principles that primarily reflect on the foundations of the EU, however, were first referred to as values of the EU in the Founding Treaties.[23] In the literature, there is no consensus surrounding a list of the general principles of EU law, nor is there an exhaustive list thereof. This is due to the fact that they were developed gradually in the jurisprudence of the CJEU. However, there is a common understanding on the issue of what the most significant general principles are. Subsidiarity, proportionality, legal certainty, equality and the protection of human rights are textbook examples of the general principles of EU law. These principles are also referred to as constitutional principles or principles regarding the scope of the EU law.

As described above, solidarity is considered to be a value of the EU, by all means, but further examination is necessary to elaborate whether solidarity is a general principle of the EU law and, as such, a source of EU law itself. To answer this question, the point of departure is Article 4(3) TEU, *i.e.* the loyalty clause that serves as a basis of several judgments of the CJEU that transformed the obligation of loyalty into a principle that funda-

---

19   Id.
20   Bogdandy & Bast (eds.), 2011, p. 53.
21   Id.
22   Lenaerts & Van Nuffel (eds.), 2011, p. 147.
23   A Treaty establishing constitution for Europe, at https://europa.eu/european-union/sites/europaeu/files/docs/body/treaty_establishing_a_constitution_for_europe_en.pdf.

mentally contributed to the legal framework of the EU. This provision is also referred to as the solidarity clause[24] that binds both the Member States and the institutions of the EU. It is driven by solidarity as a factor of cohesion, mandating either an active or a passive stance of the Member State or institution, depending on the subject matter at hand. Following Ross' approach by pointing to solidarity as the main underlying concept behind Article 4(3) TEU, it is important to note that the CJEU used the solidarity clause as a reference point in developing the concepts of both direct effect and indirect effect. The solidarity clause also served as a basis for the liability of Member States for breaching EU law.[25] Some scholars argue that the provision in the Treaties regarding the services of general economic interest (Article 107 TFEU) are also based on solidarity which were enacted as a part of the shared values of the Union. As a consequence of the above, Ross may validly claim that solidarity is a constitutional principle greatly affecting the whole legal framework of the EU.

20.2.3   Further Aspects of the Notion of Solidarity

References in the Founding Treaties do not give further guidance on the substance of solidarity but refer to the notion as a stand-alone one.[26] There are also references to solidarity in the Treaties with additional meanings such as political solidarity.[27] The concept of solidarity in a normative sense refers primarily to the relationship between the Member States; yet, several further meanings of solidarity are also represented in the Treaties: solidarity between generations,[28] solidarity [...] among peoples,[29] solidarity which binds Europe and the overseas countries,[30] solidarity between Member States, which is fair towards third-country nationals [...] stateless persons shall be treated as third-country nationals.[31] The different perspectives of solidarity expressed in the Treaties adumbrate the complex meaning of solidarity that, at the same time, allows for a wide scope of interpretation.

Wolfram Lamping emphasizes the significance of the concept of 'welfare state' in interpreting the meaning of solidarity. The core constitutive elements of the welfare state are the benefits that the state provides for its citizens by way of reallocation systems and public services that cannot be made equally available to everyone due to their costs but

---

24   Malcom Ross, 'Promoting Solidarity: From Public Services to the European Model of Competition', *Common Market Law Review*, Vol. 44, Issue 4, 2007, p. 1060.
25   Judgment of 19 November 1991, *Joined Cases C-6/90 and C-9/90, Andrea Francovich and Danila Bonifaci and Others v. Italian Republic (Francovich)*, ECLI:EU:C:1991:428, para 36.
26   Preamble of TEU, Article 3(3) TEU, Article 24(3) TEU, Preamble of TFEU, Article 67(3) TFEU.
27   Article 24(2) and (3) TEU that are among stipulation of the specific provision for the CFSP.
28   Article 3(3) TEU.
29   Preamble of TEU, Article 3(5) TEU.
30   Preamble of TEU.
31   Article 67(2) TFEU.

only to a certain community. In the welfare state, common identity is taken for granted based on the common language, cultural and historical heritage; thus, citizens undertake the additional costs of maintaining the social benefit systems. However, as Lamping points its out, overemphasizing the social element of the EU may entail risks. Given that the EU aims to achieve some of its socially orientated development of welfare state standards without the same level of cohesion within the EU, some justification may be necessary.[32] Similarly to Lamping, Clemens M. Rieder also raised the question of maintaining solidarity in a sustainable way in respect of health care services.[33]

According to the understanding of solidarity described above, if the level of solidarity increases within a given community, the ability of solidary commitment will decrease towards the members of other communities. Strengthening the relationship within a community may lead to isolation from the external environment.[34] The more the resources and possibilities are utilized in order to facilitate the process within the community, the fewer opportunities will be made available outside the community. In my view, the inward dynamics of solidarity could work the other way around as well. There may be a situation where, if the level of solidarity rises in a given community, it may result in a stronger capability of responsibility sharing with others.[35] Thus, if a relationship of strong solidarity develops among the EU Member States, it may render the EU more capable of cooperating in policy areas for the benefit of other regions such as overseas countries, third countries or even undocumented persons. Solidarity is also mentioned as a basis for the EU external relations. The EU's solidarity towards certain regions of the world, such as development cooperation,[36] humanitarian aid[37] and the EU's conflict prevention and peacemaking missions in the framework of the CFSP,[38] requires solidarity between the Member States as a prerequisite. This kind of solidarity could manifest itself in many different ways such as financial solidarity or building the common military command chain. We should note, however, that solidarity may operate differently since certain directions of development mutually reinforce each other or lead to mutual decline. It would be hardly sustainable for

---

32 Wolfram Lamping, 'Limits and Perils of Institutionalising Post-National Social Policy', *in* Ross & Prebil (eds.), 2010, pp. 46-48.

33 Clemens M. Rieder, 'When Patients Exit, What Happens to Solidarity?', *in* Ross & Prebil (eds.), 2010, pp. 122-135.

34 Id. pp. 134-135.

35 *See* the *solidarity clause* enacted in the Lisbon Treaty, Article 222 TFEU: "The Union and its Member States shall act jointly in *a spirit of solidarity* if a Member State is the object of a terrorist attack or the victim of a natural or man-made disaster. The Union shall mobilise all the instruments at its disposal, including the military resources made available by the Member States […]." (emphasis added).

36 Articles 208-210 TFEU.

37 Article 214 TFEU.

38 Articles 41-42 TFEU.

example, to provide equal access to the most developed health care service to everyone while maintaining its quality and standard at the same time.[39]

To answer all the questions in connection with the possible interpretations and the limitations of solidarity is beyond the scope of this paper, yet to understand solidarity exclusively from the perspective of access to benefits of the welfare state leads to a restrictive interpretation. In my view, focusing on the value element of solidarity instead, is what would be beneficial for European integration.

20.3 THE APPLICATION OF THE SOLIDARITY PRINCIPLE IN EU LAW

20.3.1 References to the Principle of Solidarity in the Communication of the Institutions and the Meaning Thereof

In the documents of the institutions, the meaning of solidarity is a complex notion, as we have seen on the example of the Founding Treaties. In the Commission's communications, solidarity is mainly related to the social dimension of the EU and, lately, the emphasis shifted towards the solidarity between the Member States in the wake of the migration crisis. Two communications of the Commission deal directly with the potential of solidarity regarding social aspects within the EU. In its communication issued in November 2007,[40] the Commission takes the first step to create the vision of a social Europe, while in its communication issued in July 2008,[41] the Commission already provides an action plan for building a social agenda. Both documents are rich in interpreting the meaning of solidarity and contain a diverse solidarity-concept,[42] mainly referring to it in relation to opportunities and access. The latter communication points out that the shared societal values play an important role in strengthening European identity – itself an important element of the European project from its very inception. According to the Commission's position, the renewed social agenda is based on a threefold, mutually interconnected aim of creating

---

39 Communication from the Commission to the European Parliament, the Council, the European Economic and Social Committee and the Committee of the Regions entitled 'Solidarity in Health: Reducing Health Inequalities in the European Union', COM(2009) 567 final.

40 Communication from the Commission to the European Parliament, the Council, the European Economic and Social Committee and the Committee of the Regions entitled 'Opportunities, access and solidarity: towards a new social vision for 21st century Europe', COM(2007) 726 final.

41 Communication from the Commission to the European Parliament, the Council, the European Economic and Social Committee and the Committee of the Regions entitled 'Renewed social agenda: Opportunities, access and solidarity in 21st century Europe', COM(2008) 412 final.

42 Catharine Barnard distinguishes between the following solidarity notions used by the Commission in the communications: solidarity as an aim, interpretative medium, notion, process and tool. See Catherine Barnard, 'Solidarity and the Commission's "Renewed Social Agenda"', in Ross & Prebil (eds.), 2010, pp. 94-98.

opportunities, providing access and demonstrating solidarity. In line with the directions
of solidarity as gleaned from the Founding Treaties, the Commission articulates that

> "Europeans share a commitment to social solidarity: between generations,
> regions, the better off and the less well-off and wealthier and less wealthy
> Member States. Solidarity is part of how European society works and how
> Europe engages with the rest of the world."[43]

Regarding the notion itself, the Commission emphasizes that

> "[s]olidarity means action to help those who are disadvantaged – who cannot
> reap the benefits of an open, rapidly changing society. It means fostering social
> inclusion and integration, participation and dialogue and combating poverty.
> It means giving support to those who are exposed to temporary, transitional
> problems of globalization and technological change."[44]

Accordingly, the concept of solidarity in the Commission's understanding is not a community or societal organizing principle, rather a moral commitment expressing mainly social-oriented aspects.

The Commission refers to solidarity also in its communication that aims to give an adequate answer to the challenges that workers face in the wake of global challenges.[45] In line with the 'Renewed Social Agenda', the document summarizes the possibilities for helping workers adjust to changes and lists the tasks for the re-training of workers in a vulnerable position. In line with this policy the decision for establishing a Community Program for Employment and Social Solidarity, called 'Progress' was adopted.[46] The Program aims to fund the implementation of EU objectives in the fields of employment and social affairs, as set out in the Commission Communication on the Social Agenda, thereby contributing to the achievement of the Lisbon Strategy goals in those fields.[47]

---

43   *See* COM(2008) 412 final, p. 7.

44   Id.

45   Communication from the Commission to the European Parliament and the Council entitled 'Solidarity in
the face of Change: The European Globalisation Adjustment Fund (EGF) in 2007 – Review and Prospects',
COM(2008) 421 final.

46   Decision No 1672/2006/EC of the European Parliament and of the Council of 24 October 2006 establishing
a Community Program for Employment and Social Solidarity – Progress. The Decision was amended by
Decision No 284/2010/EU of the European Parliament and of the Council of 25 March 2010.

47   Decision No 1672/2006/EC of the European Parliament and of the Council, Article 1(1).

Important references are included in the opinion of the European Economic and Social Committee with regard to the relationship between energy policy and solidarity.[48] The Committee observes that legal tensions can be expected between the EU and its Member States in view of the disjuncture between the supranational task of liberalizing and/or harmonizing key aspects of the functioning of the energy market in Europe and the national task of protecting social well-being.[49] However, the Commission believes the contrary, namely that cooperation between the Member States will enhance national security.[50] The document adopts this position and reaffirms the Commission's view by declaring

"[s]ocial cohesion must be maintained as far as possible, so as to safeguard solidarity rights as regards access to energy of both the economically weakest population groups and of vulnerable and disabled people."[51]

With regard to the external relations of the EU, some further legal documents should be mentioned for taking stock when it comes to solidarity-related legal developments. The implementation of the 'solidarity clause'[52] took place in a Council Decision.[53] Pursuant to Article 222(1) TFEU, the Union and the Member States are to act jointly in a spirit of solidarity if a Member State is the object of a terrorist attack or the victim of a natural or man-made disaster.[54] According to this legislative act, solidarity is the obligation of a Member State towards another Member State. A different level of solidarity is demonstrated in the communication of the Commission[55] reflecting on the preparatory document on the establishment of a European Voluntary Humanitarian Aid Corps (EVHAC)[56] after its stipulation under the Lisbon Treaty.[57] The Commission defines humanitarian action as "a fundamental expression of the European value of solidarity", accordingly, the Commission sees it as a unique opportunity "to express EU citizen's solidarity through volunteering" that "could equally contribute to the development of a more cohesive European society by creating new opportunities for participation for European citizens, especially younger

---

48 Opinion of the European Economic and Social Committee on 'The EU's new energy policy: application, effectiveness and solidarity'.
49 Id. General Comments, 3.3.2.
50 Id.
51 Id. General Comments, 3.3.3.
52 Article 222 TFEU.
53 Council Decision No 2014/415/EU of 24 June 2014 on the arrangements for the implementation by the Union of the solidarity clause.
54 Id. Article 2.
55 Communication from the Commission to the European Parliament and the Council entitled 'How to express EU citizen's solidarity through volunteering: First reflections on a European Voluntary Humanitarian Aid Corps', COM(2010) 683 final.
56 Id.
57 Article 214 TFEU.

ones."[58] A new direction for the understanding of solidarity is manifested in the solidarity between generations.[59] It is meant foster solidarity and cooperation between generations and to pursue specific objectives related to active ageing and intergenerational solidarity.[60]

It is outside the scope of this paper to analyze the functioning of solidarity retrospectively in certain policy areas, nevertheless, it is necessary to underline that there are areas with respect to solidarity between the Member States that were seriously challenged following the multiple crises EU integration has experienced recently, in particular in the areas of monetary policy and asylum policy. According to Peter Hilpold's interpretation,[61] solidarity is a distinctive principle-based reciprocity, in certain policy areas that are "islands of solidarity".[62]

20.3.2   The Case-Law of the CJEU

In the case-law of the CJEU, the principle of solidarity, beyond its constitutional significance demonstrated above, is primarily relevant in the field of competition law and citizenship of the Union. Hereinafter, I provide a brief outlook on the relevant case-law and shed light on some implications of the CJEU's understanding of solidarity.

The Court made its first reference to the principle of solidarity in an early joint case lodged for the annulment of legislation that prevented undertakings from selling below a minimum fixed price in the coal and steel industry. In this case, a fine was imposed on an undertaking for selling concrete bars below the fixed minimum prices.[63] With the fine, the Commission put a higher burden on the more competitive undertakings, since, according to its interpretation – confirmed by the Court in the judgment –, the fixed minimum price was justified to secure the supply. Indeed, by adopting a fixed minimum price at Community level, less competitive undertakings could survive and stay on the market. In the judgment, the CJEU found that, in the coal and steel industry, the crisis-prevention policy is underpinned by the fundamental principle of solidarity between the undertakings.[64] The Court

---

58   *See* COM(2010) 683 final.
59   Decision No 940/2011/EU of the European Parliament and of the Council of 14 September 2011, on the European Year for Active Ageing and Solidarity between Generations (2012).
60   Id. Article 2.
61   Peter Hilpold, 'Understanding Solidarity within EU Law: An Analysis of the 'Island of Solidarity' with Particular Regard to Monetary Union', *Yearbook of European Law*, Vol. 34, Issue 1, 2015, pp. 257-285.
62   Id. *See* the comprehensive analysis concerning development aid and development cooperation, cohesion policy, EU law and asylum policy, European Monetary Union.
63   Judgment of 18 March 1980, *Joined Cases 154, 205, 206, 226 to 228, 263 and 264/78, 39, 31, 83 and 85/79, SpA Ferriera Valsabbia and Others v. Commission of the European Communities (SpA Ferriera)*, ECLI:EU:C:1980:81.
64   *Joined Cases 154, 205, 206, 226 to 228, 263 and 264/78, 39, 31, 83 and 85/79, SpA Ferriera*, para. 6 of the summary of the judgment.

referred to the Preamble of the ECSC Treaty that declares the principle of solidarity and, according to the CJEU, its practical implication was manifested in other Treaty articles as well.[65] The normative aim of Article 61 ECSC Treaty that served as a legal basis for the price determination was to help the Community to become capable of overcoming the economic crises through the application of the principle of solidarity.[66] In the Court's line of reasoning, solidarity should be understood as a principle competing with the principle of proportionality. Declaring that some undertakings need to bear higher burden than others, based on the European solidarity, the Court found that the Commission did not place a disproportionate burden on the plaintiffs.[67]

In addition, in the field of EU competition law, the principle of solidarity provides a limitation to the extensive interpretation of the concept of undertaking, thereby also limiting the scope of application of competition law.[68] In the *Kattner* case,[69] the Court declared that a body such as the employers' liability insurance association to which undertakings must be affiliated in a particular branch of industry and in a particular territory for being insured against workplace accidents and occupational diseases is not an undertaking. It fulfils an exclusively social function, since this a body operates within the framework of a scheme that applies the principle of solidarity and is subject to state supervision.[70] The Court examined on the application of principle of solidarity on its merits in the *Poucet* case which related to the operation of a social security system.[71] The question arose whether certain entities managing the sickness and maternity insurance scheme for self-employed persons in non-agricultural occupations, qualified as an undertaking under the Treaties.[72] In the social security system at issue self-employed persons in non-agricultural occupations were subject to compulsory social protection, including those provided by autonomous statutory schemes, in particular the sickness and maternity insurance scheme.[73] The Court observed that schemes pursuing a social objective embodied the principle of solidarity.[74] According to the Court, the principle of solidarity within the sickness and maternity scheme

---

65   The Court refers to the following articles of the ECSC Treaty: Article 3 (priority accorded to the common interest, which presupposes a duty of solidarity), Article 49 (a system of financing the community-based levies), Article 55(2) (general availability of the results of research in the technical and social fields), Article 56 (reconversation and readaptation aids) and Article 53 (making financial agreements).
66   *Joined Cases 154, 205, 206, 226 to 228, 263 and 264/78, 39, 31, 83 and 85/79, SpA Ferriera*, para. 87.
67   Id. para. 119.
68   Richard Wish, *Versenyjog*, HVG-ORAC, Budapest, 2010, pp. 84-85.
69   Judgment of 5 March 2009, *Case C-350/07, Kattner Stahlbau GmbH v. Maschinenbau- und Metall- Berufsgenossenschaft (Kattner)*, ECLI:EU:C:2009:127.
70   *Case C-350/07, Kattner*, para. 1. of the summary of the judgment.
71   Judgment of 17 February 1993, *Joined Cases C-159/91 and C-160/91, Christian Pouchet v. Assurances Générales de France and Caisse Mutuelle Régionale du Languedoc-Roussillon (Pouchet)*, ECLI:EU:C:1993:63, paras. 8-12.
72   Id. para. 2.
73   Id. para. 7.
74   Id. para. 8.

is manifested in the fact that the scheme is financed by contributions proportional to income, whereas the benefits are identical for all those who receive them.[75] In the old-age insurance scheme, solidarity is manifested in the fact that the contributions paid by active workers are used to finance the pensions of retired workers.[76] Finally, the Court declares that solidarity applies across the various social security schemes as well, since schemes that produce a surplus contribute to the financing of those with structural financial difficulties. The CJEU points out that solidarity entails the redistribution of income between those who are better off and those who, in view of their resources and state of health, would be deprived of the necessary social cover.[77]

In the *Viking*[78] and *Laval*[79] cases the Court acknowledged the collective actions based on solidarity between employees and workers' unions and, quite remarkably, the CJEU accepts the right for collective action as a justification for restricting market freedoms. More precisely, the Court recognizes collective action as a competing interest to the fundamental freedoms.

In the *Grzelczyk* case[80] the Court assessed a national provision in connection with students' right of residence. The national legislation guaranteed a minimum subsistence allowance (minimax) only for nationals. The Court concluded that EU law

> "accepts a certain degree of financial solidarity between nationals of a host Member State and nationals of other Member States, particularly if the difficulties which a beneficiary of the right of residence encounters are temporary."[81]

Consequently, according to the judgment, making the minimax allowance for a non-national EU citizen conditional upon the worker status was a breach of EU law. This form of financial solidarity reaffirmed by the Court may entail serious financial burdens for Member States, the Court therefore further refined the content of the obligation in its case-law. In the *Bidar* case[82] the Court referred, on the one hand, to the *Grzelczyk* case by reaffirming that "the Member States must, in the organization and application of their social assistance systems, show a certain degree of financial solidarity with nationals of other

---

75   Id. para. 10.
76   Id. para. 11.
77   Id. para. 12.
78   Judgment of 11 December 2007, *Case C-438/05, International Transport Workers' Federation and Finnish Seamen's Union v. Viking Line ABP and OÜ Viking Line Eesti (Viking)*, ECLI:EU:C:2007:772.
79   Judgment of 18 December 2007, *Case C-341/05, Laval un Partneri Ltd v. Svenska Byggnadsarbetareförbundet and Others (Laval)*, ECLI:EU:C:2007:809.
80   Judgment of 20 September 2001, *Case C-184/99, Rudy Grzelczyk v. Centre public d'aide sociale d'Ottignies-Louvain-la-Neuve (Grzelczyk)*, ECLI:EU:C:2001:458.
81   *Case C-184/99, Grzelczyk*, para. 44.
82   Judgment of 15 March 2005, *Case C-209/03, The Queen, on the application of Dany Bidar v. London Borough of Ealing and Secretary of State for Education and Skills (Bidar)*, ECLI:EU:C:2005:169.

Member States", yet it also limited the scope of application of this financial solidarity. Namely,

> "it is permissible for a Member State to ensure that the grant of assistance to cover the maintenance costs of students from other Member States does not become an unreasonable burden which could have consequences for the overall level of assistance which may be granted by that State."[83]

In the *Bidar* case, the Court ruled that it is incompatible with EU law for a national provision to grant students the right to assistance covering their maintenance costs only if they are settled in the host Member State and to precluding nationals of other Member States from obtaining the status of settled person as a student. This is the case where that national is lawfully resident in the host Member State and consequently established a genuine link with the society of that State.

Finally, as far as financial solidarity of Member States with respect to the free movement of persons and EU citizenship is concerned, the Court declared that the citizen may expect "a certain degree of financial solidarity",[84] and the Court established equal access to social benefits whenever there is "a certain degree of integration".[85] However, in recent cases, the court seems to be setting limits to the scope of financial solidarity. In the *Dano* case,[86] the Court interpreted a lack of intention to integrate into the host Member State as an obstacle to the genuine link between the EU citizen and the host State, grounds for limiting the financial solidarity of the Member State. Some commentators even suggest that the clear shift in the Court's case-law, which could be interpreted as a limitation on the level of solidarity, is a consequence of the political tension arising from the phenomenon of 'social tourism'.[87]

From the numerous references made by the Advocate Generals regarding the notion of solidarity, I recall here the definition given by AG Fennelly[88] who observed that "[social] solidarity envisages the inherently uncommercial act of involuntary subsidization of one social group by another".

---

83   *Case C-209/03, Bidar*, para. 56.
84   *Case C-184/99, Grzelczyk*, para. 44.
85   *Case C-209/03, Bidar*, para. 57.
86   Judgment of 11 November 2014, *Case C-333/13, Elisabeta Dano and Florin Dano v. Jobcenter Leipzig*, ECLI:EU:C:2014:2358.
87   Dion Kramer, 'Earning Social Citizenship in the European Union: Free Movement and Access to Social Assistance Benefits Reconstructed', *Cambridge Yearbook of European Legal Studies*, Vol. 18, 2016, pp. 270-301 and 289; and Laura Gyeney, 'A szociális turizmus kérdése az Európai Unió Bíróságának joggyakorlatában' *Létünk*, Vol. 46, Issue 2, pp. 170-171.
88   Opinion of Advocate General Fennelly delivered on 6 February 1997, *Case C-70/95, Sodemare SA, Anni Azzurri Holding SpA and Anni Azzurri Rezzato Srl v. Regione Lombardia*, ECLI:EU:C:1997:55.

20.4   CONCLUDING REMARKS

In this paper, I sought to conceptualize the principle of solidarity within the legal order of the EU and to derive some general conclusions regarding the meaning of solidarity. The subject, however, needs further research, since the paper does not reflect on the significance of solidarity in the EU policy-making system. Moreover, a more complex understanding of solidarity would benefit from a theoretical assessment of the notion presented in connection with the legal implications of the principle.[89]

With regard to the special role of solidarity in the EU constitutional system, it is not an overstatement to speak of a so-called 'solidarity acquis' coined by Malcom Ross,[90] who identifies the transformative effect of solidarity in five areas: the consistent reference to solidarity by the CJEU; the implications of solidarity in fundamental rights protection; most importantly solidarity as one of the possible justifications for restricting the market freedoms; financial solidarity with regard to the citizenship of the EU; and, finally, drawing the limits of the concept of undertaking in competition law. Consequently, the main significance of the notion of solidarity is, on the one hand, to reinforce the relationship between the different levels and members of the Community as such, and to strike the balance between the market-orientated principles and the social aspects of the legal order in the common interest or for well-being of EU citizens. This is one of the substantive aims of the EU specified in the Treaties.[91] Moreover, solidarity may be understood as a general principle of EU law. The CJEU seems unwilling to further develop this understanding of solidarity unless Member States are clearly willing to deepen integration in most areas of cooperation. The legal basis for this would be the concept of solidarity as developed in the constitutional traditions of the Member States. While the significance of solidarity varies in the different Member Sates' legal traditions, solidarity is seen as an integral part of the European constitutional heritage.[92]

Finally, it should be noted that any research conducted in connection with the notion of solidarity is closely related to the question how the values of the EU are understood in general. Values as other identity-related issues are often cited as conditions for the success of European integration as such. Hence, further developing the understanding and appli-

---

89   In the field of the services of general economic interest, *see* Communication from the Commission to the European Parliament, the Council, the European Economic and Social Committee and the Committee of the Regions of 12 May 2004 entitled 'White Paper on services of general interest', COM(2004) 374 final, and 'A Quality Framework for Services of General Interest in Europe', COM(2011) 900 final.

90   Malcom Ross, 'Solidarity – A New Constitutional Paradigm for the EU?', *in* Ross & Prebil (eds.), 2010, p. 41.

91   Article 3(1) TEU.

92   Ross 2010, p. 43.

cation of solidarity in EU law and decision-making, will be an important element in the discourse surrounding the future of the EU.

21   KEY FACTORS OF THE DEVELOPMENT AND RENEWAL OF THE SOCIAL MARKET ECONOMY IN THE EU

István Kőrösi*

Keywords

Europe 2020 strategy, social market economy, eco-social market economy, social welfare systems, EU structural funds

Abstract

The purpose of this study is to present the principles, strategy and operation of the social market economy, based on legal, political and economic considerations. The first social market economy, West Germany – followed by Austria, the Netherlands, as well as other countries in Northern and Western Europe –, mustered a positive overall performance from the post-World War II years to the early 1970s. Since then, however, we have been witnessing the erosion, distortion and decline of efficiency of the social market economy. There are four main issues to be addressed: *(i)* What are the main theoretical and conceptual, 'eternal' elements of the social market economy? *(ii)* What economic policy was built on this theoretical foundation and why did the system work well in Western Europe after World War II? *(iii)* What factors eroded this system? *(iv)* Can social market economy be renewed in the second decade of the 21st century and, if it can, what are the preconditions of it? In my analysis, I highlight some key areas: EU policies, Lisbon Agenda and Europe 2020 strategy, growth, financial disequilibria and competitiveness, innovation and employment, the relation of state and market.

21.1   INTRODUCTION

The social market economy is an economic and social policy system whose theoretical, strategic, social and economic policy objectives form the basis of long-term sustainable development. The main objective is to ensure the competitiveness of the economy through the proper functioning of the market economy, enforcement of performance and fair

---

*   István Kőrösi: associate professor, Pázmány Péter Catholic University, Budapest; senior research fellow, World Economic Institute of ERRC of the Hungarian Academy of Sciences.

competition. Ensuring social peace in the society requires the realization of the objectives of subsidiarity and solidarity. It should be mentioned that, unfortunately, there are serious negative tendencies in the economy, in the society and in the environment that threaten the existence of humanity. The basic principle of social market economy is that market freedom must be linked to social compensation. In parallel to the synthesis of these two, they wanted to achieve good economic performance and social well-being based on the principle of performance, social justice and fair redistribution. They said yes to justice, but egalitarianism was rejected. Both the centralized planned economy and the 'laissez-faire' capitalism were rejected. According to the creators, the social market economy is an economic system that seeks to achieve economic efficiency based on the principles of performance and social justice through redistribution. This concept is based on the well-being and integrity of individuals and companies in a fair competition. Individual interests and public good are compatible. The means of coordination is fair competition, the rules of which are fixed, monitored and guaranteed by the state (competition law and competition policy).

The results of the social market economy of the developed countries in the period 1950-1973 were relatively fast economic growth, relatively high employment level, improvement of living standards, modernization of the economic structure and social growth. However, since the early 1970s, deepening of the crisis, escalation of economic and financial imbalances, rise in social tensions, very high level of unemployment, decline in labor income to new added value gave rise to the erosion of the social market economy. The reports of the Club of Rome state that humanity endangers its own survival and future by over-exploiting natural resources. The factors of the social market crisis are still present. What are the most important ones? Reaching the fundamental goals of the system was based on free initiative, performance enhancement and social development. These goals cannot be achieved without adequate growth and financial stability. The impact of globalization is coming from the outside world, from the global economy, and within countries where the TNC's global optimization strategy crosses or contradicts the country, it has had a very negative impact on the established system of social market economy. The implementation of both elements (order and freedom) of the social market economy has become very difficult and contradictory in many European countries. The 'order' was covered by the crisis, and freedom was limited by the 'stability culture' crisis. Previously, competition was more balanced, it was later replaced by the overcrowding, overweight and dictating role of multinational companies.

Globalization is a major challenge for Europe. The American technological superiority has not only survived but has intensified since the mid-1970s to the present day. Exports from China and emerging countries show an extraordinary expansion, and this continues. Europe's spatial loss has become a constant trend in the world economy. The realization of national economic policies is greatly hampered by the forces of globalization. The functioning of the European social market economy is costly and, of course, greater than that of the US, China and the Far East, where social welfare systems spend much less. (The deployment of social systems has also begun in the mentioned countries, which will mean increasing costs for them in the future). Financing social welfare systems in Europe is costly, but it is worth spending these costs in the interests of a greater prosperity and social security. International law, European law and national legal systems play an important role in regulating these processes.

21.2   ESTABLISHING THE SOCIAL MARKET ECONOMY

The system of social market economy was elaborated during World War II. Christian social teaching, the Freiburg School and the Ordoliberal System of Ideas were developed by Müller-Armack, Eucken, Röpke, Rüstow and their peers. Social market economy is both a 'systems theory' and a 'systems policy' *(Ordnungstheorie und Ordnungspolitik)*. The implementation of the system's strategy in Germany can be attributed to Konrad Adenauer and Ludwig Erhard. The construction of the social market economy in the 1950s and 1960s was ubiquitous in the western part of Europe, and its implementation was linked to the welfare state, which became an important element of the system of social market economy. Different models of the social market economy and the welfare state have emerged: the Rhine model (especially in Germany, the Netherlands, Austria), the Scandinavian, the Anglo-American and the Southern European models.[1] The social market economy and welfare systems have been incorporated into the constitutions and legal systems of these regions and countries, forming their core element. The legal framework at the level of the EU is incorporated into certain provisions of the TEU.[2] The direction of the further development of the social market economy is increasingly pointing towards an eco-social market economy, which makes actions in international dimensions indispensable.[3]

---

1   For a detailed analysis, *see* Katalin Botos, 'Globalizáció és szociális piacgazdaság', *Heller Farkas Füzetek*, 2011/1, pp. 3-13; László Csaba, 'Életképes modell-e a szociális piacgazdaság?', *Távlatok*, Issue 80, 2008, pp. 79-81; István Kőrösi, 'A fenntartható fejlődést ösztönző állam', *Polgári Szemle*, 2010/2, pp. 95-111; Béla Tomka, *A jóléti állam Európában és Magyarországon*, Corvina, Budapest, 2008, p. 115.
2   Articles 3(3), 5(1) and (2) TEU.
3   Article 21(2)(d)-(f) TEU.

21.3   EU Policies

The development of EU policies is a key area for the successful renewal of the EU and the social market economy.[4] In terms of content, EU policies can be divided into constitutional, regulatory, distribution and redistribution policies. In these areas, legal regulation is becoming more sophisticated, since political, economic as well as financial aspects need to be enforced. Regional, structural and cohesion development have high priority in the EU, which is supported by separate funds. These are the European Regional Development Fund (ERDF), the Cohesion Fund, the European Social Fund (ESF), the European Agricultural Fund for Rural Development (EAFRD), the European Maritime and Fisheries Fund (EMFF), the EU Solidarity Fund and the Instrument for Pre-Accession Assistance (IPA).

The main objective of ERDF is to strengthen economic and social cohesion by reducing regional disparities. The grants are focused on four main areas: innovation and research, digitalization, support for small and medium-sized enterprises, low carbon management.[5]

The Cohesion Fund is currently supporting those Member States where the GNI per capita is below 90% of the EU average. It aims to reduce economic and social disparities and promote sustainable development. Between 2014 and 2020, a total of 15 Member States will benefit from its support.[6]

The European Social Fund is the oldest of the Structural Funds: its creation dates back to 1960. In the period 2014-20, the ESF focuses on four main objectives: *(i)* promoting employment and supporting labor mobility, *(ii)* combating poverty and strengthening social inclusion, *(iii)* investing in education, training and lifelong learning, and *(iv)* improving the capacity of the institutions and the efficiency of public administration.[7]

The EU Solidarity Fund[8] was created in 2002 in response to major floods. Since then, there have been 80 cases of disaster relief: granting aid to those affected by major floods, earthquakes, forest fires, storms and droughts.[9]

---

4   An excellent summary analysis of these is provided by Marcel Szabó *et al.* (eds.), *Uniós szakpolitikák*, Szent István Társulat, Budapest, 2014, p. 260.

5   Regulation (EU) No 1301/2013 of the European Parliament and of the Council of 17 December 2013 on the European Regional Development Fund and on specific provisions concerning the Investment for growth and jobs goal and repealing Regulation (EC) No 1080/2006.

6   Regulation (EU) No 1300/2013 of the European Parliament and of the Council of 17 December 2013 on the Cohesion Fund and repealing Council Regulation (EC) No 1084/2006.

7   Regulation (EU) No 1304/2013 of the European Parliament and of the Council of 17 December 2013 on the European Social Fund and repealing Council Regulation (EC) No 1081/2006.

8   Regulation (EU) No 661/2014 of the European Parliament and of the Council of 15 May 2014 amending Council Regulation (EC) No 2012/2002 establishing the European Union Solidarity Fund.

9   *See* Petra Lea Láncos, 'Az európai strukturális és kohéziós politika', *in* Marcel Szabó *et al.* (eds.), 2014, pp. 229-242.

In 2007, under the Instrument for Pre-Accession Assistance (IPA), community programs and financial instruments received by candidate and potential candidate countries were merged (former PHARE, ISPA, SAPARD, CARDS programs). During the 2014-2020 period, IPA II entered into force as a legal framework and financial support system.[10]

Among the EU policies, the EU's Common Commercial Policy, Competition Policy and migration policy are of paramount importance for the development of the EU and for the progress of its external relations.

21.4   THE LISBON AGENDA AND THE EUROPE 2020 STRATEGY

The current processes of the world economy take place in four areas: *(i)* globalization, *(ii)* integration, *(iii)* upgrading of regionalism and sub-regionalism, and *(iv)* crucial change in the role of the state, especially in its activity in the economy.

The active adaptation and its quality and effectivity, as well as the enhancement of competitiveness have been upgraded. Nowadays, there are basic negative tendencies in both the operation of the state and that of the economy. There is a need for genuine structural reforms in order to put an end to these tendencies.

At the beginning of the 21st century we are the witnesses of the upgrading of human resources. In most part of the 20th century the key elements of development were the capital and its materialized form, the investment. After both world wars, there was an obvious lack of the dollar. The main obstacle of growth was the lack of capital, the scarcest factor in production. Therefore, it had to be paid on the highest level. Due to this fact, the share of capital-owners increased and remained high as for the value of production.

Nevertheless, as early as the mid-60s, the lack of dollar transformed into an over-abundance of dollar and financial capital. A sort of international financial 'balloon' had been created. Due to this fact, the dollar lost its value, the trust in it diminished, and these processes led to the crisis of the Bretton Woods system, and later on to several other crises on the financial market. In the developed countries, the market of standard consumer goods became saturated, the possibilities for profitable investments decreased, the rate of net profit decreased several times, taxes and incidental charges increased. All these negative tendencies created negative effects. The fall in real investments and an increasing rate in unemployment caused a significant withdrawal of working capital in most industrially developed countries, especially in those EU countries which were rich in capital. Problems have been worsened by the fact that on long term the net, after-tax profit reached in the real economy by investment, was much lower than the result of investments in the specu-lative, financial market. These investments bear more risk but may bring more yield. This

---

10   *See* the legal framework of IPA at https://ec.europa.eu/regional_policy/en/funding/ipa/framework/.

fact can be well observed at the events of the autumn of 2008. Actually, interests and dividends can/could be paid only from profits and incomes produces in the real economy. Therefore, it is impossible to overcome financial crisis without them.

There are four crucial areas which are undeniable for the development of economy and human resources: human resources, health care system, education, infrastructure and environment policy. The quality and the development tendencies in these four areas determine changes in each country concerning their future, quality of life and competitiveness on the world market. Countries which develop in a normal way can concentrate on these areas and thus, they can increase their competitiveness, while underdeveloped or regressing countries will be in a hopeless situation for a long period. Therefore, financing these areas should be increased in absolute value; moreover, their relative proportion in the national budget has to be grown. It is an essential condition for development and catching-up.

The Lisbon Agenda[11] accepted in March 2000 set the ambitious goal for the EU to "be the most competitive, knowledge-based economy of the world on the global market" by 2010. Certain economic policy makers and media experts interpret it as reaching the American economy. Nevertheless, in my opinion, the above-mentioned aim cannot be interpreted like that. (Comparison with the US did not even appear in the original concept.) In order to reach the crucial aim of competitiveness, all of Europe's competitors had to be taken into consideration with a special attention to Japan, China, India, the small, Far Eastern countries as well and other regions too.

In 2001, the strategy of the Lisbon Agenda has been elaborated in the Lisbon Program and the requirement of sustainable development was added. In 2004, following the Sapir and Kok reports the revision of the Lisbon process was initiated and, in 2010, completed in the framework of the Europe 2020 strategy. The completion of the Lisbon Agenda with the national action plans for catching-up was also accepted.

The four strategic areas of the Europe 2020 strategy are the following:[12] (i) extension of knowledge and innovation, (ii) realization of a homogenous inner market, (iii) creation of new workplaces and a new European social model and (iv) stabilization policies for the macroeconomy. The enhancement of competitiveness based on the knowledge-based economy could be the only basis on which the decrease of the role of Europe can be reversed.

This approach requires the elaboration of a totally new and steady economic policy in the EU countries. These policies are able to ensure sustainable development, renewal of institutional network, financing and creation of new models for socially sensitive market economies which meet the requirements of the 21st century. Obtaining the goals of

---

11   *See* www.europarl.europa.eu/summits/lis1_en.htm.
12   *See* https://ec.europa.eu/info/business-economy-euro/economic-and-fiscal-policy-coordination/eu-economic-governance-monitoring-prevention-correction/european-semester/framework/europe-2020-strategy_en.

development is essentially influenced by the changes of power factors in world politics and economy.

The main aims of the Europe 2020 program are: *(i)* creation of knowledge-based community, *(ii)* dynamic economic growth by enhancing achievement in macroeconomy, *(iii)* ensuring the economic competitiveness on the global market of the world, *(iv)* sustainability of the economic growth with attention to the environmental aspects and *(v)* social integration including full employment as much as possible, and the creation of a new European model for social welfare.

In the framework of the Lisbon Agenda, common targets were set up in areas determining future development, which earlier had not been included in the regulation of the integration. These are the following: education, R+D, innovation, stimulation of enterprises, labor market and social security. In these areas, coordinated cooperation was targeted instead of central regulation.

Basic structural reforms are needed in the following areas in order to realize the development set-up in the Lisbon Agenda and the Europe 2020 program: *(i)* capital and goods market, *(ii)* investments in the knowledge-based economy, *(iii)* transformation of the labor-market, *(iv)* environment policy and *(v)* social welfare policy and institutions. The main strategic aims, the key areas of the program and the crucial reforms are closely intertwined with each other, but it is difficult to realize all of them at the same time, because, due to scarce resources, controversial tendencies can appear when determining the priorities in development. Basically, both making the programs tangible and implementing them can be realized on a national level according to the different and unique economic and financing policy of each member country. Nevertheless, the EU community policy projects, R+D framework programs can contribute significantly to the above-mentioned processes.

21.5   Growth, Financial Disequilibria, Competitiveness – The Role of Human Resources

Nowadays, crucial social and economic issues are closely connected with each other. The pace, quality and structure of economic growth, the way of tackling financial disequilibria, perspectives of their decrease, the changes in competitiveness, as well as gaining or losing ground in the world economy depend mainly on the quality of human resources.

If we look at the following line: demography – training of human resources – ability to generate income, we will face the problems concerning the prospects of economic development and the ways of tackling financial disequilibria on a long term.

Demographic processes determine the human resources and the proportion of different age groups. Due to the decrease in birth, the number of students will also decrease, first in elementary schools, then in the secondary and higher education. Therefore, the number of new employees also falls, thus, the capacity of human resource also diminishes hindering future development.

The quantity, quality and structure of human resource and its ability to generate income determine the basis on which sustainable development can be founded. Human resource is crucial and undeniable, but it is not enough for development. It has to be combined with the implementation of high technology and innovation. Moreover, there would be a need for a social and economic policy focusing on human resource development. It is also necessary to create a well-functioning institutional network, as well as a suitable, steady legal system, and its effective implementation with a community control.

In order to understand the above-mentioned factors, we should add some basic remarks. The words 'growth' and 'development' appear very often as synonyms in analyses, strategies and programs. Statistics always show the growth of GDP, although production and consumption may have either useful or harmful effects. For example: the pollution of environment or the usage of non-renewable energy cost more than the value of production itself. It is the same case when statistics show growth in consumption if there is a growth in petrol consumption due to traffic jams. However, it is a harmful consumption because it spoils the quality of life and welfare. Nowadays, there are index systems which reflect very well the quality of life and environmental influences. Nevertheless, it is difficult to create short-term indices, and they are hardly ever available on time only with a significant delay especially on an international level. From the point of view of economic strategy, we accept only such a real growth which means a sustainable, environmentally friendly development enhancing the quality of life. Any other type of development can be considered as a harmful one.

As for the financial disequilibria, there is a worry about their absolute size and proportion in comparison with the income-growth of the economy, not to mention the dramatic speed they are growing by. There is a big gap between real and financial economy. Creating money by speculation and its flow have multiplied as compared to the production and the trade of goods and services.

Competitiveness is a crucial element from the point of view of the success of national economies, companies, and employees. Competitiveness as a category has been interpreted many times and in many ways. Another interpretation suggests that competitiveness expresses

> "who is able to produce the best product, who has the disposal of the best educated workforce with the best knowledge, who is on the top-list concerning investments in machines, equipments, R+D, and infrastructure, who is the best

organizer, whose institutions (government, education, business) lead the worldwide list of effectivity."[13]

Competitiveness shows how effectively a nation can make use of the available human, financial and natural resources.

Gaining and losing ground in the world economy are the result of the influence of several factors. In my opinion, the evaluation by the world market is expressed by two excellent indicators: *(i)* the changes in exchange rates indicate that the international market upgrades or underrates the work of a nation and *(ii)* the growth or fall of the export on the international market on mid-term and long-term (it can be indicated in national economies, branches of economy and products). At the same time, I should mention that in case of fuels, enhancement and gaining ground can happen without improving competitiveness as a result of scarceness of natural resources, fluctuation and growth of demand, speculation and exploitation of oligopol situations.[14]

The Lisbon process focuses on the enhancement of competitiveness in the EU. In the 21st century, the key element of it is the development and utilization of human resource. However, it is more difficult to map and analyze the notion of human resource than other key elements. Human resource can be interpreted as the collectivity of people who create values in a society, cooperate with each other, represent a value system, have an appropriate knowledge and skills which they utilize in their work during their economic and social activity. Accumulated knowledge, heritage of the past, achievements of culture and civilization, know-how, inventions and patterns, ability for innovation and its usage, they all belong to the human capital of the society. It is not only the sum of individual knowledge but the multiplication of it. One of the main characteristics of the human resource is that it improves during the usage, instead of being consumed. Therefore, the improvement of human resource is a key element in sustainable development and employment policy. Thus, it is a key factor in enhancing competitiveness according to the aims of the Lisbon process.

21.6   INNOVATION AND ITS CONNECTION WITH EMPLOYMENT

The direction of development in the EU labor market is aimed at the creation of workplaces which have special advantages in location and unify highly qualified workforce with advanced technology.

---

13   For definition and further analysis *see* György Csáki, *A nemzetközi gazdaságtan és a világgazdaságtan alapjai*, Napvilág, Budapest, 2006, p. 156.
14   Concerning the factors of competitiveness and the role of human capital, *see* Magdolna Csáth, *Honnan-hová?*, Kairosz, Budapest, 2013, p. 382.

R+D costs in the EU make 1/4 of the whole innovation costs. Other innovation costs require three times the R+D expenses until it has a success on the market. It is a proof of the fact that R+D activity is a crucial but not sufficient element in technical-economic development. The share of R+D costs has decreased in the innovation expenses, but the share of technological development and preparation of production has increased.

Data procession will be on the top of innovational investments (even) during the next years. Then, automation of production, introduction of new technologies and development of new functions for old products follow each other on the list. The introduction and spread of communication technology results in developing communication systems which work within the company and between companies. It is expected that the integration of data processing, information and communication technologies will strengthen the technical position of the EU on the international market.

The state policy of research-development can take only a smaller risk in innovation; therefore, the main task falls to companies. The main direction of the policy for technical development in the EU is supposed to provide the most favorable framework for the technical-economic development in order to enhance the spread of technical-economic information towards the participants of the economy to help them to improve their ability to cope with the risks. Besides, it is important to give the most precise picture of orientation about the possible future of technical development and opportunities on the market. It is completed by a diffusion-oriented stimulation in the technical development, which uses project-orientation as a medium.

Analyses about economic policy expect that the improvement of the framework of economic policy in the field of innovation activity may strengthen the position of technical development and competitiveness of the EU countries on the international market. It is also expected that fiscal and competition policies can regulate the activity which helps to enhance the effectivity of technical development.

Modernization and employment partly depend on the multinational companies, partly on regional and local institutions, because new workplaces are created mainly by small and medium-sized companies. These companies provide work for 70% of the employees in the developed EU-15 countries.

The EU provides resources for obtaining technologies needed for modernization, and its homogenous inner market is the main target for the export of the companies of the EU countries. The import following the operating assets from the 15 old EU countries domi-nates the structure of the production and the export. Concerning the export, the importance of return must be emphasized. The need for modernization and transformation of work-places has extremely increased after the accession to the EU.[15]

In the Central and Eastern European countries, including Hungary too, the quality of workforce is relatively high, the human resource is comparatively developed, but its utilization is far below the EU average, and far from the requirements of a stable, knowledge-based society. This situation is worsened by the problems of the health care system and the education. Therefore, we get far away from creating a knowledge-based society or from the realization of the Lisbon Agenda. It is a worrying fact that, in several transition countries – including Hungary –, R+D expenditures have been seriously affected by the transformation crisis and their proportion as compared to the GDP, has fallen dramatically. The Lisbon Agenda proposes 3% expenditures in comparison with the GDP. However, only the Scandinavian countries surpass it, the EU average is far below of this goal. This proportion is nearly 3% in the US and much more than 3% in Japan. In Hungary, the proportion of R+D expenses in comparison with the GDP does not reach 2%, although the R+D expenditures of the foreign companies are also included. This feature stabilizes our dramatic backwardness.[16]

Fiscal policy and changes in taxes and other additional charges play an important role in the realization of the Lisbon Agenda and in the improvement of competitiveness. In the Central and Eastern European countries, the policies stimulating investments preferred mainly the investments of multinational and foreign companies. It resulted in positive effects for the foreign operating assets, stimulated the modernization of technology. However, the small and medium-sized companies have remained at a disadvantage, moreover, their backwardness has strengthened, their integration as suppliers has not been realized (except for some well-known examples). The implementation of the Lisbon Agenda requires complex, far-reaching technological and structure-developing programs. When elaborating the requirements of changes in the economic structures, several factors have to be taken into consideration, such as the priority of the development and effective utilization of the human resources, as well as the requirements of a stable, future-oriented profitable employment and the fact that these factors can be provided only by an effective improvement of education, professional training and adult education. The active role of the state is undeniable in this development, because future-oriented investments cannot be increased if public financing does not appear in education and professional training.

The Lisbon process and strategy focuses on the improvement of public administration, health care system, usage of Internet, development of infrastructural networks, especially

---

15   The effects of foreign trade on growth and development are analyzed in detail by Péter Farkas, *Behind the Figures. The Main Foreign Trade-Related Factors Affecting World Economic Growth Since 1990*, Institute of World Economics, Budapest, 2007, p. 25.

16   The R+D data are detailed in international comparison at www.oecd.org/sdd/08_Science_and_technology.pdf.

in transport and communication. These areas are given high priority in financing. According to past experiences, the countries which gave high priorities to these areas developed quickly and got in the forefront. The countries which neglected them degenerated on long-term. A knowledge-based society can be built only by healthy and educated population. Modernization and up-to-date structural changes can be realized on the basis of the development and effective utilization of human resource.

Research-development and the improvement of innovation can be realized on the basis of excellent higher education and scientific training. The participation of companies with solid capital in the R+D expenses should be raised, but basic researches at universities and research institutes should not be damaged, moreover, they should be strengthened. In the EU-28 the companies have 55 % share in the R+D expenditures, but this proportion is much lower in the Central and Eastern European countries. The US and Japan are able to involve their companies in R+D in a much higher proportion.

In order to realize the Lisbon aims and to improve human resource, it is necessary to harmonize the increase of labor productivity and employment. As for the allocation of resources, there is a need for an increasing efficiency. Enhancing labor productivity requires the development of technology instead of providing less workforce for the same production. The increase of competitiveness means that the participants of the market should invest more in the innovation of the product and the production procedure. The markets of services definitely have to be developed. However, it is not enough to open the markets, but the accession has to be regulated in a sensible way. It means that it is necessary to create a reasonable, public regulation of competition.

In the EU, the number and proportion of those who take part in training and professional training has been increasing. This fact has a significant influence on economic growth, labor productivity and partly on employment. Lengthening the average time of public education with one year can provide a steady 0.3-0.5 % growth of the GDP. In the EU an average 5% of the GDP is spent on education expenditures, in budgets it has about 10-11% share. Quickly developing countries have performed a much higher proportion.

The appropriate utilization of human resource and reaching the Lisbon aims for competitiveness can be realized only by an active labor market policy and it obviously requires institutional reforms. Finland, Sweden, and Denmark could unify active labor market policy with the system of education and adult education, labor exchange and creation of R+D workplaces.

21.7   DEVELOPMENT OF RESEARCH, HUMAN RESOURCE, INNOVATION AND COMPETITIVENESS

In the 21st century, human resource, education, training, professional training and especially development of research and innovation have been upgraded among the key factors of economic development. The proportion of innovation in increasing added value, the competition of patterns, the competition for employing the best scholars and researchers (worldwide brain-drain) have increased. In this area the US was and still is in the best position due to its financial resources, research possibilities and institutions. On the other hand, Europe is a constant loser in this process, because its scholars and leading researchers, whose education costs a huge amount, are obtained and utilized by the US, while it means a continuous financial loss for Europe.[17]

The scientific and technical development is quicker and quicker and thus, both in relative and absolute number there is a lack of leading scholars and researchers as compared to the requirements.

Good organization of R+D activity, shortening the way from research to innovative investments are determining elements in the improvement of economic performance. At the beginning of the millennium, the good utilization of R+D, the strengthening of innovation and competitiveness in Scandinavia, the Benelux countries and Ireland can be explained by the above-mentioned approach.

The most important factors which determine the effectivity of R+D activity are the following: the number of employees working in the area, their qualification and creativity. The number of scientists and engineers is more than one million in the EU. European researchers have had outstanding achievements in the field of discoveries.

In R+D, the role of the state has changed, it should put emphasis on the induction of technical development, creation of operational framework based on indirect stimulation. Direct state expenditure is realized in regional support, as well as in some big projects of high risk and public projects with special goals (for example environment protection, management of water supplies, waste liquidation and recycling).

The basic dilemmas of innovations are rising innovation costs and shorten life cycles on the market. Because of the shorter life cycles of the new products, companies have to get returns of their expenditure more and more quickly. The growth of per-unit expenses creates a better situation for the big companies with lots of capital in the fields which require much technology. Meanwhile, the general use of developed technologies improves the chances for the closing-up of small and medium-sized firms.

---

17   The global competitiveness is presented in a comprehensive manner annually at www3.weforum.org/docs/GCR2018/05FullReport/TheGlobalCompetitivenessReport2018.pdf.

In the EU, information-technology (data processing) is on the first place in innovational investments. Automation of production, implementation of new manufacturing technologies, developing the functions of existing products complete the list in company planning. The integration of data processing, information and communication technologies is expected to strengthen the position of the EU on the international market, what can significantly moderate the former disadvantage of medium-sized companies. Moreover, some of these drawbacks can even disappear in some areas.

Future-oriented technological development requires more and more cooperation between developers and users. Time and expenditure can be diminished significantly in case of developments requiring lots of research if there is a cooperation. The capital and know-how of certain companies are often not sufficient to realize alone their projects. Cooperations for long-term contractual technological developments are mainly led by big companies.

The technical development policy of the EU contributes significantly to overcome obstacles and risks in innovation. According to some data, support of innovation in the manufacturing industry of the EU is very important both in size and sphere of activity, although the market operates as a liberal one. Beside an indirect, market-oriented support, there is a high proportion of direct project support that refers to the fact that the means of development are not distributed by the 'watering can' idea, *i.e.* distributing the same amount to everybody, but instead, they are distributed after investigating the aims of development. Technical development is more and more based mainly on innovational investments of private companies. However, basic research, financing and developing the infrastructure of research and education are carried out mainly by public (state) means.

Nowadays and in the near future, the main direction of modernization is the technological investment in informatics and communication. Investments in information technology are especially high in the production of office and informatics equipment, as well as at banks and in the insurance business. Branches of industry coping with problems try to overcome their difficulties by investing in informatics more and more vigorously.

Europe has lost ground during the last twenty years, mainly because it was not able to provide dynamic and attractive conditions neither for R+D, nor for the quick realization of innovations, especially not in structural changes of technology, as it has happened in the US.

In these areas, the US and the multinational companies have gained ground not only by using their power of capital, but by using their strategic superiority in spreading capital and technology, while Europe has fallen behind.

In the 21st century, we have arrived at a new technological turning point. Nowadays, not only the conditions of development are changing, but there are also new opportunities for closing-up concerning technological competitiveness. In the globalization process, there is a must for adaptation, we can also observe in this process that innovation-friendly environment, community and economy policies, as well as R+D and highly qualified workforce are appreciated. Therefore, countries which are able to react to the changes will be able to find a point to break free and to rise. As the above-mentioned factors depend mainly on economic, R+D and technology-development policies, countries which are small and not rich in traditional resources for production can also have a chance for development. In the framework of the European integration, regional R+D policies are more and more appreciated on the markets of goods, capital and services.

Since we can find national policies and systems in education and professional training, the education system works basically in a national framework. Therefore, its content and its stage of development are different in each country. As traditional production possibilities and conditions are getting closer and closer, and markets are unifying gradually in the European countries, therefore, the importance of the most effective factors in competition has increased, namely the importance of the human capital and that of the potential of technology and development. Thus, it is a crucial question for Hungary too if it would like to improve its international competitiveness, whether it is able and willing to concentrate on the development of human capital in its economic and development policy and in its choice of priorities.

The R+D policies of the European countries are different from each other not because of the volume of expenses and its proportion compared to the GDP, but because the creation of innovation-friendly environment, the organizational level of R+D possibilities, the existence or non-existence of an innovation chain and its quality are very different in each country. The success of technological development depends more and more on different relationships, the quality of forward and backward relationships and the diffusion of R+D and innovation.[18]

Enhancing the competitiveness of Europe requires the liquidation of several disadvantages. There is a serious backwardness in general use of information and communication technologies in comparison with the US. It is partly due to the fact that the tangible means of ICT are not widely spread (density of PCs, electronic trade, news service, telecommunication). Partly, it is also due to the facts that the human resource is not qualified enough, the economic policy is rigid and there are also structural disadvantages. These problems should be tackled.

Since the role of innovation has been upgraded, the relationship among R+D policies, effectivity of technical development, ability for innovation in the economy and the position on the international market become more and more important during the period of 1998-

---

18   The EU's research and development and innovation policy is analyzed in detail at https://rio.jrc.ec.europa.eu/en/library/research-innovation-and-economic-growth-rd-policy-reforms-and-strategies.

2017. The EU countries spend different amounts on R+D compared to their GDP, the effectivity of research development is even more different.

In the last twenty years, the technical development of the EU has fallen behind the achievement of the US and Japan in the global competition. It is not necessarily caused by the lack of initiatives in innovation, because there are several inventions in Western Europe, especially in the machine industry, production of vehicles and chemical industry. The causes of backwardness are much more likely the relatively lower R+D expenses, the lower number of employees in the R+D sector, the heterogenity of investments, the different regulation system, the lack of synergy, the low growth rate in the first part of the 1990s and the integration program of Eastern Europe. These factors contributed to the backwardness of the EU and, in many cases, it meant that the region has become dependent on the big competitors.

Certainly, there is a mixed situation in Europe. The United Kingdom, Finland, Ireland, Sweden and the Netherlands have a good performance due to good capital provision, effective human resource, and state policy, as well as initiatives of companies. The lack of any of the abovementioned elements worsens the chances of catching-up for the other member states. Thus, in the EU, a double aim has been set: it is important to improve the competitiveness of the EU on the international market, and to liquidate the technological gaps inside the EU at the same time.

Increasing R+D expenditures and provision of human resources for R+D are very important elements, but not enough at all. It is undeniable in the Central and Eastern European countries to enhance the utilization of R+D expenses and to implement the achievements more quickly. One of the main problems of the Central and Eastern European countries is the slow introduction of innovations.

Improving the environment for investments, reliable and steady economic policy have a crucial role in closing-up of the Central and Eastern European countries. More and more emphasis have to be put on the effects of new technologies and their acceptance. Acceleration of the technical development can result in significant saving of workforce. Therefore, if future-oriented, steady workplaces are not created successfully, the issue of unemployment will become very serious. Due to the crisis of 2008-2009, there is a significant rise in unemployment, what means that in the Lisbon Agenda the aim to extend employment has failed.

The R+D potential of the EU has grown significantly by the accessions, not in the fields of expenses, but due to scientific capacity and human capital working in R+D. All these elements are the 'dowry' of the Central and Eastern European countries.

The backwardnesses of the new member countries are less in education, professional training and adult education than in the production of GDP per capita. Moreover, there are some disadvantages in some fields in comparison with some old member countries. Qualitative and quantitative improvement of human capital is the most important factor in economic closing-up, therefore, it should be given high priority both in economic policy and finance. Education and training of human capital have a key role in the rise of the Central and Eastern European countries, and thus, the enhancement of the quality of workforce is the base of steady growth. One-year increase in education can increase the labor productivity with an average of 6% in the EU, but we can find even higher numbers too. In order to improve competitiveness, beside economic conditions, there is a need for the acceptance of innovation in the society, for an open environment and for a value-oriented society.

21.8   The Relation between State and Market – Priorities of Economic Policies and Their Application

Social market economy assumes a strong and active state. In many fields, self-regulating markets function badly, or do not function at all. Market competition, even with proper competition policies, can function properly only if the following criteria are met: *(i)* there is a great number of producers and consumers, *(ii)* there is no unilateral market supremacy and vulnerability, *(iii)* there are proper information- and decision-making possibilities, and *(iv)* the control of actors and the bargaining positions among them are balanced. In principle, the state should intervene only if any one of these conditions is missing. In the past decades, there has been a substantial deterioration of these factors. The power of transnational companies has drastically increased, and the growth of oligopolistic relations has shaken the foundations of social market economy.

For the sake of public welfare, the state should increase its role in public health, education, R+D, the protection of environment or the development of public infrastructure. As the share of these sectors is fortunately increasing, this should be reflected in the financing of the state budget. It would be appropriate to both keep and place a part of the public services or some of the infrastructure into public ownership. The state has system policy duties, and it should be a matter of concern how these can be better served.

In social market economy, the state has an eminent role in finances, development policies or policies related to external relations and integration. An active cyclical policy has particular importance. According to Müller-Armack, cyclical fluctuations are necessary concomitants of any development. Since the crises of the 1970s, the state has been less able to influence these changes.[19] In the development of infrastructure, a larger state role would be needed. The best examples for this are road constructions, the development of public transport or energy systems (gas and oil pipelines, electric networks *etc.*)

---

19   Alfred Müller-Armack, *Wirtschaftslenkung und Marktwirtschaft*, Verlag Wirtschaft und Finanzen, Hamburg, 1947, p. 144.

The achievements of the most important economic policy objectives cannot be simply left to market automatisms, and this is especially the case nowadays. The transparency, reliability and consistency of economic policies have rather deteriorated, and, in the EU countries, this contributed to the deepening of the crisis both in the 1970s and after 2008. It is no question that this calls for the renewal of social market economy. Various elements of economic policy (price policy, market policy, trade policy, agricultural policy, monetary policy) should be harmonized with one another; they should follow the same principles and should constitute a unified whole that is free of internal contradictions and does not eliminate itself.[20]

The principal theoretical and economic policy content of social market economy is unambiguous, although there are differences among its theoreticians and economic policymakers. The differences are particularly substantial on which countries can be considered social market economies. Germany is the model state, followed by Austria and the Netherlands. Scandinavia is a special case, particularly due to its individual welfare models. France, and in general Western Europe, can be considered as a social market economy, but in terms of the extent, proportions and directions of state intervention, there are great differences. The EU defines itself as a social market economy, and since 2007, the idea of the globally competitive social market economy has been fixed in the Lisbon Treaty. Beyond this commitment, the practical question still remains whether divergence or convergence is greater among the 28 countries. In order to answer this question, one needs to consider whether differences in the systems are more important than those in the levels of development.

The question arises as to what the main causes of erosion and recent unsatisfactory functionings of social market economy are.

21.9 The Factors of Erosion and the Crisis of Social Market Economy

The main internal reasons for the loss in dynamism of social market economy were the following: the slowing down of economic growth, particularly the reduction of the rate of growth of productivity, and the emergence of the deficit of state budgets leading to an internal debt which was due to an increase of the extent and burdens of social contributions, particularly that of wage contribution. The costs of administration in state expenditures accelerated, while the efficiency of state investments decreased. The increase of individual and company real incomes slowed down. As a result, by the first part of the 1970s, serious and permanent crisis issues emerged both in the German economy and all over Europe.

---

20 Wilhelm Röpke, *The Moral Foundation of Civil Society*, Transaction Publishers, New Brunswick-London, 1996, p. 239.

In the world economy, a new era started independently of the 1973 oil price explosions, which only provoked and aggravated the crisis processes.

The crisis factors of social market economy have remained with us ever since. The system was built on free initiatives, the increase of performance and social progress. These, however, assume a satisfactory economic growth and financial stability. In their absence, social market economy is doomed to failure. From the outside, the impacts of globalization had the same negative consequences. The global optimization strategies of TNCs are in contrast to national social strategies and policies. The two key elements of social market economy (order and freedom) have been eroded. Order was replaced by crises, and freedom was reduced by the crisis of 'culture of stability'.[21] The formerly more-or-less balanced competition was limited by the excessive power of TNCs, sometimes dictating market conditions. Globalization created a trap for Europe, and Europe's losing ground became a long-term trend. The competitive advantages of the US remained, while Europe had to face growing expansion and competition from China and the other emerging countries.

Under globalization, the scope and possibilities of national economic policies have been greatly reduced.[22] The unit costs of the functioning of social market economy have greatly increased, and have proved to be much higher than that of the US, Chinese or Far Eastern economies, where the costs of the social security systems are minimal or much lower. The gradual building up of these systems has already started, and these costs will continue to grow in the future. Europe was forced to pay these costs, which reduced the competitiveness of the Continent in sectors with lower value added. This constraint can be made advantageous, but under the conditions of low economic growth it is by no means easy.

As a program of the humanization of society, the elimination of poverty, the treatment of migration or the role of social policy has always received a great emphasis in the policy of social market economy. The Freiburg School considered labor as important in two aspects: as sources of value creation on the one hand and as an area of human development and self-realization on the other. They attributed particular importance to individual entrepreneurs and family-owned and small companies in the humanization and development of the economy. In practice, however, the possibilities of self-employment were reduced by the expansion of big industrial and service companies, and the possibilities of increasing productivities and income were diminished.

---

21   Walter Eucken, *Grundsätze der Wirtschaftspolitik*, Francke und Mohr Verlag, Tübingen, 1952, p. 396.
22   Botos 2011, pp. 3-13.

21.10 The Prospects and Conditions of Renewing Social Market Economy – In the Context of Globalization and National Interests

The key factor of the renewal of social market economy is the creation of a knowledge- and work-based economy and society. One of its main and most challenging tasks is the harmonization of individual and public welfare. Economic growth and fiscal balance should be jointly secured; they need an interactive approach. Instead of the former unilateral economic policies, *i.e.* prioritizing either demand or supply, emphasis should now be placed on their balancing and simultaneous implementation. Technology policies can play an important role of how companies can identify and then satisfy the new possibilities of markets. Sustainability needs a complex approach; the economic, financial and environmental aspects should be harmonized, combined with social acceptance.

The badly deteriorated balance between the real economic and financial spheres can be gradually restored only through the total mobilization of all the means of social market economy. This assumes a return to performance-orientation and the oppression of speculation, particularly in those financial sectors which were the starting points of the crisis. Emphasis should be given to national policies, and the building of the Europe of Nations can only be carried out through policy coordination. This coordination should be achieved through the acceptance and recognition of differences in cultures, national traditions, historical heritages and values. The basic principle of social market economy is the humanization of economy.

Social market economy is not an artificially created ideology or a fabricated construction. It is a pragmatic and value-oriented approach, built upon the analysis of circumstances and necessities of our age. Instead of artificially constructing a system, it focuses on the motivations of human attitudes and action, on the accepted values of society and on the policies aiming to harmonize the aspects of economic development and social justice. It tries to mobilize the primary movers of development and to keep them in motion. The final objective is not an ideal state, but rather a gradual progress in responding to the actual possibilities and requirements. Economy is not just for itself; it should serve the individual.

The social market economy of the 21st century is still based on market factors, but it rejects the omnipotence of the self-regulatory automatisms of the markets. It accounts for the limitations of market forces; it considers it important to keep its destructive forces in check. The role of the state has remained unchanged in the regulation and maintenance of market order, in defense of the collective social aspects and public welfare, and in the generation of modernization. This assumes the combination of direct or indirect interventions depending on conditions. Direct interventions can be preferred when it is obvious that public solutions are more advantageous than private ones. Subsidiarity and solidarity are unchanged principles.

The renewal of social market economy depends to a large extent on the restoration and strengthening of value systems. New and consistent economic strategies and economic policies are needed, similarly to those which proved to be the engines of development in the middle of the 20th century. We are faced with multiple deficits which hinder development, and which should be eliminated. What are these obstacles and deficits? In the Hungarian economy and society these multiple deficits are numerous, and they are inherited from the period before the systemic change. According to Béla Kádár's inaugural lecture at the Hungarian Academy of Sciences, these deficits were rooted

> "in the low functional efficiency and irrationality of state-owned economy, in a related resource scarcity, in the relative expansion of consumption aiming at forgetting 1956 and the legitimization of the regime ('goulash communism'), which lead to heavy external indebtedness. The per capita external debt was the highest in the region, and it was twice as high as the regional average."[23]

Later, Hungary integrated into the global economy, and the integration of the financial sector was particularly rapid.

Globalization is the main characteristic and determining factor of our age. We are experiencing a rapid and fundamental transformation in world politics, world economy, international power relations, the growth of population, technological progress and the relation between humanity and the environment. From the perspective of the development of social market economy, the fundamental changes were the following: the emergence of transnational companies, changes in the international financial system, the acceleration of global capital flows and the loss of control over speculative financial movements. The share of the speculative financial sphere has expanded in extraordinary proportions, particularly in relation to real economy. The gains from financial speculation were far above the possible net profits realized in the sectors of real economy. In the 21st century, this is an acute problem; it is a crisis factor which largely threatens the normal functioning of economies (international financial bubbles).

Economic policy has decisive impacts on competitiveness, catching up and welfare. From this point of view, the participation of Hungary in the European integration had extraordinary importance. As it has been indicated, the balance of membership in terms of the exploitation of factors of convergence and the success of adjustment was largely dependent on the quality and efficiency of economic policies.[24]

As a result of liberalization in the GATT and other trade organizations, international markets have become more open, while the parallel development of international institu-

---

23   Béla Kádár, 'Deficitjeink', *Pénzügyi Szemle*, 2008/2, p. 172.
24   Tibor Palánkai (ed.), *The Economics of Global and Regional Integration*, Akadémiai, Budapest, 2014, p. 409.

tional and regulatory mechanisms was lagging behind or, often, they were simply missing. The TNCs and the big banks were strongly counter-interested in the development of any international regulation, and neo-liberalism (ultra-liberalism) served the political and ideological background. It became clear that the basic elements of the Washington Consensus were contrary to the requirements of 21st century development. The reduction of the role of the state (de-etatization) contradicts social market economy, as it calls for a rational, well-functioning and strong state. No one denies that an oversized and exuberant state is undesirable and creates more damage than good, but there are broad fields which call for rational regulation. The connection of global information networks should be technologically, legally and economically regulated.

In terms of international integration, the renewal of social market economy should be closely connected to the revitalization of the European model, originally supported by Konrad Adenauer, Robert Schuman or Alcide de Gasperi among others. The principle of performance and social justice should be once again related to one another, whether it is the economy, the legal system or governance. In the 21st century, these require more complex and better composed policy mixes than any time before.

In the 21st century, rationally regulated and, in terms of the provision of public services, well-functioning market economies are needed. All the main state functions have been unambiguously ameliorated. The regulatory functions have remained important (legal, economic or institutional aspects of market regulation). Service provision is supported by the growing role of public services. Development function, among others, serves the renewal and operation of broad fields of public infrastructure. Cohesion is important from the point of view of strengthening the social character of market economy through solidarity and redistribution. Between 1970-2017, as a result of the increasing role of the state, the share of redistribution in the GDP increased in all of the developed countries.

From the point of view of development, what matters, in fact, is not the size, but the efficiency of state regulation. With regard to the process of the renewal of social market economy, the question arises as to how the state can efficiently operate under the conditions of the challenges of globalization. Under the circumstances of open markets and the free flow of capital, the importance of efficiency of national policies has greatly increased. The favorable international economic positions of Scandinavian countries demonstrate the importance of good economic and development policies, which has made possible the maintenance of financing a highly developed social service system. Experiences of the consolidation of the Swedish budget, as result of the correction of the negative anomalies of the welfare state in the middle of 1990s.

According to Béla Kádár, "the main driving forces of development in our age are not the natural resources or the abundance of capital, but the availability of human capital."[25]

---

25   Kádár 2008, p. 173.

European or Hungarian economies should be built on a value- and knowledge-based economy, and on the qualification of labor. The quality of human resources has an utmost importance. It depends basically on the quality of education and training and the existence of networks of initiatives and innovation. Europe and Hungary were successful primarily in the quantitative development of general and higher education, while in qualitative improvement they lagged behind. Education and training are investments into the future; they equally serve the enrichment of the individuals, the family or the whole of society. Those who fall out of education are usually pushed out of the labor market as well.

For the sake of promotion of human development, human ecological aspects should be particularly stressed: the relation of man and nature and the protection of the living environment. This type of attitude would support the objectives of sustainable development as well. In the process of increasing the value creating capacities of human capital, the state, the companies or the individuals have an equal role and responsibility.[26]

In research and development, a large part of Europe is behind the US, Japan or South Korea. In this respect, only the Scandinavian countries have a good international position. Hungary's lagging behind is larger in terms of the level of human resources than in material production. Within transformation into information society, man, culture and creativity are more important than technologies or financing. The content, quality and strength of the value system are the most important components of social capital. In this respect, the deficits are serious. Besides the elimination of the deficiencies of the education and health system, the quality of development policies and governance ('good governance') is equally important. Social and economic problems can only be solved together. The upgrading of human capital is a key factor of the renewal of social market economy. According to Kahane, "Information and knowledge are new production factors. They are unlimited, renewable, infinitely inter-changeable and re-usable resources."[27] Development no longer depends on average labor and capital, rather on knowledge and well-trained human resources.

In our age, the performance and prospects of countries (economic growth, inflation, employment or financial position) are primarily determined by the impacts of global integration and systems of international economic relations. Therefore, the success of the renewal of social market economy, to a great extent, is dependent on the success of integration into the system of international economic relations. In this process, the quality of national economic strategies and policies can play a decisive role. In our age, social market economy should be competitive under the conditions of global and regional integrations. It is by no means accidental that several elements of the European models have now been

---

26 Kőrösi 2010, pp. 95-111.
27 Yehuda Kahane, 'Technological Changes, the Reversal of Age Pyramids and the Future of Retirement Systems', *European Papers on the New Welfare*, Issue 4, 2006, pp. 17-47.

introduced in the US or China (the extension of health care and pension systems, the development of social institutions *etc.*).

The erosion and crisis of social market economy were caused by the misfunctioning of the state and the market. From the 1970s, the consequences of growth and financial deficits lead to a substantial change in the course of economic policies and thinking. In the EU, the control of inflation became a priority even before the introduction of the euro. Following the 2008-2009 crisis, the consolidation of state households became unavoidable. In the years after 2010, in many countries, the reduction of budget deficits did start successfully, but the consolidation of accumulated indebtedness takes more time. The deficit of the state household is still striking in France, Italy, Britain or Spain, not to mention the unsustainable indebtedness of Greece. In terms of indebtedness, Central Europe is in a better position than Western Europe. The stock of debt of the Visegrad countries (except Hungary) is below 60% of the Maastricht threshold. Hungary was also successful in the reduction of deficit after 2010. The share of indebtedness to the GDP is around 72% in 2019, which is below that of several other EU countries. From the point of view of the future of social market economy in Europe, the reduction of financial imbalances and remaining on the path of durable and sustainable economic growth is a basic criterion.

The globalization, integration, regionalism and transformation of the economic role of the nation state are processes of fundamental importance in 21st-century Europe. The impacts of external factors are increasing as the global factor plays a growing role. Regionalization is based on the exploitation of organic energies, and it contributes to increasing competitiveness in Europe. The increase of competitiveness assumes joint impacts in human capital, modernizing investments, exploitation of local advantages and good infrastructure. Economic policy favoring training and education, encouraging innovation and securing quality human capital are the main factors of development. The role and responsibility of such policies in generating development is increasing.

In the second half of the 20th century, the former European models of social market economy gave adequate answers to the challenges of the epoch. The resumption of a new and viable model of social market economy in the 21st century requires for the coordination of values and development demands of states, civil organizations or individuals. It assumes the professional analysis of crisis factors how they can be reduced and eliminated. The different demands of subsidiarity, solidarity and competitiveness should be harmonized desirably in a way that they end in a positive sum game.

21.11 FEDERATION – CONFEDERATION – EUROPE OF NATIONS?

The policy of integration, the dimension of the policies, economy and law, affect both. It is very much up to political and economic advocacy and rational reconciliation at the beginning of the 2020s. There are three main directions of the concepts of the further development of integration: federalism, confederalism and the concept of Europe of nations. There is a further version and a partial concept of these. Elements of all three basic trends can be found in both policy strategies and legislation. These fundamentally affect the levels and distribution of community decision-making and the exercise of competences.

Federalism appears in supranational decision-making, elements of confederation appear among others in the management of Community policies and intergovernmental decisions, and the 'Europe of nations' concept manifested itself in national powers and decision-making competences. The fundamental issues of further development of integration and the enlargement of the EU are decided at the summits of the heads of state or government; EU law takes into account the fundamental fact that several decisive areas of the operation of nation states are of strictly national character. National economies are interconnected but they are independent entities. Redistribution of the GDP produced, education, health care and pension systems are basically operated through national policies, but they are increasingly interlinked. Within the framework of international education, training and R+D cooperation programs, countries cooperate, recognize each other's diplomas, and acknowledge and record the pension entitlements acquired in different Member States. The federalists support the expansion of the EU's centralized decision-making powers and the extension of the scope of supranational decisions. Their ultimate goal is a centralized EU that takes the form of a political union.

Confederalists want to build a more relaxed alliance of sovereign nation states according to specific criteria. In the confederation, Member States delegate certain elements of their sovereignty to the Alliance, but the participating countries retain their international legal personality. Famous examples of the Confederation in history include Switzerland (especially between 1291-1848), the Polish-Lithuanian Union (between 1447-1492 and 1501-1569), the German Confederation (between 1815-1866) and the Confederate States of America (1861-1865). The Europe of Nations – a wording coined by Charles de Gaulle – suggests that nation states are the primary subjects and drivers of integration. Europe must express the interests, values, political will and legal relations of the participating nations.

One of the causes of Brexit, one of the most serious problems of our days in the EU, is the fundamental differences between common law and continental law. These differences have deep political, governmental, decision-making roots. A good combination of sovereignty and interdependence can best be achieved in a Europe of nations, according to the advocates of this concept. The advocates of the further development of integration argue primarily for the advantages of economic and financial openness, but this can be done well in a Europe of nations because the parallel process of breaking down barriers and representing and protecting national interests can be well-linked. *E.g.* euro accounts can be set up outside the Euro zone as well, and contracts can be signed, and sums paid in Euro, and there is no obstacle to the free flow of capital.

21.12 Future Implications – The EMU and Its Future

On 25 March 2017 (the 60th anniversary of the signing of the Treaty of Rome), White Paper on the future of Europe (the 27-member EU's road map to 2025) was adopted.[28] This summarizes five possible paths for Europe by 2025.

i. *Carrying on.* The EU continues to focus on economic growth, job creation and investment. The Community will strengthen the single market and increase investment in digital, transport and energy infrastructure. The EU will strengthen the supervision of financial markets, ensure the sustainability of public finances and develop capital markets.

ii. *Nothing but the single market.* In this case, the EU is increasingly focusing its efforts on deepening the single market. The single market for goods and capital is at the heart of the development of integration.

iii. *Those who want more do more.* One group of member states builds closer cooperation on some issues. In such areas, common legal and financial regulations are adopted. These are likely to be: defense, internal security, taxation and social policy.

iv. *Doing less more efficiently.* The EU-27 focuses its attention and limited resources on a few selected areas. The EU deals more with areas such as innovation, trade and defense. It focuses on excellence in research and development. State aid control is transferred to national authorities to a greater extent. They are investing in new EU projects in the area of digitalization and environmental protection (*e.g.* reducing carbon dioxide emissions).

v. *Doing much more together.* In this scenario, the EU decides to implement much more in all policy areas. The text mentions the EU, but in fact it is the EU Member States who have to decide what new powers they have and how much they have transferred to the EU. The proposal states that "cooperation between all Member States goes further than ever before in all domains."

The Maastricht Treaty signed on 7 February 1992 is of paramount importance for the development of integration, as it created the EU as a continuation of the European Community. I would like to emphasize the importance of economic and monetary union. The Maastricht criteria for financial stability clearly fix the requirements that must be met.

---

28   White Paper on the Future of Europe, COM(2017)2025, at https://ec.europa.eu/commission/sites/beta-political/files/white_paper_on_the_future_of_europe_en.pdf.

In 1988, the Council of the EU invited a committee chaired by Jacques Delors to draw up a program for the establishment of the Economic and Monetary Union and the introduction of the single currency. The Delors Report was completed, and then EMU was implemented in three stages.[29]

The creation and use of a single currency (since 1999 as account money and since 2002 as cash) is of great economic, monetary and legal importance. Numerous analyses have been prepared on how adequately the euro is playing its role. Taking into account the experience of the euro area, it can be concluded that it cannot be considered an optimal currency area according to Mundell's criteria, primarily due to economic divergences and lack of real convergence. One of the fundamental problems of the EMU is that there is a clear tension between the two main areas of finance. Monetary policy is common in the euro area, but fiscal policies are different and predominantly national, their harmonization is not yet envisaged. It is also hardly conceivable because Member States stick to their national fiscal competences. This can be considered justified as national economic policies compete with each other and the existence and pursue of national fiscal policies is an important factor influencing the international competitiveness of countries. Therefore, the money created under the EMU by the ECB is mainly spent within nation-state frameworks.

As far as the general budget of the EU is concerned, it can be stated that net contributors do not intend to pay more than 1% of their GNI. With the withdrawal of the United Kingdom, the revenues of the general budget will shrink by nearly 10 percent. In the current financial regulation, the main focus is on the joint banking supervision, the common regulation of the safe operation of banks and the single deposit insurance system in order to ensure the good functioning of the banking union. After the banking union, the next major step will be the creation of a capital market union. In order to better integrate capital markets, the legal framework for risk management in financial markets needs to be strengthened: the macro-prudential legal toolbox. Overall, in the field of price stability, the euro area and the EU have performed well over the past 20 years, but there are serious deficiencies in public deficits and debt developments. In the period 2013-18, Central and Eastern European countries performed better concerning fiscal discipline and debt management than most Western European countries. In Central and Eastern Europe, the debt-to-GDP ratio is also below the euro area average. Indebtedness in Hungary is also much lower than the euro area average and at the same time the debt-to-GDP ratio has continuously and substantially decreased over the past five years. In the EU, sustainable fiscal policies that promote sustainable development and responsibility are needed because the

---

29   Jacques Delors, 'Report on Economic and Monetary Union in the European Community', presented 17 April 1989, p. 38, at http://aei.pitt.edu/1007/1/monetary_delors.pdf.

renewal and good functioning of the social market economy require real economic development and simultaneous financial stability.

21.13 The Renewal of Social Market Economy – Conclusions

The renewal of social market economy is a long-term objective, but it requires permanent short-term management (taking into account the different time horizons of politics and economic policy decisions). Nowadays, economic structures to a large extent are shaped by the decisions of transnational companies. In order to renew the system, the role of national strategies and policies should be increased. In a well-functioning social market economy, a responsible and ethical way of thinking and action on all levels of the individual, companies or states are indispensable, and that is the only way by which public confidence can be restored. Social market economy can be renewed only on the basis of realities and fundamentals, by strengthening the human and civil value systems and the role of families in the society.

The basic idea of an eco-social market economy is to change the relationship between production and market, the direction of economic policy, the formation of costs and prices. Production technologies, products and management procedures that are compatible with the principle of sustainability should be given priority. The practical application of this principle means, first and foremost, that *(i)* the full costs of using and polluting the environment must be included in the prices, *(ii)* the 'ecologicalization' of the tax system, *(iii)* precise product declarations and *(iv)* comprehensive international co-operation in the field of environment protection. The negative externalities of the exploitation of the environment must be internalized and the full costs must be incorporated into prices. In addition to strict legal requirements, ecological standards must be enforced with economic-financial regulations and incentives. Legal and economic measures play an interdependent, common role in solving these tasks.

The 'ecologicalization' of the tax system means that tax burdens should be reallocated in a way that fosters sustainable development: labor should be taxed less, but the fiscal burden of the use of natural resources and capital income should be increased. Renewable resources must be taxed less than non-renewable ones. Accurate environmental product declarations contribute significantly to health and consumer protection, environmental management and fair competition.

Ecological aspects should be consistently applied in the fields of tax loads, subsidies and development. Revenues from environmental taxes should be redistributed in a rational way, so that, besides environmental considerations, the requirements of economic development and social justice can also be taken into account. The basic types of capital are natural capital, physical and financial capital, as well as human capital. Until the advent of the 21st century, both economic policy and investors focused on the development and increase of physical and financial capital. In the 21st century, the role of human and natural capital has grown enormously in ensuring sustainable development and building an eco-social market economy. The role of human capital can also be detected in the rise or decline of countries. The eco-social market economy is a European model. The most successful types are the Rhine model (German, Austrian, Benelux), Swiss and Scandinavian ones. The eco-social market economy is being challenged by globalization and global problems (in particular migration, terrorism), so we need to find the right answers to the destruction caused by globalization.

Building an eco-social market economy is a long and difficult process both in Europe and Hungary. The original goal of the social market economy was "Prosperity for all!".[30] The motto of today's eco-social market economy is "A better quality of life for everyone!" – which can, of course, only be attained gradually. Its feasibility depends on economic, social, cultural values as well as factors of civilization, environmental policy and, at the same time, responsiveness to external impacts.

The model of the social market economy of the 21st century has remained viable and renewable.[31] The objective should not be utopian and idealistic; it should aim the creation of a "humanistic economy and humanistic society", as it was defined by Röpke.[32] We should bear in mind, however, that the economic and social circumstances of the present are fundamentally different from those prevailing in 'classical' times. The negative impacts of globalization should be consciously mitigated, and economic policies should find ways of rational assertion and the protection of national interests both in the European integration and, generally, in the system of international relations.

A clear relationship between the legislative, executive and judicial branches of government, their separation and autonomy is currently more important than ever before. Therefore, the quality of the functioning of the EU and national legal systems is even more decisive. Structures, institutions and human behavior are regularly and extensively analyzed by various schools. The combined knowledge and interconnection of the results of structuralism, institutionalism, and behaviorism can play an important role in bringing together legal and state sciences, economics and public administration for an effective reconciliation of well-functioning states representing national values, based on a solid set of common rules of law.

The renewal of the social market economy and the development of European integration are closely interlinked. In this, the development of politics, law and economy has an important, interconnected role. Europe has its roots and core values in the more than

---

30   Ludwig Erhard, *Wohlstand für Alle*, Econ-Verlag, Dusseldorf, 1957, p. 390.
31   László Csaba, *Európai közgazdaságtan*, Akadémiai, Budapest, 2014, p. 198.
32   Röpke 1996, p. 239.

2000-year old Christianity and an organic development of its culture, civilization, a common system of fundamental values, as the basis of development. Maintaining and enforcing the fundamental values is essential for preserving European identity.

PART IV
HUNGARIAN STATE PRACTICE

22   In Unchartered Waters?

The Place and Position of EU Law and the Charter of Fundamental Rights in the Jurisprudence of the Constitutional Court of Hungary

*Márton Sulyok – Lilla Nóra Kiss**

Keywords

Constitutional Court of Hungary, Charter of Fundamental Rights, preliminary ruling procedure, constitutional dialogue, CILFIT criteria

Abstract

This paper examines the perception and position of EU law in the jurisprudence of the Constitutional Court of Hungary within the constitutional arrangements brought to life after 2012. In this context, the inquiry addresses the changes regarding the status of EU law in constitutional case-law amounting to what is identified here as the method of 'resourceful engagement'. Under this approach, the paper also examines the extent and frequency of the use of human rights reasoning based on the Charter of Fundamental Rights of the EU in the proceedings of the Constitutional Court (2015-2019), focusing mostly on constitutional complaints procedures. The paper briefly mentions the controversial nature of the 'Implementation Dilemma' regarding the Charter and its application in Member States' constitutional court proceedings. As a corollary, in light of domestic procedures examined in the *Repcevirág Szövetkezet v. Hungary* judgment (April 2019) of the ECtHR, it examines whether the Constitutional Court could eventually start acting as a court of referral under Article 267 TFEU in such proceedings where the protection of fundamental rights under the Charter would require the interpretation of EU law. This would mark a shift from the earlier 'context of non-reference' to an approach of 'resourceful engagement' suggested by this paper.

22.1   Introduction

In many respects and from several aspects of EU law, Hungarian constitutional jurisprudence is to some extent still unchartered territory waiting to be mapped out, many of the

---

*   Márton Sulyok: senior lecturer, University of Szeged; FRA MB. Lilla Nóra Kiss: junior research fellow, University of Miskolc.

competences in this context still raise questions rather than answers. This is true regardless of the significant reforms carried out in parallel with the changes made to constitutional arrangements in 2012.

The new Fundamental Law of Hungary and the new Act on the Constitutional Court (HCCA)[1] entered into force on 1 January 2012. The Fundamental Law, with its own approach regarding the position of EU law in the national legal order based on its Articles E and T (analyzed below) answered some questions regarding the position of EU law in the national legal order, but it also left many issues open.[2] These have been approached by the jurisprudence of the Constitutional Court analyzed below. In another article, we have used the mathematical metaphor of Euclidean distance[3] to describe the attitude of the Constitutional Court towards EU law.

As the title of the book written by Zoltán Szente and Fruzsina Gárdos-Orosz duly recognizes, the 21st century poses many 'New Challenges to Constitutional Adjudication in Europe',[4] especially with regard to (i) the migration crisis; (ii) the often complicated dynamics of multilevel constitutionalism;[5] (iii) European constitutional dialogue[6] regarding, e.g. infringement procedures in front of the CJEU; (iv) the convergence of European human rights frameworks,[7] in particular in this context; and (v) the application of the EU Charter of Fundamental Rights[8] as a frame of reference or as a substantive argument, in Member State Constitutional Court proceedings, such as the case of the Hungarian Constitutional Court.

---

1   Act CLI of 2011 on the Constitutional Court (HCCA), and the Fundamental Law of Hungary.
2   See e.g. Nóra Chronowski (ed.), *Szuverenitás és államiság az Európai Unióban*, ELTE Eötvös, Budapest, 2017; Csongor István Nagy (ed.), *The EU Bill of Rights' Diagonal Application in the Member States*, Eleven International Publishing, The Hague, 2018.
3   The so-called 'Euclidean distance' measures the distance (*i.e.* the length of a segment) connecting two points in either the plane or 3-dimensional space. *See* Ondrej Hamulak *et al.*, 'Measuring the 'EUclidean Distance' between EU Law and the Hungarian Constitutional Court – Focusing on the Position of the Charter of Fundamental Rights', *Czech Yearbook of International and European Law*, 2019 (in print).
4   Zoltán Szente & Fruzsina Gárdos-Orosz (eds.), *New Challenges to Constitutional Adjudication in Europe: A Comparative Perspective*, Routledge, Abingdon, New York, 2018, 324 p.
5   *See* Chronowski (ed.), 2017.
6   For a more recent overview of dominant theories on constitutional dialogue in Europe *see* Anne Meuwese & Marnix Snel, 'Constitutional Dialogue: An Overview', *Utrecht Law Review*, Vol. 9, Issue 2, 2013, pp. 123-140.
7   As signified with the metaphor of a 'Luxembourg-Strasbourg corridor', *in* Erzsébet Szalayné Sándor, 'Uniós jog Strasbourgban – a koherens alapjogvédelem új rendje Európában', *Magyar-Román Jogtudományi Közlöny* (Kolozsvár), 2011/3-4, p. 97.
8   In this regard, a very concise and informative handbook has been prepared by the Fundamental Rights Agency of the EU (FRA). *See Applying the Charter of Fundamental Rights of the European Union in law and policymaking at national level. Guidance*, FRA, 2018, at https://fra.europa.eu/sites/default/files/fra_uploads/fra-2018-charter-guidance_en.pdf. This handbook, however, might not completely be applicable to Member State Constitutional Courts in all aspects, as will be argued below.

By introducing the 'friendly relationship'[9] between EU law and the Hungarian Constitutional Court, and through enlightening some of 'the twilight zones'[10] in the jurisprudence of the Constitutional Court regarding the Charter and violations of fundamental rights (especially) in complaints proceedings, this paper intends to answer the following questions: *(i)* How can the friendly attitude of the Constitutional Court towards EU law be described as 'resourceful engagement'[11] through samples from its case law (also relevant to the position of the Charter therein), and *(ii)* in this context, could the Hungarian Constitutional Court become a court of referral in preliminary ruling procedures before the CJEU regarding violations of fundamental rights also protected under the Charter?

22.2   The Position of EU Law in the Case-Law of the Hungarian Constitutional Court after 2012

There are all too many less optimistic accounts regarding the 'unleashed potential' of the case-law of the Hungarian Constitutional Court incorporating EU law following Hungary's EU accession.[12] Some scholars characterize the Constitutional Court's jurisprudence as "falling between ideals and reality", scrutinizing its sensitivity to EU law despite its "lack of similar rigor regarding similar constellations".[13] Categorizations of the various EU-law related jurisprudence[14] are set up,[15] leading to the conclusion that a very basic fact lies at

---

9   Endre Orbán, 'Uniós jog az Alkotmánybíróság gyakorlatában', *Alkotmánybírósági Szemle*, 2018/2, pp. 36-45. Orbán also summarizes relevant academic literature on the subject, but we would like to mention a few key authors on the topic here, *e.g.* Attila Vincze, 'Az Alkotmánybíróság stratégiái az uniós és a belső jog viszonyának kezeléséhez', *in* Balázs Fekete *et al.* (eds.), *A világ mi magunk vagyunk... Liber Amicorum Imre Vörös*, HVG-ORAC, Budapest, 2014, pp. 597-611; Márton Varju & Flóra Fazekas, 'The Reception of European Union Law in Hungary', *Common Market Law Review*, Vol. 48, Issue 6, 2011, pp. 1945-1984; László Trócsányi & Lóránt Csink, 'Alkotmány v. közösségi jog: az Alkotmánybíróság helye az Európai Unióban', *Jogtudományi Közlöny*, 2008/2, pp. 63-69; Nóra Chronowski, 'Az Európai Unió jogának viszonya a magyar joggal', *in* András Jakab *et al.* (eds.), *Internetes Jogtudományi Enciklopédia*, at http://ijoten.hu/szocikk/az-europai-unio-joganak-viszonya-a-magyar-joggal (2019).
10   László Blutman, 'Szürkületi zóna: az Alaptörvény és az uniós jog viszonya', *Közjogi Szemle*, 2017/1, pp. 2-14.
11   *See* Hamulak *et al.* 2019.
12   Building on these and making her own conclusions, *see* Fruzsina Gárdos-Orosz, 'Preliminary Reference and the Hungarian Constitutional Court: A Context of Non-Reference', *German Law Journal*, Vol. 16, Issue 6 (special issue), 2015, pp. 1569-1590.
13   Attila Vincze, 'Odahull az eszme és a valóság közé: az árnyék az szuverenitás-átruházás az Alkotmánybíróság esetjogában', *MTA Law Working Papers*, 2014/23, pp. 1-2.
14   Set out in detail by Orbán 2018, p. 36 (with further references). For details on constitutional review of secondary EU law, *see* Gárdos-Orosz 2015, pp. 1575-1584.
15   *E.g.* Vincze 2014, pp. 4-12. His very illustrative categorization regarding the Hungarian Constitutional Court's dealings with EU law uses succinct metaphors tailored to specific anomalies he identifies in the case law: *(i)* "*omphaloskepsis or navel-gazing*" (*e.g.* regarding the 2004 referendum of EU accession); *(ii)* "*life-lie*" (*e.g.* regarding the Hungarian Lisbon-decision [Decision No. 143/2010. (VII. 14.) AB or the Fourth

the heart of the problems. Namely, that the Hungarian Constitutional Court cannot insert EU law into its schematic thinking about its own competences and on the hierarchy of legal norms and this leads to incomprehensible inconsistencies not signaling an outward openness towards EU integration, which would otherwise be mandated under Article E of the Fundamental Law.[16]

These categorizations and approaches inform more recent opinions, which, however, are less inclined to sound alarm bells and feature the Constitutional Court's dominant (and current) approach as 'restraint and seclusion'.[17]

Vincze argued in 2014 that there needs to be a judicial dialogue between national courts and the CJEU, either spontaneously or instrumentalized in the form of preliminary ruling procedures. The Hungarian Constitutional Court, he posited, could contribute to this dialogue creatively, through interpretation by participating in the interactive processes of cooperative constitutionalism and *Verfassungsgerichtsverbund*.[18] We can fully agree with these statements. His corresponding argument, however, was that the Constitutional Court was unwilling to play its part in these processes. We concede that it might have been true at the time, but we are convinced that with the passing of time, his statements need to be revisited and refined – as shown by our findings below.

Recent trends in the Hungarian Constitutional Court's jurisprudence (described later) that might seem as 'delaying or diversion tactics' to the naked eye, upon a closer look turn out to be carefully and resourcefully constructed means of engagement with EU law. Through these, the Hungarian Constitutional Court indeed declares an intention to participate in European constitutional dialogue exactly by suspending some of its proceedings in high-profile cases (*e.g.* '*lex* CEU', civil society organizations) that have parallel counterparts before the CJEU. This way, the input received from the CJEU as a result of relevant EU-level proceedings can be directly channeled into constitutional reasoning, signaling the way forward.

Unfortunately, due to the lack of many high-profile cases (in the proceedings relevant to our inquiry) with an EU law aspect, the Hungarian Constitutional Court faces another issue. An issue that is a (necessary?) boundary of its competence: being bound to the content of the petitions filed with it (otherwise known as the *non ultra petita* rule). Therefore, we shall also look at cases from the aspect of some of the petitions, and at some of the argu-

---

Amendment of the Fundamental Law [Decision No. 12/2013. (V. 24.) AB)]; *(iii)* "*sabotage*" (*e.g.* regarding the EAW in Decision No. 32/2008. (III. 12.) AB and regarding the 'forced retirement' of judges in Decision No. 33/2012. (VII. 17.) AB], *(iv)* "*blind man hitting the mark perchance*" (*e.g.* regarding different proceedings involving civil and public servants due to modifications of relevant Hungarian laws [Decision No. 8/2011. (III. 18.) AB and Decision No. 29/2011. (IV. 7.) AB]. *See* Vincze 2014, p. 4.

16   Vincze 2014, p. 13.
17   Orbán 2018, pp. 38-39.
18   *See e.g.* Andreas Voßkuhle, 'Multilevel Cooperation of the European Constitutional Courts. Der Europäische Verfassungsgerichtsverbund', *European Constitutional Law Review*, Vol. 6, Issue 2, 2010, pp. 175-198.

ments, petitioners have used regarding EU law and the Charter to shed light on one very important conclusion. References to EU law in the fundamental rights context, and more specifically to the Charter, are superficial at best, which – given the restriction of the Hungarian Constitutional Court's legroom in these cases – does not facilitate the conduct of in-depth analyses of the arising EU-law issues, especially regarding the protection of fundamental rights under the Charter.

Being bound by the content of the petition is also an issue regarding preliminary ruling procedures. If the petition does not contain a request to the Constitutional Court to engage the CJEU in such a proceeding, then it does not have the power to do so under the domestic law specifying its powers. This issue will also be dealt with in detail in the last part of the present paper regarding a very recent case,[19] in which the complaint did contain such a request, with which the Hungarian Constitutional Court refused to comply.

Vincze raises this issue as well, stating that the 'constitutional command' of Article E assures primacy to EU law, obliging the Hungarian Constitutional Court to initiate preliminary ruling procedures in all cases where there is doubt in this respect (*i.e.* regarding the primacy of EU law, which poses – in these cases – a question of constitutional interpretation).

He mentions this specifically in the context of constitutional complaint proceedings serving the protection of fundamental rights, regarding any doubts raised as to the correct interpretation of EU law. He admits, however, that while this interpretation is "obviously very advantageous from the point of view of EU law, it is not completely compatible with the constitution."[20] Below, we shall also address whether the Hungarian Constitutional Court could serve as a court of referral, building on a pre-existing 'context of non-reference', first identified by Fruzsina Gárdos-Orosz in 2015.[21]

Based on recent domestic and international developments in this domain, we shall verify whether the statements of the past will become the truths of the future, or whether the present situation changes the course of the constitutional assessment on this issue.

Let us start our inquiry with one statement of the past then, taken from the Hungarian Lisbon-decision, since it was the Lisbon Treaty that afforded legally binding force to the Charter of Fundamental Rights relevant to our paper. Decision No. 143/2010. (VII. 14.) AB,[22] declared that the Lisbon Treaty (attributing a legal value to the Charter equivalent

---

19 Decision No. 3165/2014. (V. 23.) AB.
20 *See* Vincze 2014, p. 14. (for 'constitutional command'), and p. 15. (regarding compatibility with the constitution).
21 *See* Gárdos-Orosz 2015.
22 What can be characterized as the *second Lisbon decision* is the one that is mostly dubbed 'Identity decision' [Decision No. 22/2016. (XII. 5.) AB] in academic literature, detailing the relationship of EU law and Hungarian constitutional law from the points of view of 'sovereignty control' and 'identity control' also applied by the German Constitutional Court in its 2010 Lisbon judgment. Damien Chalmers, 'A Few Thoughts on

to that of the Treaties) was formally approved by an Act of Parliament[23] and is thus "a norm that has a meritorious content within the national legal system".[24]

The increasing number of references to the Charter as a whole, or to specific provisions thereof over time in the petitions filed to the Hungarian Constitutional Court is possibly due to the above statement (as will be analyzed below in the context of what makes a constitutional complaint petition 'admissible' also in terms of Charter-references).

From the case-law after 2010, but before the entry into force of the Fundamental Law, Decision No. 29/2011. (IV. 7.) AB should also be mentioned briefly. In this respect, Vincze referred to the Hungarian Constitutional Court as a "blind man hitting the mark perchance". The basic statement of the case was that under the effective legal framework at the time, the Constitutional Court did not have legal grounds (competence) to examine whether Hungarian laws violated EU law, therefore, it refused to carry out the review also based on the Charter.[25]

Following the 2011 'constitutional turn', it was the new Article E (probably referring to the first letter of Europe) of the Fundamental Law that determined the formal position of EU law, building significantly on the previous Article 2/A with some key additions.[26] Most importantly for us, Article E(3) sets forth that EU law may lay down generally binding rules of conduct. Article T in turn specifies that "[g]enerally binding rules of conduct may be laid down in the Fundamental Law or laws", and defines laws as Acts of Parliament, Government and ministerial decrees (including the Prime Minister's decree), decrees of the Governor of the National Bank, decrees of the heads of autonomous regulatory bodies, and local (government) decrees. *Prima facie*, EU law is not considered as 'law' within the meaning of Article T, albeit it may take the form of a generally binding rule of conduct in light of Article E. Article T specifies that laws must be adopted by a body having legislative competence and specified in the Fundamental Law, promulgated in the official gazette. In addition, Article 24(2) of the Fundamental Law sets forth that the Constitutional Court:

"

---

the Lisbon Judgment', *in* Andreas Fischer Lescano *et al.* (eds.), *The German Constitutional Court's Lisbon Ruling: Legal and Political Science Perspectives*, ZERP Diskussionspapier, 1/2010, pp. 5-11.

23 Act CLXVIII of 2007 on the promulgation of the Lisbon Treaty.

24 *See* Decision No. 143/2010. (VII. 14.) AB, Reasoning III. 2.

25 Decision No. 29/2011. (IV. 7.) AB, Reasoning, III.5.

26 For a concise comparison of the two 'Europe clauses' and their development, *see* Nóra Balogh-Békési, 'Szuverenitásféltés és alkotmány', *MTA Law Working Papers*, 2014/57, pp. 7-13, and Nóra Balogh-Békesi, *Az Európai Unióban való tagságunk alkotmányossági összefüggései az esetjog tükrében*, Pázmány Press, Budapest, 2015, Chapters 5 and 6; or Allan F. Tatham, *Central European Constitutional Courts in the Face of EU Membership*, Martinus Nijhoff, 2013, pp. 156-159.

b   shall, at the initiative of a judge, review the conformity with the Fundamental Law of any law applicable in a particular case as a priority but within no more than ninety days;

c   shall, on the basis of a constitutional complaint, review the conformity with the Fundamental Law of any law applied in a particular case;

d   shall, on the basis of a constitutional complaint, review the conformity with the Fundamental Law of any judicial decision;

e   shall, at the initiative of the Government, one quarter of the Members of the National Assembly, the President of the Curia, the Prosecutor General or the Commissioner for Fundamental Rights, review the conformity with the Fundamental Law of any law;

f   shall examine any law for conflict with any international treaties."

It is possible, that these provisions read together led the Constitutional Court in the past to declare an absence of competence to nullify generally binding rules of conduct taken in the form of EU law under Article E. The Constitutional Court's competence to conduct the control of conformity of laws (*i.e.* generally binding rules of conduct) with the Fundamental Law (under Article 24) only extends to laws adopted in accordance with Article T.[27]

In its more recent case-law, the Hungarian Constitutional Court echoed its earlier conclusions made in 2011, referenced above under Decision No. 29/2001. (VII. 7.) AB. This was reiterated and clarified in respect of its own competences under the new 2012 HCCA in Decision No. 3143/2015. (VII. 24.) AB. The Constitutional Court rejected the constitutional complaint of the petitioner financial institution challenging select provisions of a law (Act of Parliament)[28] for reasons of unconstitutionality. In this decision rendered on the merits of the case, the petitioner argued that the contested law, as well as its provisions, are

"contrary to the respective provisions of the Charter of Fundamental Rights of the European Union – *ergo* the law of the European Union. The Constitutional Court hereby [...] repeatedly points out that based on provisions of the

---

27   This issue of EU law was brought under a new light in the so-called EPC (European Patent Court) decision of the Hungarian Constitutional Court [Decision No. 9/2018. (VII. 9.) AB]. This 'new light' being that the issue of 'enforced cooperation' is the intended framework in which the EPC shall exist, which is – by definition – not a "generally binding rule of conduct" under Article E of the Fundamental Law, as it only "generally binds" the parties who submit to such 'enforced cooperation'. The decision is also interesting and novel in its approach as it examines the issue of the EPC from the aspects of both Article E and of Article Q defining the relationship of domestic and international law.

28   Act XXXVIII of 2014 on settling certain questions regarding the decision for the uniformity of law handed down by the Curia in the matter of consumer loan contracts by financial institutions.

Fundamental Law and the Act on the Constitutional Court, the Constitutional Court does not have the competence to examine the collision of any laws with the law of the European Union, therefore, the relevant elements in the petition are refused under Section 64, point *a)* of the Act on the Constitutional Court."[29]

22.3 The Position of the Charter in the Hungarian Constitutional Court's Jurisprudence – Un-Chartered Territory?

In describing what the above factors entail for the Constitutional Court's jurisprudence and proceedings, on which the Charter may have a bearing, it is first important to highlight some very important issues. In constitutional complaint proceedings, the fundamental rights contained in the Charter cannot be directly referenced by private parties and economic operators as a legal basis. To be more specific, they could, but standing on their own, they will not lead to any conclusive result. The HCCA clearly sets forth that petitioners (persons or organizations) should allege and prove either that *(i)* "their rights enshrined in the Fundamental Law were violated" [Sections 26(1)a) and 27a) of the HCCA]; *(ii)* "due to the application of a legal provision contrary to the Fundamental Law, or when such legal provision becomes effective, rights were violated directly, without a judicial decision". [Section 26(2)a) of the HCCA]. The nature of the action or omission complained against is tied – on the level of the HCCA – to the Fundamental Law. Therefore, when the Constitutional Court decides on the admissibility of the complaints under the current legal framework, it will take into account the constitutionally relevant violations, not the connections of the violations to rights otherwise included in the Charter.

In this regard, it is important to mention that the Charter primarily concerns EU institutions and Member States when they implement EU law (Article 51).[30] Here, another issue arises: namely, whether the Hungarian Constitutional Court is a Member State institution that implements EU law. We have discussed what we there called the 'imple-

---

29   Decision No. 3145/2015. (VII. 24.) AB, Reasoning [56].
30   From the CJEU case-law *see* Judgment of 26 February 2013, *Case C-617/10, Aklagaren v. Hans Akerberg-Fransson*, ECLI:EU:C:2013:105, later first confirmed by the judgment of 26 September 2013, *Case C-418/11, Texdata Software GmbH*, ECLI:EU:C:2013:588. On the scope of the Charter, *see* from a vast body of literature, *e.g.* Petra Jeney, 'The Scope of the EU Charter and its Application by the Hungarian Courts', *Hungarian Journal of Legal Studies*, Vol. 57, Issue 1, 2016, pp. 59-75; Lukasz Bojarski *et al., The Charter of Fundamental Rights as a Living Instrument*, Rome-Warsaw-Vienna, 2014, pp. 77-93; Xavier Groussot *et al.*, 'The Scope of Application of Fundamental Rights on Member States Action: In Search of Certainty in EU Adjudication', *Eric Stein Working Paper*, No. 1/2011. More recently a creative interpretation regarding the application of the Charter was given by Jakab, *see* András Jakab, 'Application of the EU Charter in National Courts in Purely Domestic Cases', *in* András Jakab & Dimitry Kochenov (eds.), *The Enforcement of EU Law and Values*, Oxford University Press, 2017, pp. 252 and 255-257.

mentation dilemma' at length in another recent paper,[31] but a short summary of our main findings on the issue is in order here, as discussed below.

While the argument that the Charter "applies to the Member States only when they act as the EU's agents (*i.e.* when they implement EU law)"[32] is correct; two contradicting aspects therein are hard to reconcile in the context of the proceedings of the Constitutional Court: *(i)* the Member States act as the EU's agents; and *(ii)* they (only) act as agents when they implement EU law.

Member States normally do not act as agents of the EU when they create constitutional avenues for the protection of fundamental rights or for constitutional review based on the national constitution.

Therefore, one would be remiss to jump to the conclusion that constitutional courts can easily, and in every case, be considered 'agents of the EU'. The reason for this is that *by* their nature they do not 'implement EU law'. Member State constitutional courts can only exercise those competences, engage those procedures, and implement those protections that have been afforded to them in the national constitution and national constitutional procedural law. We have demonstrated this with a brief presentation of the relevant restrictions of the Hungarian Constitutional Court.

In the context of fundamental rights, consequently, any protections afforded to fundamental (human) rights by the Charter may inform this decision-making of the Constitutional Court, through influencing interpretation or argumentation rooted in the national constitution. Yet it normally goes no further – as will be seen in some of the cases presented below. Regardless of the reception of our interpretation of the 'implementation dilemma', there are many references to the Charter in numerous proceedings of the Constitutional Court (judicial initiatives, review and complaint petitions). If we ventured to apply different categories to these 'chartered' references, the following categories could be created:

i. *References* by the Hungarian Constitutional Court to the Charter regarding the merits of the case [in decisions (mainly through concurring or dissenting opinions) or orders]. In short, based on our desk research focusing on the past 5 years (2015-2019),[33] the Constitutional Court has so far included Charter-specific remarks in over two dozen cases,[34] most recently in March 2019[35] in a case regarding collective expulsion and the interpretation of Article E regarding the transfer of competences to the EU.[36]

---

31   Hamulak *et al.* 2019.

32   Csongor István Nagy, 'The EU Bill of Rights Diagonal Application to Member States 2018', *in* Nagy (ed.) 2018, p. 8.

33   For more details, *see* Hamulak *et al.* 2019.

34   The most famous among these being Decision No. 22/2016. (XII. 5.) AB – for a detailed analysis of the relevant aspects of the case *see* Hamulak *et al.* 2019.

35   Decision No. 2/2019. (III. 5.) AB.

36   In the majority argumentation – under para. [49] of the decision –, a reference to "interpretation in light of the Charter" comes up one time regarding an EU directive, specified in the context of constitutional

ii. *Suspension* of proceedings (through orders, with regard to any on-going proceedings before of the CJEU, in the spirit of constitutional dialogue and 'resourceful engagement' with EU law).[37]

iii. *References* to the Charter, included in the petitions[38] (or their summaries) that are part of any eventual decision or order on the matter at hand. (The most common outcome in these cases being refusal due to failure to meet admissibility criteria set up by the HCCA and the relevant jurisprudence of the Hungarian Constitutional Court.) The problem with these petitions has been described above in the context of the Constitutional Court's competences regarding the content of the petitions.

The main conclusions that can be drawn from the sample cases are the following. *(i)* It is not only the responsibility of the Constitutional Court to resourcefully engage with EU law, but *(ii)* such engagement also presupposes 'well-rounded' petitions in terms of EU law, specifically with regard to the protection of fundamental rights. In other words, petitioners and their legal representatives are also responsible for finding points of connection with the EU, resourcefully engaging with protections afforded thereby. *(iii)* Charter-based reasoning (extending far beyond mere references to the Charter as a whole or to certain provisions on the level of what they state) should be embedded in the relevant constitutional reasoning. This is especially true in constitutional complaints where 'victim status', *i.e.* being personally affected by the violation or a causal link between the violation and the act or omission complained of should be substantiated as admissibility criteria.

However, even if the level of constitutionally anchored Charter-relevant argumentation were to improve, the lack of competence to review the compatibility of Hungarian law with EU law under current constitutional and statutory arrangements is the main obstacle before the Charter gaining more solid ground. Another reason for the slow penetration

---

interpretation. This aside, references to the principle of constitutional dialogue inside the EU and to *Europafreundlichkeit* (namely the constitutional commitment of Hungary to contribute to European unity under Article E are also made. Two dissenting opinions (Czine and Juhász, under paras. [91]-[92] and [109] respectively) also reference the Charter.

37 Order No. 3220/2018. (VII. 2.) AB (regarding the VAT Act – reason for suspension: preliminary ruling procedure in progress), Order No. 3199/2018. (VI. 21.) AB and Order No. 3200/2018. (VI. 21.) AB (the so-called *'lex CEU'* case), Order No. 3198/2018. (VI. 21.) AB (regarding the Act on civil society and non-profit organizations) – in the three cases the reason for suspension has been the relevant infringement proceedings in progress in front of the CJEU. For a detailed description of these arguments *see* Hamulak *et al.* 2019.

38 Please note that at the time of writing this paper there are no official statistics available due to the absence of filtering tools enabling the court to assess all incoming petitions for a measure of Charter-references. Thus, we have compiled a sample of 10 cases from the period specified as the window of our desk research. All cases in this selection resulted in refusal orders due to the reasons described above. The cases in the sample are: Order No. 3179/2017. (VII. 14.) AB, Order No. 3090/2017. (IV. 28.) AB, Order No. 3272/2016. (XII. 20.) AB, Order No. 3143/2016. (VI. 29.) AB, Order No. 3164/2015. (VII. 24.) AB, Order No. 3019/2015. (I. 27.) AB, Order No. 3020/2015. (I. 27.) AB, Order No. 3141/2015. (VII. 9.) AB, Order No. 3082/2015. (V. 8.) AB, as well as the most recent case – Order No. 3034/2019. (II. 12.) AB.

of the Charter into the jurisprudence of the Constitutional Court is that the Court is tied to the content of the petitions, which are – as presented above and elsewhere[39] – normally 'deficient' in making the Charter legally relevant for constitutional reasoning.

However, we can always refer to the guiding hand of other constitutional jurisdictions for comparison, which – owing to differences in the legal framework or in the legal system itself – can and do use the Charter as a decisive argument in major constitutional issues.

In Austria, in a 2014 same-sex marriage case (*cf.* B 166/2013), the Constitutional Court of Austria (ACC) took a look at the Charter (Article 21 – non-discrimination) and

"recalled that, in the scope of application of the Charter [...], the rights guaranteed by the Charter may be invoked as constitutionally guaranteed rights, provided that the guarantee enshrined in the Charter is similar in its wording and purpose to rights that are guaranteed by the Austrian Federal Constitution, as is the case with Article 21 [...]. However, the [ACC] found that the national provisions relevant to the case did not implement EU law within the meaning of Article 51.1 [...], as interpreted by the Court of Justice of the European Union in its settled case-law; consequently, Article 21 [...] proved to be inapplicable in the present case. The Constitutional Court added that, even if the Charter were applicable, the provisions at issue [...] would not violate Article 21 [...], owing to the wide margin of appreciation granted to the Contracting States [...]."[40]

Interestingly, a few years later in 2017, the Constitutional Court of Austria overturned this decision, with no reference and regard to the Charter, establishing the right for same-sex couples to marry in Austria.[41]

Romania could be mentioned as another example, where the *Curtea Constituțională* (RCC) went further and initiated a preliminary ruling procedure before of the CJEU regarding same-sex relationships. It suspended its proceedings in which the preliminary ruling procedure arose, awaiting feedback from Luxembourg on the interpretation of the notion of spouse under EU law with regard to free movement (*cf.* constitutional dialogue). Once the CJEU handed down its judgment in the *Coman* case in June 2018,[42] the RCC

---

39   Hamulak *et al.* 2019.
40   *Cf.* Website of the Constitutional Court of Austria, at www.vfgh.gv.at/medien/_Wiederholung__der_in_den_Niederlanden_geschlossenen.en.html.
41   *See* Decision G 258/2017 by the ACC. On the analysis of the case *see* Árpád Lapu, 'Házasság mindenkinek – az osztrák Alkotmánybíróság decemberi döntése', *Fontes Juris*, 2018/1, pp. 67-72.
42   Judgment of 5 June 2018, *Case C-673/16, Relu Adrian Coman and Others v. Inspectoratul General pentru Imigrari and Ministerul Afacerilor Interne (Coman)*, ECLI:EU:C:2018:385. For a detailed description of the issues of the case *see* Márton Sulyok, 'Une photo de famille. Pillanatkép a családi élet és a házastársfogalom Európai Unió Bírósága általi elemzéséről', *Európai Tükör*, 2018/3, pp. 117-131.

resumed its proceedings one month later and incorporated the findings of the CJEU in its decision. The RCC's decision is unique – from the point of view of constitutional law – for the following reasons.

i. The RCC declared[43] that Romania violates the positive obligations doctrine[44] flowing from Articles 7 and 8 of the Charter when avoiding any form of legal and formal recognition of same-sex relationships, joining states such as Bulgaria, Latvia, Lithuania, Poland or Slovakia.[45]

ii. The RCC also reiterated its doctrine of "cumulative [dual] conditionality" referring to its well-established case law, as follows:

> "applying a provision of the EU law in a constitutional review, as a provision interposed between the EU law and the basic one, pursuant to Article 148 (2) and (4) of the Constitution of Romania,[46] implies a cumulative conditionality: on the one hand, this provision has to be sufficiently clear, precise and unambiguous by itself or its meaning had been clearly defined by the Court of Justice of the European Union and, on the other hand, the provision has to be circumscribed to a certain level of constitutional relevance, for its normative content to support the alleged violation by the national law of the Constitution – the sole direct provision of reference within a constitutional review. From such a hypothetical perspective, the reference of the Constitutional Court [...] is different from a mere application and interpretation of the law, a competence conferred upon courts of law and administrative authorities, it also being different from possible issues relating to the legislative policy advanced by the Parliament or by the Government, as the case may be."[47]

(iii) As a result of the preliminary ruling procedure, the RCC found that the above conditions meet Article 21(1) TFEU and Article 7(2) of the Directive 2004/38/EC (subject to the *Coman* case) and determined that same-sex relationships fall into the category of private and family life under the Charter (Articles 7 and 8).[48]

---

43 Decision No. 534 of 18 July 2018, on the unconstitutionality of the provisions of Sections 277.2 and 277.4 of the Civil Code (*Coman* decision). Published in the Official Gazette of Romania No 842 of 03.10.2018. For an introduction of the constitutional argumentation of the case *see* Sulyok 2018, pp. 126-129.

44 The doctrine originates from the jurisprudence of the ECtHR, meaning that States have positive obligations to create meaningful legal rules to effectively protect the enjoyment of the rights protected by the ECHR. For a detailed overview on how this doctrine applies also to issues of private and family life *see* Jean-François Akandji-Kombe, *Positive Obligations Under the European Convention on Human Rights*, Human rights Handbooks No. 7, 2007, DG Human Rights, Council of Europe, especially pp. 36-48.

45 *Coman* decision, para. 29.

46 The Romanian 'integration clause'.

47 *Coman* decision, para. 38.

48 Id. paras. 39-40.

These examples lead us to the next section of our paper: mapping the possibilities of the Hungarian Constitutional Court for becoming a court of referral.

22.4   THE STATUS OF THE HUNGARIAN CONSTITUTIONAL COURT AS A COURT OF REFERRAL – EXTRACTING THE RULES OF ENGAGEMENT WITH EU LAW FROM A 'CONTEXT OF NON-REFERENCE'

As presented in the introduction, Fruzsina Gárdos-Orosz has first identified what she called a "context of non-reference" regarding the Hungarian Constitutional Court's stance on matters of EU law in 2015. She described this context as a missed opportunity in defining its "proper role in achieving the constitutional aim of contribution to the European rule of law integration."[49] She then goes on to argue that

> "the institution of the preliminary reference may be of help for the Constitutional Court in finding a cooperative solution that is acceptable both for observing the Hungarian constitutional identity and promoting common constitutional goals as the Member States of the Union."[50]

Gárdos-Orosz was also right in arguing that with the new rules of the HCCA the Constitutional Court "has definitely diminished the chance of avoiding situations where considering a referral is unavoidable".[51] The different legal, political and constitutional debates of the recent past on the European and international level are sufficient evidence that the Hungarian Constitutional Court, just as any other constitutional court, can no longer seek comfort in seclusion.[52] On the contrary: if an issue triggers a response, it shall start engaging with EU law with increasing frequency and significance.[53] One possible path to choose in this effort is to start acting as a court of referral in the sense embodied in Article 267 TFEU and the relevant CJEU jurisprudence. This issue may be obvious to some, but the question is not whether the Constitutional Court can be considered a court of referral

---

49   Gárdos-Orosz 2015, p. 1571.
50   Id. p. 1572.
51   Id. p. 1575.
52   As an example for such debates in the context of examining the role of the Hungarian Constitutional Court, we can mention the infringements procedures currently on-going against Hungary as well as the so-called 'Article 7' proceedings regarding a 'systemic breach' of the rule of law based on the Treaties. The context of current European debates, however, is much vaster, and this paper is not about these, thus they shall not be mentioned in the following. The role of national (constitutional) identity and the role of the state are central to these debates as is the role of national constitutional courts in engaging with the CJEU. This was one of the main motivators behind writing the present paper as well.
53   On the complicated relationship of the Hungarian Constitutional Court and EU law, *see* Orbán 2018.

under relevant EU rules. This is, indeed, obvious. The question is much rather whether the Constitutional Court should start acting as a court of referral in light of its recent position and status in its cases related to EU law, especially when it comes to the protection of fundamental rights.[54]

Since the CJEU's 1997 decision in *Dorsch*,[55] we know that

> "in order to determine whether the body making a reference is a 'court or tribunal' [...], which is a question governed by Community law alone, the Court takes account of a number of factors, such as whether the body is established by law, whether it is permanent, whether its jurisdiction is compulsory, whether its procedure is *inter partes*, whether it applies rules of law and whether it is independent."

In the more recent 2008 landmark *Cartesio*[56] case referred by a Hungarian court, the CJEU extended this definition by recognizing the court responsible for maintaining the commercial register as a

> "court or tribunal which is entitled to make a reference for a preliminary ruling [...], regardless of the fact that neither the decision of the lower court nor the consideration of the appeal by the referring court takes place in the context of inter partes proceedings."[57]

Initiating preliminary ruling procedures is the obligation of national courts aimed at ensuring the uniform interpretation of EU law. Therefore, the national court or tribunal before which a dispute is brought takes the sole (discretionary) responsibility for determining both the need for a request for a preliminary ruling and the relevance of the questions it submits to the CJEU. Sole discretion is of key importance in this regard. Subject to certain criteria determined in the jurisprudence of CJEU,[58] national judges have a *de facto* margin

---

54 An interesting account is given by Dimitry Kochenov and Matthijs van Wolferen on the relationship of the CJEU and Member States' top courts, including constitutional courts as well, regarding the role of the preliminary ruling procedure in building what the authors call 'dialogical rule of law'. *See* Dimitry Kochenov & Matthijs van Wolferen, 'Dialogical Rule of Law and the Breakdown of Dialogue in the EU', *EUI Law Working Papers*, 2018/1, pp. 11-15.

55 Judgment of 17 September 1997, *Case C-54/96, Dorsch Consult Ingenieurgesellschaft mbH v. Bundesbaugesellschaft Berlin mbH*, ECLI:EU:C:1997:413.

56 Judgment of 16 December 2008, *Case C-210/06, CARTESIO Oktató és Szolgáltató bt*, ECLI:EU:C:2008:723, paras. 55-56.

57 Id. para. 125.

58 *See e.g.* Judgment of 8 September 2015, *Case C-105/14, Criminal proceedings against Ivo Taricco and Others (Taricco)*, ECLI:EU:C:2015:555; Judgment of 11 March 1980, *Case C-104/79, Pasquale Foglia v. Mariella Novello (Foglia v. Novello)*, ECLI:EU:C:1980:73.

of discretion in deciding whether the interpretation of EU law is necessary to decide the case before them.

Applying these factors to the Hungarian Constitutional Court, if the issue (petition) at hand can be decided in light of the national constitution and national law – without the interpretation of EU law, then discretion may point into the direction of no reference. Also, whether the exercise of discretion will lead to a preliminary ruling procedure, depends on relevant petitions to that effect and on the limitations set by national constitutional law.

In the *CILFIT* case,[59] the CJEU had ruled that

> "it follows from the relationship between the second and third paragraphs of Article 234 [previously Art. 117] that the courts or tribunals referred to in the third paragraph have the same discretion as any other national court or tribunal to ascertain whether a decision on a question of Community law is necessary to enable them to give judgment. Accordingly, those courts or tribunals are not obliged to refer to the [CJEU] a question concerning the interpretation of Community law raised before them if that question is not relevant, that is to say, if the answer to that question, regardless of what it may be, can in no way affect the outcome of the case."[60]

Thus, national court judge(s) shall decide whether the interpretation of EU law is necessary for them to render a judgment, and it is necessary when it is relevant and is amenable to affect the outcome of the case. While this may be considered a kind of 'interpretation of EU law', the line is extremely narrow.

In *CILFIT*, the CJEU provided a framework for the level of discretion of national courts by enabling them to interpret EU law regarding its relevance and impact on the case before them. On the issue whether an effect on the outcome of the case is tangible, different approaches may be found. *Melica* confirms the CJEU's wording in *CILFIT* in that 'not necessary' means that there is no way EU law could affect the outcome of the case.[61]

In the *Foglia v. Novello* case, the CJEU expressed that it accepts only 'genuine disputes', therefore an 'artificial expedient of arrangements' does not fall within the jurisdiction of the Court. Deciding whether the relationship of the case with EU law is genuine may be hard to decide in light of the margin of discretion of the national court on the one hand and the interpretation of EU law on the other.

---

59   Judgment of 6 October 1982, *Case C-283/81, Srl CILFIT and Lanificio di Gavardo SpA v. Ministry of Health (CILFIT)*, ECLI:EU:C:1982:335.
60   Id. para. 10.
61   *See* Luigi Melica, 'The Unconstitutional Development of the European Legal Framework', *Diritto Pubblico Comparato et Europeo*, 2018/3, pp. 581-630.

In the *Taricco* case, the relationship of EU law and the case before the Italian court seemed to be in a great Euclidean distance from each other, therefore some[62] argued that the questions referred by the national court were indeed inadmissible. The relationship of the case with EU law was not clear and not close. The Italian law in question gave rise to a situation that affected the financial interests of the EU. The interdependence between the case law and the preliminary ruling procedure is, clearly, not based on a supposed conflict between norms, but on a conflict between two different general interests related to two different political choices.

Despite this, the CJEU found that it was sufficient that a national court assumed that national provisions did not meet those requirements of EU law which foresaw that measures to counter VAT evasion must be effective and dissuasive. And since national courts

"have to ensure that EU law is given full effect, if need be by disapplying those provisions [...] without having to request or await the prior repeal of those articles by way of legislation or any other constitutional procedure",

the Italian Court's reference was declared admissible.[63] It is not obvious in every case whether the outcome is affected by the interpretation of EU law or not, and consequently, whether there is an obligation to refer or not.

Traditionally, constitutional courts (due to their competences as outlined above based on the Hungarian example) do not instinctively refer cases to the CJEU given the usual (constitutional) nature of cases they encounter and given the fact that their primary point of reference is the national constitution.[64] This situation is, of course, subject to change in the EU, especially when we talk about the context of protecting fundamental rights, with protections guaranteed both in the national constitution and the EU Charter of Fundamental Rights. As we have shown above, there are many approaches to choose from also at the disposal of the Hungarian Constitutional Court when (re)defining its relationship to EU law and the fundamental rights it protects.

According to the CJEU's own statistics,[65] the number of preliminary procedures referred by constitutional courts is (relatively) low: 5 requests from the *Verfassungsgerichtshof* (Austria); 1 request from the *Conseil constitutionnel* (France); 2 requests from the *Bun-*

---

62 *Case C-105/14, Taricco*, para. 28.
63 *See* Melica 2018, p. 589.
64 For a discussion of the role of constitutional courts in a preliminary ruling procedure, with special focus on the German Federal Constitutional Court, *see* Monica Claes, 'The Validity and Primacy of EU Law and the 'Cooperative Relationship' between National Constitutional Courts and the Court of Justice of the European Union', *Maastricht Journal of European and Comparative Law*, Vol. 23, Issue 1, 2016, pp. 151-170.
65 *Annual Report of the CJEU (2018)* at https://curia.europa.eu/jcms/upload/docs/application/pdf/2019-04/_ra_2018_en.pdf, p. 146.

desverfassungsgericht (Germany); 3 requests from the *Corte Costituzionale* (Italy); 2 requests from the *Konstitucinis Teismas* (Lithuania); 1 request from the *Cour constitutionnelle* (Luxembourg); 1 request from the *Trybunał Konstytucyjny* (Poland);[66] 1 request from the *Ustavno sodišče* (Slovenia); 1 request from the *Tribunal Constitucional* (Spain); and finally 38 requests from the *Cour constitutionnelle* (Belgium).

Please note that the latter, relatively large number in the Belgian case is probably due to the transformation of the *Cour d'Arbitrage* into the Constitutional Court, a process finalized in 2007. Two additions need to be made to this list compiled by the CJEU: *(i)* The RCC's reference in the *Coman* case mentioned above, and *(ii)* the most recent filing from the Slovakian Constitutional Court in C-378/19 (*Prezident Slovenskej republiky*) on 14 May 2019.[67]

As we have argued above, it is obvious that the Hungarian Constitutional Court *(i)* is established by law, *(ii)* functions permanently, *(iii)* has a jurisdiction that is compulsory *erga omnes, (iv)* applies the rules of law, and *(v)* is independent.

The question before us now is merely, whether the Constitutional Court could be classified as a court of the last instance,[68] in proceedings that see it having to decide petitions that require the interpretation of the Charter or similar EU legal acts regarding protections for fundamental rights. According to some commentators,

> "[a] national court of the last instance within the meaning of Article 267(3) TFEU does not have a duty to refer a question on the interpretation of EU law to the Court of Justice in the ruling of the Court would have no bearing on the final decision."[69]

---

66   Judgment of 7 March 2017, *Case C-390/15, Rzecznik Praw Obywatelskich (RPO)*, ECLI:EU:C:2017:174, by which the Polish Constitutional Court (PCC) is kind of a pioneer among V4 countries in 'resourceful engagement' with EU law. The PCC questioned the validity of the reduced rate of VAT for books and other publications, as provided for under EU law, regarding which the CJEU ruled that the examination of the questions referred has disclosed no factor of such a kind as to affect the validity of point 6 of Annex III to Council Directive 2006/112/EC of 28 November 2006 on the common system of VAT. This issue, however, was never intended to be the subject of this paper.
67   The only publicly available data so far amounts to the subject matter, which is defined in four areas: freedom of establishment, freedom to provide services, approximation of laws and energy. *See Case C-378/19, Request for a preliminary ruling from the Ústavny súd Slovenskej republiky (Slovakia) lodged on 14 May 2019.*
68   *See* Flóra Fazekas Flóra, *A magyar Alkotmánybíróság viszonya a közösségi jog elsőbbségéhez egyes tagállami alkotmánybírósági felfogások tükrében*, PhD dissertation, Debrecen, 2009, pp. 175-181. However, things have changed due to the Fundamental Law that provided new competences for the Hungarian Constitutional Court. By those, the Constitutional Court qualifies as a court of referral under Article 267 TFEU according to Gárdos-Orosz 2015, p. 1574.
69   Jan Gregor *et al.*, 'Reference for a Preliminary Ruling Procedure as An (In)Effective Tool of Judicial Harmonisation of European Union Law', *THEMIS 2018*, Thessaloniki, pp. 9-10.

Based on this logic, is it plausible that a judgment of the CJEU clarifying the application of the provisions of the Charter would have a bearing on the final decision of the Hungarian Constitutional Court?[70]

An important decision also involving the dismissal of two requests for a preliminary ruling on the above grounds (referring the issue of obligation to refer and to deny such requests) has been recently brought before the ECtHR in a Hungarian case, *Repcevirág Szövetkezet v. Hungary*, on 30 April 2019.[71]

We have not included the underlying Hungarian Constitutional Court's case initially into our sample period of the previous five years (2015-2019, starting from the 'context of non-reference'), as it was decided in early 2014. However, in the recent ECtHR judgment confirming the Hungarian point of view, the Court also reflects on the Constitutional Court's decision to refuse a constitutional complaint requesting that the Constitutional Court turn to the CJEU with a preliminary reference. This makes the case relevant to this last part of our inquiry.

In refusal Order No. 3165/2014. (V. 23.) AB, the Constitutional Court refused to admit a constitutional complaint against a decision of the Curia, and therefore precluded turning to the CJEU in a preliminary ruling procedure. The order was based on the following:[72]

In the case underlying the complaint, the Tax Authority determined a large amount of unpaid tax owed by the petitioner and imposed a tax fine and interest for late payment. This decision came as a result of a tax deduction applied by the petitioner after the purchase of agricultural machinery of significant value, which he later gave to certain companies to operate, free of charge. Under the current regulation, the petitioner believed to have legal cause to apply the VAT-deduction and consequently paid less taxes. This was found unlawful by the Tax Authority; which decision was also confirmed by the then Supreme Court of Hungary (now Curia of Hungary).

As a result, the petitioner filed a lawsuit against the Supreme Court for damage caused in a judicial capacity, arguing that the Supreme Court did not take into consideration effective domestic and EU rules (*i.e.* Directive 77/738/EEC), which led to the damages incurred. He also requested that the trial court, in this case, turn to the CJEU for a preliminary ruling. The court denied both petitions, and on appeal, the trial court's decisions were approved on both accounts.

The petitioner then filed a constitutional complaint alleging the violation of Article XXVIII of the Fundamental Law on the right to a fair trial and argued that the Curia failed to comply with its obligation to initiate a preliminary ruling procedure by arbitrarily

---

70   Given the title of our paper and the extensive literature regarding the status of EU law in general in the jurisprudence of the Hungarian Constitutional Court, we will only focus on the issue of preliminary ruling procedure in the fundamental rights context through a very recent 2019 case study.

71   *Repcevirág Szövetkezet v. Hungary*, No. 70750/14, 20 April 2019.

72   Decision No. 3165/2014. (V. 23.) AB, Reasoning [3]-[6].

declining the request to that effect, without professional, objective and sufficiently detailed justification. In this aspect, the petitioner also referenced the *CILFIT* and *Köbler* cases of the CJEU and the criteria defined therein[73] and added 13 references to the Charter. The petitioner argued,

> "in reference to Article 47 of the Charter that the Curia, by unlawfully discarding the reference for a preliminary ruling procedure, violated the right to a fair trial. Based on Article 51 of the Charter, the Charter was unquestionably applicable in the proceedings, because [*sic!*] the Curia (should have) applied Article 267 TFEU."[74]

The petitioner also made a secondary claim in his complaint, requesting that the Hungarian Constitutional Court turn to the CJEU in a preliminary ruling procedure. In the grounds put forward for substantiating the refusal,[75] the Hungarian Constitutional Court argued that the petitioner founded the alleged violation of the right to a fair trial on the supposition that the trial court in the case regarding damage caused by judicial action refused to turn to the CJEU. The Constitutional Court first recalled that in terms of its well-established case law regarding the criteria for admissibility, certain factors need to be considered in the instant case. First of all, the complaint serves as a means of 'constitutional appeal'[76] regarding any unconstitutionality that may influence the judgment of the court on the merits or alleging that there is a fundamental question of constitutional significance arising in the case, and that therefore, the Constitutional Court may not serve as a forum to re-adjudicate the issue de novo, or to re-examine the general direction of the judicial decision or reassess the evidence.[77]

Besides the above general points, the refusal of the preliminary ruling procedure initiative was based on a multi-tiered reasoning.

i.   The Constitutional Court agreed with the Curia's argument regarding the fact that questions posed by the petitioner in the case do not relate to the interpretation of the Treaties or a decision on the validity of the legislative acts of EU institutions [in a broad sense], but concern the re-examination of a judgment by a Member State court, which is consequently outside the purview of the CJEU. (For a decision by the CJEU would have had no bearing on the decision.)

---

73   Judgment of 30 September 2003, *Case C-224/01, Gerhard Köbler v. Republik Österreich*, ECLI:EU:C:2003:513, para. 59.

74   *See* p. 8 of Petition No. IV/507/2014 as part of Order No. 3165/2014. (V. 23.) AB.

75   Order No. 3165/2014. (V. 23.) AB, Reasoning [13]-[20].

76   Márta Dezső *et al., Constitutional Law in Hungary*, Kluwer Law International, 2010, pp. 197-198.

77   In detail, *see* Order No. 3003/2012. (VI. 21.) AB, Order No. 3028/2014. (II. 17.) AB, Order No. 3110/2014. (IV. 17.) AB and Order No. 3231/2012. (IX. 28.) AB.

ii. The Hungarian Constitutional Court stated that in examining the conformity of judicial decisions with the constitution, it refrains from making any determinations regarding special branches of law and relevant issues of legal interpretation.

iii. The Constitutional Court argued that it sees the essential content of the right to a fair trial in the enforcement of procedural rules that have constitutional significance, and any elements of judicial proceedings beyond that – such as a discretionary decision by the Curia to refuse a request for a preliminary ruling procedure – are not regarded as questions that have a constitutional bearing. In this case, the Hungarian Constitutional Court held that it has no jurisdiction to decide *in lieu* of trial courts whether they have an obligation to initiate a preliminary ruling procedure. (Whether the decision of the CJEU would have a bearing on the case in front of trial courts, is an issue within the proceeding court's sole discretion.)

iv. The Constitutional Court emphasized, upon reflection on the petitioner's claim to the Hungarian Constitutional Court *to* initiate a preliminary ruling procedure, that the petitioner can only request the court to nullify the court judgment complained of in proceedings under Section 27 HCCA, but this in no way extends to requesting a referral instead.

Against this domestic procedural background, the ECtHR decided the case arriving at the following conclusions[78] through an analysis reflecting on Article 6 ECHR:

(i) The applicant alleged a violation of his right to access to the CJEU through the Curia's refusal to request a preliminary ruling procedure, in which regard the ECtHR argued that:

> "The Court reiterates that it is not competent to assess the merits of the interpretative stance [of the Curia] in the light of European Union law in the first set of proceedings, in particular, whether or not it was in line with the CJEU's case-law [...]. The Court's competence is confined to assessing whether or not these reasons are arbitrary or manifestly unreasonable."[79]

(ii) Against this background, the ECtHR came to the reassuring conclusion that the Curia

> "could have explained more explicitly why it refused to make a preliminary reference. However, implicit reasoning can be considered sufficient [...] The Court, therefore, does not consider arbitrary or manifestly unreasonable the reasons given [...] for not making a reference to the CJEU."[80]

---

78 *Repcevirág Szövetkezet v. Hungary*, No. 70750/14, 20 April 2019, paras. 54-62.
79 Id. para. 56.
80 Id. paras. 58 and 60.

(iii) as far as the Hungarian Constitutional Court's refusal of the complaint for lack of jurisdiction is concerned, the ECtHR also made an important point finding no violation of Article 6 ECHR:

> "61. In so far as the Constitutional Court's reasoning is concerned, this court provided reasoning in reply to the request of the applicant company which complained [of the Curia's] refusal to approach the CJEU, consisting in holding that it lacked jurisdiction in this respect. Such a position cannot be considered arbitrary or manifestly unreasonable either. It is not for the Court to challenge the Constitutional Court's finding that requests for a preliminary reference to the CJEU should be made before the ordinary courts and that it lacked jurisdiction to review such decisions. The Court would stress in this context that Article 6 § 1 does not require a supreme court to give more detailed reasoning when it simply applies a specific legal provision to dismiss an appeal on points of law as having no prospects of success, without further explanation […]."

This Strasbourg judgment brings to light the fact that the role and position of the Constitutional Court in the Hungarian justice system sparks intensive debates in Hungary triggering a response from international judicial fora as well.

Regarding the role of the Constitutional Court in protecting fundamental rights through complaints procedures, we should mention that the ECtHR has very recently declared in *Szalontay v. Hungary*[81] that the constitutional complaint proceedings now qualify as a necessary and effective remedy[82] in terms of the admissibility test of individual ECtHR applications. This only reinforces our arguments about the role of the Hungarian Constitutional Court in protecting fundamental rights.

In this context, there might come a time when the relevant use of Charter-arguments in the proceedings of the Constitutional Court will lead to similarly important results, but until then, the only way to see what lies ahead of us is to map out what we consider to be the cornerstones of the Hungarian Constitutional Court's 'resourceful engagement' with fundamental rights under EU law.

---

81   *Szalontay v. Hungary (dec.)*, No. 71327/13, 4 April 2019.
82   Under para 39. of the decision, the ECtHR has concluded that in the case at hand "either a constitutional complaint under section 26(1) coupled with a complaint under section 27 against the impugned legislation […] or a constitutional complaint solely under section 27 against the judgments given in allegedly unfair proceedings, were accessible remedies offering reasonable prospects of success." Declaring that the applicant has failed to exhaust the domestic remedies at his disposal indicates necessity and the reference to the reasonable prospects of success is an inference to effectiveness.

22.5 Conclusions on a Roadmap towards a 'Resourceful Engagement' with EU Law and the Charter

Above, we examined the strengths and weaknesses of the jurisprudence of the Hungarian Constitutional Court in light of EU law and the Charter, and we have presented some foreign examples as well for comparison. Below, we should address some of the opportunities and challenges on the road ahead.

As the ECtHR's most recent decision in *Repcevirág* demonstrated, the refusal of a request for preliminary ruling by the Hungarian Constitutional Court already passed the tests of the Strasbourg system of human rights protection against arbitrariness, but this case only shows that the issue of the Hungarian Constitutional Court serving as a court of referral is expected to garner yet more attention.

Another very recent development of EU law possibly influencing Member States' constitutional courts' 'resourceful engagement' with EU law may also be mentioned from among the case-law of the CJEU, with implications regarding the Charter.

In *C-235/17, Commission v. Hungary,* infringement proceedings were initiated concerning alleged violations of the right to property through national legislation. National provisions extinguished without compensation the rights of usufruct over agricultural and forestry land. In its judgment, finding Hungary in non-compliance with its obligations under EU law, the CJEU held that the compatibility of the contested provisions with EU law

> "must be examined [in light of] the exceptions thus provided for by the Treaty and the Court's case-law, on the one hand, and of the fundamental rights guaranteed by the Charter, on the other hand (*see*, to that effect, judgment of 21 December 2016, AGET Iraklis, C-201/15, EU:C:2016:972, paragraphs 65, 102 and 103)."[83]

With above, the CJEU basically stated that when a Member State intends to justify the limitation of a fundamental right, the compatibility of the provision in question with EU law shall *(i)* not only be compared to the exceptions provided for under the Treaties but *(ii)* also be in relation to the rights protected by the Charter.

Such rules bring protections afforded to fundamental rights on the EU level to a full circle, seemingly limiting the legroom of constitutional courts in figuring out ways to avoid engaging with the Charter. We have seen above that some countries (Austria, Romania) already have landmark cases with Charter-implications in their jurisprudence, but for any

---

[83] Judgment of 21 May 2019, *Case C-235/17, Commission v. Hungary*, ECLI:EU:C:2019:432, para. 66.

constitutional court to become a court of referral it is not only the provisions of Article 267 TFEU that are quintessential, but the different perceptions and structures of preliminary reference in the different legal systems. Preliminary references normally stay within the system of 'ordinary courts' as issues of interpreting EU law normally arise in the context of first- or second instance proceedings. If in these cases requests are accepted and filed with the CJEU, then by the time the case reaches the Hungarian Constitutional Court through 'constitutional appeal' (*i.e.* a constitutional complaint), the issues relevant to the interpretation of EU law will have already been clarified.

It is firstly up to the petitioners to shed light on such fundamental-rights-related issues in their cases that would prompt or at least challenge the Hungarian Constitutional Court to conduct an actual in-depth analysis of Charter-relevant human rights arguments. In these cases, then, the Hungarian Constitutional Court may easily find itself in a position where it will be required to 'resourcefully engage' with EU law. Individual action in protecting individual fundamental rights could thus induce an adequate response. This path, so far, has been less beaten, and navigating is difficult on a terrain made up of real issues of *ratione materiae* competence and sovereignty, as well as complicated perceptions of EU law emerging at every turn, making headway slow. However, at least, progress is tangible.

23   FAIR TRIAL UNDER SCRUTINY

*Ágnes Czine**

Keywords

right to a fair trial, Constitutional Court of Hungary, Article 6 ECHR, Article XXVIII of the Fundamental Law of Hungary, Hungarian Code of Criminal Procedure

Abstract

The right to a fair trial has an eminent position in the Fundamental Law of Hungary both because of the importance of the right and the great number of applications and jurisprudence it has been the subject of. This study presents the legal background of fair trial and its place in the Hungarian legal system, analyzing the jurisprudence of the Hungarian Constitutional Court on the right to fair trial, and in particular, the obligation to adjudicate within a reasonable time. While the Constitutional Court has developed a consistent practice in this regard, there are nevertheless new issues that may make the amendment of certain pieces of legislation necessary. This paper presents a case-study on a new development in the Constitutional Court's practice on the issue of deciding the case within a reasonable time.

23.1   INTRODUCTION

Defining the concept of the fair trial is not an easy task, notwithstanding the vast volume of scholarly work dedicated to this concept. László Sólyom, former president of the Hungarian Constitutional Court wrote that the fair trial principle is a complex term. That is the reason why the Constitutional Court accepted as a methodological approach that the fair trial must be considered as a whole, because in spite of the fairness of the detailed rules, the procedure as a whole may still prove to be unfair.[1]

The substance and the elements of this principle already appeared in various international legal documents in the middle of the last century. In 1948 the Universal Declaration of Human Rights set out the principle of fair trial in its Articles 10 and 11. According to the Protocol II of the Geneva Conventions of 1949 adopted in 1977, fair trial must be

---

*   Ágnes Czine: justice, Constitutional Court of Hungary.
1   László Sólyom, *Az alkotmánybíráskodás kezdetei Magyarországon*, Osiris, Budapest, 2011, p. 554.

afforded even in armed conflicts. The ICCPR, which was adopted in 1966 and entered into force in 1976, declares in Article 14 that

> "All persons shall be equal before the courts and tribunals. In the determination of any criminal charge against him, or of his rights and obligations in a suit at law, everyone shall be entitled to a fair and public hearing by a competent, independent and impartial tribunal established by law."

23.2 FAIR TRIAL IN HUNGARIAN LAW

Article 6 ECHR lays down the substance of a fair trial when it states that in the determination of his civil rights and obligations or of any criminal charge against him, everyone is entitled to a fair and public hearing within a reasonable time by an independent and impartial tribunal established by law. The right to a fair trial is particularly prominent in the ECHR, both because of the importance of the right and the great number of applications and jurisprudence is has attracted.[2]

The statutory guarantees of a fair criminal procedure examined by the Constitutional Court of Hungary (and analyzed in detail in this paper) are regulated by Act XIX of 1998 on criminal proceedings (Code of Criminal Procedure) till 30 June 1998,[3] but the introductory provisions of Act XXXIII of 1896 on the Penal Procedure already provided for the right to a fair trial.[4] The constitutional requirement of fair trial was formulated by Article 57(1) of the former Constitution, which was in force until 31 December 2011. It stated that

> "Everyone is equal before the law and has the right to have the accusations brought against him, as well as his rights and duties in legal proceedings, judged in a just, public trial by an independent and impartial court established by law."

As regards the substantive content of the constitutional provision of the fair trial, Article XXVIII(1) of the Fundamental Law of Hungary that entered into force on January 1, 2012, is identical to Article 57(1) of the former Constitution. It stipulates that

---

2   David Harris *et al., Harris, O'Boyle and Warwick: Law of the European Court of Human Rights*, Oxford University Press, Oxford, 2014, p. 370.

3   The New Code of Criminal Procedure (Act XC of 2017) entered into force on 1 July 2018. The Constitutional Court has no case-law concerning the new Code yet, and for this reason in this paper I examine the case-law concerning the former Code of Criminal Procedure (Act XIX of 1998).

4   Nándor Bernolák, *A bűnvádi perrendtartás és novellái*, Büntetőjogi Törvénytár, Budapest, 1928, pp. VII-VIII.

"Everyone shall have the right to have any charge against him or her, or his or her rights and obligations in any litigation, adjudicated within a reasonable time in a fair and public trial by an independent and impartial court established by an act."

According to the scholarly approach cited above, in case of the former Constitution, the source of the right to a fair trial was the right to human dignity and the right is closely connected to the right to equal treatment. Yet from this right flow several other requirements that are to be applied not only in the judicial process, but in other type of procedures as well.[5]

The Constitutional Court summarized in its Decision No. 6/1998. (III. 1.) AB[6] the main elements of the right to fair trial. Based on the relevant international documents – in particular, the ECHR – the Constitutional Court elaborated an open-ended list, because the fair trial concept also contains further elements, such as the equality of arms that was not included in the text of the ECHR. This solution is similar to the approach followed by the ECtHR, because in contrast with other guarantees, the right to a fair hearing provides an opportunity for adding other particular rights not listed in Article 6 ECHR that are considered to be essential to a fair hearing.[7]

The relevant excerpts of the Fundamental Law and the former Constitution seem to be identical. In my opinion that, however, there is an enormous change in regulation and the difference can be discerned from the substance of the right to a fair trial. This change arises on the one hand, from the spirit of the Fundamental Law and, on the other hand, the shift of emphasis brought about by the legal institution of constitutional complaint. The jurisprudence of the Constitutional Court also shows that the assessment of the right to a fair hearing within a reasonable time – as an element of a right to a fair trial – is particularly different from the former concept of the right.

For the first time after the entry into force of the Fundamental Law, the Constitutional Court compared in its decision the content of the relevant provisions of the former Constitution and the Fundamental Law.[8] The result of this comparison was that there was no obstacle to the applicability of the arguments and findings developed in earlier Constitutional Court decisions. Consequently, the Constitutional Court considered the former constitutional jurisprudence elaborated in connection with the fundamental right to a fair trial to be applicable also for future cases.

---

5   Nóra Chronowski *et al., Magyar alkotmányjog III. Alapjogok*, Dialóg Campus, Budapest-Pécs, 2008, p. 270.
6   Decision No. 6/1998. (III. 1.) AB, ABH 1998, 91.
7   Harris *et al.* 2014, p. 409.
8   Decision No. 7/2013. (III. 1.) AB, Reasoning [24].

Following the Fourth Amendment of the Fundamental Law (25 March 2013) – which repealed the Constitutional Court decisions rendered prior to the entry into force of the Fundamental Law – with respect to the aspects laid down in Decision No. 13/2013. (VI. 7.) AB in connection with the applicability of the former Constitutional Court's decisions, the Constitutional Court re-examined whether the case-law related to the right to a fair trial could be applied in future. As a result of its assessment the Constitutional Court found – in its Decision No. 7/2013. (III. 1.) AB – that there is still no obstacle to the rely on the earlier jurisprudence of the Constitutional Court in relation to the fundamental right to a fair trial.[9] The later Constitutional Court decisions connected to Article XXVIII(1) of the Fundamental Law were upheld in this spirit.

The Parliament has placed the right to a fair trial among judicial procedural guarantees regulated by Article XXVIII of the Fundamental Law. A fair procedure as a requirement, however, is set forth under Article XXIV(1) of the Fundamental Law. This latter provision explicitly sets out the requirement of fairness in respect of public administrative procedures. Meanwhile, in respect of court proceedings, the procedural guarantee enshrined in Article XXVIII(1) of the Fundamental Law is the correct reference. When it comes to criminal proceedings, it is worth noting, that the right to a fair trial is not the only provision of Article XXVIII that the Constitutional Court typically examines. Other paragraphs of Article XXVIII provide for other procedural safeguards in such proceedings. These procedural guarantees are *(i)* the presumptions of innocence [Article XXVIII(2)]; *(ii)* the right to defence [Article XXVIII(3)]; *(iii)* the principle of the *nullum crimen sine lege* and *nulla poena sine lege* [Article XXVIII(4)]; *(iv)* the *ne bis in idem* principle [Article XXVIII(6)]; *(v)* the right to legal remedy [Article XXVIII(7)].

The fairness of proceedings in the ordinary sense also includes the enforcement of the judicial procedural guarantees as referred to in Article XXVIII(2) to (7) of the Fundamental Law, fulfilling the requirements set out in Article XXVIII(1) on the right to a fair trial. The significant difference is that while the procedural guarantees set out in paragraphs 2 to 7 are examined by the Constitutional Court on the basis of the general rule of necessity and proportionality, the requirement under paragraph 1 requires a specific assessment.

In the jurisprudence of the Constitutional Court the right to a fair trial is an absolute right over which no other fundamental right or constitutional purpose can be considered, since it is itself the result of discretion and as such, the right to a fair trial cannot be restricted. However, it is possible to examine within the meaning of fair proceedings the necessity and proportionality of restrictions in respect of certain partial rights pertaining to the right to a fair trial. Partial rights can be restricted, which together guarantee the fairness of the procedure in their entirety.

---

9   *See e.g.* Decision No. 8/2015. (IV. 17.) AB, Reasoning [57].

The content of the right to a fair trial was formulated by the Decision No. 6/1998. (III. 1.) AB and these elements were confirmed by the Constitutional Court later in a number of decisions.[10] By interpreting Article XXVIII(1) of the Fundamental Law, the partial rights pertaining to the right to fair trial could be formulated. According to the jurisprudence of the Constitutional Court, these are the following: *(i)* the right of access to court; *(ii)* the fairness of the hearing; *(iii)* the requirement of a public hearing and the public announcement of the judicial decision; *(iv)* the court established by law; *(v)* the requirement of judicial independence and impartiality; *(vi)* the requirement that the decision made within reasonable time. *(vii)* The rule is *de facto* not set, but according to the interpretation of the Constitutional Court, it is part of a fair trial to ensure the equality of arms in the proceedings.[11] *(viii)* According to the practice of the Constitutional Court, the right to the reasoned judicial decision must also be regarded as a part of the right to a fair trial.[12]

The Constitutional Court has found in Decision No. 7/2013. (III. 1.) AB that there was no obstacle to applying the arguments and findings laid down in earlier decisions regarding the right to a fair trial, therefore, the Constitutional Court considers them to be applicable also in future cases involving the right to a fair trial. In accordance with its jurisprudence based on the provisions of Article 24(2)(d) and 27 of the Fundamental Law, the Constitutional Court expressly stated that the constitutional requirements arising from the right to a fair trial, as elaborated in its earlier practice, not only flow from the regulatory environment, but also from the individual judgments.[13]

My opinion is that in these cases, when a judicial decision itself is assessed and the final decision can be annulled, the Constitutional Court should exercise this right with particular care and examine whether the petitioner's claim has a relevance from the perspective of fundamental rights. If so, it must be assessed whether the judicial decision constitutes such a serious violation of this right that it can justify the annulment of the judicial decision under scrutiny. Procedural violations emerging in judicial proceedings, may, by way of exception, be of fundamental right nature and this circumstance raises the possibility of a violation of the right to a fair hearing.

The statistical data[14] provided by the Constitutional Court and compiled in Table 23.1 clearly shows the changes that have taken place in respect of references made to allegedly violated substantive provisions.

---

10   *See* Decision No. 5/1999. (III. 31.) AB, ABH 1999, 75; Decision No. 14/2002. (III. 20.) AB, ABH 2002, 101, 108; Decision No. 15/2002. (III. 29.) AB, ABH 2002, 116, 118-120; Decision No. 35/2002. (VII. 19.) AB, ABH 2002, 199, 211.
11   Decision No. 8/2015. (IV. 17.) AB, Reasoning [63].
12   Decision No. 7/2013. (III. 1.) AB, Reasoning [34].
13   Decision No. 7/2013. (III. 1.) AB, Reasoning [27].
14   *See* https://hunconcourt.hu/statistics/.

Years	Article B(1) in complaints	Article XXVIII(1) in complaints
2012	294	164
2013	112	117
2014	460	563
2015	1426	1566
2016	288	571
2017	224	1171
2018	157	436
Total	2961	4588

From the data it can be gleaned that, while in 2012 the reference to Article B(1) in constitutional complaints far exceeded references to Article XXVIII(1) of the Fundamental Law, in 2014 references to the violation of the right to a fair trial were much more frequent and in the 2017 the number of references to Article XXVIII(1) was five times more than the number of references made to Article B(1). In my view, this shows that the concept of the right to a fair trial is consolidated and that the content of this fundamental right is consistently applied by the judges and the citizens seeking redress.

It is also worth reviewing how many times further paragraphs of Article XXVIII of the Fundamental Law have been referred to in comparison with Article XXVIII(1) since the Fundamental Law entered into force.

Years	Article XXVIII(2) in complaints	Article XXVIII(3) in complaints	Article XXVIII(4) in complaints	Article XXVIII(5) in complaints	Article XXVIII(6) in complaints	Article XXVIII(7) in complaints
2012	13	16	4	0	1	135
2013	7	7	5	0	0	83
2014	14	14	7	3	3	384
2015	19	15	9	0	0	360
2016	38	14	18	2	5	281
2017	27	35	17	1	7	288
2018	20	16	15	2	4	237
Total	**138**	**117**	**76**	**8**	**20**	**1768**

The statistics provided by the Constitutional Court show that most of the constitutional complaints referred to Article XXVIII(7) of the Fundamental Law, which stipulates the right to a legal remedy. This significantly exceeds the number of references to other fundamental rights, such as the right to defence or the presumption of innocence, but still remains firmly under the number of references to the Article XXVIII(1) of the Fundamental Law, which guarantees the right to a fair trial.

23.3   Obligation to Adjudicate within a Reasonable Time

I would like to highlight and explain in detail one case from among a number of the petitions based on a violation of the right to a fair trial and the related constitutional proceedings and decisions. Decision No. 2/2017. (II. 10) AB is of great importance in the practice of the Constitutional Court for the purpose of enforcing the obligation to adjudicate within a reasonable period of time.

The Fundamental Law defines explicitly the right to examine everyone's case within a reasonable time in the meaning of Article XXVIII(1), contrary to Article 57(1) of the former Constitution. Respecting to it the Constitutional Court has held that the right to adjudicate the dispute within a reasonable time is guaranteed by the Fundamental Law, the violation of which constitutes grounds for submitting a constitutional complaint.[15]

Following the entry into force of the Fundamental Law, several complainants have pleaded in their constitutional complaint the delay in the litigation and therefore the violation of their right to adjudicate within a reasonable time. The Constitutional Court mostly rejected complaints based on the breach of these fundamental rights, for example, because of the lack of exhaustion of judicial remedy or lack of competence.[16] However, the Constitutional Court also dealt with well-founded substantive considerations in breach of that partial right of the right to fair trial. In the specific case the prolongation of the main proceedings was largely due to objective reasons independent of the proceedings bodies.[17]

In Decision No. 3024/2016. (II. 23.) AB the Constitutional Court established that it could not effectively perform its fundamental duty as the main body for the protection of the Fundamental Law in respect of the right to a fair trial within a reasonable time. There is no legal consequence available to the Constitutional Court which could be used to remedy the injury occurred.[18] However, in its decisions, the Constitutional Court has usually drawn attention to the fact that the complainant may have a specific claim for damages against the court concerned to enforce his right to a fair trial and to the disposal of his case within a reasonable time.[19]

In its most recent Decision No. 2/2017. (II. 10.) AB on the requirement of deciding the case within a reasonable time the Constitutional Court laid down a constitutional

---

15   *Cf.* Order No. 3174/2013. (IX. 17.) AB, Reasoning [18].
16   Order No. 3309/2012. (XI. 12.) AB, Reasoning [5], Order No. 3174/2013. (IX. 17.) AB, Reasoning [20]-[21].
17   Decision No. 3115/2013. (VI. 4.) AB, Reasoning [30].
18   Decision No. 3024/2016. (II. 23.) AB, Reasoning [18].
19   *See e.g.* Order No. 3174/2013. (IX. 17.) AB, Reasoning [20]-[21].

requirement in connection with the application of Section 258(3)(e) of the Code of Criminal Procedure. Accordingly, when applying the provision referred to above, the constitutional requirement stemming from Article XXVIII(1) of the Fundamental Law is that in case the court decreases the sentence due to the prolongation of the proceedings, the reasoning of its decision should determine the fact that proceedings were of extensive length, and it should provide for the mitigation of the punishment and the degree of penal relief.

According to the reasoning of this decision the right to examine the case within a reasonable time is a partial right pertaining to the right to a fair trial. Consequently, when examining this partial right, a constitutional approach must be applied in which the whole of the court proceedings and certain parts of the court proceedings must be assessed simultaneously in order to determine the court's intention to decide the case within a reasonable time.

If it can be inferred from the case and the trial history that the court did not keep in mind the reasonable time requirement, then violation may be found irrespective of the length of the criminal proceedings and of the inactivity of the court concerned.

Accordingly, short-term criminal proceedings may also be extended in case the facts of the criminal proceedings cannot be established, notwithstanding the efforts made by the courts to take the decision as quickly as possible with due regard to the requirements of fair trial. The duration of criminal proceedings, even if the law on criminal proceedings is complied with, violates Article XXVIII(1) of the Fundamental Law if there are unjustified inactive periods attributable to the courts, and the excessive length of the criminal prosecution cannot be justified by the complexity of the case.

According to the standpoint of the Constitutional Court, however, the violation of the Fundamental Law due to the prolonged criminal proceedings can be remedied in the framework of the imposition of the sentence.

If it can be inferred from the reasoning of the judgment that the court has imposed a lenient penalty or measure because of the length of proceedings, the defendant may not refer to the breach of the right to be heard within a reasonable time. In order to be clearly established by the defendant that the purpose of mitigating the sentence was to remedy the violation manifested in the excessive length of the procedure, the Constitutional Court considered it necessary to lay down the above constitutional requirement related to Section 258(3)(e) of the Code of Criminal Procedure.[20] The right to a fair hearing stipulated in Article XXVIII(1) of the Fundamental Law is not covered by the right of defence [Article XXVIII(3)], but the right of defence in criminal proceedings is the cornerstone of a fair trial.

---

20   Decision No. 2/2017. (II. 10.) AB, Reasoning [82], [88], [99]-[100].

23.4   RIGHT TO EFFECTIVE DEFENCE

The Constitutional Court established in its Decision No. 15/2016. (IX. 21.) AB the unconstitutionality of Section 344(1) of the Code of Criminal Procedure and the provision was annulled with *pro futuro* effect. The annulment of the provision was based on an infringement of the right of the defence.

In the concrete case, the Constitutional Court examined whether the provision governing the bearing of criminal costs regulated in Section 344(1) of the Code of Criminal Procedure restricts the right to defence of the defendant in a proceeding conducted upon the initiative of a substitute private accuser. Pursuant to Article XXVIII(3) of the Fundamental Law, "a person subject to criminal proceedings shall have the right to defence at all stages of the proceedings. [...]." The Constitutional Court stated in its Decision No. 8/2013. (III. 1.) AB that

> "in the course of interpreting the right to defence laid down in Article XXVIII(3) of the Fundamental Law the Court considers those constitutional provisions on defence to be applicable, which were elaborated in its former jurisprudence. [...] At the very beginning of its activity, the Constitutional Court ruled that [...] the criminal procedure's basic constitutional principle is the right to defence that is manifested in numerous detailed rules governing the proceedings. The right to defence is enforced through those rights of a person subject to criminal proceedings and in those obligations of the public authorities, which ensure that they are aware of the criminal charge against them, to present their point of view, to raise their arguments against the charge, to submit their observations and suggestions concerning the activities of the authorities, as well as assisting the defendant. The essence of the right to defence is captured by the procedural rights of defence and the obligations of public authorities which provided for the defence."[21]

It follows from the right to defence that the method of defence, its strategy and tactics – in compliance with legal provisions – are determined by the interest of the defendant. The free choice of defence includes, in the absence of mandatory protection, the waiver of the right of defence, but also the defence of the defendant in person or by way of an attorney or both. In certain cases defined by law, defence provided by an attorney is mandatory. However, the defendant may decide at his own discretion whether to accept the counsel

---

21   Decision No. 25/1991. (V. 18.) AB, ABH 1991, 414, 415. For the case-law after 2012 *see* Decision No. 8/2013. (III. 1.) AB, Reasoning [25]-[26].

appointed by the authority or choose another advocate, provided that they have the necessary financial means.

The detailed rules of criminal proceedings relating to criminal charges are therefore interconnected with the right to an effective defence, since the regulation of the bearing of criminal costs creates the financial condition for exercising that right. Consequently, the principle of the right to defence should also be manifested in the detailed rules governing the enforcement of criminal charges. The expenses and the fee incurred by the legal representative of the defendant are criminal costs, even if such costs had not been advanced by the state.[22] In the event of an acquittal, the fee and verified expenses of the officially appointed counsel for the defence is paid by the state.[23] However, the regulation is controversial with regard to the fee and the expenses of the authorized defence attorney.

Based on a comparison of the relevant provisions of the Code of Criminal Procedure, it was established that the fee and the expenses of the authorized defence attorney were to be reimbursed only in the proceedings initiated by the prosecutor in case the state lost the lawsuit.

According to the general rule, pursuant to Section 344(1) of the Code of Criminal Procedure, if the defendant was dismissed or the proceedings were terminated, the substitute private accuser shall bear the costs of the criminal charges regulated in Section 74(1) since they represented the charge. However, Section 74(1) did not regulate the fee and expenses of the authorized defence attorney. It merely refers to the costs and fee of the officially appointed counsel for the defence. Section 339(3) of the Code of Criminal Procedure states, however, that in case the charge is represented by the prosecutor and the court dismisses the defendant or terminates the proceedings because of the withdrawal of the charge, the state will pay the costs incurred by the accused. This will take place within thirty days from the date on which the decision becomes final, including the payment of their counsel's costs that had not been advanced during the procedure. From the comparison of these provisions, it can be stated that in case the substitute private accuser is unsuccessful, the fee and the expenses of the authorized defence attorney must be borne by the defendant. Sections 74(1) and 339(3) of the Code of Criminal Procedure excluded the authorized counsel for the defence's fees and expenses from the scope of criminal costs from reimbursement when the substitute private accuser does not prevail. This fact significantly restricted the defendant's right of defence in these kinds of criminal proceedings. The contested provision restricted the defendant's right to defence because of the fact that the choice of counsel for the defence as a fundamental right was subject to the financial capacity of the defendant in a proceeding where the nature of the proceedings necessitates an increased need for legal expertise and effective defence.

---

22   Section 74(1)(c) of the Code of Criminal Procedure.
23   Id. Section 74(3)(c).

The Constitutional Court has not been able to uncover any constitutional purpose that would justify the necessity of the restriction: it was not justified by the related legislative environment or the related legislative activity.

On the basis of the above connection between the enforcement of the right of defence and the rules governing the bearing of criminal costs, the Constitutional Court concluded that the provision in Section 344(1) of the Code of Criminal Procedure unnecessarily restricts the defendant's right to defence regulated in Article XXVIII(3) of the Fundamental Law. Due to the unnecessary restriction, the Constitutional Court did not continue with the assessment of the proportionality issue. The Constitutional Court held that, for the reasons detailed above, Section 344(1) of the Code of Criminal Procedure was contrary to Article XXVIII(3) of the Fundamental Law. It therefore decided to annul the contested legal provision.

After the announcement of the Constitutional Court's above described decision on 21 September 2016, the Minister of Justice responsible for drafting criminal laws presented the amendment to the Code of Criminal Procedure and the Parliament enacted and promulgated Act CX of 2016 on 4 November 2016 which modified the rules governing criminal costs. The amendment prompted by the Constitutional Court decision was drafted by the Minister of Justice in a way as to introduce the same rules for the prosecution by the state, the private prosecution procedure and the substitute private prosecution procedure in the Code of Criminal Procedure. Therefore, the Parliament amended Sections 344(1) and 514(6) which entered into force on 1 January 2017. The Parliament accepted the position of the Minister that the regulation is controversial and the problem persists in private prosecution procedure, too. The judicial initiative submitted in relation to the criminal costs thus led to the amendment of several provisions of the Code within a short period of time. The new Code of Criminal Procedure, which entered into force on 1 July 2018, already contains the new provisions cited above.[24]

---

24   Act XC of 2017 on Criminal Procedure, Sections 782 and 813.

24 CONTENT NEUTRALITY AND THE LIMITATION OF FREE SPEECH

The Relevance of an American Principle in the Case-Law of the Constitutional Court of Hungary

Bernát Török[*]

Keywords

Constitutional Court of Hungary, limitation of free speech, freedom of expression, content neutrality, external boundary

Abstract

Content neutrality is arguably the most frequently mentioned principle of free speech doctrine both in legal theory and in legal practice. While it is well-known how important it is in the jurisprudence of the US, it generally remains obscure whether content neutrality is of true relevance for European jurisdictions. This article argues that the Hungarian doctrine of freedom of expression urges us to answer affirmatively. The case-law of the Hungarian Constitutional Court from the last three decades clearly demonstrates that although along with serious challenges to be responded to, content neutrality is a fundamental element of constitutional adjudication in the Hungarian doctrine. With its key concept of 'external boundaries of free speech', the Constitutional Court builds on the principle that restrictions should not be based on the fact that the content of speech is unacceptable, unworthy or wrong, and limitation on speech should be justified not by referring to its content alone but by referring to its context. After exploring the relevant case-law of the Constitutional Court and identifying the challenges this principle is facing in Hungarian doctrine, this article aims to construe valid theses of content neutrality in Hungarian law.

24.1 INTRODUCTION

It became a commonplace to say, even among international experts of freedom of expression, that while the US free speech doctrine is built on the strict rule of content neutrality,

---

[*] Bernát Török: associate professor, National University of Public Service, Budapest.

this principle is not of relevance at all in European jurisdictions. The importance of the distinction between content-based and content-neutral interventions, the argument follows, is simply a result of an optical illusion for European eyes due to the predominance of US literature, and European legal theory is actually built on different foundations. As it is usually the case with commonplaces: although it speaks about a real phenomenon to some extent, we can clearly demonstrate that it is a misleading oversimplification of the subject – at least in terms of the Hungarian jurisdiction.[1]

The truth is that an in-depth study of the principle of content neutrality is not only helpful but simply unavoidable when clarifying the Hungarian free speech doctrine. There are several reasons for this. Above all, of course, the case-law of the Hungarian Constitutional Court itself, according to which the content neutrality of restricting communication is a fundamental element in constitutional adjudication. We will see that the issue in question is just the area where the Hungarian practice has incorporated more from the US approach. It is certainly still not to say that the Hungarian doctrine would construct the practice of freedom of expression in the same way as it has been done overseas, but it is absolutely clear that the Hungarian argument has introduced a test focusing on content neutrality more, than the European average.

It is a completely separate issue that those who criticize the thesis of content neutrality are quite right that in the Hungarian case-law it is faced with powerful challenges. According to the concurring opinion written to Decision No. 95/2008. (VII. 3.) AB, this thesis in the Hungarian practice is "objectionable from a methodological point of view" and resulted in a 'distortion' in the decisions of the Constitutional Court.[2] The concurring opinion rightly points out that

> "besides decisions based on the principle of content neutrality, there are also decisions in the relevant case-law of the Constitutional Court that follow the principle of content-based restriction".[3]

However, the fact that it is challenging to clarify the exact meaning of content neutrality in the Hungarian doctrine does not mean that the principle is not of high relevance. The academic discussion overseas is encouraging in this regard: even in the US where content neutrality is without doubt the starting point for all free speech assessment, the correct place of this principle is strongly debated. It suffices to refer to some telling conclusions in literature. Geoffrey Stone argues that the hardest issue in contemporary free speech

---

1   This article is an adapted version of a book chapter on the subject published in Hungarian: Bernát Török, *Szabadon szólni, demokráciában. A szólásszabadság magyar doktrínája az amerikai jogirodalom tükrében*, HVG-ORAC, Budapest, 2018.

2   Decision No. 95/2008. (VII. 3.) AB, Concurring opinion by Miklós Lévay, I.1., ABH 2008, 804.

3   Id. I.2., ABH 2008, 804.

doctrine is the difference between content-based and content-neutral restrictions.[4] Steven Shiffrin sets out as one of the first honest starting points for building the right methodology of free speech that while the doctrine teaches that freedom of speech means that the government has no power to restrict expression because of its content, "any assessment of the legal regulation of communication must begin with the recognition that government does have power to restrict expression because of its content."[5] And then it is not surprising that some, such as Martin Redish, find it timely to rethink and, as a result, get rid of the approach based on content neutrality.[6]

Because of these challenges, trying to find the true meaning and place of the principle mentioned consistently also in Hungarian case-law and legal literature is a matter of urgency. This article first explores the relevant case-law of the Constitutional Court, then construes the findings in light of the most influential literature, and finally enumerates the valid theses of content neutrality in Hungarian law.

24.2   THE CONCEPT OF 'EXTERNAL BOUNDARY'

That the arguments regarding content neutrality of restrictions in the Hungarian practice of freedom of expression would play an important role seem predictable from the outset. Decision No. 30/1992. (V. 26.) AB stated as the fundamental thesis of distinguishing between incitement to hatred and group defamation that the right to free expression protects opinions regardless of their value and veracity. According to the classic Hungarian formulation of content neutrality,

> "freedom of expression has only external boundaries; as long as it does not interfere with such a constitutionally drawn external boundary, the opportunity and fact of expression itself is protected, irrespective of its content".[7]

---

4   Geoffrey R. Stone, 'Content Regulation and the First Amendment', *William and Mary Law Review*, Vol. 25, Issue 2, 1983-1984, p. 189.

5   Steven Shiffrin, 'Defamatory Non-Media Speech and First Amendment Methodology', *UCLA Law Review*, Vol. 25, Issue 5, 1977-1978, p. 955.

6   Martin H. Redish, 'The Content Distinction in First Amendment Analysis', *Stanford Law Review*, Vol. 34, Issue 1, 1981-1982, p. 114. For a comprehensive overview of Redish's theory, *see* Martin H. Redish, *The Adversary First Amendment. Free Expression and Foundations of American Democracy*, Cambridge University Press, 2013. There are others joining Redish in his radical conclusion, *see* R. George Wright, 'Content-based and Content-neutral Regulation of Speech: The Limitations of a Common Distinction', *University of Miami Law Review*, Vol. 60, Issue 3, 2005-2006, p. 364.

7   Decision No. 30/1992. (V. 26.) AB, Reasoning V.3., ABH 1992, 167, 179.

According to this logic, the Constitutional Court's decision stated that while incitement to hatred collides with the external boundaries of freedom of expression, such an external boundary could no longer be drawn constitutionally when it comes to group defamation.

What seemed only very likely that time, later became obvious: the above arguments have turned into the central consideration of the Hungarian doctrine of free speech, making content neutrality a crucial element in constitutional adjudication. First, the thesis of the 1992 reasoning quoted above became a well-established formula of subsequent decisions: to all intents and purposes, we do not find an important decision that would not refer to it in some form.[8] Second, it is obviously not just a revered reference, since the interpretations of the Constitutional Court analyzing freedom of expression and freedom of the press in a more encompassing manner, almost without exception add a novel twist to the previous passages. For example, according to Decision No. 57/2001. (XII. 5.) AB, freedom of expression means "the opportunity of communication that does not depend on its content or its potentially harmful, offensive nature".[9] Decision No. 95/2008. (VII. 3.) AB argues that "a constitutional democracy does not repress extremist voices simply because of their content."[10] In the formulation of Decision No. 7/2014. (III. 7.) AB, the right to individual expression is unthinkable without "anyone having the freedom to disclose his or her opinions and thoughts to others without any restriction of content",[11] while Decision No. 13/2014. (IV. 18.) AB states, in the context of political speech, that this freedom applies to all members of the political community, regardless of content.[12] In addition, in the field of press freedom, Decision No. 19/2014. (V. 30.) AB summarizes previous references as

> "the range of protection for the freedom of the press is independent of the content of the opinion; it does not protect the content of the opinion but the process and means of communicating opinions".[13]

All these examples show that the content-related assessment of restrictions is a significant element of Hungarian doctrine. The most important point in the chain of decisions in this respect is the requirement of 'external boundaries' to restricting freedom of expression and the press. In practice, the method of separating content-based and content-neutral restrictions in domestic practice is to identify the external boundary: in the case of a con-

---

8   Examples of literal reference are included, *inter alia* in Decisions No. 36/1994. (VI. 24.) AB, 18/2004. (V. 25.) AB, 75/2008. (V. 29.) AB, 95/2008. (VII. 3.) AB, 96/2008. (VII. 3.) AB.
9   Decision No. 57/2001. (XII. 5.) AB, Reasoning II.6., ABH 2001, 484, 492.
10   Decision No. 95/2008. (VII. 3.) AB, Reasoning III.3.4., ABH 2008, 782, 789.
11   Decision No. 7/2014. (III. 7.) AB, Reasoning [39].
12   Decision No. 13/2014. (IV. 18.) AB, Reasoning [25].
13   Decision No. 19/2014. (V. 30.) AB, Reasoning [55].

stitutionally identifiable external boundary, the restriction of free speech can be justified, while in the absence of this, the restriction cannot be justified. Therefore, in order to assess the relevance of content neutrality in Hungary, we first have to look at what the term 'external boundary' covers.

24.3   Limits Truly Independent of Content

First of all, it is worth starting the clarification of Hungarian doctrine by examining what is not covered by this term. We must admit that a significant part of our 'content neutrality' would clearly be considered a strict limitation of content overseas. Finding the external boundary in the most important cases of Hungarian case-law often arises in a context that the consensus of the US discourse on free speech treats as an area of content-based interventions. While in Hungary the standard of incitement to hatred, focusing on the foreseeable consequences of speech, is the textbook example for the external boundary; the more stringent clear and present danger test of the US case-law is the constitutional exception to otherwise prohibited content-based interventions.[14] The Hungarian concept of content neutrality thus unsurprisingly differs from its classic definitions in US literature. It is clear that the Hungarian test for incitement meets Ely's criteria is triggered only in case of an audience that understands the language of the speaker,[15] and it is also obviously not independent of the communicative effect of speech, already considered by the majority of theorists as the most important aspect of content-based restrictions.[16] Thus, the observer of Hungarian legal practice must admit that, in many cases, the external boundary is not a standard that can be determined irrespective of the content or communicative effect of speech. When the domestic doctrine separates internal/content-based limitations and external/content-neutral limitations from each other, it in fact calls for a careful consideration of other aspects.

It does not follow, of course, that the concept of 'external boundary' would not include, in the first place, restrictions that are truly independent of the content of speech. Yet analysis of the Hungarian practice does not pay much attention to this aspect, since petitioners have not turned to the Constitutional Court with such cases, so the concept of the external boundary has attracted more attention where its interpretation causes a more

---

14   The clear and present danger test is also considered a content-based restriction in the freedom of expression handbooks. *Cf. e.g.* Geoffrey R. Stone *et al., The First Amendment (Fifth Edition),* Wolters Kluwer, New York, 2016.

15   John Hart Ely, 'Flag Desecration: The Case Study of Categorization and Balancing in the First Amendment Analysis', *Harvard Law Review,* Vol. 88, Issue 7, 1975, pp. 1495-1498.

16   Laurence H. Tribe, *American Constitutional Law,* The Foundation Press, Mineola, NY, 1978, § 12-2, § 12-3, § 12-20; Stone 1983-1984.

serious headache. Nevertheless, we can find two important decisions, which for us are now sufficient examples of restrictions that do not refer to content at all.

Decision No. 75/2008. (V. 29.) AB examined the law of assembly that required prior notification of public gatherings, allowing the police to prohibit the event if it would seriously jeopardize the smooth functioning of representative bodies or courts, or disproportionately compromise the order of traffic.[17] Confirming a previous decision of the bench,[18] it found that this form of notification obligation – as a necessary solution for the police in order to perform public order related tasks – is not unconstitutional. According to the central rationale of the reasoning, the statutory system mandating prior notice of assemblies is based on content neutrality, and considerations of the content of the expression presented at the event may not be taken into account by the authorities.[19] Given the fact that the reference to the functioning of both the representative bodies or the courts and the order of traffic completely lack aspects of the content or impact of expressions to be articulated at the assembly, the restriction in question is a clear example of an external boundary independent of content. The Constitutional Court has subsequently remained consistent with the interpretation of the law on the passages of the Act on Assembly, and in Decision No. 14/2016. (VII. 18.) AB, in terms of the merits of the case, annulled the court decision extending the grounds for a preliminary prohibition.

Although the reasoning of the constitutional justices in our other example did not touch upon the issue of content neutrality, we may still reveal interesting aspects from the case decided in Decision No. 3208/2013. (XI. 18.) AB. The regulation challenged by the petitioners amended the rules on the placement of public billboards, allegedly aiming to improve road safety. In this amendment[20] we typically find provisions that restrict this channel of communication, irrespective of the content of the message placed on the advertising media: the legislator *(i)* explicitly forbids the placement of advertisements on the road's structures, accessories, public lighting, electricity and telephone columns, and *(ii)* the exceptions for sections outside residential areas have been reduced: earlier it was possible to place, beyond a certain distance from the road, any advertising sign; after the amendment that exemption applied only to advertising boards not exceeding 4 m^2. The Constitutional Court's decision identified the amendment as a rule only affecting commercial advertisements. With this assessment the Constitutional Court failed to put the case into the correct constitutional context: the legislation in question reduced the room for communication to a wider extent than for commercial ads, thereby also affecting electoral campaigning. However, if we look at the case with this correction, we can identify one of

---

17   Former Act III of 1989 on the right to assembly (was in force till 2018, replaced by Act LV of 2018), Sections 6(8) and 8(1).

18   Decision No. 55/2001. (XI. 29.) AB, ABH 2001, 442.

19   Decision No. 75/2008. (V. 29.) AB, Reasoning IV.5.2., ABH 2008, 651, 667.

20   Act CLXXII of 2010 on Amendments to Certain Traffic Laws.

the newest content-neutral restrictions in the regulations examined in recent years, irre-spective of the messages conveyed.

24.4   THE CONTENT AND THE MANNER OF SPEECH

Owing to its special character and significance, it is worth discussing a typical attempt of the Hungarian legal practice to consider certain restrictions of speech as content-neutral on the basis that they only refer to the form and manner of expression. Of course, it is not just a domestic invention to distinguish, and evaluate less strictly, restrictions on the manner of expression. Indeed, in the US Supreme Court, for example, since the 1940s,[21] there has been the category of time, place and manner standards as the main category of content-neutral limits. However, in the practice of the Constitutional Court, this attempt has led to extremely confusing results.

Restrictions on the manner and form of speech in a narrower range, where they are presented without reference to the content of communication, may indeed be distinguished from content-based interventions.[22] In this context, the manner of expression is interpreted as a means, channel, and medium of communication. Such restrictions include the above-mentioned cases of content-independent intervention, rules concerning the traffic-dependent location of assemblies, or the physical carriers of public messages (billboards), where clear boundaries can be drawn between different ways of expressions by means of communication platforms (such as street speakers *v.* national television channels). By way of further examples, this may include quiet laws in residential areas or provisions that enforce cleanliness of public spaces. Also, the Constitutional Court did not apply the strictest test to an otherwise public discourse, because the punishment for spraying private property "touched only on the appearance of communication alone in the outside world".[23]

However, the Hungarian practice typically calls for a distinctive aspect of 'manner', actually referring to the style and phrasing of communication. Decision No. 33/1998. (VI. 25.) AB examined the provision of the organizational and operating rules of the Local Government of the Municipality of Debrecen, according to which the General Assembly may impose a fine on its member who uses a term that is offensive to others or unworthy

---

21   *Cantwell v. Connecticut*, 310 U.S. 296, 304 (1940), *Cox v. New Hampshire*, 312 U.S. 569, 575 (1941).

22   In the US practice, the *Clark v. Community for Creative Non-Violence* case has outlined the test used until today, according to which, in order for a restriction to be included in this circle, it is first and foremost necessary to be justifiable without reference to the content. 468 U.S. 288, 293 (1984).

23   Decision No. 3132/2018. (IV. 19.) AB, Reasoning [32]. However, the statement of reasons for the decision emphasizes that the form in which the communication is published may not be limited by the fact that other means of communication were available (Reasoning [40]). It should be noted that examinations concerning the external appearance of the communication can easily lead us to the question of the scope of freedom of expression.

of the body. The Constitutional Court stated as a basis for its decision that a clear distinction should be made between the freedom of expression and the form of expression. While freedom of expression enjoys enhanced constitutional protection, the General Assembly, as an autonomous community, has the right to make restrictive provisions on how an opinion is presented, in order to guarantee the smooth functioning of the body. According to the Constitutional Court, the exclusion of expressions that are offensive to others or unworthy of the body is to ensure smooth operation.[24] Perceiving the difficulty of demarcation itself, the Constitutional Court added that although its decision was based on the separation of the right to expression and the form and manner in which that right is exercised, it does not mean that there is no relationship between the two: "In an extreme case, the manner in which the opinion is expressed may have a direct effect on the exercise of the human right to expression". If the local bylaw "keeps the manner of expression unreasonably strict", it would directly hinder the exercise of the right to freedom of expression.[25]

The same reasoning was used by the Constitutional Court in reviewing the disciplinary rules of the Parliament. Decisions No. 3206/2013. (XI. 18.) AB and No. 3207/2013. (XI. 18.) AB have examined the provisions of the House Rules, which foresee disciplinary measures for both committee meetings and the Plenary Session, if the speaking MP uses a term that is strikingly offensive to the prestige of the Parliament. The Constitutional Court confirmed what was explained 15 years earlier, stating that it is a limitation of the external representation and the manner of expression, in which the House Rules set the boundaries for ensuring the proper functioning of the body.[26]

It is worth mentioning that the reasoning of the Constitutional Court uses the term 'manner of expression' in the meaning of the relevant case-law of the ECtHR. The Strasbourg Court attributed importance to similar arguments in its blasphemy-related case-law. According to the thesis in the *Otto-Preminger-Institut v. Austria* judgment, although religious people are obliged to tolerate criticism and competing worldviews, the manner in which religious beliefs are opposed may raise the responsibility of the state to guarantee the right to peaceful enjoyment of the freedom of religion.[27]

The Constitutional Court (and the ECtHR) in essence argues that any content related to the political debate (critical or hostile to religions) may be expressed if it is uttered in a fair, non-controversial style, suitable for a dispute. However, we must see that this argument, which seeks to consider restrictions on the 'manner' of expression as content-neutral, confuses the evaluation of content-based and non-content elements. In these judgments,

---

24   The Constitutional Court annulled the qualifier "unfounded", since it perceived it as exaggerated.
25   Decision No. 33/1998. (VI. 25.) AB, Reasoning III.3., ABH 1998, 256, 261.
26   Decision No. 3206/2013. (XI. 18.) AB, Reasoning [24]-[26], and Decision No. 3207/2013. (XI. 18.) AB, Reasoning [22]-[24].
27   *Otto-Preminger-Institut v. Austria*, No. 13470/87, 20 September 1994, para. 49.

the Constitutional Court bases its assessment on non-existent distinctions. While the manner of expression as a means, channel, and medium of communication can be separated from the content of speech, the same cannot be said if it is understood as the style and phrasing of communication. The reasoning of the Constitutional Court takes the view that the content and the style of expression may be separated. It believes that if we limit only the form, the manner of expression, then the content may remain intact. Emphasizing the distinction between content and style presupposes that all statements may be expressed in an offensive or non-offensive manner without any substantive change of meaning. However, this cannot be generalized; in fact, typically the content of the opinion and the style of the expression are closely intertwined, and together form the expression of the opinion itself. Although the analogy is somewhat limp, it can be said that it is also difficult to defend artistic freedom claiming that everyone should be free to compose, but only the way that Mozart or Bartók did, because the rest would hurt our ears. A wide range of expressions are not harsh or even outrageous in order to insult others, but to express the views of the speaker in tune with his mood. The style of communication cannot be interpreted as anything other than the product of cultural patterns reflecting content, so their separation cannot be defended in logical terms.[28]

These examples support our doubts more than anything else: what else could be the content of the expression, if not the use of 'offensive, unworthy, inappropriate terms'? An in-depth examination of content-based restrictions cannot be avoided by attempting to pass off the regulation of style and phrasing as a content-neutral standard.

All in all, we can definitely state that the method based on the distinction between expression and its manner is not suited to justify the relevant aspects of free speech assessment, and, in particular, leads to a false result when referred to as a substantive element of content neutrality.

24.5   EXTERNAL BOUNDARIES NOT INDEPENDENT OF THE CONTENT

As mentioned earlier, content neutrality in the Hungarian jurisprudence, *i.e.* the concept of the external boundary, at the time of its conception, actually referred to restrictions not fully independent of the content of communication. Decision No. 30/1992. (V. 26.) AB identified a constitutional external boundary for incitement to hatred, but at the same time, as the majority view in the free speech literature shows, the clear and present danger-type tests are the most widely accepted examples of content-based limitations. These formulae obviously do not function independently of the content of the communication,

---

28   Robert C. Post, 'Cultural Heterogenity and Law: Pornography, Blasphemy, and the First Amendment', *California Law Review*, Vol. 76, Issue 2, 1988, p. 309.

because it is their very essence to examine the effect they cause, and the effect of a communicative act may not be evaluated regardless of the content of the communication. For example, in the case of the Hungarian standard of incitement, an aspect of content is that the extremist speech in question must have an impact on emotions. An expression of opinion influencing emotions – as opposed to persuading the mind – means appealing to instincts and emotions. Its mobilizing power is generally more serious and dangerous for people than the speech that tries to influence other people's thinking with a series of even demagogic arguments, obviously also having an emotional side-effect. Incitement directly stimulates visceral feelings and is therefore an emotional anteroom for violence. While this approach is clearly supportive to freedom of expression, since it is intended to narrow down the scope of intervention, it is undoubtedly of a content-based nature.

Initially, the analysis of incitement to hatred still harbored the opportunity for an interpretation that made the 'external' nature of the boundary visible. A standard focusing on the dangerous consequences of incitement inevitably draws attention to the specific external factors of the individual communicative situation. In addition to some of the content-components of the speech, the main emphasis of legal assessment is on the actual risks that can be identified where and when the speech is made. It can be said that separation from the content is facilitated by the fact that, in these cases, the harmfulness of the speech lies in the externally manifested consequences. The test of incitement therefore does not turn on the value or extremity of the communication in question, but on the actual dangerous circumstances of the speech. Interestingly, this relationship is most aptly described in Decision No. 165/2011. (XII. 21.) AB, which, by the way, as a decision examining media law provisions, typically uses standards that follow another logic. In one part of the reasoning, summarizing its practice on free speech and press freedom, the Constitutional Court concludes that the restriction of the freedom of the press primarily focuses on the intended effect rather than the content of the words.[29]

However, this initial interpretation was not followed by later practice, and the concept of the external boundary was also applied to an area that expanded beyond the manifest dangerous consequences of speech. The roots of this latter direction, by the way, can be traced in Decision No. 30/1992. (V. 26.) AB itself, which, while arguing for the unconstitutionality of group defamation, sees the absence of an external boundary in that it is not possible, or at least extremely uncertain, to identify the violation of another right – contrary to incitement where individual rights are threatened.[30] Following this, one of the striking lines of relying on an external boundary has been to conceive of such rights within the protection of the personality. According to the reasoning in Decision No. 36/1994. (VI. 24.) AB relating to the possibility of criticizing public figures, although freedom of

---

29   Decision No. 165/2011. (XII. 21.) AB, Reasoning V.2., ABH 2011, 478, 524.
30   Decision No. 30/1992. (V. 26.) AB, Reasoning V.3., ABH 1992, 167, 179.

expression extends to value judgements independently of the content (value, veracity, rationality) of the opinion, human dignity and reputation may be an external boundary even to value judgments.[31] It is a separate issue that personality protection tests are different in the public debate and beyond – but they function as an external boundary to freedom of opinion.

Later on, domestic case-law further widened the concept of external boundaries. It is not just the case that, over the years, decisions have been made that adopted rules which increasingly respond to 'intrinsic harms' instead of external consequences,[32] but also the Constitutional Court has adapted the formula itself to these interpretations. Decisions No. 3206/2013. (XI.18.) AB and No. 3207/2013. (XI. 18.) AB, following the logic and key words of Decision No. 33/1998. (VI. 25.) AB, rely on the external boundary understood in a wider sense, extending the protection, in addition to the protection of human dignity and good reputation, to the dignity of the Hungarian nation, and national, ethnic, racial and religious communities.[33] Decision No. 14/2016. (VII. 18.) AB, by making an important clarification of the term 'dignity of the communities', captures the external boundary of incitement to hatred, but at the same time refers to the protection of constitutional fundamental values. According to its reasoning, the issue to be considered on a case-by-case basis is whether the assembly performs a hate speech or whether it is against "the democratic rule of law, *i.e.* the existing constitutional order, the fundamental values of state organization".[34] It is noteworthy that, in the latter issue, the Constitutional Court also relies on the interpretation given by the ECtHR. Namely, on the basis of the prohibition of the abuse of rights, freedom of expression may not be invoked by those whose purpose is the introduction of a dictatorship and the abolition of the rights guaranteed by the Convention.

Based on the above, we can definitely draw a clear conclusion: the category ('external boundary') that can be used not only for the protection of personal rights but against communications contrary to the dignity of communities or constitutional values cannot be a suitable methods for separating content-based and content-neutral restrictions. The test of the external boundary, which has never been free from the evaluation of certain substantive elements of speech in domestic case-law, has become an overarching concept of the restriction of content. We have to ask the question: should we abandon this approach completely? Is content neutrality meaningless in the Hungarian concept of free speech? In the following, I argue that the answer is 'no' to both questions; moreover, and interestingly enough, the serious internal contradictions in the concept of the external boundary

---

31   Decision No. 36/1994. (VI. 24.) AB, Reasoning III.2., ABH 1994, 219, 230.

32   Robert C. Post, 'Blasphemy, the First Amendment and the Concept of Intrinsic Harm', *Tel Aviv University Studies in Law*, Vol. 8, 1988, pp. 293-325.

33   Decision No. 3206/2013. (XI. 18.) AB, Reasoning [24]-[25], and Decision No. 3207/2013. (XI. 18.) AB, Reasoning [23].

34   Decision No. 14/2016. (VII. 18.) AB, Reasoning [38]-[40] and [44].

may in some way help us explain the more complex reality. We can thus say that the appeal for content neutrality makes the most important aspects of the content-related analysis unavoidable, at the same time, we are not (nor have we ever been) locked into these aspects, which in turn can increase our sensitivity to further relevant circumstances.

24.6 Clarifying the Relevant Theses of Content Neutrality in Hungarian Law

Our investigation into the external boundary as a special, central category of restrictions on free speech revealed that the practice has, over time, put restrictions for the rights of others, for the dignity of certain communities, and for the protection of fundamental constitutional values in its conceptual framework. In the face of the breadth of these categories, one could not only conclude that the external boundary is not a precise test for separating content-based and content-neutral restrictions, but even that it lacks any serious aspects of content neutrality. I argue that this is not the case and that crucial considerations of the principle have not collapsed under the weight of the contradictions inherent in the 'external boundary' concept. At the same time, however, we need to clarify at what point it is worth going beyond the strict content test. In what follows, I will summarize those considerations laid down in the abovementioned decisions that may be understood as the valid theses of content neutrality in the Hungarian doctrine.

First of all, we have to start by saying that the above challenges to the protection of free speech in no way undermine the strength of the theorem that the scope of free speech covers all communication within the public dialogue, irrespective of their content.[35] The issue of inclusion in the scope cannot be made dependent on the content elements of the specific speech. Any speech that is part of the public dialogue is subject to freedom of expression, and its constitutional significance is ensured in this light. It is precisely declared in the reasoning of Decision No. 30/1992. (V. 26.) AB that freedom of expression does not *relate* to its content.[36] The concurring reasoning to a later decision attempted to resolve the contradictions of the content neutrality by stating that content neutrality is meant only for determining the scope of fundamental right situations and not for assessing the constitutionality of the restriction.[37] Although we see important considerations for further constitutional adjudication as well, there is no doubt that the idea of content neutrality must

---

35 For the distinction between scope and protection, *see* Frederick Schauer, 'Categories and the First Amendment: A Play in Three Acts', *Vanderbilt Law Review*, Vol. 34, 1981, p. 265; Eric Barendt, *Freedom of Speech*, Oxford University Press, 2005, pp. 74-78; Robert C. Post, 'Participatory Democracy as a Theory of Free Speech', *Virginia Law Review*, Vol. 97, Issue 3, 2011, p. 477.
36 Decision No. 30/1992. (V. 26.) AB, Reasoning V.3., ABH 1992, 167, 179.
37 Decision No. 4/2013. (II. 21.) AB, concurring opinion by András Bragyova, [83].

prevail most consistently with regard to the scope of freedom of expression. The Hungarian doctrine in this respect is strongly opposed to the previously analyzed Decision No. 3206/2013. (XI. 18.) AB, which addressed the issue of the use of expressions that violate social groups by simply excluding them *ab ovo* from the protection of the fundamental right of expression. Hate speech offensive to communities, in the broader sense, is subject to freedom of expression, with all its manifestations. Indeed, the scope does not depend on anything else than the type of communication to which it belongs is undoubtedly linked to the constitutional values of freedom of expression. Political speech affecting social groups is always linked to public discourse, and it is always meant to shape public opinion.

Second, and closely connected to this, but already focusing on the protection (not the scope) of free speech, we can state that the Hungarian practice, by elaborating the concept of 'external boundary', maintains the approach that seeks justification for restrictions not in the content itself, but in the context of communication. This statement is perfectly substantiated by the fact that the domestic doctrine does not adopt the strict position of content neutrality, and formulates a valid message: although the provisions restricting speech do not fail the test of constitutionality simply because they evaluate content elements, they must be rooted in additional circumstances of the communication in order to stay alive (in force). Restrictions on free speech should not in themselves refer to the worthlessness, inaccuracy or inadmissibility of the content of expression. Although majority opinions of the Constitutional Court have never made this clarification sufficiently clear, two judges have drawn the above conclusion. According to one of them, there is no opinion that, irrespective of its context, could be restricted purely on the basis of its content – the constitutionality of the restriction of rights depends in any case on the circumstances as a whole.[38] The other one points out that "somewhere, someday, irrespective of its content, every opinion must be capable of being expressed – even if the place, manner, time *etc.* may be restricted."[39]

This logic is reflected, for example, in the regulation of audiovisual media content. Using the most vivid example: while the Constitutional Court has consistently prevented the general punishment of group defamation, it has already considered the media authority's pursuit of the same content constitutional. Decision No. 1006/B/2001. AB accepted as a legitimate objective the prevention of "the radio and the television being the amplifier of those pursuing hatred that is offensive, racially motivated, hateful and call for discrimination". In this case, the Court relied on the media law argument as a circumstance beyond content, that

---

38   Decision No. 14/2000. (V. 12.) AB, dissenting opinion by István Kukorelli, ABH 2000, 108.

39   Decision No. 4/2013. (II. 21.) AB, concurring opinion by András Bragyova, Reasoning [83] (emphasis in the original).

"the opinion-forming effect of radio and television broadcasting and the convincing power of motion picture, sounds, and live reports have many times the impact on thought as other information society services".[40]

However, the special regulation of audiovisual media is just one of the most comprehensive examples of the contextual approach, and its significance extends to the full scope of free speech. From this point of view, the Constitutional Court has missed the opportunity for clarification when in Decision No. 4/2013. (II. 21.) AB on the criminal law provision prohibiting the use of symbols of authoritarian systems it failed to explain aspects relevant to the freedom of opinion. Had it done so; it could have pushed the legislator more vigorously to prosecute only those situations where there is a conscious weakening of fundamental democratic values.

Third, keeping the external boundary principle in the doctrine also warns us not to confuse two very different issues: On the one hand, that, the Hungarian practice had, in exceptional cases, considered the view expressed, too, when setting the limits. On the other hand, the most important requirement of content neutrality, the prohibition of state intervention in selecting viewpoints, is still one of the guiding principles of domestic doctrine. The thesis of protecting opinions irrespective of their value or veracity makes this clear, and this thesis has not lost its validity due to the narrow exception made in practice for the protection of fundamental constitutional values. With the help of the relevant literature, we can try to resolve this contradiction. We have seen that the key notion of the Hungarian concept, the category of external boundaries, does not distinguish between restrictions referring to content and those that are completely independent of content. Considering this, it can be said that the domestic doctrine displays a concept of content neutrality which does not primarily focus on the risk of taking content into account *per se*, but on other threats. The Hungarian practice may be explained quite well if we join the line of theoretical discourse according to which the focus of the constitutional assessment should not be so much on the issue of content, but rather on the motivation of the intervening state.[41]

Hence, fourth, the guiding principle regarding content neutrality in Hungarian practice may be to focus our attention above all on the motivation for limiting freedom of expres-

---

40 Decision No. 1006/B/2001. AB, Reasoning III.5.2., ABH 2007, 1366, 1374.
41 Frederick Schauer, 'Cuban Cigars, Cuban Books, and the Problem of Incidental Restrictions on Communications', *William and Mary Law Review*, Vol. 26, Issue 5, 1984-1985, p. 780; Ashutosh Bhagwat, 'Purpose Scrutiny in Constitutional Analysis', *California Law Review*, Vol. 85, Issue 2, 1997, p. 297; Barry P. McDonald, 'Speech and Distrust: Rethinking the Content Approach to Protecting the Freedom of Expression', *Notre Dame Law Review*, Vol. 81, Issue 4, 2005-2006, pp. 1352-1353.

sion.[42] It is not decisive in itself whether legislative intervention affects the content or the message of communication, but whether the reasons behind the intervention are constitutionally permissible or not.[43] An advanced doctrine of free speech inevitably demands this more complex approach.[44] On the one hand, it is true that content restrictions often suggest that the intention of the state is to distort democratic public discourse; on the other hand, it is plausible that in a few narrowly tailored cases supported by political consensus, protecting the most fundamental of constitutional values is justified. If we look at the most challenging decisions, such as the desecration of national symbols, the use of totalitarian symbols, or even the denial of crimes committed by the nazi or communist regime, it is comprehensible why these restrictions have been approved. However, in the absence of such extraordinary circumstances, the government's unjustifiable intention to distort or restrict public discourse rears its head.

This is palpable in Decision No. 1/2013. (I. 7.) AB, which examined, *inter alia*, the constitutionality of the rule that allowed only the public service media to publish political ads during the campaign period. Considering that the provision would have eliminated one of the most important tools of political communication to the widest audience, the Constitutional Court carefully examined the purposes that such an amendment could serve and, after considering all the circumstances of the case, ruled out the arguments that sought to justify this intervention.[45] For example, in the context of the campaign silence for the undisturbed expression of the electorate's will, the Court considered that the law in question was about to eliminate the institution of campaign silence. In this respect, the case of the legislator was radically weakened. It is just as voluble where the reasoning rejects the argument that the restriction serves to keep campaign costs under control, serving the purity of the elections. According to the Constitutional Court, this could not motivate the legislator in the case, as it did not regulate the cost-reducing use of other campaign tools, nor did it foresee any new regulations for the total cost of the campaign. After excluding these reasons, the chances of the government's motivation for other, hidden, indefensible restrictions to the freedom of expression radically increases. This played an important role for establishing the unconstitutionality of the rule under review. The suspicion of the presence of an indefensible motivation in this case is also reinforced by the aspect that we can add to the question, as compared to the reasoning of the Constitutional Court's decision:

---

42   Understanding the motivational aspects under the Hungarian fundamental rights dogma, through examining the legislative objectives (the legitimate aim in the Strasbourg terminology) is definitely an element of constitutional review.

43   Robert C. Post, 'Viewpoint Discrimination and Commercial Speech', *Loyola of Los Angeles Law Review*, Vol. 41, 2007-2008, pp. 173-174.

44   Robert C. Post, 'Recuperating First Amendment Doctrine', *Stanford Law Review*, Vol. 47, 1994-1995, p. 1249.

45   Despite the fact that the European approach gives much more room for setting the legal framework for campaigning than the US constitutional practice.

the examined regulation, although it covers all political advertising, cannot be considered as fully neutral, at least if the term is used in its broader sense as developed in literature. According to this, arguments against viewpoint-based restrictions may be used to some extent, even if a seemingly neutral rule actually distorts publicity to a disproportionate extent, *i.e.* certain viewpoints or certain speakers are clearly disadvantaged. I am convinced that, in the case of any regulation of political advertising, there are serious arguments to be made, that this is the case. The voice of the acting government necessarily resounds louder in the political discourse given a non-hostile media environment, which in addition may be exploited particularly effectively with conscious government action and communication during the campaign period. In such an environment, the political opposition seeking to replace the government is in greater need of sending messages to the electorate through paid political advertisements.[46] A radical reduction or even loss of this opportunity therefore affects its campaign communication capabilities more severely than that of the government, which plays the main role in everyday communication. And since the justifiable motivations have already collapsed, there is a great chance for the emergence of an unjustifiable one: the radical reduction of the possibility of political advertising is actually a measure to prevent the effectiveness of opposition campaigns.

Finally, fifth, and one of the most important conclusions of our excursion into content neutrality: if we place the motivation rather than the content of the restriction into focus, we can avoid the dichotomy implied in the content-based/content-neutral analysis. Instead, we can conduct a rigorous freedom of expression assessment beyond that dichotomy. To examine motivation, content neutrality may be an important pillar, but it should never become the exclusive method. In other words, a seemingly perfectly neutral regulation must be judged by the strictest standards if the state's intention to silence others is suggested by the circumstances.

The previous example of restricting political advertising has already brought these aspects to light, but it is even more interesting to identify them in a case that we have previously mentioned as an example of intrinsically independent intervention. The regulation examined in Decision No. 3208/2013. (XI. 18.) AB amended the requirements for the placement of public billboards allegedly in order to improve road safety. As mentioned above, these are typically provisioning that narrow this channel of communication, irrespective of the message placed on the advertising media (for example, the ban on advertising placement on a pylon or restricting the placement of bulletin boards of a certain size). The Constitutional Court considered the narrowing of advertising opportunities to be mere

---

46   It is an advanced approach to content neutrality to evaluate whether a given regulation affects the flow of thoughts equally, or if it may disrupt the spread of certain views disproportionately. Susan H. Williams, 'Content Discrimination and the First Amendment', *University of Pennsylvania Law Review*, Vol. 139, 1990-1991, p. 658.

advertising restrictions and therefore, constitutional in view of the fact that improving the safety of road traffic (in view of the protection of life and property) is a legitimate reason for restricting the freedom of commercial expression. Moreover, the legislator had found a proportionate solution when it banned advertising boards, most likely to distract drivers.[47] However, first, this regulation did not only concern commercial communications, and second, there could have been legitimate doubts about the legislator's motivation. Such doubts also arose in the minority of justices. According to the dissenting opinion, the constitutional purpose of the restriction may not be established, for taking all circumstances into account, the legislator could not have been guided by the intention of increasing road safety. The argument seeks to refute in detail any assumption of the legislator's justifiable motivation. First, it points out that, under the Act, even before the amendment under review, it was only possible to place any billboard, typically with an official license, that did not jeopardize traffic safety, and that non-compliant boards could be removed. Second, if the legislator had actually sought to increase safety by eliminating circumstances that distract drivers, such as reducing the number of visual information sources within the driver's field of vision, this should have been done for all visual information of the same type. However, while no advertisement may be placed on lampposts, they can indeed be placed on advertising columns placed near the roadside, at the drivers' eye level, which are even more in their field of vision. If it is true that billboards placed along public roads are distracting for drivers then this is true of all advertising signs and other visible formations within the traffic participants' field of vision, without discrimination. In contrast, the amendment banned the placement of certain billboards and did not restrict any other advertising in or even more in the driver's field of vision, and did not prohibit advertisements placed on buses, trolleybuses or taxis moving on the road, even though, according to common sense, due to their mobile nature and because of their placement, these may be even more confusing than the newly banned advertisements alongside the road. An additional argument against the credibility of the motivation to improve road safety is that the change allows the placement of some smaller billboards that are harder to see and can only be read for a shorter period of time. Meanwhile, the larger ones were no longer permitted, even though they are easier to read and as such are less distracting.[48]

Agreeing with the above arguments, we can say that in this case the presumption of a legislative intent to improve road safety has been refuted. As far as our study of freedom of expression is concerned, this means that the amendment in question has restricted democratic public discourse to a much wider extent than advertisements, such as election

---

47   Decision No. 3208/2013. (XI. 18.) AB, Reasoning [107].
48   András Bragyova's dissenting opinion, to which four other judges (László Kiss, Péter Kovács, Miklós Lévay and Péter Paczolay) joined, [128]-[140].

posters, without any reasonable justification, alongside other motivations that are either irrelevant or inexcusable from the perspective of the freedom of opinion.

We can clearly declare that this change of approach, which evolved from the principle of content neutrality, not only proves necessary, but also promises extraordinary benefits for the enforcement of constitutional requirements. In the area of freedom of expression and press freedom, it is less common these days to encounter textbook-type content-based restrictions, and the regulator more frequently attempts to influence the medium and structure of communication. It is crucial that this not be allowed without constitutionally justifiable grounds – even if the legislators are well prepared with justifications that seem to fair and acceptable on their face.

24.7 Conclusions

The inconsistency of the 'external boundary' doctrine does not erase the significance of content-based scrutiny. Besides relevant elements of content-based scrutiny, however, it should be clarified how to transcend it. The relevant theses of content neutrality in the Hungarian doctrine are the following: *(i)* Communication belonging to public social interaction is covered by freedom of speech irrespective of its content. The scope of free speech is independent of the content of speech in question. *(ii)* Restriction of speech should be justified not by referring to its content alone but by the context of the expression. Restrictions should not be based on the fact that the content of speech is unacceptable, unworthy or wrong. *(iii)* Viewpoint neutrality is a central requirement in Hungarian case-law. *(iv)* The Hungarian doctrine of content neutrality does not focus on the risk raised by a content-based rule alone but rather on other dangers: it drives our attention foremost to the motivation behind speech restrictions. *(v)* It is not decisive in itself if the regulation affects the content or message of the speech. The more important question is whether the reasons for the regulation are constitutionally justifiable or not. *(vi)* The government's intention to restrict or distort public discussion can be revealed with appropriate scrutiny. *(vii)* Stringent constitutional examination should not be confined by the content-based/content-neutral dichotomy: seemingly completely content-neutral regulations should be assessed with the most rigorous standards if the government's improper motivation is identified. *(viii)* The approach transcending the dichotomy of content-centered analyses is more suitable for new regulations on speech: legislators more and more often try to influence not the content but the structure of public communication. It is crucial that they should be allowed to do so only on justifiable grounds.

25 "LAND OF CONFUSION"

Social (Fundamental) Rights and the Provisions of the Fundamental Law in Light of the Practice of the Constitutional Court of Hungary

*István Hoffman**

Keywords

Constitutional Court of Hungary, social rights as fundamental rights, right to social security, state goals, social security system of Hungary

Abstract

Modern welfare democracies developed different approaches to social rights. This paper briefly reviews the different models for the institutionalization of social rights as fundamental rights in modern democracies. In Hungary, the approach to social security has been significantly transformed by the Fundamental Law. For this reason, the paper reviews the approach of the Hungarian constitutional system to the right to social security between 1989 and 2011 and introduces the current position of social rights in the Hungarian legal system. This is done through and assessment of the provisions of the Fundamental Law and the current case-law of the Constitutional Court of Hungary.

25.1 INTRODUCTION

The majority of the Hungarian population is affected by social rights: Hungarians receive lots of social benefits and services during their life. Therefore, social expenditures are high in Hungary, amounting to approximately 6000 billion HUF per annum.[1] The approach to social security has been significantly transformed by the Fundamental Law of Hungary. The entire Hungarian population has been affected by these changes and by the interpretation of the relevant rules (especially by the Constitutional Court), therefore, it is worth taking a look at the new rules. Firstly, I analyze the different interpretations and approaches to social rights. Since the transformation of the Hungarian social security system cannot be understood without a brief excursion to the approach reflected in the Hungarian con-

---

* István Hoffman: professor of law, ELTE Law School, Budapest.
1 Marianna Fazekas, 'Előszó', *in* István Hoffman & Gréta Mattenheim (eds.), *Nagykommentár a szociális törvényhez*, Wolters Kluwer, Budapest, 2016, p. 13.

stitutional system between 1989 and 2011, I will touch upon the relevant rules of this period as well.

25.2 SOCIAL RIGHTS – APPROACHES AND INTERPRETATIONS

Different approaches to social rights have been developed in modern welfare democracies. One approach states that considering social rights as fundamental rights is a feature of post-socialist states.[2] It is therefore important to first review the main approaches to the interpretation and role of social rights.

25.2.1   Approaches to, and Institutionalization of Social Rights

A simple assessment of the various definitions and interpretations of social rights could be the subject of an entire monograph. It should be highlighted, that social rights have been re-institutionalized as fundamental rights by the vast majority of modern states.[3] Balázs Krémer noted that modern countries may be considered as welfare states, however their approach to welfare services and the role of the state are relatively different.[4]

There are different models for the institutionalization of social rights as fundamental rights in modern democracies. The first approach is an indirect institutionalization which is based on the institutional protection of fundamental rights. Social rights are normally not defined as fundamental rights by national constitutions, but they are institutionalized through the practice of constitutional courts and supreme courts. In this model social rights are considered to be part of the institutional protection of other fundamental rights which are enumerated by the constitutions. The basic rights from which social rights are derived are first and foremost the right to life and human dignity, the prohibition of discrimination and the right to equal treatment, but other fundamental rights (for example the right to property) may also serve as a basis for social rights. This approach first emerged in the US. Social rights are not defined and regulated by the US Constitution and its amendments; nevertheless, these rights exist. The interpretation of these fundamental rights is based on the practice of the US Supreme Court. This practice is mainly based on the prohibition of discrimination and the concept of social justice developed in the Supreme

---

2   András Jakab, *Az új Alaptörvény keletkezése és gyakorlati következményei*, HVG-ORAC, Budapest, 2011, pp. 19-22.

3   L. D. M. Davis, 'Socio-Economic Rights', *in* Michel Rosenfeld & András Sajó (eds.), *The Oxford Handbook of Comparative Constitutional Law*, Oxford University Press, Oxford, 2012, pp. 1021-1023.

4   Balázs Krémer, *Bevezetés a szociálpolitikába*, Napvilág, Budapest, 2009, pp. 103-120.

Court judgments forms the core of social rights guaranteed in the US.[5] Constitutional guarantees of social rights based on this approach are weaker, since these rights are not directly based on a provision of the (national) constitution, but on the practice and interpretation of the constitutional courts and supreme courts. Hence, these rights may be changed without amending the constitution.[6]

The second approach means the institutionalization of social rights as fundamental rights by the constitutions. Social rights are second-generation human rights, as such, the evolution of these rights begun at the end of the 19th century. Firstly, the social security was linked to the equality before the law and to the rule of law. It was suggested by several German scholars that the aforementioned principles should be guaranteed through the vehicle of social security benefits provided by the state. This concept was influenced by the Bismarckian social security reforms in late 19th century Germany.[7] The 'Golden Age' of social rights commenced following World War II, with the development of welfare states. The actionability of these rights defined by the national constitutions is controversial, nevertheless, the obligation of the state to provide welfare services is uncontested.[8] The principle of the social welfare state – supplementing the principles of democracy and the rule of law – is enshrined in the national constitutions of several European countries.[9]

The characteristics of this model may be best illustrated through the German approach and interpretation. This is built on the Bismarckian social model, namely, on the concept of the 'social citizen' and on the institutionalization of the welfare (social security) system.[10] The Bismarckian social model relies on social insurance, offering solid protection for social contribution payments guaranteed under the German constitution and the judgments of the Federal Constitutional Court *(Bundesverfassungsgericht)*. The latter protection derives

5   Charles R. Epp, 'Courts and the Rights Revolution', *in* Kermit L. Hall & Kevin T. McGuire (eds.), *The Judicial Branch (Institutions of the American Democracy)*, Oxford University Press, Oxford, 2005, pp. 350-365.

6   The practice of the US Supreme Court is a vivid example for this phenomenon, transformed several times in the course of the last decades. The interpretation of these rights has changed flexibly. The constitutional background for these transformations was that the principle *stare decisis* could not be applied to judgments of the Supreme Court. Thus, after the social rights (social justice) revolution of the 1960s the accessibility and the constitutional guarantees for welfare benefits and services changed in the 1970s. A good example for this transformation is the *Califano v. Westcott* judgment [443 U.S. 76 (1979)] limiting access to family benefits. Marisa Chappel, *The War on Welfare. Family, Poverty and Politics in Modern America*, University of Pennsylvania Press, Philadelphia, 2010, p. 156.

7   Eberhard Eichenhofer, *Soziale Menschenrechte im Völker-, europäischen und deutschen Recht*, Verlag Mohr Siebeck, Tübingen, 2012, pp. 53-56.

8   Davis 2012, pp. 1025-1026.

9   Article 20(1) of the German Federal Constitution *(Grundgesetz)*, Article 1 of the French Constitution (passed in 1958), Article 1(1) of the Spanish constitution (passed in 1978), Article 2 of the Portuguese constitution (passed in 1976).

10   Thomas Meyer & Maren Eichhart, 'Sozialstaat', *in* Thomas Meyer (ed.), *Theorie der Sozialen Demokratie*. VS Verlag für Sozialwissenschaften, Wiesbaden, 2011, pp. 319-321.

from the right to property.[11] It is clear, that the constitutional approach to social rights is strongly influenced by the social model of the given country. This will be the subject of the next chapter.

25.2.2 Approach to Social Rights and the Welfare Model Followed by the Country

As of yet, social law only has a brief history, because it evolved in European countries in the second half of the 19th century. Consequently, its legal dogmatics are still in flux and are strongly impacted by the welfare systems. The main characteristics of these systems will be analyzed in this article. The following overview of the different models is based on the classification of Gøsta Esping-Andersen.[12]

The welfare model of common law countries is considered by Esping-Andersen to be a liberal one. This model is followed primarily by the US and Ireland, but several characteristics of the model may be observed in other common law countries. The state plays a limited role in this model, which is based on self-care. Here, state functions as the 'lender of last resort', intervening only where self-care is not possible and the beneficiary is worth helping.[13] As I mentioned above, social rights are not directly enshrined in the national constitutions or constitutional rules, these rights are derived from the prohibition of discrimination and the equality before law. The right to equal opportunities is gleaned from these two fundamental rights. The 'Third Way' of the British Labor party is based on this approach. In this model, the state operates as the guarantor of equal opportunities: services are provided by the state through which the social opportunities are equalized. Hence, this approach focuses on services and not benefits.[14] Another approach based on the Anglo-American common law (liberal) welfare model is the 'Workfare State'. This approach hinges on the merit of the beneficiary. The Workfare State claims that the work has a priority, and it focuses more on sanctions where the beneficiary who is able to work chooses not to participate in the labor market.[15] The different welfare systems have been impacted

---

11   Eberhard Eichenhofer & Constanze Janda, *Klausenkurs im Sozialrecht. Ein Fallbuch*, C.F. Müller, Heidelberg, 2014, pp. 5-9.
12   On the aspects of classification *see* Gøsta Esping-Andersen, 'Towards the Good Society, Once Again?', *in* Gøsta Esping-Andersen (ed.), *Why We Need a New Welfare State?* Oxford University Press, Oxford, 2002, pp. 13-18.
13   Id. p. 15.
14   Dagmar Schiek, 'Re-Embedding Economic and Social Constitutionalism: Normative Perspectives for the EU', *in* Dagmar Schiek *et al.* (eds.), *European Economic and Social Constitutionalism after the Treaty of Lisbon*, Cambridge University Press, Cambridge, 2011, p. 30.
15   Jamie Peck, 'Local Discipline: Making Space for the 'Workfare State'', *in* Paul Edwards & Tony Elger (eds.), *The Global Economy, National States and the Regulation of Labour*, Mansell, London-New York, 1999, pp. 64-72; Marianna Nagy, 'A közszolgáltatás-szervezés intézmény- és elmélettörténete', *in* Marianna Fazekas

significantly by the Anglo-American (common law) approach in the last decades, and in particular, by the principle of self-care. For example, in the continental and Nordic systems social services are regulated by private law and funded through private resources (e.g. private insurance). This tendency can even be observed in the Hungarian legal system.[16]

The second major approach Esping-Andersen identifies is what he refers to as the conservative approach, a system based on the Bismarckian welfare model. In this model the social welfare system is founded on (mandatory) social insurance, as such, social security is governed by the state and public law. Although solidarity is a crucial principle in these systems, the social welfare is nevertheless based on an insurance system. Here, the constitutional guarantees of social rights are linked to the protection of the right to property. It should be noted that the constitutional notion of property is construed more broadly than the concept of property under private law.[17]

The third model distinguished by Esping-Andersen is the Nordic welfare model. The model may be described on the basis of the Swedish welfare system. It foresees universal services and benefits protected by the national constitutions[18] Principles of insurance and self-care are a part of this model however, they are only supplementary principles. While the system is based universal benefits, the main aim of these services and benefits is to encourage employment.[19]

A specific model has evolved in the Southern European countries. It is characterized by a tension between the applicable provisions and the actual characteristics of the welfare system. This tension developed in the wake of the Italian constitutional rules passed in 1946, and the same problems emerged in Greece, Portugal and Spain. These countries were formerly governed by right-wing authoritarian governments. Their political system was transformed during the 1970s and the basic – and in part, individually enforceable – social rights as fundamental rights were determined by and enshrined in the new constitutions of the Democratic transition.[20] The constitutional rules were based on the Nordic model, yet the economic and social structures were different in the Southern European countries. Traditional – family and small community-based – social care is still prevalent

---

(ed.), *Közigazgatási jog. Általános rész II. A közszolgáltatások szervezése*, ELTE Eötvös, Budapest, 2017, pp. 47-48.

16   Balázs Tőkey, *Az egészségbiztosítási szerződés*, ELTE Eötvös, Budapest, 2015, pp. 12-16.

17   Ferdinand Kirchhof, 'Finanzwesen der Sozialversicherung', *in* Josef Isenssee & Paul Kirchhof (eds.), *Handbuch des Staatsrechts der Bundesrepublik Deutschland. Band V Rechtsquellen, Organisation, Finanzen*, C. F. Müller, Heidelberg, 2007, pp. 1445-1459.

18   *E.g.* Article 2(2) of the first part of the Swedish Constitution (The Instrument of Government) states that "[t]he personal, economic and cultural welfare of the individual shall be fundamental aims of public activity. In particular, the public institutions shall secure the right to employment, housing and education, and shall promote social care and social security, as well as favorable conditions for good health."

19   Esping-Andersen 2002, p. 14.

20   Article 47 of the Spanish constitution states that Spanish citizens have the right to housing, and Article 50 ensures the right to old-age pension.

in these countries, and the Bismarckian model exerts a significant influence. A special feature of the social insurance system of these countries is that the principle of solidarity plays a very important role in the insurance systems, meaning that the social insurance model is of an egalitarian nature.[21] Universal services only play a supplementary role in the actual functioning of systems: for example health care is based on a universal model in Spain.[22]

In a similar vein, a special model emerged in the Eastern and Central European – post-socialist – countries during the democratic transition. After the fall of communist regimes social welfare systems faced major challenges which had to be resolved within a short timeframe. Welfare services and social law had to be renewed at short notice, because the former communist model was based on the provider role of state-owned employers' services and the social insurance financed by the state. These systems were mainly based on the Bismarckian model – which was adopted by these countries before World War II – but several ad hoc solutions were also introduced which were based on different models of welfare services. Following the economic crises of 2008/2009, the welfare model of these countries was strongly influenced by the common law model, especially by the principle of the self-care and the concept of Workfare State.

25.3 SOCIAL RIGHTS IN THE CONSTITUTION OF HUNGARIAN DEMOCRATIC TRANSITION (1989-2010)

As an amendment to the former communist constitution, Act XXXI of 1989 dramatically transformed the chapter on the fundamental rights in the Constitution. A new article was incorporated into that chapter: the article on the right to social security. Although this right was regulated by the Constitution, the article was a short one. Therefore, its interpretation by the Constitutional Court was highly important. I now turn to the constitutional rules governing social rights and the new approach to social security.

25.3.1   The Constitutional Reform of 1989/90 and the Evolution of Social Law

In the course of the drafting of the constitution during the 1989/90 democratic transition, the issue of social fundamental rights was a highly controversial one and could not be

---

21 Esping-Andersen 2002, pp. 18-19; Martin Rhodes, 'Southern European Welfare States: Identity, Problems and Prospects for Reform', in Martin Rhodes (ed.), *Southern European Welfare States. Between Crisis and Reform*, Routledge, London-New York, 1997, pp. 2-8.
22 István Hoffman, 'A területi közszolgáltatások szabályozási modelljei az egészségügyben', in Tamás M. Horváth (ed.), *Kilengések. Közszolgáltatási változások*, Dialóg Campus, Budapest-Pécs, 2013, pp. 199-201.

decided through the codification of the amendment to the constitution. This was owed firstly to the fact that the procedure was strongly impacted by the welfare reform of the former Communist state, especially by the welfare reforms of the late 1960s to 1980s. These reforms brought about universal services for Hungarian citizens. Secondly, the codification of the new constitutional rules was influenced by (West-)German constitutionalism, in accordance with which a wide range of social rights were guaranteed and protected. Therefore, a very specific regulation was passed. First of all, the preamble of the amended Constitution stated that the aim of the newly formed Hungarian Republic is to build a social market economy. The amended Constitution contained two sections which were directly linked to social rights. Article 70/D stipulated the right to (physical and mental) health. Article 70/D(2) foresaw that this right be implemented through the welfare system.

The *sedes materiae* of social fundamental rights was Article 70/E of the amended constitution. Article 70/E(1) provided that

> "[c]itizens of the Republic of Hungary have the right to social security; they are entitled to the support required to live in old age, and in the case of sickness, disability, being widowed or orphaned and in the case of unemployment through no fault of their own."

Based on the above, the right to social security was defined as a right to welfare services. These services were to be provided in the case of several, constitutionally determined social risks. The beneficiaries of this fundamental right were Hungarian citizens thus, foreigners were not covered by the provision. The right to social security as a right to *services* reinforced by Article 70/E(2), which stated that "[t]he Republic of Hungary shall implement the right to social support through the social security system and the system of social institutions." Hence, the Constitution provided that the social welfare system shall have a social insurance subsystem.

There were also other Articles of the Constitution related to social rights. It should be highlighted, that Articles 16 and 17 – not as individual rights but as state goals[23] – guarantee the protection of the interests of young people and support for those in need "through a wide range of social measures". It was important that Article 70/A declared the prohibition of discrimination and the possibility for equal opportunities actions. A crucial element of Hungarian constitutional regulation was the right to life and human dignity, guaranteed by Article 54.

There was a tension inherent in the constitutional rules of the democratic transition. The preamble of the Constitution and Articles 16 and 17 were based on the concept of the social welfare state, on the concept of social rule of law state *(sozialer Rechtsstaat).* At the

---

23   János Sári, *Alkotmánytan II. Alapjogok*, Osiris, Budapest, 2000, p. 236.

same time, it was clear, that individually enforceable rights could be hardly derived from Article 70/E of the amended Constitution.[24] Therefore, the interpretation of the Constitutional Court was required to define the nature of Hungarian social rights.

25.3.2   The Interpretation of the Constitutional Court

As I mentioned above, there was a tension within the Constitutional rules that was waiting to be resolved. Early on, the Constitutional Court was faced with this problem. It stated in 1990 that the provision of preamble declaring social market economy cannot be construed to give rise to individually enforceable rights, and Hungary cannot be considered a *sozialer Rechtsstaat*.[25] This judgment was a landmark decision because it was consistently stated by the Constitutional Court, that the principle of social welfare state is not guaranteed by the Constitution. Therefore, this concept cannot be invoked independently. Hence, it was established that the right to social security declared under Article 70/E was not an individually enforceable (actionable) right. The existence of a – functional – state welfare system, including a social insurance system was guaranteed by Article 70/E.[26]

In the state socialist period – partly because of the full employment guaranteed by the socialist state and partly because of the ideology-driven denial of the existence of poverty[27] – the social insurance system was organized by the government. The first social reforms of the democratic transition focused on the social insurance model. The landmark decisions from the early jurisprudence (1990-1994) of the Constitutional Court were related to these provisions. One of these landmark judgments was Decision No. 26/1993. (IV. 29.) AB, which stated that pensions are purchased services, thus, social rights connected to pensions are directly linked to the protection of the right to property. Although it is a purchased service, the pension system is partly based on the principle of solidarity, therefore, it was not unconstitutional that the growth of higher pensions was smaller. At the same time, the Constitutional Court emphasized that the nominal amount of pensions cannot be decreased.[28] After economic stabilization in 1995 (carried out by the so-called 'Bokros package') the Constitutional Court stated that the amount of several other social insurance benefits (*e.g.* the sick pay) may be decreased by the legislature. Thus, the amount of the benefits was not been guaranteed by paying contribution, but it is a constitutional

---

24   Gábor Juhász, '70/E. § [A szociális biztonsághoz való jog]', *in* András Jakab (ed.), *Az Alkotmány kommentárja II.*, Századvég, Budapest, 2009, pp. 2581-2583.
25   Decision No. 772/B/1990. AB, ABH 1991, 519.
26   Decision No. 32/1991. (VI. 6.) AB, ABH 1991, 146.
27   Krémer 2009, pp. 117-129.
28   Sári 2000, pp. 202-204.

requirement, that the amount of the benefit should be proportional to the paid contribution.[29]

The same decision contained important findings on the constitutional guarantees of universal benefits. Before 1990, family allowance and maternity allowance were deemed to be social insurance benefits. The system was transformed by Act XXV of 1990 which transformed the nature of these benefits, which became universal benefits. The reform bill of 1995 changed the system yet again, transforming them into means-tested benefits. The same decision of the Constitutional Court stated that the principle of the rule law must be observed by these reforms, meaning that an adequate period for preparing for these changes is required. This was to be the longest interval between adoption and entry into force of the law as foreseen under Hungarian private law, 300 days. The next landmark decision on universal benefits was made following the economic crisis of 2008/2009. The judgment found the taxation of family allowance to be unconstitutional, because the relevant regulation was not sufficiently clear amounting to a violation of the principle of the rule of law.[30]

It was clearly stated by the Constitutional Court, that the right to social security gave rise to the requirement of a functional welfare system. Therefore, the constitutional basis for the means-tested benefit was primarily the right to life and human dignity, forming part of the institutional protection of these core fundamental rights.[31] This approach was also applied in Decision No. 42/2000. (XI. 18.) AB. The Constitutional Court declared that the right to housing could not be derived from Article 70/E of the Constitution. However, there is a constitutional requirement that a welfare system should be operated which provides accommodation for homeless people to prevent an immediate threat to life.

The Constitutional Court also resolved the tension within the regulation of the right to social protection. It stated that the main requirement that can be derived from the Constitution is to organize a functional social welfare system including a social insurance system. The social insurance system is protected under the right to property, yet the principle of solidarity should also be applied when carrying out the constitutional control of the legislation. In addition, the regulation of universal and means-tested benefits must comply with principle of rule of law. The basis for means-tested benefits is the institutional protection of the right to life and human dignity, as a constitutional minimum of the welfare system.

This approach was confirmed in the beginning of the 2000s but has been radically transformed by with the entry into force of the new Hungarian constitution, the Fundamental Law.

---

29   Decision No. 56/1995. (IX. 15.) AB, ABH 1995, 260.
30   Decision No. 127/2009. (XII. 17.) AB, ABH 2009, 1056.
31   Decision No. 32/1998. (VI. 25.) AB, ABH 1998, 251.

25.4 Transformation of the Right to Social Security by the Fundamental Law of Hungary

25.4.1 The New Framework of Hungarian Social Policy

The framework of Hungarian social policy was radically transformed after 2010. However, the roots of this change go back to 2008 and the reforms were greatly influenced by the common law approach to the welfare system. This transformation is particularly conspicuous in the field of means-tested benefits. The principle of merit became acquired an important role, when the labor test of the means-tested benefit was strengthened.[32] It was not only the means-tested benefits that were impacted by the reforms: restrictions emerged in the social insurance system as well. The constitutional framework of this social policy reform was created through the transformation of the relevant provisions of the Fundamental Law, since these reforms would not have been in compliance with the earlier practice of the Constitutional Court.

It is very interesting that as a tool for accelerating social reforms was inserted into the constitution after the publication but before the entry into force of the Fundamental Law: Act LXI of 2011 inserted a new paragraph 3 in Article 70/E of the Constitution. The paragraph set forth that the right to pension is constitutionally guaranteed only for those who have reached the retirement age applicable to them. The new provision also stated that the amount of the pension due to those who have not yet reached the retirement age may be reduced and the pension could be transformed into universal or means-tested social benefits.

This amendment was the constitutional basis for the social legislation of 2011. The new social legislation entered into force already in 2011, while the Fundamental Law only entered into force on 1 January 2012. Consequently, the application of the approach of Decision No. 26/1993. (IV. 29.) AB and Decision No. 56/1995. (IX. 15.) AB was directly excluded by the amended rules of the (old) Constitution. The amount of several special pensions (*e.g.* the special pensions for soldiers, police officer *etc.*) were thus reduced, and the rehabilitation benefit and the disability pension of those who had not yet reached the retirement age applicable to them were transformed into a special, partly means-tested social benefit: the benefit available to those with altered work ability.

The main elements of the transformation were foreshadowed by these changes: the decreasing role of the social insurance system and the diminishing guarantees of social security. We can conclude that the common law approach greatly influenced the system.

32　*See* in detail István Hoffman, 'Az önkormányzati segélyezési rendszer változásai Magyarországon – különös tekintettel a 2015-ös reformokra', *Közjogi Szemle*, 2016/1, pp. 21-23.

25.4.2   State Goal – Instead of a Fundamental Right: The Transformation of the Fundamental Law's Provisions

The social security paradigm was transformed by Article XIX of the Fundamental Law, the *sedes materiae* of the constitutional regulation of social rights. The Fundamental Law declares that "Hungary shall strive to provide social security to all of its citizens". Consequently, social security is not a fundamental right, but a state goal. Hungary will only aspire to provide social security, which is not guaranteed by the constitutional rules. The definition of social risks has also been partly amended: a new element in the list is disability. Benefits for persons living with a disability were formerly provided by the state: the common framework for these benefits is Act XXVI of 1998 on the Rights and Equal Opportunities of Persons with Disabilities, and the benefits for children with disabilities are regulated by Act LXXXIV of 1998 on Family Support. Another new risk was maternity, which used to form a part of sickness risks. Hence, the new laws shaped a novel constitutional framework for social security, in particular with the new concept of social rights deemed to be a state goal instead of a fundamental right. As a consequence, the earlier jurisprudence of the Constitutional Court had to be revised, as well. This revision however, was not a full one, because the earlier landmark decisions of the Constitutional Court were not only based on the section on the right to social protection but on other fundamental rights as well, for example on the right to life and human dignity and on the protection of the right to property. Therefore, several elements of the earlier approach could be applied following the entry into force of the Fundamental Law.

A more important transformation was carried out by Article XIX(2). The new provision does not contain rules on the social insurance system. This may be interpreted in two ways: firstly, that the social insurance system was – incorrectly – interpreted by the constitutional regulation as a 'social institution'. The alternative is the Fundamental Law does now guarantee an independent social insurance (sub)system.[33] It is clear that the constitutional rules offer greater leeway to transform the social system, and the former Bismarckian-type social system may also be transformed. Social insurance benefits may be transformed into means-tested (or universal) benefits and the proportionality of annuity and contribution may also be given a different interpretation by the legislature. Although the legislator enjoys has great freedom in defining social benefits, the protection of the right to property has remained the final boundary for the legislation. As mentioned above, several social insurance benefits were transformed into partly means-tested benefits, for example the former disability pensions. Similarly, the balance of benefits and paid contributions has been changed significantly due to the reform of Act IV of 1991 on job assistance and

---

33   Gábor Juhász, 'Államcélok, paradigmaváltás és aktuálpolitikai alkotmányozás. Szociális jogok védelme az Alaptörvényben', *Esély*, 2015/1, pp. 14-15.

unemployment benefits. The duration of the unemployment benefit was radically curtailed (to 90 days), its maximum amount reduced significantly. Finally, a labor test was also introduced by the reform. Hence, the social insurance nature of this benefit was weakened by these reforms.

The third novelty introduced by the Fundamental Law was the transformation of the framework of the means-tested benefits: Article XIX(3) introduced a commitment-oriented system.[34] This reform was influenced by the common law concept of social welfare system, and in particular by the merit control of social benefits and the concept of the 'Workfare State'. Article XIX(4) states, that

> "Hungary shall contribute to ensuring a life of dignity for the elderly by maintaining a general state pension system based on social solidarity and by allowing for the operation of voluntarily established social institutions."

This provision has a clear message. Firstly, it states that the main goal of the pension system is to ensure a life of dignity for the elderly. Thus, pensions for the non-elderly (*e.g.* the widow's pension and orphans' benefits) are not guaranteed under the constitution. These benefits are interpreted as pensions based on a compulsory social insurance system guided by the traditional Bismarckian approach.[35] As mentioned above, this was the constitutional basis for the transformation of benefits for persons with altered work ability into a partly means-tested, partly health insurance-type benefit.

It is an important element of the regulation that the pension system is defined by the Fundamental Law as a general state pension system based on social solidarity. Hence, the opportunity to maintain a mandatory private pension system is excluded (practically prohibited) by the Fundamental Law. Solidarity as a central element of the pension system is crucial: it is a limitation of the applicability of the protection of the right to property, because pensions are not merely purchased services, but solidarity benefits as well. The incomes of the pension system have been transformed on the basis of this regulation: the role of taxes – instead of contributions (which are partly covered by the protection of the right to property) – has been strengthened.[36] Only the 'operation of voluntarily established social institutions' is allowed under the new regulation, as such, private insurance may have an important role as supplementary system.

Article XIX(4) of the Fundamental Law introduced a new preferential rule. It reads: "[a]n Act may lay down the conditions for entitlement to state pension also with regard to the requirement for stronger protection for women." This provision was the constitu-

---

34   Id. pp. 15-16.
35   Raimund Waltermann, *Sozialrecht*, C. F. Müller, Heidelberg, 2011, pp. 173-175.
36   Juhász 2015, pp. 16-17.

tional basis for the special pension women with more than 40-year pension entitlement are eligible for (regulated in detail by the Act on the Social Insurance Pension).

There are other fundamental rights and state goals which regulate social fundamental rights. Articles XVII and XVII (guaranteeing the right to work and the rights of the child) and Article XX (on the right to health) are important elements of the new constitutional approach. The Fundamental Law contains the prohibition of discrimination and the right to property is also strongly protected fundamental right. It is an important element of the regulation that according to Article XVI(4) "[a]dult children shall be obliged to take care of their parents if they are in need". This rule is based on the common law concept of the self-care, and it could be the basis for the reduction of state provided benefits and services.

The transformed social policy of Hungary was mapped by the regulations of the Fundamental Law: social security became a state goal – instead of a fundamental right. The constitutional guarantees of the social insurance system have been weakened by the new rules and the merit principle was introduced besides the means-tested benefits. We may conclude that the Bismarckian elements of the Hungarian social welfare system have been weakened, because the new model was strongly influenced by the common law (liberal) welfare concept. But the short constitutional provisions were not always sufficiently clear, and the potential for different interpretations to evolve on the basis of the new rules existed.

25.4.3   The Interpretation of the Transformed Social Rights: The Landmark Decisions of the Constitutional Court

Because of the short constitutional provisions and the possibility of different interpretations given to social rights, the Constitutional Court played an important role. The landmark decisions were partly based on the new competence of the Constitutional Court, on the 'genuine' constitutional complaint which could be submitted by the party who could substantiate the violation of his or her individual rights. In several cases the procedure was initiated by courts or by the ombudsman.

The first landmark decision was Decision No. 40/2012. (XII. 6.) AB, which was initiated by the ombudsman. The decision stated that social security is a state goal and not a fundamental right. Hence, actions could not be based on this right. While those parts of the motion which were based on Article XIX were dismissed, Section 7(4) of the Act on the benefits of persons with altered work ability was annulled. The annulment was based on the violation of the prohibition of discrimination (Article XV of the Fundamental Law) and on the infringement of the principle of the rule of law [Article B(1)]. Although the

Constitutional Court partly applied the erstwhile dogmatics, it was a major change that the Court did not establish the violation of human dignity.[37]

This approach was followed by Decision No. 23/2013. (IX. 25.) AB as well. The decision expressly stated that there is only one constitutionally guaranteed social benefit, the pension of persons who have reached the retirement age applicable to them. The definition of other social benefits belongs under the competence of the legislator and – partly – the Government. It was confirmed that social legislation should comply with the principle of the rule of law. Thus, the transformation of earlier special pensions for people who have not yet reached the retirement age applicable to them (*e.g.* soldiers' and police officers' pensions) was declared to comply with the Fundamental Law.

It seemed, that the Constitutional Court followed the Anglo-American (common law) model in its interpretation of social law. However, there were exceptions. The decision of the Curia to authenticate the documentation of a planned referendum on the preferential pension for men who have more than 40 years pension entitlement was annulled by Decision No. 28/2015. (IX. 24.) AB. The resolution was based on that idea that the preferential pension for the women defined under Article XIX(4) is a constitutionally guaranteed right, as such, it cannot be the subject of a referendum. Hence, the interpretation of a social right as a state goal has been partly transformed, because the fundamental right nature of the social rights was (partly) recognized by the Constitutional Court.

The Constitutional Court changed its approach to some degree in Decision No. 21/2018. (XI. 14.) AB. The justification is very interesting, because the main approach has not changed: social rights are still interpreted as a state goal and not as fundamental rights. But the logic of the decision is very similar to the approach characteristic of the judgments of the social justice revolution decided by the US Supreme Court. The state goal nature of the right to social security is confirmed, but the Constitutional Court set the proportionality of reforms as a constitutional requirement. This requirement was based on the principle of the rule of law and on the rules of international law.

Decision No. 30/2017. (XI. 14.) AB was based on the principle of the rule of law. An important element of the reasoning[38] was the restriction on the applicability of Article XIX(3) of the Fundamental Law. Accordingly, only such conditions may be regulated by acts of Parliament which are linked to social benefits and have social characteristics. Similarly, the prohibition of discrimination (Article XV) was applied in the decision.

The Constitutional Court's approach to the constitutionality of the means-tested benefits and to social care was originally based on its earlier jurisprudence, but it has been transformed in part after 2012. Although the right to human dignity was not referenced

---

37   Andrea Szatmári, 'A szociális biztonsághoz való jog az Alaptörvényben az Alkotmánybíróság értelmezése szerint', *Közjogi Szemle*, 2018/1, pp. 65-66.
38   Decision No. 30/2017. (XI. 14.) AB, Reasoning [29]-[30].

in the reasoning of Decision 40/2012. (XII. 6.) AB and Decision No. 38/2012. (XI. 14.) AB, the Constitutional Court stated that the right to human dignity is violated in case the legislator prescribes the mandatory use of social care services and benefits. This decision was based on the common law approach to social services, which states, that the use of these services is primarily voluntary. The new approach reflecting the priority of self-care was interpreted by Decision No. 27/2013. (X. 9.) AB. The obligation of adult children to support their parents was found to be compatible with the Fundamental Law. However, a constitutional requirement was introduced, namely, that the alimony obligations towards minor children may not be jeopardized by this obligation.[39] Hence, the Constitutional Court originally followed the common law approach, yet this approach has partly changed. After the 7th Amendment of the Fundamental Law a new petty offense (misdemeanor) was introduced by an Act of Parliament which prohibited living in public spaces, practically banning homelessness. Homeless people were forced to use the social care system. Decision No. 19/2019. (VI. 18.) AB stated that this regulation is compatible with the Fundamental Law, because of the changes made to the constitution with the 7th Amendment. It merely established the constitutional requirement that the sanction be used only in case the care was actually provided for homeless people. The decision was highly controversial. Although the 7th Amendment has a rule prohibiting residing in a public space, but there were dissenting opinions[40] which emphasized that the forced use of services is not really compatible with the right to human dignity, according to the approach established in Decision No. 38/2012. (XI. 14.) AB. The new decision follows a different, paternalistic view of social rights, formerly not applied by the Constitutional Court. It does not comply with the main models governing the use of social services in modern welfare states.

25.5 CONCLUDING THOUGHTS

The Fundamental Law entered into force following the transformation of social policy after 2010. The Bismarckian nature of the Hungarian welfare system was weakened and a special model was introduced which is heavily relies on the common law welfare approach. This approach has been mainly endorsed by the decisions of the Constitutional Court. The decisions were not based on the right to social security, but on other fundamental

---

39   The decision was not unanimous. Elemér Balogh and Miklós Lévay wrote dissenting opinions. They stated that the right to human dignity is violated by the definition of the fee discount based solely on the resources of the provider of the social care institution. István Stumpf stated in his dissenting opinion that the guarantees for the fee discount are not regulated, therefore, it violates the principle of the rule of law. It was underlined by László Kiss, that the principles defined in the Decision No. 32/1998. (VI. 25.) AB were applicable.

40   Decision No. 19/2019. (VI. 18.) AB, dissenting opinions by Ágnes Czine, Ildikó Hörcherné Marosi, Balázs Schanda and Péter Szalay.

rights, because the right to social security was interpreted by the Constitutional Court as a state goal, which could not be directly invoked. Although the majority of the Constitutional Court's decisions were based on this liberal approach of self-care and regulatory freedom of the legislator, there are some curious decisions, as well. These decisions – in particular, the one on the referendum on the preferential pension system for men and on the misdemeanor of the homelessness – follows another approach. These differences are difficult to explain, the reasons for them seem to be extrajudicial.

26 A MULTIPOLAR SYSTEM FOR THE PROTECTION OF FUNDAMENTAL RIGHTS IN PRACTICE

Unjustified Dismissals of Government Officials in Hungary

Zsuzsanna Szabó[*]

Keywords

Multilevel constitutionalism, right to an effective remedy, unjustified dismissal of government officials, Constitutional Court of Hungary, European protection of fundamental rights

Abstract

Today, within the European multi-level and cooperative constitutional area the ECHR, the constitutional values enshrined in the EU Treaties together with the EU Charter of Fundamental Rights, as well as the constitutions of the EU Member States function as parallel constitutions. The legal remedies offered by international forums are subsidiary by nature, since it is desirable that legal issues of human rights be solved by the states at national level. The obligation to exhaust domestic legal remedies as a procedural precondition is necessary to afford the national level the opportunity to remedy the violation of human rights within its own legal system. This paper focuses on Section 8(1) of Act LVIII of 2010 on the legal status of government officials, which states that the employer has the right to terminate the contract of government officials with a two months' notice period without justification. This research is of considerable interest because the dismissed officials – who, in my opinion, *de facto* suffered injury for the violation of their human rights – were forced to turn to international fora due to the fact that the Hungarian legal system was unable to grant them proper relief. Therefore, the analysis also evaluates the current level of fundamental rights adjudication and jurisprudence related to fundamental principles in Hungary.

---

[*] Zsuzsanna Szabó: assistant lecturer, University of Debrecen.

26.1 Introduction

As European integration widened into a political process, the European constitutional area was transformed into a multi-level system. In this constitutional area, the ECHR, the provisions of the founding treaties of the EU concerning constitutional values, interpreted in conjunction with the EU Charter of Fundamental Rights, as well as the constitutions of the EU Member States function as parallel constitutions.[1] The differentiation of the legal system necessarily results in a so-called congestion of norms, an increase in the number of conflicts between the norms, as certain conditions of life are regulated by several groups of norms, in particular, when it comes to fundamental rights.[2] This means that it is the cooperation of the three forums that determines the opportunities that emerge in the area of the protection of individual fundamental rights. Lawyers largely depend on their own national constitution – although it is true that the application of national law may be modified by the infiltration of international human rights and fundamental law standards. Nevertheless, the ultimate foundation of the protection of fundamental rights will still be the national law and the national system for the protection of rights.[3]

The European constitutional system is shaped and operated by the jurisprudence of the Luxembourg- and Strasbourg-based, as well as the ordinary and constitutional courts of the Member States, which continuously build and enrich European constitutionalism through the 'dialogue' traceable in their case law.[4] The work of the ECtHR may be characterized by the concept of living instrument, which helps to develop the above-mentioned conversation ensuring the evolving nature of the interpretation of the ECHR. The Convention's provisions are interpreted by the ECtHR in light of modern-day standards to reflect today's realities and challenges.[5]

Based on the interpretation reflected in the judgments of the ECtHR, the obligation to exhaust domestic legal remedies as a precondition for launching proceedings is crucial partly because the national forums should preserve their opportunity to remedy violations of human rights within their own legal systems. This way, the international regime for

---

1   Nóra Chronowski, 'A többszintű alkotmányosság többszintű könyve', *Közjogi Szemle*, 2013/1, p. 68.
2   *Cf.* László Blutman, 'A jogrendszer nemzetköziesedése (Normák kapcsolódásai, konfliktusai a mai alkotmányos rendszerben)', *in* Miklós Kocsis & Judit Zeller (eds.), *A köztársasági Alkotmány 20 éve*, PAMA, Pécs, 2009, pp. 351-352.
3   Márta Dezső & Attila Vincze, *Magyar alkotmányosság az európai integrációban*, HVG-ORAC, Budapest, 2012, p. 489.
4   Chronowski 2013, p. 68.
5   *Regulation of Migration Processes in Eurasian Space*, Speech of the Special Representative of the Secretary General on Migration and Refugees, at www.coe.int/en/web/special-representative-secretary-general-migration-refugees/-/speech-at-the-international-round-table-regulation-of-migration-processes-in-eurasian-space-.

legal protection becomes supplementary to that on the national level.[6] It was pointed out by the Venice Commission that the legal remedy provided by the ECtHR is, by nature, subsidiary, as it is desirable that human rights issues be settled by the Member States on a national level, through the means of 'real' constitutional complaints, for instance.[7]

This study presents the practical implementation of the concept of multilevel constitutionalism. Its starting point is the theory of multilevel constitutionalism developed by Ingolf Pernice, based on a contractual approach on how political institutions are established and organized by those they are designed to serve.[8] Multilevel constitutionalism focuses on the correlation between national and EU law, from the perspective of the relationship between the state and the individual. It rests on the hypothesis that the right to exercise state power vested in both the national and the EU institutions originates from the citizens in modern democracies. Therefore, the two levels of constitutionalism are complementary elements of a system that serves the interests of the citizens.[9] According to this theory, the EU and the Member State levels of legal protection promote the enforcement of fundamental rights by mutually complementing each other. This is in line with the dual nature of the EU citizen's and Member State citizen's status, as well as the double task of national judicial and administrative bodies to apply both Member State law and EU law.[10]

It is an inherent feature of international legal norms protecting human rights that, as a general rule, they affect relations within the state. Traditionally, the decision on how international law is enforced within the national law of the state is traditionally assigned to the states. With the growing number of international norms, however, the situation has somewhat changed. The international community became interested in how international commitments are met.[11] The state continues to be the primary guarantor of the protection of fundamental rights but only if the system of legal protection implemented on the national level is fully functional.

The adoption of judgments related to fundamental rights is primarily the responsibility of ordinary courts in Hungary. However, with the introduction of 'real' constitutional complaints, these courts share this function with the Constitutional Court. As a result, the

---

6   *Neshkov and Others v. Bulgaria (dec.)*, Nos. 36925/10, 21487/12, 72893/12, 73196/12, 77718/12 and 9717/13, 27 January 2015, para. 177.

7   Zoltán Tóth J., 'Az egyéni (alap)jogvédelem az Alkotmányban és az Alaptörvényben (II. rész)', *Közjogi Szemle*, 2012/4, p. 29; European Commission for Democracy through Law (Venice Commission), *Opinion on Three Legal Questions Arising in the Process of Drafting the New Constitution of Hungary*, para. 63, at www.venice.coe.int/webforms/documents/?pdf=CDL-AD(2011)001-e.

8   Ingolf E. A. Pernice, *Multilevel Constitutionalism in the European Union*, at http://whi-berlin.de/documents/whi-paper0502.pdf.

9   Ingolf E. A. Pernice, 'The Treaty of Lisbon: Multilevel Constitutionalism in Action', *Columbia Journal of European Law*, Vol. 15, Issue 3, 2009, p. 372.

10   Attila Vincze, 'Osztott szuverenitás – többszintű alkotmányosság', *in* Kocsis & Zeller (eds.), 2009, p. 370.

11   Erzsébet Szalayné Sándor, 'Alapjogok (európai) válaszúton – Lisszabon után', *Jogtudományi Közlöny*, 2013/1, p. 17.

institutional and competence system of the courts becomes two-tiered.[12] Owing to the introduction of the 'real' constitutional complaint into the Hungarian legal system in 2012 the Constitutional Court, whose foremost task was to control the legislator, now supports the ordinary courts by providing guidelines, which are more and more often requested, or even unrequested.[13] Despite this, the Constitutional Court does not replace ordinary courts in protecting fundamental rights. With this new responsibility, however, it can now adopt judgments related to specific fundamental rights issues.[14] For the appropriate enforcement of fundamental rights by the ordinary courts, it is necessary that they base their judgments directly and in substance on the rules set out in the Constitution, as the case may be, even where lower level statutory provisions do not reflect the substance of the constitutional norm.[15] The concept of multilevel constitutionalism requires that courts take both constitutional level rules and the interpretation of international human rights courts into account when adopting their judgments, as long as the subject of the case is the interpretation of fundamental rights.

My research focuses on Section 8(1) of Act LVIII of 2010 on the status of public servants (Public Servants Act, PSA). This provision stipulated that the employment relationship of a government official may be terminated by the employer through dismissal, with a two-monthly notice period, without justification.[16] In my view, this regulation shattered the foundations of exercising the fundamental right to legal remedy in Hungary. If the former government official concerned is not entitled to hear the reasons for his dismissal, which he may challenge on valid grounds, this official's right to legal remedy has become meaningless, as there remains nothing on which he could base his claim challenging the dismissal before the labor court.[17] In the following part of my paper, I am going to present a few of the proceedings that were launched by former government officials for legal remedy of the disadvantage they had suffered.

This research is related to the topic of multilevel constitutionalism in that the former government officials whose rights were violated were compelled to turn to an international legal forum, in addition to the respective national fora, since the Hungarian legal system could not grant them appropriate relief. The cases of unjustified dismissals are therefore excellent examples for illustrating the dialogue or rather, the lack of dialogue between the fora participating in the multilevel constitutional cooperation. Namely, each of the three

---

12 Bernadette Somody et al., *Az alapjogi bíráskodás kézikönyve*, HVG-ORAC, Budapest, 2013, p. 32.
13 Dalma Dojcsák, 'Beszűrődő alapjogok – alapjogi bíráskodás és annak hiánya a rendesbíróságok gyakorlatában: ki védje az alapjogokat?', *Fundamentum*, 2016/1, p. 75.
14 Bernadette Somody, 'A rendőrarcképmás-ügy mint az alapjogi ítélkezés próbája', *Fundamentum*, 2016/1, p. 105.
15 Somody et al. 2013, p. 31.
16 This was in force between 6 July 2010 and 31 May 2011.
17 István Turkovics, 'A jogorvoslathoz való jog az Alkotmánybíróság gyakorlatának tükrében', *Pro Publico Bono: Magyar Közigazgatás*, 2013/2, p. 40.

fora, *i.e.* the Hungarian Constitutional Court and the ordinary courts (national level), the CJEU (EU level) and the ECtHR (international level) had the chance to investigate this legal issue. The study presents the procedures in a chronological order, according to the individual types of proceedings. Meanwhile, it also assesses how far fundamental rights and fundamental principles related jurisprudence has progressed in Hungary. The group of constitutional issues surrounding the law under review also suggests that the multipolar system offering legal protection is by far not perfect, although it seems to be multi-layered like a 'crowded house'.[18] The central question of the case studies shown below is what the former government officials can expect on an individual level and in general from the different fora of legal protection and their cooperation.

26.2   The First Decision of the Constitutional Court: Decision No. 8/2011. (II. 18.) AB

Already the provisions set out in Section 8(1) PSA, which ensured the employer the right to dismiss without giving reasons, thus depriving the government official from his right to successfully challenge this decision before the court, were clearly unconstitutional, in my view. The Constitutional Court was of the same opinion, and in the context of an abstract *ex post* norm control, it annulled this provision in Decision No. 8/2011. (II. 18.) AB[19] with effect from May 31, 2011, that is, *pro futuro*.

Pursuant to Decision No. 47/2003. (X. 27.) AB, the reasons for annulment with *pro future* effect are on the one hand, to ensure the predictable functioning of the rule of law until the new law to be created takes effect, and on the other hand, to make sure that keeping the unconstitutional law in temporary effect jeopardizes the integrity of the rule of law to a lesser extent than immediate annulment.[20] The Constitutional Court chooses the *pro futuro* option over the *ex nunc* or *ex tunc* effect annulment when it wishes to give the legislator an opportunity to create the appropriate rule, thus avoiding the development of a legal loophole and ensuring the general interest of legal certainty.[21] In the case under review, annulment of unjustified dismissal would have left dismissal of government officials temporarily unregulated. From this perspective, *pro futuro* annulment may seem to be a rational choice from the part of the Constitutional Court, however, in light of Decision No. 47/2003. (X. 27.) AB, this is disputable. One of the two preconditions required in the

---

18   Pedro Cruz Villalón, 'Rights in Europe – The Crowded House', *King's College London Working Papers in European Law*, 2012/1, p. 3.
19   Decision No. 8/2011. (II. 18.) AB, ABH, 2011, 49.
20   Decision No. 47/2003. (X. 27.) AB, ABH 2003, 525, Reasoning IV.1.4.
21   *See* also Decision No. 4/2013. (II. 21.) AB, Decision No. 20/2013. (VII. 19.) AB, Decision No. 6/2015. (II. 25.) AB.

above-mentioned decision was not fulfilled, since the very option of dismissal without justification jeopardizes the "predictable functioning of the rule of law." In my view, the right decision here would have been *ex tunc* annulment: this would have ensured appropriate legal protection for those affected by excluding dismissals based an unconstitutional section of the law.

The unconstitutionality of the given section of the act was based on the fact that it violated the principle of the rule of law, the right to work, the right to hold a public office, the right of access to justice, as well as the right to human dignity.[22] From among the breaches of fundamental rights, which gave rise to unconstitutionality, I will only like to discuss the "right of access to justice", which is relevant for my paper.

In its decision, the Constitutional Court derived the requirement of efficient court protection from the right of access to justice.[23] Namely, it explained that

> "legal rules should be framed in a legal environment in which the court can meaningfully assess the rights enforced, the right of access to justice is not sufficiently met by providing procedural guarantees. In lack of an obligation to provide justification, and in the lack of rules governing the assessment of the lawfulness of the dismissal, the scope of those cases in which the government official may seek justice in the hope of success (annulment of the dismissal, running counter to the prohibition of dismissal, violation of equal treatment, abuse of rights) is restricted. Limiting meaningful judicial protection of rights does not provide genuine, efficient legal protection for the employee against a voluntary, improper decision taken by the employer."[24]

The Constitutional Court presented the relevant legal interpretation given by the Strasbourg court.[25] According to this, general guarantees of judicial protection regulated by Article 57(1) of the former Constitution are also required by Article 6(1) ECHR. However, to support its own arguments, it mostly referred to the ECHR and other international human rights documents[26] as a comparative legal basis. After listing the relevant international legal instruments (Article 30 of the EU Charter of Fundamental Rights, Article 24 of the Revised European Social Charter), it simply concluded that the provisions set out in Sections

---

22 Decision No. 8/2011. (II. 18.) AB, Reasoning IV.6.
23 Article 57(1) of the former Constitution: "Everyone has the right to defend his rights and duties in legal proceedings, judged in a just, public trial by an independent and impartial court established by law."
24 Decision No. 8/2011. (II. 18.) AB, Reasoning IV.6.
25 *Frydlender v. France*, No. 30979/96, 27 June 2000; *Vilho Eskelinen and Others v Finland*, No. 63235/00, 19 April 2007; *Iordan Iordanov and Others v. Bulgaria*, No. 23530/02, 2 July 2009; *Delcourt v. Belgium*, No. 2689/65, 17 January 1970; *Barbera, Messegué and Jabardo v. Spain*, Nos. 10588/83, 10589/83, 10590/83, 6 December 1988.
26 Szalayné 2013, p. 17.

89(2)-(3) of the Hungarian Labor Code that were effective at that time also provide protection from the voluntary termination of employment in line with these requirements.[27]

In his concurring opinion, Mihály Bihari would have regarded it possible to establish
the violation of a constitutional fundamental right not specified in the majority position.
In his view, in the case under review, Article 57(1) of the previous Constitution (right of
access to justice), should have been interpreted with regard to, and in conjunction with
the provision set out in Article 57(5) (right to a legal remedy) of the same regulation. He
drew attention to the earlier conclusion drawn by the Constitutional Court, according to
which the possibility for legal remedy is a key substantive element of the constitutional
fundamental right to legal remedy, *i.e.* that legal remedy includes the remediability of a
violation of a right both conceptually and substantially. According to the concurring
opinion, in the case under review, the violation of the constitutional right was manifested
in the lack of an efficient legal remedy, and the lack of remediability of the violation that
occurred.[28] From my part, I fully agree with this argumentation. In my opinion, in its
judgment on the case, the Strasbourg court would also have established the violation of
the right to efficient legal remedy guaranteed under Article 13 ECHR (in the case of *K.M.C.
v. Hungary* to be explained below) had the applicant referred to it. However, as the ECtHR
is only entitled to investigate the violation of a specifically quoted fundamental right in its
proceedings, in line with its consistent judicial practice, this was out of the question.

26.3   DECISION OF THE ECtHR: K.M.C. v. HUNGARY

In its judgment of 10 July 2012,[29] the Strasbourg court decided a case of dismissal without
justification. The anonymous complainant, K.M.C. submitted their application to the court
on 22 March 2011, *i.e.* after the Constitutional Court had established the unconstitutionality of the provision allowing for unjustified dismissal in its above decision on 18 February
2011. K.M.C. was working as a public official at a state administration supervisory organ.
On 27 September 2010, they were given notice without any justification, by applying the
provisions set out in Section 8(1) PSA. K.M.C. did not challenge this measure in court, as
they thought that in lack of justification, they stood no chance of successfully suing their
former employer. K.M.C. complained that their unjustified dismissal made it impossible
for them to exercise their right of access to justice, meaning a violation of their fundamental
right set out in Article 6(1) ECHR.[30]

---

27   Decision No. 8/2011. (II. 18.) AB, Reasoning IV.3.
28   Decision No. 8/2011. (II. 18.) AB, concurring opinion by Mihály Bihari, 4.
29   *K.M.C. v. Hungary*, No. 19554/11, 10 July 2012.
30   "In the determination of his civil rights and obligations, everyone is entitled to a fair [...] hearing [...] by
     a tribunal established by law."

The most important observation of the Hungarian government, for my research, was that the applicant had not exhausted the legal remedies available in Hungary, as they had not launched a labor law case against their former employer. Had they done so, they could have challenged the binding decision made against them in a lawsuit before the Constitutional Court. Namely, the Constitutional Court stated in its Decision No. 35/2011. (V. 6.) AB that a law found to be unconstitutional shall not be applied in a lawsuit which is in progress before an ordinary court.[31] Reading this decision in conjunction with Decision No. 8/2011. (II. 18.) AB, the Constitutional Court would definitely have adopted such a decision which would have excluded the application of the unconstitutional law in the applicant's case and the applicant could have requested that the labor case be reopened in the wake of the decision. Furthermore, if such labor case of the applicant had been in progress, then the labor court would have been obliged to initiate proceedings before the Constitutional Court in line with the above-mentioned Constitutional Court decision for the establishment of the inapplicability of the unconstitutional law in this ongoing lawsuit.[32] (It is obvious from the Constitutional Court decisions[33] to be explained later, that the government's concept was far removed from reality, since the applicability of an unconstitutional law was not excluded by the Constitutional Court in any specific case.)

The arguments of the government were not accepted by the ECtHR which pointed out that a claim in which the applicant should have challenged his dismissal, the reasons for which dismissal, however, were completely unknown to him, could only have been a formal motion.[34] Thus, the application was not deemed inadmissible for lack of exhausting the Hungarian legal remedies.

As regards the merit of the case, the arguments presented by the court suggest that the right specified in Article 6(1) ECHR is not absolute, but can be subjected to restrictions without prejudice to the relevant content.[35] Here, the states have a certain margin of discretion.[36] The court's test assessing this was geared towards finding out whether the restriction applied restricts or reduces the individual's access to justice in such a way or to such an extent which already violates the core idea of the right in question. Furthermore, no such limitation of rights can be applied; finally, the restriction applied should be proportionate.[37]

---

31 Decision No. 35/2011. (V. 6.) AB, ABH 2011, 205, Reasoning IV.4.2.
32 *K.M.C. v. Hungary*, para. 23.
33 Decision No. 34/2012. (VII. 17.) AB and Order No. 3167/2013. (IX. 17.) AB.
34 *K.M.C. v. Hungary*, para. 28.
35 On the relevant content of fundamental rights, *see* Zoltán Pozsár-Szentmiklósy, 'Megismerhető-e az alapjogok lényeges tartalma?', *Magyar Jog*, 2013/12, pp. 714-722.
36 On the right of discretion, *see* Sándor Szemesi, *A diszkrimináció tilalma az Emberi Jogok Európai Bírósága gyakorlatában*, Complex, Budapest, 2009, p. 64; Andrew Legg, *The Margin of Appreciation in International Human Rights Law: Deference and Proportionality*, Oxford University Press, Oxford, 2012.
37 *K.M.C. v. Hungary*, para. 32.

According to the court, the ECHR "is intended to guarantee not rights that are theoretical or illusory but rights that are practical and effective",[38] and the maintenance of the right to access the labor court in Hungarian law in itself does not ensure that turning to the court will be effective in case this option is deprived of all substance and all hope for success.[39] It was also noted by the court that the Constitutional Court, whose approach was partially based on the relevant case law of the ECtHR, annulled the underlying Hungarian provision in harmony with the spirit of the EU Charter of Fundamental Rights and the Revised European Social Charter, based on similar considerations.[40] In its judgment, the court established a violation of the right of access to justice and it granted the applicant an amount of 6000 euros for non-material damage, and 3000 euros for costs and expenses.[41]

26.4   THE SECOND DECISION OF THE CONSTITUTIONAL COURT: DECISION NO. 34/2012. (VII. 17.) AB

After the adoption of Constitutional Court decision No. 8/2011. (II. 18.), several motions were filed with the Constitutional Court, in which judges proposed the exclusion of the applicability of provisions set out in Section 8(1)(b) PSA for cases in progress before them.[42] In the specific lawsuits that generated the motions, the government official claimants disputed the measures taken by the employer defendants, in the context of which they terminated their legal relationships as public officials without justification, on the basis of the above-mentioned provision of PSA. In the lawsuits, the claimants primarily applied for the establishment by the court of the unlawful termination of their legal relationships as public officials, their reinstatement into their original positions, as well as the payment of their missed allowances and other remuneration.[43] Thus, these former government officials chose to challenge these unjustified dismissals before a national forum. In their motions, the judges who asked for the procedure of the Constitutional Court argued that by applying the provision of PSA in question, such norms must be applied in the lawsuits whose unconstitutionality has already been established by the Constitutional Court and this would run counter to their constitutional obligations.

In the assessment of these motions, the above-mentioned Decision No. 35/2011. (V. 6.) AB played a very important role. In this decision, the Constitutional Court pointed out

---

38   Id. para. 38.
39   Id. para. 33.
40   Id. para. 34.
41   *See* for further detailed analysis, Péter Csuhány, 'Az Emberi Jogok Európai Bíróságának ítélete a kormánytisztviselők indokolás nélküli felmentéséről: a bírósághoz fordulás joga és a közszolgálati jellegű jogviszony indokolás nélküli megszüntetése', *JeMa*, 2012/4, pp. 74-86.
42   Decision No. 34/2012. (VII. 17.) AB, Reasoning [11].
43   Id. Reasoning [12].

that one of the key objectives of its responsibility of protecting the Constitution is to ensure that no unconstitutional norm be enforced in the legal system. A judge can fulfill his constitutional obligation as per the provisions set out in Article 50(1) of the former Constitution[44] if he makes a decision on the legal disputes brought before him through the application and interpretation of the constitutional law. Thus, the connection between the two decision-making judicial fora is established by guaranteeing the constitutionality of the applicable law, the means for which is an initiative taken by the judge in an ongoing procedure.[45] In this decision, the Constitutional Court concluded that according to its rules on competence, it has two options in the case of initiatives taken by the judges: it may establish the prohibition of the application of the unconstitutional law in general, with regard to each ongoing legal procedure, or it may decide on declaring a specific prohibition to apply the law in the case of an earlier established instance of unconstitutionality.[46]

In its Decision No. 34/2012. (VII. 17.) AB, the Constitutional Court established that although Decision No. 35/2011. (V. 6.) AB in fact allowed the courts to exclusively initiate the declaration of the prohibition of application, this only applied where the earlier decision established unconstitutionality on the basis of a judicial initiative and ordered a prohibition to apply the law in the specific cases affected by the judicial initiative.[47] The Constitutional Court did not extend the possibility to independently initiate the ban on applicability the law to such cases where a Constitutional Court decision was made on a law in effect, in an abstract norm control procedure.[48] Based on this, the forum drew the conclusion that since Decision No. 8/2011. (II. 18.) AB was adopted in an abstract norm control procedure and not on the basis of a judicial initiative, it is excluded from the start that the Constitutional Court will declare a ban on the applicability of an unconstitutional law in a specific case. Based on these reasons, it rejected the motions for the exclusion of the application of the provisions set out in Section 8(1) PSA in the ongoing labor court cases.

However, the Constitutional Court added that its conclusions do not affect the right of the courts proceeding in the individual case (*i.e.* those initiating the procedure) to independently assess the fact, in judging the lawfulness of the dismissal, that the unconstitutionality of the law that allows such dismissals and the date of it losing effect had already been established by the Constitutional Court, in the lawsuit on the legal relationship of a public official terminated by giving notice as per Section 8(1) PSA, which had already been

---

44 "The courts of the Republic of Hungary shall protect and uphold constitutional order, as well as the rights and lawful interests of natural persons, legal entities and organizations with no legal personality, and shall determine the punishment for those who commit criminal offenses."
45 Section 38(1) of the former HACC.
46 Decision No. 34/2012. (VII. 17.), Reasoning [41].
47 Id. Reasoning [42].
48 Id. Reasoning [45].

declared unconstitutional but which was still in effect.[49] As such, the responsibility to take a decision was assigned by the Constitutional Court to the proceeding judge by adding that the latter should use their own discretion in the case before them.

From my side, I fully agree with István Stumpf's concurring opinion on the question of the prohibition to apply the law, in which he explains why he disagrees with rejecting a ban on applicability. His following arguments should be highlighted:

In case unconstitutionality is established in the context of an abstract *ex post* norm control procedure, no prohibition to apply the law may be declared on a conceptual basis, for lack of a specific case in Decision No. 8/2011. (II. 18.) AB. Nor can it be declared in the future, in case unconstitutionality is established in the context of *ex post* norm control. Thus, rejecting the declaration of a prohibition to apply a law in a specific, subsequent case on the basis that this did not happen in the first case (*ex post* norm control), sets an impossible condition for those who later make judicial proposals or file constitutional complaints that flies in the face of remedying the infringement.[50] The majority opinion also referred to Order No. 1813/B/2010. AB,[51] according to which a *pro future* annulment involves the possibility, and at the same time, the obligation to apply the law that runs counter to the Fundamental Law of Hungary for a definite period. This applies to every party involved. When the Constitutional Court defines a future date for the unconstitutional law to lose effect, what it essentially does is it extends the duration of the application of the unconstitutional law itself, which will also bind the court proceeding in the case in question.[52]

Stumpf is of the opinion that the above conclusions should not have been followed as a precedent by the Constitutional Court, since at the time of their adoption, it was the former Constitution and the former Act on the Constitutional Court (former HACC) that were in effect. As consequence of the taking effect of the Fundamental Law of Hungary on January 1, 2012, in Stumpf's opinion, the role of the Constitutional Court changed: from the abstract, preventive protection of the constitutional rule of law, it shifted towards the subsequent remedying of individual constitutional infringements, as well as the enforcement of the rights ensured in the Fundamental Law of Hungary in specific cases. The relevant section of Act CLI of 2011 on the Constitutional Court (new HACC), on the other hand, expressly allows for the exclusion of applicability to be initiated widely.[53]

According to the concurring opinion, the Constitutional Court should have examined whether the conditions for ordering the prohibition to apply a law as specified in Section 45(4) of the new HACC were even fulfilled. These conditions foresee that the Constitutional

---

49   Id. Reasoning [55].
50   Id. concurring opinion by István Stumpf, [77].
51   Order No. 1813/B/2010, ABH 2011, 2936.
52   Decision No. 34/2012. (VII. 17.), concurring opinion by István Stumpf, [80].
53   Id. [79].

Court may determine the inapplicability of the annulled law in general or specific cases in a way that diverts from the general rule (*i.e.* from the *ex nunc* annulment and *ex nunc* prohibition of application) if this is justified by the need to protect the Fundamental Law of Hungary, legal certainty or a particularly important interest of the party launching the procedure.[54] In such cases too, Stumpf deems it necessary to examine, individually in each case, what the reason for defining a future date for annulment was and whether it is the need to protect the Fundamental Law of Hungary, legal certainty or a particularly important interest of the party launching the procedure that justifies the Constitutional Court decision to delay the prohibition on applying the law between the publication of the decision on annulment and the losing of effect of the law.[55]

26.5 THE THIRD DECISION OF THE CONSTITUTIONAL COURT: ORDER No. 3167/2013. (XI. 17.) AB

In the next case study, we have yet again a former government official seeking remedy for dismissal without justification. The former official launched a case against his employer at the Budapest Labor Court for the establishment of the unlawful termination of an employment relationship of a government official. He stated that pursuant to Decision No. 8/2011. (II. 18.) AB, the law that substantiates the official's unjustified dismissal is unconstitutional and as this was not annulled by the Constitutional Court with *ex nunc* effect, he requested that the labor court consult the Constitutional Court and apply for the exclusion of the applicability of the unconstitutional provision set out in the PSA in his case. The Budapest Labor Court rejected the claim, with reference to the fact that the norm was annulled by the Constitutional Court *pro futuro*. This is why the employer's measure that had previously been taken on the basis of this law was not unlawful.[56] The Budapest Capital Regional Court approved the judgment in the second instance.[57]

It is worth comparing the application of the claimant in the *K.M.C. v. Hungary* case with the comment made by the Hungarian Government. The government took it for granted that in similar cases, the judges would turn to the Constitutional Court, since,

"if such a labor court case had been in progress, the labor court would have been obliged to launch a procedure before the Constitutional Court for an

---

54   Id. [81]-[82].
55   Id. [83].
56   Budapest Labor Court 15.M.2304/2011/14.
57   Budapest Labor Court 51.Mf.635.021/2012/4.

investigation into the inapplicability of the unconstitutional law in this ongoing court case, based on the decision of the Constitutional Court of 6 May 2011."[58]

However, in this case, the Budapest Labor Court did not turn to the Constitutional Court, although the exclusion of the application of the law that runs counter to the Fundamental Law of Hungary must be initiated before the Constitutional Court in the specific legal dispute between the parties, as per Section 25 of the new HACC. This is why the Budapest Capital Regional Court also took the wrong step, since it should have repealed the judgment owing to this omission of the Labor Court.[59]

After the adoption of the judgments, the former government official turned to the Constitutional Court with a constitutional complaint. His motion contained two applications. Based on the so-called 'old type' constitutional complaint, he asked the Constitutional Court to establish that the statutory provision that had been applied in his case [Section 8(1)(b) PSA] violated the Fundamental Law of Hungary,[60] and to exclude the applicability of such law with retrospective effect. In his 'real' constitutional complaint, he secondarily sought that the court establish that the judgment adopted by the Municipal Court of Budapest had breached his fundamental rights, and that it ran counter to Article Q(2) of the Fundamental Law of Hungary, which guarantees the harmony between international commitments of Hungary and the country's domestic law. Based on these, he applied for the annulment of the first and second instance decisions adopted in his case.

The applicant was of the view that a distinction should be made between the cases dismissed before and after the adoption of Decision No. 8/2011. (II. 18.) AB. He argued that in his case, his employer must have been aware that he was applying an unconstitutional law, for at the time of his dismissal, the unconstitutionality of the law that allowed such a dismissal was already established by the Constitutional Court. In his view, the *pro futuro* annulment of the law did not render the unjustified dismissals communicated in the period between 18 February and 31 May 2011 constitutional.

In connection with the constitutional complaint, the Constitutional Court examined whether its assessment depended on whether the judicial decision that the complaint was about was adopted before or after publishing Decision No. 8/2011. (II. 18.) AB.[61] The Constitutional Court established that in the judicial decisions adopted before the publication

---

58   Decision No. 35/2011. (V. 6.) AB; *K.M.C. v. Hungary*, para. 23.

59   BDT 2012. 2675, Szekszárd District Court 3.Mf.20.061/2011/3.

60   Due to the violation of the right to work, the free choice of work and occupation, the right to hold public office, the right to effective judicial protection, as well as the right to human dignity [Article XII(1), Article XXIII(8) and Article XXVIII(1), as well as Article II of the Fundamental Law of Hungary]. Furthermore, the applicant indicated that the provision ran counter to the requirement of the rule of law stipulated in Article B(1) of the Fundamental Law of Hungary, as the principle of the dependence of state administration on the law was disregarded by the unconstitutional law applied in the case.

61   Order No. 3167/2013. (IX. 17.) AB, Reasoning [23].

of the above-mentioned decision, the judge was obliged to apply the provisions set out in the PSA, as it was the law in effect, but this obligation of the judge also remained following the publication of this decision.[62] Then the Constitutional Court referred back to one of its earlier decisions. In Decision No. 3302/2012. (XI. 12.) AB, it was stipulated on the basis of a judicial initiative for the proclamation of a prohibition of application of a law that had been annulled earlier, with *ex nunc* effect:[63] if an earlier decision did not order a prohibition of application in a specific case and it did not have to adopt a decision on a judicial initiative or a constitutional complaint, then the legal relations that arose from a similar factual basis and that were generated from the same right may receive a similar assessment before the ordinary court if the Constitutional Court does not stipulate the inapplicability of the law on the basis of an initiative launched subsequently.

Based on this, what is relevant for the case under review is that Decision No. 34/2012. (VII. 17.) AB assessed judicial initiatives aimed at the exclusion of the application of the very Section 8(1) PSA and rejected these very motions.[64] In the opinion of the Constitutional Court, the assessment of the dismissal by the employer based on Section 8(1) PSA before the publication of Decision No. 8/2011. (II. 18.) AB, as well as that of the constitutional complaint challenging the judicial decision that became binding in the case of a subsequent lawsuit cannot be judged differently in the current case than the judicial initiatives submitted after declaring these laws unconstitutional. Namely, with the Constitutional Court having indicated the losing of effect of the unconstitutional law at a date set in the future, what happened was that in the case in question, the duration of the application of the unconstitutional law was extended, without defining any exceptions, and the judge was bound to apply the unconstitutional law.[65] On these grounds, the constitutional complaint was rejected by the Constitutional Court.

István Stumpf attached a dissenting opinion to the order, according to which the complaint should have been accepted and assessed on its merits. Stumpf was of the view that the courts acting in the case made a mistake, since the unconstitutionality impacting the judicial decision could have been avoided if at the time of establishing the unlawfulness of the dismissal, the court would have considered properly the fact that at the time of giving notice, the unconstitutionality and the date of losing effect of the law that allowed the dismissal had already been established by the Constitutional Court. The courts could have acted in harmony with the Fundamental Law of Hungary in the application of the rule contained by the provision that had been deemed unconstitutional.[66]

---

62   Id. Reasoning [24].
63   The law in question was annulled by Decision No. 42/2008. (IV. 17.) AB, ABH 2008, 417.
64   Order No. 3167/2013. (IX. 17.), Reasoning [25].
65   Id. Reasoning [26].
66   Id. dissenting opinion by István Stumpf, [57].

Since in the current case the Constitutional Court repeated its arguments presented in Decision No. 34/2012. (VII. 17.) AB, criticized by István Stumpf in his concurring opinion attached to the decision, in my view, what was asserted by István Stumpf in that case holds true for this case too. In my view, the crucial interest of the party initiating the procedure should have been taken into account here as well, *i.e.* that his fundamental constitutional rights had been violated by excluding the prohibition of application.

Péter Kovács also attached a dissenting opinion to Decision No. 3167/2013. (IX. 17.) AB, which points out the deficiencies in the aspects of multilevel constitutionalism in the Hungarian practice. In Kovács's opinion, the constitutional complaint should in fact have been accepted and reviewed on its merits. In his view, the complainant's reference to the *K.M.C. v. Hungary* case was valid.[67] I fully agree with the arguments set out in the dissenting opinion. According to justice Kovács, the Hungarian legal practitioner was put in an impossible situation, as it is very difficult to fulfill two contradictory obligations at the same time: on the one hand, to apply Hungarian positive law, and on the other hand, to take into account the Constitutional Court decision that declared unconstitutionality but established it with *pro futuro* effect, as well as declaring the law to run counter to the ECHR.[68]

Péter Kovács recalls Decision No. 61/2011. (VII. 13.) AB, according to which, in the case of some fundamental rights, the Constitution defines the key substance of the fundamental right in the same way as it is set out in an international treaty (such as the ICCPR or the ECHR). In these cases, the level of protection of fundamental rights ensured by the Constitutional Court can never be lower than the level of international legal protection (typically applied by the Strasbourg court). Thus, arising from the principle of *pacta sunt servanda* [Article Q(2)-(3) of the Fundamental Law of Hungary], the Constitutional Court has to follow the Strasbourg legal practice and the level of protection of fundamental rights defined therein even of this would not necessarily flow from their own earlier precedent decisions. In his view,

> "the judges of the Hungarian judicial system are faced with a situation whereby, in the current case, positive Hungarian law, international law (the *pacta sunt servanda* principle) and EU law, what is more, all of these in the light of the judicial practice followed by Strasbourg and Luxemburg, cannot easily be harmonized in the case described in the present constitutional complaint. This incoherence is of such an extent that it would have justified the acceptance and meaningful examination of the complaint."[69]

---

67   Id. dissenting opinion by Péter Kovács, [59].
68   Id. [60].
69   Id. [63]-[64].

The elimination of the incoherence indicated by Kovács is very desirable, in my view. This can be done through emphasizing and treating as a priority the protection of individual fundamental rights among the criteria applied during the norm control procedure of the Constitutional Court. Thus, I deem it possible to fulfill the expectation arising from our obligations under international law that the primary scene of the protection of fundamental rights should be the domestic law and that international protection should merely play a supplementary role. Progress has been made by the introduction of 'real' constitutional complaints, as there was a major shift in emphasis in the activities performed by the Constitutional Court. In the individual cases, it is not the norm control function of the constitutional complaint that is dominant any more but the legal remedy nature through the constitutionality review of judicial decisions.[70] With this, the constitution-makers redefined the place of fundamental rights in individual legal protection, putting the constitutionality review of individual cases to the forefront.[71] With regard to the fact, however, that the *pro futuro* or even *ex nunc* effect annulment adopted in the abstract *ex post* norm control procedure excludes that persons affected later request a prohibition of application independently, in the form of a constitutional complaint, this means that only an annulment with *ex tunc* effect may ensure legal remedy for those concerned.[72]

Order No. 3167/2013. (IX. 9.) AB under review does not represent the spirit of protecting individual fundamental rights.[73] The prohibition of application is excluded in the majority decision. From my part, I disagree with this standpoint, for this way, the Constitutional Court renounces the legal remedy that may be provided to the victims running counter to the Fundamental Law of Hungary. It thereby violates its international obligation, to provide effective legal protection to individuals. This way, the complainants similar to K.M.C. are compelled to turn an international forum.

26.6 Decisions of the CJEU: Nagy and Others and Weigl Cases

The matter of the unjustified dismissal of government officials could not go unnoticed by the forum of the EU either, as the complainants, presumably as a kind of *ultima ratio*, referred in the judicial proceedings to the violation of the provisions set out in the Charter of Fundamental Rights. The proceeding judge made a request for a preliminary ruling regarding the interpretation of the Charter of Fundamental Rights to the CJEU in two

---

70 Georgina Naszladi, 'Veszélyben az alkotmányjogi panasz jogorvoslati jellege', *Fundamentum*, 2013/1, p. 82.
71 Zoltán Tóth J., 'Változások a magyar alapjogi bíráskodásban: Normatív és jogszociológiai elemzés', *Jogelméleti Szemle*, 2016/1, pp. 130-131.
72 Naszladi 2013, p. 82.
73 *See* Order No. 3042/2013. (II. 28.) AB.

such cases. The CJEU can play a significant role in the protection of fundamental rights when it works together with the national courts in close cooperation to make national courts more conscious of their joint responsibility for legal protection in the EU.[74]

Since the Lisbon Treaty took effect on 1 December 2009, there have been roughly twenty court decisions in Hungarian judicial practice, adopted in cases which were concluded with a binding effect through the proceedings of the Curia or high courts of appeal, that contained references to the fundamental rights enshrined in the Charter.[75] In the majority of the cases, the claimant who stated that his fundamental rights had been violated, referred to the articles of the Charter (besides indicating other legal grounds too). However, the courts adopted their decisions in substance not by reference to these legal grounds. Neither of the decisions established the violation of fundamental rights directly on the basis of the provisions set out in the Charter.[76]

The matter of the unjustified dismissal of government officials first became the subject of a preliminary ruling procedure since some former government officials filed a claim against the decisions adopted in respect of their unjustified dismissals at the Debrecen Labor Court, for the court to establish the unlawfulness of the termination of their employment. Some of the claimants requested that their employment in their earlier position be resumed. They also made financial claims of various amounts, while the others applied to the court for lump sum settlements amounting to their average salaries of twelve months, as well as the lost remuneration. The Constitutional Court rejected the motion filed by the Debrecen Labor Court for the exclusion of the application of provisions set out in Section 8(1) PSA. It was then that the judge turned to the CJEU in the case of *Sándor Nagy and Others*.[77] According to the referring court, it arises from the interpretation of Article 30 (on protection against dismissal without justification) and Article 51 of the Charter (on the scope of application of the Charter) read together that from the aspect of applicability, Article 30 has direct effect, *i.e.* it should be applied in the procedures before ordinary courts. The referring court asked the CJEU to interpret Article 30 of the Charter, in order to decide whether Section 8(1)(b) PSA should be applied in the case of disputes regarding fundamental rights.

Pursuant to Article 51(1) of the Charter, Member States are addressees of the provisions set out in the Charter only to the extent that they enforce the laws of the EU. Article 6(1) TEU, just like Article 51(1) of the Charter, makes it clear that the provisions set out in the latter do not in any way extend the competences of the EU as set forth in the founding

---

74   Ingolf E. A. Pernice, 'Die Zukunft der Unionsgerichtsbarkeit – Zu den Bedingungen einer nachhaltigen Sicherung effektiven Rechtsschutzes im Europaischen Verfassungsverbund', *Europarecht*, 2011/2, p. 167.

75   Zsófia Varga, 'Az Alapjogi Charta a magyar bíróságok előtt', *Jogtudományi Közlöny*, 2013/11, p. 554.

76   Id.

77   Order of 10 October 2013, *Joined Cases C-488/12, C-489/12, C-490/12, C-491/12 and C-526/12, Nagy Sándor and Others v. Hajdú-Bihar Megyei Kormányhivatal and Others*, ECLI:EU:C:2013:703.

treaties. It was established by the CJEU that fundamental rights-related disputes do not affect the interpretation or application of EU law outside the Charter and they are in no connection whatsoever with the national regulation that enforces the EU laws on the basis of Article 51(1) of the Charter. However, if a certain legal situation does not belong under the scope of application of the EU laws, the Court will have no competence for assessing such situation, and the provisions of the Charter that may have been quoted cannot in themselves establish this competence. Based on these, the CJEU declared that it had no competence to answer these questions.[78]

On the second occasion, it was the Curia that launched a preliminary ruling procedure in review proceedings that were started in a similar case, based on arguments that were the same as those put forward by the Debrecen Labor Court.[79] The application filed by the Curia did not bring about any meaningful changes in the cooperation of the EU forum and the national forum. This is because the CJEU repeated its arguments that it had elaborated in the *Nagy and Others* case, concluding that it had no competence to answer the questions posed by the Hungarian court. Following the adoption of the decision, the Curia was compelled to assess on its own whether the termination of the government officials' employment without justification is unlawful, as long as it is done with reference to a law whose unconstitutionality has already been established. Finally, the Curia decided to maintain the effect of the decision adopted by the second instance labor court, which regarded the dismissal without justification to be an instance of improper legal practice.[80]

In my view, the CJEU had in fact no competence to answer these questions. The CJEU cannot provide protection by breaching its own competence rules even if the national forums are helpless, since this is not the function of the preliminary ruling procedure. Even though the legally binding EU Charter of Fundamental Rights does not standardize the level of the fundamental rights protection ensured by the Member States,[81] Advocate General Cruz Villalón is of the opinion that the review of actions performed by the Member States' executive power enjoying a certain discretion usually affects the states themselves, according to their respective constitutional orders and their international treaties, in the correct interpretation of the fundamental constitutional structure qualified as a European *Verfassungsverbund* constituted by the Member States and the EU.[82]

The approach typically taken in the cases above, *i.e.* that the CJEU is not a human rights court and is not responsible for acting as a last resort in the case of helpless national forums,

---

78   Id. paras. 17-18.
79   Order of 16 January 2014, *Case C-332/13, Ferenc Weigl v. Nemzeti Innovációs Hivatal*, ECLI:EU:C:2014:31.
80   EBH 2014.M.11, Curia Mfv.I.10.082/2014.
81   Zsófia Varga, 'Az Európai Bíróság végzése a közszolgálati jogviszony indokolás nélküli megszüntetésével kapcsolatban: az EU Alapjogi Karta alkalmazási köre: C-488/12, C-491/12, C-526/12', JeMa, 2014/1, p. 62.
82   Opinion of Advocate General Cruz Villalón, Delivered on 12 June 2012, *Case C-617/10, Aklagaren v. Hans Akerberg Fransson*, ECLI:EU:C:2012:340, para. 35.

was confirmed by *Opinion No. 2/13*[83] on the accession of the EU to the ECHR. The Opinion pointed we cannot jeopardize the structure of EU law just for the sake of 'deepening' the protection of human rights.[84]

26.7   CONCLUSIONS

This exploration of the deficiencies of the protection of fundamental rights in the Hungarian legal system may contribute to answering the question who the Hungarian complainants seeking justice may expect to comply with the international standards in the case of a violation of their fundamental rights. It should be acknowledged, that the individual levels of the multipolar system provide different 'services' to those seeking justice and as the primary guarantee for the protection of fundamental rights would be the flawless operation of the Hungarian legal system, both legislation and legal practice should aspire to avoid mistakes. In my opinion, however, the dialogue between the individual levels is missing. At the same time, cooperation between the different judicial forums would also contribute to the correction of the deficiencies inherent in the individual systems: would national constitutional courts be willing to apply international standards, this would help bridge the problem of enforcement. Meanwhile, international organs would ensure, through their legal practice, that national bodies responsible for legal protection justify their own practices and at the same time, offering the opportunity to change these.[85]

However, the legal position of certain international courts' and tribunals' decision in the Hungarian legal system is different,[86] although this would be a fundamental criterion for channeling international case-law standards into the Hungarian system. International judgments fail to become a part of the internal legal system pro forma, thus, it is unclear whether the Hungary-related case law of the ECtHR is a mere source of information without any binding force in the sense of formal law for the Hungarian legal practitioners, or just the opposite, *i.e.* whether it creates an obligation for the Hungarian courts and other authorities to interpret and apply individual fundamental rights in harmony with these (the lack of which would mean a breach of international law).[87]

Hungarian legal literature has no uniform opinion in this respect either. Gábor Halmai takes the position that in Hungary, not even the Constitutional Court is obliged to follow

---

83   Opinion of the Court, 18 December 2014, *Case Opinion 2/13*, ECLI:EU:C:2014:2454.
84   Petra Lea Láncos, 'A Bíróság 2/13. számú véleménye az Unió EJEE-hez való csatlakozásáról', *Pázmány Law Working Papers*, 2015/1, p. 8.
85   Dezső & Vincze 2012, p. 490.
86   Tamás Molnár, 'Két kevéssé ismert nemzetközi jogforrás helye a belső jogban: a nemzetközi bíróságok döntései, valamint az egyoldalú állami aktusok esete a magyar jogrendszerrel', *Közjogi Szemle*, 2012/3, p. 5.
87   Id. p. 2.

the Strasbourg practices. One can find examples where the Hungarian judges assessed a problem contrary to, or at least differently from ECtHR case-law.[88] Other authors stress that the Hungarian Constitutional Court usually refers to the decisions adopted by international forums, in the spirit of constitutional cooperation.[89] The Constitutional Court itself has declared in several of its decisions that the level of protection of fundamental rights that it can provide can never be lower than the level of international (mostly Strasbourg) legal protection. As has been pointed out in the dissenting opinion expressed by Péter Kovács, presented above, arising from the constitutional principle *pacta sunt servanda*, the Constitutional Court should follow the ECtHR legal practice even if this does not necessarily derive from its own earlier decisions.[90]

However, if one follows the legal practice, a contrary situation seems to be unfolding. Although the Constitutional Court declared that the approach of the ECtHR shapes and obliges Hungarian legal practice,[91] the cases analyzed in this paper are evidence that the Court attached little significance to this obligation in its interpretation of the Constitution. Were w trying to find out today which body is the primary protector of fundamental rights in Hungary, most people would definitely mention the Constitutional Court. In my view, however, this is the wrong answer. Although it would be very welcome if the practice of the Constitutional Court shifted in this direction in the future, the decisions presented here show that at the moment, this is not what the Constitutional Court regards as its primary goal.

The Constitutional Court is the main body for the protection of the Fundamental Law of Hungary,[92] it is the guardian of our constitutional identity. Besides this function, the protection of individual fundamental rights has been of secondary importance to the Hungarian Constitutional Court to date. István Stumpf is of the view that as consequence of the taking effect of the Fundamental Law of Hungary, the role of the Constitutional Court has changed: from the abstract, preventive protection of the constitutional rule of law, it has shifted to the direction of the subsequent remedy of the infringements of individual fundamental rights, as well as the enforcement of the rights guaranteed by the Fundamental Law of Hungary in individual cases.[93] In my view, this conclusion rests on an idealistic approach, as the majority position in the decisions presented here clearly follow another mentality. In the European constitutional space, I find it desirable that the Hungarian Constitutional Court be proactive in the individual protection of rights, thereby

---

88 Gábor Halmai, *Alkotmányjog – emberi jogok – globalizáció. Az alkotmányos eszmék migrációja*, L'Harmattan, Budapest, 2013, p. 69.
89 *See* László Blutman *et al., A nemzetközi jog hatása a magyar joggyakorlatra*, HVG-ORAC, Budapest, 2014.
90 Decision No. 61/2011. (VII. 12.) AB, Reasoning V.2.2.
91 Order No. 3167/2013. (IX. 17.) AB, dissenting opinion by Péter Kovács, [62].
92 Article 24(1) of the Fundamental Law of Hungary.
93 Decision No. 34/2012. (VII. 17.) AB, concurring opinion by István Stumpf, [79].

undertaking the role that is rightfully expected of this forum as the guarantor of the protection of fundamental rights according to European constitutional traditions.

Although the Constitutional Court itself points it out that pursuant to the new HACC, in its decision establishing unconstitutionality, it is relatively free to determine the legal consequences, and in individual cases, it may also weigh the criteria of legal certainty, the protection of individual rights and the protection of the Fundamental Law of Hungary,[94] in light of the decisions presented here, we may conclude that the Constitutional Court clearly fails to make use of these options. It is the criticism of this approach that is expressed in the dissenting opinion that Miklós Lévay expressed in Decision No. 6/2015. (II. 25.) AB. Lévay takes the position that

> "however, annulment in the future does not mean that the forum could not have decided to declare the prohibition of application besides the general interest of the enforcement of legal certainty on the basis of a critically important interest of the party who launched the procedure, which was made obvious in the concrete case."[95]

Thus, in the priority list of the Constitutional Court, the requirement of legal certainty still precedes the obligation to protect fundamental rights.

I share the opinion that in today's Hungary, court decisions concerning fundamental rights are in the hands of ordinary courts, which, however, do not feel authorized to interpret and apply the Fundamental Law of Hungary, or the very fundamental rights included therein, directly. According to the most commonly applied technique, proceeding judges may only enforce fundamental rights specified in the Fundamental Law of Hungary indirectly, through the vehicle of referencing general rules of the laws.[96] Article 28 of the Fundamental Law clearly prescribes that judges carry out their interpretation in line with the Fundamental Law (interpretation in conformity with the constitution).

The clear reluctance to adopt judgments on fundamental rights is excellently illustrated by a judgment adopted by the Budapest Administrative and Labor Court and annulled by the Constitutional Court. In the grounds, it is explained in relation to the references to fundamental rights specified in the claim and the references to the requirement of proportionality of the restriction of fundamental rights, that as the freedom of press and the freedom of expression are protected constitutional rights expressly mentioned in the Fundamental Law of Hungary, they cannot be directly enforced before the court. In this

---

94   Decision No. 34/2012. (VII. 17.) AB, Reasoning [53].
95   Decision No. 6/2015. (II. 25.) AB, dissenting opinion by Miklós Lévay, [60].
96   Szalayné 2013, p. 18.

respect, fundamental right-related arguments and the explanations based on the decisions adopted by the Constitutional Court were not examined at all.[97]

The legal practice of the ordinary courts in the field of applying international standards brings up further important questions, the application of the ECHR at ordinary judicial forums cannot be called general practice for the time being, in light of the cases presented. As the Constitutional Court concluded, although the ECHR and its case law cannot be applied directly, the courts should adopt their judgments in harmony with the relevant Strasbourg case law.[98] It can be concluded from the cases presented that this requirement for harmonization does not have a binding force. It is here that we should repeat the above mentioned position taken by Péter Kovács: the Hungarian legal practitioner finds it hard to obey several contradictory commands at the same time, *i.e.* to apply Hungarian positive law on the one hand, and to apply the decision declaring unconstitutionality in the case in question on the other hand, as well as the legal interpretation of the ECtHR.[99]

This legal problem, which is well illustrated by the case studies presented in this paper, cannot be resolved without the readiness to compromise on the side of Hungarian legal practitioners. The ordinary courts could benefit from considering the concept to be shown now, which was basically developed for the relationship between EU law and national laws, but which has an immanent content that can also be converted to the multipolar system that I have analyzed. Multilevel constitutionalism as conceptualized by Ingolf Pernice does not only mean placing constitutional systems next to each other, *i.e.* renouncing their hierarchical relationship but it also sets expectations for legislators and legal practitioners. Namely, that in the multipolar system, going beyond positivism and the closed concept of legal positivism, the conflicts between the different players are resolved by focusing on the efficient enforcement of rights, as well as involving constitutional and supranational values.[100]

Pál Sonnevend finds that the ECHR increasingly functions as a parallel constitution and takes the place of constitutional guarantees.[101] The ECHR can be called as a 'shadow constitution' in the European states (Belgium, France, Switzerland, the United Kingdom) that serve as a standard for others, since it was included in the national legal structures of these countries in such a way that it can be directly referred to.[102] However, in the Hungarian

---

97 Decision No. 3/2015. (II. 2.) AB, Reasoning [85].

98 Kriszta Kovács, 'Az Emberi Jogok Európai Egyezménye és az uniós jog szerepe az alapjogi ítélkezésben', *in* Bernadette Somody (ed.), *Alapjogi bíráskodás – Alapjogok az ítélkezésben*, L'Harmattan, Budapest, 2013, p. 159.

99 Order No. 3167/2013. (IX. 17.) AB, dissenting opinion by Péter Kovács, [60].

100 Tímea Drinóczi, 'Többszintű alkotmányosság az Európai Unióban', *Közjogi Szemle*, 2008/4, p. 65.

101 Presentation at the Budapest conference held in 2013 on the International Day of Human Rights, at www.jogiforum.hu/hirek/30866.

102 Helen Keller & Alec Stone Sweet (eds.), *A Europe of Rights. The Impact of the ECHR on National Legal Systems*, Oxford University Press, Oxford, 2012, p. 686.

judicial system, except for a few rare exceptions, it did not become general practice for ordinary courts to base their justifications directly on Strasbourg case law.[103] Meanwhile, this is in fact a statutory obligation for judges, taking into account that the ECHR also became a part of Hungarian law with its promulgation. Furthermore, Section 13(1) of Act L of 2005 on the procedure regarding international treaties requires that the "the decisions adopted by the organ that has jurisdiction for deciding the legal disputes related to the international treaty in question" be taken into account in the interpretation by the courts of the international treaties.

However, the current situation is that ordinary courts tend to refer to domestic positive law rather than international law. In the case of dismissals without justification, it was the requirement of proper legal practice as per Section 4(1) of Act XXII of 1992 (the former Hungarian Labor Code) with reference to which the Curia established the illegal nature of the dismissal in the case described in the previous chapter of this paper. It did so despite the fact that at the time it was examined, Decision No. 8/2011. (II. 18.) AB, which required the application of this law (declared unconstitutional with *pro futuro* effect), had already been adopted.[104] The Curia decided in a way that was contrary to the requirement set out in the Constitutional Court decision, which was correct, in my opinion. However, it is also worth mentioning that, as the legal interpretation of the ECtHR was already known at the time of the adoption of the Curia's decision, from my part I miss the reference to the case *K.M.C. v. Hungary* from the Curia's decision. In light of this, it can be concluded with regard to the role of ECHR in Hungarian judicial practice, that ordinary courts clearly apply Hungarian law in the case of a conflict between the Hungarian laws and the provisions set out in the ECHR.[105]

In my view, the concept of multilevel constitutionalism does not only require communication between the national and international levels but close cooperation is also expected of the internal forums within the national level. It is the judicial initiative of the Constitutional Court procedure that creates the link between the Constitutional Court and ordinary courts in Hungarian law. It means progress that today, if this is missing in the appeal procedure, it will lead to the voiding of the judgment due to the violation of the law.[106]

From the cases presented, it can also be concluded that in the constitutional handling of the issue of dismissals without justification, the application of a type of procedure whose function is to further cooperation between the Constitutional Court and ordinary courts, and which may have contributed to the inclusion of the international standards into the

---

103   For a counter-example *see* Budapest Regional Court of Appeal 5.Pf.20.738/2009/7. Nóra Chronowski & Erzsébet Csatlós, 'Judicial Dialogue or National Monologue? The International Law and Hungarian Courts', *ELTE Law Journal*, 2013/1, p. 18.

104   Curia of Hungary Mfv.I.10.082/2014.

105   Halmai 2013, p. 68.

106   BDT 2012.2675, Szekszárd District Court 3.Mf.20.061/2011/3.

judicial proceedings, was missing. The procedure was institutionalized by Section 32(2) of the new HACC. This means that the judge, suspending the judicial procedure, initiates a Constitutional Court procedure if he has to apply a law which, in his view, runs counter to an international treaty, during the assessment of the individual case before him.

In my view, since the Strasbourg court adopted the judgment in the case *K.M.C. v. Hungary*, the fact that Section 8(1) PSA ran counter to the international treaty was proven beyond the shadow of a doubt. In this case, Section 13(1) of Act L of 2005 also applies, which specifically requires that in the interpretation of the international treaty, the earlier decisions of the body with jurisdiction for deciding the legal disputes related to the treaty should be taken into account.[107] Thus, the application of the ECHR and the reference to its provision acknowledging the right to effective legal remedy by the ordinary court would have involved the case law of the Strasbourg court in the proceeding.

The Constitutional Court would have had an excellent opportunity to apply the procedure specified in Section 32(2) of the new HACC in the following case, however, the breakthrough did not happen. In Decision No. 6/2015. (II. 25.) AB, the judge initiating the procedure, with reference to Section 25(1) of the new HACC, applied to the Constitutional Court for the annulment of a norm that went against the Fundamental Law of Hungary, since he found that one of the provisions of Act II of 2007 breached the Fundamental Law of Hungary and another ran counter to an international treaty. In order to support this opinion, he referred to Articles XV and Q of the Fundamental Law of Hungary. During the assessment of the motion, the Constitutional Court, in a rather questionable way, remained within the framework that it defined for itself earlier and it only annulled the provision in question with *pro futuro* effect, on account of the provision violating the Fundamental Law of Hungary, however, it disregarded examining its compatibility with the international treaty. I share the dissenting opinion of Béla Pokol, according to which

> "the technical problems of the decision' argumentation stem from the fact that although the subject of the motion is the establishment of the violation of an international treaty, except for mentioning a more general Fundamental Law declaration, Article Q, it disregarded the analysis of the special rules of the Fundamental Law concerning the examination of conflicts with international treaties."[108]

In summary, it can be concluded that in the domestic and international protection of human rights, all the 'pillars' mentioned in this paper are needed. The European multilevel system of rights protection is composed of layers of protection, that complement each

---

107 Kovács 2013, p. 159.
108 Decision No. 6/2015. (II. 25.) AB, dissenting opinion by Béla Pokol, [64].

other, instead of layers that are neatly separated according to their origin (constitutional, EU or international).[109]

But the decisions adopted by the individual forums have different legal consequences. For example, the ECtHR will never reinstate a complainant into his job position, given the attractive amount of compensation, as it is only the Hungarian justice system that has exclusive authority to do so. In my opinion, it is the ordinary courts that should change their attitude and shift to the direction of judicial practice related to fundamental rights and they should not stick to positive law to such an extent that they cannot come to a lawful decision governed by a natural sense of justice. As it stands, they lack the courage to step out of the usual framework based on national positive law. In my view, the possible solution lies in the change of approach of Hungarian ordinary courts: these forums should consistently undertake to base their justifications directly on the judgments of the Strasbourg court, taking on performing the judicial activities related to fundamental rights, which was entrusted to them from the start.

Based on the above case study, the Constitutional Court is rather the guardian of the Fundamental Law of Hungary and formal legality. If it gets into a situation in which a decision should be made on whether the protection of fundamental rights should take priority over formal legality, it is definitely not the criterion of the protection of fundamental rights that wins. However, the priorities may change and the Constitutional Court's interpretation of its own role, in view of its recent judgments, gives reason for optimism. The genuine function of protecting fundamental rights in individual cases can also be discerned in Decision No. 3/2015. (II. 2.) AB. It is stipulated in the decision that as long as the court acts in a case that is relevant for fundamental rights without taking into account such relevance, and the legal interpretation elaborated by this court is not compatible with the constitutional content of the law, then such a court decision violates the Fundamental Law of Hungary.[110]

---

109   Jörg Polakiewicz, *Europe's Multi-layered Human Rights Protection System: Challenges, Opportunities and Risks*, Lecture at Waseda University Tokyo, 14 March 2016, at www.coe.int/en/web/dlapil/speeches-of-the-director/-/asset_publisher/ja71RsfCQTP7/content/europe-s-multi-layered-human-rights-protection-system-challenges-opportunities-and-risks.

110   Decision No. 3/2015. (II. 2.) AB, Reasoning [18].

27   THE NEW HUNGARIAN PRIVATE
INTERNATIONAL LAW CODE

Something Old and Something New

*Katalin Raffai**

Keywords

private international law, codification, general part of the New Hungarian International Law Code, legal institutions in the New Hungarian Private International Law Code, EU private international law regulations

Abstract

Since the adoption of Law Decree No. 13 of 1979 on Private International Law (Old Code) both the legal environment of the EU and the Hungarian legal and social background have undergone substantial changes. Without questioning its progressive character, it must be stated that the Old Code wore the imprints of the era in which it was drafted. With the fall of the socialist system, the necessary amendments were made to the system of the Old Code, accelerated by Hungary's accession to the EU. All the above played an important role in the Government's order to begin work on the comprehensive modernization of the Old Code. The Act XXVIII of 2017 on Private International Law (New Code) entered into force on 1 January 2018. The present study focuses on the following topics: the reasons for the revision of the Old Code, the presentation of the relationship between the New Code and EU regulations in the system of legal instruments, and the review of legal institutions in the general part, with special attention to the major changes undertaken compared to the Old Code.

27.1   INTRODUCTION

It is characteristic of private international legal relations that they have an international element that relates to the laws of two or more states. The function of classical private international law is to resolve this conflict of laws and determine which national laws must

---

*   Katalin Raffai: associate professor, Pázmány Péter Catholic University, Budapest; member of the Private International Law Codification Committee.

be applied. Pursuant to the theory of private international law that evolved by the 20th century, the courts proceeding in such conflicting situations applied the rules of their domestic private international law to determine the applicable law. With the Treaty of Amsterdam this traditional method has been fundamentally altered in respect of the Member States of the EU. The Treaty gave legislative powers to certain institutions of the European Community (today the EU) and created the legal bases for the adoption of several secondary sources of law in private international law.[1] This change substantially reframed the rules of private international law of the Member States. EU regulations have taken over the role of national legislation in several fields, defining uniformly the applicable law, for example in the field of international law of obligations, dissolution of marriages, maintenance and succession. The rules of jurisdiction have also been standardized in civil and commercial matters, as well as in family matters concerning divorce, legal separation, the annulment of marriage, and parental responsibility. The new regulations narrowed down the substantive competence of Member States' national legislations to matters of so-called residual competence.

Since the adoption of Law Decree No. 13 of 1979 on Private International Law (Old Code)[2] both the legal environment of the EU and the Hungarian legal and social background have undergone substantial changes. Without questioning its progressive character, it should be pointed out that the Old Code that it wore the imprints of the era in which it was drafted. With the fall of the socialist system, the necessary amendments were made to the system of the Old Code, accelerated by Hungary's accession to the EU. All the above played an important role in the Government's order to begin work on the comprehensive modernization of the Old Code. The purpose of recodification was to create a new, up-to-date private international law act in line with European and international sources of private international law.[3] The need to revise private international law is not unprecedented. Meanwhile, this complex change affected the entire Hungarian private law and launched a wave of new legislation: the new Civil Code[4] and the New Code of Civil Procedure[5] were adopted and the rules of arbitration were renewed as well.[6]

---

1 On the questions raised by the influence of the EU on the private international law of Member States, *see* Mátyás Császár, 'Az uniós jogforrások hatása a nemzetközi magánjog általános részére', *Magyar Jog*, 2013/11, pp. 669-679.
2 For the non-official translation of the Old Code, *see* Jürgen Basedow *et al.* (eds.), *Encyclopedia of Private International Law*, Vol. 4, Edward Elgar Publishing, Cheltenham, 2017.
3 Government Decree No. 1337/2015. (V. 27.) on the Codification of the new Hungarian Private International Law and on the Foundation of the Private International Law Codification Committee.
4 Act V of 2013 on the Civil Code.
5 Act CXXX of 2016 on the Code of Civil Procedure.
6 Act LX of 2017 on arbitration. For a detailed description on the new Act on Arbitration, *see* István Varga, 'Az új választottbírósági eljárásjog újraszabályozása Magyarországon', *Közjegyzők Közlönye*, 2018/4, pp. 5-22.

The codification work started in the autumn of 2015 with the elaboration of the concept of the law.[7] Act XXVIII of 2017 on Private International Law (New Code)[8] was adopted by the Parliament in the spring of 2017, entering into force on 1 January 2018.[9]

The purpose of this study is to illustrate how EU regulations have set the framework for the New Code and what changes were brought about in the general part of the New Code compared to the Old Code. The part on general provisions is of paramount importance because there is no EU regulation for the conflict of laws concepts regulated under this chapter. Moreover, when EU regulations govern such general conflict-of-law concepts (*e.g.* public policy, overriding mandatory rules *etc.*), they are filled with the meaning gleaned from Member States' private international laws.

27.2   RELATIONSHIP BETWEEN THE NEW CODE AND EU REGULATIONS

In the period since the entry into force of the Treaty of Amsterdam, several EU private international law regulations have been adopted on issues of conflict of laws of obligations,[10] family law,[11] and succession,[12] as well as in the field of jurisdiction and procedural rules

---

7   The Concept of the New Private International Law Act, at www.kormany.hu/download/c/cf/c0000/NMJ%20TV%20KONCEPCI%C3%93.pdf.

8   For the non-official translation of the New Code, at http://njt.hu/translated/doc/J2017T0028P_20180102_FIN.pdf.

9   For a detailed description of the process of creating the New Code, *see* Katalin Raffai, 'A magyar nemzetközi magánjog megújulása – néhány észrevétel a nemzetközi magánjogi törvény újrakodifikálásáról, különös tekintettel a törvény általános részére', *Külgazdaság – Jogi melléklet*, 2017/5, pp. 53-67. (Raffai 2017a); Imre Mátyás, 'Az új nemzetközi magánjogi törvényről', *Publicationes Universitatis Miskolciensis Sectio Juridica et Politica* 2017, Tomus XXXV, pp. 355-357; Lajos Vékás, 'Az új nemzetközi magánjogi törvényről', *Jogtudományi Közlöny*, 2018/10, pp. 413-414; László Burián, 'Az általános részi jogintézmények szabályozása a régi és az új nemzetközi magánjogi Kódexben', *Közjegyzők Közlönye*, 2018/3, pp. 5-6. (Burián 2018a).

10 Regulation (EC) No 864/2007 of the European Parliament and of the Council of 11 July 2007 on the law applicable to non-contractual obligations ('Rome II'). Regulation (EC) No 593/2008 of the European Parliament and of the Council of 17 June 2008 on the law applicable to contractual obligations ('Rome I').

11 Council Regulation (EU) No 1259/2010 of 29 December 2010 implementing enhanced cooperation in the area of the law applicable to divorce and legal separation ('Rome III').

12 Regulation (EU) No 650/2012 of the European Parliament and of the Council of 4 July 2012 on jurisdiction, applicable law, recognition and enforcement of decisions and acceptance and enforcement of authentic instruments in matters of succession and on the creation of a European Certificate of Succession ('Succession Regulation').

in civil and commercial law,[13] family law,[14] maintenance and succession[15] laws. These regulations were adopted pursuant to the authorization laid down in Article 81 TFEU. EU regulations are secondary sources of law of general, binding and directly applicable effect that have priority over national private international laws of Member States: they supersede national private international rules on matters falling within its scope. Their emergence brought on an obligation of deregulation for the Member States, irrespective of whether national rules have a similar or different content from these EU regulations.[16]

National legislations thus retain a so-called residual legislative competence, which shall only be applicable in issues of international private law: *(i)* that are explicitly excluded from the substantive scope of the regulations (*e.g.* violation of personality rights are explicitly excluded from the scope of the Rome II Regulation; these rules are to be found under Section 23 of the New Code); *(ii)* that are not regulated by EU regulations (legal gap); [there is no definition, *e.g.* for certain concepts, such as a person's habitual residence; this is defined in Section 3(b) of the New Code]; *(iii)* the main object of which has not been regulated by an EU regulation (general conflict of law institutions, for example, such as classification – Section 4 of the New Code –, or international law on rights *in rem* – Sections 39 to 47 of the New Code); *(iv)* where the Regulation itself authorizes the enactment of supplementary rules (Article 7 of Rome II Regulation; Section 59 of the New Code stipulates that in cases of claims arising from non-contractual obligations, the choice of law can be made not later than in the preparatory stage of the civil procedure); *(v)* where the provisions governing jurisdiction, recognition and enforcement apply only to Member States; thus, the relevant provisions of the New Code are applicable to third States (*e.g.* recognition of a Canadian judgment in Hungary); and *(vi)* rules Hungary does not participate in, in the framework of enhanced cooperation; here again, the domestic rules of private international law must be applied (Hungary is not a party to either the rules on matrimonial property or those on registered partnership property).[17]

---

13 Regulation (EU) No 1215/2012 of the European Parliament and of the Council of 12 December 2012 on jurisdiction and the recognition and enforcement of judgments in civil and commercial matters (recast) ('Brussels I Recast').
14 Council Regulation (EC) No 2201/2003 of 27 November 2003 on jurisdiction and the recognition and enforcement of judgments in matrimonial matters and the matters of parental responsibility repealing Regulation (EC) No 1347/2000 ('Brussels IIbis').
15 Council Regulation (EC) No 4/2009 of 18 December 2008 on jurisdiction, applicable law, recognition and enforcement of decisions and cooperation in matters relating to maintenance obligations ('Maintenance Regulation').
16 Réka Somssich, 'Az új nemzetközi magánjogi törvény és a nemzetközi magánjogi tárgyú európai uniós rendeletek viszonya, kapcsolódási pontjai', *Közjegyzők Közlönye*, 2018/3, p. 30.
17 Council Regulation (EU) No 2016/1103 of 24 June 2016 implementing enhanced cooperation in the area of jurisdiction, applicable law and the recognition and enforcement of decisions in matters of matrimonial property regimes. Council Regulation (EU) No 2016/1104 of 24 June 2016 implementing enhanced cooperation in the area of jurisdiction, applicable law and the recognition and enforcement of decisions in matters of the property consequences of registered partnerships.

EU private international law rules have various effects on the private international laws of the Member States, depending on whether they are conflict-of-law, jurisdictional or mixed regulations. EU conflict-of-law regulations have a universal nature *(erga omnes)*, meaning that the regulation is uniformly applicable *(loi uniforme)* in a given area. It means, that they are mandatorily applicable to all EU and third-state cases, irrespective of any circumstances affecting the factual situation. This results in the same facts being treated according to the same substantive law in the context of EU and non-EU relations, eliminating unjustified duplication of conflict of law rules. Domestic conflict of law rules can only be applied here as 'gap fillers'. By contrast, jurisdictional and procedural rules require only a link with the EU to apply EU regulations, which allows for parallel national procedural rules: different jurisdictional, recognition and enforcement rules can apply within and outside the EU. Some of the regulations, however, lay down rules of universal jurisdiction, not only applicable in relation to EU Member States [*e.g.* Regulation (EU) No 650/2012 of the European Parliament and of the Council – the so-called Succession Regulation]. Yet, the rules on recognition and enforcement apply only to EU Member States, thus there still is a two-way regulatory system on these issues.[18]

The New Code therefore focuses on issues not covered by EU legal instruments of private international law and by international treaties. This is stated in Chapter I of the New Code, under General Provisions. Pursuant to Section 2, the provisions of the Act shall apply in matters that do not fall under the scope of a directly applicable legal act of the EU with general application or an international treaty.[19] This is a formal change compared to the Old Code, which stated its secondary character only in relation to international treaties.[20] The question of how to express the priority of EU instruments was raised by the Codification Committee. The codification methods of Member States do not follow a uniform pattern. The Codification Committee finally decided that the priority of EU regulations needs to be stated in a general way at the beginning of the New Code, thus avoiding the future necessity of incorporating new EU regulations into the text of the Act.

The integration of EU law into the rules of private international law of Member States has also had an effect on the direction of changes. It was expedient to align the national connecting principles of private international law with those contained in EU regulations in order to avoid divergence. On the other hand, legislation remaining within the competence of the Member States was also to be aligned with EU fundamental freedoms (non-discrimination, free movement, freedom of establishment and to provide services *etc.*),

---

18   The Concept of the New Private International Law Act, paras. 19-21; Vékás 2018, p. 415; Somssich 2018, p. 35.
19   New Code, Section 2 "The provisions of this Act shall apply in matters that do not fall under the scope of a directly applicable legal act of the European Union with general application or an international treaty."
20   Old Code, Section 2 "This Law-Decree shall not apply to any questions regulated by an international treaty."

and it shall be the task of the CJEU to examine the compatibility of these rules with EU law.

The aforementioned factors affected the direction of Hungarian international private law legislation. In line with EU regulations and multilateral treaties established by the Hague Conference on Private International Law, as well as with the changes in the theory of private international law, the New Code took a different approach to several issues. It affords, for example, greater autonomy to parties (choice of law), defending the weaker party (overriding mandatory rules,[21] special jurisdiction rules) and judge's discretion (the principle of the closest connection). On the other hand, it retains the traditions of the Old Code, where justifiable, like in the case of nationality being the main principle of a person's personal law. Finally, it also retains the principle of place of registration for defining the personal law of legal persons.

There is also a mixture of tradition and novelty in the structure of the New Code; the structure follows that of the Old Code. Namely, the New Code is also divided into three major parts: General Part, Special Part and Jurisdiction-Recognition-Enforcement Part. There is, however, a significant change in the structure, owing to the structure of the Civil Code, where the provisions on family law follow the chapter on persons, in contrast with the Old Code, where they were placed at the end of the Special Part. Regulation on guardianship was placed into the chapter on the law of persons, from the chapter on family law, and the intellectual property rights follow the part governing the rights *in rem*. The rules for *de facto* and registered partnerships have been included in a separate chapter. The section on jurisdiction, recognition and enforcement has also changed: the procedural provisions are followed by the rules on the immunity of the State,[22] and those are followed by the rules of jurisdiction. Finally, this part is concluded by provisions on the recognition and enforcement of foreign judgments.

Old and new elements thus alternate in the system of the New Code, and it is to be considered a positive feature that in contrast with the old, strict regulation, the New Code is more flexible, as it gives more flexibility to the parties' choice of law, providing also a broader scope for judicial discretion.

---

21   It is debated in the legal literature whether provisions simply protecting private interests may be overriding mandatory provisions. *See* Laura M. van Bochove, 'Overriding Mandatory Rules as a Vehicle for Weaker Party Protection in European Private International Law', *Erasmus Law Review*, Vol. 7, Issue 3, 2014; Katalin Raffai, 'Protection of Public and Private Interests in the Rome I Regulation – Observations on the Interpretation of Overriding Mandatory Provisions', *Studies in International Economics – Special Issue of Külgazdaság*, 2015/2, pp. 15-33.

22   In the Old Code, the regulation of the state's immunity with regard to the law of persons was placed in Section 17, the rules regarding exclusive jurisdiction were to be found under Section 62/A and the preclusion of jurisdiction was placed under Section 62/B.

27.3   General Part

The following part briefly reviews the main changes in the General Part, especially the new provisions not covered by the Old Code.[23] It should be emphasized, that the Hungarian legislator had in the course of legislation almost the biggest room for maneuver when drawing up the rules of the General Part. The main reason for this is that EU regulations, without exception, regulate two major fields: *(i)* issues specific to the special part of private international law (the law applicable to contractual and non-contractual obligations, divorce, maintenance *etc.*); and *(ii)* jurisdictional, recognition and enforcement issues (civil and commercial matters, divorce, insolvency *etc.*).

In these regulations, general conflict-of-law legal institutions are only regulated indirectly and partially, on a complementary basis (*i.e.* public policy clause, overriding mandatory rules, states with more than one legal system *etc.*). Some of these are only regulated through an exclusion clause (*i.e.* renvoi accepted only under the Succession Regulation). There have been calls for a so-called Rome 0 Regulation to uniformly regulate the general conflict-of-laws legal institutions in the EU. However, research has shown that there is no uniform legislative policy background in the Member States that would support this, without which this aspiration is devoid of reality.[24]

The General Part includes rules of the scope of the law, interpretative provisions, classification, *renvoi*, states with multiple legal systems, rules on the application of foreign law, choice of law, a general escape clause, a general auxiliary rule, a public policy clause, overriding mandatory rules, and provisions on the change of the applicable law. A novel feature of the New Code is that similar to the structure of EU regulations, it placed the definition of basic concepts considered of substantial importance at the beginning of the Act, among the interpretative provisions. Section 3 defines the interpretation of three concepts in the context of this Act: the concepts of court,[25] habitual residence and domicile.[26]

---

23   *See* also Burián 2018a; Tamás Szabados, 'The New Hungarian Private International Law Act: New Rules, New Questions', *Rabels Zeitschrift*, 2018/4, pp. 979-985; Katalin Raffai, 'The New Hungarian Private International Law Act – a Wind of Change', *Acta Univ. Sapientiae, Legal Studies*, Vol. 6, Issue 1, 2017, pp. 124-128. (Raffai 2017b).

24   *See* in detail Stefan Leible & Hannes Unberath (eds.), *Brauchen wir eine Rom 0-Verordnung? Studien zum Internationalen Privat- und Verfahrensrecht.* JWV, Jena, 2013; László Burián, 'Gondolatok az uniós nemzetközi magánjog általános szabályai megalkotásának lehetőségéről és szükségességéről', *in* László Burián & Sarolta Szabó (eds.), *Arbitrando et curriculum bene deligendo. Festive publication in Honor of Éva Horváth's 70th Birthday*, Pázmány Press, Budapest, 2014, pp. 31-44.

25   The court shall mean all authorities which have competence in matters pertaining to the scope of the Act.

26   In the Old Code, it was nationality and residence that were relevant in defining a person's personal law. The principle of residence lost its central in the New Code. The New Code uses the definition of domicile in accordance with the Brussels I Recast regulations, mainly in the framework of rules of jurisdiction in matrimonial property cases. Residence is the place where the individual person resides permanently or with the intention of permanent settlement.

From among these concepts, the principle of habitual residence is of paramount importance, because it is one of the most frequent connecting factor both in EU regulations and in multilateral private international law treaties, and yet, none of these have provided a definition for habitual residence. At the same time, certain judgments of the CJEU have set criteria governing the determination of habitual residence in cross border legal relationships.[27]

The New Code defines the concept of habitual residence to facilitate the application of the law, and it is obvious that the definition was inspired by the judgments of the CJEU. According to the New Code, the habitual residence of a person is the place where the actual center of the individual's life is. When determining the center of life, the facts indicating the intention of the individual concerned shall be taken into account. The legislator attributed a decisive role to habitual residence as a connecting factor in the field of personal law, protection of personality rights, family law, civil and registered partnerships, ensuring herewith the conformity between Hungarian and EU law that was absent earlier on.

27.3.1 Legal Institutions Used in the General Part of Both the Old and the New Code

27.3.1.1 Classification (Section 4)

Classification (characterization, *qualifikation*) is a complex process that must be performed by the acting forum (*i.e.* the court) when applying the law. The problem of classification is hidden in the hypothesis of the conflict-of-law rules. It is for the court to decide when assessing the private international law case what legal relationship it corresponds to, and which legal system governs its terminology. The difficulty stems from the fact that the different legal systems refer to the same legal institutions with different terms which may be classified into different categories. These discrepancies affect the connecting factors and ultimately determine the applicable law. A classic example of classification is whether the surviving spouse's right to usufruct on a property is a matter of matrimonial property or one of succession.

---

27   The relevant CJEU case-law consists mostly of cases regarding family law and construing a child's habitual residence. For more details *see* Katalin Raffai, 'Az ember személyes jogára vonatkozó szabályok a nemzetközi magánjogi törvényerejű rendeletben és javaslatok a hatályos szabályozás átalakítására', *in* Barna Berke & Zoltán Nemessányi (eds.), *Az új nemzetközi magánjogi törvény alapjai II.*, HVG-ORAC, Budapest, 2016, pp. 48-51. [Berke & Nemessányi (eds.), 2016b].

Most legal systems rely on the principle of *lex fori*, that is, the terminology of national law, which is what both the Old[28] and the New Code[29] impose. This rule was similar in both Codes. The *lex fori* classification is the starting point, yet the new rules are more differentiated than the previous ones. In practice, the biggest problem of classification arises when the Hungarian legal system does not know the given legal institution. The Old Code treated such cases quite vaguely, nevertheless, both scholarly literature and case-law applied the principle of *lex causae* to such situations.[30] Sections 4(2) and (3) of the New Code clarify the application of this legal institution, saying that if a legal institution is unknown to Hungarian law or its function or purpose is different from those under the Hungarian rules, it shall be applied pursuant to the foreign law regulating that legal institution, with special regard to its function and purpose under the foreign law. Section 4(4) draws attention to other instances of classification: "Paragraphs (1) to (3) shall apply accordingly to the determination of jurisdiction and the recognition and enforcement of foreign decisions."

27.3.1.2   Renvoi (Section 5)

Renvoi[31] is one of the most controversial institutions of private international law. The rules of *renvoi* have changed significantly compared to the rules of the Old Code,[32] mainly due to the fact that *renvoi* is excluded in the EU regulations (exclusion of *renvoi*), with the exception of the Succession Regulation. On the other hand, *renvoi* is a convenient tool for pursuing the homeward trend because it gives the court the opportunity to prioritize the application of the *lex fori* principle. The Old Code[33] accepted partial *renvoi* only, that is, foreign law referring back to Hungarian law, a typical case of the homeward trend (see above).[34] The New Code, however, only regards *renvoi* as an exception. It requires both

---

28   Old Code, Section 3(1) "If the legal qualification of the facts or relationships to be judged in a legal dispute from the aspect of the determination of the applicable law is disputed, the interpretation of the rules and concepts of Hungarian law governs."

29   New Code, Section 4(1) "When deciding which conflict of law rule is to determine the law applicable to the factual situation, the concepts of Hungarian law shall be followed."

30   Raffai 2017a, p. 63; Vékás 2018, p. 417; László Burián, 'A hazafelé törekvés a régi és az új nemzetközi magánjogi kódexben', *in* Ádám Boóc & István Sándor (eds.), *Studia in honorem Gábor Hamza*, Közjegyzői Akadémia Nyomdája, Budapest, 2019, p. 43.

31   The word *renvoi* comes from the French 'send back' or 'to return unopened'. *Renvoi* means that the private international rules of the applicable law refer back to the laws of the original state, while directing means that the addressed law refers to the laws of a third state.

32   Old Code, Section 4 (Second phrase) "If, however, the foreign law refers back to Hungarian law in the question concerned – taking into account this rule – Hungarian law shall apply."

33   Burián 2019, pp. 41-50.

34   For more details on *renvoi* see László Burián, 'A vissza- és továbbutalás szabályozása az új nemzetközi magánjogi törvényben', *in* Péter Darák & András Koltay (eds.), *Ad astra per aspera – Festive Publication in Honour of Pál Solt's 80th Birthday*, Pázmány Press, Budapest, 2017, pp. 75-86.

back and forward referral in cases where nationality is the connecting factor to determine the applicable law, and therefore it accepts the whole *renvoi*.[35]

27.3.1.3 Application of Foreign Law and Establishing Its Content (Sections 7 and 8)

There is no significant change in the application of foreign law in the New Code.[36] Like the Old Code, it treats foreign law as a matter of law and to be applied *ex officio*. However, the Old Code did not provide appropriate guidance as to the criteria to be taken into account by the court when applying foreign law, generating several uncertainties in case-law. Hungary's accession to the London Convention ('European Convention on Information on Foreign Law') relieved much of the difficulties. As the Council of Europe summarized it,

> "Under the terms of the Convention, the Parties undertake to supply information, when problems of foreign law arise into course of legal proceedings, concerning their law and procedure in civil and commercial fields as well as on their judicial system."[37]

In accordance with the London Convention, a new provision was added to the provision on *ex officio* application in the New Code, according to which the provisions of foreign law should be examined by the court in the context of that foreign law, including the legal practice of that foreign legal system.[38] It is the court's responsibility to determine the content of foreign law.

There is no major change regarding evidence on the content of foreign law. The New Code also allows the judge to use different means of proof, such as parties' submissions, expert opinions, or addressing the Ministry of Justice with requests for information. If the content of the foreign law cannot be established within reasonable time, Hungarian law shall be applied as auxiliary law. A newly introduced flexible element of the New Code is that in case the foreign law of unknown content cannot be considered properly under

---

35 New Code, Section 5(2) "If, by virtue of this Act, the applicable foreign law is determined on the basis of nationality and the conflict of law rule of the foreign law *a)* refers back to Hungarian law, the Hungarian substantive law shall apply; *b)* refers onwards to a different foreign law, the substantive law rules of that law shall apply."

36 For more details on application of foreign law *see* Sarolta Szabó 'Az új nemzetközi magánjogi törvény egyes általános részi kérdéseiről', *Jogtudományi Közlöny*, 2018/11, pp. 451-456.

37 The full text of the Convention is available at www.coe.int/en/web/conventions/full-list/-/conventions/treaty/062.

38 New Code, Section 7(2) "The court shall interpret the foreign law in accordance with the rules and practices of that foreign law."

Hungarian law, then the closest foreign law to the applicable law should be used as a substitute.

27.3.1.4   Public Policy (Section 12)

The purpose of the public policy (public order, *ordre public, Vorbehaltsklausel, öffentliche Ordnung*) clause in private international law is to protect the fundamental values of domestic substantive law and to ensure the opportunity to refuse the application of a foreign rule that collides with national values. In this case, the domestic law (*lex fori*) shall be applied. Therefore, public policy is a general clause, filled with content by the court enforcing the law.[39] The Old Code did not give a definition for public policy; however, for cases where foreign law proved to be contrary to Hungarian public policy, it automatically mandated the application of Hungarian law.[40] The provisions of the New Code are no different on public policy, however, by clarifying the scope of fundamental values to be protected by public policy – with the protection of constitutional principles expressly among them –, it serves and supports the court that applies the law.[41] Section 12(2) of the Code specifies that the provisions of Hungarian law shall only apply as a substitute in case the violation of public policy cannot be averted in any other way.

It should be mentioned that the earlier provision prohibiting the unsubstantiated disapplication of a right ensured under a different social and economic system has been omitted from these rules. As an awareness-raising provision, this earlier rule bore the mark of the political ideology of the socialist legal system. Thus, with the loss of its former function it was only appropriate to omit it from the New Code.

27.3.2   *New Legal Institutions Introduced in the General Part of the New Code*

27.3.2.1   Interterritorial Conflict of Law Rules, States with Multiple Legal Systems (Section 6)

There are states where multiple legal systems are in parallel use, especially in federal states, where the separate territorial entities have their own legal systems (*e.g.* the US or Canada). In these states, the facts of private international law cases may be connected to multiple territorial units, which may cause inner collision. As the Old Code did not provide for

---

39   For a detailed description, *see* Katalin Raffai, 'A közrendi klauzula a nemzetközi magánjogi törvényerejű rendeletben és javaslatok a hatályos szabályozás átalakítására', *in* Berke & Nemessányi (eds.), 2016b, pp. 18-27.

40   Old Code, Section 7(1) "The application of foreign law must be disregarded if it violated Hungarians public order.", Old Code, Section 7 (3) "In place of the disregarded foreign law, Hungarian law shall apply."

41   New Code, Section 12(1) "The foreign law determined by this Act shall be deemed contrary to Hungarian public policy and therefore shall not be applied if the result of its application in the given case would clearly and seriously violate the fundamental values and constitutional principles of the Hungarian legal system."

such cases, it was for the proceeding court to decide which law was applicable. Section 6 of the New Code filled this void by introducing a completely new provision which regulates the so called interterritorial and interpersonal conflicts related to states with multiple jurisdictions. Given that these are not genuine collisions in terms of private international law, the solution to these cases is to apply the national conflict of law rules of the affected state.

There are also states where different laws apply to different groups of persons, which is the so-called interpersonal conflict. In states that apply religious rights (*i.e.* Israel or Muslim states), individuals have different rights to personal status. In such a case, the conflict of law rules of that state determine which law is applicable to that person. In the event that the interterritorial or interpersonal resolution of the conflict is impeded, like where a particular issue is not regulated at all, or its application would not lead to a satisfactory result, the law of the state with the closest connection to the facts applies.

27.3.2.2 General Choice of Law Clause (Section 9) and General Escape Clause (Section 10)

In this section, I briefly introduce two legal institutions that have several similarities in common. Both connecting factors were originally applied in the field of the law of obligations and transposed from there to the General Part, their scope extended. The Old Code allowed both the choice of law clause and the escape clause to be applied with a more limited scope, in the field of contracts only. However, since the drafting of the Old Code, private international law has allowed the parties much more autonomy, who therefore have a much broader opportunity to choose the applicable law.[42] The opportunity for choice of law within a limited scope is provided in family law and law of succession. This approach is followed by the New Code, which, as a novelty, places the clause into the General Part, as a general concept, without restricting its application to the law of obligations. This provision is in line with new trends in private international law and EU regulations. Pursuant to the Rome I Regulation, the act requires that the choice of law must be explicit – and the parties must name the applicable rules unambiguously.[43] However, the autonomy of the parties may not violate the rights of third persons.[44] Another new element

---

42 *See* Miklós Király, 'A személyek és a felek autonómiája az új nemzetközi magánjogi törvényben', *Jogtudományi Közlöny*, 2018/12, pp. 509-516.

43 New Code, Section 9(1) "Unless otherwise provided by this Act *a)* the choice of law shall be explicit, *b)* the law of the state which would be applicable to the given relationship should the choice-of-law agreement be established and valid, shall apply to the establishment and validity of that agreement; however, the choice of law shall also be deemed established and valid if it complies with the law of the state where the agreement has been concluded."

44 New Code, Section 9(2) "The choice of law may not violate the acquired rights of third parties." *See* Lajos Vékás, 'A törvény szerkezetéről és néhány általános részi kérdésről', *in* Barna Berke & Zoltán Nemessányi (eds.), *Az új nemzetközi magánjogi törvény alapjai I.*, HVG-ORAC, Budapest, 2016, p. 29.

in the General Part of the New Code is the general escape clause (*Ausweichklausel*), which in a nutshell means that if the judge decides that the facts of the case have a closer connection with another law, he has the possibility to apply that law instead of the originally applicable law.[45] The parties also have the right to request this, in which case it is up to the judge to decide whether to accept and apply the clause. The previous Code only used the escape clause in the chapter on obligations, as an auxiliary connecting factor. Its regulation as a general clause gives more leeway to the court to consider the application of the law that is properly connected to the case. The only limitation to the freedom of the judge guaranteed by the general escape clause is the choice of law by the parties; in such an event, the general escape clause is not applicable.

27.3.2.3   General Auxiliary Rule (Section 11)

One major innovation of the New Code is the introduction of the general auxiliary rule, which allows the court to determine the applicable law even if it is not defined in the Code (legal gap). Its similarity with the general escape clause is that in both cases the law closest to the fact shall be applied. There is a significant difference between their respective functions: in the case of a general escape clause, judicial discretion makes it possible to derogate from the law applicable as the main rule, while in the case of the general auxiliary rule, the judge must fill the legal gap.

27.3.2.4   Overriding Mandatory Provisions (Section 13)

Similarly to the public policy clause, overriding mandatory rules (*Eingriffsnormen*) are also meant to have a protective function. The aim of these substantive rules is the protection of public interest, and there shall no deviation from them. These substantive rules are applied in the service of fundamental political, economic, and social political interests of the relevant country. Therefore, their application is mandatory not only in domestic relations but also in relations affected by foreign facts. If the court finds that the issue of international relevance affects the public interest in Hungary, it disapplies the connecting factors, and automatically applies the overriding mandatory provisions of Hungarian law. The previous Code did not cover the overriding mandatory rules;[46] thus the New Code had to fill this gap, complying also with the EU law (mainly with Rome I and Rome II Regulations).[47] However, the solution of the New Code shows differences in comparison

---

45   Derogation from EU regulation; in contrast to those rules, it is defined in a general manner, and it is not placed among the rules of the law of obligations.

46   *See* Katalin Raffai, 'Néhány gondolat az imperatív normák szabályozásának szükségszerűségéről', *in* Berke & Nemessányi (eds.), 2016b, pp. 28-44.

47   New Code, Section 13(1) "Irrespective of the law determined by this Act, those provisions of the Hungarian law shall apply, from the content and purpose of which it can clearly be established that they are subject to unconditional enforcement in legal relationships falling under the scope of this Act (imperative rules)."

with the Rome I and Rome II Regulations as to the application of overriding mandatory provisions. Section 13(2) of the New Code allows the court to take another state's overriding mandatory rules into consideration as well if they have a close connection to the case and the case could not be decided in their absence.[48]

27.3.2.5   Change in the Applicable Law (Section 14)

Change in the circumstances determining the applicable law is a phenomenon where a substantial circumstance changes in the factual situation of the case and this results in a change in the applicable law. The Old Code did not contain general provisions for a change of circumstances. In the Special Part of the Old Code, however, in the law of persons, in family law, and the law of rights *in rem* for example, there were special provisions governing cases of changes in the applicable law. The New Code contains rules of general character on changes in the applicable law.[49]

27.3.3   *Legal Institutions Missing from the General Part of the New Code*

A significant change in the New Code is that certain legal institutions of general character from the Old Code were discarded, such as the rules on reciprocity, fraudulent connection (*fraus legis*, evasion of law, *fraude á la loi*), and parties' common request to disregard the applicable foreign law. The Old Code assumed as a general rule that the application of foreign law was not subject to reciprocity, but an Act could, in exceptional cases, provide for considering the question of reciprocity.[50] This somewhat controversial rule has not yielded significant case law, and with the disappearance of the socio-political background that accounted for its introduction at the time,[51] it was no longer justified to keep these rules in the New Code.

Fraudulent connection means that the parties artificially change an element in the factual situation in order to circumvent the law otherwise applicable. The Old Code sanctioned such deceptive behavior by applying the law otherwise applicable. At the same time, it also served by way of a rule of exception as an instrument of the homeward trend. If fraudulent behavior led to the application of Hungarian law, then the Old Code did not

---

48   New Code, Section 13(2) "The provisions of the law of any other state subject to unconditional enforcement may be taken into account if they are closely connected with the factual situation and are of decisive importance regarding its assessment."

49   New Code, Section 14 "Change in the circumstances determining the applicable law shall only have effect on legal relationships established validly according to the law applicable prior to the change if this Act expressly provides so."

50   The antagonism between the socialist and capitalist legal systems generated several specific regulations both in the General Part and the Special Part of the Old Code. *See* reciprocity at Section 6(2); public policy at Section 7(2).

51   Vékás 2016, p. 24.

sanction fraudulent connection (in that case, Hungarian law had to be applied). The views on fraudulent connection vary in the different jurisdictions, with the connection being mainly sanctioned by the Latin legal systems. Before the adoption of the Old Code this institution was unknown to Hungarian case-law. Being difficult to prove and having no tradition in the Hungarian legal system, the courts did not apply it very often. This justifies why it is not regulated in the New Code.

In civil law legal systems, the application of private international law rules to international situations has always been mandatory for courts, and that can never be optional. This principle contradicts the former Section 9 of the Old Code, which stated that if the parties jointly requested the court to ignore the application of the originally applicable foreign law, Hungarian law should be applied instead.[52] Section 9 was a genuine 'Hungaricum', standing apart from the European legal systems, which all apply the principle of mandatory application of law. This provision is also contrary to EU law where the application of foreign law is not optional; moreover, it is a typical case of the homeward trend.[53] For all these reasons, the Codification Committee decided not to incorporate this institution in the New Code.[54]

27.4   FINAL REMARKS

As mentioned in the Introduction, the goal of recodification was to create a new Act on Private International Law which is up-to-date and in line with European and international sources of private international law. With this objective in mind, the Codification Committee set out to combine traditional elements of Hungarian private international law with modern ones in the General Part. As such, it was the drafting of the General Part of the New Code that meant the most complex legislative task for legislators. In short, legislative change affected three aspects: obsolete rules have been omitted, long-lasting rules have been retained and harmonized with EU law, and several new elements (approaches) previously unknown to Hungarian international private law have been incorporated.

---

52   Old Code, Section 9 "If the parties request disregard of the foreign law applicable in accordance with this Decree-Law together, in its place Hungarian law – or in case of possibility of choice of law, the law chosen – shall apply."
53   For more details *see* Vékás 2016, pp. 26-28; Vékás 2018, pp. 420-421; Szabados 2018, pp. 990-991.
54   Burián 2018a, pp. 9-10.

28   THE RIGHTS OF THE VICTIM IN HUNGARIAN CRIMINAL PROCEEDINGS

*Anna Kiss**

Keywords

rights of victims, code of criminal procedure in Hungary, victims in criminal procedure, Directive 2012/29/EU, rights of vulnerable persons

Abstract

In the course of the development of criminal law victims lost their former leading role in the procedure and were pushed to the periphery of justice. Legal experts have come to realize that this tendency is tremendously unfair to the victim. European documents on the legal position of the victims increasingly called the attention of the legislature to the need of bringing about changes. In Hungary, the relevant new law was passed in June 2017. The Code came into effect in July 2018 and confirmed the victim's procedural position. Since July, there are three groups of victims' rights in Hungarian Criminal Proceedings: provision of information and support; participation in criminal proceedings; protection of victims and recognition of victims in need of special protection. In addition to describing the rights, the study also draws attention to the fact in light of the principle that all rights are worth upholding it is not enough to regulate the rights of victims. The study also warns that although the rights of victims are important, we should not forget the guarantees concerning suspects' rights, which must also be ensured.

28.1   INTRODUCTION

In 2017 the Hungarian Government adopted the draft law put forward by the Minister of Justice on the new concept of criminal procedure. The new law was passed in June 2017. The Code came into effect in July 2018 and reaffirmed the victim's procedural position. The rules for vulnerable persons have been given a separate chapter in the new act on criminal procedure, as opposed to incorporating them into various chapters and subheadings. The provisions are founded on a stronger emphasis on individualization and the specific needs of persons requiring special treatment.

---

*   Anna Kiss: senior research fellow, National Institute of Criminology, Budapest.

Since July 2018, there are three groups of victims' rights in Hungarian criminal procedure, as Table 28.1 shows:

Provisions of information and support	Participation in criminal proceedings	Protection of victims and recognition of victims in need of special protection
(i) Right to understand and to be understood;	*(i)* Right to make a declaration;	*(i)* Right to protection;
(ii) Right to receive information from the first contact with a competent authority;	*(ii)* Right to be heard;	*(ii)* Right to avoid contact between victim and offender;
(iii) Right of victims when making a complaint;	*(iii)* Rights in the event of a decision not to prosecute;	*(iii)* Right to protection of privacy;
(iv) Right to receive information about their case;	*(iv)* Right to safeguards in the context of restorative justice services;	*(iv)* Individual assessment of victims to identify specific protection needs;
(v) Right to interpretation and translation	*(v)* Right to legal aid;	*(v)* Right to protection of victims in need of special protection during criminal proceedings;
	(vi) Right to reimbursement of expenses;	*(vi)* Right to the protection of child victims during criminal proceedings
	(vii) Right to the return of property;	
	(viii) Right to decision on compensation from the offender in the course of criminal proceedings	

28.2 VICTIM'S ROLES IN THE CRIMINAL PROCEEDING

Hungarian criminal procedure follows three phases: investigation, indictment, and the court proceedings/trial. The criminal procedure in Hungary begins with the investigation of the crime, usually carried out by the police under the supervision of the public prosecutor. When the investigation is over the public prosecutor decides whether charges should be brought and whether the case should be brought to court for trial or – if there is insufficient evidence or if it is established that the offender should not be punished – the case should be closed at this stage. When the case is brought to court for trial, the court examines the evidence collected and decides on the guilt of the defendant.

28.2.1   Who Is a Victim?

According to the relevant EU Directive, 'victim' means a natural person who has suffered harm, including physical, mental or emotional harm or economic loss which was directly caused by a criminal offence; family members of a person whose death was directly caused by a criminal offence and who have suffered harm as a result of that person's death.[1]

The term 'injured party' is used in Act XC of 2017 on the Code of Criminal Procedure. According to Hungarian law, a victim (injured party) is the party whose rights or lawful interests have been violated or jeopardized by the criminal offence. Therefore, according to Hungarian criminal procedure, it is not only a natural person who may be a victim, but also a legal person (*e.g.* a company). However, Hungarian law does not consider indirect victims (*e.g.* family members) to be victims. Nevertheless, in the case of the death of the victim the relative in direct line, the brother or sister, the spouse or common-law partner of the victim and the legal representative of the victim may exercise the rights of the victim.

28.2.2   Victim's Position

The victim is a many-faceted party. The victim, as the aggrieved party, can assume different positions in the process of the administration of justice. According to their legal position, they can be a 'simple' victim, a 'denunciator' who reports the crime, a 'private complainant', a 'witness', a 'private party', a 'private prosecutor', or a 'substitute private prosecutor'. According to Erika Róth, the victim is either on the side of the state helping to enforce its criminal claim or acts as its substitute in the criminal procedure.[2]

i. *Simple victim.* According to Hungarian criminal procedure, the victim's name in Hungarian is "injured party", and as such has the right to receive information and protection.

ii. *Denunciator and private complainer (reporting of crimes).* According to the Directive:

> "In order to encourage and facilitate reporting of crimes and to allow victims to break the cycle of repeat victimization, it is essential that reliable support services are available to victims and that competent authorities are prepared to respond to victims' reports in a respectful, sensitive, professional and non-

---

1   Directive 2012/29/EU of the European Parliament and of the Council of 25 October 2012 establishing minimum standards on the rights, support and protection of victims of crime, and replacing Council Framework Decision 2001/220/JHA, Article 2(1)(a).

2   Erika Róth, 'What is the Real Interest of the Victim?', *in Special Edition of the Proceedings of Criminology. New Tendencies in Crime and Criminal Policy in Central and Eastern Europe. Proceedings of the 65th International Course of the International Society for Criminology, 11-14 March 2003, Miskolc.* Hungarian Society for Criminology, Bíbor Publishing House, Miskolc, 2004, p. 396.

discriminatory manner. This could increase victims' confidence in the criminal justice systems of Member States and reduce the number of unreported crimes. Practitioners who are likely to receive complaints from victims with regard to criminal offences should be appropriately trained to facilitate reporting of crimes, and measures should be put in place to enable third-party reporting, including by civil society organizations. It should be possible to make use of communication technology, such as e-mail, video recordings or online electronic forms for making complaints."[3]

In criminal proceedings, the investigation is based on information about how the offence was committed. This may be data obtained by the investigating authority such as the official, but it may also be data from the report and the private indictment. In Hungary, in most cases the crime is reported by the victim.

iii *Victim-witness.* Those victims may be heard as a witness, who may have knowledge of the facts waiting to be proven.

iv *Private party.* The private party is the victim enforcing a civil claim in criminal proceedings. The private party may enforce the civil claim against the defendant, arising out of the offense forming the subject of the indictment.

v *Private prosecutor.* According to the law in force, the victim can act as a private prosecutor. Unless provided otherwise by the relevant Act, in case of an assault, invasion of privacy, violation of secrecy of correspondence, libel, defamation, and irreverence, the prosecution shall be represented by the victim as a private prosecutor, provided that the offender may be prosecuted upon private motion.

vi *Substitute private prosecutor.* In criminal proceedings when according to the law the charge shall be represented by the public prosecutor, in case of passivity on the part of the prosecutor, the victim may represent the charge as substitute private prosecutor. The victim can act as a substitute private prosecutor in three instances: if the prosecutor drops the charge; if the prosecutor or investigation officials reject the denunciation; or if the prosecutor or investigation officials terminate the investigation. The victim can be a substitute private prosecutor, or in the case of the victim's death, immediate relatives, the spouse, companion or legal representative can continue with the proceedings. The roots of substitute private prosecution go back to the end of the 19th century. The laws of the time allowed the victim to act as substitute private prosecutor in case of inactivity on the public prosecutor's part.

---

3   Directive 2012/29/EU, Recital (63).

28.3   VICTIM'S RIGHTS

28.3.1   Right to Ask for Information

Victims have the right to ask for information about the justice system, about services available to them, and about the progress made in their case and the status of the person who harmed them. The wish of victims as to whether they want to receive information shall bind the competent authority, unless that information must be provided due to the right of the victim to actively participate in the criminal proceedings.[4]

28.3.2   Right to Protection

Victims have the right to have their security and privacy considered, and to receive reasonable and necessary protection from intimidation and retaliation. Victims can ask that their identity not be publicly released. According to the law, in order to protect the life, physical integrity, or personal freedom of the witness, as well as to ensure that the witness fulfils the obligation of giving testimony and to ensure that the testimony is given free from any intimidation, the witness should be afforded protection.

Concerning the confidential treatment of the personal data of a witness *(i)* the court, the prosecutor and the investigating authority proceeding in the case shall ensure that the data of the witness is treated confidentially and may not become known via other data of the procedure; *(ii)* the court, the prosecutor and the investigating authority ensure that the identity of the witness may not be become known by way of examining documents suitable for identification; and *(iii)* the confidential treatment of the witness' personal data may only be terminated with the consent of the witness.

From the time of ordering the confidential treatment of the witness' personal data, the copies of documents containing such personal data may only be given to participants in the criminal proceedings without this data. A witness may be declared specially protected in case *(i)* his/her testimony relates to the substantial circumstances of a particularly serious case; *(ii)* the evidence expected by his/her testimony cannot be supplemented; *(iii)* the identity, the place of stay and the fact that he/she is intended to be heard by the prosecutor or the investigating authority is not known by the accused and the defence counsel; *(iv)* the exposure of the identity of the witness would seriously jeopardize the life, health or personal freedom of either the witness or his relatives.

In exceptionally justified cases, the chairperson of the panel of the court proceeding in the case, the prosecutor, or the investigating authority may initiate that the defendant,

---

4   *See* Directive 2012/29/EU, Article 6(4); Act XC of 2017 on the Code of Criminal Procedure.

the counsel for the defendant, the victim, other interested parties, the representative of the victim and other interested parties be protected. The request may be submitted to the court, the prosecutor or the investigating authority proceeding in the case, while a verbal request should be recorded in a report.

The president of the court, the head of the prosecutor's office, and the head of the investigating authority or the commander of the penal institution, respectively, may initiate the personal protection of the staff of the court, the prosecutor's office, the investigating authority and the penal institution or another person in connection with the above.

The documents pertaining to personal protection shall be kept together with the documents of the criminal case. With the exception of the decision on the request and initiation, the documents shall be handled confidentially.

The participation of the defendant, victim and witness in the witness protection program specified in a separate act[5] shall not affect their respective rights and obligations related to the criminal proceedings; and in respect of the participants of the program, the provisions of the act shall apply with the following derogation: *(i)* persons participating in the program shall be summoned or notified by the body responsible for their protection, further, official documents to be served on such persons may only be delivered by the body responsible for their protection; *(ii)* persons participating in the program shall state their original personal identification data during criminal proceedings, but give the address of the body responsible for their protection as their place of residence or stay; *(iii)* no one – including the authorities – may be provided with a copy of documents containing the personal data of persons participating in the program and any information regarding such persons, unless they hold the permission of the body responsible for the protection of such persons; *(iv)* costs incurred in connection with the appearance and participation of persons participating in the program may not be accounted for as costs of the criminal proceedings; *(v)* the witness may refuses to give testimony regarding data that imply his/her new identity or new place of residence or stay.

28.3.3   *Right to Participation*

Victims have the right to present victim impact statements and have them considered. Victims' views about decisions that affect their rights must also be considered.

---

5   *See* Act LXXXV of 2001 on regulations pertaining to victims participating in the witness protection program.

28.3.4   Right to Seek Restitution

Victims have the right to have the court consider making a restitution order for their financial losses and to have any unpaid amount enforced through a civil court.

28.3.5   Right to Interpretation and Translation

Criminal proceedings are conducted in Hungarian, but victims can use their native, regional or minority language or any other language they choose both verbally and in writing. If the use of their native language would lead to undue difficulties, the use of another language known to them will be prescribed. They are entitled to an interpreter free of charge.

If a person, whose native language is not Hungarian, intends to use his/her native language in the course of the proceedings, or – pursuant to and within the scope of an international agreement promulgated by law – their regional or minority language, an interpreter shall be employed. If the use of the native language involves unreasonable difficulties, the use of another language defined by the person not commanding the Hungarian language, shall be arranged with the assistance of an interpreter.

28.3.6   Criminal Charges (Reimbursable Victim Expenses)

In a criminal procedure, the following costs and expenses may be reimbursed: *(i)* travel and accommodation expenses; *(ii)* costs of the expert invited by the victim with the consent of the prosecution/court; *(iii)* expenses of full or partial video or audio recordings of the proceedings/stenography; *(iv)* expenses for one copy of the case files; *(v)* communication expenses (phone, fax, post); *(vi)* representative's fee.

28.3.7   Applying for Mediation

The victim may propose at any stage of the proceedings to refer the case to penal mediation if the conditions for such a procedure are fulfilled. Mediation is applied only once in the course of proceedings: for certain crimes against the person, crimes against property or traffic offences, or if the crime is punishable with a maximum of five years' imprisonment; with the victim's and the offender's consent.

The meeting of the perpetrator with the victim can play a significant role in the perpetrator's ability to evaluate the consequence and damage that he/she had caused, while it assists the victim in processing the events and finding peace. While most restorative programs in other countries of Europe take place outside of prison, in recent years there have been many experiments which examined how restorative justice could be implemented within the walls of prisons and whether it is possible to develop a prison regime which is entirely based on restorative principles and values (*e.g.* the MERESP Project in Hungary).[6]

In the National Institute of Criminology (OKRI) during 2008 and 2009, a focus group project was carried out to examine the lessons of the mediation procedure from the side of the prosecutors' practice.[7] (Mediation, as one of the tools of restorative justice, will be discussed later.)

28.3.8   Additional Rights

Should the victim be a minor, they have some additional rights. *(i)* If the victim is under 14 years of age, they may be heard as a witness only if their evidence cannot be supplemented. He/she may be subjected to confrontation only if this will not cause him/her anxiety; they are to be given special attention by the victim support reference persons operating at county police headquarters and the Budapest police headquarters. *(ii)* If the victim is under 18 years of age, they have the right to have their parents/legal representatives/custodian present at their interview (the person accompanying the victim is entitled to the reimbursement of the same expenses as the witness). *(iii)* If the minor is a victim of domestic violence, the minor has the right to be heard in the presence of a psychologist, and at special premises if possible. *(iv)* If the minor does not have the financial resources to pay for a lawyer, they have the right to free legal representation under all circumstances.

28.4   Victims' Rights after the Directive

According to the requirements of the Directive, in 2015 criminal procedural law was modified in Hungary. The following changes were made. *(i)* In the case of the death of the victim the relative in direct line, the brother or sister, the spouse or common-law partner of the victim, and the legal representative of the victim may exercise the rights of the victim. *(ii)* The victim is entitled to know whether the defendant is at large or has been released. *(iii)* The victim is entitled to be represented by legal aid counsel in all criminal proceedings. *(iv)* The victim is entitled to clear communication both verbally and in writing in all criminal proceedings. *(v)* The victim is entitled to not meet the defendant if it is possible. *(vi)* The victim is entitled to not have to repeat the procedural actions related to them if it is possible. *(vii)* For all victims, it is necessary to examine whether there is a case of special treatment; in the case of special treatment there is a need for greater protection of the victim.

---

6   Andrea Tünde Barabás, *Áldozatok és igazságszolgáltatás*, OKRI, Budapest, 2014, p. 166.
7   Andrea Tünde Barabás, 'Restorative Justice in Hungary: A Rapidly Growing Field of Practice', *Restorative Justice*, Vol. 3, Issue 3, pp. 387-395.

(viii) In the case of a sexual offence, the victim may request to be heard by a person of the same sex as the victim. *(ix)* In all cases, interrogation of a witness under the age of 14 must be recorded with a video camera. *(x)* Proceedings involving the victim may include the adult person identified by the victim who emotionally supports the victim. *(xi)* In the case of a victim requiring special treatment, it is possible to have a closed hearing (ex-camera trial).

28.4.1 The Victim Has New Rights

Based on the relevant EU rules, there are new rights of victims in criminal procedures.

i. *Victim statement.* The legislator, taking into consideration the recommendation of the European Commission on victim protection, created a new legal institution – the victim statement. According to this, the victim is entitled at any time during the criminal proceedings to declare what kind of physical, psychological harm, financial disadvantage they have suffered as the result of the criminal offence, whether they wish that the guilt of the defendant should be declared and the defendant to be punished. As such, the victim statement is a forward-looking opportunity for victims to ensure that their interests are taken into account by authorities, so that proceeding bodies consider them not only as additional actors in the criminal proceedings, but as persons who had suffered harm.

ii. *Waiver.* In light of the Directive, the new code determines that if the victim no longer wishes to exercise their rights in criminal proceedings, they may make a declaration at any time to this end. Naturally, this statement shall not prevent the victim being questioned as a witness, if it is deemed necessary. Therefore, the victim must still fulfil their obligation to testify and the statement does not exempt them from the obligation to appear in person for certain procedural actions. The victim may revoke the statement at any stage of the criminal proceedings. The text, however, clearly states that if the statement is withdrawn, the victim cannot exercise their rights retroactively. This may namely delay the proceedings.

28.5 RIGHTS OF VULNERABLE PERSONS

The rules for the protection of vulnerable persons have received a separate chapter in the new act on criminal procedure. Earlier, they could be found under various chapters and subheadings. The provisions put an emphasis on aspects of individualization and the individual needs of persons requiring special treatment.

The new act defines those persons that may be the primary recipients of special treatment: the victim, the witness and sometimes the defendant. The act concretely enumerates those cases when it is compulsory for the acting bodies to provide special treatment. In such cases, special treatment is enforced without a separate decision. The code includes the following cases: *(i)* if the person concerned has not yet reached the age of 18; *(ii)* they are a disabled person; *(iii)* they have been the victim of a sexual offence.

There are two groups of measures: the first group contains measures which have the aim of facilitating the proper exercise of the rights of those concerned, as well as to ensure their careful treatment: *(i)* increased caution when communicating with the person concerned; *(ii)* increased caution in order to protect the privacy of the person concerned; *(iii)* the execution of certain procedural acts without delay; *(iv)* the requirement to avoid unjustified repetition of the procedural act; *(v)* the carrying out of the procedural act in a room designed for that purpose or in any other suitable place *etc.*

The second group covers protection measures that may in a particular case restrict the rights of other participants in the criminal procedure. These legal tools are restricted to cases where, the participation of the person requiring special treatment in the criminal proceedings threatens their life, physical integrity or personal freedom. These measures may also be geared towards helping the person concerned to exercise their rights and fulfil their obligations without intimidation or influence. Soft measures can naturally also be applied where providing protection becomes necessary.[8]

28.6 Mediation

Mediation is one of the tools of restorative justice that seeks to resolve the criminal offence as a special conflict. It is not a novel legal institution: it has existed since 1 January 2007. Council Framework Decision of 15 March 2001 on the standing of victims in criminal proceedings prescribed the introduction of this legal instrument into Hungarian law. The experiences of 10 years since its implementation prove that its application has been successful. The new code reformulated this legal institution; the new provisions followed the tendency of the extension of scope. The legislature kept the basic requirements, at the same time, it introduced significant changes in several aspects.

The goal of the reformulated mediation of the new act on criminal procedure is defined through its purpose. The aim of the institution is to establish an agreement and reconciliation on the basis of the voluntary participation of suspect and victim, promoting also the suspect's future lawful behavior. The mediation process has a desirable reach beyond the criminal proceedings; therefore, the law has extended its application far beyond its earlier scope. Not only active repentance can be applied in the context of terminating substantive

---

8   Ákos Kara, *The Rights of the Victim in the New Hungarian Criminal Procedure (Conference Presentation),* 4th Annual Conference of Balkan Criminology, Budapest, 21-24 September 2017.

punishability or other concessions, but other means as well, as long as the purposes of the mediation process is upheld. It is also an important modification that there is no need to clarify the facts with sufficient certainty for the prosecution because the evidence can be complemented following a possible unsuccessful mediation process. The public prosecution's office can only suspend proceedings within the deadline for the investigation. The public prosecutor may offer the application of a measure or decision before initiating the mediation process. One of the most important issues of the codification process was the shift in the attitude towards the defendant's cooperation. The legislator has set up a new integrated system for the cooperation of the defendant in which the mediation procedure was incorporated. This is the systemic reason why the judge cannot apply mediation in the trial phase.[9]

28.7   THE RIGHTS OF THE VICTIM IN EU MEMBER STATES

Three basic models of victim representation can be identified in Europe: the French, the German and the English model.

i.   *The French model.* In those countries which have adopted the French civil party approach, victims are entirely independent of the prosecution and enjoy important procedural rights. These include the right to require the launch of a prosecution or specific investigatory acts by the authorities, access to the dossier, representation through counsel at all hearings and the resolution of claims for civil damages against the defendant by the trial court. This system clearly empowers the victim, who is able to exercise considerable influence over the conduct of proceedings.[10]

ii. *The German model.* In the German model, the victim plays an active role. In the drama called criminal procedure, they are not only the victim of the crime, but also an actor of the process. In this model, victims of serious crimes are entitled to act as subsidiary prosecutors (*Nebenkläger*) alongside the public prosecutor.[11]

iii. *The English model.* The English model is called the 'service rights' system. Here, victims are only entitled to information and the right to offer the court a 'Victim Impact Statement'. However, they have no right to determine the course of the procedure, unless they are involved in a private prosecution.[12]

---

9   Krisztina Farkas, *Az eljárás gyorsításának lehetőségei a német, a svájci és az olasz büntető igazságszolgáltatásban*, PhD dissertation, Miskolc, 2016. *See* the thesis in English at http://phd.lib.uni-miskolc.hu/document/22696/17210.pdf.

10   Richard Vogler & Barbara Huber, *Criminal Procedure in Europe*, Duncker and Humblot, 2008, p. 23.

11   *See* Michael Kaiser, *Die Stellung des Verletzten im Strafverfahren: Implementation und Evaluation des "Opferschutzgesetzes"*, Freiburg, 1992, p. 53.

12   Vogler & Huber 2008, p. 24.

According to Vogler, these different models

> "illustrate perfectly the conflicting pressures on the criminal justice reform in Europe. On the one hand the powerful international victims' rights movement, backed by measures from the Council of Europe and the EU is pressing for an increased participation for victims, whilst on the other hand; the move towards adversariality suggests their restriction to mere service rights."[13]

28.7.1   Minimum Standards

To ensure a minimum level of victims' rights in all Member States, the EU adopted several EU legal instruments setting up common rules aimed at protecting and assisting victims of crime. These are horizontal instruments dealing with victims' rights in general, more specific instruments governing protection measures and financial compensation to victims of crime and substantive law instruments regarding trafficking in human beings and child sexual exploitation.

Directive 2012/29/EU establishing minimum standards on the rights, support and protection of victims of crime ensures that persons who have fallen victim to crimes are recognized, treated with respect and receive proper protection, support and access to justice. The Directive replaces the 2001 Framework Decision[14] on the standing of victims in criminal proceedings and considerably strengthens the rights of victims and their family members to information, support and protection, including victims' procedural rights in criminal proceedings. The Directive also requires that Member States ensure that officials who are likely to come into contact with victims receive appropriate training regarding victims' needs. Finally, the Directive encourages cooperation between Member States and coordination of national services' actions regarding victims' rights.

EU Member States were to implement the provisions of the Directive into their national laws by 16 November 2015. The EU has adopted two instruments for strengthening the protection of victims of crime that ensure recognition of protection measures issued in other EU countries. These are the 2011 Directive on the European Protection Order[15] and the 2013 Regulation on mutual recognition of protection orders in civil matters.[16] Thanks to these instruments, victims or potential victims can rely on restraint or protection orders

---

13   Id.
14   2001/220/JHA Council Framework Decision of 15 March 2001 on the standing of victims in criminal proceedings.
15   Directive 2011/99/EU of the European Parliament and of the Council of 13 December 2011 on the European protection order.
16   Regulation (EU) No 606/2013 of the European Parliament and of the Council of 12 June 2013 on mutual recognition of protection measures in civil matters.

issued in any EU country if they travel or move to another EU country. Both instruments are applicable throughout the EU since 11 January 2015.[17]

The transposition of the Framework Decision into national laws was unsuccessful in many respects, since a number of Member States did not implement it entirely. Nevertheless, they revised and supplemented their criminal procedures and transposed the Directive. Today, we are witnessing common problems in the EU. It is up to national judicial systems to face them and find a solution, including the instrument adopted in 2015, where the Member States reinforced the rights of the victim.

28.7.2   The German and Italian Justice Systems

Following the presentation of the Hungarian criminal procedure, I would like to present the rights of the victim in the German and Italian justice systems. Germany and Italy belong to the civil law system and as a result, they have common roots and demonstrate several similar and comparable features. There is a close interrelationship between the Hungarian and German legal systems: many Hungarian legal institutions have German roots. An assessment of the Italian criminal proceeding is also important because of the role of the Justices of Peace.

Mediation in its original sense, *i.e.* a proceeding between the offender and the victim to resolve their conflict by a mediation process is possible in the German and Hungarian criminal justice system alike. In the Italian criminal justice system, conciliation occurs in a specific way, by means of a specific legal institution, the so-called Justice of Peace (conciliation).

28.7.2.1   Germany

The victim can take part in criminal proceedings as a witness or take on a more active role by formally becoming a private prosecutor or private accessory prosecutor and thus benefit from a variety of rights available to them. As a private prosecutor, they will take the place of the public prosecutor; as a private accessory prosecutor, they will take part in the proceedings alongside the public prosecutor. Victims have the following rights: *(i)* to be informed about their rights in the summons, including the possibility of receiving assistance; *(ii)* to refuse to testify if they are or were married or engaged to the suspect (the same applies to registered same-sex partnerships) or they are the victim's close relative; *(iii)* to refuse to answer specific questions if they might lead to the victim or victim's relatives being prosecuted; questions that might dishonor the victim or pertain to their private life may be asked only if absolutely essential; *(iv)* to be accompanied by a person of trust, unless

---

17   *See* https://e-justice.europa.eu/content_victims_of_crime_in_criminal_proceedings-66-en.do?init=true.

that person's presence would jeopardize the purpose of the investigations; *(v)* to be accompanied by a lawyer, who may be excluded if it makes the hearing of evidence difficult; *(vi)* to be supported during questioning by a lawyer at public expense in case the victim is unable to exercise their rights on their own; *(vii)* to have following expenses reimbursed if they apply within three months of their questioning to the authority questioning them: travel costs, expenses incurred, loss of time, disadvantages in housekeeping or loss of earnings (subject to limitations); however, they ordinary police questioning does not give rise to reimbursement claims.

The German term for mediation is offender-victim mediation *(Täter-Opfer Ausgleich)* which is a legal institution applied in both substantive and procedural law, as such, it is the subject of complex regulation. The legislator distinguishes between the offender-victim mediation in its original sense, and reparation in the sense used by substantive law exclusively and the legal conditions for their application. Otherwise, the law defines the same legal consequences for both forms of mediation. The main characteristics of the legal institution in substantive law appear in the effort of the offender to achieve reparation, in the communication process between the offender and the victim, in the redress of the damages caused by the crime and in the order of the three alternatives of fulfilment. Namely, as the case may be, the offender restores the whole damage; they restore it in part or made a serious effort of restoration. The legislator placed reparation outside the framework of the offender-victim mediation, in the course of which it requires that reparation for the offender shall mean a substantive personal fulfilment or a personal renouncement, in addition to the reparation of the damage as a whole or to a substantial degree. The procedural provisions prescribe extra obligations for the prosecution and the court, because they shall examine the possibility of coming to an arrangement between the offender and the victim in each phase of the proceeding. Where such an arrangement becomes possible, they shall try to implement it. In mediation, it is possible not to file formal charges with conditions or to drop the proceeding with conditions, which amounts to an arrangement combined with diversion.[18]

28.7.2.2   Italy

The victims play an important role in criminal proceedings. There are a number of rights, which they may exercise in the criminal procedure. They may participate as a victim (offended party) without a specific legal status or play a more active role by officially bringing a civil action against the offender. In Italy, victims have the right: *(i)* to be informed about their rights; *(ii)* to receive information relating to the status of proceedings, and of entries in the Official Registry of Reported Offences; *(iii)* to be informed of a request to

---

18   Farkas 2016.

close proceedings; *(iv)* to receive information about their case; *(v)* to be reimbursed for the costs of participating in the criminal proceedings; *(vi)* to be assisted by an interpreter and to the translation of important documents *etc.*

The proceedings before the Justices of Peace is a special legal institution that offers diverse possibilities to dispose of a group of less serious crimes. This procedure can be considered one of the main innovations of Italian criminal law: "a soft and effective criminal law". On the one hand, it has the goal of reducing the caseload of Italian criminal courts, on the other hand – in the case of the majority of less serious crimes – to create an alternative judicial criminal system. In this procedure, the obligation of conciliation to resolve the conflict between the parties, the alternative resolutions for the disposal of cases and the special sanction system play a significant role. The alternative criminal procedure covers three solutions: the waiver of the criminal claim because of the lack of importance of the crime, the expiry of culpability due to compensation and the conciliation between the parties. In these cases, there is usually no trial, so the procedure may be conducted more rapidly, and courts can be unburdened. Conciliation and compensation often take more time, but since they take place outside the court proceeding, they have an acceleration function as well.[19]

28.8   SUMMARY

Recently, the position of the victim has been the subject of an increasing number of surveys. During the course of the development of criminal law, victims lost their former leading role in the procedure, and were pushed to the periphery of justice. Legal experts have come to realize that this tendency is drastically unfair to the victim. To quote the well-known song by the Doors, "they are riders on the storm, swept away by sand."

It is not easy to understand this, especially when day-to-day criminal chronicles influence us. An increasing number of people fall victim to crime every day, and this experience often has grave psychological, social, and financial implications. In many cases, the administration of justice fails to restore the damage caused by the offence. Victims are severely disregarded during criminal proceedings, and the possibilities for the enforcement of any compensation are very limited. Consequently, the government must provide victims with other types of assistance.

Recently, similarly to the beginning of the 20th century, more and more people have been calling for a restoration of the victim's proper place and role in the drama we call criminal procedure. This is only possible by expanding the rights of the victim. To address

---

19   Id.

this situation a rising number of specialists have turned the spotlight on the victims of crime.

Consequently, the question arises: should we restore the former leading role of the victim in the pursuit of crime? By no means. This is not the solution. A solution is only possible if the victim's rights increase, and if guarantees for the enforcement of victims' rights are built into the criminal procedure.

European documents on the legal position of the victim increasingly call attention to the need for bringing about changes in legislation. However, we still have problems concerning the improvement of the victim's situation for several reasons. In the early 90's the aim was to develop jurisdictions which respect the principles of fair trial, and the state was too busy to deal with victim's rights. Later, this aim was replaced by a more practical way of thinking. The new goal was to provide effective justice through faster and simpler criminal proceedings. The situation of the courts of justice, which are at the limit of their functioning abilities, may actually be made easier by rendering the procedures less complicated. But simplification and acceleration of the procedure alone are not enough to ensure effective justice. Legislators should also consider human rights issues, because simplified procedures lacking guarantees do not work out in the long run. Human rights apply not only to the defendant but also to the victim, and most victims are dissatisfied with the performance of law enforcement authorities (police, prosecution, courts). Meanwhile it is very important to maintain that it does now suffice to regulate the rights of victims, because of the principle that all rights are worth upholding. I agree with Erika Róth who warns us of the following:

> "Without challenging the necessity of victims' protection and assuring the victims' rights in the criminal procedure and out of it, I would like to emphasize that we should not forget the guarantees concerning the suspects' rights, which have to be accepted as well."[20]

---

20   Erika Róth, 'Position of Victims in the Criminal Procedure in the Context with Requirements of the European Union', *European Integration Studies*, Vol. 9, Issue 1, 2011, pp. 109-120.

PART V
CASE NOTES

29   Fiscal Equalization among the Hungarian Local Governments – Autonomy v. Equity

Decision No. 3383/2018. (XII. 14.) AB of the Constitutional Court of Hungary

Gábor Kecső[*]

Keywords

European Charter of Local Self-Government, financial resources of local authorities, fiscal equalization, solidarity levy, Constitutional Court of Hungary

Abstract

The 2017 budget of Hungary contains a regime on fiscal equalization among local governments that distracts funds from the municipalities with relatively high taxing power within the country. The respective norms were reviewed by the Constitutional Court from the perspective of international law, since Hungary is one of the member parties to the European Charter of Local Self-Government. This note highlights the essence of the abovementioned decision and discusses some underlying issues of allocating public tasks and funds between the governmental layers in a unitary country where the per capita revenue of local taxes is very divergent.

29.1   The Facts of the Case

The Hungarian Parliament adopted the Act XC of 2016 on the 2017 Central Budget of Hungary (2017 Budget) that laid down a new arrangement for equalizing the revenues of municipalities. The top governmental layer of the capital city and the counties are beyond the scope of the regulation. The fiscal equalization regime can be summarized as follows.[1]

Complex rules provide for diverting some intergovernmental grants from local governments the hypothetical taxing power of which is above 32,000 HUF per capita. The grants covered are expressly defined by the 2017 Budget. Hypothetical means in this context that local taxing power is calculated as if the municipalities levied the local business tax at a

---

*   Gábor Kecső: senior lecturer, ELTE Law School, Budapest; counselor, Constitutional Court of Hungary.
1   Based on Budget 2017, Annex 2, Point V.

525

rate of 0.55%. Therefore, the calculation is irrespective of the actual facts, *i.e.* whether the municipality actually taxed at that rate or not. (The rate is capped at 2% in the central act on local taxes.)

If the hypothetical taxing power is higher than the intergovernmental grants covered, the margin shall be paid by the local governments to the central budget. This payment is called 'solidarity levy' in the 2017 Budget. The equalization ratio and the rate of the solidarity levy increases as the hypothetical taxing power grows. 2017 saw 166 municipalities obliged to pay the levy in a total sum of 26.5 billion HUF, meanwhile the overall sum of the intergovernmental grants given to the 3178 Hungarian municipalities[2] exceeded 700 billion HUF in the same year.[3]

The equalization regime provides for extra funds for municipalities with under 10 000 HUF per capita hypothetical taxing power. The 2017 Budget implemented the net method of fiscal equalization, since an additional fund for the aforementioned local governments comes from the solidarity levy. Nevertheless, it should be noted that the solidarity levy is not only meant to finance municipalities with a low hypothetical taxing power, but to finance the central budget. In other words, the regime blends horizontal (local-local) and vertical (local-central) fiscal equalization.

The Members of Parliament initiated the annulment of the diversion rules including the provisions on the solidarity levy before the Constitutional Court. The petitioners asserted the violation of Article 9 of the European Charter of Local Self-Government (Charter) on the Financial resources of local authorities. Hungary has signed and ratified the full text of the Charter.[4] The petitioners argued, on the one hand, that the fiscal equalization regime restricts local autonomy, because it diminishes the discretion local authorities may exercise within their own sphere of responsibility. On the other hand, the Charter states that local authorities' financial resources shall be commensurate with the responsibilities provided for by the constitution and the law. In contrast with this rule, the Hungarian regime equates local financial resources with the hypothetical taxing power. While fiscal equalization is mentioned by the Charter, it cannot be construed as a justification for the solidarity levy, because the Charter does not allow local governments' net payments to the central budget.

---

2   Hungarian Central Statistical Office: Gazetteer of Hungary 2018, Budapest, p. 19.
3   Act LXXXIV of 2018 on the Discharge of the Budget 2017, Annex 1, Point IX.
4   It applies from 1 July 1994 to Hungary. Act XV of 1997 on the Implementation of the Charter, Section 3.

29.2   The Decision of the Constitutional Court

According to the Fundamental Law of Hungary, the Constitutional Court shall examine any law for a conflict with international treaties.[5] Proceedings of the Constitutional Court may be initiated by – among others – one quarter of Members of Parliament.[6] The petitioners complied with this condition, however, their petition did not contain an express request in full. Therefore, the petition was not appropriate to review the fiscal equalization regime in light of the full text of Article 9 of the Charter. Nevertheless, it made it possible for the Constitutional Court to decide on the petition in respect of Article 9(1), (2) and (5).[7] The decision was made unanimously before Christmas of 2018, without any concurring or dissenting opinions.

The Constitutional Court has taken into account the Explanatory Report to the Charter and attributed high importance to the revenue inequality among Hungarian municipalities. Approximately half of the tax base of local business tax is at the disposal of municipalities whose inhabitants make up merely 20% to the Hungarian population. According to the ministerial explanation to the 2017 Budget, this is why the legislator aimed to reduce fiscal differences. Furthermore, since certain public tasks were centralized in Hungary after 2010, the financial resources were to follow the costs. This means that the solidarity levy is considered to be a component of the reallocation of revenues within the public household (sector general government).

The decision emphasized the concept of the ministerial explanation and recalled that the regime allocates extra funds to municipalities with a low hypothetical taxing power. Consequently, the fiscal equalization system is not contrary to the Charter. Article 9(5) expressly says financial equalization procedures or equivalent measures are necessary in order to mitigate the differences in the distribution of financial resources among local governments. The decision concludes that restricting this system would be a violation of Article 9(1) and (2). Nevertheless, these paragraphs do not require that the sum of the horizontal fiscal equalization grant reach the sum of the solidarity levy. In other words: these Charter rules do not prohibit that the solidarity levy flow partly into the central budget. The Constitutional Court stated that since the Hungarian regime is sufficiently

---

5   Article 24(2)(f) of the Fundamental Law.

6   Act CLI of 2011 on the Constitutional Court, Sections 52(1) and (1b).

7   The text of these paragraphs is the following: "(1) Local authorities shall be entitled, within national economic policy, to adequate financial resources of their own, of which they may dispose freely within the framework of their powers. (2) Local authorities' financial resources shall be commensurate with the responsibilities provided for by the constitution and the law. [...] (5) The protection of financially weaker local authorities calls for the institution of financial equalization procedures or equivalent measures which are designed to correct the effects of the unequal distribution of potential sources of finance and of the financial burden they must support. Such procedures or measures shall not diminish the discretion local authorities may exercise within their own sphere of responsibility."

refined – meaning that it charges only the municipalities with outstanding per capita taxing power and supports municipalities with a low per capita taxing power – the fiscal equalization is in line with the abovementioned two paragraphs of the Charter.[8]

29.3 COMMENTS

What is notable about the abovementioned decision? In my view, three reasons are worth mentioning. Firstly, this is the first case in which the Hungarian Constitutional Court interpreted Article 9(1), (2) and (5) of the Charter. As such, it may contribute to the primary sources of academic literature on fiscal equalization among local authorities from a Hungarian perspective.[9] Secondly, the decision dealt with the status of the Explanatory Report. It does not have binding effect. Instead, it belongs to the context in which the Charter must to be interpreted by the sovereign national bodies according to Article 31 of the Vienna Convention on the Law of Treaties. In Hungary, the Constitutional Court has empowered to interpret international treaties when the question is whether domestic law violates rules of international law. Finally, the decision confirmed the validity of the fiscal equalization regime within a unitary state where the taxing power of local governments differ to a large degree.

It is well known that local autonomy results in outstanding differences in various respects, including taxation. Yet this room for divergence is not without limits. Equity among the constituents of the nation (*e.g.* citizens, families and local governments) must also be respected. Buchanan's thoughts on equalization are on point, were we to, for the purposes of our topic, replace 'states' with 'municipalities':

> "The mere acceptance of the equity principle in discussions concerning the fiscal problem of federalism can yield important results. First of all, upon its acceptance inter-area transfers do not represent charitable contributions from the rich to the poor and are not analogous to the concept of ability to pay in

---

8 Decision No. 3383/2018. (XII. 14.) AB, Reasoning [35]-[37].
9 Fiscal equalization is a frequently discussed topic in the literature. *See e.g.* Peter Swan & Gerald Garvey, *The Equity and Efficiency Implications of Fiscal Equalization*, Sydney, Mimeograph, 1992; Ehtisham Ahmad & Jon Craig, 'Intergovernmental Transfers', *in* Teresa Ter-Minassian (ed.), *Fiscal Federalism in Theory and Practice.* Washington, 1997, pp. 73-108; Hansjörg Blöchliger *et al.*, 'Fiscal Equalisation in OECD Countries', *OECD Working Papers on Fiscal Federalism*, 2007, No. 4; Robin Boadway, 'Fiscal Equalization: the Canadian Experience', *in* Núria Bosch & José M. Durán (eds.), *Fiscal Federalism and Political Decentralization*, Edward Elgar, 2008, pp. 109-139; Jeffrey Petchey & Sophia Levtchenkova, 'Fiscal Capacity Equalization and Economic Efficiency: The Case of Australia', *in* Jorge Martinez-Vazquez & Bob Searle (eds.), *Fiscal Equalization: Challenges in the Design of Intergovernmental Transfers*, New York, 2007, pp. 13-30; Daniel Bergwall *et al.*, 'Intergovernmental Transfers and Decentralised Public Spending', *OECD Network on Fiscal Relations across Levels of Government*, 2006/3.

the inter-personal sense. The principle establishes a firm basis for the claim that the citizens of the low-income states within a national economy possess the «right» that their states receives sums sufficient to enable these citizens to be placed in positions of fiscal equality with their equals in other states. A transfer viewed in this light is no sense a gift or subsidy from the citizens of the more favored regions."[10]

Finally, we should not forget that the Hungarian regulation reviewed by the Constitutional Court has a special feature. Fiscal equalization extends beyond the horizontal level. The solidarity levy – at least in part – serves vertical fiscal equalization purposes, from the local governments to the central government. This element may be puzzling for the theorists, even though the decision itself is unambiguous. Theoretically, one can argue that the scope of the review was restricted owing to the deficiencies of the petition (lack of express request). If all rules of the Charter and the 'spirit' of the Charter would have been taken into account, the Constitutional Court could have rendered a different decision.

---

10   James M. Buchanan, 'Federalism and Fiscal Equity', *The American Economic Review*, Vol. 40, Issue 4, 1950, p. 596.

30   MAGYAR JETI ZRT. V. HUNGARY

Judgment of the ECtHR Concerning the Imposition of Liability for Posting Hyperlinks to Defamatory Content

*Renáta Gyalog**

Keywords

freedom of expression, defamatory content, liability of online press, Article 10 ECHR, hyperlinks

Abstract

The article aims to introduce the judgment of the ECtHR on the case *Magyar Jeti Zrt. v. Hungary*. Although in this Hungarian case the ECtHR dealt with a special provision of the Hungarian Civil Code that – under the interpretation of the domestic courts – imposes objective liability for posting hyperlinks which lead to third-party online content, the judgment can be considered as a big improvement compared to the previous decisions of the ECtHR concerning the freedom of expression. The judgment offers legal certainty and guidance for journalists who post hyperlinks by determining five relevant questions to be taken into account when deciding whether the liability of a press organ can be established for contents cited from other websites over which they have no control. Becoming the best ECtHR judgment of the year 2018 under the yearly vote announced by Strasbourg Observers blog portal also emphasizes the importance and the relevance of this decision for the digital media.

30.1   INTRODUCTION

On 4 December 2018 the ECtHR delivered its judgment on the case of *Magyar Jeti Zrt. v. Hungary*, which decision was declared to be the best ECtHR judgment of the year 2018 under the yearly vote announced by Strasbourg Observers, a blog portal that aims to raise awareness on the latest judgments of the ECtHR and to assess recent legal, political and social developments in Europe by introducing the case-law of the ECtHR.[1] This category winner case concerned the freedom of expression guaranteed under Article 10 ECHR.

---

*   Renáta Gyalog: assistant judge, Békéscsaba District Court, Hungary.
1   *See* https://strasbourgobservers.com/about/.

Based on Article 10 ECHR, the ECtHR examines three requirements in order to decide whether the interference of the state can be considered as lawful. The three requirements, which justify the restriction on freedom of expression are lawfulness, legitimate aim and necessity in democratic society.[2] When the ECtHR finds that even one of these three requirements were not fulfilled it will hold that freedom of expression under Article 10 ECHR was violated.[3]

However, freedom of expression under Article 10 ECHR is not only a right in itself but is essential for protecting other rights guaranteed by the ECHR, as well. Furthermore, as the ECtHR has already concluded in its early case-law, "freedom of expression constitutes one of the essential foundations of a democratic society and one of the basic conditions for its progress."[4] Moreover,

> "it is applicable not only to 'information' or 'ideas' that are favorably received or regarded as inoffensive or as a matter of indifference, but also to those that offend, shock or disturb the State or any sector of the population. Such are the demands of that pluralism, tolerance and broadmindedness without which there is no 'democratic society'."[5]

In other words, without freedom of expression there is no democratic political process or development of human beings. Thus the function of Article 10 ECHR is to protect any expression, altogether its content disseminated by any individual, group or type of media.[6] As it was first emphasized by the ECtHR in *Lingens v. Austria*, the press is a 'public watchdog', thus it has a special status to enjoy the freedom of expression under Article 10 ECHR. The press has an important democratic function when it imparts information and ideas on political issues and opens the way for political and other debates of public interest.[7]

However, the digital environment and the use of new technologies, such as Internet, as a new field of communication affect the work of journalists as well, and the protection of the freedom of expression on the Internet becomes a more and more pertinent issue. Although the Internet expanded the possibilities of the media, it also reproduced the problems of the 'original' platform of the media, and created new challenges.[8] Since only

---

2   Judit Bayer, 'Az Emberi Jogok Európai Bíróságának 10. cikkel kapcsolatos joggyakorlatának egyes súlypontjai', *Állam- és Jogtudomány*, Vol. 58, Issue 4, 2017, p. 120.

3   The same 'three-part test' is applied by the ECtHR in cases relating to Articles 8, 9 and 11 as well.

4   *Castells v. Spain*, No. 11798/85, 23 April 1992, para. 42.

5   *Handyside v. the United Kingdom*, No. 5493/72, 7 December 1976, para. 49.

6   Dominika Bychawska-Siniarska, *Protecting the Right to Freedom of Expression under the European Convention on Human Rights – A Handbook for Legal Practitioners*, Council of Europe, Strasbourg, 2017, p. 12.

7   Id. p. 87.

8   András Koltay, *Új média, új szerkesztők és a sajtószabadság alapjoga*, HTE MediaNet, Vol. 70, Kecskemét, 2015, p. 10.

a limited number of regulations have been adopted relating to the digital challenges, national and international judges, as well as judges of the ECtHR play an important role in establishing the main standards.[9]

30.2   Relevant ECtHR Case-Law Concerning the Freedom of Expression

As the ECtHR emphasized it in its early case-law, the right to access to Internet and participating in the information society is inherent in the right to freedom of expression. The ECtHR first pointed out in *Ahmet Yildirim v. Turkey* that

> "the Internet has now become one of the principal means by which individuals exercise their right to freedom to receive and impart information and ideas, providing as it does essential tools for participation in activities and discussions concerning political issues and issues of general interest."[10]

This case set an important precedent relating to the exercise of the right to freedom of expression online, as it was the first case concerning blocking access to Internet, dealing with blocking access to the entire domain of Google sites by a blanket blocking order, since it hosted a website containing content which was deemed offensive to the memory of Atatürk. In its decision the ECtHR noted that "Google Sites is a Google service designed to facilitate the creation and sharing of websites within a group and thus constitutes a means of exercising freedom of expression."[11] The ECtHR held that there had been a violation of Article 10 ECHR as

> "the measure in question produced arbitrary effects and could not be said to have been aimed solely at blocking access to the offending website, since it consisted in the wholesale blocking of all the sites hosted by Google Sites. Furthermore, the judicial review procedures concerning the blocking of Internet sites are insufficient to meet the criteria for avoiding abuse, as domestic law does not provide for any safeguards to ensure that a blocking order in respect of a specific site is not used as a means of blocking access in general."[12]

In this judgment the ECtHR concluded that if the restrictions on freedom of expression do not meet with the conditions required by Article 10(2) ECHR, freedom of expression

---

9   Bychawska-Siniarska 2017, p. 108.
10   *Ahmet Yildirim v. Turkey*, No. 3111/10, 18 December 2012, para 54.
11   Id. para 49.
12   Id. paras. 68-69.

under Article 10 ECHR will be violated. On the other hand, the ECtHR also concluded that free speech is not an absolute right, thus it cannot enjoy greater protection than other fundamental rights. However, taking into account the risks carried by the Internet, it is more likely that freedom of expression may be limited on the online platform than in the non-digital environment.[13]

Another important decision on this topic was delivered in *Cengiz and Others v. Turkey*. In this case the ECtHR emphasized the importance of YouTube in the exercise of freedom of expression by observing that "YouTube is a video-hosting website on which users can upload, view and share videos and is undoubtedly an important means of exercising the freedom to receive and impart information and ideas."[14] In this case the ECtHR held that blocking YouTube violated Article 10 ECHR as

> "the authorities should have taken into consideration, among other aspects, the fact that such a measure, by rendering large quantities of information inaccessible, was bound to substantially restrict the rights of Internet users and to have a significant collateral effect."[15]

As the ECtHR concluded in these two decisions, blocking online services widely used by Internet users (Google Sites and YouTube) as platform for user-generated content that allegedly commit a crime cannot be permitted, as it violates the other users' right to freedom of expression by rendering them unable to use these services.[16]

In *Kalda v. Estonia,* the ECtHR dealt with granting prisoners' access to the Internet in particular circumstances. In this case a prisoner was not allowed to access three Internet websites run by the state and the Council of Europe which contained legal information.[17] In this case the ECtHR considered that

> "Article 10 cannot be interpreted as imposing a general obligation to provide access to the Internet, or to specific Internet sites, for prisoners. However, [...] in the circumstances of the case, since access to certain sites containing legal information is granted under Estonian law, the restriction of access to other

---

13   Oreste Pollicino, 'European Judicial Dialogue and the Protection of Fundamental Rights in the New Digital Environment: An Attempt at Emancipation and Reconciliation: The Case of Freedom of Speech', *in* Sonia Morano-Foadi & Lucy Vickers (eds.), *Fundamental Rights in the EU. A Matter for Two Courts*, Hart Publishing, 2015, p. 106.
14   *Cengiz and Others v. Turkey*, Nos. 48226/10 and 14027/11, 1 December 2015, para. 52.
15   Id. para 64.
16   András Koltay, 'Az internetes kapuőrök és az Emberi Jogok Európai Egyezményének 10. cikke – A sajtószabadság új alanyai', *Állam- és Jogtudomány*, Vol. 58, Issue 4, 2017, p. 136.
17   *Kalda v. Estonia*, No. 17429/10, 19 January 2016, paras. 6-9.

sites that also contain legal information constitutes an interference with the right to receive information."[18]

The ECtHR found that security and cost implications as reasons for not allowing the applicant prisoner to access the required Internet sites had not been sufficient to justify this interference, thus Article 10 of ECHR had been violated in this case.[19]

The ECtHR had to deal with cases concerning the liability for online user-generated content as well. In *Delfi v. Estonia*, the domestic courts held liable Delfi AS – a company that run an internet news portal on a commercial basis – for the offensive comments posted by its readers under one of its online articles about a ferry company. According to the decisions of the domestic courts, Delfi AS had to remove the offensive comments.[20] The ECtHR found that the nature of the comments was extreme and the comments were posted in reaction to an article published by Delfi AS on its professionally managed news portal run on a commercial basis. Thus, the domestic courts imposed liability on Delfi AS on relevant and sufficient grounds without the violation of Article 10 ECHR.[21] In other words, in this case the ECtHR found that protecting the reputation of individuals ranks among the objectives that can justify a limitation on freedom of expression.[22]

However, a different conclusion was reached by the ECtHR in *Magyar Tartalomszolgáltatók Egyesülete and Index.hu v. Hungary*. In this case a self-regulatory body of Internet content providers and an internet news portal were held liable by the domestic courts for offensive and vulgar online comments posted by their readers on their websites relating to the publication of a critical opinion on the practice of two real estate websites.[23] According to the ECtHR, in this case there had been a violation of Article 10 ECHR, since the exercise of the domestic courts was not balanced properly between the right to freedom of expression of the applicants and the right to respect regarding the commercial reputation of the real estate websites as competing rights. The ECtHR also found that the internet service providers did not operate for profit and the comments did not contain hate speech.[24]

As we can see in these two cases the ECtHR decided on the question of violation of Article 10 ECHR by examining the offensive content of the comments.[25] In other words,

---

18   Id. para. 45.
19   Id. para. 53.
20   *Delfi AS v. Estonia (GC)*, No. 64569/09, 16 June 2015, paras. 11-32.
21   Id. para. 162.
22   Oreste Pollicino & Marco Bassini, 'Free Speech, Defamation and the Limits to Freedom of Expression in the EU: A Comparative Analysis', *in* Andrej Savin & Jan Trzaskowski (eds.), *Research Handbook on EU Internet Law*, Edward Elgar Publishing, 2014, p. 508.
23   *Magyar Tartalomszolgáltatók Egyesülete and Index.hu v. Hungary*, No. 22947/13, 2 February 2016, paras. 5-25.
24   Id. paras. 89-91.
25   Bayer 2017, p. 120.

if the offensive content of the comment goes over a certain limit, the Internet content provider can be held liable for the infringement.[26]

In *Times Newspaper Ltd v. the United Kingdom,* the ECtHR dealt with the responsibility of publishers of internet archives containing materials that violated the right to reputation. During the libel proceedings against the applicant newspaper, it was required to add a notice to both articles in its Internet archive indicating that they were subject to libel litigation.[27] The ECtHR concluded that this requirement had not been disproportionate, thus, there had been no violation of Article 10 ECHR.[28]

The ECtHR had to deal with the question of liability for information obtained from Internet as well. The case of *Editorial Board of Pravoye Delo and Stekel v. Ukraine* concerned defamation proceedings against a local newspaper and its editor-in-chief for publishing a letter downloaded from the internet alleging that senior local officials were corrupt and involved with a criminal gang.[29] In this case the ECtHR found that the domestic courts imposed the applicant's liability without proper legal basis, since

> "given the lack of adequate safeguards in the domestic law for journalists using information obtained from the Internet, the applicants could not foresee to the appropriate degree the consequences which the impugned publication might entail. This enables the Court to conclude that the requirement of lawfulness contained in the second paragraph of Article 10 of the Convention was not met."[30]

As the ECtHR concluded in this decision, states have a positive obligation to create adequate laws for preventing and dealing with online infringements of law, since the Internet cumulates and increases the risk of certain challenges already known before.[31]

As it was introduced, concerning digital challenges the ECtHR has already had to deal with cases relating to the blocking the access to Internet, the liability for online user generated content, the liability for publications on the Internet and the liability for publication of information obtained from the Internet. However, in the case *Magyar Jeti Zrt. v. Hungary* the ECtHR had to deal with a totally different and more complex question: whether someone can be found objectively liable for using hyperlinks to refer to online content over which they have no control at all if this online content later was declared to be

---

26   Koltay 2017, p. 138.
27   *Times Newspaper Ltd v. the United Kingdom,* Nos. 3002/03 and 23676/03, 10 March 2009, paras. 5-8.
28   Id. para. 49.
29   *Editorial Board of Pravoye Delo and Stekel v. Ukraine,* No. 33014/05, 5 May 2011, paras. 4-20.
30   Id. para. 66.
31   Koltay 2017, p. 136.

unlawful, in other words whether the press organ is objectively liable for the veracity of the contents cited from third parties.

30.3   BACKGROUND OF THE CASE IN QUESTION

The applicant of the case before the ECtHR was Magyar Jeti Zrt., a Hungarian company that operates a Hungarian news portal called 444.hu. This news portal publishes approximately 27 articles per day in several topics such as politics, sports, technology and it has approximately 250,000 unique users per day.[32] On 6 September 2013 an article was published on this online news portal about the following incident.

On 5 September 2013 a group of probably drunk football fans who travelled by bus to a football match stopped at an elementary school in Konyár, a Hungarian village, near the Romanian border. The fans got off the bus and started singing while waving flags and throwing beer bottles. Furthermore, they chanted and shouted racist remarks at the mostly Roma students playing outside in the playground of the school. One of the fans even urinated in front of the school building. The teachers took the children inside the school building, and to keep them safe, they made them hide under tables and called the police. After the police arrived, the group got back on the bus and left.[33]

On the same day, the leader of the Roma minority local government in Konyár, Mr. Gy. gave an interview about the incident to Roma Produkciós Iroda Alapítvány, a media outlet focusing mostly on Roma issues. In his interview he accused the Hungarian right-wing political party called Jobbik of the incident and stated that "Jobbik came here [...] they attacked the school, Jobbik attacked it [...] Members of Jobbik, I add, they were members of Jobbik, they were members of Jobbik for sure." A video of this interview was also uploaded on Youtube.[34]

The applicant company published an article about this incident on the 444.hu news portal under the title "Football fans heading to Romania stopped to threaten gypsy pupils." The article was written by one of the journalists of the news portal and started with the following paragraphs:

> "By all indications, a bus full of Hungarian football fans heading to a Romania-Hungary game left a highway in order to threaten mostly Gypsy pupils at a primary school in Konyár, a village close to the Romanian border. According to our information and witness statements, the bus arrived in the village

---

32   *Magyar Jeti Zrt v. Hungary*, No. 11257/16, 4 December 2018, para. 6.
33   Id. para. 7.
34   Id. para. 8.

Thursday morning. The fans were inebriated and started insulting Gypsies and threatening the pupils. Teachers working in the building locked the doors and instructed the smallest children to hide under the tables. Mr. Gy., president of the local gypsy municipality, talked to us about the incident. A phone conversation with Mr. Gy. and a parent has already been uploaded to Youtube."[35]

As we can read in this extract, in the description of the incident the article referred to the football fans only and the political party Jobbik was not mentioned at all. The article only indicated that a phone conversation with Mr. Gy. and a parent had already been uploaded on Youtube. However, the words "uploaded on Youtube" were highlighted in green and were activated as a hyperlink, which took the readers clicking on it to the Youtube video about the interview with Mr. Gy. Three other websites operated by other media outlets also activated a hyperlink to this Youtube video.

On 13 October 2013 the political party Jobbik started defamation proceedings at Debrecen Regional Court, Hungary. Amongst the eight defendants were Mr. Gy., Roma Produkciós Iroda Alapítvány, Magyar Jeti Zrt. and the other media outlets that activated hyperlinks to the Youtube video. The political party Jobbik claimed that the defendants infringed its right to reputation under Section 78 of the Civil Code not only by naming and accusing Jobbik for the incident but even by creating hyperlinks to the Youtube video.

According to the relevant Hungarian legislation, personality rights such as the right to reputation are protected by the Civil Code and the relevant rules are applicable not only to private individuals but to legal personalities as well. Regarding defamation, the Civil Code states that statements or even the dissemination of a falsehood relating to another person can violate the right to reputation and establish defamation. Untrue statements or giving untrue information influencing the public's way of thinking about a person violate the right to reputation. In case that these statements or information influencing the public's way of thinking are not the expression of objective reality, they are in infringement of the right to reputation, regardless of whether they were done in good or bad faith, thus, they can be imputable to the infringer.[36]

30.4   LEGAL PROCEDURES BEFORE THE DOMESTIC COURTS

As we mentioned before, the political party Jobbik brought defamation proceedings before the Debrecen Regional Court against eight defendants including Mr. Gy., Roma Produkciós

---

35   Id. para. 9. The full article in Hungarian can be read at https://444.hu/2013/09/06/romaniaba-tarto-szurkolok-alltak-meg-cigany-diakokat-fenyegetni.

36   Ferenc Petrik, *A személyiségi jog védelme. A sajtó-helyreigazítás*, HVG-ORAC, Budapest, 2001, p. 89.

Iroda Alapítvány, Magyar Jeti Zrt. and the other media outlets that uploaded the video about the interview with Mr. Gy. or activated hyperlinks to it.

The Debrecen Regional Court found that Mr. Gy. violated the plaintiff's right to reputation in the interview given by Roma Produkciós Iroda Alapítvány and later uploaded on Youtube, by suggesting the untrue impression that the incident on 5 September 2013 in Konyár was committed by the political party Jobbik and that the people who participated in it were members of Jobbik. The regional court also found that the defendants who uploaded this interview containing these false statements, as well as the defendants who disseminated it by activating the hyperlink to the Youtube video violated the political party Jobbik's right to reputation.[37] Thus, the defendants who uploaded the video were obliged to publish an excerpt of the decision of the regional court on their websites, and the other defendants – including Magyar Jeti Zrt. – were obliged to delete the hyperlinks from the articles. Furthermore, Mr. Gy. was also obliged to pay non-pecuniary damages to the political party Jobbik.

In the judgment the regional court pointed out that although Article IX of the Fundamental Law of Hungary protects and guarantees the right to expression, it does not mean that this right is without any restrictions because even while practicing this right, the right to reputation cannot be violated. Relating to Mr. Gy, the regional court found that when he falsely suggested that the political party Jobbik was involved in the incident in Konyár and the participants of the incident were members of Jobbik, defamation was established since the political party Jobbik could be recognized through the content of the interview without any question. With his interview Mr. Gy. falsely conveyed the impression that the political party Jobbik committed a threatening, racist and aggressive act against the Roma students and his statements could negatively influence the public opinion about the political party. Relating to the other defendants, the regional court highlighted that under the relevant sections of the Civil Code, the violation of the right to reputation can be realized not only by making untrue statements but also by publishing or disseminating these untrue statements, regardless of whether it was made in good or bad faith or whether the infringement can be imputable to the person who committed it.[38]

In other words, relating to Magyar Jeti Zrt., the regional court established that when they made the Youtube video available by creating a hyperlink to it, they infringed the plaintiff's right to reputation, because through the hyperlink they publicly disseminated the defamatory statements of Mr. Gy. The regional court also pointed out that, although the defendants who activated hyperlinks to the video published their reports about the incident in the most realistic way and using the available information and presenting all the contradictory opinions – thus, acting with the necessary precision for to the responsible

---

37   Debrecen Regional Court 6.P.21.359/2013/24.
38   Id.

practice of their work – under the relevant Hungarian legislation, they are still objectively liable for disseminating the defamatory statements. Since this lack of imputability leads to the lack of subjective liability, these defendants – unlike Mr. Gy. – were not obliged to pay non-pecuniary damages.[39] The regional court concluded that there were four conjunctive conditions to indemnify non-pecuniary damages. The violation of personal rights shall be unlawful, the violation must be imputable to the person who committed the infringement, non-pecuniary disadvantage must be suffered and there must be a causal link between the violation of personal rights and the non-pecuniary disadvantage. In the case of legal persons, non-pecuniary damage includes some kind of non-pecuniary disadvantage or loss in the public opinion about the legal person, in the legal person's participation in its business or in other relations.[40]

Six defendants including Magyar Jeti Zrt. appealed to the Debrecen Regional Court of Appeal claiming that in the interview Jobbik was mentioned not as a political party but as a group of people with anti-Roma ideology. Nevertheless, it had been publicly known that the political party Jobbik embraced anti-Roma ideology and was involved in hatred-inciting activities. The increasing popularity of the political party Jobbik could be linked to its activities relating to this ideology, thus, the content of the interview could not be defamatory to it. Public opinion identified Jobbik more as a collectivity of organizations with anti-Roma ideology than as a political party. The interview contained the opinion of Mr. Gy. that the ideology of participants involved in the incident could be identified as similar to the ideology of the political party Jobbik. Thus, the interview of Mr. Gy. did not contain statements but only opinions which stayed within the framework of freedom of expression. In relation to those defendants who activated hyperlinks to the Youtube video, it was also emphasized that they did not identify with the content of the video, only made it available by creating a hyperlink, which act did not establish dissemination.[41]

The Debrecen Regional Court of Appeal upheld the decision of Debrecen Regional Court. The regional court of appeal did not accept the argument of the defendants that the interview of Mr. Gy. did not contain statements, only opinions, which stayed within the framework of freedom of expression. The regional court of appeal pointed out that statements and opinions must be distinguished as follows.

Claiming that something has happened establishes the statement of facts, which is an objective category having the content of reality, while opinions express an ideology, criticism or way of thinking, which is a subjective category. A statement of fact can be proven true or false. In the case of an opinion, however, this is not possible, since people can merely

---

39   Id.
40   Id.
41   Debrecen Regional Court of Appeal Pf.I.20.289/2014/7.

identify with it.[42] Furthermore, statements must be examined by their contents, which must be evaluated in complexity, being aware of the public opinion of the society.[43] When a statement can be evaluated in more than one ways and an injurious meaning may be connected to it, violation of personal rights can be established.[44] Thus, the content of the interview of Mr. Gy. can be qualified as a statement of facts, as it can give the impression to the average audience that the participants of the incident were members of the political party Jobbik.

Regarding the defendants who activated hyperlinks to the Youtube video, the regional court of appeal pointed out that defamation can be realized by making an untrue statement available via a link, even if the disseminator does not identify with the content. Under Section 78 of the Civil Code, dissemination occurs by sharing the information, which makes the content available to anyone and, thus, the disseminator has objective liability.[45] Since dissemination is realized by sharing information, which results in objective liability, it does not matter what the aim of the sharing was, whether it was acted in good or bad faith, what the scope of publicity or the gravity of the infringement was.[46]

Two defendants, including Magyar Jeti Zrt. lodged a petition for review with the Curia of Hungary, arguing in essence that the judgment of Debrecen Regional Court of Appeal restricted the freedom of press in an unnecessary manner, as the defendants only reported on an event of public concern and acted with the necessary precision relating to the journalistic practice. It was maintained that the interview of Mr. Gy. contained opinions and not statements of facts, since the expression "Jobbik" referred to the behavior of the football fans and not to the political party. Dissemination cannot be established, since the defendants did nothing more than fulfil their journalistic obligation of reporting. Furthermore, as the lower-level courts established in their judgments, the reports of the defendants were balanced and in compliance with the journalistic tasks.[47]

The Curia of Hungary upheld the judgment of Debrecen Regional Court of Appeal. It agreed with the lower-level court in that the interview of Mr. Gy. contained statement of facts that linked the political party Jobbik to the incident with the football fans. The lower-level courts had to examine the veracity of this link which should have been proven by the defendants, and which the defendants could not prove.[48] Relating to dissemination, the Curia of Hungary recited its previous decisions,[49] emphasizing that dissemination could

---

42   Id.
43   Supreme Court of Hungary PK 12.
44   Budapest-Capital Regional Court of Appeal 2.Pf.20.732/2012/3.
45   Debrecen Regional Court of Appeal Pf.I.20.289/2014/7.
46   Curia of Hungary BH 2013.266.
47   Curia of Hungary Pfv.20.011/2015/3.
48   Id.
49   Curia of Hungary Pfv.II.930/2011/7., Curia of Hungary Pfv.IV.21.968/2012/6.

be realized by sharing information or making it available in a way that anyone could have access to it. Internet is only one possible platform for publishing where dissemination can be realized, meaning that information and facts are shared by computer network. The hyperlink in an article becomes an attachment and it makes the content of the attachment accessible and readable by one click. In case of dissemination the Civil Code established objective liability, regardless of whether the disseminator acted in good or bad faith. The Curia of Hungary held that requiring media outlets not to make accessible any injurious content did not restrict the freedom of press or the freedom of expression, since this requirement was not of the kind which could not be in compliance with journalistic practice.[50]

Magyar Jeti Zrt. lodged a constitutional complaint against the judgment of the Debrecen Regional Court of Appeal under Act CLI of 2011 on the Constitutional Court. The company did not argue that, under Section 78(2) of the Civil Code, even dissemination can establish the violation of the right to reputation. However, judicial practice interpreted this section in a way which resulted in that the press organ was objectively liable for the veracity of the contents cited from third parties. Thus, violation can indeed be established when a press organ reports on an event of unclarified circumstances in an unbiased and balanced way, and in compliance with the journalistic tasks. This interpretation creates an undue burden for the press organs as they could only publish information the veracity of which is beyond any doubt, making it impossible to report on controversial events.[51] Magyar Jeti Zrt. also found the judicial practice unconstitutional, as it did not examine whether the conduct of the press organs was in compliance with the ethical and professional rules of journalism, only the veracity of the disseminated information was examined.[52]

The Constitutional Court dismissed the constitutional complaint, emphasizing that distinction must be made between reports on public figures' press conferences and reports on events, which the press presents according to its own assessment. In the case of public figures' press conferences, if the report was objective and unbiased and if the statement concerned a matter of public interest, the publisher gave the source of the statement and enabled the person to whom the statement was injurious to react, thus, dissemination could not be established, as press organs neither made their own statements nor intended to influence the public opinion with their own thoughts.[53] However, in the case of the football fans, the press report was not about providing up-to-date information on statements of third parties of a public debate or at a press conference, but about summarizing the

---

50 Curia of Hungary Pfv.20.011/2015/3.
51 Decision No. 3002/2018. (I. 10.) AB, Reasoning [26].
52 Id. Reasoning [27].
53 Id. Reasoning [75].

contradictory information relating to an event of public interest. Thus, creating a hyperlink to the Youtube video established dissemination.[54]

After exhausting domestic remedies, on 23 February 2016 Magyar Jeti Zrt. lodged an application with the ECtHR arguing that the domestic courts restricted its freedom of expression under Article 10 ECHR by finding it liable for publishing a hyperlink leading to an interview containing defamatory statements.

30.5 Application to the ECtHR

Magyar Jeti Zrt. claimed that, although under Section 78(2) of the Civil Code, dissemination of injurious and false content establishes liability, no legislation or case-law can be found that would state that using hyperlinks could be considered as dissemination.[55] It emphasized that the hyperlinks did not convey but merely point to the information, and the domestic courts made their decisions without paying attention to this special aspect of hyperlinks. Establishing objective liability for using hyperlinks would result in the establishment of dissemination even if the hyperlinked website, at a later time, modified its content to defamatory falsehoods that originally were not included.[56] The rule of objective liability as the domestic courts applied it rendered the domestic courts unable to consider the purpose of the dissemination or whether Magyar Jeti Zrt. had acted in good or bad faith. Objective liability rules were incompatible with the case-law of the ECtHR and not necessary in a domestic society.[57] Magyar Jeti Zrt. also claimed that the right to reputation of the political party Jobbik should not have prevailed over the applicant company's right to expression.[58] It emphasized that a greater degree of tolerance to criticism was required from politicians.[59] The applicant company maintained that even domestic courts had found that the report of the applicant company was balanced and in compliance with the ethic and professional rules of journalism. Using a hyperlink in its article had been a technique of reporting which enabled the applicant company not to identify with the content of the Youtube video. Magyar Jeti Zrt. also noted that if the use of hyperlinks were to automatically establish objective liability for defamation, online news portals would be unable to use hyperlinks in their articles, which would restrict the cross-referential system of the Internet and, thus, would restrict the users' access to information.[60]

---

54 Id. Reasoning [77].
55 *Magyar Jeti Zrt. v. Hungary*, No. 11257/16, 4 December 2018, para. 38.
56 Id. para. 39.
57 Id. para. 41.
58 Id. para. 42.
59 Id. para. 40.
60 Id. para. 43.

The Hungarian Government maintained that, according to the applicable sections of the Civil Code, defamation could be realized by stating or disseminating an injurious falsehood relating to another person, and that the protection of the personality rights of others, such as the right to reputation, prevailed over the right to freedom of expression.[61] In its view, the applicant company did not act with due care when hyperlinked the Youtube video, as Mr. Gy. used definite terms in the interview that could not be interpreted as an opinion but only as a statement of facts, which allowed for a negative influence on the public opinion about the political party Jobbik. Thus, acting in good or bad faith was irrelevant in establishing the infringement of the political party's right to reputation.[62] It emphasized that distribution could be realized by making unlawful contents accessible in any way, which could impose objective liability on the distributor. This could enable preventing serious violations of human rights without any sanctions. The Government argued that this would mean a limitation of freedom of expression or would impose an undue burden on the publishers.[63] In the view of the Government, the judgments of the domestic courts held a fair balance between the competing rights of the applicant company and the political party Jobbik.[64]

Regarding third-party views, there must be a distinction between using a hyperlink to another website and publishing the content of a linked webpage. Hyperlinks are for navigating readers to a content that had already been published somewhere else, thus, it would be difficult to find or to access to information without hyperlinks. It was emphasized that the content of the linked website could be changed later anytime without the awareness of the user of the hyperlink, thus, establishing liability for third-party content would mean that a wide range of groups could be held liable for content over which they have no control and that would reduce the Internet users' access to information.[65] Using hyperlinks had several benefits for the public interest both on the journalists' and the readers' side. For instance, it allows to deliver content faster, which in turn facilitates the journalistic process and allows readers to check the original content of journalistic sources. It also promotes public debate as information and opinions can be reached and expressed more freely. However, it was also accepted that there could be cases when the liability of journalists could be realized regarding the use of hyperlinks, such as when they refuse to remove a hyperlink which leads to content that was found illegal by a court judgment.[66] It was added that Internet was based on the idea of linking information freely, allowing readers to navigate to and from information, thus, hyperlinks did not serve the purpose of endorsing

---

61   Id. para. 45.
62   Id. para. 46.
63   Id. para. 47.
64   Id. para. 49.
65   Id. para. 50.
66   Id. para. 51.

one publication or another. Without using hyperlinks, alternative instructions would be needed so that readers can find more information.[67] In addition, if online publishers were found liable for the linked content, that would impose an undue burden on civil societies and minorities combating racism, thus, strict liability rules would provide protection only for those who are against the minority groups.[68]

30.6 Judgment of the ECtHR

In its judgment, the ECtHR first noted that there was no dispute between the parties whether there had been an interference by the decisions of the domestic courts relating to the applicant company's freedom of expression stated by Article 10 ECHR. Since such kind of interference can be accepted only if it was prescribed by law, if it had at least one legitimate aim described by Article 10(2) ECHR and if it was necessary in a democratic society, the ECtHR had to examine these criteria in order to decide whether there had been a violation of Article 10 ECHR.[69]

Regarding lawfulness, the applicant company argued that the interference with its freedom of expression would be prescribed by law, since, in its opinion, under Hungarian law it was not foreseeable that dissemination could be realized by posting hyperlinks. However, the Government stated that under the relevant articles of the Civil Code the liability of the applicant company could be established.[70] The ECtHR emphasized that the expression 'prescribed by law' must have a legal basis in domestic law and must be accessible to whom it concerns with foreseeable effects.[71] The ECtHR also noted that concerning the admissibility and limitations of hyperlinks, neither explicit regulation nor case-law could be found in the domestic law and practice.[72]

Relating to legitimate aim, the ECtHR could accept that the interference with the freedom of expression in the present case served the protection of the rights of others as the Government submitted.[73]

In the question whether an interference with freedom of expression can be held necessary in a democratic society, the ECtHR referred to its case-law which established the following fundamental principles. Journalists who report on issues of general interest must act in good faith and on an accurate factual basis. Furthermore, they must provide reliable

---

67   Id. para. 53.
68   Id. para. 55.
69   Id. para. 56.
70   Id. para. 58.
71   Id. para. 59.
72   Id. para. 60.
73   Id. para. 62.

and precise information in compliance with journalistic ethics. Without fulfilling these requirements, Article 10 ECHR cannot be applicable in their case.[74] ECtHR also needs to examine whether the domestic authorities could hold a fair balance in cases when the values guaranteed by the ECHR such as freedom of expression and right to reputation of others are in conflict with each other and need to be protected.[75] Relating to Internet, it was highlighted that it had an important role in providing access to news for the public and in disseminating information. However, the particular nature of Internet makes the risk of violating human rights and freedoms higher compared to the press, thus, the duties and responsibilities of Internet news portals may differ from the duties and responsibilities of traditional publishers. Although in certain cases Internet news portals can held liable for user-generated content even if they do not publish third-party comments in a traditional way.[76] In its case-law, the ECtHR also dealt with the responsibility of information society service providers (ISSPs) having the function to store information, that is provided by a recipient of their services. The ECtHR found that ISSPs cannot be found liable for content of third parties excepted when they do not remove contents declared to be illegal.[77]

The ECtHR considered that in the present case, it must be examined what the duties and responsibilities of an Internet news portal are in a situation where a hyperlink, that is included in an online article, leads to content, which later was found to be defamatory. Since the domestic courts found the applicant company objectively liable for hyperlinking the defamatory content, the ECtHR had to decide whether the interference in the freedom of expression under Article 10 ECHR was based on sufficient and relevant reasons, and whether it was necessary in a democratic society.[78]

The ECtHR emphasized that the role of hyperlinks was to make information accessible by navigating Internet users from one page to another, thus, linking news and information to each other.[79] For this reason, we must distinguish hyperlinks and traditional acts of publication, since hyperlinks direct Internet users to content that can be found somewhere else on the Internet with the sole purpose to call the attention of the users to the existence of news or information on another website.[80] It was also highlighted as difference that activating a hyperlink never means to have control over the content of the website where the hyperlink leads and this content can change later anytime. Due to the particularities of hyperlinks, the ECtHR could not agree with the domestic courts, which found that if a

---

74   Id. para. 64.
75   Id. para. 65.
76   Id. para. 66.
77   Id. para. 67.
78   Id. para. 69.
79   Id. para. 73.
80   Id. para. 74.

hyperlink disseminated defamatory content it could automatically establish the liability of the person who had activated the hyperlink for the defamatory content.[81]

To decide whether the liability of Magyar Jeti Zrt. as a publisher of a hyperlink that navigated to defamatory content can be established, the ECtHR found the following questions relevant:

> "*(i)* did the journalist endorse the impugned content; *(ii)* did the journalist repeat the impugned content (without endorsing it); *(iii)* did the journalist merely put an hyperlink to the impugned content (without endorsing or repeating it); *(iv)* did the journalist know or could reasonably have known that the impugned content was defamatory or otherwise unlawful; *(v)* did the journalist act in good faith, respect the ethics of journalism and perform the due diligence expected in responsible journalism?"[82]

Concerning these questions, the ECtHR first noted that the hyperlink in question only linked the article with the Youtube video containing the interview of Mr. Gy. In the article itself there was no further comment nor repetition of any parts of the video. The article did not mention the political party Jobbik at all, only noted that a video about the interview with Mr. Gy. was available on Youtube.[83] Furthermore, the article did not state that the statements in the video were true, it did not approve the hyperlinked content and did not accept any responsibility for it. Thus, the ECtHR concluded that the article did not endorse the content of the Youtube video.[84] The ECtHR also concluded that since the article only posted the hyperlink, it did not repeat any parts of the defamatory content.[85] Relating to the question whether the applicant company knew or could have reasonably known that the hyperlink led to defamatory content, the ECtHR noted that the domestic courts – except the first instance court – did not find this relevant and did not examine it. The ECtHR also pointed out that in the case of politicians and political parties, there are wider limits of acceptable criticism compared to private individuals.[86] For this reason, the ECtHR found that the journalist in the case of Magyar Jeti Zrt. could reasonably assume that the content to which the hyperlink in the article provided access would remain in the acceptable limits of criticism relating to the political party mentioned in the interview.[87] Furthermore, the ECtHR emphasized that since the domestic courts held that hyperlinking resulted in

---

81   Id. para. 76.
82   Id. para. 77.
83   Id. para. 78.
84   Id. para. 79.
85   Id. para. 80.
86   Id. para. 81.
87   Id. para. 82.

the dissemination of information, which established objective liability, the interpretations and decisions of the domestic courts did not make any balancing possible between the right to reputation of the political party Jobbik and the right to freedom of expression of the Magyar Jeti Zrt., which were the two competing rights in the present case. In the view of the ECtHR, this kind of objective liability could have negative effects on the flow of information on the Internet, as it would make publishers and article authors refrain from using hyperlinks to content over which they could not have any control. Since all of this could have direct, moreover, chilling effects on freedom of expression on the Internet, the ECtHR held that there was a violation of Article 10 ECHR in the case of Magyar Jeti Zrt.[88]

30.7 Conclusion

Although in the case of *Magyar Jeti Zrt. v. Hungary,* the ECtHR dealt with a special provision of the Hungarian Civil Code, the judgment itself is undoubtedly helpful for journalists to decide whether or not to use hyperlinks to navigate to other content over which they have no control.

In the judgment the ECtHR pointed out that there are four crucial characteristics of hyperlinks to decide whether they establish dissemination. The ECtHR concluded that hyperlinks have *(i)* a navigational function,[89] *(ii)* they are referencing tools,[90] furthermore, *(iii)* hyperlink providers do not exercise control over the content to which a hyperlink leads[91] and last but not least, *(iv)* hyperlinks do not create new content.[92] Highlighting these specialties, the ECtHR demonstrated a clear understanding of the important role of hyperlinks on the Internet. Contrary to the Hungarian courts, the ECtHR found that dissemination of defamatory information or statements cannot be realized automatically by using hyperlinks. To investigate whether to impose liability for the use of a hyperlink, the ECtHR posted the following five relevant questions to take into account: whether the journalist endorsed the impugned content, whether he repeated it without endorsing it, whether he merely put an hyperlink to the impugned content without endorsing or repeating it, whether he knew or reasonably could have known that the impugned content was defamatory or otherwise unlawful and whether the journalist acted in good faith, respected the ethics of journalism and performed the due diligence expected in responsible journalism.[93]

---

88   Id. para. 83.
89   Id. para. 73.
90   Id. para. 74.
91   Id. para. 75.
92   Id. para. 75.
93   Id. para. 77.

Providing the aforementioned relevant aspects, the Magyar Jeti Zrt. judgment offered guidance and legal certainty regarding the potential liability for posting hyperlinks to defamatory content. After dealing with cases about blocking the access to Internet, the liability for online user-generated contents, the liability for publications on the Internet and the liability for publication of information obtained from the Internet, the Magyar Jeti Zrt. judgment can be considered as a big improvement compared to the previous judgments of the ECtHR on the freedom of expression concerning digital challenges. Becoming the best ECtHR judgment of the year 2018 under the yearly vote announced by the Strasbourg Observers Blog,[94] it also emphasizes the importance and the relevance of this decision for the digital media.

---

94   See https://strasbourgobservers.com/2019/02/25/the-best-and-worst-ecthr-judgments-of-2018-are/.

PART VI
CONFERENCE REPORTS

31 EUdentity – European Conference on Constitutional Identity

Report on the 'Constitutional EUdentity 2019' Conference Organized by the Constitutional Court of Hungary, 8 March 2019, Budapest

Attila Szabó[*]

At the invitation of the President of the Constitutional Court of Hungary, Koen Lenaerts, President of the European Court of Justice and Andreas Voßkuhle, President of the Federal Constitutional Court of Germany both visited Budapest on 8 March 2019 to speak at the conference organized by the Hungarian Constitutional Court. In addition to the attending dignitaries of international law, the constitutional courts of Austria, the Netherlands, the Czech Republic, Latvia, Luxembourg, Italy, Switzerland and Slovenia were also represented at presidential or vice-presidential levels.

The conference 'Constitutional EUdentity 2019' was attended, besides foreign guests, by the President of the Republic, the President of the Constitutional Court and the Minister of Justice of Hungary, by Hungarian public law dignitaries, constitutional jurists, public administration professionals, as well as members of academia. This professional event of major significance even at an international level had as its venue the Great Hall of the Hungarian Academy of Science.

As the focus of the conference President of the Constitutional Court Tamás Sulyok chose a topic that created the opportunity for participants, beyond discussing topical issues of the legal profession, to respond to everyday challenges faced by constitutional courts. The optimal way to meet this demand proved to be to examine the problem of European and national identities from several aspects. Already in its title, the conference implied the main points of connection between European and national identities; the way these 'types of identity' affected each other; the elements and sets national identities shared when compared to one another and the way national identities affected European identity. The conference provided an exceptional opportunity for participants to strengthen the dialogue between constitutional courts, which is essential for efficient cooperation.

The President of the Republic János Áder welcomed attendees quoting Ferenc Deák (Hungarian Minister of Justice in the 19th century, known as the 'Wiseman of the Nation'). The President said that the effort to define the constituents of European constitutional

---

[*]   Attila Szabó: chef de cabinet, Constitutional Court of Hungary.

identity was not made easier by the fact that the concepts of identity, sovereignty and loyalty were often mixed up in various lectures and studies. Quoting Tamás Sulyok, the President of the Republic recalled that under the concept of constitutional identity the Hungarian Constitutional Court understood Hungary's constitutional self-identity. János Áder added that the Federal Constitutional Court of Germany, a frequent point of reference for constitutional courts, pointed out in one of its decisions that the primacy of EU law was fundamentally restricted by the constitutional identity of the *Grundgesetz*.

The President of the Constitutional Court Tamás Sulyok emphasized in his welcome address that globalization and the new challenges Europe faced called for a redefinition of the essence of European identity. The conference aimed to contribute to the clarification of the legal content of the concepts of European and national identity. The common historical past was the strongest link among European nations, the president added. It depends solely on us whether our common European identity will be shaped by conflicts or a constructive dialogue. A bridge would have to be built between our Europeanness and our national identities, in a way that a balance is found between our 'global' and 'local' self-understanding. This was what made an intensive dialogue between judicial forums operating in the European space, based on mutual recognition, especially topical, he said.

The President of the European Court of Justice Koen Lenaerts emphasized that European identity reinforced national identity; moreover, European identity was comprised of the Member States' common values. The EU was based on the equality of the Member States, who retained their rights to shape their respective national identities. In areas not regulated by EU law Member States enjoy a wide margin of discretion to create their own legislation.

Andreas Voßkuhle, President of the Federal Constitutional Court of Germany underlined in his address that the concept of constitutionality could be different from Member State to Member State but there are some common points and values (human dignity, liberty, acquired rights) that formed a strong constitutional basis. In the EU the precise content of European identity has not yet been defined and it is our common responsibility to make up for this, he said. The President of the German Constitutional Court emphasized the importance of dialogue between the Member States and the EU noting that maintaining the balance between national constitutional identity and European values was of key significance.

The Minister of Justice of Hungary László Trócsányi said in the EU, too, there was need for mutual respect and communication as well as for the equal partnership between the parties. All these are indispensable for maintaining and developing integration and for creating an ever-stronger EU in the global area.

The above was followed by contributions from the representatives of national judicial and constitutional forums. Presentations were delivered (in order of speaking) by Peter M. Huber, Justice of the Federal Constitutional Court of Germany, János Martonyi Former Minister of Foreign Affairs, Brigitte Bierlein, President of the Austrian Constitutional

Court, István Stumpf, Justice of the Hungarian Constitutional Court, Maarten Feteris, President of the Supreme Court of the Netherlands, Tamás Sulyok, President of the Hungarian Constitutional Court, Pavel Rychetsky, President of the Constitutional Court of the Czech Republic, András Varga Zs., Justice of the Hungarian Constitutional Court, Marta Cartabia, Vice President of the Italian Constitutional Court, Ineta Ziemele, President of the Latvian Constitutional Court, Rajko Knez, President of the Constitutional Court of Slovenia and Martha Niquille, Vice President of the Federal Supreme Court of Switzerland.

The two panel discussions were chaired by Christoph Grabenwarter, Vice President of the Austrian Constitutional Court and Francis Delaporte, Vice President of the Constitutional Court of Luxembourg.

These outstanding professional contributions can be summarized as follows. The EU's value catalogue's success is primarily owed to democratic constitutionality. These common values are, at the same time, not abstract but actually practical values, of which some outstanding ones comprise the core values binding each Member State. National constitutional courts are the forums that determine the value content of these values. A collision between national and EU values is possible, in which case, however, there are no simple solutions for solving the situation. Therefore, where possible, the emergence of such collisions should be avoided. This is why regular dialogue between constitutional courts is so urgently needed, especially on contentious issues where the future of the EU's value community (fairness, honesty, diversity, subsidiarity) can be ensured. Some questions, too, were formulated with reference to the value community and the cooperation of constitutional courts: there is no agreement between Member States as to where the boundaries of common core values exactly are. The question what institutional preconditions are required from the side of constitutional courts in the Member States to enable the efficient functioning of the Association of European Constitutional Courts is also in need of further elaboration. The systematic, efficient and purposeful sharing of Member State information should not be underestimated. A further question is whether the components of the core of constitutionality can precisely be identified and if so, what these are. What are the components, by contrast, that make up national identity? The question also arises who or what bodies are entitled to identify its constitutive elements. The Member States alone or the Member States' constitutional courts, or would it be useful in this respect, too, to strive for and identify the contents of national identity in the course of a dialogue? It is characteristic of the EU that it is a region regulated by national legal systems, EU law and international treaties, where constitutional courts are in the space between national and EU legislations. It is here that they perform their activities based on their exclusive competence to interpret national legislation. It is in this respect that it emerged as an important argument that the EU was required to consider national characteristics, *i.e.* national identity. It also arose as a possibility that national constitutional courts should try to define a common language to facilitate communication.

As the summary and conclusion of the conference it was pointed out that dialogue between Member States' constitutional courts – for which this conference was an example – created the opportunity to reduce the number of difficult-to-formulate and express, very delicate and open questions. Meaningful dialogue makes it possible to reach an agreement between Member States on certain issues, while in questions where a uniform stance is not feasible, the common goal may be to try and bring positions closer and find a common denominator as a compromise solution.

32   Conference on the Evaluation of Legislation

Report on the 'Evaluation of Legislation' Conference Organized by Pázmány Péter Catholic University, 3 May 2019, Budapest

*Noémi Suri**

The Pázmány Péter Catholic University (PPCU) hosted a conference with the title 'Evaluation of legislation' on 3 May 2019. The roundtable discussion organized by Petra Lea Láncos (associate professor at PPCU) and the Ereky Public Law Research Center of PPCU as co-organizer focused on the issue surrounding the broad topic of evaluating legislation. The presenters of the workshop shared their experiences, ideas and research results on questions of national and EU law-making practices from Belgium, Hungary, Portugal and the United Kingdom to promote quality in legislation. The conference provided space for assessing the direction of the development of European legislation with special regard to scrutinizing the relevant role of the European Commission.

Following the opening thoughts of Petra Lea Láncos, András Zs. Varga (justice of the Constitutional Court, professor of law at PPCU) held the first keynote presentation of the conference's plenary session with the title 'Constitution as a limitation of legislation'. Participants were given a brief overview of the codifications of procedural law in Hungary in recent years, the goals defining criminal and civil law-making, the methodological tools employed in support of these goals, and an evaluation of all the above. The report focused on three key issues: the role of the constitution in the hierarchy of norms (in the Kelsenian sense), the interpretation of the relationship of EU legal supremacy and the constitutions of Member States, as well as the methodological issues of the current form of legislation.

In her presentation entitled 'Legislative elements of post-legislative scrutiny', Helen Xanthaki (professor of law at University College London) focused on the measurability of the quality of legislations. In her starting argument she highlighted the institution of law as a tool for good legislation, and thus proceeded towards the specific criteria of quality legislation. In her view, good legislation means effective legislation; the type, extent and level of which is defined by the government. Xanthaki showed that measuring the quality of legislation requires a principled method capable of re-assessing the link between policy, legislative text, and regulatory results.

---

*   Noémi Suri: assistant professor, Pázmány Péter Catholic University, Budapest.

The next presenter, Joao Silveira (associate professor at Universidade de Lisboa) delivered his speech on 'Cutting edge tools for legislative assessment'. The analytical assessment of the communication from the European Commission[1] on the Regulatory Fitness of EU legislation was the central theme of his presentation. Silveira demonstrated the advantages of the so-called REFIT program (Regulatory Fitness Platform) of the Commission through practical examples, but besides highlighting the toolbox of intelligent legislation, he also talked about the assessment of the inter-institutional agreement about the improvement of the quality of legislation between the European Parliament, the Council of the European Union and the European Commission. In his concluding thoughts, he pointed out that the scope, procedures and methods of impact assessment are still not standardized. Innovative, 'top-notch' tools, specific trends and approaches may further improve the quality of assessment. Nonetheless we still have to face challenges in terms of the use of IT innovations, and the integration tools used to scrutinize policies.

Following a coffee break Patricia Popelier (professor of law at Universiteit Antwerpen) continued the morning session of the conference with her talk on the 'Evaluation of legislation and judicial review'. Popelier was looking for the answer to the question of what role the courts play in the *ex ante* and *ex post* evaluation of legislation. After considering legitimacy and efficiency concerns, and dogmatically clarifying the so-called institutional isomorphism, the participants of the roundtable discussion lined up their arguments for why it is not advisable to ignore the role of courts in the evaluation of legislation by reviewing the issue from both the legislators' and the government's perspective.

Participants of the conference learned about measures taken by the EU in the last fifteen years to improve the quality of legislation from William Robinson (researcher at the Institute of Advanced Legal Studies). In his presentation entitled 'The European Commission's tools for better law-making, in particular consultation, impact assessment and evaluation', Robinson drew attention primarily to the fact that in the course of applying measures to improve legislative quality, it is vital not to ignore the basic principles of EU law such as the requirement of the rule of law, the principle of subsidiarity, the importance of dialogue and consultations and the preparation of reports on the financial position of the EU.

The morning session of the conference was concluded by Rui Lanceiro's (associate professor at Universidade de Lisboa) presentation on 'Administrative simplification assessment in legislative evaluation'. The presenter approached the applicability of administrative tools used to evaluate the quality of legislation from the point of view of costs. Lanceiro defined two categories of costs: so-called substantive, *i.e.* actual costs, and administrative costs. From the given cost factors the costs of impact assessment and the costs of communication between citizens and the government were compared. Based on

---

1   EU Smart Regulation Agenda, COM(2010) 543 and COM(2012) 746.

the analysis of OECD and EU reports in the field, he drew the conclusion that the applicability of certain tools depends a great deal on the economic performance of the given country, which is further complicated by globalization.

Presenters of the afternoon session of the 'Evaluation of Legislation conference' took stock of the application and experiences of the use of different tools to assess the quality of Hungarian legislation through unique case studies. The talk delivered by Lóránt Csink (counselor at the Constitutional Court, associate professor at PPCU) and entitled 'Evaluation of legislation in Hungary: approach, system and methods' set the tone for the debate by focusing on the importance of decision-making processes. Csink emphasized three necessary requirements for law-making: goal setting (defining long-term goals upon value choice), strategy/methodology (defining the tool to achieve long-term goals) and execution (the importance of administration). In his view, during the evaluation of legislation the following questions must be answered: *(i)* What is the impact of the legislation? *(ii)* What side-effects occur as its result (legal, political, social)? *(iii)* Is it applicable to the society from the point of view of comparative law? *(iv)* Where and how is it applicable?

Balázs Gerencsér (director of Ereky Public Law Research Center, associate professor at PPCU) held a presentation summarizing the major research projects conducted during the last 8 years in the Ereky Public Law Research Center, founded at the Department of Administrative Law of PPCU in 2011 and reorganized as a research center in 2014. His talk on 'Pilot projects and evaluation' primarily focused on the results of the research project carried out between 2011 and 2013 with regard to model experiments conducted to develop public administration. As a result of this research project the team examining model experiments defined the possibilities, methodology and standards of public administration modelling by analyzing pilot technologies of foreign states and international organizations based on a unified set of criteria.[2]

The closing presentation of the conference was delivered by Krisztina Rozsnyai (ministerial commissioner, Ministry of Justice, associate professor at ELTE Law School) with the title 'Preliminary evaluation of the new Hungarian Law on Administrative Procedure'. Rozsnyai reported on the results of the codification processes in administrative procedures in progress since 2010. In her speech, she elaborated on the goals of renewing administrative procedures, the tools to reach these goals, the procedure of law-making and the work methods used during the codification. After a review of the background for establishing administrative procedures, participants were given detailed information about the role of administrative court proceedings in the Hungarian legislation with regard to administrative procedures, and the tools ensuring effective, fast and professional adjudication (the

---

2   *See* further at https://jak.ppke.hu/kozigazgatasi-jogi-tanszek/en/research/research-on-pilot-projects-2011-2013.

importance of autonomous decision-making mechanisms) in lawsuits in public administrative matters.

In conclusion, we can clearly state, that all three branches of power have significant responsibilities when it comes to assessing legislation and, ensuring the necessary quality thereof. The legislative power is responsible for adopting legislation conforming to the hierarchy of norms as well as the legal environment and suitable for triggering the appropriate political and social impact. The judicial branch exerts an impact on improving the quality of legislation through the application and interpretation of law. The government is tasked with defining the goals, levels and scope of legislation as well as facilitating the execution thereof. All the presenters agreed, that if we wish to define the requirements of high-quality legislation, it is largely dependent on the economic performance of the given country, in which the principle of efficiency, the applicability of administrative tools, and the practicability of IT innovations play a key role.

33 FROM INTERNATIONAL LAW IN BOOKS TO INTERNATIONAL LAW IN ACTION

ELTE Law School's Jessup and Telders Victories in 2019

Gábor Kajtár – Katalin Sulyok[*]

> "We are not unmindful of, nor are we insensible to, the various considerations of a non-juridical character, social, humanitarian and other, which underlie this case; but these are matters for the political rather than for the legal arena. They cannot be allowed to deflect us from our duty of reaching a conclusion strictly on the basis of what we believe to be the correct legal view."[1]

33.1 INTRODUCTION

As the ICJ put it in 1966 in the *South West Africa* cases "Law exists, it is said, to serve a social need".[2] This short paper aims to give an overview of the many levels on which the above statement of the ICJ holds true.

Hungary had an outstanding year in 2019 in terms of international law moot court competitions. ELTE University Faculty of Law, the oldest and 1st ranked law school in Hungary, has won the two biggest international law moot courts in the same year. With these historic wins, Hungary is the 4th European country in the 60-year history of the Philip C. Jessup International Law Moot Competition that won the International Championship Round held in Washington D.C. Also, ELTE University is the first in the world to

---

[*] Gábor Kajtár: associate professor, ELTE Law School, Budapest, and coach of ELTE Jessup Team since 2010 as well as coach of ELTE Telders Team since 2016. Katalin Sulyok: senior lecturer, ELTE Law School, Budapest, and co-coach of ELTE Jessup Team in 2015, 2017 and 2019; co-coach of ELTE Telders Team in 2019. The authors are deeply indebted to Prof. Pál Sonnevend, Head of Department of International Law and Dean of ELTE Law School for his dedication to the Philip C. Jessup International Law Moot Competition as a former agent, coach and Vice Dean for international relations. Special thanks go to Dr. Réka Somssich, Vice Dean of ELTE Law School. ELTE Law School could not have achieved this outstanding success without its fantastic students and especially our exceptional Jessup Alumni community.
1 Joint dissenting opinion of Sir Percy Spender and Sir Gerald Fitzmaurice, *South West Africa cases*, 1962 ICJ Reports, p. 466.
2 *South West Africa cases (Ethiopia v. South Africa, Liberia v. South Africa)*, Second phase 18 July 1966, 1966 ICJ Rejorts 6, para. 49.

win the Telders International Law Moot Court Competition in the same year as winning the Jessup competition.

This piece provides a detailed narrative of the above successes of ELTE Law School. To shed light on the wider context of these achievements, it will demonstrate the ways in which international law moot courts are beneficial not only to the mooting students, but also to those having an academic interest in public international law. What is more, the philosophy and overall message of international law moot courts may become ever more important in times when the global world order and international multilateralism experiences efforts challenging the international rule of law.

33.2   Hungarian Moot Court Successes in 2019

ELTE Law School has a long history of participating in the world's biggest and most prestigious moot court competitions. The last couple of years have already seen some outstanding results on the international plane. Yet the achievement of the year 2019 will mark most probably the year, when Hungary has irrevocably been put on the map of international law moot court competitions.

33.2.1   Winning the Jessup World Cup

The Philip C. Jessup International Moot Court Competition was founded by Harvard Law School in 1960 and ever since, it has become the biggest and most prestigious international moot court in the world, where approximately 700 universities participate from more than 100 countries every year.[3] At present it is administered by the International Law Students Association (ILSA).[4] After the national rounds organized in each country, the best teams qualify to attend the International Final Round held in Washington D.C. The one week-long Finals usually take place in the beginning of April at the Hyatt Regency Hotel. The Final Round is typically attended by roughly 750 students who had all been working on the same Jessup Problem since September, which features an elaborate legal conflict between two fictitious States that decide to bring their dispute before the ICJ.[5] During the competition, agents of the teams represent the applicant and the respondent before a panel of three judges. First, they have to prepare a typically 60-pages long written memorial on behalf of both the respondent and the applicant State. These arguments are then be presented in

---

3   See Jessup history at www.ilsa.org/jessup-history/.
4   About ILSA see www.ilsa.org/what-we-do/.
5   For this year's Jessup case see www.ilsa.org/Jessup/Jessup19/2019%20JESSUP%20FINAL%20COMPRO-MIS%20with%20CandC.pdf. Problem Authors: Michael Peil, Hannah Zhao and Douglas Pivnichny.

the national rounds as well as in the International Final Round in a 45-minute long oral pleading on each side.

ELTE Law School has been participating in the competition for 30 years. In the last 10 years ELTE Jessup Team was coached by Gábor Kajtár, associate professor of international law. During these years ELTE Law School has always qualified for the International Final Round and in the last couple of years, its team, representing Hungary, achieved outstanding results in Washington D.C. In 2014, Dávid Surjányi was the Third Best Oralist and in 2015, Dániel Pap was named Second Best Oralist out of 700 students. In 2018, ELTE Jessup Team (Gergő Balázs, Barbara Bazánth, Zolta Buda, Olívia Németh and Dzsenifer Orosz) won the award for the best combined memorials not only at the International Rounds in Washington D.C. (Alone E. Evans Award First Place), but also out of the more than 700 competing universities from all around the world (Hardy C. Dillard Award First Place).[6] Notably, Dániel Pap and Barbara Bazánth were chosen as best non-native oralists in 2015 and 2018 respectively, both receiving the International Law Institute's scholarship to attend a summer school at Georgetown University.[7]

Hungarian law schools provide a five-year training program, during which Public International Law is a 2 semester long compulsory course. This year's Jessup team was composed as follows. Team members: Zolta Buda (in the 5th year of his law studies), Gábor Bazsó (in the 3rd year of his law studies), Marcell Koncsik (in his 2nd year of law studies) and Vanessa Szép (in the 5th year of her law studies). Their coach was Gábor Kajtár and co-coaches were Katalin Sulyok and Dániel Pap.

In the Preliminary Rounds that take place in the first three days of the International Final Rounds, the Hungarian team met with teams representing China, Romania, Ireland and Panama. By being ranked in the top 32 teams from among the participating 143, the ELTE Jessup Team qualified to the Advanced Rounds. Here, it won against a team representing Russia, and then proceeded to the Octofinals, where it competed with the team of Ukraine. In the quarterfinals it met with the team of the Philippines, a former world champion. In the semifinals its counterpart was the team of Singapore Management University, also a multiple former world champion. In the final Championship Round, ELTE Law School competed as respondent against Columbia Law School as applicant, a team which is a four times World Champion, and hence one of the most successful teams in the history of Jessup. The bench of the Championship Round comprised Hugh Adsett (Global Affairs Canada), S. James Anaya (former UN Special Rapporteur, dean of University of Colorado Law School), and Andrew B. Loewenstein (partner at Foley Hoag LLP).[8]

---

6   See www.ilsa.org/Jessup-history/Jessup-2018/.
7   See www.ilsa.org/Jessup-history/Jessup-2015/.
8   See www.ilsa.org/Jessup-history/Jessup-2019/.

Besides winning the Championship round based on the unanimous decision of the bench, Gábor Bazsó received the Stephen M. Schwebel Award as best oralist at the Championship Round. Also, ELTE won the third-place award for the best written memorial for the Applicant, and the combined memorial scores also placed them in the Top 10 among participants of the International Final Round.

33.2.2   Winning the Telders Cup

The Telders International Law Moot Court is a European-wide competition that is organized in The Hague since 1977. Its final round is traditionally held in the Peace Palace and is presided by judges of the ICJ. Agents, *i.e.* team members are expected to prepare written and oral pleadings mimicking the proceedings of the ICJ. The memoranda are usually approximately 40-pages long and the oral presentation is about 30 minutes per side.[9]

ELTE University has participated in Telders several times and achieved its biggest success this year by winning the final round. Team members were second year law students: Dóra Balogh, Dávid Máté, Balázs Schultz and Franciska Tóth. Their coaches were Gábor Kajtár and Katalin Sulyok.

The finalists were Leiden University (applicant) and ELTE Law School (respondent). The final round judges were Judge Giorgio Gaja (ICJ) presiding, Judge David Re (Trial chamber President, Special Tribunal for Lebanon) and Maria Teresa Infante Caffi (Ambassador of Chile to the Netherlands). One of the Hungarian agents, Franciska Tóth also received the Best Oralist Award.[10]

33.3   BENEFITS OF INTERNATIONAL LAW MOOT COURTS

Mooting experience has obvious benefits for the participating students themselves, but other benefits of taking part in such competitions may not be that self-evident. In the following we comment on these often overlooked or under-appreciated aspects of participating in international law moot courts.

33.3.1   Educational Benefits

Moot courts represent an enormous added value to legal education especially in countries with civil law systems, where education is more focused on the theoretical and doctrinal

---

9   For this year's Telders case *see* http://teldersmoot.com/2017/10/06/telders-case-2019/.
10   *See* http://teldersmoot.com/2017/05/22/telders-results-2019/.

aspects of positive law rather than the pragmatic aspects of crafting persuasive legal arguments. In such education systems, moot courts represent a hands-on approach to studying
law, where students can gain some practical insights into the art and craft of preparing
effective written and oral pleadings based on an elaborate and complex set of facts.[11] The
mooting experience therefore mimics real life lawyering work of representing clients.

Preparing effective and persuasive arguments requires practical training in legal research,
legal writing and legal rhetoric. And even more importantly, moot court problems give
an excellent opportunity to face, for the first time, some of the most typical dilemmas in
legal argumentation: how one may identify legally relevant facts, how to peruse over
uncomfortable gaps in the agreed facts, how to build a persuasive litigation strategy where
none of the claims are in contradiction, but follow a tight logical order, or how to select
those arguments of the opponent that can be conceded should the judges insist upon it.
These are skills that cannot be taught in theory, only on a learning-by-doing basis.[12]

Students involved in moot courts can hone such skills during the year-around preparation, which will be a highly valuable asset on the job market. Our Jessup alumni typically
work in the private sector at international law firms in Hungary or abroad. Some of them
continued to nurture their close relationship with public international law even after the
moot court and specialized in investor-state arbitration. Increasingly, our students have
started to secure internships and employment with international judicial fora. Others have
used their Jessup experience to work in other branches of law, yet even in those fields they
benefitted greatly from the practice-oriented, sharp legal thinking they developed during
their mooting year.

33.3.2   Academic Benefits

As it may be clear by now, there are obvious educational benefits of international law moot
courts for participating students. But what is in it for junior and mid-career academics?
What can be learnt by those international lawyers who are coaching Jessup teams? Working
with the most talented and creative students has been always a privilege for us. The Latin
maxim *docendo discimus* aptly describes the co-benefits that coaches gain by teaching
those most interested in the deeper complexities of international law: 'by teaching, we
learn'.[13] Questions asked by these students may provoke new ideas for academic research
as well.

---

11   For some of the most important guidelines on preparing memorials and preparing for the oral rounds *see*
      www.ilsa.org/ilsa-other-stuff/ilsa-publications/ilsa-guide-to-international-law-moot-court-competitions/.
12   For the given year's best memorandums *see* www.ilsa.org/ilsa-other-stuff/ilsa-publications/jessup-com-
      pendium/.
13   *'Homines dum docent discunt'*, Seneca, Letters to Lucilius, Book I, letter 7, section 8.

Furthermore, moot courts can provide an important avenue for recruiting excellent prospective PhD candidates and hence they are of significant value from the perspective of the entire faculty. Lastly, but perhaps most importantly, international law moot court cases are typically written in a way as to target some of the most developing fields of international law, highlighting thereby some current problems of international law worth researching more in depth. The Jessup case does not yield to one single 'correct' solution, since international law does not provide yes-or-no type (*i.e.* lawful-unlawful) answers to legal dilemmas in these areas. International law concerning these questions (and arguably, many more) can be more adequately described as lying in a grey zone, where the legal status quo is increasingly challenged by emerging new norms. For those who have already taken part in moot courts comes as no surprise that the goal of a moot court pleading is to compile the most persuasive legal, factual, and policy arguments on both sides.

Strong arguments can be made with respect to both the applicant and the respondent side – ideally the case is balanced in a way that one of the sides will have stronger arguments in positive law, while the other may have advantage on moral grounds or policy. In fact, the Jessup problem is usually written in a way as to articulate a clash between international law as it stands today and emerging waves of legal development challenging old paradigms. Typically, one side will argue for a conservative approach based on positive law while the opponent side will have to argue based on emerging customary law and soft law instruments, representing a more progressive approach to the international law issue at hand. Researching these problems therefore brings students and coaches to the heart of the dynamically evolving questions of international law, which are marked by uncertainty inherent to law, and to international law more specifically.[14] These legal issues always provide fertile ground for further doctrinal research.

This year, for instance, the Jessup problem, the case concerning the Kayleff Yak,[15] featured several such fast developing problems. For one, the case brought up issues of the protection of biodiversity and traditional knowledge of indigenous communities concerning the use of genetic resources. To what extent are international conventions on biodiversity protection directly enforceable before an international court? How can questions of scientific proof and complex causal scenarios be adequately argued by a party to prove that a sudden decline in the Yak population was in fact caused by the respondent State's hunting, and not by natural factors, such as climate change, or the applicant's own taking that has been ongoing for millennia for cultural and religious purposes? What hard and justiciable obligations can be discerned from the Nagoya Protocol for a territorial State to share the benefits with an indigenous community of a pharmaceutical product that has been arguably developed based on the community's traditional knowledge, but was produced from an

---

14   *See* Jörg Kammerhofer, *Uncertainty in International Law: A Kelsenian Perspective*, Routledge, 2012.

15   *See* www.ilsa.org/Jessup/Jessup19/2019%20JESSUP%20FINAL%20COMPROMIS%20with%20CandC.pdf.

enzyme that was first derived by a state-funded researcher? How can the 'inventive step' be defined in practice, which would render a pharmaceutical product a patentable intellectual property, distinct from traditional knowledge entailing benefit-sharing obligations?

The most topical question regarding the extent and enforceability of human rights obligations of corporations as well as the extraterritorial application of human rights guarantees also permeated the case. This aspect entailed questions of attribution, where different international adjudicatory bodies adopt divergent standards to define the level of state control over a company giving rise to the imputability of the corporation's conduct to the State. The possibility of enforcing human rights guarantees are increasingly discussed in international case-law and scholarship. The 'orthodox' view fosters extraterritoriality strictly based on exercising effective control over the territory in question, while a more progressive approach increasingly emerges in judicial decisions and soft law documents favoring more extensive possibilities to create extraterritorial application and enforceability of human rights guarantees.

All of these issues raise yet unanswered questions in international legal doctrine and therefore inspire new frontiers of academic research.

33.3.3   Benefits for Participating Universities

ELTE Law School's outstanding performance in the Jessup and Telders competitions has significantly contributed both to the further success of our students in their career and to the various international LL.M. programs of ELTE Law School.

ELTE Jessup and Telders alumni have been admitted to best LL.M. and Ph.D. programs around the word. Our alumni earned LL.M. degrees *e.g.* from Cambridge, Oxford, Harvard, Sorbonne and Heidelberg. ELTE Law School runs three international LL.M. programs: the European and International Business Law LL.M. program, the European Human Rights LL.M. program and the International and European Taxation LL.M. program. The visibility of these programs is also enhanced by the university's successes on the world's mooting stage.

The European and International Business Law LL.M. program is designed to prepare an international group of legal practitioners for the global challenges of the 21st century. At a time when globalization and European integration are on the agenda, an intercultural approach to law and its application, in other words, comparative legal studies are indispensable for a sound analysis of legal issues and the settlement of legal disputes. The course concept links theory to real world business. The high-level curriculum offers solid grounding in the institutional fundamentals of the European economic integration and an introduction to international business law.[16]

The European Human Rights LL.M. program started in September 2016 and focuses on complex and creative problem solving in the field of human rights law and wishes to enable students to take new approaches in human rights litigation on various European fora. Globalization has prompted interest in a deeper understanding of the relationship between human rights and traditional areas of law. Important efforts have already been made by various international organizations to disentangle the links between ethics, human rights, development and economics. Human rights advocates can provide a rights-based approach not only to strive for higher level protection, but also to bring about better economic and developmental results, thereby instrumentalizing human rights values and concepts.[17]

The International and European Taxation LL.M. program is designed to give students the knowledge necessary to understand the ongoing tax issues of the world we live in. The program ensures a well-balanced education in terms of theory and practice. An advantage of the program is that it is run in association with market leader tax advisor companies. Top managers and partners of Hungarian Big4 provide the students with practical knowledge.[18]

33.3.4   Benefits for the International Community (of Lawyers)

The Jessup also provides benefits for a wider community of international lawyers, by creating a worldwide network of future international law practitioners. The competition also fosters mutual understanding and respect for students coming from other countries. The philosophy of the competition avowedly and openly nurtures a belief and associated world view where real life disputes between states can be mediated if not resolved through adjudication and legal means. As it has been repeatedly emphasized by speakers at opening ceremonies, the Jessup is organized in the hope that it will help educate a future generations of lawyers, who are committed to the cornerstones of international law, such as the equality of states, international rule of law, respect for human rights, and the peaceful resolution of inter-state disputes.

'Ubi societas ibi ius' – 'wherever there is society, there is law'. Evidencing this fact, the Charter of the UN and the Statute of the ICJ signaled the beginning of a new world order based on the peaceful settlement of disputes rather than wars, and ultimately 'Faustrecht'. As Judge Jessup has famously put it in 1948 "the ultimate function of law, which is the

---

16   For more information see www.elte.hu/en/european-and-international-business-law-llm.
17   For more information see www.elte.hu/en/european-human-rights-llm.
18   For more information see www.elte.hu/en/international-and-european-taxation-program-for-lawyers-llm.

elimination of force for the solution of human conflicts."[19] Judge Jessup steadfastly believed that "law is indeed a human necessity"[20] and, that conflicts should be solved peacefully based on the rule of law. '*Ubi ius ibi remedium est*' – 'wherever there is a law, there is a remedy'.

Admittedly, "international law is not rules. It is a normative system" as the former president of the ICJ, Rosalyn C. Higgins has famously put it.[21] These rules are not just an accumulation of past decisions, as judges must constantly decide between competing legal arguments when making decisions.[22] Along the same lines, the essence of the judicial task was summarized by Hersch Lauterpacht as a choice "not between claims which are fully justified and claims which have no foundation at all but between claims which have varying degrees of legal merit."[23] Thus, law in action and especially in adjudication is not a black-white logical formalism but "judicial discretion as governed by law".[24]

Hersch Lauterpacht's words are worth reproducing in full here:

> "The salient factor in most situations is that the legal merits of a case are seldom so obvious as to permit the elimination of the necessity to balance the conflicting or competing legal considerations – all of which are relevant to the case and all of which, though in different degrees, are worthy of consideration. [...] It is, as a rule, a question of giving effect to a better right against a right of less compelling legal merit."[25]

International moot courts like Jessup and Telders are great opportunities to demonstrate the processes of international law. The cases are usually written in a way where clear-cut legal answers are impossible to give. Also, competing legal considerations between applicant and respondent reveal two other challenges: how to accommodate policy and humanitarian considerations into the law, into a legal argument. Striking a good balance between the two extremes of international law in splendid isolation detached from the realities of international relations and being hollowed out by purely policy arguments and *Realpolitik*, a good Jessup or Telders agent has to keep in mind the words of the ICJ:

---

19   Philip C. Jessup, *A Modern Law of Nations*, The Macmillan Co., 1948, p. 2.
20   Id. p. 3.
21   Rosalyn Higgins, *Problems and Process. International Law and How We Use It*, Oxford University Press, 1995, p. 1.
22   "Subject to that overriding primacy of the existing law, they bring to mind the fact that the necessity of choice between conflicting legal claims is of the very essence of the judicial function, whether within the State or in the international sphere." Hersch Lauterpacht, *The Development of International Law by the International Court*, Cambridge University Press, Cambridge, 1982, p. 399.
23   Hersch Lauterpacht, *The Development of International Law by the International Court*, Cambridge University Press, Cambridge, 1996 (reprinted), p. 398.
24   Id. p. 399.
25   Id. pp. 396-397.

"The Court must now turn to certain questions of a wider character. Throughout this case it has been suggested, directly or indirectly, that humanitarian considerations are sufficient in themselves to generate legal rights and obligations, and that the Court can and should proceed accordingly. The Court does not think so. It is a court of law, and can take account of moral principles only in so far as these are given a sufficient expression in legal form. Law exists, it is said, to serve a social need; but precisely for that reason it can do so only through and within the limits of its own discipline. Otherwise, it is not a legal service that would be rendered. Humanitarian considerations may constitute the inspirational basis for rules of law. [...] But the existence of an 'interest' does not of itself entail that this interest is specifically juridical in character. [...] An interest, no doubt; but in order that this interest may take on a specifically legal character, the sacred trust itself must be or become something more than a moral or humanitarian ideal. In order to generate legal rights and obligations, it must be given juridical expression and be clothed in legal form."[26]

A good Jessup or Telders problem thus teaches students and reminds their professors of the essential relationship between law and policy and between law and ethics that cannot be avoided.[27] Indeed we must deal openly with these factors both in teaching and in the practice of international law. Overall, international law moot court experience allows law students to face the complexities and even the weaknesses of the normative system of international law, making them better equipped for legal advocacy and lawyering in every branch of law.

---

26 *South West Africa cases (Ethiopia v. South Africa, Liberia v. South Africa)*, Second phase 18 July 1966, 1966 ICJ Reports 6, paras. 49-51.
27 Higgins 1995, p. 5.

PART VII
REVIEW OF HUNGARIAN SCHOLARLY LITERATURE

34 Vanda Lamm (ed.): Emberi Jogi Enciklopédia (Book Review)

Zénó Suller[*]

Vanda Lamm (ed.), Emberi Jogi Enciklopédia [Encyclopedia of Human Rights], HVG-ORAC, Budapest, 2018, 748 p, ISBN 978-9632583457

The unique Encyclopedia of Human Rights is the remarkable outcome of a project coordinated by Professor Vanda Lamm, full member of the Hungarian Academy of Sciences and President of the International Law Association Hungarian Branch. The Encyclopedia contains more than 100 studies written by 67 leading Hungarian scholars, all of them experts their respective topics presented in the Encyclopedia. The studies encompass not only the first, second and third generation human rights but also evolution of human rights as such, its historical antecedents, the organizational and institutional framework of the protection of rights, certain treaties and documents of outstanding relevance, as well as legal concepts related to the subject of human rights. Finally, the encyclopedia includes some non-traditional rights and contested fundamental rights as well.

There are some reference works on the international book market, like the epic Encyclopedia of Human Rights.[1] This vast work presents human rights in five separate books. The Hungarian Emberi Jogi Enciklopédia is more modest in length, however, it already plays a significant role in the Hungarian legal literature, since this is the very first comprehensive lexicon-like summary of human rights containing almost all aspects of the field. The title may be somewhat misleading. In most cases the word encyclopedia refers to a codex containing definitions and pure facts on broad general topics or a specific area. This book, however, contains scholarly studies on the different issues and institutions of human rights. Yet the structure follows the classical encyclopedia style: the chapters are organized in alphabetical order instead of categorizing them under chapters of the same or similar content.

The preface, written by the editor Vanda Lamm, explains the need for and the volume of the work. She explains that national and international laws and rules concerning human rights expanded to such a scale that it is not easy to navigate them. She emphasizes that since human rights were created following World War II, several domestic and international

---

[*]   Zénó Suller: PhD student, Pázmány Péter Catholic University, Budapest.
[1]   David P. Forsythe (ed.), *Encyclopedia of Human Rights*, Oxford University Press, 2009.

protection and monitoring mechanisms and bodies have been set up. It is a huge achievement, says the editor, that human rights issues no longer fall under the exclusive competence of the states.

The chapters cover several fields of law, but strong emphasis is put on international and European law. Although this is almost inevitable due to the international character of human rights and the unique role of human rights within Europe, it may have been adequate to view human rights from a domestic law standpoint since the book is only available in Hungarian. As such, it is primarily a useful tool for Hungarian lawyers and comparative lawyers. Nevertheless, it is an important merit of the book that some of the chapters concern new branches of law and new challenges of human rights which are have not yet received much scholarly attention, or at least not in Hungarian legal literature. Due to the length of the encyclopedia it is not possible to provide even a rough analysis or all the chapters. Therefore, this review will only highlight those chapters that are unique or special in some way.

The most surprising chapter in a human rights encyclopedia is definitely the 'Issue of animal rights'[2] written by Balázs Majtényi. At a first glance, animal rights surely fall outside the scope of such a book since the special focus of human rights is *sine dubio* on rights of the person, *i.e.* members of the human race. However, if we consider the topic from a more progressive, development theory perspective, animal rights also fit into this picture. The tendency is that fundamental rights and legal protection cover more and more groups of individuals. First, fundamental rights only entitled white male nationals, eventually and gradually extended to women and all races of the one and undivided human species. And now as environmental consciousness is starting to gain ground, we are becoming more and more aware that we are not the only valuable habitants of our globe and that the other habitants also deserve legal protection for their very existence. This chapter, however, also presents other theories which deny that animals can have legal capacity, denying herewith also the need for animal rights. This way of thinking is often referred to by animal rights activists as speciesism, resulting in discrimination against animals simply because they are a different species. The conclusion, however, is that this approach is no longer sustainable, a view that is supported by a range of international agreements and norms as well as national laws.

András László Pap's chapter on 'Ethnic profiling'[3] deals with a more traditional field of human rights. Minority protection and the prohibition of discrimination based on nationality or ethnicity have been considered the core of human rights since World War II and it is enforced to an increasing degree in practice nowadays. This paper therefore is not outstanding for raising a new issue, but rather because of the relevance of one dimension

---

2   Vanda Lamm (ed.), *Emberi Jogi Enciklopédia*, HVG-ORAC, 2018, pp. 52-56.
3   Id. pp. 232-235.

of ethnic discrimination. Ethnic profiling is a real danger, not only against Afro-Americans in the US, but in Hungary against Roma groups and increasingly against Arab communities within Europe owing to recent terror threats. Ethnic profiling emerges in the context of law enforcement, namely police and investigative work. It describes a procedural treatment in the framework of which criminal profiling is based on ethnicity. It means that possible perpetrators or future criminals are inspected and monitored mainly because they are members of a national or ethnic community within which the criminal rate tends to be higher or the majority presumes it to be higher. Often the reason behind ethnic profiling is prejudice, racism or xenophobia on behalf of proceeding officers. The author admits that there may be some empirical grounds of ethnic profiling since the crime rate is many times indeed higher within these groups and effective law enforcement and crime prevention is an appreciable goal. However, he draws the conclusion that experience, and surveys show that ethnic profiling does not result in more effective prevention, investigation or enforcement and is certainly not more cost-efficient. The essay also emphasizes that collective criminality is unacceptable and only individual circumstances may be considered during criminal proceedings. Another moral argument against ethnic profiling is that it can raise serious tensions between law enforcement bodies and the given ethnic group. A just and efficient justice system, however, can create a strong bond between the state and individuals from all ethnic backgrounds.

The question of sexual orientation and gender identity is an issue receiving growing attention mainly in the political field. Legal systems – even in developed Western societies – are not catching up with the social discourse on the equality of homosexual and bisexual people. Since the legislation cannot provide adequate answers, – and often is unwilling to do so –, it is mainly up to judicial interpretation and scholarly work to help fill the gaps in legislation. This is why Eszter Polgár addresses the topic of 'Sexual orientation and human rights'.[4] According to the author's definition, sexual orientation refers to the capacity of a person which determines which gender (man, women or both) one can relate to emotionally and sexually. This definition suggests that sexual orientation is not a question of choice or an illness, but it is irreversible and unchangeable. This approach means that it is unacceptable to criminalize relationships between homosexual or bisexual persons which is still the case in many states today. At the same time, the author states that the LMB community does not seek additional rights, but equal rights and equal treatment. This has two dimensions. Firstly, the decriminalization of same sex relations and secondly, to open the institution of marriage and child adoption. Legal development in this respect varies in from state to state, even in Europe. The chapter provides a detailed collection of case law on the development of equality mainly within the Council of Europe, which according to her can be considered as the pioneer of LMB rights.

---

4   Id. pp. 655-662.

While LMB rights concern a minority of people, the right to access water is definitely of interest to every individual and every nation. This is especially true in light of climate change, global warming and the increasing occurrences and vast scale of droughts in Africa. This is why Melinda Szappanyos' chapter on the 'Right to water'[5] is an essential contribution to the topic. She points out that the right to water may not be traced as far back as other aspects of human rights, but it is becoming increasingly relevant to deal with the problem. The right to water has not always been a right of its own and it is still rarely included in international treaties as such. Yet it is considered to be an evident and indispensable part of the right to life and the right to health. The paper also provides a general introduction to the content of the right to water. It should be mentioned that the author presented the two most relevant questions of access to water. Hydro-conflict refers to legal disputes between states regarding water reservoirs, while the privatization of water supply raises questions regarding the role and duty of the state in case a private entity owns and manages the water supply system.

The encyclopedia contains numerous other studies from various fields discussing a wide range of issues concerning human rights. While the present book review cannot give a glimpse into the wealth of human rights issues raised in the volume, it may encourage the reader to get acquainted with this ambitious project. To summarize, this ambitious scholarly work covers almost all aspects of human rights and constitutes a valuable source for both academics and practitioners. Since it is written in a simple, intelligible language, and as such, may also be interesting for individuals who seek legal protection or are simply interested in legal topics.

---

5   Id. pp. 735-740.

35 PÉTER MEZEI: COPYRIGHT EXHAUSTION – LAW AND POLICY IN THE UNITED STATES AND THE EUROPEAN UNION (BOOK REVIEW)

*István Harkai**

Péter Mezei, Copyright Exhaustion – Law and Policy in the United States and the European Union, Cambridge University Press, Cambridge, 2018, 211 p, ISBN 978-1107193680

Copyright Exhaustion is Péter Mezei's fourth monography and the first one written in English. The book fits into the row of his scientific oeuvre launched with Digital Sampling and Filesharing,[1] followed by Filesharing Dilemma – Litigations are Slow, the Internet is Fast[2] and the Exhaustion in Copyright Law.[3] In these works he keenly seeks answers to the question whether new technologies raise challenges to copyright law on international, European and national level.

Copyright Exhaustion covers the legal instrument of the exhaustion and first-sale doctrines in the EU and the US, and as such, it is a very timely book.

The Introduction covers the definitions of the exhaustion (*Erschöpfung*, first-sale doctrine) doctrine. The author also presents the different interests at play in property rights and copyright, as well as the detailed theoretical and legal framework of exhaustion with special regard to the International and European norms, such as the TRIPS Agreement and the WIPO Internet Treaties. The norms of parallel import – the rules under which the copyright protected works enter into the circulation of goods in the given country – are also evaluated. In the European Economic Area, the common market, the free movement of goods foresees that states abstain from adopting regulations which can potentially hinder the principle of exhaustion. Thus, the EU decided to follow the principle of regional exhaustion.

In Chapter 2 the author summarizes the results of an in-depth analysis of the relevant rules of the European copyright regime as well as the relevant case law of the member states and the European Court of Justice. The historical development of the exhaustion

---

* István Harkai: assistant lecturer, University of Szeged.
1 Péter Mezei, *Digitális sampling és fájlcsere*, Szeged, 2010.
2 Péter Mezei, *A fájlcsere dilemma – a perek lassúak, az internet gyors*, HVG-ORAC, Budapest, 2012.
3 Péter Mezei, *Jogkimerülés a szerzői jogban*, NMHH, Budapest, 2016.

doctrine is clearly presented through court decisions *(Deutsche Grammophon, Coditel, Cinétèque, Basset, Membran, Patricia, Corbusier, Blumquist, Warner Brothers v. Christiansen)* and the rules of the significant body of law of European copyright-related directives (Software Directive, Rental and Lending Rights Directive, Database Directive, InfoSoc Directive). From this remarkable deduction the author concludes that according to European copyright norms only tangible goods fall under the scope of the regional exhaustion doctrine. This finding is relevant since intangible goods are conveyed to the public within the framework of license agreements, which must be considered as services. The exhaustion doctrine can be applied only to the distribution of tangible copies based on sale contracts, gift or exchange agreements, which result in the transfer of ownership. Exhaustion is not applicable to the service-type distribution of works, such as rental and lending agreements, public performance, communication to the public, retransmission by cable and making available to the public.

The doctrine of exhaustion is one of those legal institutions which developed in parallel in Europe and in North America. In Chapter 3 the author examines the legal nature of the first-sale doctrine before and after the USCA by examining the relevant norms of the US Copyright Act of 1976 with special regard to the terminological uncertainty characteristic of it. He continues his assessment with the limitations on the first-sale doctrine by introducing the reader to the reasons why and how the first-sale doctrine was limited in the case of sound recordings and software, including the special case of film rental.

The well-known *droit de suite* is introduced not only in Chapter 2 but in Chapter 3 as well, but this time in the context of American copyright law. The complex topic of parallel import is also elaborated on. The relevant case law is sorted into three main groups. The author first introduces cases where works are produced abroad with the purpose of selling in the country of production, but later on they are exported to the US *(Nintendo of America v. Elcon Industries, Scorpio, Starks, Harms, Red Baron, BMG v. Perez, Omega v. Costco Kirstsaeng)*. As a second group those cases are mentioned, where products are produced and distributed in the United States but are later on exported and then re-imported to the US *(Cosmair, Neutrogena)*. The third group covers products that had been also produced in the United States with the explicit purpose of exporting to a third country where they should have been sold exclusively, but were then re-imported *(Sebastia, Quality King v. L'anza)*.

In Chapter 4 the author examines leading cases in the field of digital copyright law. In *UsedSoft* the CJEU had to decide whether the right of distribution of the plaintiff Oracle is exhausted, if the computer programs are made available not on a tangible data carrier but in downloaded a digital format. It also had to be decided whether the license-key of the program had been exhausted after having been sold by the respondent. In *ReDigi* – a case from the US – phonograms were re-sold in a digital music store. The court had to decide whether this activity would result in the exhaustion of the right of reproduction.

Next, the author brings the reader's attention back to Europe by giving a brief introduction to the legal practice of the German and Dutch courts regarding the re-sale of audio and e-books.

After analyzing the case law, Mezei criticizes the differences between license and sale contracts, as well as distribution and making available as a form of communication to the public. The migration of files and forward-and-delete technologies are also mentioned. As he puts it: the place of digital exhaustion does not depend on the type of the work, but rather on the type of data carrier, on which the work was distributed in the first place.

In Chapter 4 the main question is formed: do we really need digital exhaustion, or "[...] isn't it only a hype?" To answer this question, he assembles traditional and constructive approaches and arguments. As a conclusion, he puts his money on digital exhaustion by arguing that in a globalizing world, in order to maintain predictable competition and equality of rights, it is necessary to recognize a wide, international digital exhaustion.

All in all, Péter Mezei's book on exhaustion in copyright law is highly relevant, in particular in light of the hiatus in the relevant literature in the field of digital exhaustion. This gap is now filled with a work putting forward an insightful, modern, progressive point of view. His work also reminds us, that the difficulties in the 21st century can only be overcome, if all the fields of the given problem – in our case the right of distribution and the exhaustion doctrine – are revised with due consideration to the new social, economic and technical circumstances.

36   Csongor István Nagy (ed.) – Investment Arbitration and National Interest (Book Review)

Tamás Szabados[*]

Csongor István Nagy (ed.), Investment Arbitration and National Interest, Council on International Law and Policy, Indianapolis, 2018, 236 p, ISBN 978-0-985815684

The book Investment Arbitration and National Interest edited by Csongor István Nagy raises fundamental questions about international investment protection law, which are answered by various experts at different levels, in the global and regional context.[1] The central question of the book is the legitimacy of the current system of investment protection characterized by uncertain substantive standards, intransparent dispute settlement procedures and a lack of consistent decisions.

The first part of the book introduces the most topical issues of the current investment protection regime in a global context. The outstanding opening contribution by Frank Emmert and Begaiym Esenkulova 'Balancing Investor Protection and Sustainable Development in Investment Arbitration – Trying to Square the Circle?' describes the legitimacy crisis of international investment arbitration enumerating the reasons and illustrating the issues with cases from the more recent arbitration practice: the disregard for state sovereignty, the overprotection of investors' interests, as well as the uncertainty and unpredictability of decisions rendered by arbitral tribunals. The trust of states, regional organizations, such as the EU, and the public in international investment arbitration is dissipating. The authors advocate for a paradigm shift by applying the requirement of sustainability in investment protection law that can respond to the above challenges. Sustainability requires striking a balance between the protection of the investors' interests and the interests of other stakeholders. Sustainable development objectives should be taken into account when negotiating investment treaties and the interests of various stakeholders can be included in the dispute settlement mechanism through different channels, such as the involvement of a public interest attorney in investor-state dispute settlement proceedings or *amicus curiae* submissions. More predictability could be ensured by establishing a

---

[*]   Tamás Szabados: senior lecturer, ELTE Law School, Budapest.
[1]   The book is available at https://static.wixstatic.com/ugd/8e15a8_51c30de1fd9f4207b1406635f7872f89.pdf.

multilateral investment court. In their study, Dalma Demeter and Zebo Nasirova outline the 'Trends and Challenges in the Legal Harmonisation of ISDS'. The authors put investment protection law in the broader context of public international law. The general tendency of the increasing role of non-state actors in public international law and the accompanying bottom-up regulatory approach is revealed in the field of international investment protection law. This tendency is convincingly illustrated by the *Phillip Morris v. Australia* investment protection dispute concerning the Australian tobacco plain packaging legislation that was challenged by the investor.[2] Investment claims provoked such a public outcry that the Australian government decided to exclude investor-state dispute settlement provisions from investment treaties.

The second part of the volume addresses further legitimacy issues. In his study titled 'Abuse of Process' and Anti-Arbitration Injunctions in Investor-State Arbitration – An Analysis of Recent Trends and the Way Forward', Wasiq Abass Dar examines abuse of process in the context of investor-state arbitration and the potential room for anti-arbitration injunctions. Abuse of process is defined as the bringing of multiple or parallel investment protection proceedings by the investor before different arbitral tribunals for the same claim against the same respondent state in order to increase the chances of success in the legal dispute either relying on different investment treaties or splitting a claim. To prevent abuse of process, certain courts issue anti-arbitration injunctions as a remedy upon the request of the respondent state. This practice has been, however, criticized in the legal literature contesting the authority and the interventionism of national courts when issuing anti-arbitration injunctions. This approach considers such injunctions as a form of denial of justice in breach of the investment treaty. After having overviewed the differences between civil law and common law approaches towards anti-arbitration injunctions, the study draws the conclusion that despite scholarly debates the fact remains that national courts are unwilling to give up the possibility to issue anti-arbitration injunctions and as such, anti-arbitration injunctions should be granted with caution only under exceptional circumstances by the seat court or supervisory court.

Rebecca E. Kahn deals with 'Third Party Participation by Non-Governmental Organizations in International Investment Arbitration: Transparency as a Tool for Protecting Marginalized Interests'. Using the example of the extractive industry, the contribution examines the appearance of the interests of indigenous peoples and environmental considerations in investor-state dispute settlement. Although we find instances where tribunals allowed the participation of NGOs representing indigenous peoples or environmental NGOs, their submissions were usually only considered to a limited extent. Arbitral tribunals

---

2   *Philip Morris Asia Limited v. The Commonwealth of Australia*, UNCITRAL, PCA Case No. 2012-12, Award on Jurisdiction and Admissibility, 17 December 2015.

enjoy a wide discretion as to allow third party participation and whether to take into account their submissions in the award.

The study written by Bálint Kovács poses the question to what extent investor-state dispute settlement mechanisms can serve small and medium-sized enterprises (SMEs) with the title 'Access of SMEs to Investment Arbitration – Small Enough to Fail?'. Although investment protection rules do not distinguish between SMEs and larger companies, owing to their size SMEs are less capable of negotiating the conditions of their investments or to protect the investments they make. Because of their vulnerability, SMEs are exposed more to harms resulting from state intervention. Some tribunals interpreted the concept of investment narrowly that may exclude certain investments made by SMEs from the scope of application of the International Centre for Settlement of Investment Disputes (ICSID) regime. Investor-state dispute settlement mechanisms are less available for SMEs because of the costs of these proceedings. Therefore, it is proposed to adopt specific rules and procedures tailored to SMEs, which make it possible to settle their investment disputes at lower costs and in a shorter time. A formalized framework of assistance, including financial assistance and information on how to bring investment claims, could help SMEs assert their rights.

The third part of the book presents the most recent regional perspectives and developments of investment protection. Most studies deal with the interaction between EU law and international investment protection law. In his contribution 'The Promotion, Protection, Treatment and Expropriation of Investments under the Energy Charter Treaty – a Critical Analysis of the Case Law', Dildar F. Zebari describes thoroughly the relevant case law related to Article 10 (promotion, protection and treatment of investments) and Article 13 (expropriation) of the Energy Charter Treaty. The study 'Opinion 2/15 of the European Court of Justice and the New Principles of Competence Allocation in External Relations – A Solid Footing for the Future?' written by Balázs Horváthy explains how *Opinion 2/15* on the conclusion of Free Trade Agreement between the EU and Singapore contributed to the clarification of the division of competences between the EU and the Member States.[3] The Opinion of the CJEU is relevant in terms of determining the scope of the common commercial policy competence and the division of competences between the EU and its Member States concerning the new generation of trade and investment agreements. *Opinion 2/15* distinguishes between direct and indirect (portfolio) investments and defines the concept of direct investment. Non-direct investments and other issues, such as the investor-state dispute settlement rules, do not fall under the scope of the common commercial policy. The CJEU concluded that the EU-Singapore Free Trade Agreement is a mixed agreement requiring ratification by the Member States. In the author's view, the requirement of ratification by the Member States can contribute to the legitimacy of the

---

3   Opinion of 16 May 2017, ECLI:EU:C:2017:376.

agreement and similar new generation agreements. Csongor István Nagy analyses extra-EU BITs under EU law with the title 'Extra-EU BITs and EU Law: Immunity, "Defense of Superior Orders", Treaty Shopping and Unilateralism'. The study centers on three questions. The first one is the applicability of Article 351 TFEU to extra-EU BITs. The second question raised is whether Member States can use a defense of superior orders when a state act is required by EU law. The third issue analyzed by the author is whether investors from the EU can rely on extra-EU BITs by incorporating a company in a third country following the *Achmea* judgment of the CJEU.[4] Pavle Flere discusses 'The Arbitrability of Competition Law Disputes in the European Union – Balancing of Competing Interests'. He states that the arbitrability of competition law has become widely accepted in practice as part of *lex mercatoria* and arbitrators have an implied duty to apply EU competition law rules *ex officio*. The recognition and enforcement of an arbitral award may be denied if it disregards antitrust rules in cases of manifest and hard-core violations of EU competition law.

The fourth part addresses enforcement and recovery. Yue Ma's contribution analyses the 'Execution of ICSID Awards and Sovereign Immunity' and presents how sovereign immunity pleaded by a respondent state, as a 'last bastion', can inhibit the execution of ICSID awards. She describes the obstacles to the execution of ICSID awards in light of the legislation and court practice of certain forum states (US, UK, France and China) other than the investment host state as well as in the host state. The author warns that the difficulties concerning the execution of ICSID awards may gain more significance in the future due to the growing backlash against investment arbitration. Orsolya Toth turns the readers' attention toward the New York Convention with her study on 'The New York Convention – Challenges on its 60th Birthday'. Despite the success of the New York Convention, the author describes three challenges as far as the application of the Convention is concerned. First, as more and more countries have acceded to the Convention, there is an increasing risk that national courts apply the Convention favoring their own nationals or conflating the provisions of the Convention with domestic law. A second challenge is the increasing involvement of states in arbitral proceedings, while the third one is the difference in the treatment of awards set aside in the seat state in terms of their enforcement in other countries.

The closing part of the book focuses on institutional issues, and in particular, the investment protection regime set up by the EU-Canada Comprehensive Economic and Trade Agreement (CETA). In their study, Zoltán Víg and Gábor Hajdu introduce the substantive and procedural rules of the CETA related to investment protection with the title 'Investment Protection under CETA: A New Paradigm?'. The authors are critical, because the CETA follows to a large extent American solution, and most notably the model of NAFTA. They put forward several *de lege ferenda* proposals to amend the provisions

---

4   Judgment of 6 March 2018, *Case C-284/16, Slovak Republic v. Achmea BV*, ECLI:EU:C:2018:158.

of the CETA. Although the CETA recognizes the right of the host state to adopt legislation affecting investments for legitimate policy objectives, it is suggested by the authors that the appropriate balance between the interests of the host state and those of the investors should be struck by the introduction of the necessity test. It is proposed that the standard of fair and equitable treatment should be concretized more by enumerating the relevant cases in an exhaustive list. Interestingly, in the authors' view, companies owned or controlled by third-country citizens or companies should be excluded from the concept of investor within the meaning of the CETA and thus, from its scope of application.

In summary, this thought-provoking volume offers readers an outline of the most current issues of investment protection law and arbitration. Remarkably, most of the contributions put forward proposals to answer the challenges that investment protection law faces. It will be interesting to see whether investment protection law will develop along these forward-looking ideas in the future.

37 ANDRÁS JAKAB – DIMITRY KOCHENOV (EDS.) – THE ENFORCEMENT OF EU LAW AND VALUES. ENSURING MEMBER STATES' COMPLIANCE (BOOK REVIEW)

Petra Lea Láncos[*]

András Jakab & Dimitry Kochenov (eds.), The Enforcement of EU Law and Values. Ensuring Member States' Compliance, Oxford University Press, Oxford, 2017, 510 p, ISBN 978-0198746560

In light of Brexit, the stubborn resistance to the implementation of EU asylum law, as well as the creeping downgrading of democratic and constitutional structures (backsliding) in individual Member States – to name only a few of the integration challenges – is a comprehensive volume on the enforcement of EU law and values most welcome. In particular, the initiation of Article 7 proceedings against Poland – that means the use of the so-called 'nuclear option' and its possible failure – sheds new light on the enforcement of Union values, rendering the edited volume all the more topical.

In fact, the editors[1] sought to overcome the traditional scientific perspective and broaden the analysis of enforcement by capturing both legal compliance issues and adherence to European values. A complex analysis suggests that instances of occasional resistance from Member States are merely symptoms of profound issues of political or economic mismanagement, a long-term national political strategy, or problems inherent in weak states. In line with this broad approach, the volume is both thematically and methodologically broadly conceived, including theoretical, comparative and Member State-specific explorations in areas of law, politics and economics. The volume is divided into four comprehensive, complementary parts that discuss different perspectives of the enforcement problem: 'Theoretical Issues', 'Instruments and Methods', 'Comparative Outlook' and 'Case Studies'.

---

[*] Petra Lea Láncos: researcher, Deutsches Forschungsinstitut für öffentliche Verwaltung, Speyer; associate professor, Pázmány Péter Catholic University, Budapest.
[1] András Jakab & Dimitry Kochenov, 'Introductory Remarks', *in* András Jakab & Dimitry Kochenov (eds.), *The Enforcement of EU Law and Values. Ensuring Member States' Compliance*, Oxford University Press, Oxford, 2017, pp. 1-5.

The first theoretical part describes the context and outlines the main normative approaches to ensure compliance in the Member States. It starts with Kochenov's contribution and sets out the central problems of the enforcement of Union values. He classifies the values of the EU as enforceable legal principles under Article 2 TEU and distinguishes them from state goals by teleological, historical and systematic interpretation. He criticizes the separation of the acquis from values in Article 2 TEU, as well as the restrictive approach advocated in the literature that the latter should only be enforced through the highly political procedure of Article 7 TEU. He even argues that the enforcement of values should play a key role in the enforcement of EU law.[2] The next author defines the enforcement of values as a matter of choice between different interpretive scales in order to grasp the meaning of the rules to be applied. In his contribution, Itzcovich differentiates between two major approaches to interpretation: *Wertjurisprudenz* and *Geseztespositivismus*, which in turn are shaped by respective social, political and institutional conditions.[3] Avbelj investigates the issue of the 'systemic defiance', that is, the serious breach of Union values in the pluralist structure of the Union. He concludes that, if the Member State cannot provide functioning 'endogenous' mechanisms to enforce Union values, the option remains from a pluralistic perspective, to discipline these Member States incremental remedies and sanctions or even expel them from the Union. However, this is an inadequate solution: young democracies and established right-wing states need time and comprehensive, effective mechanisms to live up to EU ideals.[4]

The second part, 'Instruments and Methods of Enforcement', is a multi-faceted section that discusses both existing tools and their potential for improvement, as well as new solutions and mechanisms. Accordingly, the pieces authored by Gormley[5] and Wennerås[6] are dedicated to exploring the traditional instrument of infringement proceedings, encouraging their more extensive use and interpretation. In his contribution on preliminary ruling proceedings, Broberg criticizes the fact that while the procedure is the most important instrument for enforcing EU law, it does not realize its full potential in the judicial protection of individual rights.[7] Norbert Reich, former director of the *Bremer Zentrum für europäische Rechtspolitik* (Centre of European Law and Politics, University of Bremen ZERP) and former Dean of the Bremen Faculty of Law, to whose memory this volume is dedicated, examines the *Francovich* case law on state liability for non-compliance

---

2 Dimitry Kochenov, 'The Acquis and its Principles: The Enforcement of the 'Law' versus the Enforcement of 'Values' in the EU', *in* Id. pp. 9-27.
3 Giulio Itzcovich, 'On the Legal Enforcement of Values. The Importance of the Institutional Context', *in* Id. pp. 28-43.
4 Matej Avbelj, 'Pluralism and Systematic Defiance in the EU', *in* Id. pp. 44-60.
5 Laurence W. Gormley, 'Infringement Proceedings', *in* Id. pp. 65-78.
6 Pål Wennerås, 'Making Effective Use of Article 260 TFEU', *in* Id. pp. 79-98.
7 Morten Broberg, 'Preliminary References as a Means for Enforcing EU Law', *in* Id. pp. 99-111.

with EU law and the effectiveness of such legal action as an instrument for the enforcement
of EU law. Following a detailed analysis of the relevant case-law, he concludes that national
courts interpret the criterion of 'sufficiently serious' in respect of *Francovich* actions
restrictively, and, in particular, that actions in the field of social law are unsuccessful.
Therefore, the infringement procedure is indispensable for the full enforcement of EU
law.[8] In his contribution, Besselink criticizes both the restrictive interpretation of the
Article 7 procedure by the Council and the view that any control by the Member States
should be confined exclusively to the implementation of EU law. In order to give the procedure the necessary bite, he advocates for the exercise of the Council's powers of control
even before the preventive procedure is initiated, calling for a full review of national conformity.[9] In the context of economic policy coordination in the framework of the European
Economic and Monetary Union, Amtenbrink and Repasi analyze the so-called 'Six Pack',
the 'Two Pack', European Stability Mechanism and European Fiscal Compact from a
compliance perspective. They conclude that current mechanisms for ensuring conformity
have failed. In case a Member State involuntarily violates the stability requirements, disbursements will cease, with the result that the respective state is pushed into an even deeper
economic crisis. At the same time, sanctions in this area are ineffective as the Council is
reluctant to apply them. The authors plead for capacity building at the national level as
well as greater involvement of national parliaments and the EP in developing and monitoring the implementation of the Stability Framework.[10] Cseres describes the decentralized
implementation of European competition law, examining CJEU case-law on the distribution
of cases and the concept of trade impact. Her conclusion: the decentralized system creates
parallel competition systems that lead to a fragmentation of enforcement and unequal
legal protection in the competition area.[11] Stefan gives insight into the diversity of EU soft
law measures and their various forms of enforcement. She emphasizes the benefits (voluntary compliance, socialization aspect) and functions of soft law (interpretive aid, execution
of binding law); at the same time, she stresses that the diversity of Union soft law leads to
a variety of enforcement, creating problems of legitimacy, legal certainty and legitimate
expectations.[12] Von Bogdandy *et al.* deal with the criticism and further development of
the Reverse Solange doctrine, highlighting the shortcomings of the EU framework to
strengthen the rule of law and the rule of law dialogue. In addition to the judicial instrument

---

8   Norbert Reich, 'Francovich Enforcement Analyzed and Illustrated by German (and English) Law', *in* Id.
     pp. 112-127.
9   Leonard Besselink, 'The Bite, the Bark and the Howl: Article 7 TEU and the Rule of Law Initiatives', *in* Id.
     pp. 128-144.
10   Fabian Amtenbrink & René Repasi, 'Compliance and Enforcement in Economic Policy Coordination in
     EMU', *in* Id. pp. 145-181.
11   Katalin J. Cseres, 'Rule of Law Values in the Decentralized Public Enforcement of EU Competition Law',
     in Id. 182-199.
12   Oana Ştefan, 'Soft Law and the Enforcement of EU Law', *in* Id. pp. 200-217.

of Reverse Solange, they also advocate for the establishment of a Systemic Deficiency Committee. This independent committee of experts within the Commission would monitor developments in the Member States and publish a report on compliance with Article 2 TEU.[13] Jan-Werner Müller elaborates on his proposal for the establishment of a Copenhagen Commission and addresses the criticism of unnecessary institutional multiplication, technocratic rule and the (il)legitimacy of committee activities. The proposed commission would resemble the German Office for the Protection of the Constitution, itself a necessary element of the militant democracy. Müller sees the advantage of the proposed institution in its authority, which, in contrast with the CJEU or the Commission, would be comprehensive and unrestricted.[14] András Jakab, co-editor of the volume, argues in favor of a creative, teleological interpretation of Article 51(1) of the Charter of Fundamental Rights, to ensure that the Charter rights are enforced through the application of Article 2 read together with Article 7 TEU before the national courts. The advantage of this solution would be that since illiberal governments usually only pack the highest courts with their cadres, a true community of values may emerge through the fundamental rights dialogue between national courts and the CJEU.[15]

The comparative section provides insight into the enforcement solutions of various federal states and international organizations. It starts with a contribution by Hanschel on the enforcement of federal law against the German states. He describes the autonomous enforcement instruments of the Federal Government, the heteronomous judicial review and the *Federal-Länder* dispute before the General Constitutional Court (*BVerfG*). He emphasizes that, owing to the interdependence of politics and cooperative federalism, it is rare for such enforcement instruments to be used, instead, in conformity with public expectation, the instruments of uniform and efficient administration and political negotiation are used.[16] Romainville and Verdrussen describe Belgium's 'dynamic', 'bipolar' federal system. Although the system contains a number of principles for the solution of institutionalized defiance (exclusive competences, implicit competences and primacy of federal law *etc.*), conflicts are resolved through dialogue, compromises, that is, the inclusion of minorities and cooperation agreements in complex policy areas. The Belgian Constitutional Court tasked with overseeing the relationship between levels of government, also contributes to the ongoing development of the system.[17] López-Basaguren describes the historical

---

13 Armin von Bogdandy *et al.*, 'Protecting EU Values: Reverse *Solange* and the Rule of Law Framework', *in* Id. 218-233.
14 Jan-Werner Müller, 'A Democracy Commission of One's Own, or What it Would Take for the EU to Safeguard Liberal Democracy in its Member States', *in* Id. pp. 234-251.
15 András Jakab, 'Application of the EU CFR by National Courts in Purely Domestic Cases', *in* Id. pp. 252-262.
16 Dirk Hanschel, 'Enforcement of Federal Law against the German *Länder*', *in* Id. pp. 265-282.
17 Céline Romainville & Marc Verdrussen, 'The Enforcement of Federal Law in the Belgian Federal State', *in* Id. pp. 283-299.

unification of the regions in Spain and the sovereignty claims of the autonomous regions of Catalonia and Basque Country. He describes the role of the Constitutional Court and the criminal classification of possible independence aspirations of the affected regions, such as rebellion and criminal disobedience as crimes against the Constitution and public order.[18] In his contribution, Tushet reports on the enforcement of federal law *vis-à-vis* US states in a culturally homogeneous, but ethnically and demographically diverse context. He points out that the enforcement of federal law is straightforward, as the national government can act directly on citizens, through or in cooperation with state governments and courts, and through injunctions and damages claims. Meanwhile, the balance between federal and state levels is ensured through the principle of and the anti-commandeering principle and the conditional preemptive effect of federal law.[19] Lambert explores the execution of ECtHR judgments and concludes that, while the reasons for Member States' refusal to comply are diverse (*e.g.* financial, competence-related reasons, governed by public opinion or the extent of the reforms required, and even political considerations), the general strategy of the Council of Europe is to prevent non-compliance, motivating signatory states to act by persuasion, support, exchange of good practices and cooperation, instead of relying on sanctions.[20] Antonella Tancredi's contribution stands out, especially because it compares the enforcement mechanisms of the WTO in detail with those of the EU. She emphasizes that the WTO's mixed diplomatic enforcement instruments defined by reciprocity and bilateralism, offer more room for maneuver to achieve consensual dispute settlement than available EU solutions.[21] Couzigou examines the possibilities for executing ICJ judgments and resolutions of the Security Council. Her analysis shows that the instruments available are used by biased organs in an imprecise and inconsistent manner, rendering the system highly politicized and non-transparent. She proposes the setting up of a judicial institution tasked with monitoring implementation in accordance with common standards and making recommendations to the UN Security Council publicly available in order to improve the predictability and transparency of the system.[22] Closa compares democratic conditionality in the practice of regional organizations. He emphasizes that although the majority of regional organizations had gradually introduced democratic conditionality, imposing the customary sanction of suspending voting rights revealed

---

18   Alberto López-Basaguren, 'Regional Defiance and Enforcement of Federal Law in Spain: The Claims for Sovereignty in the Basque Country and Catalonia', *in* Id. pp. 300-315.

19   Mark Tushet, 'Enforcement of National Law against Subnational Units in the US', *in* Id. pp. 316-325.

20   Elisabeth Lambert Abdelgawad, 'The Enforcement of ECtHR Judgments', *in* Id. pp. 326-340.

21   Antonella Tancredi, 'Enforcing WTO Law', *in* Id. pp. 341-362.

22   Iréne Couzigou, 'Enforcement of UN Security Council Resolutions and of ICJ Judgments: The Unreliability of Political Enforcement Mechanisms', *in* Id. pp. 363-378.

regulatory shortcomings, arbitrary decision-making and the ensuing lack of legal certainty in the relevant organizations.[23]

The last part, 'Case Studies in the Context of the EU', deals with different cases of EU enforcement failures in individual Member States. This section kicks off with Mayer's contribution on the case law of the German Federal Constitutional Court regarding European integration (*Solange I and II, Maastricht, European arrest warrant, Honeywell, Lisbon and OMT* judgments). His analysis shows that the position of the Federal Constitutional Court hovers between Europe-friendliness and resistance, with the court alternating between a tight and a loose grip in applying ultra vires and identity control. Mayer arrives at the conclusion that the verdicts ultimately reflect the composition of the chamber rendering the judgment.[24] Ziller describes in detail the events that led to the empty chair crisis and the resulting Luxembourg compromise, which had a strong impact on the functioning of the Commission and the Council. He points out that France has brought both the functionalism of Schuman and Monet and the intergovernmentalism of De Gaulle into integration – the empty chair policy was an example of the latter. He emphasizes that both the empty chair as resistance and the Luxembourg compromise as a solution were extra-legal instruments.[25] Lachmayer explains the rise of the FPÖ (Freedom Party of Austria), their perception as a threat to European values and the measures taken by the 14 other EU Member States. The well-known failure of these measures led to the report issued by the 'Three Wise Men', which in turn resulted in the refinement of the system for the enforcement of European values through the development of Article 7 TEU and the establishment of the EU Fundamental Rights Agency. However, Lachmayer points out that the attempted restrictions on minority rights and corruption in Austria under Haider's government had already thrown light on the inadequacy of these solutions, evidenced yet again by the handling of recent events in Hungary.[26] Szente draws the road Hungary travelled from being the democratic pioneer of the former socialist states of Central Europe through facing the challenge of integration to the transformation of the legal and administrative system during the second and third Orbán government. He emphasized that, although various EU and Council of Europe institutions had tried to provide political and legal solutions to halt violations of democracy and the rule of law in Hungary, surprisingly little has been achieved. One explanation for this could be the broad support of the government among the Hungarian population, as well as the fact that the EU was not interested in deepening this internal conflict during the financial crisis. In the absence of powerful enforcement tools, there is a risk that the idea of 'illiberal democracy' will spread to other EU Member

---

23 Carlos Closa, 'Securing Compliance with Democracy Requirements in Regional Organizations', *in* Id. pp. 379-401.
24 Franz C Mayer, 'Defiance by a Constitutional Court – Germany', *in* Id. pp. 403-421.
25 Jacques Ziller, 'Defiance for European Influence – the Empty Chair and France', *in* Id. pp. 422-435.
26 Konrad Lachmayer, 'Questioning the Basic Values– Austria and Jörg Haider', *in* Id. pp. 436-455.

States as well.[27] Ioannidis describes Greece as a 'weak member' of the EU and points out that the lack of capacity and the widespread corruption in Greek administration and the judiciary resulted in a deficient implementation of EU law, which in turn threatened the enforcement of the rule of law in the sense of Article 2 TEU. He outlines EU financial and technical support requirements as examples for solving Member State defiance that is not political, rather structural and budgetary in nature.[28] The concluding contribution by Łazowski reflects on the possible forms of resistance on the part of the United Kingdom in the context of Brexit. While there are still open questions, the options cited by the author, such as the repeal of the 1972 European Communities Act, the core principles of supremacy, direct effect and CJEU jurisdiction have not been decided on to date. Nevertheless, these considerations continue to be relevant for possible future withdrawals by other EU Member States.[29]

The volume, with its collection of select contributions, brings the reader up to date on European law scholarship regarding the enforcement of Union values and provides an outlook on relevant national and supranational solutions. However, the abrupt conclusion leaves the reader with a sense of puzzlement: it would have been worth summarizing the more promising solutions or even the dead ends in enforcement attempts and analyze them in the context of the EU. Delineating the different implementation contexts and their challenges, staking out national political or legal forms of resistance would also have contributed to a better understanding of the enforcement problem. As it is, however, it is left up to the reader to draw the conclusions from the findings of this volume.

---

27   Zoltán Szente, 'Challenging the Basic Values – Problems in the Rule of Law in Hungary and the Failure of the EU to Tackle Them', *in* Id. pp. 456-475.
28   Michael Ioannidis, 'Weak Members and the Enforcement of EU Law', *in* Id. pp. 476-492.
29   Adam Łazowski, 'Inside and Out, The UK and the EU', *in* Id. pp. 493-510.

38   INTER ARMA CARITAS – REVIEW OF THE MEMORIAL VOLUME ISSUED TO COMMEMORATE THE 90TH ANNIVERSARY OF THE BIRTH OF GÉZA HERCZEGH (BOOK REVIEW)

*Tamás Török**

Gábor Béli et al., Emlékkötet Herczegh Géza születésének 90. évfordulója alkalmából [Studies in the Honor of the 90th Anniversary of the Birth of Géza Herczegh], Studia Europaea, Pécs, 2018, 275 p, ISBN 978-615-5457-85-2

According to the popular *bonmot*, the age of polyhistors is over: 'omniscience' exists only in terms of the society, but no individual can now be omniscient. This statement is true both in general and for the specific fields of science as well, therefore, readers might show due caution when they come across a book, which is about to challenge the above. Precaution is even more justified if the field of science concerned is a complex one, such as law, in particular public international law: incorporating several exotic topics from martial law to space law – less known and even less used by the professionals themselves. Moreover, the genre of memorial volumes bears the risk of the authors exaggerating the merits of their fellow scholar and being liberal about any problematic element of the oeuvre. Taking the foregoing into account, the lecturers of the University of Pécs undertook an almost impossible challenge when they decided to publish a complex professional volume commemorating the 90th anniversary of the birth of Géza Herczegh, who passed away in 2010 and who has left an exceptionally rich and colorful heritage to posterity.

Modicity and credibility. These are the two principles the editors had to build on, and according to the result achieved, their endeavor has been successful. The volume recalls Géza Herczegh as one of the most talented lawyers of the 20th century, who received, already during his life, the position he had well deserved in the domestic and the international public life of the profession. As an outstanding expert of legal theory, he was a university professor, a member of the academy, a consultant of international law and an author

*   Tamás Török: PhD candidate, University of Pécs.

of several scholarly documents. However, he was never satisfied with merely the static theoretical work: as a professional of practice, he had contributed to the elaboration of the Geneva protocols of 1977, then he was the director of the Institute for Legal Studies of the Hungarian Academy of Sciences, dean of the Faculty of Law of the Janus Pannonius University (today the University of Pécs), as well as justice and vice-president of the Hungarian Constitutional Court, member of the Venice Commission and of the ICJ. Still, what made him so exceptional was not his imposing career, but the 'polyhistor attitude' he applied to reinterpret several fields of international law.

The book presents Géza Herczegh as a 'value-driven realist' who honestly believed in the idea, which serves as the basis of humanitarian law and, which is also used as the motto of the ICRC: *inter arma caritas* – in war, charity. Indeed, as a professional, he was capable of stepping over the rigid, positivist legal framework and of assessing the international relations as complex psycho-socio-economic structures built on historical determinations, thus he was always able to see in a teleological way any situation or any given problem. To borrow the words of János Martonyi,

> "He knew exactly that international law had its own limitations. He knew that international law also had very special potentials. He also knew that international law had a serious responsibility, too. He could think freely about international law, yet he knew that beyond the limits and the potentials there was something much more important: values."

He laid down his international lawyer's *ars poetica* summarizing the above as early as in his first book: "The international community is on the way of becoming really universal and encompassing the whole of humanity irrespectively to races, languages and economic systems."[1]

The book paints an authentic picture of how the existence in minority experienced as an ethnic Hungarian in Upper Hungary, the family traditions of knowledge and the love for the scholarships of law and history, as well as the desire to know the world well, all made Géza Herczegh an innovator and an indispensable figure of international law in Hungary. The volume presents the image of the polyhistor and the heritage of his work on 275 pages, in three main chapters. The structure goes beyond a mere reflection on the practical necessities of the book's content and its edition: it conveys a consciously formed message. The present discourse in Hungary about public international law is an organic system based on the joint work of three generations. The heritage of Géza Herczegh and his coeval scholars, the work of the present community of lawyers leaning on the profes-

---

1   Géza Herczegh, *The Colonial Question and International Law*, Közgazdasági és Jogi Könyvkiadó, Budapest, 1962. p. 7.

sional and the human values of their predecessors, and the introduction of the next generation of professionals, form – even within the book – integral units built upon each other.

The first chapter ('Teacher, Researcher and Judge – Memories of Géza Herczegh') recalls through personal reminiscences the worldwide renowned and acknowledged scholar of international law, the colleague, the mentor and the friend.

Elisabeth Sándor-Szalay, in her personal laudation starting off the volume, remembers the educator, mentor, consultant and friend, who lives in the collective memory of the members of the invisible college of international lawyers. By way of his human sociability, his exceptional intelligence and as a native-level speaker of four languages, he could always understand and attentively listen to his colleagues – be it freshmen of the faculty of law or the justices of the Constitutional Court or the ICJ.[2]

The subsequent pages of the chapter contain laudations by three fellow-justices of the ICJ. As recalled by Gilbert Guillaume in his confession of personal tone: Géza Herczegh was naturally determined by his court and university experiences to see the merits of every case with the eye of a judge, but at the same time to always take into account the principles and the rules of international law as well. For him, value-based adjudication also meant the unconditional protection of the court's dignity; therefore, he held that conscientiousness and the seeking of consensus were of primary importance during his work. Gilbert Guillaume added: due to his perfect command of the French language, it was a constant joy to listen to him speak.[3] Rosalyn Higgins QC primarily focused on the analysis of his professional career in The Hague. Géza Herczegh joined the court when its workload started to increase swiftly. He participated in the hearing of almost thirty cases, including the adjudication of several (among others, *East Timor* case, *Lockerbie* case, *Legality of the use of nuclear weapons in armed conflict* case, the *Case of delimitation between Qatar and Bahrain*, *Gabčíkovo-Nagymaros* case), which had an overarching effect in time. The aim of Géza Herczegh was to support the work of the court and to maintain its good reputation without presenting any ideological or theoretical perspective in his dissenting opinions. Thus, over nine years, he only wrote four declarations and one longer opinion – the latter was related to the *Gabčíkovo-Nagymaros* case.[4] His successor in the office, Peter Tomka mainly concentrated on examining his professional heritage, primarily with regard to the *Lockerbie* case, the *Legality of the use of nuclear weapons in armed conflict* case and the *Gabčíkovo-Nagymaros* case. He underlined and illustrated with examples that, although the exceptional material and dogmatic knowledge of Géza Herczegh, as well as his systematic approach,

---

2   Erzsébet Szalayné Sándor, 'Laudáció – Herczegh Géza Gábor tiszteletére', *in* Gábor Béli *et al.* (eds.), *Emlékkötet Herczegh Géza születésének 90. évfordulója alkalmából*, Studia Europaea, Pécs, 2018, pp. 9-12.
3   Gilbert Guillaume, 'Géza Herczegh, juge à la Cour internationale de justice', *in* Id. pp. 13-16.
4   Rosalyn Higgins QC, 'Reflections on Judge Geza Herczegh', *in* Id. pp. 21-23.

fundamentally determined the foundation of the merits of the above decisions, he never attempted to put himself into the forefront by issuing concurring or dissenting opinions.[5]

To close the chapter, János Martonyi and Iván Gyurcsík, as coeval scholars and friends, share their personal memories with the reader. Both of them underline the special approach that determined Herczegh's way of thinking. The world as we know it today is the result of history, of cultural heritage, and of different cultural environments; therefore, a scholar of international law with a responsible thinking must be aware of the above. With the words of János Martonyi:

"Of course, we always say that he was an international lawyer, as well as a historian; but I think that the point is that he saw the whole, not just parts of it. In the background of international law, he was able to see and to understand the world and its great network of connections."[6]

Iván Gyurcsík writes very expressively about the heritage of his roots in Upper Hungary; the experience of being the member of an ethnic minority and the spirit-forming effects of a stormy history:

"We were forced to call the start of a new servitude liberation, to call democracy a dictatorship, to call the revolution a counter-revolution, and the intervention force defeating it a revolutionary one. We have to learn to call things by their name, because failing that, we cannot set the rules, hold someone accountable for not complying with them, and thus we cannot prevent politics to become a labyrinth of mischiefs of a narrow faction."[7]

In the second chapter ('Self-determination, Humanitarian Law, Protection of Minorities – Studies in the Primary Fields of Research of Géza Herczegh') there are studies related to the two focus areas of the scientific interest of professor Herczegh in which nine members of the Hungarian community of scholars of public international law lay down their thoughts about the current dilemmas of legislation and application of the law related to humanitarian international law and the to the protection of minorities under public international law.

János Bruhács took on the challenge of providing an analysis of the relation between the Third World and international law by focusing on the changes that occurred in the past decades in the field of the nations' right to self-determination, as well as its elements

5   Peter Tomka, 'Judge Géza Herczegh – The First Hungarian at the International Court of Justice', in Id. pp. 29-39.
6   János Martonyi, 'Köszöntő', in Id. pp. 41-43.
7   Iván Gyurcsik, 'Derűvel, bölcsességgel – Jogainkért Herczegh Géza emlékére', in Id. pp. 45-49.

of guarantee developed by today. By focusing on the relation between political and economic independence, the study underlines the serious deficit in the terms of the latter, aggravated further by the present system of institutions of international investment law, in particular the role of investment protection agreements and the international courts of arbitration.[8]

Péter Kovács examined the relationship between the development of humanitarian international law and the sanctioning of its violation, with special regard to the often difficult questions connected to the international acceptance and the national non-acceptance of the Statute of Rome. He argues, with a rich illustration of examples, for the *raison d'être* of the international criminal court, and he also presents the – often legally and politically absurd – arguments used by certain countries against the ratification of the Rome Statute. The study is also a manifesto for humanitarianism: as emphasized by the author, there are imperatives of international humanitarian law that we must always hold to.[9]

Gábor Sulyok also discussed the field of humanitarian international law, he examined the state of humanitarian interventions after the turn of the millennium. After reviewing the most important related military actions of the past decade, he concludes that, as a continuing tendency that started in the last decade of the past century, the repression of the serious and mass violations of human rights and humanitarian law usually takes the form of multilateral actions. However, it is beyond doubt that if the latter was not an option for any reason, the states would again resort to the tool of unilateralism. At the same time, the selectivity of humanitarian interventions is a serious problem: although there is often more than one country intervening in a conflict, for different motivations, a comprehensive intervention to primarily help the ones in need does not take place.[10]

Gábor Kajtár emphasizes in his study about the right to self-defense that, by now, its own concepts of necessity, proportionality and imputability apply, therefore, its specific legal institutions may be clearly distinguished from one another. The general prohibition of the use of force between states and the right to self-defense [Articles 2(4) and 51 of the Charter of the UN] form a unified norm, which is – in his opinion – at the same time, a *ius cogens*. The normative clauses of the two articles are inseparable: if we increase the extent of the right to self-defense, it shall automatically reduce the personal, material and temporal effect of the general prohibition of the use of force. Therefore, if we did not consider the right to self-defense a *ius cogens*, then, with the amendment of a simple norm of customary law, an acknowledged – indeed, particularly important – *ius cogens* norm could be modified.[11]

---

8   János Bruhács, 'A harmadik világ és a nemzetközi jog Herczegh Géza gondolatainak fényében', *in* Id. pp. 53-64.

9   Péter Kovács, 'A humanitárius nemzetközi jog fejlesztésének és megsértése szankcionálásának összefüggései Herczegh Géza írásai alapján, a Római Statútumra történő kitekintéssel', *in* Id. pp. 65-84.

10   Gábor Sulyok, 'Humanitárius intervenció az ezredforduló után', *in* Id. pp. 85-118.

11   Gábor Kajtár, 'Az önvédelem jogának jus cogens természete', *in* Id. pp. 119-127.

Zsuzsanna Csapó presented the collision models of the ICC and of the African International Criminal Court established with the Malabo Protocol, amalgamating the models of the ECtHR and CJEU as well as of the two courts in The Hague, but which remained a plan in the absence of signatory states. Though the study examines hypothetical cases, it elaborates a test connected to setting up regional criminal courts. At the same time, the author counts with the fact that, although the regional courts of human rights have not derogated the concept of universal human rights, this analogy is not applicable to criminal courts because of the fact that the primary interests of the states are at stake.[12]

Bence Kis Kelemen examined the connection between the application of a living shield and international humanitarian law. The author presents in detail the current legal debates related to the application of a living shield that focus primarily on loosening the principles of proportionality and precaution, as well as the challenges raised by asymmetric conflicts. In a reassuring way, the author concludes that, although the inclusion of the principle of proportionality poses an inherent danger to the enforcement of the principle of humanity, the example of living shields is a good example of how this principle is able, together with the precautionary requirements, to restrict the principle of military necessity and thus the international humanitarian law as well.[13]

Elisabeth Sándor-Szalay's essay provides a complex overview – with historical, sociological and policy elements, in addition to the legal ones – of the system of international protection of the rights of national minorities, with a special emphasis on the relevant activity of the Council of Europe. According to the analysis, the most important result in the past decades was that the integration of minority rights and freedoms – based on the Framework Convention for the Protection of National Minorities – into the system of the wider protection of human rights under international law implied the possibility of a dynamic interpretation of the law for the independent Advisory Committee engaged in the monitoring, and sometimes even the overwriting of ideas that the states' parties had when signing the convention. Thus far, the framework character of the convention combine with its 'living instrument' nature, offered a possibility for the document to fulfil a real standard-setting function and to be able to develop levels of expectation in terms of the specific minority rights.[14]

Norbert Tóth discusses the emergence and the identifiability of the conceptual elements of national minority in terms of customary international law: although in these days, multilateralism experiences a serious crisis, the methods of proof necessary for the devel-

12   Zsuzsanna Csapó, 'Afrikai Nemzetközi Büntetőbíróság versus ICC? Egy esetleges regionális nemzetközi büntetőbíróság felállításának gondolata', *in* Id. pp. 129-146.
13   Bence Kis Kelemen, 'Az élő pajzs és a humanitárius nemzetközi jog, avagy átütheti-e a katonai szükségesség a humanitás elvének pajzsát?', *in* Id. pp. 147-164.
14   Erzsébet Szalayné Sándor, 'A nemzeti kisebbségek jogainak védelme – mint a nemzetközi együttműködés körébe tartozó emberi jogok védelmének szerves része', *in* Id. pp. 165-174.

opment of norms of customary law are present in the practice. As a tool for it, the author presents the International Law Commission's Draft conclusions on identification of customary international law and with its help he provides an overview of the possible manifestations of the state practice, laying down the foundations for customary law in terms of rules of international minority law and of the *opinio iuris*.[15]

The third chapter ('Tribute to the works of Géza Herczegh – studies by members of the college for advanced studies') offers a chance for the next generation of lawyers to pay tribute to the past and to introduce themselves: we can read the studies prepared by a team of students of the Óriás Nándor College for Advanced Studies of Pécs in the fields of legal history, diplomacy history and humanitarian law.

Instead of a summary, it is worth recalling the thoughts of János Martonyi, which faithfully summarize the message of the memorial volume: a work of consistent structure, high professional quality, not only commemorating the past, but also laying great emphasis on the future:

> "[…] there are great changes ahead and it would be very good to have with us today, tomorrow and the day after tomorrow the wisdom, the joy, the standard, the objectivity, the reservedness and the truth-telling of Géza Gábor Herczegh, and of course, above all, a very-very strong Hungarian and moral commitment that he represented."

Though the celebrated scholar is no longer among us, the book is a testament of these values being the legacy for both the present and the future generations of lawyers, from which they may profit in the practice as well.

---

15   Norbert Tóth, 'A "nemzeti kisebbség" fogalmi elemei a nemzetközi szokásjogban – a szokásjogi norma azonosításának lehetősége', *in* Id. pp. 189-204.